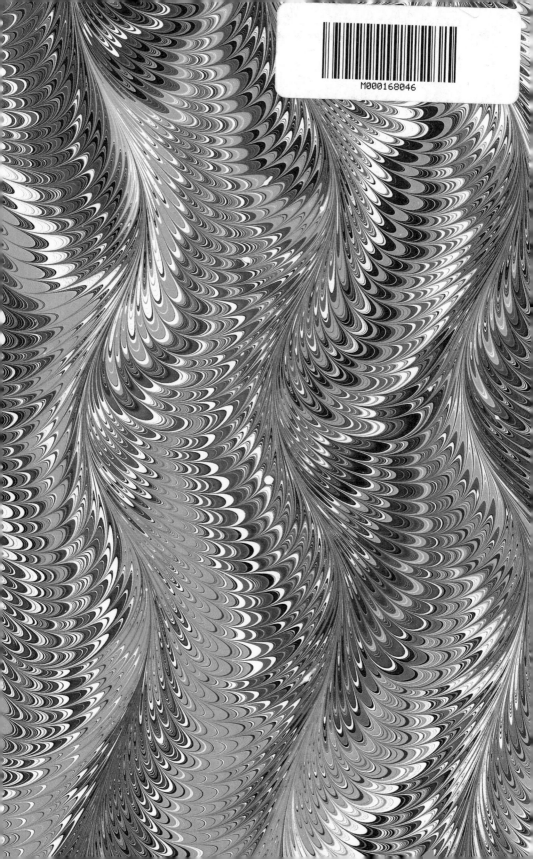

German Anti-Partisan Warfare in Eurpope
1939-1945

German Anti-Partisan Warfare in Europe

1939-1945

Colin D. Heaton

Schiffer Military History
Atglen, PA

DEDICATION

This is book is dedicated to everyone who has fought and died for freedom, regardless of nationality and ideology, in particular my grandfather, 1ˢᵗ Lt. Charles Harris, United States Army, killed at Metz in October 1944. It is also in remembrance of my grandmother, Virgie Heaton, who passed away before she could witness my eventual completion of the Ph.D., Celidh Balloch, my mother Linda, father, Doug Sr., and the rest of the family. Without their support, this would never have been possible.

Especially for my son, Maximillian Hunter Joseph Heaton.
One day you will know the truth and understand all things.

A special dedication to my good friend, the late Lt. Col. Leonidas Damianov Maximciuc, USAAF (Ret.), Prince of Bessarabia, grand-nephew of Czar Nicholas II of Russia. Leo fought for freedom his entire life. You will be missed.

Book Design by Ian Robertson.
Copyright © 2001 by Colin D. Heaton.
Library of Congress Control Number: 2001091482

Printed in the United States of America.
ISBN: 0-7643-1395-9

We are interested in hearing from authors with book ideas on related topics.

Published by Schiffer Publishing Ltd.
4880 Lower Valley Road
Atglen, PA 19310
Phone: (610) 593-1777
FAX: (610) 593-2002
E-mail: Schifferbk@aol.com.
Visit our web site at: www.schifferbooks.com
Please write for a free catalog.
This book may be purchased from the publisher.
Please include $3.95 postage.
Try your bookstore first.

In Europe, Schiffer books are distributed by:
Bushwood Books
6 Marksbury Avenue
Kew Gardens
Surrey TW9 4JF
England
Phone: 44 (0) 20 8392-8585
FAX: 44 (0) 20 8392-9876
E-mail: Bushwd@aol.com.
Free postage in the UK. Europe: air mail at cost.
Try your bookstore first.

Contents

Introduction

This research project will examine several factors: the actions undertaken by the armed forces of National Socialist Germany in countering the escalating partisan and guerrilla threats to their occupation forces in Europe during World War II; the rise and activities of the underground movements in specifically researched regions of Europe, and the Allied efforts undertaken to identify and support those resistance factions deemed reputable and viable in their domestic struggles against *Nazi* oppression. Why the German policy was adhered to and how it became counterproductive is not very well known. What is less known is the true nature of the guerrillas and partisans of Europe, which groups were truly successful, both militarily and politically, and the fact that nearly four million Europeans voluntarily served within the political and military structure of Hitler's Germany.

This fact was particularly important in the eastern provinces, where the brutality exhibited by both sides redefined "total war" as we understand it today. There are various factors involving partisan and guerrilla uprisings, such as nationalism, economics, religion, politics, simple fear, and the Allied efforts to recruit, train and supply partisans. The latter became the blueprint for the modern method of counterinsurgency and witnessed the creation of special operations units specially designed for this purpose.

Of further importance is the analysis of the German failure at effectively dealing with insurgencies, or to even create an active and timely program regarding partisans and guerrillas potentially friendly to Germany's cause, or at the very least in opposition to Stalin's Communism.[1] The application of social, political, and personal interests in the welfare of a target population to serve a greater self-interest came to be known a generation later as a "hearts and minds" campaign. The activity of war must have a clear and definite purpose with clearly defined goals, as well as pursuing a logical and legitimate conclusion. In this regard the indigenous populations must be considered a crucial component for eventual success, and thus treated fairly and with understanding.

It may also be agreed that such an endeavor, either by the initiating or the defending belligerent, must adhere to the accepted rules of engagement and established legal and universally accepted moral doctrine. These parameters assist in determining the difference between *jus ad bellum* and *jus in bello*.[2] The application of psychological and political persuasion, long considered justifiable weapons of war becomes especially important with regard to the German war waged against the populations of the Soviet Union and Balkans. Regarding the Soviet Union, that nation was primed for an internal revolt against domestic tyranny when German forces crossed the frontier on 22 June 1941. The Russian people were long suffering under the oppression of Stalin's rule and the subsequent purges of collective groups, including the military. The recent history of that nation bears out the potential success of a massive German propaganda and recruiting campaign that would have more than likely turned the tide in Hitler's favor.

During the Stalinist purges prior to World War II, three of the five marshals, thirteen out of nineteen army commanders, and over half of the 186 division commanders were killed, including their entire families being either murdered or exiled to Siberian labor camps.[3] It is interesting that, according to Josef Goebbels[4] and Hans Baur, Hitler[5] believed "Stalin must be mad" once the news had come through Berlin regarding the murders of the most competent members of the Soviet military. However, the military were not the only victims of Stalin's pograms, such as the estimated 10,000,000 Ukrainians starved to death—or killed outright—between 1929-1938 for failing to subscribe to the radical Five Year collectivization programs, or the slaughter of the White Russians and Chechens who wanted to break away and form a democratic republic. The Ukrainian farmers had their seed and crops stolen, unable to plant, with 4, 200,000 deaths in 1933 alone.[6] Kazakhstan also suffered, with the nomads and farmers thrown into camps to starve and die, with 1,700,000 estimated deaths, "almost half the population of the republic, perished in the most wretched conditions.[7] The gulags and fields of Russia were filled with the broken bodies and captured spirits of millions of people who simply wanted to be free. Hitler failed in exploiting this reality and it cost him an empire.

Military historians will find this project important in that it explores the events that established various post-war counterinsurgencies, usually labeled as wars of "national liberation" and anti-terrorist doctrines that remain in effect to this day. Much of this doctrine was a direct result of the post-war analysis regarding the German methods, and the resulting failure and the utilization of both former German operatives as well as ex-freedom fighters by the post-war Allies. This study and evaluation includes the partisans and guerrillas who fought against German oppression, fighting for freedom only to be betrayed by their powerful western allies and continue their respective struggles against the Soviet occupation of their homelands.

The United States Army took an intense interest in the German counterinsurgency experience and conducted exhaustive post-war interrogations and interviews with hundreds of persons, especially *Generalmajor* Reinhard Gehlen of the *Abwehr*.[8] The OSS (Office of Strategic Services) and U.S. Army CIC (Counterintelligence Corps) collected vast amounts of information regarding the conduct of counterinsurgency warfare doctrine and policy during and after the war. This information seemed invaluable given the growing threat of the Soviets during and soon after the end of hostilities. With the deterioration of the Allied coalition the data collected became the blueprint for future American and British counterinsurgency operations around the world. The future application of this knowledge and the ideals of democracy supporting the internal opposition to totalitarianism allowed the cultivation, support and expansion of friendly irregular forces during the four decades of the Cold War, thus assisting the western struggle for global stabilization.

This project was conducted through the utilization of primary and secondary sources, enhancing the currently available literature through reviews of post-war interrogations, archive documents, as well as lengthy interviews conducted with the men who operated in and commanded the dreaded *Kommandotruppen*, as well as the regular and specialized *Waffen SS* formations (for a complete listing of all *Waffen SS* units see *Appendix B*). This study will also illustrate what their respective capabilities and responsibilities were in each theater of the war depending upon the level of the insurgency threat as it was then evaluated by German intelligence in the rear and by the field commanders at the front. In order to understand the counterinsurgency campaign as waged by the special units of the Army, *Luftwaffe, Freiwilligen, Waffen SS, SS Polizei, Kriminalpolizei* and *SD,* we must first evaluate the conditions that fostered the creation of partisans, guerrillas and their supporters, as well as their hunters.

The great expense and time consuming operations utilized by the Germans against irregular forces will be explained in detail as to why it met with success on a limited scale, yet failed in the overall strategy, which was an ever changing and flawed concept as discussed by the participants interviewed for this project.

As this book is being published, certain British intelligence files have become available, primarily SOE and Foreign Office documents, and a second edition of this book will be released in due time incorporating the new material, as well as additional interview sources, whose collective information will also be included.

Foreword

Among writings on military history in the United States, the literature of insurgency and counterinsurgency warfare is disproportionately thin. American military historians have mirrored the tendency of the United States Army itself to prefer preparation for and study of conventional war—to say nothing of waging it—far above examination of irregular war.

The years of the Cold War never produced an actual Soviet eruption out of the East to shape a massive contest of armored forces across the North European Plain, but even as the prospect for such an event grew increasingly remote, American soldiers preferred to contemplate it, rather than wrestle with the complexities of the types of irregular war that frustrated them in Vietnam. Today, with the Cold War gone, the occasions for military action truly likely to involve the United States tend yet more toward the irregular and small-wars end of the spectrum of combat, yet enthusiasm for the study of the historical roots and parallels of current counterinsurgency tasks remains underwhelming.

From Colin Heaton, military historian and veteran of the United States Special Operations Command, we have in *German Anti-Partisan Warfare in Europe* what we can hope may be the beginning of a corrective. The military tasks awaiting Americans will probably be mainly those of counterinsurgency warfare; Heaton gives us an invaluable historical guide to them.

Like the military tasks in which we are already engaged, those awaiting us may especially lie in Balkan countries that are among the German arenas Heaton examines. For recounting that German history, Heaton offers special qualifications, both in his knowledge of German documentary sources and beyond that in his remarkably wide circle of acquaintanceships with surviving German participants in WWII and ability to win their confidence and apply it in interviews. His reporting of German counterinsurgency doctrine, tactics, and experience is admirably authoritative.

We Americans should study counterinsurgency war more than we have, but we must particularly grapple with one of the lessons that Heaton has to offer. To wage counterinsurgency war poses dauntingly intractable problems. Insurgents thrive on all kinds of instability—economic, political, social. Anything that aggravates instability tends to benefit them. Given the nature of military force, however, efforts to subdue insurgency by means of force tend themselves to worsen instability. Colin Heaton offers no ready escape from this dilemma; the dilemma usually undid the Germans. But he explores the problem thoroughly, to permit us to ponder it and other issues of counterinsurgency as they deserve.

Russell F. Weigley

Acknowledgments

This project was only possible due to the assistance of many persons. The historical narrative would have been possible with the use of the all-important primary and secondary sources and supplemental documentary evidence. However, it was the collection of lengthy and extensive interviews over the years and the personal recollections of the participants, including letters, diaries, journals, and photographs that created the unique collection that is this project.

The German veterans and their allies who fought the Communists and nationalist insurgencies and participated in the partisan/guerrilla war at the tactical, strategic and operational level, as well as the civilians who also assisted with this project with research over the years are duly noted (* indicates deceased before completion):

Germany

Sturmbannfuehrer Rudolf Maximillian von Falkenhahn,* *Gruppenfuehrer* Otto Kumm, *Oberst* Willi Fey,[9] *Sturmbannfuehrer* Willi Jaehde, *Oberleutnant* Otto Carius, *Obergruppenfuehrer* Karl Wolff,* *Gruppenfuehrer* Max Wuensche, and *Generalleutnant* Johannes* and Frau Ursula Steinhoff, *Generalmajor* Hannes* and Frau Marga Trautloft, *Generalmajor* Dietrich* and Frau Marion Hrabak, Angelica Bruggemann-Wrobbel, *Oberst* Hajo Herrmann, Heidi Galland, *Generalleutnant* Adolf* and Frau Heidi Galland, *Generalleutnant* Gunther Rall, *Oberst* Bernt Freytag von Loringhoven, Hermann Boschette, *Oberfeldwebel* Albert Kerscher, *Oberleutnant* Paul Egger, *Militaerarchiv* Freiburg, *Bundesarchiv* Koblenz and Berlin-Lichterfelde, University of Muenster Library, University of Duesseldorf Library, University of Bonn Library, University of Munich Library, University of Cologne Library.

Greece

Panikos Panay, Harry Kiriakides

11

Netherlands
Astrid Reyns, Paul Leuw

Denmark
Hans Paul Linus, Haaken Klineman, Gabriele Laken.

Norway
Damien Larsfeld, Nils Andersson, Thorvald Thorsson, Olaf Greldfed.

Belgium
Oberfuehrer der Waffen SS Leon Degrelle*

Bessarabia
Lieutenant Colonel Prince Leonidas Damianov Maximciuc-USAF (Ret.)*

Former Soviet Union
Colonel Anna Nikolina, Captain Gregor Koronov, Dr. Naille Sidtikova, Boris Kolokov

Ukraine
Fedoric Valiskorovo

France
Pierre Deshayes, Thomas Daschle, Louisa Dumont, Francois Tarlet

Former Yugoslavia
Lothar Pankosk, Milo Stavic

United Kingdom
Gerry Dorian (Glasgow), Glen Stokes (Glasgow), Celidh Balloch (Glasgow), Charles Messenger (London), Imperial War Museum Library, Public Records Office.

United States
Colonel Aaron Bank, U.S. Army,* Lieutenant General James H. Doolittle, USAF,* General Curtis E. LeMay, USAF,* Jeffrey L. Ethell,* General Maxwell Taylor, U.S. Army,* Brigadier General Charles B. Yeager-USAF (Ret.), Jon Guttman, Kevin Hymel, Ray Denkhaus, Michael Haskew, Carl von Wodtke, John A. Donatelli, Gregory M. Kopatch, Brian Rigg, Lieutenant Colonel James N. Rowe-U.S. Army Special Forces,* Robert Gerd Ridgeway, Norman Melton, Staff Sergeant Edward E. Ford-USMC Force Recon, General Matthew B. Ridgeway- U.S. Army,* United States National Archives, Library of Congress, Hoover Institution for Peace Studies, General of the Army Omar Nelson Bradley,* JFK Special Warfare Center Library at Fort Bragg, North Carolina, Dr. Kenneth P. Slepyan, Transylvania University, Dr. Reina Pennington, Norwich University, Timothy A Wray.

Finland
Eino Jutilainen-Finnish Air Force (Ret.), Heidi Wennerstrand-Hand.

Italy
Capitano Mario Antonucci

Republic of South Africa
Pieter Krueler, Pieter van der Brugge

Czech Republic
Lothar Esporabst

Academic Institutions
Temple University, Philadelphia, Pennsylvania
Dr. Russell F. Weigley, Dr. Richard Immerman, Dr. Dennis A. Rubini, Dr. Jay Lockenour, Paley Library, Chong Rim (South Korea), Gerry Muzinzki, Ola and Sofie Carsberg (Sweden).

University of North Carolina at Wilmington
Dr. Larry E. Cable, Dr. Bruce Kinzer, Dr. Larry Usilton, Dr. John Haley, University Chancellor Dr. James A. Leutze, Dr. Melton A. McClaurin

University of Strathclyde, Glasgow, United Kingdom
Prof. Conan Fischer, Dr. Arthur McIvor, Professor Tom Tomlinson, Dr. Mary Heimann, Mrs. Alison Armour, Mrs. Jo Aspinwal, Professor Hamish Fraser, Dr. David Moon.

University of Freiburg, Germany
Rolf Gebaur

1

Objectives

The first aim and end (of tyrants) is to break the spirit of their subjects.
                                                    - Aristotle, *Politics.*

Foremost among the questions answered in this book is the necessity to provide a complete understanding as to the actual roles and importance of the relevant resistance groups, as well as the proper contextual definitions of the terms *partisan* and *guerrilla*. Included in this study is a contrasted analysis between the western and eastern European irregular forces, their various agendas, as well as the historical accuracy regarding their true roles during the war.

Equally important and inclusive in the body of this project is the study of the failure of the German military to effectively control the partisan and guerrilla groups within their domain. The argument provided is that German forces, not unlike all other traditional military elements involved in the global conflict of World War II failed primarily through a lack of understanding as to the requirements of unconventional warfare. This was especially true during the German occupation in the east, where the failure to effectively subvert (or at least convert) the majority of these factions within the most palatable tenants of the National Socialist paradigm proved costly, thereby reducing German military stability. However, the failure must also lie with the political leadership in Berlin, and especially Adolf Hitler.

Many of the problems facing the German military during the war became disasters that could have been averted, had Hitler implemented the proper damage control measures and exhibited the type of leadership necessary for a successful and homogenous military dictatorship, he may have better managed the insurgency problems facing his military. Although the *Gestapo* and *SD* successfully maintained the domestic scene under internal control, the conditions beyond Germany's borders were a completely different story. With regard to Germany's failure to properly administer their domains, both politically and militarily, the recipe for disaster in handling the rising insurgency problems throughout occupied Europe was already in motion.

Due to the relatively few enlightened, although experienced, officers within the German military, to include select members who would at one time serve on the General Staff and witnessed the need for an immediate application of legitimate counterinsurgency policy, these men would discover what their predecessors already knew: Adolf Hitler, in utilizing an anti-bureaucratic method of governmental administration very distinctive from the military structure, and his lack of consultation with his truly enlightened military and political advisors created situations that would escalate beyond his control. Hitler, according to Ian Kershaw in *The Nazi Dictatorship,* was "uninterested in what he regarded as trivial matters of administrative detail beneath his level of concern."[10] Kershaw also correctly asserts that Hitler only intervened "after all parties concerned had already resolved their differences."[11] This disinterest and inattention to matters outside his areas of interest illustrate the failure of Hitler as an intelligent and cogent leader.

In attempting to create and implement a viable policy to answer the growing partisan and guerrilla problems facing German soldiers and their allies throughout Europe, the field commanders, unable to have their desperately needed audiences with the *Fuehrer* were forced to implement their own individual methods of counterinsurgency warfare as they saw fit. These random methods would create immense problems, since no two adjacent units dispatched on counterinsurgency duty would have the same operational plan until late 1942. This lack of coordination, absence of logical doctrine and the fragmented approach to counterinsurgency warfare (especially between the Army, *SD, Freiwilligen* and the *Waffen SS*)[12] would still persist following the acceptance of a universal counterinsurgency doctrine, and this fact would plague the *Wehrmacht* until its final defeat in 1945.

The investigation becomes an involved process, especially where the Germans were concerned due to the secret nature of many of the operations and the fact that soldiers' letters home were heavily censored, with "postal service becoming sporadic, almost non-existent as the war progressed, thus lowering morale within the ranks and increasing the debilitation and ineffectiveness of the units."[13] Other factors effecting the morale of the Germans were the standard conditions of prolonged combat, exhaustion without relief and the constant fear of death, injury, or even worse, capture. The weather, terrain and climate also played their part on lifting or lowering morale. Soldiers in the far north of the front were affected by the months long polar nights and days, where perpetual winter and summer days took their toll upon morale, as did lice, disease, food shortages, and long periods without leave or relief.

Soldiers surviving prolonged fighting in dense forests, whether against irregular or conventional forces were rapidly drained of strength and required lengthy rest periods, forcing reserve forces to be brought forward and rotated on a regular basis. The same is true of soldiers who operate for extended periods in limited visibility where the psychological strain of nocturnal combat wears heavier than in daylight operations. The Germans did begin to realize this and night operations were highly restricted to defensive operations for the most part, except in unusual circumstances. Due to the use of heavy equipment, the reliance upon support hardware and the necessity to observe indirect fire support for better accuracy limited the rate of advance and proved detrimental. Panic and confusion may more easily debilitate a unit, especially with younger troops or those not specifically trained for the type of combat operations of the particular environment. The irregular insurgent, usually having no such considerations was within his element; he moved quickly at will, often knowing the terrain far better than his adversary and was able to dictate the terms of battle functioning at his advantage.

The primary source documentation is almost non-existent regarding the minute details of German counterinsurgency operations in comparison to records concerning conventional engagements. This is due to the fact that the *Waffen SS* and *Wehrmacht Heer* reports regarding counterinsurgency were not always maintained within their own archive, but rather collected and preserved by the *SD* in their respective departmental offices that were segregated by provincial responsibility under the *Gauleiteramt*. Most of these missing and precious documents were destroyed at the end of the war under the admitted direction of *SS Obergruppenfuehrer* Karl Wolff, since they were usually inclusive of *Sonderkommando* and *Einsatzgruppen*[14] operations in the round up and execution of Jews and political commissars throughout Europe.[15] Fortunately, many of the separated *Einsatzgruppen* records were preserved and published, and may be located at the respective archives in Germany and the United States.

German anti-partisan forces, under the pretext of legitimate partisan interdiction by *Waffen SS* and Army units (primarily the *Sonderkommando* and *Einsatzgruppen*) following behind the advancing front-line forces used this cloak as a method to eradicate the selected "enemies of the state," even at the direct refusal of specific front-line commanders to allow their men to be seconded to these murderous groups once their presence was established. Such was the case of *General der Infanterie* Friedrich Olbricht, who witnessed the atrocities in Poland between 6 September 1939-5 October 1939 while assigned to the *24th Infanterie* Division, and later in Russia, increasing his personal resistance activities against Hitler.[16]

This reluctance to actively engage in these operations by a select few senior officers occurred throughout the war, yet this is overshadowed by the widespread assistance offered by many other division commanders to allow these units to function without hindrance, often with troops supplied as auxiliaries from their units as an "anti-partisan" force. One secondary work that effectively deals with this problem is *Ordinary Men: Reserve Police Battalion 101 and the Final Solution in Poland,* by Christopher Browning.[17] Browning's examination into the unit and its activities identifies many of the problems regarding morale and perceived legitimacy among some of the men assigned to these duties, as detailed in several of the interviews conducted. Another secondary work (although of minimal significance) regarding this topic is *Forgotten Soldier,* by Guy Sajer.[18] Although an important contribution to the literature on World War II in general from the personal perspective, the book illustrates how this ad-hoc process functioned. Sajer, an Alsatian by birth was assigned to the *Wehrmacht's Panzer* Division *"Grossdeutschland"* as an infantryman and medical specialist. During his tenure as a combat soldier he spent the entire period on the Eastern Front and was involved in a counterinsurgency operation while seconded to an *SS* unit while returning from leave. The scenes he describes are noteworthy, although brief and limited to a single action, and the emotional reconstruction is not unfamiliar to anyone who participated in close quarters combat against either regular or irregular forces.

It is crucial to military history in general, and the present military and diplomatic peacekeeping efforts regarding the Bosnian/Croatian crisis in particular, to have an unambiguous understanding of the people who become partisans or guerrillas; grasping their motivations, fears, plans, and hopes. Also of interest and worth remembering is the ongoing crisis between Russia and the Chechens. Understanding the recent history with regard to Moscow's attitude towards these people may help resolve the issues facing that ever-escalating quagmire. Just as the Germans were easily able to recruit multitudes from the Soviet empire to fight against their long time oppressor, the Chechens were also reluctant to volunteer for military service; thousands flooded the German ranks as the Caucasus became a battleground. Most of this hatred was fueled by the intentions of Levrenti Beria, who persuaded Stalin to send in the *NKVD* under the ruse of a military exercise. As stated by Overy:

> The crowds were suddenly surrounded by *NKVD* troops and the deportation orders read out to them. Scuffles broke out as unarmed Chechens fought to escape. Some were shot down. The rest ordered to pack at once, no more than a hundred pounds of baggage per family. Heavy snowfalls and frost hampered the operation, but within twenty-four hours most of the Chechen population was loaded into trucks and trains, destined for Siberia. In one township those left behind were gunned down, buried in pits and covered with sand. It says much for the invincibility of the national spirit that the Chechens retained their identity in exile and rebuilt their national homeland when they were finally allowed to return home after 1956.[19]

The result of over 1,500,000 people being dislocated, and entire families destroyed had a lasting impression upon the people, and this hatred is still evident today. These factors become crucial in the attempt to correctly interpret the ambitions of irregular forces that, by their activist nature and challenge to established authority, are also pretenders to statehood. The Germans failed to control these irregular forces through a complete tunnel vision approach, despite the extensive anti-Communist support network they enjoyed throughout Europe, including the complete destruction of every national conventional military force by the German armed forces from 1939 through 1942, with the exception of the Red Army.

The study at hand is also essential to understanding the continuing political and ethnic instability confronting specific ethnic groups throughout Eastern Europe today, in particular the endless strife in the former Yugoslavia. This region of Europe has, for the last several centuries, remained a hot bed of political and social instability, culminating in the genocide of the mid 1990s, drawing all of the major powers in Europe as well as the United States of America into the all consuming flames since 1914. The German failure to pacify and contain these unstable factions during the war is evident, even when forging alliances and establishing friendly military and political organizations among specifically targeted indigenous personnel.

What is also essential to this study is the evaluation of what situations actually *created* a partisan movement in the respective regions of Europe, whether it was pro or anti-German in nature in each theater of World War II Europe. Without question the invasion and occupation of another country will stir the population into some form of action. However, the aggressor can measure the level and intensity of resistance according to the treatment of the target audience. The confiscation, occupation or defilement of arable land necessary for sustenance, the destruction of homes and villages, and especially the targeting of a particular group (if not the entire population) for extermination or forced labor are prime motivations. When historians observe the history of resistance throughout Europe the evidence points to the fact that the greatest levels of insurgency activity occurred in Russia and the Balkans, where the German occupation was the harshest and military control was tenuous.

Identifying and properly categorizing these various resistance groups with regard to their proper status as either partisans or guerrillas is not a simple process for the conventional opposition leadership, although understanding this difference becomes absolutely necessary. The problem becomes one of arguable context, such as the evolution of the respective terminology in the secondary literature over the last two centuries. Here another dilemma arises: how to properly label these groups through the historiography, of which there is a sparse selection dedicated to the topic in general. What has surfaced thus far in the pursuit of the secondary literature is quite varied and interesting, therefore dissemination and inclusion becomes the responsibility of the researcher and author of the present document. In the case of this work the definitions and methodology of separately identifying partisans and guerrillas according to their respective *modus operandi*, both operationally and politically, have been affixed following specific guidelines drawn upon the relevant and available historical and political considerations and evidence. The evaluation regarding these separate definitions also stems from personal experience during the 1980s with the United States Special Operations Command. The following data in this book was accumulated over the years through various methods, as detailed in the text and was deemed relevant.

The term *partisan* is in this work denotes an irregular force politically motivated into paramilitary action against an armed external aggressor, imbued with limited military or paramilitary capabilities and dedicated to waging unconventional warfare through small localized units on an individual as well as collective basis. This differs slightly from the generic term for *guerrilla*, which simply refers to an individual or collective group following the same pattern of armed paramilitary defiance similar to partisans against a numerically superior force, while also following a domestic political agenda aimed at the domestic as well as intrusive governments. In both cases, the partisan and guerrilla run the very real risk of being labeled a "terrorist" organization by their conventional opponent in order to de-legitimize their activities due to the very nature of their type of war. The insurgent is nearly always outnumbered, hence the necessary stealth and secrecy of his movements and organizational framework. It is the *method* of resistance rather than the *presence* of resistance that plays a large role in how the insurgent is both viewed and handled. The "terrorist" labeling method of propaganda is the most useful tool in the conventional government's arsenal, since the term "terrorist" strips away both the protection afforded to legitimate combatants and pretenders to legitimacy and alters the domestic and world-wide opinion against the cause of the freedom fighter.

The difference between a partisan and a guerrilla may be stated thus: *guerrillas* are a force that offer resistance to *either* a foreign *or* domestic nation state or pretender to statehood, or an incumbent national regime that operates contrary to the ideology and wishes of the irregular force in general, hence the initiation of a *guerrilla* campaign to overthrow that government. In most cases an irregular force that also passes *as* a pretender to statehood through the application of a domestic political and paramilitary agenda counter to the existing establishment may also be accurately labeled as a *guerrilla* force.

Partisans fight as a paramilitary force to expel a foreign invader, supporting a threatened or denounced government and the representative military, hoping to gather external alliances and support deemed necessary for long term survival. The partisan is not a *guerrilla* attempting to impose his will or establish a new order domestically, but rather defending and attempting to restore what he or she perceives to be a legitimate political system under siege. Most members of partisan organizations may be labeled as "nationalists" who are maintaining the status quo. However, in order for a force to be legitimately labeled a "terrorist" organization it must perform several acts contrary to the proper application of either conventional or unconventional warfare. Since insurgents cannot afford the luxury of open conflict with a conventional force, they must adapt their methods according to the same criteria as their opponent: mobility, surprise, ruthless efficiency in the attack and rapid dispersion and egress. Despite the cause or the perceived righteousness of the movement (since a guerrilla or partisan war is a "people's war") the irregulars conducting operations must understand that their activity out of uniform (especially if operating *in the name* of a nation state whose government has legitimately surrendered to the outside belligerent) may be in direct violation of accepted international law.

The same is true of the guerrilla who often fights to overthrow the existing government, in which case he is legally a civil insurrectionist and subject to domestic as well as international law. This is primarily due to the fact that guerrillas and partisans both fight and live among the people, even if they proffer different long term political agendas, thus assuring their anonymity while increasing the likelihood of enemy retribution. Such activity by the invader only furthers and legitimizes the irregular's cause. The only supportive consideration regarding their legitimacy is if they are identifiable upon capture by wearing some form of distinctive clothing, especially a uniform, such as Tito's resistance fighters who have been labeled "partisans," yet are legitimately "guerrillas." The adherence of these conditions may still not protect the insurgents from legal reprisal, an enforcement of the rules as opposed to prosecuting a conclusion to hostilities, such as their being labeled a "terrorist" organization. The purpose of this clause, usually initiated by the aggressor government in power or occupation force, is to demilitarize the role of the insurgent and thus provide a condition for which civil criminal penalties may be imposed. This in effect removes the international conventions from having jurisdiction over the irregulars, or even conventional forces as in the case of German POWs in the Soviet Union.[20]

In all cases, the targeting of non-combatants by irregulars qualifies as a terrorist act, whether a conventional or unconventional force performs that act. The German razing of villages and the killing of civilians should be considered a terrorist act, while the bombing of a German barracks by irregulars should not be so labeled since the targets of the aggression were legitimate targets in uniform. However, should the irregular force, regardless of the perceived righteousness of its cause target non-combatants or attempt to impose its will by force and fear then the label "terrorist" is applicable. In effect, the treatment of the civilian population is usually (but not always) dependent upon the conduct of the civilians during an occupation. To quote Michael Walzer; "soldiers must feel safe from civilians if civilians are ever to feel safe from soldiers."[21] Richard Overy illustrates this reality; "Neither German soldiers, nor the thousands of Soviet citizens who worked for their new masters, were safe."[22] The irregular must understand that his actions will have consequences, and these actions must be considered and weighed against potential reprisals.

Should the irregular force be confronted by a foreign invader, engaging that invader in unconventional warfare operations, while actively supporting the domestic national military force, in conjunction with attempting to continue the existing domestic political and social paradigm, then that force may be accurately labeled a *partisan* organization. Both partisan and guerrilla organizations will attempt to achieve perceived legitimacy in both domestic and foreign arenas, thus raising the potential for foreign support, either in lethal or non-lethal aid and direct military support if possible.[23]

The short term objective of the *guerrilla* is to instill fear and hinder the progression of the target government and its military assets by all means necessary; the ultimate objective of the guerrilla is the complete collapse of the existing political establishment through paramilitary interdiction, reduction of the target government's perceived legitimacy and effectiveness through enervation, and the eventual political upheaval resulting in the complete breakdown of the target government's credibility, both at home and abroad. Another goal of the *guerrilla* (which is not always a factor, although this is a major component of *partisan* warfare) is the desire to cultivate a relationship with an external political or military force friendly to the irregular's cause, thereby obtaining financial and military assistance in either a covert or overt fashion. This is critical in order to assist the irregulars in either re-establishing a previous regime or forming a new post war government.

Both partisan and guerrilla factions have several requirements in common, such as the distinct responsibility to wear identifying clothing, or some semblance of a uniform in order to maintain protection under the Hague and Geneva Conventions' statutes on insurgency warfare.[24] It was this failure by most of the insurgent groups throughout Europe that de-legitimized their existence to the Axis forces. However, as history has clearly proven, this adherence to the rules of land warfare by irregular forces would have probably not offered much in the way of security against reprisal and execution. Another and even more critical element to success is the necessity to foster good will among the local population, especially farmers, who are needed if the irregular forces are to survive, let alone be effective, since it would be the civilian non-combatants who would pay the price for sheltering and aiding the resistance movements.

This has been the nature of small wars and insurgencies internationally since the termination of global hostilities in 1945, as the Cold War super powers maneuvered against each other globally, initiating and supporting various insurgencies in a covert as well as overt capacity. The end result, as seen from the conclusion of the irregular operations in World War II and the collapse of Soviet Communism is a plethora of small pretenders to nation statehood, heavily armed and moderately trained with ancient rivalries tearing at the social and political fabric of their respective nations. Without the stabilizing factors of the United States and the Soviet Union as moderators and overseers, especially where the accountability of weapons, both conventional and nuclear are concerned, rational control has disappeared. The future of several newly established nations, as well as their collective populations looks quite bleak as a general rule, and the complete understanding and definitive interpretation of the partisan and guerrilla as separate and distinctively viable tools in the propagation of warfare must become a part of the standard military education for nations and soldiers world-wide.

Some secondary works are of course more effective than others in covering the activities and history of modern insurgency and counterinsurgency warfare. One of the best examples of a modern chronicle dealing with the terms *partisan* and *guerrilla* (although in the same context, despite the period in question and its non-European origin) are the collective memoirs of Colonel John S. Mosby, Confederate States of America.[25] Colonel Mosby's work, *Mosby's War Reminiscences* becomes crucial to understanding how the terms came into modern use with the United States military establishment and are characteristically (even jointly) mentioned in the same context without differentiation. Mosby frequently mentions the term "partisan" as a self-descriptive title, despite the fact that he led a legitimate uniformed contingent in open warfare using "guerrilla" tactics.[26] Similarly, the term *guerrilla* appears as a method of description, while never offering a differentiation between the two terms as a matter of simplification and historical or political identification.[27] From this context we may observe the American application of the two terms as being virtually indistinguishable.

The terms *partisan* and *guerrilla* have been redefined by this century, given the broad scope of international political and economic instability, the efforts of the superpowers to maintain client state relations in both hemispheres, and the rise of new nation states following both world wars, or at the very least the rise of pretenders to nation statehood on the international stage. The first prominent situation to ascribe the term "partisan" correctly in this century ironically occurred during the Russian Civil War, when civilian irregulars fought the forces of Admiral Kolchak and actually joined the Bolshevik cause. This action defined their position, and thus their members became *guerrillas* in their military tactics but truly *partisan* in their politics, since the Bolshevik government was, albeit forcibly, the government in power and in danger of being overthrown by the former Imperialist armed forces leaders, to include Cossacks, who felt threatened by both the Communists and the new imperialists.[28]

However, despite the descriptive nature and recent history of irregular paramilitary warfare it remains puzzling that few credible sources actually handle the historical significance of irregulars, including their distinctions, multi-faceted purposes, or their domestic and international government detractors and supporters. Also critical to having a better understanding of the role of the counterinsurgent, as well as grasping a true and unambiguous picture regarding the ultimate success or failure in tempering, fostering, or combating insurgents is the ability to make the vivid distinction between the "partisan" and "guerrilla," and this failure appears to be a common thread throughout the international military community. The Germans failed in their responsibility to examine and understand this critical and obvious component, and Hitler and his nationally driven war machine would pay the ultimate price for this transgression.

Regarding the historiography of insurgency warfare, relatively few publications have even addressed the issue of irregular forces on the modern battlefield while defining their true nature. The supportive literature regarding the study of insurgency warfare in Europe, whether based upon historical or sociological viewpoints is not vast, although it does exist. This lack of investigative interest includes the absence of any critical or analytical breakdown regarding the legitimate identification and differentiation between partisans and guerrillas, legitimate insurgent or common political criminal. The understanding that has proven to be so crucial in the successful comprehension of the various insurgent forces, including their motivations and desires, appears to have fallen into the abyss of disinterest. These important components in their entirety are virtually non-existent. It must be the platform and agenda of the insurgent rather than their respective actions alone that defines the individual groups as either *partisans* or *guerrillas* in the modern era. World War II offered the first clear example regarding the distinctions between partisans and guerrillas. The fact that this has yet to be addressed seriously is as mysterious as the Herculean legends that grew from the respective nations detailed in this project under German occupation regarding the effectiveness of their individual "partisan" movements.

Separating the currently accepted mythologies regarding partisan activity throughout Europe during the war, it becomes clear that certain geographic locations and identifiable groups were more active and successful than others. This was especially true in the east, and why this was the case among the anti-German forces appears amazingly clear: the more brutal the German program of repression and outright extermination, the more organized, dedicated, and effective the partisans became as a matter of survival and retribution.[29] As these groups became more dedicated and effective, they in turn received the attention and eventual assistance of the major Allied powers in support of their irregular activities. This fact stands as positive proof that, given the proper set of circumstances and an appropriate support network, an irregular force can successfully engage a superior opposing force with the assistance of a foreign power. This is especially true of irregular forces that fight to maintain an already identifiable and internationally accepted form of government against an external aggressor that is deemed beyond the bounds of legitimacy. Such was the case in 1990-91 when Iraqi forces invaded Kuwait, the Soviet invasion of Afghanistan in 1979 and the North Korean and North Vietnamese invasions of their respective southern borders.

Once a situation such as an invasion has occurred and the indigenous insurgents are supported by an external government and the lines of supply are maintained, the insurgent will in almost every case eventually defeat his conventional opponent. The viability and operational success potential is especially valid should the irregular forces receive active troop and materiel support; such was the case with the Red Army, SOE and OSS support of various partisan and guerrilla factions during World War II. Time is always on the side of the irregular, primarily because they, unlike an established government with a public opinion forum to consider are the political and public conscience of their perceived constituency. In addition, should the insurgency movement be supported by the masses (which is mandatory for success) then the irregulars will have the bulk of the population to draw upon for future generations of combatants, creating a never ending support network.[30]

The Germans, as well as every other conventionally minded and subsequently trained military establishment never realized this critical fact in time to alter the courses of action that undoubtedly prolonged their respective conflicts. The use of arms against an identified and legitimate opponent is only as effective as that identified target's ability to be impressed by, psychologically impaired, or physically damaged by such force beyond repair, thus preventing him from continuing operations both materially and psychologically. Foremost in the equation is their actual value to the history of the war despite the emerging national post-war mythologies. Secondly, is the amount of attention they garnered from the German occupation forces that functioned primarily in a passive and indirect counterinsurgency role in the west, as opposed to highly active operations in the east. Other factors include their collective and individual value to the Allied war effort in both tangible military terms as well as intelligence gathering.

The Norwegians were reasonably effective in gathering local intelligence, especially on German naval activity in the fjords and on the dispersal of *Luftwaffe* assets in the country, transmitting this information to the British. They were also successful in assisting with the repatriation of downed Allied airmen (even those interned in Sweden) mainly through the efforts of resistance operatives such as Bernt Balchen.[31] Several successful commando raids against the German naval and air bases took place, although these were rather random and the Royal Air Force was given the primary responsibility for managing the heavy lifting.

Another nation with a remarkable history of counterinsurgency is Finland, especially during the Winter War of 1939 against the Soviet Union when Stalin ordered the invasion on 30 November and throughout World War II until the first armistice in 1940,[32] then the second cease-fire agreement after hostilities flared up again, signed in 1943. One factor that may have expedited Hitler's timetable on invading the Soviet Union was a statement by Winston Churchill[33] on 30 November 1939, that Finland "…had exposed…the military incapacity of the Red Army."[34] This was seconded by the German General Staff handing out surveys regarding the very inadequacies mentioned by Churchill again on 31 December 1939.[35] However, given the fact that there was little in the way of civilian irregular activity in Finland, since all able bodied men were conscripted (over ninety percent are said to have volunteered, fit or not) partisan warfare in Finland does not carry a great amount of weight with regard to this project. This is despite the fact that through the efforts of Mrs. Heidi Wennerstrand-Hand, whose collective recordings of interviews with her grandfather, Kai-Olaf Wennerstrand, and the written recollections of her great uncle, Bertl Wennerstrand, both of whom fought from the Winter War forward prove invaluable with regard to the unconventional tactics employed against the Soviets. In any case, the war in Finland would fill volumes due to its complexity, and it is therefore beyond the scope of this study.

2

Background

*Weapons are an important factor in war, but not
the decisive factor; it is people, not things, that are
decisive.*

- Mao Tse Tung

The effectiveness of partisans and guerrillas from isolated independent action to full nation state support and direct sponsorship was effectively displayed in varying degrees in both the west and the east. The exponential rise of partisans can be clearly measured in the east, especially where the *Sonderkommando* (special commandos) and *Einsatzgruppen*[36] (operations groups) of the *Sicherheitsdienst (SD)* and *Schuetzstaffel*[37] (*SS*, including specific specialized units of the *Waffen SS*)[38] respectively operated with ruthless efficiency in the wholesale murder of specific target populations.[39] However, it must also be stressed that their were many pro-German partisan groups who supported not only the anti-Communist (primarily the anti-Stalinist) position of the National Socialist regime, but also fervently participated in the genocide of various target populations, especially (but not limited to) the Jews in Eastern Europe.[40]

The eastern anti-German partisans and guerrillas, in particular the Yugoslav Communist and Soviet representatives posed the greatest threat to German military authority, as well as threatening the intended collective social structure to be established within the *Grossdeutsches Reich* as perceived in Berlin. It has been estimated by several German experts, such as *Waffen SS Obergruppenfuehrer* Karl Wolff, who operated in the War Casualties Department under Heinrich Himmler's *SS Personalamt,* that between eight and twelve percent of all German military casualties were the direct result of irregular actions, with approximately eighteen percent of German war materiel falling to partisan activity. Other factors, such as the destruction of bridges, roads, vehicles, aircraft, factories, weapons and other critical components were included in the assessment.[41]

The root causes of the partisans success have many factors, not the least of which was due to the great expanse of territory and the difficult terrain the Germans were forced to patrol and occupy following the conquest of the Balkans in May 1941, and the invasion of the Soviet Union on 22 June 1941, known to history as *Operation Barbarossa.*[42] Another factor after 1942 (and in particular 1943) was the increased Red Army support of various

Ukrainian, Georgian, Moldavian, Bessarabian,[43] Kuban, Caucasian, and Belorussian partisan units, whose leaders were not only supplied with modern arms and equipment but were also given official general officer ranks, pay, military training, weapons and support. According to Richard Overy:

> By 1943, the partisan movement in the rest of the occupied areas had come of age. The growing confidence of the Red Army and the greater availability of military supplies boosted the partisan organization. The units came to resemble the regular army. Tanks, heavy artillery, even aircraft were made available. A total of 22,000 trained military experts were sent into the partisan regions, three-quarters of them demolition experts, 8 percent of them radio operators.[44]

This was also true in 1944 after the Soviets were able to reach the pro-Communist partisans in the Baltic States, especially the anti-German partisans in Lithuania,[45] Latvia, and Estonia. The purpose of including these various groups into the military matrix was two fold: it offered legitimacy to these groups under the Geneva Conventions[46] (which was of little concern to the Red Army or the Germans, especially where POWs were concerned) and placed Communist Party members within the ranks, complete with political officers attached to the units in order to control and direct their activities, as well as cultivate a collective pro-Moscow attitude.[47] It is of no little interest that during the U.S. 7th Army Interrogation of *General der Infanterie* Eduard Glaise von Horstenau, the captured officer stated that it was Hitler's intention to "denounce the Geneva Conventions regarding POW treatment had the war lasted another three months."[48] According to Horstenau, everyone on the General Staff and in the government present opposed the plan, with the sole exception of Goebbels. Hitler even stated that Germans in Allied hands would have to expect the same fate.[49] Even the notorious Party Secretary Martin Bormann was apparently opposed to the suggestion.[50]

The ulterior and primary motive for Red Army support was to emerge after the war: following hostilities with Germany the Red Army would be in a better position to later disarm and, if necessary, eliminate their allied insurgents once their services were no longer deemed necessary.[51] This policy of internal cannibalization would become necessary in order to effectively dominate and manage the newly acquired nations under the umbrella of Stalinist "protection," since most non-Russian partisan groups were promised their own respective nation states in a "carrot and stick" application by the Germans, while the same application may have been implied by the Soviets to non-Soviet irregulars. This elimination of the insurgents proved necessary following the war when the Ukrainian Insurgent Army (UPA) decided to fight for the Germans in 1941, but then turned against them following several massacres and the failure of the Germans to agree on the terms of post-war independence. Many of these men later served with Vlasov, and it was in fact UPA guerrillas who ambushed and killed Marshal Nikolai A. Vatutin near Rovno in February 1945. Following the war, the UPA fought a vicious guerrilla campaign against the Red Army that lasted until the early 1950s.[52] The harsh reality regarding Allied support was displayed by the Soviets in 1944 during the Second Warsaw Uprising, when Red Army forces allowed the Polish partisans to be slaughtered without offering any military assistance, despite the fact that Marshal Ivan Konev's advance Tank Guards Army was sitting just over twenty miles away.[53] The Soviet plan to occupy and replace Poland with a Communist controlled government was not clearly evident to the Western Allies at that time. However, the failure to support an active, successful, and legitimate insurgency network that had the capability of actively enhancing the conventional intervention force is indefensible and defies military logic.

The fact that Stalin supported the plan of genocide and forced labor among the German civilians (7,000,000 in Hungary, Czechoslovakia, Romania, and Yugoslavia, with another 9,000,000 collectively in Soviet Russia, Poland and Eastern Germany)[54] trapped behind the advancing Red Army simply allowed the partisan/guerrilla problem that had haunted the German occupation forces to re-ignite, especially among the pro-German partisans who had escaped Communist decimation. After Stalin's decimation of his own population numbering into the tens of millions, the response of the ethnic Germans and anti-Communists should have come as no great surprise, right along with the guerrilla actions against the Red Army in Eastern Europe at the end of hostilities.

Unlikely alliances developed in several regions with irregulars from opposite political poles who previously tried to eradicate each other suddenly found themselves fighting for a common cause. This was the same condition that faced all irregulars fighting against the Germans; right and left wing groups working together (if they could jointly work at all) against the common threat. The ensuing refugee problem, such as the 500,000 people who fled East Prussia in late 1944-45 was exacerbated by homelessness and the unbelievable atrocities committed by Red Army troops against both Germans and non-Germans alike, along with the hate propaganda issued by Ilya Ehrenberg to soldiers in the field.[55]

This betrayal by the Soviets came to light during several interviews with former partisan and guerrilla members, all of whom openly admitted that following the removal of the German presence many insurgency groups turned on their former Soviet allies, waging a lengthy guerrilla war of survival against the occupying Red Army, especially once the Soviets decided to force the peasantry into state sponsored collectivization.[56] Such was the case throughout the nations of Eastern Europe, particularly in Hungary and Romania,[57] after the blatant disregard by Stalin of the Potsdam Conference where the Soviet Union agreed in principle to allow free democratic elections in the former occupied nations, and Germany was divided.[58] This did not transpire and the occupied nations adopted "constitutions" mirroring that of the Soviet Union.[59] The feeling of betrayal, especially among those insurgents who had served faithfully against Germany and the fascist partisans erupted into full-scale rebellion in Romania, Bulgaria, the Caucasus and Ukraine.

Much of this insurgency was fostered by the ensuing economic hardship placed upon the local populations as they were "liberated," when the Soviets began stripping each nation of everything of value not damaged and sending the spoils east, thus reducing the value of the national currencies.[60] The Soviet occupation forces had managed to starve the population of Hungary; something the Germans had never even attempted, creating further tensions. Romanians were forced to pay Moscow $300,000,000 in war reparations as well as grow extra food to feed their hosts.[61] Land was distributed in a reform movement (land collectivization) giving the peasants fifty hectares each, yet still imposing reparations that meant starvation subsistence for the population.[62] Hungary was given a similar condition, another "carrot and stick" application, but this time it was delivered Stalin style. The Hungarians "elected" their government in the fall of 1945, placing Ferenc Nagy and the Small

Farmers Party in power. However, Communists still controlled local government, with representatives such as Janos Kadar in Budapest answering to Moscow.[63]

The wheel of insurgency for survival, bypassing politics and nationalism had turned full circle, and President Harry S. Truman[64] of the United States, long suspicious of Stalin's real intentions towards the occupied nations after meeting him at Potsdam stated: "I believe that it must be the policy of the United States to support free peoples who are resisting attempted subjugation by armed minorities or outside pressures."[65] It was perhaps the fear of a Communist insurgency, or at least a continuation of radical action against the Western Allied occupation forces as had been seen in Eastern Europe that fostered this support. The adoption of the Marshall Plan to rebuild Germany (as well as Japan) and stabilize the economy, while instituting a democratic form of government was focused upon these very real concerns.[66] Although the assistance was open to all (including the Soviet Union) Moscow declined, and applied direct pressure to its new satellites to follow suit. Stalin wanted no continued contact with the western democracies, especially the financially and militarily powerful Americans.[67]

Much of the insurgency trouble late in the war arrived after the Soviets failed to establish new governments or hold fair elections, since the validity of the elections held were challenged by the Western Allies.[68] The pro-democratic factions felt betrayed after fighting *Nazism,* while many of the pro-Communists were selected for liquidation once the war was over if their leadership seemed too far to the right of Moscow's interests.[69] The socialists were already targeted, thereby increasing their resolve and insurgency activity against the new occupation force. The suppression of these "freedom factions" and the resulting "People's Courts" by the Soviets equaled (and in many cases surpassed) the most ruthless activities of the Germans.[70] Future events, such as the 1956 Soviet invasion of Budapest, Hungary[71] and the 1968 crack down in Prague, Czechoslovakia are just two post-war examples that tend to support this line of thought. However, despite the accepted mythologies arising from Western European nations regarding their own respective partisan/guerrilla operations against the German occupation forces, the facts outlined regarding selective memory and historical fact stand alone in the comparisons between these various factions. The nations of the west were virtually ineffective against the German occupation (with a few exceptions) when compared with their Eastern European counterparts.

This is especially true even when the western partisans were being constantly supplied with arms and advisors by both British Special Operations Executive (SOE)[72] and the American Office of Strategic Services (OSS), despite the fact that both governments were diametrically opposed to Communism. The fact was that both organizations (especially SOE) supported anyone concerned with combating the German occupation forces; Communists, nationalists, and monarchists unilaterally and often without question as to their ultimate objective. It is also worth noting that this support was not limited to individual or collective groups fighting the Germans; many instances of SOE offering greater support to non-Communist entities meant greater assistance to the detriment of the other unpalatable groups, an arrangement that was to hopefully pay dividends. The better armed and successful the anti-Communist forces the least likely a successful Soviet dominated government would be installed once the war was finally won. Since the Communist ideology was especially prevalent within the ranks of the French *Maquis* who were constantly supported by the British to some degree, the eastern and Balkan insurgents fought virtually alone with weapons stolen from the Germans in raids and ambushes until supported by the British, Americans, and Soviets mid-war, and even this application of unilateral aid was ad-hoc.

Part of the problem was the attitude of the regular officers within the United States military and the British forces in particular, who were as ideologically opposed to the concepts of Communism as they were to the ideals of *Nazism*. This was true of the majority of the conservative American population in general who did not actually understand the dogma of Communism or even Marxism. Yet, the U.S. military was clearly and accurately representative of that population, both socially and politically, although according to Jill Caruthers; "...the Soviet Union and Stalin were viewed favorably. Statistics showed that the public looked on Britain with more suspicion than the Soviet Union."[73] The atmosphere regarding Communism in the Franklin Roosevelt[74] administration, which was unconcerned and even trusting of Stalin and the Soviet Union, was not shared by Winston Churchill, or even by Roosevelt's successor, Harry S. Truman, who stated: "(Communists) are out to dominate the world. By betrayal, infiltration, and subversion they have taken over millions of helpless people."[75]

Aiding the Soviets with materiel for waging war against the common enemy was one thing; operating on the ground among them or their Communist contingents was a different matter, especially where the Soviets proper were concerned.[76] It is a matter of historical fact that Communists in the United States suffered purges of their own under the tenure of J. Edgar Hoover, director of the Federal Bureau of Investigation from 1919 through the 1970s.[77] This was especially true after the condemnation of the American Communist Party in their failure to denounce the German-Soviet Non-Aggression Pact of September 1939.[78] Most of this support consisted of weapons and advisors, although food rations were also a consideration, especially when special operations forces considered long term supply and reinforcement necessary. This was particularly true of the isolated groups in Yugoslavia who were constantly at war with the occupying Germans and the pro-fascist *Chetniks* (or *Cetniks*)[79] and Czechoslovakia.[80] The problem of food supplies is important, especially where morale and combat effectiveness are concerned. In order to support an effective support network for clandestine organizations certain measures had to be taken, especially with regard to the production and distribution of food. This was necessary for the sustenance of civilian irregulars already living on a starvation diet if they were expected to become and remain effective.[81]

The question regarding this dilemma is; why is there such a deeply ingrained myth surrounding the effectiveness and legitimacy of the western partisans in Europe? It is quite simple to allow the historical evidence to prove the falsehoods, yet why should this become necessary? The answers lie in the fact that, despite the post war outrage regarding the "Final Solution" against the Jewish population in Europe there were many Gentiles who simply turned a blind eye to the programs of deportation and "relocation," while having full knowledge of the ultimate fates of their friends and neighbors.[82] The guilt of those who did nothing has been replaced by a false sense of participation, and the German methods of political and military rule and complete containment, which differed between the western and eastern German acquisitions and the resulting insurgency movements will be detailed in the subsequent chapters to explain perhaps why this charade surfaced.

The role of the partisan/guerrilla has changed little over the thousands of years of unconventional warfare. It is a point of fact that, until the advent of modern military formations led by a professional cadre of officers and non-commissioned officers, supported by political nation states to pursue the various agendas of defense and offense, small unit warfare of the type engaged by irregulars was the accepted method of aggressive expansion and preservation from the age of hunters and gatherers to the present day. The classical literature, from Herodotus, Thucydides,[83] Ovid, Suetonius, and Julius Caesar's *Gallic Wars* collectively discuss the problems facing the conventional force in a partisan rich environment. Chronicled encounters with irregular forces, such as hit and run tactics of Cassivallaunus against Julius Caesar's short lived British expedition,[84] and the uprising of King Caratacus in AD 43-51 in Britain until defeated by Ostorius Scapula;[85] the revolt of the Iceni and other Britons under Boadicea until defeated by the Romans under Gaius Suetinius Paulinus (with Tacitus stating the Romans were outnumbered eight to one) in AD 61,[86] and the *Tuetoberger Wald* disaster when the 17th, 18th and 19th Roman Legions under Publius Quinctilius Varus were decimated in AD 9[87] offer some glimpse as to the established history and viability of conventional forces combating irregular forces, and the necessity to develop programs and education among the military to understand the nature of unconventional warfare.

Educated conventional commanders such as Hannibal Barca of Carthage (247-188 BCE) during his tragic and tenuous invasion of Italy have also undertaken the same application of unconventional tactics.[88] Although his forces were small and fairly unsupported they were able to instill fear and eventual distrust of the legions and the Roman Republic among its citizenry, despite the fact that his actual military value lay not in military victory (which was fleeting and virtually non-existent) but in his forcing the Romans to disperse their legions sporadically as an interdiction force, thus weakening the combined force arrayed against him. This tactic was later adopted by Publius Cornelius Scipio "Africanus" (236-190 BCE) who believed in learning from his enemies in order to defeat them. Scipio's diligence was put to use in his eventual defeat of Carthage,[89] a campaign that was one of the great inspirations of John S. Mosby.[90] Likewise, Napoleon Bonaparte's forces were constantly interdicted by the partisans in Spain during the Peninsula War, as well as the systematic decimation of his ranks and lines of supply and communication by the Cossacks following the Battle of Borodino and during the retreat from Moscow in 1812.[91] Both examples provide clear evidence as to the effectiveness of irregular warfare, and the word *partisan* is actually used in dispatches emanating from both the British and French commands to denote irregular forces, whose allegiance was dictated more by the pocket book than political ideology.

Although the words "partisan" and "guerrilla" are modern adaptations, the fact remains that irregulars have haunted the ranks of large, well established military organizations since the recorded conquests of Alexander the Great in the 4th century BCE, including his being repulsed in what is now present day Afghanistan by irregulars, a location well known to students of modern history. Again the Roman references to conflicts between irregular and conventional forces, such as the Siege of Masada in AD 73-74, a guerrilla stronghold reduced by Judean Governor Flavius Silva who commanded Emperor Vespasian's 10th Legion *(Legio X Fretensis)*; the similar Sieges of Gamala and Jotopata in AD 67,[92] and Julius Caesar's victory over Chieftain Vercingetorix of the Averni (died 46 BCE) at Alesia in 53 BC ending the Gallic Wars were available to the German professional officer corps for a historiography review.[93] Their own experience in World War I during the African campaign was also ignored during the Second World War, much to the detriment of both the Germans and the Allies.

Mosby's ability to utilize a small force (usually less than a hundred men for faster mobility) in an irregular cavalry unit was legendary to both sides of the American Civil War. So effective were his operations from 1863-64 in tying down several divisions of Union cavalry and infantry in the defense of Washington, D.C. the federal government authorized its representatives to bribe him with a blank check in order to purchase his services. This never materialized due to Mosby's character, loyalty, and political convictions, yet it illustrates just how effective an irregular force may become when competently led, supplied, and supported by a host government. The Confederate Congress was also impressed by the successes of the "partisan" units, and in conjunction with President Jefferson Davis passed the Partisan Ranger Law in 1863, "authorizing the President to issue commissions to officers to organize partisan corps."[94]

The role of the irregular has changed little since the age of spear and stone projectiles, while the capabilities of the irregular have increased exponentially given the technology made available through the course of time, and the evolutionary process that is war making. Despite the era in which we research, irregulars have always played a major role in the military planning of every competent commander during a campaign of foreign invasion and occupation. This is especially true with regard to rear area security, peripheral defense, preservation of lines of supply and communication, as well as the constant necessity to maintain a high level of morale within the conventional ranks involved. These mentioned articles are all primary targets of irregular activity. As observed through the recollections of John S. Mosby, the responsibility of the partisan is, "(being the aggressor and striking the enemy at unguarded points...thus compel him to guard a hundred points...carrying the war into the enemy's camps."[95] This maxim parallels Sun Tzu's philosophy of "deceiving the enemy as to your strength, and striking where the enemy is most vulnerable, while constantly maintaining a harassing posture and gathering information."

Also critical is the collection of "real time" intelligence, or information imminently necessary within a short span of time for the proper assessment and deployment of military assets. Such information becomes more critical and accessible through the friendly irregular who may function in the open among his enemy undetected, perhaps even being trusted. This method was effectively adapted by Mao Tse Tung in China both during the war against the Japanese as well as the following conflict against the Nationalists of Chiang Kai-Shek, and was likewise adopted by the Viet Minh against the French in Indochina and the resurgent Viet Cong effort against the United States in Vietnam a decade later.

History has proven that time is always on the side of the irregular, since he has no calendar or political elections, no annual budget concerns, nor does he suffer the strain of faltering domestic or foreign public opinion. This is only possible when the irregular is actively supported; when well supplied and led, he is perhaps the greatest threat to a conventional force due to his effect upon not only the military component, but also the domestic political stability of his intended target. This is especially true of partisan forces operating in support of regular units, such as that experienced by the Germans during the Second World War in the Soviet Union.

The methods of investigation utilized throughout this process are varied, yet uniquely interwoven as to portray the events as accurately as possible while incorporating the opinions of both pro and anti-German partisan members, as well as conventional and covert operations participants. Also included are the opinions and experiences of Allied and German operatives during counterinsurgency operations. These interviews, international in their composition and conducted over the last two decades in both Europe and the United States have proven the validity of utilizing oral testimony as an essential ingredient to the reconstruction of historic events by the actual participants. It was considered crucial to obtain the opinions of German and Allied military personnel alike, as well as European civilian participants, since objectivity and truth are the ultimate objective of this (or any) investigative research. Eliminating one or the other would only produce a biased, unbalanced product that would never hold its own against intense academic scrutiny and would prove futile in the final analysis.

However, it must be stated that the human memory is not the most reliable asset in every case, and in some instances the interviewer must be on guard as to the deliberate or inadvertent falsification of information by the participants with whom he interacts. This project and author were no exception, and only through the application of cross-referencing various testimonies, along with the evaluation of the archival documentation and personal records obtained from the participants is truth disseminated from falsehood. It is in this department that some historians take exception to many of our colleagues in the United States who, through their own technical and educational evolution assume that oral testimony offers no valid or credible evidence to the "true academic historian." A historian can completely disagree and enthusiastically and effectively argue that this line of thinking is simply the product of either honest misinterpretation, ignorance, or even abject laziness on the part of those who have neither the capacity, connections, nor interest in pursuing the interview. This may seem a harsh analysis, and this statement (among other conclusions) will undoubtedly open an interesting if not controversial debate. So be it.

True, the interview sometimes smacks of journalistic qualities, yet the oral testimony is a qualifying factor in courts of law as well as history. As stated by Mosby in several sections of his memoirs, he argues convincingly (and their may be many other examples available) that even the historical document, written at the time an event took place, despite being cherished by academic historians is not always a truthful addition to the historiography. The falsehoods regarding Mosby's actual actions and numbers in the field, fired through the communications lines of the Union Army offer conclusive proof that the written evidence, like its oral counter-part, is only as good as the corroborating sources and the credibility of the originator. Taking a primary source document at face value simply because it is supposedly a timely piece of information deemed relevant to the situation in question is as foolish as resting one's thesis statement solely upon the testimony of an individual, without investigating all avenues available for complete and thorough corroboration. In defending the oral testimony, the primary sources must also be meticulously screened for details that may support or even refute the evidence collected. It is not for the researcher to offer the "definitive" history of a topic, but rather promote debate, thought, and honest intellectual labor that will either stand or fall with the litmus test that is time. This project proposes that irregulars have been consistently misunderstood by conventional leaders, and provides examples as to how and why misunderstanding or disregarding this threat will prove fatal. The readers may decide for themselves where the faults lay. This author simply lays the facts out for examination.

The persons contacted for the research of this topic were the critical component in reconstructing the activities of partisan/guerrilla and counterinsurgency operations on the personal and unit level. During the course of the interviews the validity of the information may be rated from the most reliable to the least reliable, depending upon the perspective of each participant and the role they played during the war. These are analyzed thoroughly with the least reliable information excluded. The current release of selected SOE operational records through the Public Records Office in Kew, Surrey, United Kingdom have yielded a valuable harvest of information assisting in the compilation of relevant documentation previously unavailable.

With regard to the most reliable sources of information concerning German operations against partisans, the German officers and enlisted men interviewed were without question the best sources of supportive and corroborative testimony and documentation. The operations of specific units in the counterinsurgency role are in most cases a matter of archival record.[96] However, after action reports and operations orders, while detailing the missions and offering vital statistics regarding counterinsurgency effectiveness fail to portray the social, moral, and intellectual component of the individuals involved, as well as the importance of their actions. Some records have been proven false through investigation, where various rear echelon commanders or analysts altered reports to justify the actions of their troops. Whether the person interviewed was enlisted, commissioned or even general grade in rank, the strain, fear, and constant repetition of these exhausting operations can only be examined through the eyes, memory, letters, diaries, and post-war interrogation reports of those who participated. The investigation must delve into the operational planning and execution of counterinsurgency strategies and tactics employed by the Germans in the east and west, with both passive and active methods explained and their effectiveness evaluated.

Of the Germans interviewed, four were general grade officers of the *Waffen SS:* [97] *Gruppenfuehrer* Otto Kumm (of *2nd Waffen SS Panzer* Division *"Das Reich"* during the period in question); *Obergruppenfuehrer* Karl Wolff (former adjutant to *Reichsfuehrer-SS* Heinrich Himmler[98]), *Gruppenfuehrer* Max Wuensche (*1st Waffen SS Panzer* Division *"Leibstandarte"* and former adjutant to *SS Oberstgruppenfuehrer* Josef "Sepp" Dietrich,[99] as well as staff aide to Adolf Hitler), and *Oberfuehrer* Leon Degrelle (*28th Waffen SS Panzergrenadier* Division *"Wallonien,"*) one of the few non-German generals in the *SS*.[100] Degrelle is unique in the fact that he enlisted in the German army as a private, rejecting a direct commission in 1940, rising through the ranks and eventually creating his own battalion.[101] This battalion of *Freiwilligen* (volunteers) was later increased and designated an Army regiment in 1941, which was later absorbed into the *Waffen SS* in 1944 with Degrelle (tried and sentenced to death in absentia after the war in his native country), a university educated political scientist, intellectual, fervent anti-Communist activist, and international lawyer from Belgium as its only commander throughout the war.[102] Degrelle's unit would witness over 20,000 men pass through its ranks during the war, and only three (including and according to Degrelle, despite being wounded seven times during the war, twice severely) would survive their three years on the Eastern Front.

Others interviewed included one field grade officer, *Waffen SS Sturmbannfuehrer*[103] Rudolf Maximillian von Falkenhahn (*1st* and *2nd Waffen SS Panzer* Divisions), a shadowy character and former *Luftwaffe* enlisted *Fallschirmjaeger* (paratrooper). The enlisted ranks included *Waffen SS Hauptscharfuehrer* Hans Hossfelder (*2nd Waffen SS Panzer* Division and *8th Waffen SS Kavallerie* Division) whose recollections during the Belgrade offensive in April 1941 were previously published.[104] Interviews were also conducted with actual partisan resistance participants and leaders such as Pierre Deshayes, who took over the organization of the French Resistance in general in 1943.[105] Despite the Allied (in particular American) complaints regarding the incompetence of the majority of the *Resistance* contingents and their leadership (the *Maquisard* notwithstanding), Deshayes was the outstanding exception due to his successes in maintaining constant pressure upon German and Vichy forces.[106] His efforts, including his diplomatic skills with the Allies effectively tied down nearly twenty German divisions (roughly 300,000 men) throughout the country, although most were not front line quality troops and over half were Vichy French police units, thus preventing their deployment to other regions of Europe.[107] Although Deshayes possessed no formal military training or combat experience, his organizational skills, credibility and ability to assess situations rapidly and accurately were the keys to his success.

A major concern of the Allies was the actual position and reliability of the Vichy government in their alliance with the Germans, especially when *Operation Torch*, the Allied landings in North Africa were placed in motion in November 1942.[108] A major consideration regarding the success of the mission was the potential removal of Admiral Jean Louis Xavier Francois Darlan, the commander of the French Navy prior to the German conquest.[109]

Darlan had received support from American President Franklin D. Roosevelt, yet Churchill had grave misgivings, and in one of his more lucid moments decided the French turncoat must be removed.[110] Roosevelt had blamed de Gaulle[111] for the lack of a well coordinated French resistance effort, which was a proper assessment due to the in-fighting between de Gaulle and General Henri Giraud[112] over who should lead the French forces outside the country, although Roosevelt openly acknowledged the right-wing government of Marshal Henri Philippe Benoni Omer Petain as a counter to the Communist elements permeating the most active resistance efforts.[113] Due to de Gaulle's attempt at becoming close with the Soviet Union "as a counter-weight to British influence on the Continent de Gaulle had basically thrown away any chance for complete support from the Americans and British, except with regard to direct war aims."[114] In reciprocation Stalin stated that de Gaulle was the best person to lead the *Resistance* and offered his support,[115] which helped legitimize de Gaulle in the eyes of the world and the Communist insurgents within his own nation. Michael R.D. Foot states that:

> The kind of greatness of which his character made him capable compelled him to preserve and maintain his pride and honor; and political circumstances joined to personally compel him to adopt a fiercely independent attitude towards all other governments.[116]

It is with a certain evidentiary scrutiny that this work takes exception to this portrait of de Gaulle. De Gaulle was a non-combatant military figurehead of a defunct government relying upon the charity of Britain and the United States, a mutually beneficial condition in which France and the Allies found themselves. De Gaulle was always complaining that the "Western Allies treated the Free French as a purely military organization and ignored their political qualifications,"[117] and he even authorized French units from Syria and part of the

French Air Force, the *Normandie-Nieman Escadrille* to be dispatched to serve under Red Army command on the Eastern Front.[118] Due to de Gaulle's flexible politics and his seemingly endless ability to alter his allegiance to either east or west as his mood saw fit, as well as his ineffectual ramblings and interference with military matters in which he knew absolutely nothing, he was never considered a major player in wartime strategy making. The Allies purposely left him and the French out of the *Operation Overlord* planning due to the lack of security within the French command structure. The only organization to even accept input from him was SOE and later OSS, since French involvement and personnel recruitment was critical to overall success. SOE Colonel Gubbins found him useful and became one of his supporters,[119] despite the fact that he stated; "It is clear that we cannot build up a proper secret army in France under the aegis or flag of de Gaulle; that we must do through our independent French (i.e. F) Section, until such time as a combination is practical politically."[120]

The Communists had no apparent interest in him at all except as a vehicle to further their own agenda, since it was in fact they who had been pressing for an uprising against Germany from the early days along the lines established by Moscow. It would be this factor that would see the French Communists actually initiate the first and most successful guerrilla campaigns. The Western Allies were not immediately receptive to supporting and arming a massive paramilitary Communist insurgent force in France. Much of this wariness by Britain and the United States is the real reason why the Communists did not become active in guerrilla activities either within or beyond France's borders until November 1943, and why the French *Resistance* is actually more a myth than a reality through no fault of their own.

In actuality, de Gaulle may be labeled a true patriot of France, while also becoming an unreliable ally and political liability. In deference to the bulk of the post-war glorification of de Gaulle, especially after his election as President of France it is quite clear to the distant and lucid observer that he was a non-committed opportunist who actually cared for no one but himself. His massive ego would never allow him to admit the great debt owed by France to the Western Allies, despite the hundreds of thousands of white crosses marking the final resting places of the dead from the United States and Britain from not one, but two world wars. However, de Gaulle was at least willing to support the Allies in the liberation of France, although he was not about to dirty his own hands. With regard to de Gaulle's supporting the French Communist movement he must have found their initial demands quite reasonable, which included the arming of all French "patriots" to fight Germany; punishing all traitors and collaborators, the development of "democratic" and social programs once the war was over, with France assuming its rightful place among the Allies and the "satisfaction of the legitimate aspirations of Overseas France."[121]

Darlan's star descended as Pierre Laval[122] (denounced as the French "Quisling") muscled him out of the upper echelons of the Vichy government, thus reducing his effectiveness, although he still commanded the respect of the French Fleet at Mers-el-Kebir, Algeria. The French Fleet remained a potential threat to the success of *Operation Torch*, a fact that did not escape Roosevelt and Churchill.[123] Darlan's fluctuating position between supporting the Germans then the Allies depending upon the military climate added to the universal distrust, and therefore SOE planned his removal. The man chosen for the assassination was a twenty-year old French SOE trained expatriate named Fernand Bonnier who succeeded on 24 December 1942, yet was captured, tried and executed two days later without ever betraying his benefactors.[124]

American General and Supreme Allied Commander Dwight D. Eisenhower, while supportive of resistance activities throughout Europe was one of the most skeptical towards actively aiding the French with military personnel of the OSS (who operated in smaller "Jedburgh Teams" usually consisting of three men, with two officers and an enlisted radio operator) and SOE, both working deep behind enemy lines. Although OSS and SOE were allied in combating the Germans and supporting the insurgency movements throughout Europe, their relationship was less than harmonious. This was particularly true with regard to allocating supplies and support between the various departments, especially when section MIR was created to handle the Czech and Polish underground networks headed by Colonel Gubbins. Tensions would occasionally arise due to many factors and there was some distrust between the groups through cultural and professional differences. A sample of the divide between both organizations is stated in the following:

General Donovan has demanded a very largely increased share in Special Operations in the Balkans. There are no good reasons for opposing this demand, provided that an agreed policy is carried out. At present the OSS organization as a whole is answerable only to the United States Joint Chiefs of Staff and is entirely independent of the State Department. On the other hand, SOE carries out a policy agreed between the Chiefs of Staff and the Foreign Office. There is a definite danger that General Donovan's organization will not necessarily pursue the same policy as SOE. Such a development would obviously lead to incalculable difficulties, and should be avoided if possible.[125]

OSS and SOE would originally combine their respective talents and resources in France, later expanding their operations throughout Europe and later in Asia against the Imperial Japanese military. The differences between SOE and OSS would not become as great a threat to Allied harmony as would the later Anglo/American-Soviet relations regarding resistance support in Eastern Europe. The inability of the French partisans to maintain total mission and personnel confidentiality, as well as the constant distrust and betrayal among their various groups placed the lives of these dedicated men and women in danger. Deshayes' success at preventing leaks, organizing his troops and supplying them with a logistics and intelligence network that was rarely compromised, despite the fact that he organized most of his operations from Lisbon, Portugal is one of the great success stories of the insurgency war in Europe. His success was to ensure a constant flow of arms, advisors, munitions, and even supplemental manpower to support his efforts, efforts that paid off handsomely before, during, and after the initiation of *Operation Overlord.*

The German intelligence network, in particular the *Abwehr* under the direction of *Admiral* Wilhelm Canaris maintained an impressive collection of data on the various resistance movements throughout Europe. Canaris was always Himmler's greatest antagonist until his dismissal, imprisonment, and eventual execution at Flossenburg concentration camp for his involvement in the 20 July 1944 bomb plot to kill Hitler. Canaris had been subverting German ambitions through secret negotiations with London through Geneva and Stockholm,[126] and later *Generalmajor* Reinhard Gehlen, who would become Chief of Counterintelligence was well aware of who the primary partisan and guerrilla leaders were throughout Europe.[127] In mentioning Gehlen, it must be again stated that his uncanny knack for accuracy seemed almost supernatural to Hitler, who both despised him for his non-Aryan appearance yet envied him for his intelligence. Becoming a *Hauptmann* in 1935 Gehlen was slow to rise through the ranks until the war began. During the late 1930s he was a staff officer in Poland and Liaison Officer for the *16th Armee* in France in 1940. He was appointed Chief of Operations for Army Group East in 1941 preparing for *Barbarossa* and planning all logistical matters.[128] His succession as *Abwehr* Chief in 1944 following Canaris' demise ended his image as a nondescript intelligence officer. This new position allowed him more direct contact with the upper echelons in the German High Command, where he tried to reduce the racial attitudes towards the eastern peoples, which according to Richard Overy; "The bloodiest chapter in the history of German conquest was the subject of race."[129] Gehlen was also a primary catalyst in attempting to recruit from the occupied areas and reduce the counterproductive German methods of counterinsurgency.

Despite the plethora of documentation regarding the German attitudes toward race as a propaganda tool, the Soviets were just as relentless in their pursuit of "race" as a qualifier to incite hatred against their invaders. Already well known for anti-Semitism, the Communists provided their population with a "Stalinized" version of racial criteria, as delivered by Ilya Ehrenberg in August 1942 in the army journal *Red Star* and cited by Richard Overy:

> Now we know. The Germans are not human. Now the word 'German' has become themost terrible swear word. Let us not speak. Let us not be indignant. Let us kill. If you do not kill the German, he will kill you...If you have killed one German, kill another. There is nothing jollier than German corpses.[130]

Reinhard Gehlen was a firm supporter of the *Freiwilligen*, the recruited and trained foreigners who fell under his department's authority as well as the *Hilfswilligen* concept, the utilization of auxiliaries (mostly deserters and POWs) to serve in many civilian roles.[131] Gehlen drafted proposals to arm, equip and distribute hundreds of thousands of former POWs and defectors within the ranks of the *Wehrmacht,* and he was instrumental in creating the Russian National People's Army (RNNA)[132] and the Russian People's Liberation Army (RONA) under exclusive Russian commands, for a total of between 800,000 and 900,000 former Soviet soldiers and partisans, with many wearing German uniforms with their own insignia. Hitler was not informed of this activity until late in 1944. So popular was RONA that partisans and guerrillas from many miles away would travel through Soviet lines to join the unit.[133] It was also Gehlen who would suggest Andrei A. Vlasov as the leader for the anti-Communist forces following his capture on 12 July 1942.[134] Following the war Gehlen formed a new intelligence service, *Organization Gehlen* that became the basis for West German counterintelligence (including the counter-terrorist unit *Grenschuetzgrenz-9,* or *GSG-9*) and upon which the post-war CIA counterintelligence branch was originally modeled. Pierre Deshayes' name was foremost on the list, and the reward placed upon his head forced periodic and lengthy absences from his homeland.

Poland, although critical to the study of World War II provided insufficient resistance forces to effectively combat the German occupation. This is easily explained since Poland suffered the most heavily with regard to the decimation of its population (some conservative estimates state twenty-two percent of the population were liquidated) by German occupation forces, as well as under Stalin's occupation.[135] First we will examine the German approach to insurgency activity in the west, which will offer a contrast to the occupation in the east that would forever alter world opinion regarding the role and legitimacy of partisan and guerrilla warfare.

3

Partisans of the West

*We should support whatever the enemy opposes
and oppose whatever the enemy supports.*

- Mao Tse Tung
16 September 1939
Selected Works, Vol. II, p. 272.

The German invasions of Norway, Denmark, Belgium, France and Holland in 1940 secured vital strategic regions for Hitler, providing Germany with essential ports and air bases for the planned offensives against Britain. Occupation by German forces was considered "light duty" by comparison to future assignments in the east. Almost as soon as the defense forces of these nations capitulated a British Special Operations Executive landed a campaign to foster partisan activity against the Germans in occupation. These efforts, while noble in concept were universally futile in comparison to the Red Army support offered to the partisans in the east. However, this is not to say that the effort did not yield tangible results.

One of the greatest obstacles to be overcome by SOE and later OSS was the lack of any collective effort or unity among the various politically divided factions, which only secured the German stranglehold upon the populations and economies in the west. The investigation leads to a logical conclusion that the following was true: Western European populations were better educated and more aware of their respective national identities, thus offering an ingrained ideological understanding of government and the process of politics. This collective understanding also fostered rivalries that became as volatile as the underground insurgency itself. It was a well known fact that the Norwegian, French, Yugoslav, Greek and Soviet partisans were unable to work together or collectively (the Greek partisans were an SOE nightmare), delaying much needed Allied support, yet in later years many claimed they were ignored and virtually unassisted in their fight against the Germans.[136]

Where Allied Special Operations failed in gaining collective unity among their allies they succeeded in maintaining the essential material, political and moral support necessary to provide hope and foster a belief in eventual victory, regardless of the motivations of the respective partisan and guerrilla factions. However, the very facts that created an intelligent and educated population among the conquered nations also provided a high caliber of laborers for the German war machine. This policy differed slightly from the populations in the east, who in large had little education and were largely illiterate, living under despotic regimes, whether a Communist totalitarian dictatorship or monarchical rule. These peasant populations, agrarian in their subsistence and with little interaction with larger cities or the greater nation in general were basically ignorant or at the very least disinterested in the basic tenants of politics. These populations were even less knowledgeable with regard to world events and fought less for political motivations than reasons of economics and pure survival once the German intent was clear. Politics served with bread tends to be ingested better, and the providers were only interested in gathering manpower, not educating or providing for the population.

A major factor in the German method was that unlike in the eastern provinces, the Germans did not mandate the Western *Reich* dominions and governments directly from Berlin en masse, so the heavy hand of micromanagement was not immediately felt, although the method of control would change as the war continued. The Berlin government decided quite prudently to allow "user friendly" governments to function in place of a *Militaerischesgauleiteramt,* such as the Norwegian socialists under Vidkun Quisling,[137] although the Vichy government in southern France was the prime example until 1942. This offered at least the semblance of a domestically controlled civil government despite the fact that every western nation under German domination operated a government in exile from their havens in London.

France

Historians can do nothing less than agree that French military forces ceased to be a viable asset following the invasion and ultimate conquest by German forces in May-June 1940. The question then becomes one of when did the actual resistance efforts originate within the indigenous population, and at what point (if any) did this resistance become a serious threat to the German occupation? Any resistance is counter to the wishes, good order, and discipline of an occupation force regardless of the condition or the severity of that resistance. However, it is the contention of this thesis that the French resistance was not a viable threat until after1942, when British SOE began fostering and supporting the various resistance factions in earnest, despite their feeble attempts between 1940-41. Even when SOE was able to lend active support to the resistance elements, the Mediterranean and Balkans were first and second on the priority list with France following behind. The availability of assets, money, aircraft, and general support would be forthcoming, although not enough and too late as far as de Gaulle was concerned.

Also important is understanding the nature of the French capitulation in relation to the terms of surrender, and the occupation and the creation of the pro-German Vichy government under Marshal Henri Petain. Petain's government accepted the conditions laid down by Hitler, while the Free French who were salvaged from the beaches at Dunkirk later declared their government in exile under de Gaulle, stating that the "true French government" had actually never surrendered. These distinguishing differences become critical when determining the legitimacy of the French *Resistance* as an established and legal opposition force. If the actual French government as accepted by international law had not surrendered in 1940 then the civil resistance, both political and military factions would be considered legitimate irregulars; partisans fighting to preserve an existing government while combating an invading external force. It is important to note that four days before the armistice was signed, "one junior French general had the courage to proclaim over the BBC that he did not accept the surrender, and to invite those of his compatriots who agreed with him to join him in fighting on."[138] This "free combatant" status, once verified and supported by international law would also require that the irregulars be considered as legitimate combatants under the Geneva and Hague Conventions, both of which govern the laws of warfare, provided that the irregulars wore distinctive clothing and identified themselves as legitimate and accepted representatives of their government in exile. However, as common sense dictates, irregulars are hardly effective if they are easily identified. The aspect of anonymity is the insurgent's greatest asset, enhancing his mobility and lethality.

When analyzing the German methods of counterinsurgency in both the west and the east it is important to understand the German perceptions and attitudes toward the various ethnic peoples in these respective regions. The Western Europeans held a similar social, religious and ethnic background to the Germans despite the constant strife through the centuries of wars, politics, economics and tenuous interaction. Germans and Western Europeans mingled and interacted across their respective borders more frequently and had a long history of contact. There was a basic unilateral understanding, as illustrated in the teachings of both western history and culture, including the language instruction in the German and other national schools through university level. This was not the case with the Eastern Europeans on a large scale, where enrollments were small and dependent upon social if not political status. However, the German perception of the French is exemplified by the following passage quoted by Omer Bartov:

> Later my soldier friends and I went to a "bookstore" in Versailles. You can't imagine what junk and pornography we saw!…You can truly see that in the areas of cleanliness and morality, the French people have skidded to a new low. Such an incident is simply unthinkable and impossible in our German Fatherland. When a society is capable of reducing feminine beauty to such a level, then this society has lost its right to be called a "*grande nation*."[139] Yes, this society has lost not only its vitality but also its morality.[140]

The following entry by Bartov (citing other sources) illustrates the same soldier's attitude upon his entry into Russia: "(…the Russians)[141] fight like hired hands-not like soldiers, no matter if they are men, women or children on the front lines. They're all no better than a bunch of scoundrels."[142] The letters from German soldiers in the east, especially in Russia are quite contrasting. The attitude of the German soldier towards the French and other westerners could be considered benign in comparison, as history has shown, despite the great exploitation of these nations by Germany for labor during the occupation. However the Germans may have perceived their western neighbors, the occupied peoples were far from willing to accept the German occupation and their overtures across the board.

Perhaps one of the most interesting and disturbing selections for investigation is the actual history and operational viability of the French *Resistance* and the German response to this threat. The legitimacy of this threat is especially important regarding the creation of the *Maquisard* (or *Maquis*) whose name derived from the young men who escaped the fate of the imposed Forced Labor Act to wage a guerrilla style war on their own terms.[143] It is accurate to state that the individual cells and groups of the *Resistance,* divided not only between the Metropolitan *Resistance* and the Free French Forces, but also between the northern intellectuals and students of the *Musee de L' Homme* was quite effective. Under the leadership of activist Paul Rivet in Paris (which was limited in scope and operationally ineffective due to the strong German presence), and the direct links with the Southern Front *Resistance* the *Maquis* were the only reason to consider the French underground an active and viable entity.

Each group within the *Resistance* had its own concept of fighting the occupation, as well as what form of government the nation should have once the war was won, a problem not lost upon both the charlatan de Gaulle and the paranoid Winston Churchill. Neither of these two men were credible military leaders, although both were masters of their respective political agendas. These potential political problems were hopefully not insurmountable obstacles, yet despite these differences the *Maquisard* Communists had the greatest success against their occupiers (both passive and active).[144] Although their activities were highly varied, such as an occasional shooting of a German soldier and blowing up a train despite the misguided, fragmented and untrained groups, the ability to embark upon large scale activity such as sabotage,[145] railway disruption, [146]escape networks for downed Allied airmen and soldiers, and even passive subversion were marginally successful despite the lack of any large scale cohesive methodology, activism, or large scale support network during the period 1940-42. [147]

These units started out along the same lines; individuals gathering friends and operating loosely with ad-hoc equipment until either later joining a larger, more established group or building up their own collective. These groups, regardless of size, lack of open support and political polarity were nonetheless highly motivated in their pursuit of interdiction and harassment behind German lines, especially from 6 June 1944 forward as the Allies advanced across France, when the great myth of French *Resistance* was born.[148]

In fact the *Resistance* effort as it is commonly repeated through the post-war revisionist mythological texts only began during the spring of 1942, two years after the occupation by Germany and only increased exponentially as victory seemed certain following the Allied landings during *Operations Husky, Overlord* and *Dragoon,* and not before.[149] Lynsey E. K. Kirk's argument that the retreating German military and *Gestapo* forces lessened the risk, so that is almost impossible to meet anyone who had not been "in the *Resistance*" by the end of the war has merit.[150] This "unanimous involvement" is one of the factors that assisted the growth of the accepted post-war myths of the "great French *Resistance* movement," although the *Resistance* as defined by guerrilla warfare standards was limited in both scope and material value and was completely benign until 1943. Prior to this, the only legitimate claim to large-scale activity was the sheltering of downed Allied airmen (at which they excelled) and the production of underground anti-*Nazi* literature.[151] As Pierre Deshayes stated;

> This region was totally incapable of effective resistance until more military and logistical support could be obtained by the British and Americans. Other reasons included the large numbers of German occupation forces, the willingness of many Frenchmen to work for the *Nazi's,* and the fear of being caught or even assumed to be involved with the *Resistance*. It must also be stated that the failure of the various units to communicate caused most of the problems.[152]

For the passive French supporters, their activities included sheltering escaping Allied troops and airmen as well as fugitive partisan members, altering road signs, tearing the metro passes into "V" shapes for public display, painting the Cross of Lorraine on walls and in public places, and printing opposition papers and leaflets for distribution.[153] However, despite several sterling performances by certain factions of the *Maquisard* over the years, the truth lies in the fact that the French *Resistance* as a whole was a fairly disjointed, undisciplined, and basically ineffective rabble for most of the war, at least where organized military operations were concerned, causing the Germans little legitimate concern.[154] General Charles de Gaulle best explains the military inability of the partisans:

> All lack of skill is merely relative. Does it follow that because an army is unskilled therefore one must refrain from sending it into attack? Did the volunteers and the pressed men of the revolution hesitate to fling themselves upon their enemies?[155]

The one exception was the *Maquis*, which held most of the Communist contingents. By the definition outlined herein, the *Maquis* became effective as a "guerrilla" unit as opposed to a "partisan" force. The *Maquis*, who uniformly disagreed with the position of the forced labor draft would fight for the opportunity to have a Communist revolution in France, or at the very least a Communist majority in a new government. Their tactics would revolutionize the *Resistance* movement with the adoption of overt assassination, large-scale raids, and the open recruitment methods lacking in the other partisan factions. Pierre Deshayes explained his position with regard to the *Maquis*:

> The *Maquis* were the most effective, although they were sometimes quite reckless in their approach. They would plan attacks without consulting higher or adjacent authority, without regard to the repercussions to the surrounding civilians once the Germans arrived. This was part of their plan; to increase the collective activity and the level of retribution. This would hopefully increase their recruitment. The same method had worked for the Soviets, and they also sent advisors to France to assist and coordinate these missions. This was not done with the knowledge or even the approval of the higher Allied Command. Yes, I would say they were effective, and they provided great support for the liberation of France. However, they were a great concern to most of us. The tensions sometimes reached massive proportions, and I personally feared an internal civil war between the units. That was before Jean Moulin arrived. He was the best, and he managed to solve many of these very serious issues. We rapidly became a massive force throughout the nation by the time of the D-Day landings.[156]

Another viewpoint regarding the reliability of the *Resistance* comes from Colonel Aaron Bank, the "Father of U.S. Special Forces:"

> ...de Gaulle insisted that every OSS team entering France consist of at least one French officer being attached to it...The guerrillas had their own leaders. If we had tried to take over their operation we would have been lucky to get out

alive. Our job was to help them plan and keep them supplied. But they knew we were there to help them, so they usually did as we advised. And make no mistake about it, they were very courageous. You didn't have to kick them in the ass to make them fight.[157]

The *Maquis* drew the lion's share of recruits due to their aggressive nature and direct confrontation methods bordering on fanaticism, as revenge was the primary motivation for many of the men and women who joined. In fact, the large numbers of women joining the resistance movements is perhaps the greatest single factor contributing to the collective success of the insurgents across the continent. As stated by Simon Wiesenthal:

> Women active in the underground were the bravest of the brave, ignoring every danger to reach their aim or to die in dignity. They knew well that the odds were against them, but they felt as much as the men the responsibility to resist the oppressors and to leave a message to those who came after them; life is worth living only when lived in freedom, and this freedom is worth dying for.[158]

It could be argued that the efforts of the *Maquis* were as counter-productive as they were violent. In the town of Lomont the recruiting had been so successful the leader of the regional *Maquis* group, one "Paul" stated on 23 August 1944 that the group was too large and could sustain no further volunteers.[159] They were to become the most active group, especially in the larger cities and in direct confrontation and street fighting, especially during the Allied drive towards Paris. However, the motivation was not simply for the liberation of France and the capitol from German occupation; it was a race against time and a political power play, as Deshayes and others feared. The lack of effective coordination was primarily because new resistance organizations sprang to life without the knowledge of other more established groups, and this occurred with greater frequency as the war continued.[160] Lynsey E.K. Kirk's recitation in the dissertation supports this position of disunity through ignorance and lack of wide spread interest:

> During the approximately four year period of the occupation of France by the German *Nazis*, neither active nor moral support for the French *Resistance* were uniform. Between 1940 and 1944, both public admiration and active support for the *Resistance* increased.[161]

Much of this ineffectiveness was due to the inability for individual groups to effectively communicate.[162] Combined with the reprisals by the Germans en masse against the population, whether they were active in the *Resistance* or not broke up the cells almost as rapidly as they were formed. These divisions were even more prominent in the southern region of Vichy (the most active region for overt resistance and sabotage), where the *Maquisard* was not united into a common cause even in the most liberal sense until May 1943 during the *Conseil National de la Resistance*.[163] In analyzing the facts and reviewing the thesis statement presented by Lynsey E.K. Kirk, it must be stated that the *Resistance* was not the active, ever present nationalist and patriotic movement as claimed in the post-war mythology and representative historiography, although the lethality of the insurrection gained momentum after 1943, and proved to be of great importance to the Allied war effort, as stated by Aaron Bank:

> I first went into France in 1943, and by the end of the year my three man team had created an additional hundred or so three man cells. By the next year there were about 2,400 partisans recruited, trained and supplied by us. It created a great logistical and tactical problem for the Germans, and the delays of German units reaching the front alone was worth the effort. I completely supported the expanding of OSS, but we did have some problems with the British, who had their own political agenda. This is not to say that the SOE did not perform well. They were highly motivated and effective. It was the British government that we learned later that kept screwing things up, that was why we had to be separate from them in order to be as effective as we were.[164]

In fact, most of the notable actions of the *Maquisard* only occurred *after* three factors became apparent. First was the "Rationing Act of 1940" and then the "Forced Labor Act" (*Service du travail obligatoire*) of 1942,[165] both of which increased resentment and escalated passive resistance, including the 13 July 1942 German proclamation that "terrorists" and civilians would suffer reprisals following the killing of eighteen Germans.[166]

This revenge included women being sent to forced labor camps, children being separated from their parents and being placed in specifically oriented schools for political indoctrination, as well as the random shooting of innocent civilians. It was these measures where the Germans took the well-established step of random retaliatory murder, so common in the east although yet not so well established in the Western *Reich* until 1944.[167] It was perhaps the Deladier Decree of 26 September 1943 authorizing the arrest and imprisonment of "suspected" Communists (a broad term at best), most of whom would also perish that would propel thousands of new recruits into the *Maquisard* alone.[168] That was until the following incident.[169]

With regard to the retaliatory actions taken by the Germans, one of the most well known and controversial actions took place in June 1944, when the full fury of the *2ⁿᵈ Waffen SS Panzer* Division *"Das Reich"* was brought down upon the small town of Oradour-sur-Glane. The *Resistance* had captured and executed a battalion commander and a sniper had killed a company commander in Oradour-sur-Vayres.[170] *Sturmbannfuehrer* Otto Dickmann led his 120-man company into the wrong town, then continued on to the town of Tulle where 642 villagers were killed by shooting or burning in a building, of which 207 were children.[171] The only survivor was Madame Marguerite Roufflance, who would later tell the story.[172]

This activity sent shock waves throughout the Allied commands when the news broke. Even Himmler was appalled that such a thing had taken place in the west in full view of the population, especially with thousands of French *Freiwilligen* within the ranks of the *SS* and Army, and with over a hundred Frenchmen serving in *"Das Reich"* alone.[173] These were rather isolated events in the west, unlike in the east and were somewhat restrained. However, this act was to have grave repercussions for the Germans in the months to come, since the report of the incidents were burned into the collective conscience of the French people. However, it would be two even more important factors that would encourage and motivate the French into a more active mode of anti-German activity. First, the looming Allied invasion of the continent, which would mean being bailed out by the Americans and British twice in the same century, impugning French pride. The second factor was the *Service du Travail Obligatoire* (STO) of 16 February, 1943 that saw the upsurge of "active" partisan activity, first advertised in late 1943 as a possibility, and not before.[174]

Two reasons may be blamed for the lack of an organized and cohesive resistance: regional operations with independent agendas and leaders unwilling to work with other groups; lack of weapons and technical support until late 1942 (when Hitler ordered the full occupation of France on 10 November 1942 after meeting with Pierre Laval) to early 1943 by Allied Special Operations forces, and the increasing pressure placed upon the population by the German government for food, labor, and the forced deportation of Jews.[175] Laval later authorized the "La Releve," which allowed one French POW to be released for labor for every three skilled French civilian workers.[176] This labor provision later proved inadequate, so Laval instituted the "Compulsory Labor Service," which forced all French males of working age to support the German war effort. This latest error in judgment was to prove critical in the swelling of the ranks of the *Resistance*.[177] Although the latter was the least important factor, it did at least convince many "fence-sitters" that a side must be chosen. This became a point of contention between the left-wing and right-wing factions, with each political group wishing a different post-war future for their nation, with neither faction offering much in the way of opportunity to an already suffering and rapidly disappearing Jewish minority, which began to suffer from the 3 October 1940 "Statute of the Jews."[178]

Much of this discord was due to the opposing nationalist (supporting the Free French led by de Gaulle) and Communist *Resistance* factions (dominating the ranks of the *Parti Communiste Francais* and *Front National*) rarely working together due to mutual mistrust, multi-faceted political connections, confused ideologies and often betraying each other in the process of trying to usurp one another in meaningless power plays. The one common bond that periodically united the units in the south were the appointed Vichy representatives; German supporters who became the prime targets of *Resistance* hatred. Such is the case of former French Admiral Joseph Darnand[179] (nicknamed *"der Sturmbannfuehrer"* for his ruthless efficiency) and the French Police, the *Malice* who supported the *Gestapo* in their arrest, torture, deportation and execution of their own countrymen.[180] Darnand's rationale for rooting out the *Maquis* and other "undesirables" stemmed from the statement he made on 24 June 1942: "I hope for a German victory...because without one, Bolshevism will arise everywhere."[181] These activities would find many Frenchmen who had previously supported Vichy, maintaining their faith in Petain turn away and join the *Resistance*, although the passive support would far outweigh the active participation.[182] The extreme Right blamed the liberal Third Republic for the French military failure during *Case Yellow*.[183] As related by Lynsey E.K. Kirk;

> They saw more security for the bourgeoisie in supporting Vichy, since they feared a popular insurrection of the people if the *Resistance* was left to decide the fate of the country. The collaborative policies they used, amongst others, to repress the *Resistance* were done to preserve their own status and to prevent a Bolshevik-style revolution in this volatile era.[184]

In conjunction with the collaborationist government in Vichy under Marshal Henri Petain and his assistant, Premier Minister Pierre Laval, German control over the resistance situation would find greater success than in the east.[185] The political significance of the growing resistance movements that remained unclear in the north were quite distinct and separate further south, and their representative leadership was as eclectic as their political ideology. As previously mentioned, "Combat" (located in the south) was led by Henri Frenay,[186] while Emmanuel d' Astier de la Vigeri commanded "Liberation;" (also southern) while other units, such as "Franc-Tireur," (southern) "Liberer et Federer," and "Tremoinage Chretien" functioned independently.[187] The great collective mixture of participants included groups that went through a succession of leaders.

These various politically active groups included conservative right-wing Catholics, left-wing Catholics, socialists, Communists, trade unionists, leftist intellectuals, former army officers, white collar professionals such as doctors, lawyers, architects and engineers, university professors, Christian democrats, and many others finding their niche in partisan society. Much of this partisan leadership was leftist in orientation, and this has to do with the fact that the right-wing Vichy were hated perhaps even more than the Germans, and were therefore an unwitting catalyst for cohesive and collective activity by several factions.

In addition, due to the small numbers of German garrison troops and the great expanse of the countryside, covert and direct sabotage missions were much easier to plan and execute in the south.[188] What is ironic is that de Gaulle and his Free French were right-wing democrats opposed to the concept of replacing a German occupation with a Communist government, despite the fact that the Communists openly declared their patriotism and desire for national integration in June 1941.[189] However, despite this reality the very mechanism designed to unite the *Resistance*, the radio broadcast by de Gaulle personally on 23 October 1941 perhaps created more confusion and dissolution than those problems already existing. The BBC broadcast stated: "...the war of the French people must be led by their leaders, in other words by myself and the National Committee. All those fighting, whether in France or abroad, must follow orders to the letter."[190]

This statement led to a conflict of interest: should the local *Maquis* leaders currently remain inactive while awaiting orders, regardless of their opportunities to strike, or should they continue on their own and supplement their existing missions with new orders as they arrive from self-appointed leaders? Another conflict that helped render the *Maquisard* ineffective early in the struggle was the aforementioned political distrust and sporadic in fighting among regional leaders. In fact, Henri Frenay was not supportive of de Gaulle and believed that de Gaulle was too far removed from the realities on the ground to issue proper orders for *Resistance* action.[191] De Gaulle's self appointed leadership of Free French forces was the ultimate in arrogance, and many believed that de Gaulle would not be grateful to the sacrifices of the *Resistance* once the war was over. Even Stalin stated that;

> The trouble with de Gaulle was that this (his) movement had no communication with physical France, which should be punished for its attitude during this war. De Gaulle acts as though he were the head of a great state, whereas, in fact, it actually commands little power.[192]

This turned out to be the case in the eyes of the survivors.[193] As stated by Lynsey Kirk; "...a favorite argument of 'Combat' was that there would have been a *Resistance*, whether there had been a de Gaulle or not."[194] Some of the *Resistance* fighters felt that de Gaulle had betrayed them by fleeing with this mistress to France (his wife would arrive in Britain later) leaving them "holding the bag." As also stated by Kirk, "de Gaulle was in fact considered a deserter and convicted as such by military authorities." This branding as well as his strict autocratic method of dictating policy increased the suspicions of many within the *Resistance*.

The Communists were especially wary since they believed that de Gaulle might have been a pawn of the western capitalists working against the interests of Communism once the war ended.[195] This factor was perhaps the greatest catalyst for increasing Communist guerrilla activity, since the winners are in a more legitimate position to dictate post-war policy. As Deshayes explained:

> It is true that there were many that feared the possibility that Communists would become strong in the partisan role, and in that way they would become a post-war problem, which would lead to civil war. I must admit that I was also concerned, yet we could not lose sight of the business at hand...defeating the Germans, or at least weakening their position; lowering morale, and spreading their forces thin. The entire situation was precarious for a while; we had to prepare for the coming Allied invasion and the prospect of an all out battle with the Germans kept me awake at night. I knew that the civilian casualties would be great, and that what we had created in four years could be destroyed in as many weeks.[196]

However, there were others who understood the need to maintain an expatriate government on friendly territory capable of coordinating with the Allies for a future liberation of France. Most of these forces were also suspicious of de Gaulle's post-war plans for their country, and they could not understand how anyone so far away could issue orders based upon limited intelligence gathering and little effective contact with the insurgents on the ground. The BBC radio broadcasts were as much a morale boost as an information pipeline to the *Resistance* in particular and the population in general. This was especially true as the war progressed, denoting Allied victories of 1943 from Stalingrad,[197] North Africa, Sicily,[198] the fighting in Italy, the great battle of Kursk,[199] and the eventual announcements of the Allied invasions of France (both in Normandy and in the south) and the airborne invasion of Holland in September 1944.

De Gaulle did manage to effectively maintain French spirits during his tenure in London, and he was also rather effective in uniting French nationalist emotions and gaining British and American military support, as well as obtaining respect and recognition for the *Resistance* by 1942, which was when he was finally accepted as the "Leader" (or Commander-in-Chief) of the French *Resistance*. In Britai, he was already accepted as the legitimate spokesman and leader of Free French forces worldwide. De Gaulle's greatest problem was gaining the support of all *Resistance* groups regardless of politics in order to effectively lay the groundwork for an organized, cohesive resistance to support the planned Allied landings. De Gaulle eventually found a man through whom he could effectively consolidate both his wishes and the fragmented *Resistance* forces into a more effective unit, after he had been chosen over General Giraud on 15 May 1943 as the *Resistance* figurehead.

The man chosen by de Gaulle who would write the most colorful and tragic history of the *Resistance* was Jean Moulin.[200] By April 1943 the northern and southern *Maquis* factions were fairly cohesive, operating and communicating for greater (if not perfect) effectiveness, with most of the "ideological problems placed on the back shelf for the time being."[201] By 27 May 1943, during the first meeting of the *Conseil National de la Resistance* (CNR) in Paris, Moulin was a known man and wanted by the *Gestapo*. On 21 June 1943 he was arrested by Klaus Barbie, tortured beyond description and died from his wounds without revealing anything.[202] Moulin had arrived in France with $2,000,000 and a weapons shipment schedule courtesy of SOE to fund and organize the *Resistance*.[203] It would take a year to see the fruits of his labor, creating the *Mouvements Unis de la Resistance* (MUR) that brought the majority Communist *Maquis* into the collective.[204] This was not as difficult as first assessed, since all of the French *Resistance* organizations were unified in their desire to have their nation under French control, and an eventual (if brief) occupation of Allied forces.[205]

However, given de Gaulle's inflated post-war importance in French history texts and the plethora of post-war foreign literature (especially following his appointment as President), de Gaulle should be placed in the proper context. De Gaulle was a politician who, despite his great hero status never fired a shot in anger, commanded troops in the field or shared any of the risks, yet he galvanized his nation by his ability to use propaganda and national pride to suit his own ends and the needs of his nation. Giving de Gaulle his due, he was instrumental in organizing the Free French forces who, despite their meager numbers of 30,000 by the end of 1940 supported the Allies in every theater of operations on land, sea and in the air.[206] De Gaulle was also responsible for creating a leadership structure by late 1942 that established a clear chain of command for the resistance, with an easily recognizable figurehead beyond German reach (with himself and his hand-picked right-wing supporters as the elite leadership), although this information was top secret and known only to a few dozen of the *Resistance* members according to one of these high ranking leaders, Pierre Deshayes.[207] This single factor in conjunction with covert Allied support created a more effective organization by mid-1943, finally becoming a serious threat in the south by 1944.

This distinct political divide between the two French camps was tested in the fact that the Vichy government maintained the French Fleet in West Africa, which had been destroyed by the Royal Navy to prevent their falling into German hands for use against the convoys operating in the Atlantic. This naval operation, which took the lives of Frenchmen and sent the pride of the French Navy to the bottom of its Algerian anchorage angered both Vichy and nationalists alike. The situation between the factions was not only tenuous from a French viewpoint, further aiding the Germans in their occupation, but also divided the Allies due to the mistrust of the resistance movement in general.

This unorthodox application of French nationalism combined with collaboration was also witnessed by the "blind eye" of the Vichy officials in various southern regional districts for the first couple of years, who in some cases were even passively assisting the *Maquis*, or at the very least passively supportive. This was demonstrated during the 2 April

1943 funeral of a *Resistance* member, Paul Koepfler, when the entire town of Poligny joined the funeral procession in defiance of the standing ban. The fact that there was no great patriotic commitment to the *Resistance* must also be placed into proper perspective. According to Henri Frenay, a leader of the French *Resistance* operating in the south; "...for ninety percent of the French population, this war is not their war...what really matters to them is food, clothing and shelter."[208] This was seconded by the comments of a Clermont-Ferrand police officer in May 1941; "One can say without fear, that the chief preoccupation of the public, and this will have vital importance, is the question of food supply."[209] Conversely, Francoise de Menthen, another *Resistance* member stated: "We refused to admit defeat. We refuse even more emphatically to help Germany conquer us permanently. We can contribute to Germany's defeat, and for the French people there is no more imperious duty."[210]

The greatest problem facing the Germans throughout the war (in which the French were actually the best of all the partisan groups in Europe in this regard) was the assistance offered to downed Allied airmen. The *Resistance* was responsible for the safe return of thousands of potential prisoners of war, of which several have been interviewed for this project (see *Interview and Assistance* list). Between the efforts of the Dutch, Belgian and French underground movements over 7,000 airmen were saved from capture in a chain that stretched from the North Sea to the Pyrenees into Spain. One such airman was Brigadier General (then Captain) Charles E. "Chuck" Yeager, who was rescued by the *Maquis* after his P-51D *Mustang* was shot out from under him on a bomber escort mission. Their effectiveness is clearly stated by Yeager:

> When I was shot down the *Resistance* fighters used every method, including taking extraordinary risks to themselves to insure that I was passed safely over to the Spanish partisans across the Pyrenees. I was very impressed by their network and the secrecy with which they operated.[211]

Another point of view comes from a French partisan named Paul Bodot who spent his time destroying trains and rails, harassing German troops and whose family was successful in aiding Allied airmen. One was an Australian named "Barney" in February 1944, and another was an American named "Pierce" on 28 August of the same year.[212] This commitment to salvaging Allied aircrews was a prime avenue to ensure financial and materiel support from Britain and the United States. The saving of Allied airmen was one method of passive resistance to German authority that allowed these men to continue their war against Germany, as well as providing positive propaganda for the *Resistance* movement abroad.

One of the most successful and active groups was known as "Noah's Ark" by the Germans, since they were aware that the partisans in the group used animal names as their *nomme de guerre*. The leader, a remarkable woman and mother of two named Marie-Madeline Fourcade[213] managed an organization with 3,000 operatives covering all of France. Gathering intelligence and aiding Allied airmen, this was the most successful group and the only major French *Resistance* unit to be led by a woman.[214] The unit spied on the Germans and reported U-boat and *Luftwaffe* movements, as well as the establishment of the V-1 rocket launch sites on the Channel coast, including the first accurate reports of the V-2 ballistic missiles by one of her people, Jeanne Rousseau.[215] These reports were crucial in the *Operation Crossbow* missions to destroy these sites before Hitler could effectively bomb Britain and interdict the coming Allied invasion. These were some of the most important missions undertaken by the underground.

However, the events in the village of Remy on 2 August 1944 following the Allied invasion illustrated just how far some Frenchmen would go to show their support for the liberators of their country. On that day, twenty-two year old Lieutenant Houston L. Braly, Jr. was flying a ground support mission and was killed when his P-51 *Mustang* was damaged in the blast of the train his flight had just strafed. The villagers buried the young pilot with full honors, despite warnings from the German commander who warned that hostages would be taken if such a burial occurred.[216] Many people who never served in the resistance risked their lives to be present at the ceremony.

It was due to this one sole effective method of operation that the German government was forced through its local *Geheimstaatspolizei*[217] *(Gestapo)* offices to issue the decree of 8 June 1942 against the harboring of Allied personnel.[218] Any European civilian could (and often did) face death following the original decree of 7 December 1941[219] if caught protecting an Allied soldier or airmen (as well as Jews), yet many bravely defied this order, as discussed in the various interviews with partisan members and airmen alike. This decree also covered the harboring of Allied agents, some of whom were known to the Germans.

One such operative was United States Marine Colonel Pierre Julien "Peter" Ortiz, a former French Foreign Legionnaire of Russian and Spanish-French parentage.[220] Ortiz had ample combat experience against the Berbers and Taureg tribesmen in North Africa and in France against the Germans, and his command in varying degrees of French, Spanish, Arabic and even German brought him to the attention of the OSS. His operations code-named *Union*[221] and *Union II*[222] working with the *Maquis* placed him at the top of the *Gestapo* wanted list. One reason the Germans took a great interest in him was a visit he paid to a German occupied town's local tavern. Wearing a long trench coat and carrying a .45 caliber Colt automatic pistol he forced the officers who were seated discussing the "*Maquis* and the troublesome American" to drink a toast to Roosevelt, while opening his coat to display his Marine uniform, then he rapidly disappeared out the door. The morale boost for the local population speaks for itself.[223] Besides organizing resistance, supplying thousands of weapons and money, Ortiz kept hope alive, and his reports secured and continued Allied support for the *Maquis*, who were the most effective of the units, although still highly fragmented. However, on 14 August 1944 during a parachute drop Ortiz and his team was captured by an anti-partisan detachment commanded by a *Major* Kolb. They would spend the rest of the war as prisoners until liberated on 28 April 1945 at Marlag/Milag by the 1st Scottish Armored Division.[224]

This is without question the greatest legacy of the *Maquisard*, where effective coordination of operations was nearly impossible due to the risk of betrayal by their fellow countrymen, internal political differences, as well as the presence of well placed German agents fluent in French and various dialects, and quite savvy in the local customs in the regions to which they were assigned.[225] In fact, the first collective meeting of the *Maquis* leadership in Lyon occurred right under the noses of the local *Gestapo* in January 1944. The ultimate result was an agreement for collaboration, a decision that would increase the effectiveness of the *Resistance*. The new organization would work under the direction of General Koenig, and the forces of *Forces Francaises de L' Interieur* and *L' Armee Secrete* under General Delestraint would find their ranks swelling exponentially.[226] This would lead to even greater Allied support with both arms and advisors in support of the forthcoming *Operation Overlord*. The *Resistance* finally came to life during the D-Day invasion, and by August the resistance activity brought the expected German response, with over 40,000 people arrested and 1,000 killed in action.[227]

In analyzing the definition between partisan and guerrilla, it becomes unclear in total with regard to the *Maquisard*. It becomes simple when we distinguish between those individuals and groups that were motivated politically, thereby illustrating a partisan movement against an enemy insurgent force; e.g. Germany. However, when one looks at the partisans who actively engaged their own countrymen under Vichy dominion, from which orders for suppression, arrest, and deportation were issued against the *Resistance*, these irregulars would no doubt qualify as "guerrillas" since they were fighting an insurgency type of conflict against an "illegitimate" form of government they intend to overthrow, preferably with outside international support.

The *Resistance* members in total should be honestly remembered for such noble and critically acclaimed activities, as opposed to the plethora of post war propaganda that spawned the apocryphal legends that survive to this day. The sacrifices made by the brave men and women is illustrated in the following passage by sixteen year old Henri Fertet:

> I am going to die today for my country; I want a free France and a happy France…the soldiers are coming to get me…Judging by writing you may think my hand is trembling, but it is not. I am just using a short pencil. I am not afraid of death; I have an extremely clear conscience…but it is hard to die…A thousand kisses. Long live France.[228]

In evaluating the German methods at handling dissent, two major events were to define the ruthless suppression tactics employed by the Germans against resistance factions, as well as illustrate the vulnerability of the civilian population. Situations such as the Plateau of Glieres (also referred to as Haute-Savoie) were to redefine the previously successful passive counterinsurgency methods employed by Germany in the west. German military efforts to track down and combat partisans in the west were usually limited to passive detection, infiltration of partisan groups by informers or covert operatives, and the occasional raid against detected safe houses. Very few events would reach large scale combat proportions.

One major battle between partisans and German forces in the west would stand alone in the annals of the *Resistance* in particular, and perhaps more than any other event would assist in creating the great *Resistance* mythology; the battle of the Plateau of Glieres in March 1944.[229] The German antipathy was due to the effectiveness of the local *Maquis* in performing raids against the local German and Vichy garrisons in stealing food, weapons, fuel, and the recruitment of new partisans. This unit was politically motivated and adhered to de Gaulle's pre-war doctrine of hit and run warfare in support of large-scale military operations, and they were quite successful given their limited means:

But surprise must be organized. Not only by means of secrecy, observed in conversation, orders and reports by those who prepare plans and make decisions, and by the concealment of preparations, but also under cover of a thick veil of make-believe. In our age, when a thousand mischief-makers are mixed up in our affairs, when honor is less persuasive than money, when the press is ever on the hunt for information, when no enterprise can be carried on without telephones, wireless and typewriters, when all figures have to be deciphered, it is almost impossible to prevent information reaching the enemy. But, nonetheless, one may confuse him. If one is willing to hoodwink one's own camp deliberately, to mislead the very people one intends to employ, or by clever artifice to use all the means which are now available to each side for discovering what the other is doing, in order to spread misleading rumors, one can really hide behind falsehood.[230]

This particular partisan cell, known as the *Glieres Resistance Battalion* was commanded by Lieutenant Theodore Morel, a military officer who had planned spectacular raids against hotels for clothing and food, lodges for ski equipment and cold weather supplies his partisans required, since inclement weather had prevented air supply drops from SOE as well as the planned supply drops organized by Pierre Deshayes through Spain and across the Pyrenees from his office in Lisbon.[231] Other assistance came from the local Catholic Church, which had offered great support to *Resistance* groups throughout the country. The Abbey Jean Truffy, head of the local Catholic Church had actively assisted Morel's unit in the village of Petit Bornand.

Truffy was a remarkable man who had managed to aid the *Resistance* without arousing immediate suspicion among the Vichy or the Germans. Jean Truffy was also something of a diplomat and lawyer, successfully pleading the cases of several arrested *Resistance* members and suspected partisans who were destined for the gallows. Truffy had followed his conscience, assisting all who were in danger including Jews, while actively collecting information and gathering valuable intelligence for the partisans at great personal risk. Unfortunately, Truffy's network was unable to detect and therefore warn the partisans of the new enemy developments in time to avert disaster, and the priest was under suspicion by the time the German units had entered the region.

Although Morel was killed on the raid at the German depot at Entremont on 11 March 1944 his leadership style and established chain of chain of command allowed his force to remain formidable. The German High Command was desperate to make a statement and the end for the unit finally came on Sunday, 26 March 1944. The unit numbered 465 fighters when they were trapped on the Plateau by a battle hardened *Gebirgsjaeger* unit; the *157th Alpen* Division supported by 12,000 Vichy police and infantry. The Mountain Division had been deployed fresh from two years of fighting partisans and Red Army forces in the Caucasus, making it one of the most experienced and proficient of the anti-partisan groups.[232]

Upon deployment the Germans found the *Maquisard* had chosen a location that gave them position in terrain with complete command and control over all avenues of approach and with complete visibility to the valley below. The high, rocky, snow covered plateau cliffs projected over four hundred feet on one side and over a thousand feet above the valley on the other, with limited access to the high ground. It was from this vantage point that the partisans had launched their assaults. The Germans focused their attention upon the surrounded group, as related by Pierre Deshayes:

> It was quite difficult to logistically support all of the *Maquisard* units, so since I was in operational control for logistics and intelligence I had to make some very hard decisions. The supply flights to this particular unit was without question of the utmost importance. The Germans had managed to locate the unit, which was doing a fine job of interdicting Vichy round-ups of Jews, and their destruction of trains and rails actually saved thousands of Jews from being sent to the extermination camps over the previous year by Klaus Barbie, who was well known to us. Their efforts also provided a network for the Southern *Resistance* Command, which would later provide critical support for *Operation Dragoon,* the invasion of southern France by the Americans a few months later.[233]

The *Resistance* fighters had been forced into a retreat and this was where they made their final stand, all the while being re-supplied by the RAF with approximately 670 parachute canisters with 200,000 pounds of weapons, grenades, medical supplies, food, and ammunition. The Germans immediately took up offensive positions while the *Luftwaffe* bombed the plateau with He-111 medium bombers in a combined arms attack, softening up the partisans as the elite mountain infantry moved in. Despite making good gains under the cover of aerial bombardment, the greatest German concern was the continuous Allied airdrops that prolonged the action. The order was given for a rapid and ruthless suppression mission, and this was accomplished with virtually every partisan perishing.

The valiant defense by the *Maquisard* at the Plateau of Glieres was one of only a few such engagements, although it did constitute the largest response from the occupation forces on the Western Front. It can be safely established that this engagement more than any other in France created the accepted mythology of the cohesive, effective and ever active French *Resistance* movement, which was never completely cohesive or militarily effective due to the previously mentioned facts, such as political mistrust and regional rivalries. These facts were the primary reasons why the Germans were basically effective in suppressing the French partisans with minimal effort, as well as the reservations held by Allied leaders and operatives regarding close working and support of the *Resistance*, as stated by Aaron Bank. Bank felt that the OSS would have been more effective in their insurgency and sabotage roles without the collaboration of the local militias.[234]

Given the eventual rise of the French general population following the assistance offered by SOE/OSS and the two successful Allied invasions, *Overlord* and *Dragoon*, *Generalfeldmarschall* Gerd von Rundstedt was prompted to state that:

> From January 1944, the state of affairs in Southern France became so dangerous that all commanders reported a general revolt…Cases became numerous where whole formations of troops, and escorting troops of the military commanders were surrounded by bands for many days and, in isolated locations, simply killed off…The life of the German troops in southern France was seriously menaced and became a doubtful proposition.[235]

Norway, Holland, Belgium and Denmark

The Norwegian resistance was not as effective against the Germans directly, given the method of German troop dispositions and the lack of a widespread occupation force on the scale seen throughout the rest of Europe, although seventeen divisions were entrenched in Norway as a security force to prevent any Allied invasion and to subdue the local resistance. However, the underground was effective in mapping German ground and air force locations for Allied intelligence, coast watching for enemy ship movements (such as the battleship *Tirpitz*) on the North Sea and Skagerrak, passing this information via the "Shetland Bus," and keeping the Allies informed as to the German heavy water projects.[236] Teachers refused to lecture on the revised history as ordered by the Quisling government, and 12,000 of the 14,000 teachers resigned in a mass protest.[237] Perhaps the greatest effort put forth by the underground was the safe exfiltration of over 2,000 Jews across the border to neighboring Sweden out of German reach. This was accomplished by hiding the civilians in trucks under potatoes, clothing, coal, etc.[238] Others were walked across in dangerous forced marches during the winter, while still others forged papers and crossed the border "legitimately."

The Dutch partisans were, however, despite the active *Nazi* movement within the country[239] apparently quite effective at intelligence gathering and in conducting raids to free their citizens in German (usually *Gestapo*) hands, despite the fact that their ranks had been almost completely penetrated by German agents, as seen in the Venlo debacle in November 1939. The "Venlo Spy Trap" mission saw two British Intelligence Officers, a Major Stevens and a Captain Best planning to rendezvous with a Dutch underground contact. The mission was to meet with several unknown yet apparently disaffected enemy generals who opposed Hitler and were requesting British assistance. The team was compromised immediately since the entire mission had been a German ruse.[240] The organizer of the entire debacle was *Brigadefuehrer* Walter Schellenberg, the creator of the *Einsatzgruppen* concept that was to deploy teams to function as an intelligence/counterintelligence operation. It would be the invasion of Russia and that would see the *Einsatzgruppen* begin to function as a death squad.

Dutch farmers and worker were conscripted for labor, therefore supplying the Germans with food and animals, the building of airfields, bunkers, fortresses and roads, as well as neglect to their farms, the economy began to collapse.[241] Families were going hungry, and the occupation forces did nothing to alleviate the problem.[242] The occupation force did flood much of the southern countryside in order to prevent Allied aircraft from landing in any invasion attempt, further destroying arable farmland and personal property, creating an economically based partisan uprising as opposed to a purely politically motivated guerrilla movement. When the farmers revolted the guns began firing to make a statement.[243] It is without a doubt these factors perhaps above all else that precipitated the Dutch underground movement, despite the vast numbers of German occupation forces, even with the siphoning off of units as the war expanded eastward in 1941.[244]

One fact that salvaged the Dutch Resistance from the fate of abject atrophy and a jaundiced review by the Allies was the ability of the Communist and nationalist partisan factions (primarily among the university students and intellectuals)[245] to work together against the common enemy, despite the effective control of the nation by the Chief Commissioner for the Netherlands, Arthur Seyss-Inquart.[246] This cooperative nature assured the Dutch of two important things: continued Allied support in the form of arms and agents to assist their operations (especially in preparation for the D-Day landings on June 6 1944 and *Operation Market-Garden* in September 1944) and increased financial aid following the war.[247] The Dutch partisans were more centralized with true military factions (such as the "Shock Troopers" led by Prince Bernard)[248] and therefore confined to a more isolated geographic region than any other collective partisan group fighting the Germans with the exception of the Norwegians. Yet, despite this geographic handicap they were able to perform miracles of sabotage and intelligence gathering, much of it due to the fact that most Dutch speak and understand German as well as English. The train strike in September 1944 in support of the forthcoming Allied invasion was so effective that the Germans sent in military and civilian railroad specialists to get the railways running, unaware that the strike was the prelude to an Allied airborne invasion, and despite the great assistance afforded the Germans en masse among the railroad workers in order to keep their jobs.[249]

The result was a complete paralysis of German rail traffic, halting unit reallocations and crippling the German response time once the Anglo-American forces began descending by parachute and glider. The effect was to also reduce the deportation of forced laborers and limit the deportation of Jews, and thousands of more lives were saved as a result.[250] It may be stated that the plight of the Jews as well as the privations experienced by the population in general spurred the resistance efforts, which seems to be a common thread throughout Europe. However, despite the valiant Dutch Resistance efforts, which resulted in little material damage to the German war effort (even during the entire course of the war) the Allied operation was crushed within ten days. This was primarily due to the twist of fate that placed the *II SS Panzer Korps*, comprising the *9ᵗʰ Waffen SS Panzer* Division *"Hohenstauffen"* and *10ᵗʰ Waffen SS Panzer* Division *"Freundsberg"* under the command of *Gruppenfuehrer* Wilhelm Bittrich in the region of Arnhem for a rest and refit after almost three solid years of heavy fighting in Russia. According to Stephanie Elizabeth Mills:

> It seems, therefore, that the Dutch effort should indeed be praised, for although criticized for fragmentation and being rather low on military successes, the contribution it made to the morale of the people, as well as the help provided for the 'hunted,' is immeasurable and should never be forgotten.[251]

The experiences of the Dutch partisans were quite similar to those of other freedom fighters throughout Europe, such as the experience of Hanneke Ippisch. Her interview conducted by Roberta Donovan for *World War II* is quite interesting, and her decision to join the resistance forces was personal, not economic or political in nature. Ippisch witnessed a group of German soldiers forcing a Jewish family into the back of a truck, and as she stated, "This made a terrible impression on me, so I decided to join the underground and fight the Germans."[252] Ippisch's sense of morality combined with deep patriotism guided her conscience, offering the incentive to risk her life as an irregular. Her tenure as a partisan would include demolition, sabotage, and a variety of other operations which began at age seventeen. Ippisch's greatest contribution was the assistance of moving and hiding Jews during the great roundups of 1942-43. Ippisch was just one of thousands who actively supported her nation's cause for freedom, and in January 1945 she nearly paid the ultimate price for her bravery:

I walked into the building and that was the end of that, because the Germans were there. They had been trying to find my boss for five years. I found out later that the reason we got caught was that one member was caught the day before and he talked. He couldn't handle it and you could not blame him for that. You never know how you might react under pressure or extreme torture. The Germans found five men and me. That was the last I saw of those men. They were in jail one week, and then they were all shot. They took me to jail and I didn't know if they were going to execute me or not. But I was sentenced to life imprisonment. Actually, that wasn't too bad because we knew that the war would soon be ending.[253]

Ippisch survived to see liberation and today she lives in the United States. The deep sense of nationalism and the instinctive desire to survive both economically and literally became the greatest catalysts for underground recruitment and support. Their activities forced the Germans to enact "terrorist laws," thereby labeling the resistance as a "criminal sect" while legitimizing the wholesale extortion and slaughter of millions. The definition between "partisan" and "guerrilla" is far more simple than separating the "terrorist" from the "freedom fighter," a situation that has only increased in momentum and confusion to the present day.

Denmark

The Danish resistance movement was perhaps the smallest and least known, although the most effective in protecting its Jews from German deportation. Part of the saving grace regarding the population was primarily due to the fact that Hitler considered the Danes one of the purist of the Aryan races, and he wanted to maintain a friendly *status quo*.[254] However, despite the small footnote afforded it in history the Danish resistance movement did exist, and was sparked by the same conditions as seen in France and Holland. The forced conscription of laborers and the confiscation of agricultural products were great catalysts, yet it was the Jewish question that sparked many into irregular action.

The forced transportation of the small number of Jews from Denmark created a fervor in the towns and cities. The Danes were perhaps the most tolerant and protective of their Jewish friends and neighbors and did not collectively or readily deliver their countrymen for the slaughter. The order for the reduction of Jews in Denmark originated not from Himmler or even Hitler, but from *Generaloberst* Alfred Jodl.[255] This fact is supported in a letter from Frau Luise Jodl to Professor Peter Hoffman outlining the difficulties her husband had with forcing compliance among the local authorities.[256]

Many Danes risked their lives spiriting Jews to Sweden by boat,[257] where hundreds made it safely through the very secretive network, establishing an organization that was never effectively penetrated by the Germans. Perhaps the greatest compliment paid to the Danish resistance came from British Field Marshal Bernard Law Montgomery[258] when he called them "second to none," due to the 50,000 known active resistance personnel out of a national population of just over 4,000,000.[259]

Belgium

The German occupation forces of Belgium and Northern France were commanded by *Generaloberst* Alexander Falkenhausen (1878-1966) from 1940-44, a rather humane man who ignored repeated *Gestapo* warnings regarding his lenient treatment of the populations under his governorship. Falkenhausen, a staunch anti-*Nazi* who was friendly with the retired Chief of Staff, Ludwig Beck perhaps knew better than most that the post-war repercussions would fall heavily upon Germany. Despite his humanity he would be tried and sentenced by a Belgian court to twelve years imprisonment in 1951.

The Belgian underground was virtually ineffective as an active subversive entity due to the lack of a cohesive paramilitary background and a divided society regarding politics and the leadership of King Christian, who to his credit remained with his people as opposed to other national leaders who left to establish governments in exile. However, despite the lack of an active subversive element, the Belgians were second only to the French for the collective effort of rescuing an estimated 3,000-4,000 Allied airmen from German internment.[260] Most of these men were able to return to England within months of being shot down, as demonstrated by the experience of Chuck Yeager.

The most successful escape line for airmen was "Comet," founded in 1942 by twenty-four year old Andree de Jongh. Andree (code named *Dedee*, also known as "Postman Across the Pyrenees"), her father (a school principal) and sister were captured, with the father being executed and her sister surviving eighteen months in Mauthausen and Ravensbrueck concentration camps.[261] Andree was interned in Ravensbrueck, and both sisters would survive the war. "Comet" was so effectively organized that it ran without the de Jongh's, and in three years successfully saved over 800 airmen from capture and was taken over by Belgian Baron Jean de Blommaert following the Jongh family's capture. Blommaert increased the size of the network, extending it all the way through Paris, connecting with the French *Resistance*.[262] In Belgium, as in France, women made up a large percentage of the underground system. Working as guides, tailors and spies, they were quite effective in assisting the Allied airmen, freeing up the men for the more dangerous role of saboteur. The women in the west were usually more involved and successful at the command level within resistance groups. This reality was possible due to the German concept that women were less likely to become involved in subversion, following the orders of men if at all and usually remaining inactive politically. This stereotyping was perhaps the greatest asset affording women the success they enjoyed. Such would not be the case in the east.

4

Partisans of the East:
Eastern Europe, Poland, & the Balkans

*To be attacked by an enemy is not a bad thing, but
a good thing.*
- Mao Tse Tung
26 May 1938

When Germany invaded Poland and later the Soviet Union German forces encountered a threat far beyond their conventional military capabilities. The Polish resistance was nominal and never completely efficient, primarily due to the Soviets and Germans partitioning the country in 1939 and fragmenting the population. The other factors were the immediate collection, isolation and eventual deportation of millions of "undesirables," thus weakening the social infrastructure necessary to create a legitimate and viable underground network. Those persons who did manage to form a resistance cell could not rely upon the Red Army, who viewed their activities contrary to good order, nor could they rely upon the White Russians who hated the Communists. As stated by Vera Laska: "Our White Russian neighbors were no more merciful than the German guards."[263] These underground fighters were completely on their own.

The eventual avalanche of insurgency wreaked havoc upon the occupation as well as the front line forces on their advance across the steppes and mountains of the east. Each of the geographic locations are evaluated and include interviews with participants, the German operational plan, as well as the relevant regional political and economic backdrop that assisted in the rise of partisan/guerrilla activity.

Poland was not the first nation to be invaded by Germany, but it was the first nation to attempt a credible resistance with military force, albeit small, disorganized and easily swept away due to the combined invasions of both Germany and the Soviet Union. However, the Germans immediately saw the need for reconciling the most potent part of Polish society; the Catholic Church. Emphasizing the fact that Communism was the enemy of their faith, German commanders (with Berlin's blessing) such as Reinhardt Heydrich, his adjutant *Oberfuehrer* Heinz Jost (sacked by Heydrich on 22 June 1941 for lack of enthusiasm)[264] went to Krakow to settle the fears of the Archbishop *before* the invasion.[265] They even paid the Jesuit monastery a visit and were warmly received.[266] The German leadership may have not been experienced in counterinsurgency operations, but they were aware of the necessity for preventative maintenance.

Part of the Polish late-war and post-war disenchantment with the Communists stems not only from the failure of the Allies to assist in the Warsaw Uprisings of 19 April-16 May 1943 (Jewish)[267] and 1944(general),[268] but also in the fact that German and Soviet diplomats were deciding the fate of Poland without even consulting the Poles on the matter. This in and of itself was a violation of the Thirteenth of President Woodrow Wilson's Fourteen Points at the Versailles Conference and the following Paris Peace Treaties, which states:

> An independent Poland should be erected which should include the territories inhabited by indisputably Polish populations, which should be assured a free and secure access to the sea, and whose political and economic independence and territorial integrity should be guaranteed by international covenant.[269]

As stated by Fiona Mitchell, the treaties secured the rights of minorities, although they remained under the protection of their host nation states under Article 93, Part II, Section VIII of the Treaty of Peace (Versailles). This resolution was a recipe for disaster, given the multi-ethnic composition of Poland, hence the great interest of Hitler in bringing the over 1, 200,000 Germans within Poland under the *Reich* and into the *Volksgemeinschaft*.[270] Several points of contention would play a factor in the future partisan war: the Catholic Polish ideology contrasting with the Soviet atheistic program; the fact that the Soviets always maintained a constant feudal eye upon Poland from the Czarist era, culminating in their hatred after the Treaty of Riga in 1922;[271] Soviet influence over Lithuania preventing that nation from recognizing Polish claims to Vilna,[272] and the fact that the Soviets offered nothing in the way of assistance to a besieged Poland until their own fear of a rapid German advance forced their movement westward to protect their interests. Even the Soviet view that the elimination of Communists in Germany was purely a "domestic affair" and unimportant if Hitler was willing to negotiate with the Soviet Union to their mutual advantage."[273] This growing distrust also reached new heights when Stalin began the purges, mass murders, arrests and trials in 1936-38, thus eliminating any possible union of the European Communist Community (or *Comintern*).[274]

The Soviet military was also included in this project and the interview with former Red Army Colonel Anna Nikolina, who served as a political officer in an all male infantry unit at the capture of the *Reichstag* in Berlin in May 1945 was invaluable. Nikolina served in Poland in 1944, indoctrinating the irregulars as to the benefits and necessity of supporting the Communist cause, while supplying the partisans with weapons and assisting in operational activities in support of Red Army units. Nikolina would win immortal fame as her image was captured on newsreel film tying the Soviet flag atop the captured *Reichstag* on 1 May 1945.

The Poles were well aware that Stalin was no friend of Poland and yet they still hoped to have Western Allied assistance, even when the sword of fate was descending. Allied assistance to the Poles fell apart for the following reasons: the Western Allies had no geographical access to the Poles except by air and sea, and this was tenuous since it was not until January 1944 that American long range fighter escorts could accompany the four-engine bombers across the width of Europe. The Royal Navy was in no condition to challenge the German surface and U-boat assets in the Baltic Sea, and the strategic bombing doctrine of striking important German military and industrial targets was given priority over all else. The other reason was that Poland fell into the Soviet operational sphere, and it was expected that the Red Army would assist the Poles as they advanced crossed the Dnieper and Vistula Rivers, at least by air. This reliance proved to be a fatally flawed plan on two occasions.

The first clear failure was the inability of the Allies to assist the Jewish uprising in Warsaw in April 1943. The crisis erupted on 19 April 1943 and the Jewish partisans asked for, and were given the assurance of Red Army and Air Force assistance, as well as supply drops by Western Allied aircraft. It became quite clear that without this assistance the uprising was doomed to failure, and the German response was swift and brutal. A methodical and maniacal *SS* officer of the old school, *Brigadefuehrer* Juergen Stroop (who would later serve in Greece until being relieved and replaced by Walter Schimana)[275] commanded the counterinsurgency forces. [276]

Stroop was a hardened veteran of the Ukrainian anti-partisan campaign, perhaps the toughest theater of the war, winning the Knight's Cross for his efforts. As an on the job trained counterinsurgency specialist Stroop wasted no time in coordinating all of the conventional forces at his disposal, including armored units and combat veterans with the necessary attitude and disposition to get the job done. The result was predictable, yet despite the fact that 56,065 Jews were killed there was still hope in the minds of the few survivors that the Allied forces would do something. German losses were sixty killed and just over 1,000 wounded, seriously reducing the German myth of racial superiority against the "subhumans" in the ghetto.[277]

The second wake-up call for Poland occurred during the second Warsaw Uprising of August-September 1944, led by General Tadeusz Bor-Komorowski.[278] This time the Red Army had forward units within twenty-six miles of the city, complete with medium and heavy armored and air support. Stalin gave assurances to both the Poles and his allies that the Red Army would support the Poles in their fight. It seemed logical since Soviet forces were much closer than in 1943 and the German army was reeling from the rapid Soviet summer offensive. However, Stalin remained true to form and the Red Army would stand fast, allowing the Poles to draw even more German combat units from the front to deal with the problem. This plan served an additional purpose; Stalin did not intend to honor the agreements guaranteeing Poland free elections and autonomy. The more partisans the Germans killed the less he would have to deal with when the Soviet Union took over the country.

The Soviets maintained the same line of thinking during the second uprising, which was by all accounts a better-organized and executed rebellion against the Germans. Partisans outside the ghetto maintained a steady supply of food, weapons, ammunition, radios, medical supplies and, just as important, news on the progress of the advancing Soviet forces. The resistance fighters knew that the Red Army had managed to reach to within twenty-three miles of the city center, almost within range of General (later Marshal) Konstantin Rokossovsky's artillery fire.[279] However, according to Richard Overy regarding the Polish nationalists and their perceptions of the Soviets as potential liberators:

The Warsaw rising was instigated not to help out the Soviet advance but to forestall it. Polish nationalists did not want Warsaw liberated by the Red Army but wanted to do so themselves, as a symbol of the liberation struggle and the future independence of Poland.[280]

The Germans knew the situation as well and a flurry of orders emanated from Berlin. Himmler ordered Bach-Zelewski to "completely destroy the city," as stated by Karl Wolff:

> Once the Soviets were within striking distance of Warsaw, the order was given for the city to be leveled, including all inhabitants. Hitler had actually ordered this, and the office of Governor General Frank acknowledged receipt and understood. Himmler also ordered Kaminsky[281] to take his men in to join the operation, and the rest is history.[282]

The German plan during this second revolt was similar in nature, yet commanded by a different sort of officer, *SS Obergruppenfuehrer* Erich von dem Bach-Zelewski, a Prussian aristocrat who had no personal hatreds for the Jews, Poles or the Russians, yet was a dedicated soldier who had devoted his life to fascism, ever since he had seen first hand the result of the Communist uprisings during the 1919 rebellion. Zelewski was a combat veteran of both world wars and a highly efficient partisan hunter in Russia who understood his enemy, and even better understood the strain it placed upon the men under his command.[283] Zelewski had commanded an 11,000 strong force of *Einsatzgruppen* from July 1941, including 6,000 policemen.[284] Under Zelewski, those rounded up and killed were so collected and eliminated as "partisans", although most were simply civilians, including Jews, Gypsies and the handicapped. Villages were destroyed under orders and under Bach-Zelewski anti-partisan operations reached their early zenith:

> On a military level the operations were reasonably successful. More than two-thirds of the occupied area had no partisan activity of any significance, and in the more favorable topography of the north-west, dense forests and inhospitable swamp, thousands of partisans were rounded up and shot or publicly hanged, with placards placed around their necks, as an example to the rest.[285]

Bach-Zelewski opinions on the murder and violence against the civilians, especially his vocal opposition to the actions of the *Kaminsky Brigade*[286] (operating in Warsaw from 5-25 August 1944) and its leader belied the Iron Cross in both classes awarded to Bronislav Kaminsky by Himmler personally, and his acts of barbarity forced a change in policy by the *Oberkommando der Wehrmacht* following the successful conclusion of the suppression.[287] Bach-Zelewski was under tremendous strain at that time. His own moral conscience ate away at him, especially after the *29th Waffen Grenadier* Division *der SS "Russische Nr. 1"* and the *36th Waffen Grenadier* Division *der SS* under the sadistic and efficient *Standartenfuehrer* Oskar Dirlewanger joined the operation.[288] Dirlewanger's malcontents were even worse than Kaminsky's group, further increasing the problems of command and control as well as maintaining morale among the standard *Waffen SS* formations. These two abnormalities in uniform would carry the word atrocity to new heights.[289]

Reich Commissioner Hans Frank, the international lawyer and Governor General of Poland had issued the order that all ghettos were to be eliminated and their occupants sent to the camps for immediate extermination.[290] Bach-Zelewski was placed in the unenviable position of having to kill civilians, unlike the "open and shut case" of armed partisans in combat. Many of the victims were women and children, and the end result was Bach-Zelewski suffering a complete emotional nervous breakdown.

By the conclusion of the month long operation the casualties eclipsed the previous year's statistics: German losses totaled 26,000 killed or wounded, 15,378 partisans killed, and nearly 250,000 civilians of all ages and sexes killed. The ultimate irony is that the Soviets could have entered the city during this period and possibly assisted in ending the war months sooner by launching a drive on Berlin three months earlier than actually occurred. However, the Red Army did not enter Warsaw until 17 January 1945, although they were less than thirty miles away the entire time. The Poles had been given a display of what they could expect once their "liberators" arrived, and this factor would come to haunt American, British, German and Soviet governments alike.

Czechoslovakia

The British utilization of Free Czech troops was well underway as soon as the British condition was stabilized, as occurred with escaping nationals from most of the occupied nations with governments in exile. However, where to deploy Czech forces prior to the Allied invasion of the European continent remained a concern. For General Ingr, Commander in Chief of the Free Czech Military under the government in exile of President Dr. Eduard Benes in London.[291] Ingr suggested the bulk of the Czechs be sent to the Middle East Command, minus the 500 strong Parachute Battalion under the command of General Gak.[292] German attempts to recruit Czechs for the military were less successful in the Protectorate than in any other region of Europe, although conscription was commonplace by late 1943, as stated by Karl Wolff:

> Due to great losses on the Eastern Front we began to actively conscript Europeans to replace these losses. There had been many successes in the *Freiwilligen* operations, except in Czechoslovakia. This would later become a problem, as many Czechs deserted as soon as the opportunity arose, and naturally deserters were to be shot if captured. This reality was to only increase partisan activity against us, and increased the effectiveness of the Allied forces working with them. In hindsight, I can only say that we must have been completely blind as to the requirements regarding all European support operations.[293]

The exact desertion rate among the Czech conscripts from their German units is not known, although the Allied command received constant and regular reports regarding the defections, usually among the nationalists, as related by the example cipher telegram:

> Have news from Switzerland of presence of several hundred Czech deserters with partisan bands in Northern Italy. Also eleven battalions of Czech police troops in areas of Turin, Bologna and Lago Maggiore who are considered likely material

for subversion for either individual or mass desertions to partisans...Will be dropping Czech officers to partisans to control Czech deserters and persuade more to come over...[294]

SOE operations in Central Europe were considered critical to political as well as military success due to the large numbers of international military forces and their governments in exile. In planning for covert operations, the necessity to function successfully and effectively with paramilitary and irregular forces brought new challenges. One man who realized the necessities involved was General Ingr, who drafted a memorandum titled *Principles of Training for Special Purposes.*[295] Ingr outlined the recruiting and training requirements for the all-volunteer force.[296] Intelligence, self-reliance, psychological testing and preparation, as well as cultural and language education for non-Czech operatives was deemed essential for proper assimilation and effective command and control. Ingr also drafted the basis of training and the depth of the selection process. However, the non-Czech operatives were expected to simply function in an advisory capacity as opposed to expecting to take direct control over internal partisan operations. Ingr believed that it was necessary to establish a presence of reliability among the indigenous patriots, and chalking up a series of successful operations against the German occupation forces was at the top of the list.

The SOE trained, equipped, and deployed the Czech assassins of *Obergruppenfuehrer* Reinhard Heydrich, the ruthless and efficient Chief of the *Reich* Main Security Office (*RSHA* or *Reich Sicherheit Hauptamt*) and Bohemian administrator. Heydrich, who was the chief architect of the "Final Solution" at the January 1942 Wansee Conference offered the Free Czech government a major propaganda coup.[297] The mission also witnessed one of the most brutal reprisals ever exacted against the population of Prague in retaliation.[298] In order to operate an effective underground force, SOE would have to assimilate within the population while operating as saboteurs, intelligence gatherers, trainers, advisors, and political liaison specialists. The enormous list of critical responsibilities continued to grow, as the depth of the support operations became more apparent. In order to fill the ranks with qualified individuals Ingr submitted a list of requirements he personally considered non-negotiable. Ingr understood that the underground movement in Czechoslovakia, like every other nation in Europe was not a cohesive movement. Political conflicts between nationalists and Communists surfaced frequently, although these divisions were not to become as detrimental to the Allied effort as in Yugoslavia, Albania, Greece, or even France, where SOE and later OSS had an even stronger presence during the war. In order to ensure that the SOE and later OSS operatives fulfilled their obligations according to the wishes of the respective governments in general (Czechoslovakia in particular) the format was outlined.

Psychological testing was considered the first step, followed by loyalty checks on all prospective volunteers. Elimination of egos and delusions of heroism were critical, as was the necessary self-reliance deemed crucial for individual and team success. However, Ingr wanted men who were apolitical, yet conscious of their role in establishing good Allied relations with potential future political leaders and their agencies, the very same organizations involved in the fight they were supporting. In preparing the blueprint for SOE operations in Eastern and Central Europe, the rigorous physical and technical training need not be discussed in this thesis. However, it is important to understand the importance of the selection process, since training was an expensive and time-consuming affair where cutting corners was out of the question. According to Ingr, "They should be men of sufficiently outstanding character to become spiritual and professional leaders of local patriot groups."[299] Ingr did not want men who harbored grudges or personal vendettas, anything that may disrupt the harmony of the collective group.[300]

Ingr also wanted complete logistical support in order to assure that the partisans would believe that they were being included and funded as opposed to being used as expendable assets. As stated in a memorandum, "From our experience, it is an undeniable fact that in order to keep alive resistance, it is necessary to feed it."[301] Despite the best-laid plans of Ingr and SOE, Czech resistance was more of a hope than a reality. This fact was hammered home after a meeting between General Ingr and General Cory, when the desire to send Czech troops into action resulted in a Parachute Battalion numbering 500 men being recruited, trained, and destined for the Middle East.[302] The plans for detailing the special operations teams were also outlined, their deployment discussed, as well as the rising difficulty in disseminating between appropriate channels for field communications.

The creation of a Czech Armored Brigade was planned as a conventional force on 15 September 1943. The force, comprised of Free Czechs in Britain was to contain the following components: two armored regiments, one motorized infantry battalion, a sapper field squadron, one regiment (minus one battery) of field artillery, one battery of anti-tank artillery, a six gun compliment of light anti-aircraft artillery, five squadrons of signals, a medical unit, Provost, and a headquarters element.[303] Under the command of a General Miroslav the unit was never expected to become combat ready, with the quality of recruits questionable at best. Any possibility of tangibly supporting SOE operations with this politically motivated conventional force was also ruled out as less than feasible.[304]

As the Allies closed in on the Third *Reich* from both sides, intelligence gathering regarding German formations became much easier to obtain, and these operations became the most important activity conducted by SOE and OSS. These missions became even more problematic as the Soviets approached. The necessity to cooperate with the Red Army was evident, although the reality of such an event being successful began to diminish, especially since the Soviets were reluctant to work with underground forces that they did not control in every fashion.[305] The Allies also knew that as the Eastern Front moved westward they were liable to arouse the gravest suspicions in the minds of the Russians. However, active conventional operations were scaled back in Czechoslovakia due to the possibility of clashes with the Red Army, as indicated in the following:

> As no important military operations into Czechoslovakia are contemplated by 12 Army at this time, it is felt that rather than expending effort on small-scale sabotage, Czech resistance should give priority to the production of intelligence on enemy troop movements and dispositions in the areas covered by the resistance organizations concerned.[306]

Cracks in the partisan support network became evident in the memorandum dated 8 January 1945 that effectively reduced the capabilities of the already anemic partisan support in Czechoslovakia.[307] The inadequate numbers of supply flights and the minimal weapons and food shipments assisted in the disintegration of the indigenous insurgency, effectively assisting the Germans in their efforts to eliminate the resistance network.[308] By the time of this memorandum regarding intelligence gathering, dated 27 April 1945, the German *6th Panzer Armee* under Josef "Sepp" Dietrich had been virtually crushed, and ordered by Hitler personally to remove their prized cuff titles for their failure in halting the Soviet advance through Hungary and the Czech Protectorate. The bulk of German resistance had already collapsed with the survivors streaming west to avoid Soviet capture, surrendering to the U.S. 7th Army with Dietrich among them.[309] The raising, supplying, and control of the "Secret Army" in the Protectorate, as well as their reorganization and control soon became a "diplomatic" as opposed to a "military" concern, with President Benes attempting to control all aspects of "in country" operations, a condition well beyond his depth. Benes also decided to maintain the political balance within Czechoslovakia, as stated in the following:

> His aim had been to establish a Government of national unity embracing political opinions ranging from conservatism to Communism. He himself held no belief whatever for the Communist way of thinking, but he did feel that such Communist leaders, as there were in Czech public life, were better inside his Government than encouraged to make mischief by being excluded.[310]

This continued interference would plague special operations and hinder progress, especially regarding the projected "Czech Rising" so anticipated yet never fully culminated. Part of a Most Secret memorandum dated 2 January 1943 states:

> As you know, I have been dissatisfied, for some time, with Czech affairs, as I have doubted the seriousness of their intentions, and have been attacking General Ingr for the last six weeks....I think a strong line with Benes should get us what we want. I fear that the Czechs are very demoralized just at present. The general situation will, of course, help us with them.[311]

Despite the veneer of support offered by the superficial memoranda and letters, there is clear evidence that SOE thought the British Chiefs of Staff and the Foreign Office had little intention of massively supporting any future "Czech Rising" (this pertains also to the "Slovak Rising")[312] despite the overtures to Benes and the partisans themselves. This fact is supported by the following Top Secret outward telegram:

> Although we intend to maintain this support and even to increase it to a limited extent as weather permits, it will be confined to promoting sabotage and general resistance. We have neither the means nor the intention of supporting a general rising and the Czechoslovak government have been categorically informed of this.[313]

SOE operations would not be expanded to support the Czech resistance, and Dr. Benes was knowledgeable of this fact. However, this reality was not passed on to the resistance proper. The potential for a collapse in partisan morale was disastrous, and the distribution of this information was understandably restricted. SOE would thus become compromised on several occasions by the never-ending political struggles taking place both in London and

Czechoslovakia, strife that would assist the Germans (especially after their entry into Slovakia on 27 August 1944)[314] more than their occupation forces in limiting the role of insurrection. In order to minimize Benes' interference with the British Chiefs of Staff, thus limiting his influence over Czech SOE and OSS operations, SHAEF decided it prudent to take control of Special Operations, placing it under Eisenhower's direct command, thus eliminating Benes' ability to influence decision-making policy.[315] However, Benes' interference with SOE operations was the least of the Allied problems; the feeling within the country toward Benes himself became a matter of concern as well.[316]

The political problems within Czechoslovakia prompted SOE to take a careful position when supporting various resistance movements. An example is a Top Secret memorandum regarding information collected from a "Colonel Imro," commanding the 2nd Slovak Technical Division, following his defection to the Allies in Northern Italy in August 1944. This memorandum outlines the various resistance groups, their capabilities and potential, as well as the distrust among all other groups of the Communist Party, although certain gains had been made regarding collaboration between specific groups, such as the Agrarian Party, led by M. Ursiny and the Communists under "Sefcik."[317] It would be the rising of the political uncertainty and the internal collapse of the Czech Government in exile that would prompt General Ingr to submit his resignation as Commander-in-Chief of Czech Forces on 25 April 1945.[318]

The most active group (according to the PRO records on SOE) were the partisans located in Eastern Slovakia. Their activities included raids, sabotage, and weapons thefts, although on a limited scale, with the group numbering some 400 personnel.[319] Central and Western Slovakia were even less successful and active, numbering far less personnel despite being well organized and apparently highly motivated.[320] Part of the information collected during the intelligence gathering missions and supplied to SOE was a "Black List" of *Gestapo* agents and informers.[321] The British were also concerned about the possible post-war repercussions regarding their active involvement with resistance planning, not only in support of Patton's 3rd Army as it entered the region, but their support of anti-Communist Czech nationalists who were to be given continued support should the Soviets more actively support the Communists as anticipated. The activities of the Soviets in the region were well documented by the SOE EPIGRAM team operating in the region. The intelligence collected on the condition, efficiency and morale of the Red Army operating on limited means was quite revealing, as seen in the report.[322]

The British Chiefs of Staff were also acutely aware that the responsibility for SOE operations the Czechoslovakia may become convoluted, and this potential ambiguity was addressed on 21 April 1945 with a memorandum from SOE and distributed throughout the Allied command.[323] In addition, in order to secure the SOE position concerning their responsibilities, yet deflect any potential ill will and antagonism from the Soviets, a Top Secret Cipher Telegram issued from SHAEF to 12th Army Group, the War Office and OSS offices dated 26 April 1945 states:

> We have requested British Chiefs of Staff to place SOE operations in Czechoslovakia under Supreme Headquarters, AEF[324] control. Should British Chiefs of Staff agree to our request, which is regarded as likely, following directive regarding Czech resistance operations will come into force.[325]

The response from AMSSO to SHAEF was less than inspired, as stated in the following Top Secret Cipher Telegram dated 27 April 1945:

> We have recently considered the question of control of SOE operations in Czechoslovakia and have decided that no change is at present desirable and that there are good arguments for retention of present system of control.[326]

Western Allied concerns regarding the Soviets were becoming more evident, and SOE was to find itself operating in a covert role as an intelligence gathering service focusing upon the Red Army, with the Czech nationalist resistance groups to be included as an auxiliary collection source, although the messages transmitting through the Allied command were veiled, yet distinctly specific: "We agree that you can issue orders to Czech resistance as are necessary to ensure their cooperation with your operations."[327] One memorandum was less ambiguous regarding the Soviet/Allied relationship in Czechoslovakia:

> I am also concerned lest, if we say nothing to the Russians ourselves on this matter, but leave it to be handled entirely by Czechs, the Russians may not only conclude that we have no interest in the attachment of our officers to General Ingr's Staff and continuance of our operational contacts with occupied Czechoslovakia, but also become suspicious of activities which SOE have hitherto been carrying on there and accuse us of lack of frankness towards them.[328]

The same document also outlined the condition of the Anglo-Soviet relationship as Germany nearly expired, and control of Eastern Europe was becoming a diplomatic as well as military concern for both camps:

> Subject to your views, I see no reason why our attitude on this question need be affected by the Soviet Government's refusal to allow the Diplomatic Corps to return to liberated Czechoslovakia with the Czechoslovak Government, since the arguments about the present military situation and the lack of accommodation can scarcely be applied to our small SOE Mission, which will of course be solely concerned with military activities against the Germans in occupied Czechoslovakia.[329]

The Western Allied position with regard to the Czechs, and the overall Czech attitude towards their eastern liberators was realized by the local population when Soviet forces entered the country. This increased Allied activity prompted the eventual and much delayed Czech Rising from 30 April-5 May 1945. On 1 May a strike erupted at the Skoda Works, followed by a general uprising on 5 May initiating confrontations with the 11,000 German (predominantly *Waffen SS*) troops of Dietrich's Army remaining in Prague.[330] The atrocities committed by the *SS* in Prague were well documented, forcing mass appeals for assistance from the Czech resistance with a personal appeal by General Miroslav, while the Red Army was still 100 km to the east and Patton's 3rd Army was stalled on the Karlsbad-Pilsen-Budweis line.[331]

SOE responded by sending four teams into the area to support the advance teams already on the ground.[332] Despite the avalanche of Allied support closing in from the east and west, and with the typical increase in partisan activity heavy fighting still occurred throughout the country, and in Prague in particular through 7-8 May 1945.[333] The confusion during this period prompted a sensational response from the German commander of the surrender delegation:

> On Tuesday a message was received from SHEAF stating that General Jodl, the head of the German Military Surrender Mission, had complained to them that German troops were unable to surrender on account of the Rising, would we, therefore, send a message to the Czech Patriots instructing them to cease fighting the Germans and place all captured broadcasting transmitters in their hands in order that orders to surrender might be transmitted to German soldiers. It was manifestly impossible for SOE to send a message of this nature, and therefore, the Chiefs of Staff were once more approached in the matter. They, however, disclaimed any responsibility and stated that morning the initiation of transmission of any message affecting the nature of the resistance in Czechoslovakia had been transferred from Chiefs of Staff to SHAEF.[334]

Allied forces were concerned that the German forces that continued to fight in the face of unrelenting Czech resistance would prompt the Soviets to drive even further into the country. This potential threat prompted SHAEF to continue urgently for a message to be sent to the Czechs. If the Germans continued to fight in violation of the surrender agreement, the 3rd US Army would be forced to continue to Prague to enforce the surrender terms.[335] This in fact was the case as of 9 May, when the remaining SS forces were still heavily engaged in battle, shelling tactical points in the city in an attempt to channel the partisans and restrict their movement, while fighting a delayed withdrawal. Any intervention by SHAEF was eliminated by the following factors: Patton's forces were reported to have outrun their communications; Truman and Churchill had agreed to a strategic halt, while Eisenhower and the Soviet High Command had ratified the agreement, and the Red Army had entered Prague by that time in force.[336]

Despite the strategic military and political situation in Czechoslovakia, SHAEF was still requiring SOE intelligence summaries regarding the partisan and Red Army situation (which was unknown, since Stalin would never inform SHAEF as to where the Red Army was)[337] and the political support of nationalist Czechs. In addition to these requirements, SOE was still coordinating the activities of their agents while assessing the ever-escalating situation that was rapidly expanding beyond their control.[338] The solution to this situation was to send Colonel Perkins, Regional Head of SOE, Captain Thomas, a Czech Liaison Officer and two wireless telegraph operators to Patton's Headquarters to maintain a direct line of communication and constantly update the general on the conditions within the country.[339] The following illustrates the results of the last major SOE mission to Czechoslovakia:

> He (Colonel Perkins) has, nevertheless, since been able to penetrate as far as Prague, where he has met a Czech officer sent in by SOE in September 1944, a

Captain Nechansky, who was for some time the leader of the resistance movement in Prague itself. Colonel Perkins has also been able to contact a number of leading Czechs in Prague, and to make a tour of part of the city. He was present at the initial meeting between the Czechs and the Commanders of the Russian relief force.[340]

Perkins' mission was to lay the foundation for the Allied assessment of the Soviets towards the Czechs, and vice versa. Although thankful for the Soviet military support in forcing the Germans out the Czechs were prepared by in large to re-take control, both militarily and politically, of their nation. The Soviets had other intentions, and the addendum to the report previously cited states the following:

> 'Attitude of the Russians towards the Czechs:' The behavior of the Russians is extremely abrupt, almost as conquerors. The tone of the conference between Czech generals commanding Czech troops and the Russian Generals was one of definite command by the latter-'You will do this, or that...'[341]

The Czechs were and always had been by in large pro-west in their politics and outlook (as was Benes) and their hopes for Anglo-American support after the war began to fade into obscurity, as stated in a letter from SOE operative "M.P." to "C.D." dated 16 May 1945:

> The Czechs are not happy, they now realize they are completely sold out. Reports from the east, Brno etc. are coming in now & are pretty terrible, not only the women but also the agriculture & country is getting its dose of rape...I saw a couple of German women killed by lynching, & another example was hanging a local *Gestapo* by his feet to a lamp-post, a can of petrol and a match-rather unpleasant & really what we have been fighting against for five years. In whole of the American occupied zone no such things have occurred...There is not the slightest sign in Prague that any other country has fought this war than Russia and that hurts, when one considers the support we gave to the Benes gov. in England...it is not a true reflection of the real Czech majority, but rather forced on them from the east...by the victorious Red Army... what a rabble.[342]

Another document offers the Soviet-Czech relationship as of January 1945:

> Whilst at Huszt the Czech Delegation was virtually cut off from the rest of the world owing to the refusal of the Soviet authorities to permit the use of wireless for communication with the Czech Government in London, and their insistence that communication with the Czech Ambassador and Military Mission in Moscow was to be maintained 'en clair' through the Soviet High Command...These Soviet controlled organizations showed no desire to maintain touch with the Czech Delegation, who were thus virtually cut off from contact with the local population...Instances were known of wounded Czech soldiers, sent to liberated Czech territory for convalescence, having been arrested by the Russians for expressing pro-Czech feelings, and the Czech command had been requested to ab-

stain in future from sending wounded to Ruthenia...The majority of men called up in liberated Carpatho-Ukraine territory had been drafted into the Red Army and only very few had been permitted to join Czech military units...Soviet troops had been guilty of vandalism and looting. For example, they had transported furniture to Russia in army lorries...The Soviet authorities had not implemented the clauses of the Soviet-Czech treaty of December 1943 stipulating the handing over of liberated territories to the Czech civil administration, on the pretext that behind the operational zone full Red Army control was still necessary to safeguard the Soviet rear. Soviet commandants and other Red Army administrative representatives in the rear were stated to be subordinated to the political administration of the Red Army. The Czechs are in a weak position owing to fear of doing anything likely to strain relations with the Soviet Government.[343]

Another document dated 21 January 1945 stated similar difficulties in the Carpatho-Ukraine region between the Soviets and Czech nationalists:

Matters were further complicated by the recruiting of Carpatho-Ukrainians into the Red Army despite (Minister Frantisek) Nemec's protests. Czech officers on the spot who worked for Czechoslovak unity in Carpatho-Ukraine got into difficulties, both with the Red Army and local political leaders. The aide-de-camp of General Nizbursky, the Czechoslovak officer charged with recruiting Carpatho-Ukrainians into Czechoslovak formations, was arrested by the Russians, as were other Czechoslovak officers, on grounds of 'undue' political activity.[344]

The political situation was clear: Czech Communists, who were outnumbered by nationalists ten fold were completely supported by the Red Army, and called for the workers to be armed for the re-taking of the Sudetenland to further their political agenda, despite the agreements between Britain and the United States that the territory was already destined to be returned to Czech control. The Czech Communists were also initiating propaganda to the effect that the Western Allies had rendered absolutely no support, conventional or otherwise to the liberation of the country, stating "Cries for help are only heard in Moscow. A deaf ear in the west.[345]

The future planning for Czechoslovakia by the Western Allies had been placed on hold following the horrendous repercussions after the assassination of Reinhard Heydrich.[346] The fall out of these acts had effectively eliminated SOE activity from 1942 to 1944, forcing SOE to operate from Italian staging areas for operations in Czechoslovakia. The operational matrix was based upon the efforts of SOE in conjunction with the Yugoslav partisans and guerrillas and the French *Maquis*.[347]

Romania and Bulgaria

The German forces in Romania and Bulgaria were minimal in numbers until the forced retreat in the face of the massive Soviet offensive in the autumn of 1944. Special operations in these nations was restricted to the availability of partisan/guerrilla forces that could be managed and diverted from other areas, such as the Czech and Slovak partisans in division strength who were directed toward the Carpathians to link up with the Red Army.[348] These forces would prove very effective against the German forces, but they would later turn against the Red Army once the Soviets occupied the nations they invaded. An important person is *Kneaz*[349] Leonid Ivanovich Damianov Maximciuc who fought as a partisan after the war against the Red Army and the Romanian Communists. Maximciuc offers the viewpoint of someone who actively supported the German war effort against Stalin, although he never joined in the war effort against the Western Allies as an anti-Communist, and continued this activity through 1948.

Other Romanian nationals following a democratic ideal were Iuliu Maniu[350] and "Mihalache" who fought the Soviets under the banner of Marshal Ion Antonescu and Premier Antonescu, but were skeptical of their ally Hitler.[351] Romania did receive expert military assistance and advisors, such as *Generalmajor* Hans Doerr who had been appointed *Chef des Generalstabs* from 1941-43 and worked with both Italian and Romanian forces.[352] Doerr had commanded the 2nd Italian Army in the Balkans under General Vittorio Ambrosio as *Verbindungsoffizier* from 31 March to 30 April 1941 until the collapse of the Yugoslav government.[353] Doerr was later assigned as *Chef des deutschen Vebindungstabes,* creating the *"Kommandostellen Doerr Verbaende"* on 13 November 1943 and personally managed the 2nd and 4th Romanian Armies at Rostov and Stalingrad. His close coordination with *General der Artillerie* Constantin Contanescu, *General* Stanescu Dragalina and *Oberstleutnant* Dragomir allowed the *Panzerarmee* to escape encirclement, effectively withdraw and counter-attack despite heavy pressure from Red Army and partisan elements.[354]

Both Maniu and Mihalache were imprisoned by the Soviets in October 1947 in Bulgaria.[355] The Romanians had attempted to negotiate with the Western Allies but were met with refusal, unless the Soviets were brought into the settlement, which was considered unacceptable.[356] Churchill decided that the Romanians should negotiate a separate peace with Moscow, pull out of the war and establish a precedent for talks with Stalin and Molotov after the war.[357] King Michael then acted; arrested both Antonescus, sent the military into Bucharest to restore order on 23 April 1944 and simultaneously declared an end to all hostilities.[358] This action allowed the Red Army to run through the country, successfully pursuing the Germans while increasing the anti-fascist partisan network.[359]

This network was not placed into action against the Germans as expected, but given the task of locating and destroying those anti-Communist and nationalist partisans who had supported the Germans. This included those irregulars who had supported the fight against the Antonescu government, attacking German forces in the country, yet were still not considered by the Soviets to be "politically correct" along Moscow's guidelines. This activity would propel irregular activity to new heights even after World War II concluded; the first move in creating the Cold War in Europe. Communist partisans and other factional irregular forces erupted into action during the summer of 1943, thus prompting the new government leader Muraviev to declare his nation neutral, but to no avail. The Soviet Union declared war on Bulgaria, prompting the government to seek peaceful negotiations.[360] The Red Army invaded the nation taking the capitol and a *coup d'etat* the following day established the "Fatherland Front" as the new government. Bulgarian forces joined the Soviets against Germany, securing an armistice with the Western Allies in October,[361] while the same partisan versus guerrilla warfare seen in Romania erupted in Bulgaria.

Bulgaria's King Boris, secure in the knowledge that Hitler would not occupy the nation complied, yet the relationship was a strained one at best.[362] This situation was transformed when a "Professor Filov" established a new fascist government, with a General Mihov assuming the role of War Minister. Zahariev became the Minister of Commerce, and a man named Grabovsky, the most pro-German of them all, became Minister of the Interior.

Hungary

Hungary plays a large role in the study of partisan/guerrilla warfare despite the lack of any major resistance movement against the Germans, since it was the staunchest supporter of *Nazi* Germany next to Italy under the government of its Regent, Admiral Nicholas Horthy,[363] although Hungary offers a textbook example of lukewarm underground activity bordering on apathy.[364] This apathy was primarily due to several factors; the lineage of many German aristocratic families were rooted in the Hungarian nobility, their connection to Germany and Austria from the days of the old empire, and the German assistance in securing southern Slovakia in 1938 and northern Transylvania in 1940.[365]

The Regent of Hungary, Admiral Nicholas Horthy was a pro-fascist who feared Communism and had allowed German forces to enter Hungary on their way to attack Yugoslavia in April 1941 in the hope of reacquiring Backa province, lost to Yugoslavia after WW I.[366] Another fear held by the Hungarian government (especially Foreign Minister Bardossy) was that Romania may have the Transylvania region returned by Germany if the Hungarians did not fight as an Axis ally. However, Hungary stood to acquire southern Transylvania from Romania if their efforts were deemed worthy. Bardossy initially hesitated, then openly joined Hitler in June 1941 following the Red Air Force bombings of the Kassa border region.[367]

This is where the previously unheard Hungarian partisan forces came to life. During the first summer and winter offensives in southern Russia, Hungarian forces suffered heavy casualties as German commanders considered them expendable assets.[368] This disaffection with the war and the mandatory conscription filtered through the ranks and back home, and the pro-Communists began their campaign of domestic discontent, while the pro-fascists suddenly found themselves being used up for no apparent political, military or economic gain. Given Germany's commitment to holding Hungary due to the rich natural resources, agricultural commodities, railway network, and strategic positioning not only against the Soviet Union, but as a transportation, fighter and bomber base for offensive operations, Hitler would maintain a death grip on the nation until the final Soviet clearing of German forces in April 1945.[369] This alliance continued despite mounting public opinion urging the country to abandon the German alliance, urged forward by Ferenc Nagy and the Socialists and Small Farmers Party. This sentiment was seconded by Count Nicholas Kallay, Horthy's new Premier, urging a Hungarian withdrawal by summer 1943.[370]

Hungary's attempts at settling with the Western Allies and not the Soviets was to be expected, yet Churchill, in his characteristic myopia convinced the other Allied powers not to negotiate without the Soviets. This decision, like most of Churchill's during the war regarding dealings with Stalin (in particular the Yalta Conference, which would follow the European Advisory Commission established in Tehran in 1943, setting up zones of occupation)[371] was to have immense post-war ramifications.[372] Kallay's reluctance to move rapidly allowed Soviet forces to enter Bessarabia and cross the Hungarian frontier. Germany responded by sending tank and infantry divisions from Austria into Hungary, and the nation eventually became a bloody battleground, as stated by Albert Kerscher, commander of a King Tiger platoon of the *2nd Waffen SS Panzer* Division *"Das Reich:"*

> Hungary was important to Germany strategically; all of us understood this fact. The Soviets were pouring in millions of men and thousands of tanks and guns, and in my battalion alone we had only twelve tanks. The greatest problem for us was of course the Red Army, but they were increasing their forces with partisans every step forward. We were just as concerned with our fuel and supplies getting through the partisans in our rear as we were the massive attacks we faced from the front. This problem increased the closer the Soviets came to Budapest. We could just not kill enough or destroy enough of their hardware to make a dent in the flood. We were losing, and it was just a matter of time.[373]

The apathy into which Hungarian resistance fell during the German occupation should not have been unexpected, given the long-term political climate and the history of the people. However, there was still a glimmer of hope, as stated in the letter from Gygory Paloczi Horvath in Jerusalem (alias George Peter Howard) to Aladar Toth in Stockholm, Sweden dated 7 January 1942.[374] This letter clearly states the desire by the Hungarian Allied supporters to be so designated and identified, due to the belief that collaborators would be executed. However, despite the desire to strike back by several Hungarian groups the letter clearly outlines the potential problems of German retribution against the population should resistance increase, as well as the benefits to the Hungarians should they take that risk. As stated by Horvath:

> A *Coup d' Etat*, revolt or revolution would have the result that the *Nazis* would occupy Hungary as an enemy country. This again would have the following results:
> 1.Through the next part of the war Hungarians would not be forced to fight for Hitler.
> 2. The Germans would be forced to occupy our country with about 200,000 men.
> 3. At the time of the peace conference Hungary would not be treated as an enemy country.[375]

The Hungarians would find themselves paying a heavy price under Soviet domination and the Western Allied intelligence summaries predicted this to some degree, although no prediction could have prepared the intelligence services for the horrors that would occur. The Soviet disposition regarding the Hungarians is noted:

> The Russian attitude towards the minorities, such as the Hungarians was that they were small, insignificant people who were not responsible for their actions. Germany is the main enemy. If, however, these smaller peoples make the silly mistake of obstructing the Russian advance then they will have to pay the same penalty as the Germans.[376]

The Soviet attitude towards the Hungarians was not unique, and was in fact the universal common denominator in Stalin's treatment of all the conquered peoples. The Soviets should have learned valuable lessons from the German failures in ill-treating the masses; it cost them a war. Despite the warnings and lessons to be learned, the Soviets continued on their self-destructive path. The insurgents who had been supported and deployed by the Red Army and *NKVD* were themselves soon to be eliminated, since Stalin "regarded partisan war as a threat, something beyond the reach of the highly centralized and suspicious state apparatus,"[377] and he wanted no large groups of armed insurgents with delusions of freedom. As stated by Overy:

> In 1944 the partisan war was wound up. As the Red Army swept through the vast areas of occupation, partisan units, with their colorful names, 'Death to the Fascist' or 'The People's Avengers,' were absorbed into the regular army. One-fifth were rejected as unfit. Others were carefully scrutinized by the *NKVD* units which followed in the wake of the conquering armies. Membership in the partisans did not bring immunity from the security habits of the regime. All Ukrainian partisans, even Communists, were distrusted as a matter of course.[378]

The Soviet mentality was one of paranoia and mistrust, perhaps understandable given their recent history of slaughter (both from within and without) and the cloistered nature of the national political leadership. The Soviet policy of domination through force that had failed Hitler would see Stalin try to create an even larger empire. The people of Eastern Europe were to learn first hand the price of both fighting against Germany and fighting for Stalin, and the Western Allies knew all along the end result. The tragedy is that the future of Europe and indeed the world could have been altered and a more moderate climate established had the diplomats put forth the same effort as their fighting forces.

5

The Balkans:
Greece & Albania

*After the enemies with guns have been wiped out,
there will still be enemies without guns; they are
bound to struggle against us, and we must never
regard these enemies lightly. If we do not now raise
and understand the problem in this way, we shall
commit the gravest mistakes.*

- Mao Tse Tung
5 March 1949

The story of Greek partisan operations is an extensive yet not quite clear cut area as to all of the activities and groups involved, although of the two main resistance elements, EAM/ELAS and EDES, ELAS would prove to be the most successful organization in actual "guerrilla" warfare against the Germans prior to SOE and OSS support being thrown heavily into the EDES corner. ELAS would also become the most contentious organization with regard to both the Germans and the Western Allies. The greatest dilemma for the Western Allies would be the power struggle between the nationalist and Communist factions, both combating each other with as much ruthless abandon as exhibited against their common enemy. The fratricide committed by these groups would equal (if not surpass) the body count inflicted upon the population by the Germans during three years of occupation.

Once Mussolini's forces invaded during the winter of 1940-41 and were pushed out of Greece into Albania by the smaller Greek Army, they became immediately entangled in the quagmire of guerrilla warfare. The losses for Italy climbed to over 60,000 casualties by April 1941, and the strategic situation for Germany became precarious. The bulk of these casualties were incurred through partisan and guerrilla activity; resistance that swelled as the campaign of terror initiated by the Italians backfired, as stated in the following report:

> The Greek guerrillas are for the greater part tough mountain villagers; their ranks have recently been swelled by peasants who came into conflict with the occupying authorities and are seeking refuge in the hills. The burning of entire villages by the Italians has also had the result that a large percentage of the male population, deprived of their homes, took the mountains and thus join the *"Antartes"*[379] as these guerrillas are called in Greece. We knew of several instances where guerrillas are actually commanded by officers of the Greek regular army. Some other bands owe allegiance to certain minor left wing politicians.[380]

Hitler's ambitions did not include an invasion of the Balkans, and the bail out operation to assist Mussolini[381] would cost him valuable time for his *Operation Barbarossa* offensive, tentatively scheduled for April, then delayed until May, then again postponed until 22 June 1941. Launching *Operation Marita* in December 1940 Hitler sent his forces across the Bulgarian frontier, despite the pleas from General Iaonnis Metaxas that Greece did not want a war with Italy, let alone Germany, and the country would remain neutral. The reality of the situation was soon to be very apparent.

The German occupation would witness 40,000 people starve to death (1941-44) during the famine that gripped the country, with another 25,000 people estimated to have perished by the time of the Allied liberation.[382] However, the mass suffering and rapidly deteriorating economic conditions that would create exponential numbers of partisans and guerrillas cannot be totally attributed to the Axis occupation. True, the German invasion to assist Mussolini created greater hardships upon the nation, but it can be safely stipulated that the internal guerrilla war that had been brewing for years was also a contributor to the losses.

The insurgency movement in Greece far exceeded the percentage of resistance when compared with the general populations of other nations in Europe. Next to Yugoslavia, Greece would become the most politically unstable and sensitive region of German occupied Europe due to the multitude of independent political entities, whether these groups were pro-western, pro-eastern, left-wing, right-wing, pro-monarchists, pro-democratic, Communists, or even National Socialists. Ironically, much like in Yugoslavia, the Greek irregulars could seldom set aside their differences, even when famine swept the country. Bands of guerrillas and partisans scoured the country raiding farms and stealing what little food there was, creating animosity and fear as they stalked the land. So devastating was the famine that Mussolini kept his word to "speak with Hitler about the crisis," and he did so in a letter, stating, "Greece is on the brink of financial and therefore economic and political catastrophe."[383] The seeds for the post-war Greek Civil War would be planted as much by the Allies as the Germans themselves. Greece, more than any other nation saw their entire social and political structure at war with both their common enemy as well as each other. To quote Mark Mazower regarding the conditions in Greece, the country was "caught up in a total war, society itself became a battlefield."[384]

The ELAS (*Ethnikos Laikos Apeleftherotikos Stratos*), or Greek People's Liberation Army (the militant faction) and EAM (*Ethniko Apeleftherotiko Metopo*), or National Liberation Front (the political wing) Communist partisans were the left-wing military and political representatives led by the fanatical and brutally effective Aris Velouchiotis[385] during the war, and the Communist partisan leader General Markos Vaphiadis after the war. The EAM/ELAS combination created the largest and most effective "guerrilla" force in the nation, qualifying for this status due to their waging unconventional warfare upon the occupation forces, while also fighting both politically and militarily to institute a Communist government to replace the ousted monarchy once the German occupation was over.[386]

However, despite the huge numbers of EAM/ELAS members it would appear that Communism was never the political choice of the masses. The operational military and political structure was quite similar to the organization of the old Irish Republican Army and Sinn Fein, and was the most effective guerrilla group operating in Greece despite the fact that they received less than a third of the materiel support as the other factions. EAM/ELAS would maintain its loose yet well-defined command structure until the leadership was replaced by Nikes Zachariades, when it boasted a debatable wartime membership surpassing 1,000,000 members, although the wartime estimate as of May 1943 was 17,000 and as of July 1943 perhaps as many as 30,000 troops in the field.[387] ELAS was a guerrilla group that fought not only the Germans, but also the much smaller EDES nationalist partisans, who deserve this designation since they fought the Germans as well as the ELAS guerrillas in order to restore at least a democratic if not monarchical government once the war ended. EDES was ably led by Napoleon Zervas[388] before and during the war, continuing the struggle against the TEA (*Tagmata Ethikos Aminis*) or "Brigade of National Defense" and "Royal Greek Army" led by General Alexandros Papagos during the Greek Civil War that erupted following the end of hostilities.[389]

Much of the partisan history related to Greece also includes their fight against the Bulgarians and Albanians during the same period, which was not highly publicized and was at best sporadic. However, this activity stemmed from Bulgaria joining the Axis in March 1941, mainly out of their interest in acquiring Macedonia (also contested by Yugoslavia before the war and acquired after it) and Thrace from the occupying Germans, and eventually ceding to German overtures for greater participation against the Soviets in 1942. The total Balkans situation, with Greece as the epicenter was to smolder and erupt into the Cold War's first major contest, placing the blooded yet still inexperienced special operations communities to the ultimate test.

The Germans found themselves the unlikely inheritors of this political and military quagmire, unable to subdue the political threat and almost unwilling to admit that there was a competent paramilitary threat. The German occupation in Greece was perhaps not as bloody as that of Russia or Yugoslavia, but the end result was still far from the reasonably "peaceful" existence experienced in the west. The German reaction to partisan/guerrilla activity would follow the same traditional pattern as in Russia and the rest of the Balkans, further exacerbating an already potent problem initiated by the Italians the year before. Such activities as burning villages, taking hostages, forced labor,[390] and killing civilians occurred, although with less frequency than elsewhere, yet still enough to create concern for both the population accused of harboring irregulars and the soldiers who were ordered to participate.

The assignments of German officers such as Hans Doerr to work with Axis forces stemmed the flow of casualties and destabilized front. However, these were short-term remedies. When German forces entered the Balkans, the *12th Armee* on 6 April 1941, under the command of *Generalfeldmarschall* Wilhelm List encountered stiff partisan/guerrilla resistance, although despite this obstacle they captured the port of Salonika within three days.[391] List ordered the *1st Waffen SS Panzer* Division *"Leibstandarte"* to attack the Metsovo Pass, part of the area commanded by General Tsolakoglu's 3rd Army Corps and defeat the Greek reinforcements before they could become effective. As stated by Mazower, the German advance was so rapid the British Expeditionary Force was still sending radio messages to the already captured Greek staff, only to be answered by Germans on the other end.[392] Panikos Panay, former Greek EDES partisan and the second son of a Greek Orthodox priest also noted this situation:

> The Germans had moved very rapidly, as they were motorized and efficient. We knew that it was only a matter of time, and that the British forces were outnum-

bered and retreating, preparing for an evacuation to Crete.[393] It was a very tense time, I can tell you. Most of the men in the army were already in the process of preparing to fight a guerrilla war, and most of us already had quite a bit of experience in this type of fighting. We were mostly from the mountains, and this would play to our advantage.[394]

With Athens being approached on 18 April the Prime Minister committed suicide, while the government and King George debated the issue of his successor.[395] When the *6th Panzer* Division entered the southern suburbs of Athens on 27 April nearly all resistance from the military had ceased. The *Chef des Generalstabs,*[396] *Generaloberst* Eberhard von Mackensen began utilizing all the assets at his disposal, including the *1st* and *2nd Waffen SS Panzer* Divisions assigned to the command.[397] Greece was to be subdued quickly and without hesitation since Yugoslavia had been knocked out of the war almost two weeks earlier. The end result of a massive army living off the land while displacing the population that grew the crops,[398] basically eliminating the commercial structure during the occupation was to wreak havoc.

The people of Greece were to begin a long term of economic and personal pain with Athens suffering more than any other city in Europe. The fate of the Greeks was to create great problems for the Axis forces in occupation, as stated by Mazower: "These policies of expropriation and plunder...the reflection of an ultimately self-defeating tendency in Berlin to see the economic benefits of conquest before the political ones-had a catastrophic impact in Greece."[399] This was apparently not much of a concern to the political leaders in Berlin, as stated by *Reichsmarschall* Hermann Goering to the *Reich* Commissioners and Military Commanders of the Occupied Territories on 6 August 1942:

> In all the occupied territories I see people living there stuffed full of food, while our own people are going hungry. For God's sake, you haven't been sent there to work for the well-being of the peoples entrusted to you, but to get hold of as much as you can so that the German people can live. I expect you to devote your energies to that. This continual concern for the aliens must come to an end once and for all...I could not care less when you say that people under your administration are dying of hunger. Let them perish as long as no German starves.[400]

With the official German occupation policy being one of complete disinterest as opposed to outright genocide there were few who could logically see a clear distinction. Whether one is shot, gassed or starved the result is the same; only hunger takes a much longer time to kill and effects many more people. Even Propaganda Minister Josef Goebbels entered into his diary in February 1942: "The inhabitants of the occupied areas have their fill of material worries. Hunger and cold are the order of the day. People who have been this hard hit, generally speaking, don't make revolutions."[401]

This lack of understanding and ignorance of the facts would become the primary reason for civilians and ex-military personnel to join guerrilla and partisan movements. Striking back at the cause of the famine was deemed necessary to end it, as well as survive. However, the price for insurgency would prove high, as in the mountainous northern region when the Germans began operating counterinsurgency units there in 1943.[402] This area had by in large escaped the worst of the famine, until combat disrupted the farming activities, forcing the people to flee their land and having their homes and villages destroyed. The resistance situation in Greece would become almost a mirror image of the movement in Yugoslavia, due to the fact that both countries had "a defeated army, economic collapse, a dismembered state, a small but active Communist Party."[403]

A prime example of German retaliation for insurgency activity was the reduction of two villages named Kato and Ano Kerzilion in July 1941, when the villages were burned and over 200 men were shot.[404] On 24 October 142 people were shot after being taken hostage in reprisal for a skirmish.[405] Just in October 1941 alone 488 civilians and suspected partisans and guerrillas were executed, with 164 people taken hostage in the Salonika region.[406] Following these events the Germans noticed an increase in partisan/guerrilla activity, which only furthered their resolve to reduce the problem by compounding the error.

Perhaps the most notorious act of brutality committed by German forces of the *1st Gebirgs* (Mountain) Division[407] in Greece was the eradication of the village of Komeno on 16 August 1943, when the German troops entering the area following a "suspected" partisan attack were ordered to eliminate everything in the village.[408] The body count numbered 317 civilians killed in reprisal for harboring partisans, with the ages ranging from a "one-year-old Alexandra Kritsima to seventy-five-year-old Anastasia Kosta; they include seventy-four children under ten, and twenty entire families."[409] Even the village priest was killed by a *Leutnant* Roeser and was witnessed by a survivor, Alexandros Mallios, who hid behind the churchyard wall.[410] The Germans also looted the village, confiscating the livestock and appropriating anything that could be loaded into trucks and taken back to base.

The impact upon the Germans was varied, although certain soldiers many years later stated that the event was discussed, and that "few thought it right," and "most of the comrades were very depressed." According to Kershaw, a NCO stated that this "would be the last time I take part in something like that. That was a disgrace, which had nothing to do with fighting a war.[411] Almost none agreed with the action."[412] One of the most poignant statements follows:

> ...most of the soldiers did not agree with this action...Many said openly that it was nothing but a disgrace to shoot unarmed civilians. Others, rather fewer, took the view that they were all a potential enemy so long as they supported the partisans against us soldiers. The argument was so heated that I might almost speak of a mutiny.[413]

Kershaw states correctly that most of the units involved in the shootings of civilians were transferred from the Eastern Front, and it is quite likely that they carried that persecution mentality with them. Also stated by Kershaw, "Komeno may be described as the Greek exception, which proved the Russian rule."[414] As already mentioned the same was quite true of the men in the *2nd Waffen SS* during their march through France, as their application of reprisal tactics was demonstrated in 1944.

However, so potentially controversial was the event at Komeno the German commander falsified the report to offer the image of strong guerrilla activity and engagement, which was later filtered up through the chain of command, until by the time it reached the General Staff it was portrayed as a full fledged battle with "virtually no innocent civilians involved."[415]

The desire to cover up the incident at the grass roots level and prevent higher authority from discovering the truth speaks volumes as to the perception of the act by the local command authority. Had the German Army Command in total been a supporter and proponent of this type of activity there would have been no need to falsify anything regarding the event. In this role of interpretation, *Oberleutnant* Kurt Waldheim personally handled the final draft, offering his own opinions as to the events to which he had never even been a party into the unit war diary.[416]

The responses from several of the men who participated are interesting, and are related by Mazower. A chaplain from the *1ˢᵗ Gebirgsjaeger* Division[417] stated in October 1943 that "the mass killing of women and children during operations against the bands is producing a difficult inner burden on the conscience of many men."[418] Some soldiers believed that the villages, in their supporting the partisans and guerrillas were legitimate targets, not offered protection under the laws of land warfare. The Germans who were apparently disturbed by these events were experiencing the effects of psychological depression, a problem not recognized as being a legitimate concern among the members of the German High Command. Despite these reservations and discussions among the men as chronicled by Mazower, the orders to continue with similar activities throughout the occupation were never rescinded. In fact, the following orders from Hitler issued through *Generalfeldmarschall* Wilhelm Keitel on 16 December 1942 point out the true colors of German intentions at the higher level, and explain the methods previously described:

> The enemy had thrown into bandit warfare fanatic, Communist trained fighters who will not stop at any act of violence. The stake here is more than to be or not to be. This fight has nothing to do with a soldier's chivalry nor with the decisions of the Geneva Conventions. If this fight against the bands, in the east as well as in the Balkans is not carried out with the most brutal means, the forces at our disposal may in the near future not last out to master this plague. The troops are therefore authorized and ordered in this struggle to take any measures without restriction, even against women and children if these are necessary for success. (Humanitarian) considerations of any kind are a crime against the German nation...[419]

By issuing this order the Germans had created a situation that was irreversible, forcing the two major left and right wing factions to suspend their internal annihilation of each other in order to focus upon the common enemy. Had this order and the after effects not been present, it is quite plausible that the Germans would have been able to moderately pacify the country. Once the two insurgent factions engaged in open, widespread warfare two possibilities would most likely have occurred. First, the partisan/guerrilla problem would have eliminated itself, easing the pressure against German forces. Second, and even more likely, the mass population, suffering from being caught in the middle of a civil war would have probably found the Germans as a saving entity as opposed to a ruthless invader, thus legitimizing their presence and gaining popular support.

Yet, despite these two politically opposite factions' continuous hatred for each other they did on occasion unite and effectively coordinate operations against the Germans, and they were sometimes highly successful in the process.[420] So effective were the two groups that the Germans were forced to occupy every Greek island to prevent the landings of SOE operatives who had supported the partisans and guerrillas since September 1942.[421] Ironically, there were many areas where villagers joined the Germans simply to survive. Avoiding the repercussions of being accused of partisan/guerrilla support, as well as taking a defensive posture against guerrillas (especially the rogues under Velouchiotis) who were often just as (if not more) ruthless as the Germans in dealing with villagers. It would be this kind of activity that would turn many Greeks away from EAM/ELAS during and after the war and hasten the British and American intervention to halt Communist expansion into Greek civil and military life. It was actually due to the activities of ELAS that hundreds of villagers were forced to join the Germans for protection, thus legitimizing the German position while depriving the irregulars of much of their support network. Regaining that support would prove difficult until SOE entered the picture as a viable force in 1943, and even then it was a risky endeavor.

However, the problems facing SOE and later OSS was the inability to determine both the actual numbers of resistance fighters as well as the difficulty in deciding which groups were actually effective in the resistance and thus deserving of massive Allied support. Additional problems included deciding which groups may have been semi-collaborators or even "sunshine patriots," shifting their alliance as the situation deemed necessary for their political survival:

> It is impossible to gauge the number composing the various guerrilla bands which exist. It can be taken for certain, however, that they are not very large. For instance, Lt. Col. Myers, who collaborated with Col. Zervas who commands the guerrillas in the Ghiona Mountains, asked us to supply by air arms and equipment for 400 men.[422]

Other problems facing SOE when they began operations in 1943 was the fear of "alienating the villagers."[423] This stemmed from SOE wanting to limit the size and number of sabotage operations in order to reduce the opportunities for massive German reprisals, which may have created even greater problems for the Allies long term. This concern was also stressed to the partisan and guerrilla leaders, since their support and restraint was critical to SOE and later OSS achieving the overall plan. The irregular groups in Greece were also not as cohesive in their application of resistance as their Yugoslav or Soviet counterparts, despite the fact that many ex-Yugoslav soldiers and irregulars fled across the Macedonian border into Greece and functioned with the partisans and guerrillas.

This event was primarily due to the German supported Croat independence movement, so declared on 10 April 1941 just prior to German forces entering Zagreb, and the *Ustascha* (also spelled *Ustache, Ustasche*) who ruthlessly murdered Serbs on a scale that dwarfed the German efforts in the country alone.[424] So obviously counterproductive was *Ustascha*, Glaise von Horstenau suggested to Hitler during a September 1943 visit to the Wolf's Lair in East Prussia, that German forces "not to have too close contact with the *Ustascha*."[425] Hitler, unmoved by the situation patted Horstenau on the shoulder, and said; "You know, we really don't want all causes of friction to be removed from the Balkans…we always must have the opportunity to intervene."[426]

The inability to confirm a proactive command and control structure with an adequate head count posed great problems with the SOE missions. The intense rivalry between various irregular groups proved just as deadly to villagers as a German armored column, since feeding aiding and supplying "the wrong" group could invite a reprisal from a rival group, a method employed by Aris Velouchiotis with reckless abandon. Villagers worried about German actions against them as well as partisan or guerrilla reprisals. It is easy to understand how neither group made effective allies of the locals in the insurgency/counterinsurgency campaign. It was this reality and fear that forced many Greek civil servants (especially the *gendarmes*) working for the occupation forces to abandon their jobs and vanish from sight. This reality created problems for the Germans in operating within the country effectively, which served the Allied and guerrilla/partisan plans extremely well. The situation also helped de-stabilize the nation once the war was over, since the rivalries that forced a cessation to the national administration only enhanced the chaos following the German withdrawal in October 1944. The Cold War in Greece was receiving its first push; a nation with multi-factional political and paramilitary groups competing for control of a bankrupt country whose government stopped functioning more from turmoil initiated from within than from deconstruction originating from without.

This potential reality was taken into account when the Foreign Office decided that SOE should begin selecting the men who would try and assist the Greeks against their German conquerors; men were wanted who would be able to operate without political conviction, maintaining and transmitting the faith that the Allies would indeed come, while attempting to forge alliances among the various factions for the greater common good. Another fact was that SOE and later OSS[427] would never be absolutely sure which group was which, given the very fluid and politically unstable nature of the Greek guerrilla and partisan campaign, as stated in the following:

> So far one cannot say that the guerrillas in Greece are 'organized.' They are a hetero-geneous collection of mountain villagers, many of whom lived as bandits before. It has been recognized for some time that if their activities are to be of real use to our war effort, they should be coordinated into a strategic plan.[428]

The SOE and later OSS situation was understandably confusing. This confusion would only compound the problems facing the Western Allies following the end of World War II when the Greek Civil War erupted. The Allies discovered they were dealing with the same conditions that had plagued the Italians and Germans; both Axis nations failed to understand their target audience and therefore paid the price for inattention. The British and Americans understood the situation better, although a complete understanding of the various Greek political and social differences that divided the country would never be totally comprehended and would also cut down the lines of communication. A major problem was the resistance by the Communists of the KKE (virtually decimated as an active force by Metaxas' secret police during the occupation) and the return of King George to the throne at war's end. Churchill staunchly supported the return of the monarchy, a position that divided the insurgency forces as to their loyalties.[429]

As stated by Mazower, the future political fate of Greece "would be decided outside the country."[430] The disaffection regarding politics in lieu of combat operations against the enemy was addressed when EAM representatives, expecting growing support from the starving and maltreated populace paid Zervas a visit to negotiate joint insurgency activity. Zervas was apparently wary, and for good reason; he had already denounced EAM/ELAS as a Communist organization, much to the regret of the British, since the declaration would undoubtedly bring a Soviet response, a condition which was not anticipated or even welcome.

Zervas also had another problem that would hinder his perceived usefulness to the British; it had been rumored that he had forged an "understanding" with *Generaloberst* Hubert Lanz, *Kommandeur* of the *22nd Armee Korps* in late 1943.[431] There were some successes, such as in Thessaly, where Communists and Republicans joined to create the quite effective National Front.[432] Other actions included public demonstrations totally condemning the Axis occupation and pronouncing a Greek Communist Government, such as the rally in Athens on 28 February 1942,[433] and the police and workers' strikes throughout various cities.[434] However, these were not common circumstances, and the distrust among EAM/ELAS (and EPON, the EAM Youth Movement) and EDES would seriously hinder Allied operations, thereby allowing tens of thousands of German troops to withdraw while the Greeks fought themselves, and even their Allied supporters on rare occasions. Controlling the Greek resistance was perhaps the most frustrating element in the entire exercise:

> The only way to do this is by setting up a Coordination Committee which will have liaison officers to each group operating in various parts of the country. These officers will be carefully chosen so as to impress the leaders and exercise the necessary influence over them. Measures have already been taken to find suitable Greek-speaking British officers to be sent to Greece for this purpose. The Coordination Committee is being organized in conjunction with the Greek Deputy Premier in Cairo, who is responsible to the Greek Government for subversive activities in Greece. We hope that an organization on the above lines will be in working order by the Spring of 1943. [435]

Allied measures to create a more effective resistance movement in Greece were also hampered by the apparent misinterpretation of Allied intentions by the Greek *Gendarmerie* and the resistance forces, despite the fact that the vast majority of Greeks supported the Western Allies, believing that their intervention was their only salvation.[436] Many escaping British servicemen who either managed to avoid capture during the German invasion or SOE and Allied airmen shot down usually managed to link up with the resistance movements, thus solidifying the perception of Allied interest and continued support.[437] Villagers often protected these men at great personal risk, such as the support offered to Captain Richard MacNabb, until his daring and luck ran out and he was captured in Athens in May 1942 after a year of operating with EDES partisans.[438] The usually ruthless German response to the subversive activity is understandable, given their lack of understanding regarding counterinsurgency activity and the necessary political and social ramifications involved until too late in the war, and by too few in a position to effect a reversal. However, the Greek response was less lucid. The Greek Government and police believed that resistance and insurgency equaled a Communist conspiracy, according to the Greek Government exile based in Cairo.[439] Trying to make the Greeks in the country understand that there was not a Communist plot to infiltrate Greek governmental affairs seemed impossible, and when this was actually achieved the leftists were convinced that the Allied support would be poised to eradicate their cause once the war was completed. The tensions between the left-wing and right-wing political groups would only impede what could have been an even more successful insurgency campaign, despite the Communists rallying for an entire guerrilla campaign against the occupation forces following the launching of *Operation Barbarossa*.[440]

However, despite these problems certain spectacular acts of sabotage were effectively executed. One event was the 30 May 1942 sinking of two ships in Piraeus harbor by SOE supplied and trained Greeks, while the following day saw the destruction of a major ammunition depot in Salonika. The result was a standard German reprisal campaign, including executions and the destruction of homes.[441] The Western Allied concerns regarding the Soviet Union and the limited yet important support to Greek Communists were well founded. So concerned was the OSS and the United States Government, special mention was made on the subject:

> They desire that the Soviet Government be informed of the operations which you propose to undertake in this area, and to this end it is directed that you keep the State Department fully advised in order that they can accomplish this. The Chiefs of Staff desire that you show preference among resistance groups or prospective successor governments only on a basis of their willingness to cooperate, and without regard to their ideological differences, or political programs. Explicit instructions to these ends should be given to the personnel in these activities.[442]

The Germans had failed to understand the basic rationale of the Greek population regarding the best method of occupation, hence creating a greater problem. The Allied support mechanism was late in realizing the distinctions between the methodology and intent of EAM/ELAS guerrillas, who wanted not only the Germans out, but also wanted to establish a new Communist government. EDES was even divided between members wishing a restoration of the monarchy along greater democratic lines and those members who wished to have a democracy without a monarch. EAM/ELAS supported the people and confronted the problems facing them on a daily basis; food, sanctuary, economics, work, and the other problems created by the Axis and failed to be addressed in full by EDES. EDES approached the people from a political viewpoint, focusing upon working with the Germans only as long as it suited their purpose, while a more radical faction preached constant guerrilla warfare in order to secure greater Allied support, hoping for a Second Front in Europe to be established in Greece.[443]

Part of the Allied plan to incorporate the partisan and guerrilla factions was the execution of *Operation Animals*, the SOE controlled campaign of expanded guerrilla warfare that was to hopefully engulf Greece from every point on the compass. This would assist the Allied deception regarding the true Second Front in France, as well as feed Hitler and the *Generalstabs* erroneous information to buy the troops in North Africa and Sicily time to be reorganized and relocated. It was due to this precise fear of an Allied invasion that witnessed *Generalleutnant* Alexander Loehr, a Russian Orthodox, Austrian Eastern Front veteran who spoke the language and was *Kommandeur* of *Armee Gruppe E* being placed as

Oberbefehlshaber Suedost.[444] Loehr was one of those officers who did not follow the ideals of Hitler and was actually opposed to the implementation of political officers into his units.[445]

However, Loehr was systematic, methodical and rigidly focused upon the doctrine of conventional warfare, with little imagination regarding proper applications of counterinsurgency methods. Loehr's men would become the most responsible for the rapid increase in irregular activity, and the event of 14 July 1943 would prove this point. On this day, Loehr ordered the *1ˢᵗ Panzer* Division "to take the most severe measures," and field commanders who demonstrated "negligence or softness" would be punished.[446] Faced with these orders and a military system quite willing to execute its own, compliance was quite understandable. Loehr did have his critics, such as his Chief of Staff, *Generalleutnant* August Winter. Winter understood that the collective retribution was inadequate, stating; "When people proceed with an atonement action, they should go for the truly guilty and for hostages, rather than razing places that have nothing to do with it to the ground. That only increases the bands."[447]

This reactionary policy was mostly due to the fact that the Germans tended to equate the resistance in political and racial terms, as opposed to seeing the reality behind the actions. As stated by *General* Hubert Lanz, "On the contrary, they (German soldiers) admired the great past and lofty culture of Hellas. But how would they react to guerrilla warfare?"[448] The German inability to accept the fact that people, with or without uniforms had the inherent right to fight for their freedom under a brutal occupation, and in turn respect them as brave opponents only fostered a narrow minded and self-deprecating attitude. Even Hitler ordered that "partisans" be called "bandits" to reduce their legitimacy and soften the psychological impact upon the soldiers committing the executions. The intent was to lower their value as humans, as well as destroy any lingering doubts as to their legal status under the articles of war.[449] Certain acts committed by irregulars could justifiably support this categorization of partisans and guerrillas as "bandits," as stated by Richard Overy: "Partisans sometimes walked a thin line between military hero and gangster."[450] Hans Hossfelder stated it clearly during his interview:

It was one thing enter Russia and combat the Red Army, kill partisans and the like. We had been indoctrinated to believe that they were a subhuman culture, slightly above the status of animals, and this was not too hard for many of us to believe. I believed it. However, for the men who entered Greece before June 1941, as I was one of them, it would have been difficult too carry out or issue an order to kill people simply because they had to die. This was not the case in Russia. Now, when these troops returned from Russia and the brutal anti-partisan war in Yugoslavia, it was a different matter. Men had seen and done so much killing, it almost seemed to be just a part of the job. I do not say that it is right now, or even that it was right back then. It was only right according to the times we found ourselves in, given the particulars of the circumstance. It was very sad.[451]

One of Loehr's first actions was to issue secret orders to disarm all Italian forces in the Balkans following the coup against Mussolini should Italy surrender or change alliances, a very prudent step considering the strained German-Italian relations during the occupation.[452]

This in fact did occur, and most of the Italians were entrained and sent north to Yugoslavia and internment camps beyond. Others joined the partisans and guerrillas throughout the Balkans, including Greece, or swore allegiance to Mussolini and Hitler and continued to fight with Germany.[453] In the end many of these men deserted to the irregulars.[454] Loehr's second action was to immediately take the reigns of the counterinsurgency war, and as Mazower states, " ...the line between civilians and guerrillas had blurred almost to vanishing point."[455]

However, despite the propaganda issued from Berlin regarding the dangers of humane treatment towards the civilians, especially partisans or guerrillas (again without any distinction being made) there were documented cases where the irregulars (or *andartes*) exhibited unusually humane treatment towards their prisoners. One case is cited by Mazower, where a *Leutnant* Ludwig Guenter was captured in 1944 and was treated quite well.[456] Another case involved Hermann Franz, the chief of the paramilitary police in Greece, who stated that his men were also well-treated when captured by ELAS, although their boots were taken.[457]

Several Italian commanders made overtures to the British, such as General Mangani of the Casale Division and General Delabona, commanding the Italian 26th Corps who brought their terms to the Bishop of Jannina.[458] Much of this was possible due to the large numbers of Germans troops operating from different units and from many different military organizations. The Army worked in conjunction with the *Abwehr*, a marriage that seemed to function adequately, while the *SD* and *Waffen SS* were almost always at odds with each other, with both groups also combating the Army with regard to policy and regions of control.[459] Then there were the Italians, who were operating according to their own agenda, mindless of the German interests, although their approach in general was far more humane.

The end result was that the various German military and police organizations could never operate according to a single plan, minimizing their effectiveness while illustrating their weakness to the enemy. Had the Germans properly evaluated the political conditions in Greece and made the proper overtures to the proper segments of the population, the tragedy of the guerrilla war in Greece may well have been avoided.

Albania

Albania has always been perceived as one of the more obscure and isolated nations of the world despite being surrounded by the great states of Europe. The people had a rather long legacy of guerrilla warfare long before World War II. The resistance movement within Albania, while not very effective at first due to inadequate communications and the difficulty of operating an Allied liaison mission between various resistance factions, the mountain warriors proved themselves to be as great a threat (albeit on a smaller scale) as their other Eastern European neighbors.

Since the days of the resistance to the Ottoman Empire, most notably the campaigns of Major General Andranik Oznian, who served as an officer of the Imperial Russian Army in the Caucasus during World War I, the Albanians had a great legacy of guerrilla warfare from which to draw upon.[460] Fighting the Turks with a passion and dedication that brought him honors and notoriety, Oznian and his ally, Armenian guerrilla leader Aghbiur Serob virtually destroyed the military and political viability of the Turks and Kurds. Many of these older veterans would form the nucleus of the resistance movements in a much larger war closer to home.

The Germans were not very concerned with the Albanians, mainly due to the isolation of the country, the lack of adequate beaches and ports to support an Allied invasion, and the effectiveness of the natural mountain defenses and the pro-German guerrillas who patrolled the borders. Also, the Italians were given the country as a consolation prize after their April 1939 invasion, which became the spring board for the October 1940 Greek invasion. The subsequent long battles with high losses in the attempt to conquer the rugged country, supported with German armored support once the Italian situation had turned for the worse.[461] However, despite the fact that the Albanians hated the Italians and combated them on a regular basis, the Germans did find themselves aided by thousands of Albanians who had suffered under the Communists and who had also challenged the government of King Zog, who purged other parties and instituted a Stalinist style program of land "restructuring" and collectivization.

The Italian puppet government under Shevcet *beg* Vrlaci reduced this threat, although in the long run it was a failure, since most of the Islamic nomadic sheepherders never answered to the central government in Tirana anyway. The Germans managed to receive assistance from the fascist government under Balli Kombetar, a shadowy figure who supplied 15,000 men for a campaign of terror equal to anything witnessed in Yugoslavia and Russia.[462] The Communist guerrillas, led by Mustafa Gjinishi were a small and virtually ineffective organization that fought the Italians as well as the few nationalist Albanians under Aba Faja, who rose to the occasion. They fought each other in vicious battles that alarmed even the Italians and Germans and exceeded the carnage against the Axis powers in sheer brutality.

The anti-Communist Albanian partisans (or *Chams*) and their fighting ability brought them to the attention of Heinrich Himmler, following a report filed by *Gruppenfuehrer* (later *Oberstgruppenfuehrer*) Josef "Sepp" Dietrich, commander of *1ˢᵗ Waffen SS Panzer* Division *"Leibstandarte"* during the Balkans invasion of 1941. The end result was the creation of an Albanian *SS* unit, the *21ˢᵗ Waffen Gebirgs* Division *der SS "Skanderberg" (Albanische Nr. 1)* that fought not only in their own nation, but throughout Greece and Yugoslavia.[463] Due to their treatment at the hands of their German leadership and the apparent disinterest from the High Command the unit eventually became an ineffective and basically worthless mob, and most deserted to the British.[464]

As with most ethnic groups in the Balkans the rivalries, both ethnic and political were rife in Albania, with families fighting the Italians and random German troops on the border as often as each other. The Albanian irregulars can best be labeled as partisans *and* guerrillas, since the majority were fighting to remove the enemy from their land, although this same majority was apolitical and uncaring as to whether King Zog returned to the country or not. The main intent of the irregulars was the theft of weapons and ammunition from Italian or German troops in order to continue their own internal blood feuds.

The partisans were actively supported by the British during the war, since the country fell within the geographic region of Greece for SOE support. However, even when the situation looked bleakest the Greeks refused to join forces with the Albanians for very definitive reasons.[465] It would appear that the Greeks under King George saw the opportunity to seize control of Albania, annexing the country once the war was over due to the long history of Italian aid given the country before the war. The fact that Italy launched all of its major attacks from Albania gave the Greeks the political incentive to force the issue.

Another factor that rendered the situation interminable was the British Military Mission report stating that the Albanian resistance movement was really "no movement" at all, just a disorganized and loosely dispersed collection of individual cells that rarely managed an effective and coordinated operation.[466] However, the Communists did remain in closer contact and assist each other more than the other ideologically opposed factions, which seemed to be a common thread throughout Europe.[467] One of the most effective partisan leaders was Muslim Peza, a sworn enemy of King Zog who managed to operate the most effective and largest partisan band in the country. Soon after the German support arrived in April 1941 the National Liberation Army (NLA) was created, a force that assisted in collecting other loose bands under a united Nationalist Confederation.[468]

Despite the early reports by SOE regarding Albanian inefficiency, Winston Churchill stated in 1943: "The partisans and patriots in Yugoslavia and Albania were containing as many (German) divisions as the British and American armies put together." These were units that could have assisted Rommel in North Africa or even been sent to the Eastern Front to reverse the Stalingrad and Kursk debacles.[469] Churchill's assessment was quite true, and according to Karl Wolff "at least fifty divisions were engaged throughout the Balkans on occupation duty, primarily to check partisan activity."[470]

Keeping the partisans active and supplied was another major problem for SOE, the enemy notwithstanding. According to Major Peter Kemp in 1943: "This is not a war of liberation, but a war of Sovietization."[471] Another observer named William Maclean stated: "The average partisan, while admitting with pride that he is a Communist believes that he is fighting for an independent, democratic and popular Albania."[472] Albania would become the most insulated, isolated and xenophobic nation in Europe following the war under the tyrannical dictatorship of Enver Hoxha.

The Germans were forced to place more troops into the country during the winter of 1943-44, when Communist guerrilla leader Mehmet Shehu launched massive raids against the German and fascist government outposts and garrisons, attempting to liberate towns and villages. There was moderate initial success, although the German response was checked by a sudden explosion of a 70,000 strong guerrilla force intent on capturing Tirana, which was accomplished on 17 November 1944.[473] This activity was an ambitious plan for the Communists; to not only expel the Axis from the country, but to forcibly take control of a government in exile.[474] General Sir Henry Maitland Wilson, Commander-in-Chief Middle East "demanded that the partisans conform to the overall Allied game plan, which called for cooperative moves against the *Nazi's...*"[475]

Continued attacks destroyed many German strongholds in a domino effect as the irregulars gained numbers as they swept through the countryside, moving north from the southern region through Tirana in the center and on to Shkoder, which was captured on 29 November. All of this was accomplished without any conventional western material assistance.[476] At the invitation of Tito, Albanian guerrillas and partisans entered southern Yugoslavia, primarily ethnic Albanian regions such as Kosovo, where the Germans were still operating.[477] The NLA was now a force to be reckoned with, and every German defeat meant diminishing post-war Western Allied influence in the region. German forces were withdrawn to the more important Greek and Yugoslav regions, with Albania being written off as a bottomless pit not worth further attention.

Once the war drew to a close Enver Hoxha seized power, placing Mehmet Shehu as Prime Minister while the Allies watched and did nothing. The situation that evolved over the least several decades placed tensions upon Albanian Kosovars and Serbs, a situation that erupted in 1999, invoking images of another bloody and not too distant era.

6

Yugoslavia

*Give full play to our style of fighting-courage in
battle, no fear of sacrifice, no fear of fatigue, and
continuous fighting.*

- Mao Tse Tung
25 December 1947

The insurgency movement in Yugoslavia became legendary from the beginning of the
German invasion, with an image of savagery and unrelenting hostility that set the pace for
the future of armed insurgency for political gains long after the peace was established.
Hitler's Directive No. 25 launched the German invasion of Yugoslavia on 27 March 1941,
with Point No. 2 of the Directive stating:

> It is my intention to break into Yugoslavia in the general direction of Belgrade
> and southward by a concentric operation from the area of Rijeka-Graz on the one
> side and from the area around Sofia on the other and to give the Yugoslav armed
> forces an annihilating blow. In addition, I intend to cut off the extreme southern
> part of Yugoslavia from the rest of the country and seize it as a base for the con-
> tinuance of the German-Italian offensive against Greece.[478]

Twenty-five German and twenty-three Italian divisions invaded rapidly, supported by
an air umbrella of 1,500 German and 670 Italian aircraft as well as various naval assets.
Opposing this massive force were thirty Yugoslav divisions that were under staffed and ill
prepared for such an onslaught. The capture of Belgrade on 12 April and Sarajevo on 18
April 1941 by German forces and the subsequent armistice agreement forced the established government and leadership to evacuate to the relative safety of the mountainous
terrain.[479] Led by the Secretary General (since 1937) Josef Broz "Tito" this government,
which also formed the revised version of Guerrilla Operations Command[480] continued to
wage perhaps the most successful guerrilla campaign in all of Europe. This success came
despite the constant internal friction between the various partisan and guerrilla forces under
his control, which by 1945 eventually numbered approximately 300,000 personnel, of which
180,000 were labeled devout Communist supporters. Their configuration consisted of six
corps each with three divisions, with the balance of the total in reserve.[481]

The Yugoslav military had long expected the potential use of irregular forces within their nation, and in 1929 the Army and Navy published the *Handbook on Guerrilla Warfare*, partly a contingency plan for future operations and a continuation of planning against further conflicts with Hungarian forces.[482] The synopsis of the guidelines is as follows:

1-Guerrilla companies and units created by regular forces to operate either as the vanguard of large units or on their flanks or in the rear of the enemy, in all cases in tactical cooperation with large units, or in the rear of the enemy independently.

2-The size of a guerrilla unit may vary depending upon specific tasks when in conjunction with regular forces; in the case of independent action the organizational structure is fixed. Regardless of the unit composition or specific tasks the method of operation is surprise attacks. The success of these operations 'presupposes a friendly population and thus its support.'[483]

The Yugoslav government and Army did not actually plan on a long-term guerrilla warfare strategy should an invasion occur. In fact, the disorganized rabble that would best describe the Yugoslav resistance movement among the non-Communist groups would become glaringly obvious to not only the Germans, but the Allies as well. As recorded by Tomasevich, Colonel Branislav J. Pantic stated during the 11 November 1941 meeting between the Plenipotentiary Commanding General and Draza Mihailovic's representatives: "The Communists were the first to start the fight, whereas Mihailovic stood completely aside and was preparing to strike in the direction of Bosnia and Skandjak. He wanted to take revenge on the *Ustascha* who had tortured to death hundreds of thousands of Serbs."[484] The deep rift between the nationalist and Communist resistance groups created the best possible condition where German political ambitions were concerned. However, the reality on the ground for the occupation forces was an unparalleled nightmare.

The historical record has labeled the Yugoslav resistance as a "partisan" force, a statement that is now worthy of challenge. Given the descriptions contained within this thesis and the necessity of accurately labeling paramilitary groups according to their political agendas, Tito was in fact not in total command of a massive and completely "partisan" force, but rather a massive partisan *and* guerrilla force. Had Tito's forces been focused upon combating the Germans to restore the ousted monarchy, then his forces *en masse* could legitimately bear the title of "partisan." However, given the fact that Tito was fighting the Germans to free Yugoslavia, as well as combating the Orthodox Christians, separatists and Roman Catholics for domination of the nation, both internally and externally in order to install a Communist post-war government, his forces were in fact "guerrillas" by definition.

Tito's successes were, according to Tomasevich, successful due to the spirit and fostering of patriotism and even nationalism, despite the Communist aversion to a restoration of the previous legitimate government.[485] These activities by Tito and his Communists were critical to laying the groundwork for the Communist controlled (albeit Soviet free) Yugoslavia that would emerge following the Second World War.[486]

The internal problems between ethnic groups divided by national identity, language and religion were to become insurmountable problems for the Germans. The country had always been a hot bed of unrest, as the Sarajevo resistance to Austro-Hungarian rule and the assassinations of Archduke Franz Ferdinand in 1914 and King Alexander I in 1934 illustrate.[487] This reality was not lost upon Hitler and the members of the General Staff, prompting Hitler to send *General der Infanterie* (*Generaloberst*) Edmund Glaise von Horstenau to Agram Zagreb on 15 April 1941 as liaison officer between the *Wehrmacht* and the new Croatian State (the first independent Croatia since 1100 AD) on 11 April 1941.[488] *Generaloberst* Glaise von Horstenau would remain as Plenipotentiary General in Croatia until September 1944.[489]

Tito would emerge as the only person who could successfully control the population, regardless of ethnic, religious and political convictions through a ruthless application of internal policing and the collective inclusion of all groups within the government to maintain harmony and reduce terminate strife. This political maneuver, combined with a police state environment would secure internal pacification through Tito's death in 1980, when his ruthless genius would be lost. The bindings that held the nation together would eventually fall apart, and the Yugoslavia of Tito's era would become a collection of breakaway states, independent nations or pretenders to statehood fighting for freedom from Belgrade's control, much in the way the Yugoslavs fought for freedom from German occupation.

The German invasion saw the placement of several stellar and future high-ranking officers placed in command of units that began to feel the sting of irregular warfare almost immediately. The lessons of guerrilla warfare were to be learned the hard way in the rugged, mountainous country, where danger lay behind every tree, smiling face and within every village. German officers trained in the rigid thinking of the age were not prepared for the insurgency warfare that would soon be thrust upon them.

When the German *12th Armee* entered the Balkans and drove through Yugoslavia, one of the generals who would become perhaps the most capable of Hitler's future field commanders was *Generalleutnant* (later *Generalfeldmarschall*) Walter Model.[490] Model's career would reach it's zenith when he commanded the *2nd Panzerarmee* and *9th Armee* in the epic struggles on the Eastern Front from late 1941 to the spring of 1942, in particular while involved in the two Demyansk operations against superior Red Army and partisan forces and from January-May 1942, and again from 5 May-18 August 1943.[491] Model's direct attack and complete annihilation method of warfare earned him Hitler's respect, and the sobriquet "Hitler's Fireman" among the *Generalstabs*. Model's *modus operandi* placed him in the welcomed echelon of *Waffen SS* commanders despite his lengthy *Wehrmacht Heer* affiliation, especially since he had no moral problem with allowing the dreaded *Einsatzgruppen* and *Sonderkommando* to operate with his forces.

Another officer and veteran of the First World War was *Generalfeldmarschall* Wilhelm List, who commanded the *12th Armee*[492] units in Bucharest, Romania, Galicia and Sofia, Bulgaria from 1 March 1941 during the Balkans invasion, fighting the retreating Yugoslav forces and irregulars, finally breaking through the Metaxas Line in Greece.[493] List would find himself thrown into counterinsurgency warfare throughout Greece, Croatia, Dalmatia, Bosnia and Serbia, and in combat support with units such as *"Leibstandarte"* under Josef "Sepp" Dietrich.[494] It would also be List who would become *Wehrmachtbefehlshaber im Suedosten* by Hitler's Directive No. 31, dated 9 June 1941, following his superlative performance.

Another officer of the old school and of crucial importance in the counterinsurgency war was *Generalfeldmarschall* Maximilian *Freiherr* von Weichs.[495] Weichs began to operate with counterinsurgency units in the mountainous country of Greece and Yugoslavia in late 1940 through the spring of 1941.[496] It was during April 1941 that Weichs issued direct orders to shoot all male civilians in areas of partisan/guerrilla activity, and "guilt was to be assumed unless innocence could be proven."[497] This period would mark the beginning of the German supported death squads as well as the indigenous active military units conducting such operations.

Under Weichs' watch the level of retaliation would escalate, with the first mass killings beginning on July 15 and the first documented burning of villages and the taking of hostages.[498] Weichs' Balkans experience would prove invaluable later during the Russian campaign, where he served from 1941-45 (with a brief return to the Balkans during the retreat), especially as the numbers of irregulars exploded and German forces were diminishing in both numbers and fighting quality.[499] Weichs' greatest test against the Red Army and irregulars was probably during the period 1 January-6 May 1943 as stated in his war diary.[500] Under his command were many future anti-partisan commanders in the coming war with Russia, men who would learn quickly from their enemies and create an atmosphere that would re-define the nature of modern military and political warfare. One such officer was *Generalmajor* Hermann von Witzleben, who was also commanding troops in the Balkans and Yugoslavia, thus becoming indoctrinated in the realities of partisan warfare.[501] This experience would serve him well when he later commanded elements of the Hungarian 2nd Army during the fall and winter of 1942-43.[502] Among the ranks of his staff would rise several prominent members of the counterinsurgency warfare community.

Interviews with two former Yugoslav insurgents hammer home the depth of the partisan/guerrilla war in that nation, a nation torn apart by ethnic hatreds and political volatility. When offered the combined assistance of the British SOE, American OSS and the Red Army in 1943 and late 1944 respectively, the irregular forces already posed a threat to German forces that far exceeded their worst expectations. As soon as the Balkan nations collapsed under the weight of the German invasions, partisans who had already served several years fighting the Italians and each other rapidly shifted their point of aim to the new and more deadly threat. The partisan and guerrilla threat forced the German occupation forces to relocate thousands of civilians, some for "special treatment" and others for forced labor, since rear areas were now considered as insecure as the former front lines. The Germans would create special tactics in dealing with these partisans, which are detailed later in the chapter on German tactics.

The war against Tito took on a personal tone with Hitler. During Christmas 1942 *General* Loehr held a high level conference of all German leaders of the Serbo-Croatian districts.[503] Among these officers was *General* Lueters, commanding general of all German troops in Croatia, who issued a warrant for Tito's arrest the following spring, following the arrival of a dispatch from *Fuehrer Hauptamt*.[504] The order stated, "It was the will of Hitler to change the territory taken from Tito into a desert and not to spare anyone, women or children."[505] This order was apparently resisted by all of the *Wehrmacht* generals concerned and after a flurry of memoranda fired to Berlin, "the order was rescinded."[506] However, not all of the German generals succumbed to humanitarian logic. *Brigadefuehrer* Arthur Phleps ordered his *"Prinz Eugen"* Division into action, completely destroying four villages with the majority of the inhabitants in Northern Dalmatia in March 1944.[507] Von Horstenau's comments regarding his relationship with the *Waffen SS* units speaks volumes:

> The *SS* acted as if they were in enemy territory, led by the bad example of their commanders. Robbing and looting were wide-spread. No action was taken against any of the offenders, even more embarrassment was caused by the 1st Cossack Division,[508] brought to Croatia in autumn 1943. This division advanced from Syrmia towards Agram robbing, looting, burning and raping. Interventions did not help, because it was stated officially that there existed a lack of soldiers and nobody could be spared. The example the *SS* and Cossacks also had its influence on the regular *Wehrmacht* troops, who wondered why they could not have the same privileges. Only Pevelic looked at it all with oriental equanimity.[509]

An Italian officer, *Capitano*[510] Mario Antonucci fought as an Italian *Alpini* (Alpine soldier) in Albania, Yugoslavia, Russia and Hungary, and even combated partisans in the Carpathian Mountains of Romania. Antonucci also fought against regular and irregular forces at the Metaxas Line in Greece and again in Hungary in 1944 and 1945 respectively. Many Italians defected to the Allies and irregulars between 1943-45 when their government became unstable and the Badoglio government, in conjunction with King Victor Emmanuel III of Savoy overthrew Mussolini.[511] Antonucci's comments on the Balkan war are interesting, given the fact that he was wounded three times in Yugoslavia alone and once in Russia fighting irregulars:

> In fighting regular soldiers there are many advantages, such as easily identifying your opponent, understanding that there are accepted rules of warfare, and the knowledge that you could possibly out maneuver a conventional force. With partisans this was not the case, you never knew where you stood, and the accepted rules of war did not apply. The fact that the Germans performed the way they did made life very difficult for all of us. I hated the Balkans, and I have never returned, not even for a holiday.[512]

The Yugoslav interviews were extremely important, including a pro-German *Chetnik* who later joined the *Waffen SS* as an anti-partisan specialist serving in the *"Kroatische Nr. 1"* Division despite his Serbian origin. His story was similar to others interviewed; those persons of ethnic Germanic background hoping for a union of Germanic peoples under the expanding Third *Reich*, and the expulsion of those they considered their "enemies."[513]

The pro-German Croatian units were the paramilitary support network of the Independent State of Croatia, led by the fascist *Ustascha* Party,[514] a fanatical organization headed by Dr. Ante Pavelic. Pavelic spent most of the 1930s and 1940s exiled in Italy,[515] and came to power on 10 April 1941 with Italian and German support following the bloodless coup that ousted Prince Paul, and then began the program of "ethnic cleansing" of the approximately 1,925,000 Serbs (making up 30.6 percent of Croatia's population) within Croatia, again with German support.[516] His successful recruitment in 1943 of the Peasant Party into his new government proved advantageous and offered him legitimacy in the eyes of the Germans.[517] However, Pavelic would begin following a well-understood program, such as the persecution of Jews, Gypsies and Serbs (although some could serve in the military), all of whom would eventually become victims of hate and violence.[518]

According to Jonathan Gumz, the *Ustascha* field leader Mile Budak planned for a full one-third of the Serbs in Croatia to be exterminated, another one-third forcibly converted to Catholicism, and the balance resettled outside Croatia's borders. However, this plan was amended to a program of complete liquidation once German support was available.[519] By the end of the war approximately 200,000 Serbs would be killed by *Ustascha* along with German counterinsurgency and auxiliary support.[520]

The German reaction to these mass killings was mixed. The field commanders almost in total (in addition to von Horstenau) wanted the violence halted due to the consequences of violence begetting violence. German military officials, despite having far too few troops to handle occupation, counterinsurgency, as well as widespread police duties wanted to arrest and detain specific *Ustascha* members guilty of atrocities.[521] However, Ambassador Kasche, although openly supporting the activities of the secret police considered "the *Ustascha* horrors as an ugly though excusable reaction of revolutionary 'dynamics.'"[522] According to the post-war interrogation report on von Horstenau, "the Ambassador's policies seemed to be in contrast to the principles used in the *Reich* and in other occupied territories."[523] Eugen Kvaternik, operating as Secretary of State for Security simply answered the questions posed to him by the Ambassador regarding his tactics, stating "that these methods had been learned during a three weeks' instruction course with the *SS*."[524]

During the spring of 1942 this tacit acceptance of *Ustascha* policy was put to the ultimate test. A motorized infantry company commanded by a young officer candidate had massacred a village near Sarajevo. Von Horstenau ordered the division commander to arrest the company commander responsible, and detain all members of his company, strip them of their weapons and process them for a general court-martial.[525] Given the expectation that death sentences would be imposed Hitler was informed of the situation in total.[526] The following response from Hitler funneled through the High Command is typical of the "hands off " policy regarding atrocities committed in the field by pro-German forces, especially when it suited the overall German agenda: "The *Fuehrer* has decided that the *Ustascha* Movement represents the state-authorized movement in Croatia and that therefore it is necessary to overlook temporary offenses."[527] However, despite Hitler's apparent regard for the autonomy and activities of the Croats, the *Chetniks* were nevertheless living on borrowed time.

March 1943 saw the senior members of the Balkans command finally receive some relief regarding their distaste of the *Ustascha* and *Chetniks* who were making life more difficult as opposed to offering meaningful assistance. During the attacks launched against Tito's forces (with intelligence placing the leader with one of the groups) the order was given (supported by the Croatian government) to eliminate the *Chetniks* (who were supported and "favored by the Italians") under Mihailovic, despite their previous collaboration and the meetings held between Mihailovic and *Oberstleutnant* Rudolf Kogard, Intelligence Officer to the Plenipotentiary Command in the area of Southern Herzegovina, Southern Dalmatia and Montenegro.[528] The mission carried the German regulars, auxiliaries and half-hearted Italian forces "along the upper Narenta."[529]

The breakdown occurred when the Italians apparently warned the *Chetniks* who largely avoided the envelopment. What did occur completely by chance was that the main force of

Tito's guerrillas walked into an ambush not meant for them, and after a long and costly engagement Tito escaped. Following this event Lueters resigned his command to *Generalleutnant* Lothar Rendulic, commander of the *2nd Panzer Armee* in Serbia.[530] Shortly afterward the Italians withdrew from the Axis and the Soviet gains following Kursk forced hundreds of thousands of German troops to be returned to the Eastern Front, thus weakening an already tenuous German foothold on the region, both militarily and politically. It was at this time of German force reduction that SOE increased its activities, and with great urgency.[531]

The Italians and Germans had divided the region between them, with Mussolini maintaining control over the western portion of Croatia with Germany occupying the east.[532] The ruthless activities would initiate the exponential increase of civilians to the Tito camp from 1941 through the end of the war, and become powerful enough to garner the interest and support of British SOE and later American OSS contingents. The openly constructed murders of the Greek and Serbian Orthodox population by both Tito's guerrillas and *Ustascha* were a detrimental factor in forming an effective, responsive coalition government in any of the occupied Yugoslav territories.[533]

This factor became quite evident to the forthcoming SOE members sent to estimate the effectiveness of the movements and analyze the respective resistance groups for further assistance consideration. One such operative whose analysis became important and extremely accurate regarding the Yugoslav situation was Captain Evelyn Waugh, a former Royal Marine turned SAS officer.[534] Waugh's reluctance to embrace Tito's Communists (Churchill also distrusted Tito) was due to the reality of the purge of the Christian religions under Tito that occurred during and, as he foresaw, after the war.

Part of the ever-present problem was the religious animosity between the Roman Catholic and Orthodox Christian elements that had been stirred by the Communists in order to weaken any possible Christian coalition that may challenge their plans for a new government. As stated in Waugh's diary: "Randolph asked me to go with him to Croatia in the belief that I should be able to heal the Great Schism between the Catholic and Orthodox Churches," since Waugh was a converted Catholic.[535] SOE mission in Yugoslavia and Waugh's appointment to Croatia were considered some of the most important of the war, and Waugh's reports stating his belief that an alliance with Stalin "completely deprived the war of the crusading element," were not met with great enthusiasm by Sir Roger Keyes, Director of Special Operations, or those reading his reports in Whitehall.

Part of Waugh's complete disenchantment stemmed from his service under Randolph Churchill, renegade son of the Prime Minister who had managed to alienate much of the partisan/guerrilla support through his thoughtless and immature actions. One of his episodes included spreading a rumor (that began as a joke) that Tito was really a woman. This rumor reached London and apparently infuriated Tito, and did little to forge complete trust among the Communist partisans needed so desperately to counter the German occupation.[536]

The fact that Tito ordered the elimination of tens of thousands of Christians, both Catholic and Orthodox appears to have been recognized as faulty in retrospect by the Yugoslav leader. Tito apparently realized that if he were to control a Soviet free Yugoslavia in the post-war future he would need the support of the very people he was killing. Tito appointed bishops to the Yugoslav branch of the Orthodox Church and began to heal the fractures that would prove necessary in the not too distant future.[537] However, Tito re-evaluated the effort to continue combating the *Chetniks* and hopefully have Mihailovic killed, since this would possibly create a problem between the Soviets and British that would eventually effect his position. To give Tito due credit, he did continue to negotiate with the *Chetniks* while continuing to fight the Germans, all the while maintaining a tenuous foothold without any large-scale support from either the east or west.

Waugh managed to accomplish the near impossible; he contacted the clergy of both Christian sects, obtained valuable information, and after studying the problem wrote a detailed report that history would prove was highly accurate, and portended a grave future for the region, the Christians, and Tito's reliability. However, due to the current political climate Waugh's report regarding the less than affable conditions and the widespread murder of the clergy by the Communists was not taken seriously, and Waugh himself was faced with a court-martial. Only Waugh's reputation as a completely honest man with great insight as to problem solving and conflict resolution and his supporters within the Labor Party prevented the travesty.[538]

The British operatives discovered the same problems in containing the activities and organizing an effective allied force among the indigenous personnel that confronted the Germans: ethnic and religious strife between the major sects reducing the overall combat effectiveness of the partisan operations. The British were basically hedging their bets, sending officers to various resistance groups in order to effectively support and prosecute a greater effort against the enemy.[539] The German effort had been challenged effectively despite their large numbers of troops, including *Wehrmacht* and *Freiwilligen*,[540] and by 1943 Tito's 300,000 strong Communist guerrilla force had prompted Hitler to initiate a series of large-scale operations.

The first of these was *Operation Weiss* (White), which commenced on 20 January 1943 and witnessed thirty-seven divisions totaling 90,000 German and Italian troops, mostly *Panzertruppen* and *Gebirgsjaeger*, and comprised of the *717th* and *718th* Divisions, elements from the *714th* Division, the *7th Waffen SS* Division *"Prinz Eugen,"* the *187th* Reserve *Infanterie* Division, *369th Infanterie* Division (Croatian Legion), the Italian "Bergamo," "Marche," "Murge," "Lombardia," "Re" and "Sasari" Divisions, several Croatian brigades and an additional 12-15,000 *Chetniks* supported by *Luftwaffe* and *Reggio Aeronautica* fighters, dive bombers, artillery and armor, encircling Bihac in January 1943.[541] By March 1943 *Generaloberst* Loehr's Situation Report stated: "The battles thus far fought show that Mihailovic as a military leader has failed. By not recognizing the existing possibilities because of his lack of knowledge of the area, and the terrain, and the demands of the time, he has been chiefly responsible for the failure so far."[542] In essence, Loehr was placing the failure of subduing the Communists squarely on the very man he never adequately supplied and supported.

This mission trapped Tito and 25,000 guerrillas in a pocket that Hitler wanted reduced. The date of 17 May 1943 saw the much larger second stage directed against the Communists, code named *Operation Schwarz* (Black) that sent 117,000 Axis soldiers into a massive partisan hunt.[543] In typical *Blitzkrieg* fashion with rather unexpected large-scale German-*Chetnik* collaboration the net cordoned off a large number of partisans from the 1st, 2nd, 3rd and 7th Communist Divisions, complete with Tito and the entire resistance military leadership encircled, with 30.0 percent perishing and the 4,000 wounded being left for dead as the Communists retreated.[544] One of the most spectacular events occurred when the 1st *Gebirgs*

Division, containing five companies of infantry and heavy artillery encountered 3,000 Communists in the mountains near Kolasin. The unit commander authorized smaller detachment commanders to make liaison with the *Chetniks*, and jointly the Communists were reduced. Shortly after this episode the German High Command, upon learning about the joint operation ordered the *Chetniks* disarmed, which was done.[545] However, not all of the German operations went as smoothly.

The overall force, commanded from Belgrade by *Armee Gruppe F* and *2nd Panzer Armee* (responsible for all German units in Albania and Yugoslavia) became confused as to the command structure, especially when issuing orders and authorizing adjacent unit movements. What had worked in the conventional forum against the Western Allied ground armies and the Soviets in the early days proved to be totally detrimental in combating a strong, well-organized and cohesive insurgency movement. The German command and control fell apart almost immediately despite the initial success, and the fact that the partisans had been corralled near Dvar. This was due to the German Military Commander Southeast, *Generalfeldmarschall* Maximilian von Weichs refusing to coordinate with the *SS* units due to his disapproval of their methods.[546] It would be this development that would prompt Hitler to issue *Sturmbannfuehrer* (later *Obersturmbannfuehrer*) Otto Skorzeny the orders to capture or kill Tito; "whichever proved most plausible."[547] The pressure placed upon the irregulars would see the Allies make a greater effort to support them in their struggle. Another and equally important subject was an anti-German Serb named Milo Stavic, who served with and knew Tito[548] personally, and was entrusted with feeding the President's dog as well as planning ambush operations against German occupation and Muslim *"Handschar"* units.[549] His perceptions of the guerrilla struggle in which he participated for nearly four years are interesting to note:

> Most of us who were nationalists wanted a Yugoslavia free of the one party domination, and we were not all necessarily Communists. However, once the Germans invaded and Belgrade fell in April 1941[550] we were forced into action, as Serbs were being murdered by Croatian forces. It was this activity that created the great partisan movement, nothing else.[551]

Another perspective regarding this topic was offered by an irregular named Lothar Pankosk, who fought as a *Chetnik* supporter of the Germans and also fought against fellow Serbs (especially the forces of DRINA) supporting Tito's government:

> We as Serbs were initially opposed to the German invasion, and we *Chetniks* were nationalists who wanted a country of our own. When the Germans invaded and the war increased the divisions within our national ethnic peoples, we soon learned that Tito was requesting support for his Communists from Russia. This was not what we wanted, since we knew that any Soviet assistance meant a possible Soviet government, or at least a Soviet controlled government, and this was completely unacceptable. Our decision to fight with the Germans stemmed from our belief that we would cease to exist as nationalists if the Communists won. I have no regrets in my decision to fight the Titoists. I also fought against them after the war, and went to Greece to fight against the Communists there in the civil war.

I was not alone. It is ironic that historians discuss the Genocide of the Jews and Serbs under German rule, yet they conveniently forget the millions killed by the Communists, people killed who simply wanted to be free and determine their own destiny. We fought for our lives, our land and people. Nothing else.[552]

What both of these men have to say is highly relevant, not only regarding what was transpiring in the Yugoslavia of World War II but is continuing to this day. The liquidation of large numbers of people has always been the greatest catalyst for social upheaval and discontent with an occupation force. This fact was at least addressed by the Germans who saw the volatile nature of Balkan politics, and in Yugoslavia in particular. *Reichsfuehrer-SS* Heinrich Himmler understood the difficulties facing German occupation forces, since his *Waffen SS* units were the premier cut and thrust weapons in the counterinsurgency program, along with the Russian Security Corps under *Generaloberst* Helmuth Stieff numbering some 15,000 volunteers.[553] As stated by Gumz, Himmler stated that "it was a gross political error to think that one could exterminate two million Orthodox Serbs."[554] According to Karl Wolff regarding the Yugoslav situation:

> Yugoslavia was to become the greatest problem for the occupation forces, even more so than Russia, mainly due to the rather static and long term nature of our occupation. It is a misconception to state that German forces actually occupied the entire country. This would have been impossible. We could only occupy major cities and garrison outposts, but never the entire nation. This failure to occupy the entire nation, as well as effectively control the population was what helped create the great problems that later arose. We did not have this problem on such a great scale in other parts of Europe, and this was a question that, I think, puzzled many senior officers. I don't think that we were capable of understanding the true nature of the problem.[555]

Hitler, in his usual benign fashion regarding such matters openly stated to the Croatian leadership that his "interests in the country were purely economical,"[556] and he offered no support to his military in suppressing the Genocide, despite the fact that it was evidently detrimental to instituting a peaceful occupation. When *Generalmajor* Paul Baader, the German military commander of Bosnia brought the facts of the *Ustascha* operations to Hitler's attention during a July 1942 leaders conference, Hitler simply said, "I don't want to hear any more about it."[557] By November 1942 *Generalleutnant* Rudolf Lueters was in command of the Germans Troops in Croatia, placing him parallel to Horstenau operating in the same region.[558]

Hitler's apathy was again demonstrated by the meeting held with Pavelic on 23 September 1942, and attended by *Generalmajor* Alexander Loehr, who told Hitler about the repercussions resulting from the Croatian activities.[559] Loehr's position was that the atrocities should be terminated, and the partisan problem growing as a result of these activities should be addressed more effectively. Hitler's response, according to Gumz (citing Horstenau) was that the Croats were "only letting off a little steam."[560] Another factor that may support the fact that the German occupation of Yugoslavia, in particular the German units established for the counterinsurgency campaigns were limited in number, was the fear of weakening the Axis alliance with Italy should a stronger German presence be installed.[561] The Italians were none too pleased with the increased German presence, especially since they took a more moderate approach in dealing with the locals, which the Germans found lacking in both discipline and effectiveness.

This one factor above all else explains the necessity to recruit, train and deploy indigenous forces as *Freiwilligen* auxiliaries to police their own domain. The Germans saw the necessity to bolster the occupation forces with politically reliable and if possible battle experienced units and commanders, of which the *7th der Waffen SS (Freiwilligen) Gebirgs* Division *"Prinz Eugen"*[562] blazed a notably ruthless path throughout the country during its tenure, being assisted by aircraft and allowed possession of its own battalion of artillery. *"Prinz Eugen"*, under its first commander, newly promoted *Gruppenfuehrer* Artur Phleps (later killed in Rumania) and his replacement, *Gruppenfuehrer* Karl *Ritter* von Oberkampf would prove extremely lethal to partisans, suspected partisans and sympathizers alike. This was especially true in Yugoslavia following their deployment to the region in December 1942.[563]

The prime examples were the August 1942 massacre of Muslims at Foca with thirty-three villages burned by *Chetniks* and 400 men and 1,000 women and children previously supported by the Italians being killed; the January and February 1943 massacres of Muslims at Sandjak (by *Chetniks*); July 1943 massacre at the Muslim village of Kosutica, where people of all ages were gunned down after the corpse of a *Waffen SS* man was discovered, which only increased resentment toward the population and strengthened the ranks of the partisans and guerrillas, especially the Communists.[564] The death toll would have been higher had many not already evacuated the area, with most going to Sarajevo.[565]

Phleps was ordered by Himmler to halt such activities, since he was at that time staffing the *13th der Waffen SS* Division *"Handschar"* and the news of such an event might dampen the efforts.[566] Other examples abounded, such as the 3,000 Croatians killed in Dalmatia in late March to early April 1944, when Phleps was promoted to *Obergruppenfuehrer* and placed in command of the *5th SS Gebirgs Korps,* and Oberkampf assumed command of *"Prinz Eugen"*. Actions such as these secured a massive influx and support network for the Communists, a growth that would dwarf all other theaters of the war in comparison to the German presence. Supported by the indigenously recruited and trained *"Handschar"* (Scimitar), comprised primarily of Muslims from Bosnia-Herzegovina, as well as the Russian Protective Corps, a group of 3,000 men recruited from the exiled Russian population within Serbia in 1943, but later expanded to 11,197 men by September 1944.[567] Most of these men had been partisans or guerrillas fighting against the Italians prior to the German invasion, or were involved with the ethnic wars against their various regional enemies, as well as the border clashes against the Greeks.

Hitler forced these private conflicts into a new stage when he authorized Himmler to recruit various eastern peoples into particular units, with the emphasis placed upon actively engaging partisan units in the field. The Germans did manage to recruit the assistance of the Serbian *Chetniks* who had been warring with Tito's Communist supporters in a futile civil war and knew the terrain well, and their enemy even better. The *Chetniks* were, in effect, a rather loose confederation of "guerrillas" pursuing a "partisan" agenda that was bordering on banditry, hardly an effective collective, yet hoping to alter the political structure to their own designs and restore the monarchy, although ultimately deciding that German support would offer the greatest chances for success. The use of these irregulars would further entangled in the web of conventional versus-irregular-versus special operations in the region, and this political, ethnic, religious and economic quagmire fueled dissent that had already lasted for centuries and would only gain momentum during the war, and rise again in the 1990s.

The *Chetniks* were especially effective when it came to scouting for German units, often times even serving within their ranks[568] until they turned against the Germans under the command of nationalist leader General Mihailovic.[569] Mihailovic managed to unite several *Chetnik* and Serb factions to defeat the "true common enemy" following the belated and questionable acknowledgment by London that the British government was recognizing him as the true and *only* legitimate commander of resistance (partisan) forces at the expense of Tito.

All of this occurred while the Muslim members of *"Handschar"* had been deployed and equipped, where they excelled in the location and elimination of Jews.[570] It is interesting to note that the Jewish population in Yugoslavia was very small even before the war, and it virtually ceased to exist upon the conclusion of hostilities through the unlikely and coincidental collaboration of Roman Catholic Croatians, Orthodox *Chetniks*, Bosnian Muslims and German forces in unison. However, there is no evidence that any reasonable numbers of Jews were ever deported from the country to the extermination camps, leaving their fate to even the dullest imagination.

Most of the anti-partisan/guerrilla activity was under the command of the *XV Cossack Cavalry Corps* comprised of *Freiwilligen* that operated in both Hungary and Yugoslavia; a force that contained approximately 21,000 ethnic Russians, most of whom were former POWs who converted to the German ideology. They did eventually become the most successful of all anti-partisan groups, and they crippled an entire Soviet Army on the Hungarian side of the Danube in December 1944, surrounding three divisions until reinforced by German troops from *1st SS "Leibstandarte"* and *2nd SS "Das Reich."* This impressive force was virtually decimated, and the few thousand who surrendered to the British were handed over to the Soviets, and according to Wolff and Kumm, none are known to have survived.

The Croats were another group friendly to the German cause, long opposing the Communists and fighting their neighbors and the Tito government for an independent state. The Croats would receive the most military and financial assistance from the Germans than any other pretender to statehood, including their own fighter squadron and the creation of two *Waffen SS* Divisions, sub-titled *"Kroatische Nr. 1"* and *"Nr. 2"* respectively, with the *"Nr. 1"* being finally (and ironically) absorbed into the *13th der SS "Handschar."* Both units would serve in Yugoslavia, Russia and the Balkans later in the war, but would be primarily supported by the *22nd (Freiwilligen) Kavallerie* Division *der Waffen SS "Maria Theresia."* These units would piece-meal surrender to British forces in Austria in May 1945.

The German military and *Freiwilligen* units were augmented by a large contingent of military police units, and the contributions of *Oberst der Polizei* Karl Gaisser is of great importance.[571] As a commander of the *Gauleiter Gendarmerie* in Croatia from June 1943-November 1944, Gaisser was in local control of anti-partisan activity of specific regions.[572] Gaisser's *Polizei* detachments assisted in the eradication of partisans and guerrillas beyond any doubt, although there has yet to surface any legitimate information that either he or the men under his command participated in the genocide of the Jews, Serbs and other target populations *en masse*. Gaisser found himself caught up in the *Ustascha* pogrom against the Serbs, which undermined his mission of pacifying the districts under his command. The constant flood of refugees criss-crossing the country allowed the partisans and guerrillas to hide within their ranks, making the counterinsurgency operations almost impossible to accomplish.

The situation during the summer of 1942 came to a head when the German General Staff in occupation of Yugoslavia met with the primary *Ustascha* leaders, "including Pavelic and Lieutenant Colonel Eugen Kvaternik."[573] After securing their assurances to halt the policy (especially after Kvaternik had 200 people of the Orthodox faith murdered outright as revenge for the previous "murder" of two Croats)[574] and maintain a more moderate position regarding the Serbs, the *Ustascha* leaders reneged on their word. According to Gumz, "within three months the German *718th* Division informed *General* Baader that the *Ustascha* pillaging had grown worse."[575] The *Abwehr* and Army Intelligence blamed the explosion of partisan activity upon these actions, and this facilitated the creation of the indigenous *Freiwilligen* units in an attempt to curb the activity. Again, according to Gumz: "By midsummer 1942 Sarajevo had taken 20,000 Serb refugees from the *Ustascha*; another 10,000, according to German police officials, had gone over to Tito's Partisans."[576] Another problem facing the Germans was that *Generaloberst* Kuntze issued a directive dated 15 April 1942 that no field units could negotiate with "rebel groups or any unofficial armed units, because such dealing not only could be interpreted as a weakness on the part of the German armed forces, but also gave a legal standing to such groups."[577]

One of the commanders to be supported by Gaisser was *Generaloberst* Kurt Zeitzler.[578] Zeitzler, nicknamed *Kugelblitz* ("Thunderball") was one of the few gifted Army commanders who understood the nature, seriousness and complexity of counterinsurgency operations, as demonstrated by his lengthy and successful career as a counterinsurgency commander. Zeitzler's career began in Serbia and throughout Yugoslavia while commanding *Panzergruppe I* from 7 December 1940-1 May 1941, seeing temporary service in Bulgaria and Romania from 3 January-28 February 1941.[579] Zeitzler attempted to reign in the Croatian death squads, explaining the situation to the leadership as to the negative result and counterproductive nature of their actions. His failure to secure an agreement may have been the reason he was removed from command, although this is yet to be proved through the documentation. One explanation for his reassignment comes from Karl Wolff, who was on the planning staff for *Operation Barbarossa*:

> The planning for *Barbarossa* had been long and detailed, but it was in March (1941) that the final planning stages were in motion. We had planned for an April invasion, but Rudolf Hess' action delayed the execution.[580] Then we had the Yugoslav problem that required our attention. With the fall of Belgrade we were an occupation force, yet still pushing on to Greece, then Crete in May that further delayed *Barbarossa*. Hitler was becoming very impatient with all of these actions, wanting them completed quickly. When it came to the assigning of the various field commanders, there were many whose names were drawn due to their various areas of expertise. Zeitzler had a great amount of experience with partisans, and it was believed that as a qualified *panzer* and infantry commander he would be critical in the opening phase of *Barbarossa*.

I don't believe that Zeitzler's failure at containing the problem in Yugoslavia had anything to do with his appointment to the coming Russian campaign. If anything at all it would have been perceived as a promotion and a sign of his stature within the *Wehrmacht*.[581]

Following *Operation Barbarossa,* Zeitzler, who was openly opposed to the policy of mass reprisals (or *Suehnemassnahmen*) for partisan activity found himself stalled by the Croatian disregard to heed German authority. He was later given command of the 1st Hungarian Cavalry and 1st Hungarian Motorized Infantry units, which would become complete brigades by 1944 and operate as an anti-partisan force with some success. By this date his command would include a White Russian Tank and Cavalry Corps (later part of the Vlasov Army detailed to his command in 1944) to augment his already powerful forces.[582] From the opening salvoes of *Barbarossa* Zeitzler took the initiative in counterinsurgency activity in the south, through the Ukraine from 26 June-31 July 1941, effectively reducing these threats to his forces, lines of supply and communication.[583] Zeitzler's command in the face of stiffening partisan resistance in the Soviet Union will be discussed in the following chapter in greater detail.

It still remains as stark evidence the paranoia Hitler maintained regarding the insurgency problem in Yugoslavia, since at any given time no less than thirty divisions (of which four divisions were *SS*) were on occupation duty in the Balkans, with the bulk deployed to Yugoslavia, although the number only rose to thirty divisions in 1943 following the collapse of North Africa in May, due to fears of a possible Allied invasion of the Balkans from the Adriatic Sea from Sicily or Italy.[584] This was also the high mark of SOE activity in the country in an effort to draw more German forces from Italy to reinforce Yugoslavia, since the diversion would hopefully hasten the Allied victory following the invasions of Sicily and Italy.

It can be argued that Hitler was less concerned with the establishment of pro-German governments as he was in maintaining a firm hand of occupation, considering his "allies" more as subjects than partners. Hitler's attitude of disinterest regarding the internal stability of the Yugoslav regions was to prove his *modus operandi* throughout the rest of Eastern Europe. One factor that is evident and succinctly stated by Gumz was the German desire to end the liquidation of the Serb community by the Croats, in particular by the *Ustascha* Security Police.[585] As cited by Gumz, "the *Ustascha* state disregarded the German officials' protests against Serbian genocide, and these same officials possessed few effective means to compel Independent Croatia to follow German directives."[586] These activities and their memory would come back to haunt those opposed to Serb jurisdiction following the civil wars within the country during the 1990s.

These problems with attempting to pacify the local populations and complete their transformation from pro-Communist support to at least one of theoretical nationalism supported by Berlin (if not outright alliance) was further stifled by the inability of the German commanders (including Zeitzler) to curb the ethnic hatreds that made the pogrom against the Jews in the country seem mild. The hands off policy of Hitler and the High Command that supported political and personal in-fighting[587] also allowed the German field commanders (as well as *Ustascha*) to handle situations as they saw fit, which more often than not led to disaster. Gumz cites one example; the village of Novo Selo that saw reprisals in late 1943 when a German NCO was stabbed. The four partisans responsible were captured wearing German uniforms and executed by the commander of the detachment from the *369ᵗʰ* Division. This was a justifiable occurrence under the laws of land warfare. However, the commanding officer, *Generalleutnant* Fritz Neidholt authorized the hanging of ten men at random and the destruction of a like number of homes in complete violation of the accepted rules of warfare.[588]

It was this inability to control the aspirations and activities of the Croats by the Germans during the war that the modern United Nations and NATO politicians should keep in mind when dealing with this region in the present and future. A prime example of the *Ustascha* application of ethnic cleansing in August 1942 by the leader of the Security Service, Eugen Kvaternik, bears a strange resemblance to the mass murders committed in the country only recently. Operating under the pretext of "anti-partisan operations" the Security Service entered the region of Srem, entering the city of Sremska-Mitrovica where the police chief had detained thirty suspected guerrillas. Upon entry the force leader, Victor Tomic, arrested between 3,000 and 4,000 Serbs, and days of mass executions followed. The survivors were killed at a later date or sent to Germany as forced labor, while others were placed in a Croatian concentration camp. A few were selected to be set free.[589]

These situations prompted Baader to increase the role of the *Feldengendarmerie* to maintain control and reduce the crisis to a manageable level, and his success rating was due to a humane and strictly controlled program of lenient treatment for everyone, including Muslims, Croats and Serbs. Even the fruitless attempts at arresting the Croatian offenders to prevent further mass murders became bloody encounters, such as the battle between the *Wehrmacht* forces and *Ustascha* personnel at the Drina River on the Serb-Croatian border.[590] However, these situations were few and far between, primarily due to the German inability to spare enough occupation troops to control the Croatians, let alone ensure the peace.

According to Gumz, who states that the administrative chaos and confusion between command structures such as the *SS, Wehrmacht,* and *Polizei* added to the inability of combating the partisans that labored "without defined spheres of authority, leading to a patchwork of claims and counterclaims for authority."[591] Part of the conflict stemmed from the inclusion of the *Freiwilligen,* where the *SS* believed it had authority over the Army for the selection and recruitment of the *Volksdeutsche,* especially among the Croatians. The Croatian government and *Ustascha* believed that the recruitment of Croats undermined their self-proclaimed and German supported "independent" status, and the Army itself wanted to recruit soldiers, not uniformed executioners. All wanted to control the human assets within their domain to serve their individual purposes, and this is where the confusion was perhaps greatest.

This confusion must be analyzed not as much as an administrative quagmire unable to handle a military problem, but as the inability of German forces to perform in an unaccustomed role. The German military was an operational, combined arms conventional military force and had proven itself as such during the early days of the war through 1942. However, rather than simply state that the Germans failed in Yugoslavia due to paralyzing departmental rivalries and administrative chaos is too simplistic. The stark reality is that the German military was thrust into a role for which it was neither trained, equipped nor capable of handling. Soldiers must never be expected to accomplish missions that fall outside their defined roles and method of operation, much as a podiatrist, although a doctor, should not be expected to perform a quadruple bypass in a coronary unit. This was the true nature of the German failure and the reason for the creation of the indigenous counterinsurgency units that performed well in that role, yet were torn to pieces when they eventually confronted the conventional Red Army in strength, since their training and experience lay in the realm of counterinsurgency warfare, not open and prolonged conventional warfare for which they were neither specifically trained nor equipped.

One of the great plans envisioned by Hitler was the creation of a massive auxiliary army to supplement the German armed forces, thus expanding his *Reich* to include millions preferably loyal to National Socialism. It was primarily due to the crisis between the *Ustascha* and the Serbs that prompted Hitler to authorize the creation of auxiliary units under German commanders, in order to effectively control the population under arms according to Karl Wolff.[592] The Aryan peoples of Europe, whether Germanic or not were allowed to be incorporated into the greater *Volksgemeinschaft*, although the definition of "suitable" seemed to change depending upon the day of the week and the latest hallucination. Hitler and Himmler both believed that the long-standing rivalries of the various ethnic peoples in Europe could be turned to their advantage, and Yugoslavia was to join Russia in becoming a proving ground.

The ultimate explanation for the failure of the German occupation forces in curtailing the partisan problem in Yugoslavia was the fact that they were trained and deployed *strictly* as combat units, not as civil authorities or even as a passive occupation force. The placement of limited numbers of troops due to political and military requirements forced this responsibility upon the local and German staffed police units, who did not have the appropriate training and adequate numbers to effectively handle the insurgents, let alone control the unpredictable *Ustascha*. Germany's failure to properly address the problem, both militarily and politically and take the necessary corrective action in preventing the Croatian atrocities proved to be the greatest asset to the Communist partisans, flooding their ranks and setting the stage for an independent pro-Communist government after the war.

Generaloberst Lothar Rendulic was also faced with this disheveled situation when his *2nd Panzer Armee* entered the region in August 1943. Realizing that the Independent Croatians were unable to form a satisfactory military force he proposed to take control of the loose Croatian forces himself. He even threatened to shoot the family members of deserters in an attempt to maintain discipline, which would eventually prove expensive and erode Croatian support.[593] Hitler overrode his wishes and Rendulic withdrew his support and contact from the German occupation headquarters in Zagreb.[594]

In creating a strong anti-Communist entity German propaganda stressed such past events as the Russian Civil War of 1919-30, which divided millions of people throughout Eastern Europe into two camps, until the Bolsheviks defeated their rivals with the aid of many Eastern European Communist groups, especially the Hungarian Communists.[595] This attempt at conversion was not successful on a large scale, mainly due to the apparent fact that those peoples already engaged in discord with the various Communist organizations needed no further prodding. Himmler was accustomed to ignoring problems, and his interest in the partisan and guerrilla situation was to simply order even more executions of suspected insurgents. Only when this policy exacerbated the problem and after Hitler took an interest in actively cultivating his "Greater *Reich*" did Himmler voice any serious interest himself. This concept was explained by Himmler's adjutant and expert on Eastern Affairs, *Obergruppenfuehrer* Karl Wolff:

> The *Reichsfuehrer* was concerned with the problem of the partisans, especially in Russia and Yugoslavia where they were virtually unchecked. Our Hungarian, Romanian and Bulgarian allies were also experiencing problems with partisans, and this was what Himmler said to me: 'Wolff, do you believe that we may be successful in trying to create our own units of partisans to work behind enemy lines? Perhaps they could work with the *SS Kommando* units…it may work.' I spoke to Felix Steiner[596] and Otto Kumm about this, and they were of the opinion that it would work. The greatest problem was trying to undo the damage already done from the invasion (of Russia) forward with regard to the civilian populations, especially the mass executions, which had not been handled very well.[597]

The Yugoslav partisan support network established by SOE was a critical component to the history of the partisan/guerrilla war, since it illustrates the extent to which the British government was willing to bring the war to the Germans long before the actual invasion of the European continent and the bulk of the Western Allied forces was possible. However, although Tito was supported to some extent by the Western Allies early on, and to a lesser extent by the Soviet Union until 1944, the activities of the Soviets, once they appeared on foreign European soil shook the Yugoslav Communists' faith in the safety of their already ethnically and politically disturbed population. Tito decided to break from Stalin and adopt a Communist although separate national identity, and this decision would see Allied aid come pouring in by late 1944.

Despite the best laid efforts to convince the Soviets to assist the Western Allies, as well as the desire to bring both Communist and nationalist factions together for the common cause under Mihailovic's command (who was a professional officer), Tito would have none of it.[598] Much of this dialogue had occurred before the British became active in Yugoslavia, since Tito and Mihailovic had met before on 19 September 1941 and again on 27 October 1941 to discuss their various agendas.[599] The end result was an agreement that the two men "agreed to disagree" with regard to policy and tactics (especially with regard to the role of women),[600] despite the fact that Tito had sought out Mihailovic for his assistance due to his vast experience when the national government collapsed.

Although the British believed and openly stated that the Communists were "military amateurs,"[601] despite the fact that many Communist guerrillas were veterans of the Spanish Civil War and the fighting in the Balkans long before the German invasion, the Allied program of virtually ignoring the Titoists until 1944 due to their anti-British posture, despite their enviable combat record may have in fact prolonged the war and created even further divisions within the country. However, the realities on the ground soon forced Churchill to increase British aid to Tito, given the Yugoslav leader's softening position on hard-line Communism and his apparent ideological distancing from Stalin.[602] Tito's decision to remain the leader of a Communist yet Soviet free Yugoslavia proved astute, and his success as a guerrilla leader and ruthless politician created the most unique nation in Eastern Europe following World War II. As stated by Lothar Pankosk:

Although we had fought against Tito's guerrillas as pro-fascists (guerrillas), we could respect Tito for maintaining autonomy for Yugoslavia from all Soviet control. This showed the country that he cared about Yugoslavia rather than just the Communist Party. However, I do know that it was the activities of the Soviet military in Eastern Europe and the greedy Stalin wanting to conquer as opposed to liberate nations. These fears were proven accurate, as history shows.[603]

The successful Allied efforts to aid the partisans and guerrillas by SOE and OSS have been established by the post-war historiography, and the motivations for supporting nationalism in contrast to the rising Communist strength appear quite clear. The Red Army application of assistance to irregular forces was also successful, although the Soviet methods were apparently less subtle and usually far more direct. The Soviets apparently attempted to foster good will towards the Yugoslavs, as stated in the following report:

Manifestations of Russo-Jugoslav collaboration are made on every suitable occasion. The funeral ceremony of Russian soldiers killed on Jugoslav soil is held publicly, usually in the main square…The civil administration is left entirely in the hands of the Partisans, the only proviso being that Russian military requirements have top priority. During the early days of liberation Russian guards shared the patrolling duties, but as order was restored, and the Red Army moved further away, these duties were taken over entirely by the Partisans…The Russian attitude towards the Partisans is interesting. Their interests are on the larger issue of the war and they regard Jugoslavia as relatively unimportant. This is the general army view who think of these small countries in south-eastern Europe as stepping stones on the road to Germany. The seriousness of the Partisans was in marked contrast to the Russians…At Alibunar the divisional commander repeatedly shocked the Partisans by his frivolous behavior. When embarked on a Partisan song he would rudely interrupt them and call for a tango or a waltz. His remark on being interrupted to the Commissar was: 'What, a Partisan—No, impossible, you are too clean.' As to my future movements, they had nothing against my going just where I liked…For the first time the Russian peasant is seeing a higher civilization than that to which he is used to in Russia and in countries where some of them thought the workers were kept in chains by the capitalists. When they reach the even richer and better cultivated lands of Germany all Russians will have plenty to think about, and perhaps demand more from their own country as payment for their suffering. One thing is clear, that they expect and want the same material help which we have given during the war, after the war.[604]

As stated by Lothar Pankosk, the Soviet handling of the non-Communist partisans and the civilians within their spheres of influence promoted further resistance among irregular forces following the German defeat and withdrawal from Yugoslavia, as occurred throughout Eastern Europe. These activities did not pass unnoticed by SOE, as stated in several reports by operatives in the region.[605] The Titoists had effectively combated the Germans and their allies and effectively organized their areas of control into small, local governments with civil administrations, repairing of utilities and communications, as well as restoring religious and educational life. The proclamations by Slavonia, Bosnia, Croatia, Dalmatia, Bosnia-Herzegovina, Istria, and Gorizia of independent statehood was bolstered by nationalism among the various groups, and brought the same response from the liberating Soviets as from the conquering Germans.[606]

The greatest problem with regard to the successful application of a peaceful civil administration within Yugoslavia post-war was the same concern that plagued the Germans; racial and ethnic tensions, primarily between the Croats, Bosnians and the Serbs. These problems exist to the present day and have expanded to include other ethnic and religious groups within the Balkans. The failures of 1945 are still being handled in the present day for better or worse, and hopefully the lessons learned from the German and Soviet failures will be applied in the Balkans soon enough to prevent future outbreaks, and consume the innocent people who become the unwilling victims of mankind's brutal indifference and petty hatreds.

7

The Soviet Union
German-Soviet Relations Before the War

Give full play to our style of fighting-courage in
battle, no fear of sacrifice, no fear of fatigue, and
continuous fighting.

- Mao Tse Tung
25 December 1947

The attitude towards the Germans by the Russian people during this era is not one that a non-Russian can readily comprehend. The hatred and mistrust between the two peoples dates back through the centuries and had been propelled by propaganda. The history of tension began with military conquests driven by the promise of economic gain, motivating the Teutonic Knights during the *Drang Nach Osten* in the twelfth century forward, prompting the Prussians to invade on several occasions. The invasion by Holy Roman Emperor Frederick I *"Barbarossa"* in the twelfth century and the defeat of the Teutonic Knights by the Prince Alexander Nevsky of Novgorod at Lake Peipus on the neck of the Neva River a half century later, and the final defeat of the Teutonic Knights at Tannenberg in 1410 were distant memories. It would not be until the First World War and the defeat of the Czarist forces, and later the Great Patriotic War of 1941-45 that the anti-German sentiment would rise to unparalleled proportions.

Russian history is rich with invasions by dozens of invaders from both east and west, whether by Huns, Mongols, Turks, Tatars, Japanese, French, Swedes, Magyar, Germans, or fellow Slavs. During the Second World War the average Russian peasant was semi-literate, if educated at all, and rarely worldly or well traveled, and with a culture steeped in folklore, mysticism, religion, and a deep love of their land. The Russians were separated not only by language depending upon their dialect and geographic location, but were also separated throughout their history by successive governments, from the Czarist despots to the murderous Bolshevik and Stalinist reformations.

Despite these seemingly vast differences, the common bond for all Russians, to include Ukrainians, Bessarabians, Belorussians, Georgians, and many others was the need and love of the land, and this love and necessity would be what solidified their strength. This was true even during the German invasion of 1941, and partisan activity increased as more land was threatened and the population was relocated or eliminated. The cultural identity and economic survival of the villages and nation were dependent upon the able bodied men joining the military or acting in the role of partisans, in which the term partisan is an accurate description, since these civilian irregulars were fighting an external invader to support and maintain an incumbent regime, friendly to their individual existence or not, in order to preserve their national, political and social integrity.

The irregulars from the Soviet Union who could aptly be named "guerrillas" would find themselves fighting against the Soviet system on the side of the Germans, or fighting the Germans in conjunction with partisans, later to combat the Red Army for independent status, since their aim was to assist in the overthrow of the Stalinist regime, hoping for independence from the Soviet Union for their respective homelands. The Ukrainian nationalists and White Russians would become the greatest irregular forces of the war, acting simultaneously in the role of a pro-German guerrilla organization and anti-German partisans, and their combat record and level of achievement would be unsurpassed. It is a fact that Soviet partisans and guerrillas were separated by more than ideology, but also by their capabilities and motivation. As stated by Overy:

> Increasingly the partisans began to conscript local men and women into their bands by force. Peasants had little choice. If they resisted they were shot by their own side; if they joined the partisans they were likely to suffer the same fate at the hands of the Germans. They had no military training. Partisan units with large numbers of forced conscripts—and by 1943 they constituted from 40 to 60 per cent of most brigades—took exceptionally high casualties and were conspicuously more inept than units with a cadre of experienced guerrillas.[607]

The first large scale anti-German partisan uprisings initially sprang up during the German drives toward Leningrad in the north and Stalingrad to the south in the Don River Basin region, and these partisans also fostered the German reprisal campaign that would without doubt mark the beginning of the end of Germany's perceived legitimacy as far as the Soviet people were concerned.[608] This was a tragic series of events for the Germans as well as the Soviets, since upon hearing that German forces were approaching millions of peasants, long suffering under Stalin looked at the *Wehrmacht* as a liberating army.[609]

During this period approximately 2,000 men (many were students from Leningrad) decided to hide in the forested region of Gatchina rather than become conscripts in the Red Army. Many of these men served the Germans in rear areas, but a large percentage defected to partisan and guerrilla units later due to their treatment at the hands of their benefactors.[610] However, this was in stark contrast to the *Freiwilligen*, who had a one- percent defection rate and proved their value in battle, despite a few limited circumstances with a Cossack battalion on the southern flank of Army Group Center. It would be these few actions that would prompt Hitler to order the dissolution of the Russian volunteers and have them deported to French coal mines, with the first group deported numbering some 80,000.[611] *Generaloberst* Kurt Zeitzler's intervention managed to have Hitler limit the numbers and reduce the rate of disarming.[612]

Despite the great human assets provided by the irregular components, the Red Army was slow to exploit these partisan groups, yet by 1942 they did begin operating in conjunction with specific and well known partisan leaders, some of whom had fought for the Bolshevik cause in the October Revolution in 1917 and the subsequent Civil War. One program the Red Army embarked upon that would illustrate Stalin's callous disregard for his own people was the "strike and withdraw" tactic. This involved staging an attack upon a German unit and withdrawing to a village or town, knowing that the Germans would react with reprisal killings. This would, in theory, create even more partisans, converting many anti-Communists into Red Army supporters and alienating the Germans from the mass population. This fact was clearly stated by Captain Gregor Koronov:

> In the Pripet Marshes on the road to Leningrad, we were barely holding our own against the German attacks…we managed to use mine dogs against their tanks, but this only worked part of the time, since the dogs would become crazy from the shell fire and run under anything, German or Soviet, sometimes even running into our own troops for comfort, just to escape the hell.[613] The tilt-rod packs actually destroyed as many of our own tanks as German. Well, we knew that somehow we had to create some partisan activity, resorting to conscription in many cases, and the political commissars went around the villages trying to recruit even the old and very young. When this did not work due to the flood of refugees fleeing to the east, our commissar, Fedor "something" asked for volunteers to attack a village of "collaborators." We went in, shot the people, killing over thirty, and then took a couple of German prisoners and placed them in the street, shot them, and laid them out as if they had been part of the massacre. Later, at another time our unit had some disciplinary problems, and the men to be punished were given civilian clothes and ordered to carry grenades and bombs into German lines…this sort of activity provoked the Germans into reacting, and their predictable brutality would surpass ours, and the desired result would produce several partisan groups wanting revenge. Unfortunately for our commander, the truth was later learned about his activities against the civilians. One of the men who joined our unit had escaped the massacre, and he identified several people, and he spread the word to others. He killed our CO then deserted to the enemy. This was a very nasty business.[614]

The German and Russian soldiers had a certain commonality; hardship and brutal discipline. As stated by Richard Overy: "Soldiers were brutal because much of their experience of life was brutal and harsh."[615] Regarding the Russians: "Their resilience and stubbornness, the toughness of both men and women, were the product of a bitter climate and extreme conditions of work."[616] The collective social and political experiences of both actions wavered periodically officially, although the underlying suspicions and animosities were always present despite the apparent reconciliation prior to the Second World War. As also stated by Overy and supported by the evidence is the fact that: "the first partisans could scarcely be regarded as volunteers."[617] The aggressive nature and resilience of the insurgency movement would take time to build up, but increase it would.

One of the strange anomalies regarding the German-Soviet relationship, given their diametrically opposed political positions during both the Weimar and *Nazi* political regimes was the Treaty of Rapallo, signed on 16 April 1922.[618] The German treaty with the Soviets in August 1922 and a "second and more extensive program agreed to in March 1926"[619] allowed the technical and tactical training of the German Army and fledgling Air Force, while offering technical assistance to Soviet industry, especially in the area of mechanization and agricultural equipment. The treaty also allowed for the export of raw materials from the Soviet Union into Germany, an agreement that Stalin maintained through the first full week of the war between the two nations in June 1941.[620] The Soviets, despite their open contempt for capitalism were also dealing with the largest of the American companies in building up their own internal domestic technology. The Ford Motor Company's tractor division, supported by major American banks (at this time American banks were privately owned and not federalized until Franklin D. Roosevelt's New Deal plan in the 1930s) longing for a new economic empire.[621] The Treaty of Berlin in April 1926[622] supported the Treaty of Rapallo, thus securing a guarantee from Russia against German military aggression that would have been a clear violation of Article 16 of the Versailles Treaty.[623]

Another positive move was Germany's joining the League of Nations during the same year, considered a positive gesture by the western powers that perhaps believed that Germany was evolving into a more respectable and manageable nation. Yet, despite the current political dramas unfolding in Germany that would ultimately decide the fate of the world within little more than a decade, the *Nazi* government received assistance from an unlikely area: White Russians and other European anti-Communists who emigrated to Germany were funding the *NSDAP* and offering their services in intelligence gathering as well as supplying cash.

This assistance to Hitler by the wealthy landed aristocracy of old Imperial Russia brought the *Nazis* into a better light among the media moguls, *Junkers*, and German aristocracy as well.[624] This assistance would later assist in swelling the ranks of the eastern *Freiwilligen* during the war. It is ironic to note that Henry Ford, while working his deals with Stalin also funded Hitler, due to his own anti-Semitic belief that Jewish bankers and businesses in America were conspiring against his creation of the world's largest automobile manufacturing plant. Also lending support was Benito Mussolini and Montagu Norman, Governor of the Bank of England from 1922-1944, who was another anti-Semite with high social and economic rank.[625]

It must be stated that these political events must have remained confusing to the future partisans and guerrillas when they were deciding which side of the political fence to jump over, and especially so to the more literate who read *and* understood *Mein Kampf*, which outlined a friendship with both Britain and Italy while reducing the east and Russia, yet unmistakably placing Germany in the role of a world power while keeping a wary eye on France.[626] Hitler's political and strategic about-face, then reversing himself by invading the Soviet Union, while simultaneously fighting Britain could have only increased that uncertainty. The Leftist and Rightist Movements in 1930s Europe were both being juggled about by the ever changing alliances, treaties and trade agreements, and this did not escape the notice of the western capitalist nations who would provide most of the overt and covert support to the anti-fascist insurgents during World War II.[627]

One factor regarding Germany's continued policy toward the east would prove very disconcerting to many; the statement by British Foreign Secretary Austen Chamberlain following Germany's entry into the League: "For the Polish Corridor no British Government ever will or ever can risk the bones of a British Grenadier."[628] The British position regarding Poland became muddled, especially following the great support for Poland following the outbreak of war. The same M.P.s who condemned the Soviet Union for invading Finland in 1939 also condemned Germany and declared war upon Hitler for the same activity regarding Poland. The Soviet-German Non Aggression Pact was perhaps another puzzling development for the ruling heads of Europe, as it appeared for all intent and purpose that the two titanic despot regimes would join forces, despite their long standing historical and ideological differences. Even the Red Army-*Wehrmacht* Protocol of 20 September 1939 and the partition of Poland distorted the world view as to the true nature of the relationship, even among many Germans, although the General Staff was well aware of their country's future plans toward the Soviet Union.[629]

For the Russian people (and eventually the Germans as well) a total war for national survival existed from day one. The difference was that the Soviets realized this much sooner than their enemy, and conflict termination as the end of a struggle by any means soon replaced any realistic hope of conflict resolution through negotiation, despite Allied fears of a possible Soviet separate peace as demonstrated in World War I.

The two great national dictatorships would soon engage in a war unlike any seen before or since, and the role of the insurgent and counterinsurgent would be defined completely for all time.

8

German War Plans & the Birth of Counterinsurgency Doctrine

*This army has an indomitable spirit and is deter-
mined to vanquish all enemies and never to yield.
No matter what the difficulties and hardships, so
long as a single man remains,he will fight on.*

- Mao Tse Tung
24 April 1945

The following section deals extensively with the German method of combating partisans, in addition addressing (albeit more limited in scope) the Soviet anti-partisan method
of operations, since both military organizations suffered serious losses in men and materiel
due to the activities of irregular forces during and after the war, with the Soviets experiencing a resurgence of irregular activity against their occupation forces once peace was concluded in the east. The German perspective regarding counterinsurgency is the most extensively covered, since it is the precipitator of future counterinsurgency operations that would
later be emulated by the Soviets as the war progressed, and analyzed by the United States
and Great Britain when the war ended.

The Soviets would learn from the experience of the German special units and began
waging a ruthless war against anti-Communist and Ukrainian nationalists, elements which
fought both for and against the German occupiers at various times, such as the Ukrainian
Insurgent Army, and later the Ukrainian Nationalist Organization under Stepan Bandera
(UPA),[630] boasting 300,000 members in a conflict that lasted several years after the war
during the Soviet occupation of Eastern Europe.[631] The evaluation is also important with
regard to the post-war development of specialized counterinsurgency military forces by the
former Western Allies, who reviewed the German method to some degree, interviewing
many of the participants and progressing the concept, tailoring the methodology to fit the
new Cold War environment on a global scale.

The failure of German military forces to effectively deal with their insurgency problems stems from the entrenched linear military training, thinking, and philosophy mandated
at the *Kriegsakademie* where adherence to strict, classical applications of conventional
methods of combined arms warfare along the guidelines of *Generaloberst* Hans von Seeckt
were literally gospel.[632]

The British were also guilty of failing to exercise a continued logical approach to subversion warfare, despite the great support and success of British forces during World War I

114

in the Palestine-Middle East campaign. The guerrilla forces commanded by Major Thomas Edward Lawrence under the direction of General Allenby successfully launched covert missions against the Ottoman Empire, capturing the strategically important port of Aquaba, destroying the Turkish railway network and destroying two entire Ottoman armies, while forcing a full one-half of the entire enemy force to maintain a defensive garrison posture. Simply the act of containment alone was worth the effort, with the other successes, such as the capture of Jerusalem and Damascus becoming bonuses. This ignorance of well-established reality flies in the face of accepted conventional wisdom, as stated by M.R.D. Foot:

> Liddell Hart himself, ironically enough, did not accept this extension of his own doctrine. He held to a more conventional view of resistance forces, as adjuncts unable to exercise more than a secondary influence on a campaign; charged moreover with dangerous political implications for the aftermath.[633]

The German application of military logic would include Seeckt's concepts regarding the partition of Poland, stating "Poland's existence is intolerable, incompatible with the survival of Germany. It must disappear, and it will disappear through its own internal weakness through Russia…with our assistance."[634] Seeckt also foresaw the future of Hungary in a similar capacity, drafting a letter to Prince Ludwig Windisch-Graetz on that nation's domestic and foreign policies in June 1917.[635] Seeckt's brilliance regarding conventional military applications provided the benchmark for modern German military thought. Yet despite these innovations that were the groundwork for future German successes, the failure to include doctrinal analysis regarding irregular warfare was to haunt the army of the Third *Reich*. The one positive note in Seeckt's applications was the inclusion of foreign recruitment into German service, even if only as allies in future conflicts. Part of this plan would ensure a collection of natives who knew the people, language, customs, and the terrain; considered essential to conducting effective combat and especially counterinsurgency operations. The following description illustrates the advantage the irregular has over the foreign invader:

> We used the forest trails and our own short cuts. Except for the danger involved, it could have been a routine operation. We were familiar with every path, brook and spring, with each cave and precipice. We knew the best spots for strawberries or blueberries, the isolated farms with orchards where we could "borrow" fruit without disturbing the owners, and the noisy dogs to be avoided…the border guards were no match for us…They were like fish out of the water in the mountainous terrain that we knew as the palms of our hands from years of camping and skiing. They got easily tired and lost; on skis they made a pretty ridiculous picture.[636]

The missions by von Seeckt to Persia, Turkestan and Afghanistan in 1920-21 offered some glimpse of what was to come regarding the recruitment of the *Freiwilligen*.[637] Gustav Stresemann, the German Foreign Minister from 1923-1929 supported much of this ideology.[638] However, Stresemann envisaged a unification of all German speaking peoples into a single united Germany, including Central Europe for the greater common good, a concept adopted by Hitler and spread by the *Nazi* Party as their "original concept."[639] The main point of concern was the fact that, following the conclusion of hostilities in 1918 Germany lost thirteen percent of its territory and approximately 6,000,000 citizens.[640] This fact alone was enough to ensure a large support network for Hitler and the *NSDAP* declarations regarding the nature of the *Volksgemeinschaft* and the eventual reunification.[641] It is important to remember that much of this support came from outside the German borders of pre-1936, the same territories that would supply tens of thousands of *Freiwilligen* during the coming war.

However, the true intent of German foreign policy was to surface in the pontificating of Dr. Alfred Rosenberg,[642] a native of Reval, Estonia[643] who believed that the Eastern peoples should be relegated to serfdom in support of German economic advancement.[644] This would soon become the policy of *Nazi* Germany under Adolf Hitler, emerging as part of his great crusade against Jewry, Communists, and others within his grasp, although operating on a much larger and more radical scale.[645] The possibility of insurgency action by the subjugated peoples was, however, never addressed, and when it did occur the narrow thinking in the upper echelons of the military command would consistently label it a "Jewish Movement," whether the irregular forces were in fact Jewish or not mattered little.[646]

This narrow thinking with regard to a non-traditional military force seemed somewhat hypocritical, given the fact that the *Freikorps* during the Weimar Republic period was a collection of veterans, malcontents and the unemployed, with students making up a fair percentage of its ranks.[647] The *Freikorps*, which had a membership of approximately 70,000 men in 250 various units between 1919-1920[648] was not a cohesive military organization, unlike the *SA*,[649] which had a greater military base and a political foothold, yet through their hit and run terror tactics they were the prime reason for the destruction of the collective leftist (especially the Communist) groups within Germany until the rise of Hitler and the *NSDAP*.[650] It would be the *Freikorps* who would provide some of the highest ranking leaders within the *SS*, including the combat ranks of the *Waffen SS*, with its membership roles reflecting a "who's who" in Germany.[651] The *Nazi* elimination of the Communists would reach new heights, despite the fact that they had joined the *Nazis* in the Berlin Transport Strike in November 1932 (which included the Social Democrats) while simultaneously courting Stalin.[652]

This linear line of thought would carry over into the *Waffen SS* academies through the 1930s and early war years, severely handicapping the future leaders and soldiers who would be forced into adapting to an unconventional warfare environment and were ill prepared for what would certainly come. The *Waffen SS* would, much to their credit, surpass the Army and enhance their military academic curriculum to include situation planning, conventional and logistical support, and operational development of counterinsurgency doctrine in 1942 following the Yugoslav and Russian campaigns. This became an important factor for the *Waffen SS* units, since they were held in rather low regard by the more established German Army officer corps early in the war.

However, as the war progressed and *SS* combat units began to show their mettle in combat operations, often "saving the day" with their fanatical determination and discipline, their ranks became more respected by their allies and feared by their enemies. These combat attributes were displayed many times, such as at Belgrade in 1941,[653] Demyansk and Kholm in 1942, Kharkov and Kursk in 1943,[654] Cherkassy in March and Arnhem in September 1944,[655] and in the final defense of the *Reich*, just to name a few operations. In developing new tactics and doctrine the combat arm of the *SS* was to become legendary as well as notorious. One of the doctrines that would be developed was the handling of counterinsurgency activity, created in the field as the problem arose throughout the front. Much of this doctrine was sound in its application, although the reprisal killings against villages and civilians in regions of insurgent activity would guarantee and maintain a high number of irregulars flooding to join the ranks of the partisans and guerrillas.

These newly enacted measures would offer the German forces in the field a greater chance of survival against partisan activity, while enhancing the legendary brutality that would be attributed to the counterinsurgency units such as *"Florian Geyer,"*[656] *"Handschar,"* *"Wallonien," "Maria Theresia," "Lettisches"* (Latvian) *Nr. 1* and *Nr. 2*,[657] the *"Dirlewanger"* and *"Kaminsky"*[658] Brigades, as well as elements of *"Wiking," "Nordland," "Totenkopf," "Leibstandarte,"* and *"Das Reich."*[659] The examination of German military doctrine and their operational planning is crucial to the completion of this study. The point of fact is that the German military had experienced partisan and guerrilla activity during the First World War, such as the experience of Walther Reinhardt.

During October-November 1918 Reinhardt experienced partisan attacks in France and was at least somewhat knowledgeable in counterinsurgency operations.[660] This experience brought him into the planning operations for the *Truppenamt* with von Seeckt and August von Mackensen in 1919-20, although it would appear that his contribution in this area was neglected.[661] One area in which Reinhardt contributed was the concept of the international *Freiwilligen,* a union of various peoples for military service into a *Landesjaegerkorps,* which von Seeckt adopted with great enthusiasm in 1919.[662] The policy would expand to include the Balkans, Poland and Upper Silesia, along with White Russian volunteers included within the formations.[663] The largest of the meetings, the *Nachtkriegskaempfe Balken* (Night War Struggles Balkans) in 1918 included several wartime luminaries; *Reichfinanzminister* Erzberger, *Generaloberst* Erich Ludendorff, *General Graf* Waldersee, *General* Groener, *General* von der Goltz, *General der Infanterie* Reinhardt and *Generalmajor* Hans von Seeckt.[664] The elite group of officers met in Berlin on 2 March 1919 and history was in the making.[665]

This early forum was augmented by the most experienced irregular combat leader in the German military, *Generalleutnant* Paul von Lettow-Vorbeck, a professional soldier with a long history of service throughout Africa long before the war who commanded the German forces and irregular volunteers throughout the East African campaign.[666] Lettow-Vorbeck had devised the concept of *Freiwilligen* in 1905 similar to the British method of raising colonial troops. The difference was that Lettow-Vorbeck believed that volunteers fought better and were more reliable than domestic conscripts, and when treated well proved their value.

A member of the German volunteer contingent in Africa during World War I was a South African named Pieter Krueler, a remarkable man who had fought during the Boer War as a teenage mounted messenger for General Jan Christian Smuts, yet decided to fight against the British during the First World War, unlike his former commanding officer.[667] His comments on the German leadership offer insight into the effectiveness of Lettow-Vorbeck's methods of utilizing guerrilla units:

I had fought the British during the Boer War, and was a messenger for Jan Smuts as well. After the war the Germans began recruiting South Africans and others to serve in their colonial service, and they paid more money than most of us had ever seen. Our officers were all German, and they trained us in their standard military methods, yet they respected our hit and run cavalry techniques and were impressed by our ability to stay in the saddle as well as in the field without re-supply for long periods. We were used to living off the land, and we knew the terrain in most of South West and Southern Africa. However, in going to Eastern Africa we were in a strange environment, yet we were able to adapt. We were very successful in attacking British, French and Belgian troops who were mostly infantry and heavily tied to their routes of supply. We hardly ever engaged enemy troops directly, yet by striking at their supply lines and destroying their communications, we had perhaps inflicted more damage, by destroying morale and placing hardships upon their commands. This is the true nature of guerrilla war as we knew it.[668]

Much of this experience involved irregular operations that should have laid the groundwork for better German understanding of the future conflict that would come to haunt them. The program of recruiting and training foreign nationals to serve German interests was best exemplified by *Generalfeldmarschall* August von Mackensen during his service in Finland.[669] Mackensen planned a program of support and the creation of the Finnish Regiments: Northern *Jaeger* Battalion (I), *Lappland-Askar* Battalion (II), and Polar *Nacht* Battalion (III) from 17 June 1940-May 1941.[670] These activities laid the groundwork for what would become the most "successful failure" of German arms; an international army fighting for a common German goal. However, defeat was to be snatched from the jaws of victory.

The official policies issued by Hitler through Himmler and Reinhard Heydrich concerning the use of force against insurgents can be found in the *Einsatzgruppen Reports*.[671] This outstanding collection of correspondences between the operational death squads and the headquarters in Berlin presented in this work provides great detail concerning the effects of the flawed German counterinsurgency operations during the war, as well as the level of intensity regarding the counterinsurgency campaign proper. The following extract is a prime example illustrating the history of German reprisals in the Soviet Union for a specific and well documented incident initiated by "suspected" partisans:

Chief of the Security Police and the *SD*
Berlin, 12 July 1941. 12 copies.
(11th copy)
Einsatzgruppe B:
Location: Minsk

The industrialized areas are only slightly damaged. The town is without light and water. Political and governmental officials have fled. The population is very depressed. Many people have lost their shelter and the food situation is worsening. To protect the communication lines and prevent acts of sabotage, the Field Commander[672] ordered the arrest of all male inhabitants between the ages of 18-45. The civil prisoners are being screened at this time. The attitude of the population toward the German is one of wait and see. The Belorussians show a friendlier attitude towards the Germans. However, the entire population hopes that the occupation will enable them to live a normal life in the near future. According to the last report of *Einsatzgruppe B,* wooden houses in the western part of Minsk were set afire. Apparently the houses were set on fire by Jews who were supposed to evacuate their homes for returning Belorussian refugees. At present the population is in a mood to launch a pogrom. Their fury caused certain anti-Jewish actions. A number of Jews were liquidated for this act.

The action just described was typical of the German methods employed in combating the "partisan menace" before a tried and proven method of counterinsurgency actually existed. The following chronicle is also from the *Einsatzgruppen Reports* and reinforces the image of the reckless German method of handling the local populations in Russia proper:

Einsatzgruppe C:
Location: Rovno.
1*Actions*

On 5 July 1941 Jews were executed as reprisal for the bestial murder of the Ukrainian nationalist leader Dr. Kirnychny in Rudki. The Ukrainian population on their part set the synagogue and Jewish houses on fire. 150 Ukrainians were found murdered in Stryj. In the course of a search it was possible to arrest 12 Communists who were responsible for the murder of the Ukrainians. It concerns 11 Jews and 1 Ukrainian who were shot with the participation of the entire population of Stryj. End of message.[673]

Another example, written by a Corporal K. Suffner (as related by Omer Bartov) is as follows: "Bolsheviks and Jews have murdered 12,000 Germans and Ukrainians in a beastly manner...the surviving Ukrainians arrested 2000 Jews and exercised a frightful revenge. We swear that this plague will be eradicated root and branch."[674] The reprisals outlined in these reports were in retaliation for partisan activities, or rather "preemptive guerrilla warfare,"[675] regardless of the ethnic background of the suspected participants. As stated by *General der Infanterie* Hans von Greiffenberg:

The use of force on the part of the German occupation troops (evacuation, taking of hostages, punitive expeditions) fell far short of producing the desired results. Since the Russian partisans hardly adhered to the rules of civilized warfare, such measures were most likely to provoke reprisals against German troops and against friendly elements among the local population.[676]

What also appears to be clear was that Jews were to be made the scapegoats for every partisan act, creating and legitimizing anti-Semitic feeling within the ranks while fostering a line of thinking and conduct which fell into the same rhetoric as Hitler's misguided views on "Jewish Bolshevism" and other outrageous conspiracy theories designed to incite hatred. It was impressed upon the soldiers and German population that "The Jew was taken to be the most cunning and dangerous enemy of the German race,"[677] and these activities appeared to justify the accusation. The response by German forces to acts of sabotage and violence are well known. However, the belief as to *who* actually conducted these acts is illustrated in the following letter written by a German NCO in July 1942:

> Recently a comrade of ours was murdered in the night. He was stabbed in the back. That can only have been a Jew, who stands behind these crimes. The revenge taken for that act brought indeed a nice success. The population itself hates the Jews as never before. It realizes now, that he is guilty of everything.[678]

The *SS* and Army personnel involved in these actions rarely knew who their victims were, and perhaps the great majority did not care, since the enemy was virtually anyone posing a threat, either tangible or suspected. This was supported by the implementation of the *SD* policy against partisans, Allied Commandos and POWs, as initiated by *Obergruppenfuehrer* Ernst Kaltenbrunner, measures that did not specifically fall into the established military guidelines regarding the conduct of the war.[679] Likewise, as stated by Daniel Jonah Goldhagen in his acclaimed work, *Hitler's Willing Executioners*:

> Little is known of who the perpetrators were, the details of their actions, the circumstances of many of their deeds, let alone their motivations. A decent estimate of how many people contributed to the genocide, of how many perpetrators there were, has never been fully made.[680]

One factor must be made clear regarding the average German soldier and his participation in what may be deemed atrocities. Although the following comments are not an excuse for clear breaches of moral and legal applications during war, a certain counter-argument must be supplied. Men who are fighting for their lives, especially against a cloaked enemy hiding among the local population, uncertain as to their duty and without proper leadership and guidance seldom take the time to disseminate between friendly and hostile indigenous personnel. Regardless of the individual's thoughts and beliefs it mattered very little, for the killings of even "suspected Jews" in even the most anti-Semitic region only fanned the flames of resistance among the civilian population. Another detrimental factor was the propaganda issues facing the German, as well as the fact that the primitive living conditions of the average peasant and the seemingly endless numbers of non-European races impressed upon the Germans their own sense of cultural and ethnic superiority. The German soldier was soon to begin receiving an expensive and irrevocable education in civilian unrest that would not only challenge the *Wehrmacht* militarily, but would eventually assist in the final defeat of Germany. The average soldier was to carry this burden throughout the war, combating his personal demons and possibly questioning the legitimacy of his actions, as seen in the chapter on Greece.

The lack of a comprehensive and cohesive concept regarding counterinsurgency doctrine within the ranks of the German military was not unique among the world's great militaries. First of all, few of the high-ranking officers in primary leadership capacities worldwide had ample combat experience, let alone experience in offensive operations against insurgents. These were not skills traditionally taught at Bad Toelz, the primary *SS* officer's academy, Brandenburg Briest, West Point, St. Cyr, or Sandhurst, nor was this information to be found in the annals of the military manuals for training and leadership.[681] The German soldier was completely unprepared for warfare on the Eastern Front with regard to operations in cold weather, limited supplies, and against such superior numbers in men and materiel as would become the case after 1943. Against the insurgents awaiting him their could have been no greater fear and confusion.

The German was also psychologically unprepared for what awaited him. He was subjected to many varieties of friendly propaganda, although all forms continued to purport his racial superiority. One day he may hear that all of the sub-humans must be relocated further east, especially Jews. Later he would hear that they must be eradicated, eliminated from potentially poisoning the pure German blood supply, that they were "deemed to be a biological threat to the German people."[682] He would also be told that not all Russians were Communists, and that the German crusade was established to free the Russians from Bolshevism, while at the same time condemning all Russians for supporting the Bolsheviks, while the Jews supported and assisted the powers in Moscow. Still later, the German soldier would hear other alterations as to the true policy of his country toward the eastern peoples. If the German soldier was not completely confused by the endless alterations of state and military policy he would not have been human. Another problem facing the Germans was the fact that unconventional warfare, definitely the oldest method of waging war made conventional military thinkers very nervous. This is evident even today and may been seen in the United States military and their past views on special operations units. The German leaders and military educators at the various military academies would not incorporate the widespread concept of counterinsurgency doctrine throughout the *Wehrmacht* until mid-1944, quite late in the game for attempting to remedy the plague that was growing exponentially. Despite this fact, specific commanders developed their own counterinsurgency doctrine in the field to try to counter the threats to their men and assets. Anti-partisan units were hurriedly created in 1942 and deployed ad-hoc, since partisan resistance before the summer of that year had never been well coordinated in the Soviet Union or the west.[683]

The Germans were the ultimate practitioners of target directed paranoia when it came to the establishment of psychological and special warfare units. It would prove crucial to impress upon the soldiers that their cause was not only ethically and morally just, but also of critical military importance. Creating a desire within the men to actively kill with great enthusiasm became the main topic on the agenda. Just how to implement the actual methodology of accomplishing these goals was another matter. These skills were an alien doctrine, yet this doctrine would evolve over time from hard experience, as stated by Otto Kumm:

> Our professional officer's training, and that of the Army and *SS*, since more than half of the *Waffen SS* were comprised of former Army soldiers, did not include military action against civilian irregular forces. This was not even a concept at this time, since prior to the Second World War there had been static warfare,

much like in the First World War. With the new war it was highly mobile, covering ground more quickly, and bringing much more territory and more people under our control. Also, another and more dangerous problem was that we now had the Soviet Union to contend with, and its great mass of territory and people. It should have been foreseen that we would have future problems with (guerrilla) fighters, but this was simply an oversight that we tried to remedy too late with too little.[684]

The one exception to the rule was the brainchild of a former World War I staff officer, Theodor von Hippel, who served under the legendary *Generalleutnant* Paul von Lettow-Vorbeck during the little known yet brutal guerrilla war in East Africa.[685] Hippel later joined the *Abwehr* working under Canaris where he devised the concept of creating small elite forces called *Sonderkommando*, similar in design to the small elite teams he commanded in East Africa. This highly successful concept would be taken several steps further with the creation of the controversial *Ebbingshausgruppe* in Brandenburg. The testing and selection process culminated in the organization of the *Lehr und bau Kompanie z.b.V. 800* [686] on 15 October 1939 from the nucleus of the *Ebbingshausgruppe*, hence its official designation as the *Brandenburg Kompanie* that would later be increased to division strength.

What made the *Brandenburgers* elite and originally different from the future *Waffen SS* combat units was that the *Abwehr* recruited men who did not exhibit the typical Aryan features traditional within the *SS* or even the Army, preferring the Slavic appearance to the Nordic type, complete with the necessary language skills to effectively carry out the charade. Those recruited were to have preferably lived in the various eastern regions, thus being totally familiar with the social customs, traditions and courtesies of their specific areas. It was also considered important that the men had family, friends and reliable contacts in these regions, preferably with an anti-Communist political outlook. The *Brandenburgers* were trained in special operations warfare, with the emphasis being placed upon small teams and individual action and initiative. These qualities would later become crucial, given the nature of their future assignments, and some members of the group would become legends within the *Waffen SS* once the unit was disbanded and incorporated into the *SS* proper.

One such individual was *Waffen SS Sturmbannfuehrer Graf* Adrian von Foelkersam, one of the original *Brandenburgers* who won the Knight's Cross for leading a sixty-two man detachment into the Maikop oil fields in the Soviet Union. Dressed as *NKVD*[687] soldiers and speaking fluent Russian, Foelkersam led his covert team in while presenting himself as a "Major Truchin" from Stalingrad. After collecting a large group of deserters and convincing them to "continue the fight for Russia and Stalin," Foelkersam duped the garrison commander into effecting a withdrawal.[688] All of the Soviet soldiers followed suit and the German army entered Maikop on 9 August 1942 without a shot being fired.[689]

Foelkersam would later serve under Otto Skorzeny on various missions, such as the commando raid by *SS Fallschirmjaeger* Battalion *500* to abduct or eliminate Marshal Tito on Hitler's personal orders, missing the dictator by a matter of minutes. Their only consolation, at high cost to the *Luftwaffe* and *SS* parachutists was the killing of 6,000 partisans of Tito's Proletarian Brigade and the capture of Tito's dress uniform, later displayed in Vienna.[690] Other missions would include the kidnapping of Admiral Horthy's son on 16 October 1944 by an old *Brandenburger* group of *Waffen SS Fallschirmjaeger* commandos led by Otto

Skorzeny and Foelkersam to induce Hungary's compliance to Hitler's wishes in 1944, following Hungary's attempt at negotiating a separate peace the previous day,[691] and the *Gran Sasso* raid to free Mussolini from captivity in 1943.

The *SD* and *SS Sonderkommando* were the men who would be called upon to combat the partisans in the east and the Balkans most frequently, and most enlisted in the *Waffen SS* and served with distinction in the anti-partisan role. These men had established a new standard, although not in the same mold as Klingenberg they were the nucleus for the whirlwind operations to come. The Soviets took serious notice of this and other German successes and began to emulate their opponents by creating special units within the *GRU*, one of which later became known as *Spetsnaz.*[692]

These German counterinsurgency operations picked up momentum as the war progressed, and the Germans began to consolidate their hold on the conquered territories. However, the partisan and guerrilla activity that had been sporadic and relatively slow in picking up until the end of 1941 began to erupt with full fury all along the Eastern Front by December the following year. German armies quickly discovered that their ever-increasing supply and communications lines were exposed to these initially random but later well-coordinated partisan assaults. As stated earlier, the first large-scale partisan efforts were experienced along the Pripet Marshes near Leningrad, along with the first large scale use of Soviet cavalry units.[693]

The first actions by *Generaloberst* Kurt Zeitzler's command against partisans occurred at Kiev in the Ukraine from 27 June-16 July 1941, where his forces gained valuable if expensive experience.[694] Their operations in Rostov from 12 October-1 December 1941 offered further experience,[695] while exercising the expanding Russian *Freiwilligen* units that were originally formed and deployed from 12 April-4 August 1941.[696] *Panzergruppe I* was blooded in the combined human wave assaults and partisan activity that swept along the entire front, but especially at Bland-Lublin, Uman (from 23 June-16 July 1941), Smolensk and Libau. Army Group North approaching Leningrad received some of the most severe setbacks due to partisans and guerrillas between 24 June-16 July 1941, and set the pattern for decisive and ruthless response from the *6ᵗʰ Panzer* and the *Waffen SS "Polizei"* Divisions.[697] The German spearhead toward the Donetz and Nikolayev from 24 September-3 November 1941, and the Sea of Azov from 4-10 October 1941 produced an exponential increase in both partisan and guerrilla activity, as well as mass Soviet miliatry and partisan defections to the German side.[698]

The winter of 1941-42 and the subsequent German summer offensive saw Zeitzler's *Panzergruppe I* invading the Caucasus (meeting heavy partisan resistance near Tagenrog) during *Operation Blue* from 17 May 1941-12 August 1942;[699] the Kertch Peninsula on 12 July 1942,[700] Maikop from 13-18 August 1942,[701] and all through the following year of 1943. That year witnessed not only the expected increase in partisan activity during continued operations (which Zeitzler factored into his *Operation Zitadelle* planning for Kursk-Orel during June-July and the Kuban bridgehead operations)[702] during *Operation Wotan-Stellung* from 26 August-2 October 1943, but also was amended by the seasoned commander during the near disaster at the Korsun-Cherkassy pocket, a classic *Kesselschlacht* (Cauldron Battle) from 25 January-18 February 1944 that was similar to the Demyansk struggle in 1942, although not as long and protracted due to better planning.[703] The beleaguered German commander, *Generalmajor* Stemmermann managed to coordinate a breakout that ended in tragedy, with the general and 22,000 of his 30,000 troops perishing under Konev's artillery, armor, Cossacks, and partisans, and 8,000 Germans destined for a decade of service in the gulags and labor camps.[704]

In responding to the partisan threat no *Wehrmacht* commander was more ruthless and enthusiastic in dealing with these threats (both real and perceived) than the sadistic and egomaniacal *Generalfeldmarschall* Johann Ferdinand Schoerner, a devout *Nazi* and Hitler favorite.[705] Schoerner had served as an officer in the First World War and had written a revolutionary and well-received treatise, titled *"Tactics on Mountain Warfare"* in 1921 as a mere *Hauptmann*. It was his expertise in mountain warfare that saw his appointment as commander of the *6th Gebirgs* Division (which had previously served in Greece and the Balkans in 1941) on the Murmansk Front at Liza in the spring of 1942.[706] Schoerner was a strict disciplinarian and rabid anti-Semite who actually admitted to enjoying his status with Hitler and Himmler, by not only allowing his units to operate with the dreaded *Sonder-kommandotruppen*, but he is known to have created his own regular Army units for use in the mass murder of innocent civilians who had absolutely nothing to do with the partisan and guerrilla problems plaguing his command.

In fact, it was *Gruppe Schoerner*'s activities all through 1942 (especially at the Nikopol bridgehead)[707] and 1943 (with 25 November 1943 figuring prominently) during the counter-attacks in the south that led to a desertion of former White Russian and Ukrainian allies to the Soviets. German soldiers under orders entered several villages and burned out the in-habitants, shooting those who fled and publicly executing those who surrendered. When Schoerner was appointed *Oberbefehlshaber Sued Ukraine* on 6 May 1944 and *Nord (Kurland)* on 23 July 1944 he had managed to prove himself capable of reducing partisan activity by liquidating thousands of "potential partisans." He was later appointed by Hitler directly as *Oberbefehlshaber Heeresgruppe Mitte* on 17 January 1945 for his energetic efficiency, al-though the post-war evaluation can safely state that his activities produced greater prob-lems than they solved with regard to the civilian population, creating more partisans and guerrillas than had previously existed as his forces retreated.

Operating well behind German lines the partisans and guerrillas sabotaged virtually at will, although these attacks usually yielded little in actual material damage. These actions did, however, provoke a response from the Germans, in particular by units of the *SS* and *SD* often with Army support. Dr. Rolf Himze's record reflects German Army and *Sonderkommando* counterinsurgency operations in Sininica-Prossolovo in the summer of 1942, as well as the actions at Shisdra, Glinaja, Bjeloy, Don Basin, Stalingrad, Donetz, Bjelowodzk, Strelzovka, Starobojelsk, Rubeschnaya, Proletarsk, Lissitschansk, Rudnik-Solotoy, Bjelgorod, Kursk, Tamarowka, Borrissowka-Graiworor, and extensive counterinsurgency operations in the Dnieper.[708] The one factor that is irrefutable was that the German military needed to adopt an operational and tactical plan to handle the growing threat. The shooting of civilians was increasing the hostility towards the Germans, and this in turn provoked even greater reprisals from the occupation forces. Omer Bartov, who cites *Generalmajor* Lemelsen, commander of *XLVII Panzer Korps* illustrates this fact:

> I have observed that senseless shootings of both POWs and civilians have taken place. A Russian soldier who has been taken prisoner while wearing a uni-form, and after he had put up a brave fight, has the right to decent treatment.[709]

The fear of falling into German hands, either from fear of the Germans or the knowledge that Stalin would "handle" any Red Army troops who were captured should they be repatriated were most definitely the greatest motivations for the historical record reflecting the dogged resistance of the Red Army. The same acts of German barbarity that propelled the civilians to rise as insurgents also prompted the Soviet military to resist at all costs. These problems would only grow as the war continued; a proper working policy of counterinsurgency was desperately needed. Bartov also reflects the reality of this:

> In February 1942 the *18th Panzer* admitted that 'Red Army soldiers…are more afraid of falling prisoner than of the possibility of dying on the battlefield,' and maintained that this was manifested by the fact that 'since November last year…only a few deserters have come over to us and that during the battles fierce resistance was put up and only a few POWs were taken.'[710]

Another interesting entry illustrates the position of the *"Grossdeutschland" Panzergrenadier* Division command structure regarding the treatment of indigenous civilians following several reprisal attacks by ad-hoc groups of partisans or guerrillas:

> …all commissars-politruks-who fall into the hands of the troops are to be transferred immediately to the divisional intelligence section. Shooting by the troops after taking them prisoner is strictly forbidden.[711]

The divisional records also reflect the comments from prisoners who arrived wounded, and stated that they had been shot even after they had surrendered, a situation that was not to abate regardless of how many directives were issued. *"Grossdeutschland"* Division also issued a statement in April 1943 that proved such activity stiffened "the enemy's resistance."[712] It is safe to say that most of these orders were ignored, either through complete disobedience to superior authority (rather unlikely in the German military, especially within elite units) or a belief that the statements were simply issued for propaganda value and not meant to be taken seriously. This possibility is reflected by the proclamation that all guerrillas and partisans and their "support" were to be publicly hanged as a warning against further involvement with insurgent activity.[713] Civilians who violated the established movement orders, despite having their homes destroyed or occupied, and given little if anything in the way of rations were "either executed by the troops or given over to the *SD* for 'special treatment.'"[714] The German soldiers in Russia receiving such a wide range of orders must have been seriously confused as to which course of action was correct, constantly looking to their superior officers for guidance, which did not always provide an adequate answer.[715]

Also challenging the Germans soldier's perception of reality and truth were the changing official positions as to the actual rationale and method of the growing Soviet resistance. Prior to *Operation Barbarossa* and for several months afterward the Propaganda Ministry issued the old rhetoric that the eastern peoples were animals, unintelligent, and willing to capitulate if given the proper applications of force and incentive. The separation of criminal and acceptable conduct was an often blurred if not imaginary line. Detlev Peukert wrote that the German policy "was an integration of normality and barbarism."[716] Indeed, the nearly 6,000,000 enemy killed and captured by the advancing *Wehrmacht* before the first winter seemed to support this assessment.

However, as the first winter dragged on into the second year of the invasion the Soviet resistance, both militarily and through insurgency increased ten-fold. The German in the field must have felt perplexed at this rise in enemy activity, given the fact that so many had been killed and captured, and Berlin stated that these were not a people to resist or display such a show of force. Now the position in Berlin was that their natural enemy was cunning, brutal, and spurred on by the Jewish conspiracy that allowed the Bolshevik's to remain in power. The German soldier must have been at the very least confused and open to question the logic of these diverse explanations emanating from Berlin. This confusion was also apparent in the handling of suspected partisans, since contradicting and countermanding orders (sometimes loosely interpreted as the occasion warranted) came and went, depending upon the attitude and character of the commander involved. Later, as the fortunes of war turned against the Germans the institution of political officers within German units, to not only to carry propaganda to the front, but hold motivational and political indoctrination created an uneasy atmosphere of desperation and distrust among the rank and file.

The political officers were usually young, under thirty years of age and the product of years of propaganda and reinforcement of *Nazi* ideology. Nearly all came from the Hitler Youth and most were members of the *SS* if not the *SD*. Their loyalty lay only with Hitler and the Party, and this fact was well known among the ranks they were assigned to. Most of these "POs" were avoided by the "primary groups," and shunned by the older establishment of veterans who were perhaps not keen on the Party line. Even the more active supporters of *Nazi* doctrine often found the POs a discomfort, since the young political instructor would attempt to recruit support for his agenda from among the established members of a unit. This would not necessarily earn him credibility in the eyes of the majority of the soldiers where little if any had existed before.

In many cases these political officers would accompany units on ethnic cleansing patrols, sizing up the morale and dedication of the senior NCOs and officers, estimating the political soundness of the troops, and make reports that would usually end up in the headquarters of the *SD*. What most of these political officers could not comprehend, unless they were combat veterans, was the fact that men in battle, under the extremes of duress, fatigue, hunger, cold, and a myriad of other life threatening conditions seldom have the time or inclination to consider political ramifications, and are even less inclined to ponder their own nation's policies regarding their conduct and expectations. Men fight for each other, to stay alive, and if they kill, they do so to continue that status. This position was taken by Hans Mommsen, and is cited by Bartov:

> The picture drawn by the regime's propaganda of troops frantically fighting for the National Socialist cause, was false even concerning the elite formations of the *Waffen SS*...The mentality of the average *Landser* was characterized by soberness, rejection of the far-from-reality propaganda tirades, and by a firm will personally to survive. Certainly, under cover of the commissar order there were grave encroachments by the army against the defenseless civilian population handed over to it and against prisoners of war; the partisan war led to an unprecedented brutalization of the conduct of war by both sides. But the average soldier had little

influence on this and could hardly find a way of avoiding the escalation of violence.[717]

Killing suspected partisans and guerrillas served two definite purposes; it removed potential threats that would harm them and it hopefully sent a message to others not to engage in similar activity. This explains the constant use of euphemisms and guarded speech describing planned or executed killings of civilians. As long as the men believed they were eliminating a legitimate and viable threat, the chance of any negative psychological and morale problems was lessened.

However, the realities of the inefficiency of their actions seemed to have been lost upon the more influential members of the *Oberkommando der Wehrmacht*. The perceived legitimacy regarding their actions appear to be as individualistic as it was fragmented. Many units were less opaque in their transmission of messages regarding the handling of partisans and guerrillas, such as the *12th Infanterie* Division's instructions to have partisans and guerrillas (without stating the difference between the two groups) "sentenced by an officer on the spot." The *2nd Waffen SS Panzer* Division *"Das Reich"* developed a notorious reputation along with its sister *SS* units for similar tactics, as stated by *Hauptscharfuehrer* Hans Hossfelder:

> Many people have often wondered if we actually had standing orders to shoot women and children, and I know that there have been many denials regarding this by former *SS* members. However, it was unfortunately true. I can state that these types of orders were not as commonplace in my unit as in others, obviously. When we speak about the partisans, it must be understood that these were of course criminals even according to the Geneva and Hague Conventions, since they forfeited their non-combatant status upon taking up arms against us. Our handling of these people was considered within our right, although there were many excesses and outright war crimes committed against innocent people. This cannot be completely overlooked.[718]

With the breadth of the insurgency problem and given the vast front occupied by the German military, Bartov concludes that "very few units on the Eastern Front could have avoided taking part in such actions."[719] This statement is perhaps more true than not. The upsurge in partisan activity following these crimes was mentioned in the 31 January 1942 declaration by Army Group North:

> The recent revival of partisan activity in the rear areas…demands that action be taken…with the greatest ruthlessness. Partisans should be destroyed wherever they appear, as should their hiding places, if they are not needed by our troops for accommodation.[720]

According to Bartov's research, the *12th Infanterie* responded (as did most other units) by destroying villages and shooting (although not exclusively) the male inhabitants. The survivors were left to fend for themselves, further heightening the mood and numbers of the resistance.[721] This fact was supported by all of the Germans interviewed who participated or witnessed such activity, such as Otto Kumm:

> Naturally the destruction of villages, killing people even if proven to be partisans rapidly destroyed our credibility and increased the resistance against us. This was true all over Europe, not just in Russia. What was perhaps the worst thing for us was the narrow-minded approach we as a collective military body used in handling these problems. The lessons should have been learned much sooner, but unfortunately this was not to be the case.[722]

There were many commanders, as stated by Bartov, who felt that "their soldiers were far too lenient in their handling of the civilians."[723] Bartov cites Generalfeldmarschall von Reichenau on 10 October 1941:[724]

> Regarding the conduct of the troops toward the Bolshevik system many unclear ideas still remain. The essential goal of the campaign against the Jewish-Bolshevik system is the complete destruction of its power instruments and the eradication of the Asiatic influence on the European cultural sphere. Thereby, the troops two have tasks, which go beyond the conventional unilateral soldierly tradition. In the east the soldier is not only a fighter according to the rules of warfare, but also a carrier of an inexorable racial conception and the avenger of all the bestialities which have been committed against the Germans and related races. Therefore, the soldier must have complete understanding for the necessity of the harsh, but just atonement of Jewish sub-humanity. This has the further goal of nipping in the bud rebellions in the rear of the *Wehrmacht* which, as experience shows, are always plotted by the Jews.[725]

Reichenau also stated that "no effort should be made to put out fires started by retreating Soviet forces. The destruction of buildings was part of the 'fight of annihilation' against Bolshevism."[726] The irrational response methods employed by German forces are seen today in lucid hindsight as irrational and devoid of logic. There were very few within the military command structure who had either the talent, insight, or even the slightest interest in attempting to solve the counterinsurgency problems facing the military. Of course, a few officers decided that something needed to be done, at least on a temporary basis, and interjected as a *modus operandi*. Long term solutions were not even part of the initial planning, according to Kumm and Wolff. First, the Germans needed to see what worked, why it worked, and if it did not work discover why. In addition, as stated by Kumm, "We needed to know that in the event of success, would the same formula work in Yugoslavia as applied to Russia? These were all interesting questions and we had very little time to attempt trial and error."[727] The Office for Tactical Study headed by the *SS* and the *Abwehr* jointly undertook the planning, as stated by Karl Wolff:

> The problem had become so critical, especially where morale among the troops was concerned, that (Felix) Steiner, Bach-Zelewski and I decided that with the

British paras in training. *Imperial WarMuseum.*

British paratroopers in training. This was the preferred method of entry for SOE operatives throughout the war. *Imperial War Museum.*

Below: Still from movie footage of executions at Babi Yar. *Bundesarchiv.*

Leon Degrelle (second from left) and his Walloons on the Pomeranian Front, January 1945. *Leon Degrelle.*

Kurt Student, commander of the *Luftwaffe Fallschirmjäger. National Archives.*

German paratroopers on a King Tiger during the Ardennes Offensive, December 1944. *National Archives.*

Victorious *Fallschirmjaeger* following the capture of Eban Emael in Belgium, 1940. *National Archives.*

Standartenfuehrer Kurt "Panzer" Meyer (far left) and staff inspecting his new command, the 12 *Waffen SS Panzer Division "Hitlerjuegend"* in 1944. *Bundesarchiv.*

Still shot from a propaganda film of a reconnaissance unit from *"Leibstandarte"* during the Ardennes offensive. *National Archives.*

Generalleutnant Kurt Student congratulating his paratroops under *Oberleutnant* Rudolf Witzig for their actions at Eban Emael. *Bundesarchiv.*

Reinhard Heydrich as a *Gruppenfuehrer*. National Archives.

Kneaz (Prince) Leonidas Damianov Ivanovich Maximciuc, grand nephew of Czar Nicholas Romanov in Great Britain during 1947, following his escape from Romania and the Red Army while operating as a partisan against the Communist occupation. *Leo Maximciuc*.

A member of the *Brandenburg* detachment assigned to the *Skorzeny Kommando*, following the Mussolini rescue. *Rudolf von Falkenhahn*.

Sturmbannfuehrer Otto Skorzeny (third from right) with *Hauptsturm-fuehrer* Adrian von Foelkersam (second from right) with his Knight's Cross from the Maikop oil field capture in Budapest, following the coup d'etat in September 1944. *National Archives.*

Ju-52 loading troops in Greece for deployment to Crete in May 1941. *National Archives.*

Obergruppenfuehrer Josef "Sepp" Dietrich with his staff, which includes future *SS Gruppenfuehrer* and Hitler adjutant Max Wuensche (second from right) during the Greek campaign in April 1941. *National Archives.*

Tito and aide after being wounded during *Roesselsprung,* 1944. *Milo Stavic.*

Rudolf von Falkenhahn as a seventeen year old *Fallschirmjäger.* He would serve as a paratrooper in Norway, Belgium, and Crete, transferring to the Army with *6th Panzer Division,* then serving in North Africa. His transfer to the *Waffen SS* in 1942 was conducted by Himmler personally. Falkenhahn served as a sniper and fought most of the war in a counterinsurgency role.

SD men dressing as civilians for infiltration purposes in Russia. *Lothar Pankos.**

Tito (fifth from left) and his supporters following the capture of the town of Jajce in 1943. This became their headquarters until recaptured by German forces during _Operation Weiss_, forcing Tito to move his temporary headquarters to the caves at Drvar. _Milo Stavic._

Forward reconnaissance unit of _"Das Reich"_ during the push through Yugoslavia. This team is scanning Belgrade from across the Danube River. _National Archives._

"The Old Boy," Fritz Klingenberg, following his receipt of the Knight's Cross for his capture of Belgrade in April 1941. *National Archives*

German troops enter Sarajevo in April 1941. *National Archives.*

Otto Skorzeny following the Gran Sasso raid to rescue Mussolini. *National Archives.*

Officers of the *"Prinz Eugen "* Division during *Operation Weiss* in Yugoslavia. *National Archives.*

Tito's cave headquarters at Drvar in 1944. This was where the *SS Kommando Abteilung* landed in gliders to capture the resistance leader during *Operation Roesselsprung. Milo Stavic.*

Tito's forest headquarters in 1943. *Milo Stavic.*

Standartenfuehrer Otto Kumm following his receipt of the Oak Leaves to the Knight's Cross. He would later receive the Swords. *Otto Kumm.*

Execution of collaborators in Russia. *Robert G. Ridgeway.*

Pierre Deshayes in 1992. *Pierre Deshayes.*

Oberst Wolfgang Falck, "Father of the Night Fighters," was concerned about partisan activity in Yugoslavia, where his night fighter defenses were exposed and spread extremely thin. *Wolfgang Falck.*

Generalfeldmarschall Ferdinand Schoerner. *National Archives.*

Sturmbannfuehrer Hans Hauser after receiving his Knight's Cross. *Hans Hauser.*

Will Fey of *Panzerabteilung 502 (Schwere),* 2nd *Waffen SS Panzer Division "Das Reich."* Fey and his comrades often fought as armoured counterinsurgents, especially in the last days of the war. *Will Fey.*

German counterinsurgency forces in Russia, 1942. *National Archives.*

Germans carrying a wounded comrade during the winter of 1941/42 at Stalingrad. *National Archives.*

Left to right: Will Fey, Paul Eggar, and an unidentified tanker of *PzAb. 502 (Schwere) "Das Reich"* in front of a *PzKpfw 7* Tiger I during Operation Zitadelle, 1943. *Will Fey.*

German infantry on the Leningrad Front, 1943. *National Archives.*

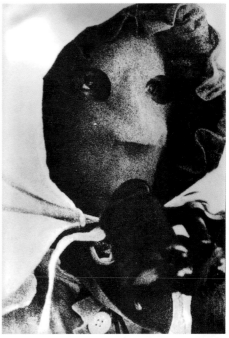

German soldier in new winter gear, 1943. These uniforms were used extensively in the counterinsurgency campaign, since extended time in the field demanded greater protection from the elements. *National Archives.*

Obergruppenfuehrer Theodor Eicke, commander of the 3rd *Waffen SS Panzer Division "Totenkopf."* executioner of *SA* leader Ernst Roehm during the "Night of the Long Knives" and former commandant of Dachau concentration camp. *National Archives.*

"Das Reich" men under fire in Russia, 1942. *Bundesarchiv.*

Oberstleutnant Dietrich Hrabak (left) in consult with *Generaloberst Wolfram Freiherr von Richthofen* in the Ukraine. Hrabak related the concerns he had regarding partisan/guerrilla activity at his airfields while serving as a pilot and commander of both *JG-52* and *JG-54* on the Eastern Front. *Dietrich and Marion Hrabak.*

Soldiers of *3rd Waffen SS Panzer Division "Totenkopf,"* captured in a still from a propaganda newsreel during *Operation Zitadelle,* 1943. A T-34 burns in the background, and the soldier drinking has probably added another tank destruction badge to his right sleeve.

Waffen SS panzer-truppen in **Russia, 1943.** *National Archives.*

Oberfuehrer Felix Steiner during his command of *"Deutschland"* Regiment. His genius created the original *Freiwilligen* concept, with the forming of the *5th SS "Wiking" Division.* National Archives

"Das Reich " moves into position during *Operation Zitadelle,* **1943 in a still from a propaganda film.** *National Archives.*

"Wiking" **Pak-40 anti-tank crew in action, Russia, 1943.** *National Archives.*

Obersturmfuehrer **Franz Vogt, one of the first recipients of the Knight's Cross for** *"Das Reich,"* **serving with Klingenberg (the reconnaissance battalion) in France in 1940.**

Leon Degrelle while living in Spanish exile. *Leon Degrelle.*

From left to *right-Sturmbannfuehrer* Leon Degrelle (receiving Knight's Cross personally from Hitler), *Obergruppenfuehrer* Herbert Gille (receiving Swords), Hitler, *Gruppenfuehrer* Herman Fegelein, and Heinrich Himmler. *Leon Degrelle.*

Women fighting at Stalingrad were not uncommon, and throughout the war they played a major role in both conventional and resistance units. *Anna Nikolina.*

Left: Hitler, Hans Baur and Martin Bormann during a visit to a military hospital in the Ukraine, 1942. *Hans Baur.*

Below: *SS* men attacking a partisan stronghold in Russia. *National Archives.*

Hans Feber (left) and Rudolf von Falkenhahn (right) during field training exercises. Both men would serve in North Africa and Russia. Feber would die in Stalingrad. *Falken-hahn.*

Standartenfuehrer Gustav Lombard, regimental commander under Fegelein in *"Florian Geyer"* (later a brigade commander) receiving his Knight's Cross for his counter-insurgency efforts. His other awards included the Iron Cross in both classes, the Wound Badge in Silver, the German Cross in Gold, and the Anti-Partisan Badge in Gold. Lombard would miraculously survive a decade of Soviet captivity with the world's top fighter ace Erich Hartmann, and Hans Baur. *Hans Baur.*

Wounded men of the *5th Waffen SS Panzer Division "Wiking"* in Russia, 1943. *National Archives.*

Sturmbannfuehrer Sylvester Stadler, who led several successful anti-partisan missions in the Soviet Union in 1943-44. *Bundesarchiv.*

Author with *Sturmbannfuehrer* Rudolf von Falkenhahn, 1984. *Colin D. Heaton.*

Propaganda Minister Josef Goebbels congratulating recently decorated survivors of the Demyansk Cauldron in Berlin. Falkenhahn is directly behind the unidentified *Gruppenfuehrer*. *Bundesarchiv.*

Preparing "bait" for Soviet snipers, a practice used by both sides. *National Archives.*

German soldiers on patrol during a counterinsurgency mission in Russia. *Bundesarchiv.*

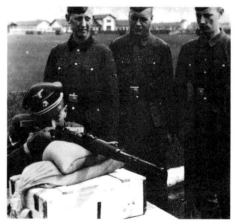

Rudolf von Falkenhahn (with rifle) at the sniper school near Berlin. Every counterinsurgency unit deployed sniper teams in the east and Balkans. *Bundesarchiv/ Falkenhahn.*

Generaloberst Hasso *Graf* von Manteuffel, who disagreed with the *SD* policies and threatened to shoot Himmler's men who wanted to recruit his soldiers for liquidation missions. *National Archives.*

Sturmbannfuehrer Wicslinzky.

Brigadefuehrer Herman Fegelein, commander of *"Florian Geyer"* after being wounded yet again during a counterinsurgency operation near Minsk, 1942. *National Archives.*

Soldiers of *"Leibstandarte"* with a captured Soviet regimental banner. *National Archives.*

Hans-Ulrich Ruedel (left) in 1943 on the Eastern Front. As a *Kommandeur* and later *Kommodore* of *Stukageschrwader 2 "Immelman,"* Ruedel had an amazing career as a tank buster. Once when he was forced to land his Ju-87 *Stuka* behind Soviet lines in 1944 his escape and evasion on foot was covered by *Jagdgeschwader 52* and *Oberstleutnant* Dietrich Hrabak, with pilots Gunther Rall, Erich Hartmann, Walter Krupinski, Johannes Steinhoff, and others. The ground attack echelon was commanded by Major Leonidas Maximciuc, flying with the Free Ukrainian Air Force. Ruedel evaded capture for three days. *Franz Kieslich.*

Gruppenfuehrer Hermann Fegelein (center with pen) with his commanders of *"Florian Geyer"* in Russia, 1943. *Bundesarchiv.*

Soviet ski patrol near Leningrad. *National Archives.*

Lieutenant Vasily Sokolovsky (left), Deputy Premier of the Soviet Council Nikolay Bulganin (center), and Marshal Georgy Zhukov (right) in 1942 during the planning for the relief of Stalingrad. Bulganin would request that partisans play a major role in the operation. *National Archives/Robert G. Ridgeway.*

Generalfeldmarschall Friedrich von Paulus (foreground left) and his adjutant, *Oberst* Wilhelm Adam (far right), surrender at Stalingrad on January 31, 1943. *National Archives.*

Still shot from the motion picture recreation of the Soviet link up at Stalingrad in November 1942. *National Archives.*

Gruppenfuehrer **Paul Hausser.** *National Archives.*

Marshal Koniev (left) on the push into Germany, January 1945. *National Archives.*

Marshal A.M. Vasilevsky, commander of the 3rd Byelorussian Front following Marshal Chernyakhovsky's death in combat. Vasilevsky coordinated the 3rd Byelorussian and 1st Baltic Fronts during the drive into East Prussia. The atrocities committed by the Red Army and partisans under his command forced thousands of non-committed civilians to join the German cause. *National Archives.*

Youthful *Freiwilligen* of the *"Legion Nederland"* being decorated in Russia. *National Archives.*

"Sepp" Dietrich (center) with Leon Degrelle (far right) in Brussels during the swearing in ceremony of the *28th Wallonien* as a full *Waffen SS* Division in April 1944. *Leon Degrelle.*

Generalleutnant **Walter Model during an inspection tour near Demyansk, 1942.** *National Archives.*

Leon Degrelle (left) decorating men of the *"Wallonien"* **at the ceremony in Brussels, April 1944.** *Leon Degrelle.*

Author with Lt. Col. Leonidas Maximciuc in Wilmington, N.C., August 1999. *Colin D. Heaton*

Gunther Rall as a *Major* following his receipt of the Swords to the Knight's Cross, 1944. *Gunther Rall.*

Above, Right: *Hauptsturmfuehrer* Joachim Peiper (right) in Russia, 1942. *Rudolf Falkenhahn.*

Right: *Oberst* Hannes Trautloft, Inspector of Day Fighters. Trautloft, along with *General der Jagdflieger* Adolf Galland witnessed many of the episodes during meetings of the General Staff, and related these to the author. *Hannes and Marga Trautloft.*

Generalleutnant Hans Baur following his release from Soviet captivity in December 1955. *Hans Baur.*

The execution of Manfred Pernass following his capture. Pernass operated as an American Military Policeman in Skorzeny's commando unit of English speakers. *National Archives.*

Adolf and Heidi Galland during a reunion in happier times. *Colin D. Heaton.*

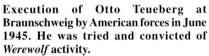

Execution of Otto Teueberg at Braunschweig by American forces in June 1945. He was tried and convicted of *Werewolf* activity.

proper analysis and experienced officers on the project we could arrive at some solution. Several plans had been tried previously, such as propaganda broadcasts and the dropping of leaflets by aircraft and artillery shells into suspected partisan areas. This was mostly a waste of time, since the partisans fighting us were not really worth trying to convert. We needed to enlist the loyalty of those who had yet been pressed into partisan or Soviet military service. Failing that, the second plan was to develop tactics for the soldiers in the field, offering better chances of success while raising their morale, which by 1943 was not as high as we would have liked to think, at least in Russia. What we derived was placed into service, and *"Florian Geyer," "Maria Theresia"* and other units were specially trained in these tactics. They worked far beyond our expectations, offering Hitler the chance to strike a new combat award, the Anti-Partisan Badge in three grades; bronze, silver and gold for fifty, seventy-five and a hundred days of such combat. The men who won these awards were few, and they wore them proudly. It was not unusual to have men in an anti-partisan unit all decorated with the Iron Cross in either of the two classes, and even higher decorations.[728]

Otto Kumm was one of the organizers and recipients of this new doctrine, and having used it operationally he concurred with Wolff on the effectiveness of the tactics:

Once we were given a plain language table of organization and equipment, with tactics outlined, we felt better prepared for tackling the partisan problem. However, we had been improvising with our own methods, and these new tactics were unique; they were handed down as a guideline, not engraved in stone, offering us the opportunity to use the new method in conjunction with the previous method. We were even encouraged to write reports on our missions and make recommendations. Another unique part of this plan was that everyone, even the lowest rank was to give his input through the chain of command, so that every perspective was covered. It was a wonderful method of waging (counterinsurgency) warfare, but it never resolved the problem of halting the constant flood of partisans that seemed to pop up like mushrooms after a summer rain. Other officers made recommendations that were finally taken seriously and placed into doctrine. This was how important Berlin finally took the partisan problem.[729]

The Red Army continued to spur the partisans on, supplying them whenever possible after 1943, knowing full well how the Germans would react, as stated earlier by Captain Koronov. This calculated strategy was intended to create further hostility toward the Germans, increasing the personal and political will of the civilian population to support the Red Army and partisans, and to strain the German military in both manpower and materiel. The Red Army's first open display of affiliation and support was to confer general grade ranks upon notable partisan leaders, legitimizing their combat activities and further incorporating the Soviet political ideology into the minds of the average Russian peasant and worker. This ingenious program solidified the Russian people behind the common objective of repelling the invaders. Once united and supported the partisan war exploded to a level that, according to several Germans interviewed, caught the German military completely by surprise.

Despite the open benevolence displayed by the Soviets toward their partisan allies, all support including arms, munitions, food, clothing and propaganda came with a price. The partisan leaders and their groups were forced to swear allegiance to Stalin and the Communist Party. This was ensured by the placing of political officers within the ranks of each partisan group, as well as *NKVD* spies. Many partisan groups actually became effective field operators with the full knowledge that to do otherwise meant an unpleasant fate. It is this factor, as well as the long history of Stalinism combined with the decrees issued against surrender that forced thousands of previously loyal Russians into the German camp.

Many of the more experienced members of the irregular forces also knew that Stalin would turn against them, especially the Ukrainians, Bukovinans, Moldavians, Azerbaijanis, Turkmeni, Armenians, Khazakhstanis, Belorussians, Bessarabians, Caucasians and even his fellow Georgians once their services were no longer needed. Once the insurgency is won there is no longer a necessity in keeping the insurgents. This fact was learned after the Russian Civil War and was practiced doctrine within the pages of Stalin's operational manifesto, fueled by paranoia. Stalin believed that the large numbers of armed, well trained and battle hardened insurgents fluent in Red Army tactics would become a problem after the war once he returned the country to business as usual. This fact was illustrated after World War II when the Ukrainian and Caucasus partisans and guerrillas began to be exterminated. This pogrom led to a long-standing guerrilla war that lasted well into the 1950s and occurred in every nation occupied by Soviet forces, with exception to East Germany. The spark of nationalism that fueled the partisan movements against Germany simply shifted their focus to a new, albeit pre-existing threat.

German propaganda played upon the inherent distrust of the political commissars believed to be rampant within the Red Army, as well as within partisan and guerrilla units, yet this program of mass de-Stalinization failed. However, the success of the German propaganda campaign was demonstrated by the fact that few Germans are known to have been swayed by enemy propaganda, believing in the superiority of their cause if not their leadership. It is interesting to note that, as the war continued and Germany's fortunes became ever more precarious, the propaganda projected to the *Wehrmacht* in the field became even more desperate and fanatic, bordering on the completely irrational, calling for personal sacrifice and National Socialist fervor to compensate for the losses of entire divisions and their collective war materiel. The primary reason this program failed in both inception and practice where the Soviet military and irregulars were concerned is stated in the post-war analysis of the topic by *Generaloberst* Erhard Rauss:

> By means of a close-meshed network of especially chosen personalities, the commissars held the entire army machine under their control and in a tight grip. The commissars were to a preponderant degree real political fanatics. They came mostly from the working class...But they also took care of the troops...However it is not true that the Russia soldier fought well only because of fear of the commissars. A soldier who is motivated solely by fear can never have the qualities that the Russian soldier of this war displayed...Unceasing propaganda has burned nationalism into his soul. And, however impervious he may be to foreign propaganda, he nevertheless has been unable to escape the engulfing waves of his own.[730]

Much in the way of the study of partisan and guerrilla strategic operations during the war have been completed, primarily through the efforts of the United States Army Counterintelligence Corps that completed a study of German and Soviet combat methods following the war. These findings were supported by the interrogations of captured high-ranking German officers with extensive Russian Front, intelligence, counterintelligence and counterinsurgency experience. Men such as Reinhard Gehlen,[731] Otto Kumm,[732] Karl Wolff,[733] and Josef "Sepp" Dietrich,[734] as well as several former insurgents who later fought the Communists and defected to the west participated to some degree. These methods of collecting information were considered critical to forging a cogent plan for counterinsurgency methodology in Europe, once the Communist threat from Soviet occupation throughout Eastern Europe created the Cold War as we understand it. Much in the way of post-war guerrilla warfare doctrine as practiced by the British and American forces in their respective small wars and insurgencies from the 1950s to the present is owed to this comprehensive study.

The Allies also made great use of the knowledge of the German commanders in captivity, and the United States Army Counterintelligence Corps and later the Central Intelligence Agency gathered 2,175 manuscripts containing a total of 77,000 pages of documentation compiled "by 501 former *Wehrmacht Heer, Waffen SS,* and *Luftwaffe* generals and eleven admirals,"[735] and leading the way was *Generaloberst* Franz Halder, Chief of the General Staff from 1938-42.[736] Through his energetic as well as egotistical approach to maintaining the war with Communism, Halder summoned the assistance of dozens of his wartime colleagues who, upon their release from Allied captivity in 1947 or later began to actively work for the United States. This occurred despite his active participation in the slave labor program assisting German industry for which he was imprisoned.

Such notable members included *General der Infanterie* Dr. Waldemar Erfurth, the German representative of the *OKH* to Finland from June 1941 until the cessation of Russo-Finnish hostilities; *General der Infanterie* Hans von Greiffenberg, Chief of Operations Section of *OKW* and Chief of Staff Army Group Center during *Barbarossa,* in which he was a major participant in the planning, and *General* Erhard Rauss, commander of both *3rd* and *4th Panzer Armee* on the Eastern Front. Also included were *SS Gruppenfuehrer* Otto Kumm, *Generalmajor* Reinhard Gehlen, *Obergruppenfuehrer* Karl Wolff, *Gruppenfuehrer* Max Wuensch, *Gruppenfuehrer* Kurt *"Panzer"* Meyer, and *Generaloberst* Hasso von Manteuffel.

9

From *Operation Barbarossa* Forward

*Thousands upon thousands of martyrs have hero-
ically laid down their lives for the people; let us
hold their banner high and march ahead along the
path crimson with their blood.*
- Mao Tse Tung
24 April 1945.

Insurgency warfare in the Soviet Union was unlike any other area of Europe, primarily due to the great expanse of the region, the difficulties and variance of the terrain, and the great numbers of personnel, both military and civilian. However, despite these irrefutable facts there is a misconception regarding the overall effectiveness of irregulars against the German invaders. True, Stalin was successful in his calling for the partisan war, and "…encouraged the partisans to the war in ideological terms; resistance was an expression of commitment to the Soviet cause and the forces of socialist progress."[737] Although German personnel losses to partisans and guerrillas throughout Europe were approximately eight percent of the total German war casualties (according to Wolff), the inherent value of the irregulars was their ability to hinder and even stall German advances on rare occasions; inhibit reinforcements, and interrupt lines of supply and communication.

Perhaps the greatest asset in hindering the German war effort, especially in the east was the forcing of the German military to detach large numbers of front-line troops to rear areas for garrison, police, and security duties, thereby reducing the overall command effectiveness of the *Wehrmacht* in the field.[738] As stated by *Generaloberst* Erhard Rauss in *Fighting in Hell: The German Ordeal on the Eastern Front:*

> A Western European army fighting in Russia is faced with conditions entirely different from those to which it is accustomed, conditions rooted in the peculiarities of Russia and its people. The most unusual characteristic of the country is the climate, which affects terrain and vegetation and determines living conditions in general.[739]

The conditions facing the German soldier in the Soviet Union have become legendary. The impact of the climate and terrain would also have a great impact upon the German prosecution of the war against the insurgents, as well as their campaign to recruit, support and foster a pro-German sentiment among the disaffected members of Stalin's "Workers Paradise." According to Overy; "No doubt the German invaders could have made more of such anti-Soviet sentiments than they did, but millions of nationalists continued to fight against the Soviet side even when the true nature of German imperialism became clear."[740] The great expanses of forests and swamps "were the natural sanctuaries for growing partisan cells and provided ideal conditions for their purposes."[741] So great would the problem become in these regions:

> Toward the end of the war the vast Russian forest areas were becoming so insecure that a special warning radio channel had to be included in the signal operation instructions of higher headquarters, to be used extensively for urgent calls for assistance in case a unit or strong point was attacked or threatened by partisans.[742]

The partisan cells swelled not only through the masses of the disaffected civilian population but also from large numbers of Soviet soldiers who joined their ranks after being encircled and cut off, unable to rejoin their units that had either been decimated, captured, or withdrawn. The utilization of the civilian force in combination with military personnel, tactical understanding, and zealous leadership provided a lethal threat to German rear areas and forward outposts.

On the Eastern Front the *SS* was dispatched to handle the partisan/guerrilla threat in a very unique way. *Generalfeldmarschall* Wilhelm Keitel, a career Army officer and devout Hitlerite instituted a seriously flawed method. Keitel ordered the *Nacht und Nebel* (Night and Fog) decrees allowing for the seizure of property and the execution without trial of all persons suspected of compromising German security in the occupied zones.[743] Keitel also issued the orders upgrading the actions against civilians and Jews, including the mass murder of all male Jews from ages 17 to 45, but soon the age limitations meant nothing.[744] The interpretation of this new regulation was left to the discretion of the respective field commanders, which according to Otto Kumm, "...little in the way of a clear definition was ever provided."[745] Various *SS* units created their own counterinsurgency teams that were usually comprised of company sized elements numbering approximately 200 men, again according to Otto Kumm.[746] These units were motorized, well armed, and would be rushed rapidly to an area of suspected partisan activity.

One of the first large-scale partisan encounters (with the insurgents operating in brigade strength) occurred at Vyazma, 145 kilometers east of Smolensk and 240 kilometers west of Moscow (the Vyazma-Bryansk Line) in October 1941.[747] The German *7th* and *10th Panzer* Divisions of *IV Panzer Armee* raced through a hole in the Soviet defenses, encircling the city and an entire Soviet army of fifty-five divisions, capturing between 463,000 and 633,000 prisoners.[748] The commander of the *10th Panzer* Division was *Generalmajor* Ferdinand Schaal, recently promoted for his successes in Poland and France. Schaal was beset by partisan problems from the start. His successor, *Generalmajor* Wolfgang Fischer found himself engaging irregulars who were linked up with the Red Army in an effort to close the quickest routes to Moscow. These events precipitated the need for immediate and direct counter-insurgency activity, which was provided, although it proved to be ad-hoc in the initial employment.

The systematic murders of the local populations that had begun in the late summer, such as the 33,711 Jews, partisans, commissars, POWs and others killed in reprisal for the bombing of the Continental Hotel, headquarters for the *6th Armee* at Babi Yar, near Kiev in the Ukraine on 29-30 September 1941 (eventually over 100,000 bodies would fill the great ravine) were a portent to what the population in general could expect.[749] The commander of the execution detail, Paul Blobel, was later ordered to "exhume Babi Yar and other mass graves to dispose of the bodies more effectively."[750] The Germans had just launched the first salvo in a self-destructive campaign of terror that would further the resolve of millions of Soviet citizens to take up arms, many of whom were potential allies against Stalin, and foil the one great opportunity to enlist the aid of the multitudes who had initially perceived the German military as a liberation force.

The German invasion unleashed a series of partisan uprisings all along the front, which are illustrated in this section. In the records of *Generalfeldmarschall* August von Mackensen, partisan actions at Dnepropetrovsk from 13-25 August 1941 and continuing with a brief pause at the bridge-head from 26 August-29 September 1941 against the *13th* and *14th Panzer* Divisions, the *1st* and *5th Waffen SS Panzer* Divisions, the *25th*, *44th*, *57th*, *60th* (motorized), *125th*, *198th*, *298th Infanterie* Divisions; the Italian *Freiwilligen* Divisions *"Pasubio," "Torino," "Celere,"* and the Slovakian *Freiwilligen* Division.[751] These units were also actively engaged against irregulars and the Red Army from 3-31 December 1941 as the irregular activity increased.

The commander of Army Group Center, *Generalfeldmarschall* Fedor von Bock recorded the partisan/guerrilla activity between 22 June 1941-5 January 1942, when at various times he commanded *Panzergruppe II, III, 4th Armee* and *9th Armee*, although his appreciation for the severity of the problem was grossly underestimated.[752] This is evident by two factors: the action taken in 1942 by *Generaloberst* Franz Halder as head of the *Fuehrerreserve des Oberkommando des Heeres (Ausschieden aus dem Amt)* on 24 September 1942,[753] and the previous surrounding of Demyansk by what was largely a Red Army supported partisan force under Lieutenant General Andrei A. Vlasov. Vlasov sent ski-equipped shock troops fresh from Moscow and Siberia, supporting the 2nd Shock Army from the Volkhov Front south of Leningrad into the fray supported by armor and air support, thus creating a gap four miles wide.[754] Seizing the opportunity opened by the partisan spearhead the Soviets pushed nearly a quarter of a million men into the salient. This bold stroke totally encircled the German forces by 12 January 1942, including the entire group commanded by *General* Georg von Kuechler, the former commander of the *18th Armee* who had replaced *Generalfeldmarschall* Wilhelm *Ritter* von Leeb.[755]

Kuechler immediately deployed his forces into a hedgehog perimeter defense, since the Soviets had encircled the collective German forces at both Kholm and Demyansk. Kholm saw partisan activity from the first day to the last, and the German defender, *Generalmajor* Theodor Scherer, a resilient World War I veteran and fieldcraft innovator maintained his forces throughout the long ordeal, much of which was hand to hand combat. Every day the defensive positions grew smaller as casualties mounted and enemy numbers increased despite the casualties suffered. Scherer was wounded twice; once seriously when steel splinters penetrated his legs during a mortar attack and again when a T-34 fired a high explosive shell into his observation post. Scherer would not give ground, relying instead upon air support supplied by *Luftwaffe Generaloberst* Alfred Keller, another First World War veteran and *Pour le Merite* recipient who commanded the transport aircraft, and the promise of relief forces.[756] For his dogged defense under incredible pressure and against great odds, Scherer received the Knight's Cross on 5 May 1942 when the siege was lifted.

Also trapped in the same region was the *9ᵗʰ Armee* only recently under the command of *Generalleutnant* Walter Model, who was appointed by *Generaloberst* (later *Generalfeldmarschall*) Guenther von Kluge.[757] Model, one of Germany's most capable infantry commanders was the former commander of the *XLI Panzer Korps* assigned to Army Group Center. Model was chosen to replace the exhausted *Generalleutnant* Adolf Strauss on 18 January 1942, and he strengthened and solidified the east flank defenses of *XXIII Korps* while the *VI Korps* protected the west, allowing the German forces to sustain horrendous human wave attacks and armored assaults with minimal supplies and munitions.

On 21 January Model issued orders from his headquarters at Vyazma sending the *1ˢᵗ Panzer* Division into an assault against the Soviet stronghold of Sychevka in an attempt to trap Red Army units at the Rshev Gap. The *1ˢᵗ Panzer* fought as infantry with *Luftwaffe* close air support, having lost all of their armor they were later augmented by *Waffen SS* units, including the Flemish volunteers who later became designated the *27ᵗʰ Waffen Panzergrenadier* Division *der SS "Langemarck"* and the battle hardened *3ʳᵈ Waffen SS Panzer* Division *"Totenkopf,"* as well as an ad-hoc collection of German, Soviet, Czech and other anti-aircraft and self-propelled guns for direct support. The battle for the Rzhev Gap would be over within thirty-six hours and Vlasov would lose an entire division. Model's foothold on the north road to Vyazma secured a German supply route for a little longer, despite increased partisan attacks. This would be Model's first major experience with such ferocious fighting and partisan units, which he dealt with ruthlessly. A man who once met Model was *Waffen SS Sturmbannfuehrer* Rudolf von Falkenhahn:

> Model was a fanatical fighter, and a real politician. He believed that to die in battle was his destiny, and he never backed down. His monocle, Scotch and premium cigars were always carried with him by his aide-de-camp. However, had Model survived the war he would have been hanged as a war criminal for his activities against civilians, even women and children. It must be understood that, even through all those years of war, I rarely met soldiers regardless of rank who actively pursued non-combatants. I did see it happen and it was wrong. It certainly expanded the partisan resistance against us, and Model was one of the most ruthless in that regard. I think that was why he and *Generalfeldmarschall* Schoerner were Hitler's favorite *Wehrmacht* commanders. I was very happy to have never been on the receiving side of his anger, which was legendary.[758]

Vlasov constantly threw his partisans and exhausted troops into the grinder, and he must have been well aware that failure to maintain pressure on the Germans would be fatal. Vlasov sent reinforced partisan units to the south along with surviving Red Army soldiers in a plan to attack Model's weak right flank held by the German *4ᵗʰ Armee* and auxiliary units. The plan was to once again punch a hole through the German defenses and run his forces through to Vyazma, dividing the German defenders who could then be attacked in a two prong operation, while the main Soviet force enveloped the German *4ᵗʰ Armee* along with partisan support. The partisans played a significant role in the fact that Major General P.A. Belov[759] took his cavalry corps into battle (large numbers of his force were partisans) and broke through on 26 January in a bid to link up with Vlasov's infantry, starting their attack from the north-east. The infantry were racing along the only hard surface road in an attempt to link up with 3,000 Soviet paratroops dropped to the south as a hammer for the enveloping anvil. Model's reconnaissance forces and intelligence foresaw the danger, counter-attacking the partisan forces with the *4ᵗʰ Armee* from their position in Gzhatsk and new members destined for the *"Wallonien"* Brigade (still attached to the Army at this time) linking up with *4ᵗʰ Panzer Armee* salvaging the anemic German supply line. The *"Wallonien"* voluteers would be soon transferred to join their unit already stationed in the Ukraine. Leon Degrelle described the hit and run battles with the Soviet and partisan forces:

> We moved all day and all night on foot, sometimes with trucks, and always looking for the next ambush. The Soviets sent artillery in to try and channel us into their killing zones, but we hit the earth and pushed through, taking casualties every time. The largest partisan fighting I was involved in was near the road, where the partisan cavalry attacked and withdrew quickly. I ordered my men not to pursue, it was not our mission. When we linked up with members of *4ᵗʰ Armee*, we felt safer. But that was just the beginning.

The Soviets began relying upon their partisan auxiliaries even more due to their massive casualties. General (later Marshal) Georgi Zhukov had been assisting with the coordination of the counter thrusts to the south of the front, primarily in the Caucasus and during the assaults on Moscow.[760] Stalin wanted to broaden the scope of the war, pulling the German reserves into the fray in order to stretch their already anemic supply lines that could be attacked by the partisans. Zhukov opposed this tactic since the Soviet forces were themselves stretched to the limit and their own supply problem was only growing. Regardless, Stalin ordered the 1ˢᵗ Shock Army into Demyansk to support Vlasov, thus abandoning Vyazma. This was a critical error that allowed Model and his headquarters to remain intact and plan a stiffer defense supported by a counterattack possibility.[761]

The road to Demyansk was so narrow it afforded only single vehicle traffic, and due to its unimproved status it was virtually unsuitable for anything other than tracked vehicles, horse drawn wagons and infantry. The Germans defended the road tenaciously and the Soviets paid heavily in men and materiel. The partisans were considered expendable and were themselves beyond their supply and communication lines and had outrun their Red Army support. Instead of the double pincer movement planned to destroy Model's forces at Vyazma, the Soviets concentrated 300,000 men in a great arcing swing north to northwest to envelop Model's *9ᵗʰ Armee* and continue on to Smolensk. Vlasov controlled the operation and succeeded in cutting Model off, but due to the restraints of supplies and ammunition, as well as the stiff opposition of the defenders the Red Army lost nearly a quarter of its troops, and the Soviet drive stalled on 27 January 1942 without any appreciable gains. Model was now facing the Red Army to the north, east, and west, with the only opening being the narrow corridor between Vyazma and Gzhatsk held by elements of the *4ᵗʰ Armee* and *4ᵗʰ Panzer Armee*. The *3ʳᵈ Panzer Armee* was located to the south covering the road to Smolensk as a buffer against a Soviet attack, which usually arrived in the form of a random tank or partisan unit. Then there was the brutal winter weather, killing and maiming as effectively as the enemy.

On 22 February Hitler issued his first *Festung Befehl* (Fortress Order) denying Model any chance of a breakout, withdrawal, and especially surrender.[762] The roads were blocked by high snow that would soon turn into a quagmire, eventually halting all movement even more thoroughly with the spring thaw. The Germans would be limited to defensive infantry actions, just as the Soviets would be slowed in the attack. This type of weather gave the partisans even greater room for maneuver since the mechanized German threat was effectively neutralized. As the weather began to turn more favorable the Germans began receiving more supplies. The drawback was that the Soviets had caught their breath and were renewing their attacks with vigor. Model knew that he had to strike quickly since the renewed partisan efforts applied great pressure on his lines of communication and threatened to isolate his command into smaller pockets that could be more effectively dealt with.

German relief forces were headed east and north, and Vlasov ordered his forces to attack and stall the enemy armor and infantry. It would be partisans *en masse* who would be given the honor due to their mobility and speed. If Model's trapped forces tried to breakout and meet the relief columns the Soviets could then counter-attack and destroy them in place. In support of the Soviet attempt Vlasov unleashed his Siberian reserve troops and untried Mongolian infantry in a swing to the south in another hammer and anvil operation.

Model's access to superb aerial photographic reconnaissance and intelligence assisted in his realizing the threat, and he allowed small units to advance in late March, forcing Vlasov to retreat against Stalin's orders. Vlasov was hoping to withdraw his conventional forces, thereby luring the Germans into a pursuit while the partisans harassed and attacked the German flanks. However, Model did the opposite and pulled his forces back (also against Hitler's orders) maintaining unit integrity and control of his supply routes. He did send his armor and supporting infantry south to check the partisan threats, meeting the Soviet force coming from the opposite direction. The resulting battle lasted for three weeks, with the first German reinforcements arriving the first week of April. This fresh German force included the battle hardened *1ˢᵗ Waffen SS Panzer* Division *"Leibstandarte"* under the command of *Gruppenfuehrer* "Sepp" Dietrich. Other units brought into the battle against the Red Army and partisans were *3ʳᵈ Waffen SS Panzer* Division *"Totenkopf"* commanded by *Gruppenfuehrer* (later *Obergruppenfuehrer*) Theodor Eicke,[763] *5ᵗʰ Waffen SS Panzer* Division *"Wiking,"*[764] *4ᵗʰ Waffen SS* Division *"Polizei,"* as well as *Panzer Grenadier* Division *"Grossdeutschland"* commanded by *Generalleutnant* Hasso von Manteuffel, which absorbed much of *"Langemarck."*[765] After crushing an entire partisan and cavalry regiment the outnumbered Germans effectively halted Vlasov's ambitions, due to his having to send forces north in an attempt to relieve Leningrad.

The Soviet 2ⁿᵈ Army under the command of General Kiril A. Meretskov pushed through sixty miles into the front of *Generalleutnant* Georg Lindemann's *16ᵗʰ Armee* and soon found itself over extended. Meretskov expected to be either relived or reinforced with the spring thaw, but the Germans exploited his weak flanks, and on 19 March 1942 encircled the Soviets. Vlasov managed to break out of the trap briefly on 27 March and link up with Soviet forces still fighting to reach him. This retrograde operation failed, and the *SS* and

"Wallonien" replacements that cut his avenue of retreat sealed his fate. Vlasov relieved Meretskov, whose men had been fighting without food, ammunition and medical supplies for a month, and a typhus epidemic had swept through the ranks, further reducing the force by a full third. These events forced Vlasov to take personal command of the 2nd Shock Army.

Vlasov began relying more heavily upon the partisan forces and asked Stalin for permission to withdraw, to link up with a stronger force of fresh reserve troops and partisans and then counter-attack. Stalin refused, and the fly, mosquito, and disease infested marshes continued to claim lives and morale. Vlasov blamed Stalin for the loss of good soldiers and civilians due to his fanatical inflexibility, lack of military knowledge, and total disregard for his citizens' lives. Stalin did send an aircraft into the pocket to extract Vlasov, fearing his death or even worse his capture, but Vlasov refused, stating, "we leave together or die together." Stalin did finally issue the order to withdraw on 5 May, but only when it was too late. Lindemann's forces penetrated the pocket on 20 May once the last major partisan groups had been destroyed, trapping Vlasov and sixteen of his divisions with supporting elements. It may have been these series of events that formed Vlasov's decision to turn against Stalin long before his capture in July 1942, but this will never be known for certain.

The "Demyansk Cauldron" would be relieved by German forces on 5 May 1942 although pitched battles continued, establishing German positions from Novgorod to Yam Tezero where Vlasov, wounded by a forward sentry was captured while recuperating in a barn on 12 July by *Oberleutnant* Oliver Thoring with the remnants of a platoon of redirected troops from *28th "Wallonien"* who had been separated from their unit for weeks.[766] The Germans had been searching for Vlasov for several weeks believing that he had been shot, and in fact burying his aide Vinogradov, who had been mortally wounded and suffering from what was diagnosed as malaria.[767] When he died they believed he *was* Vlasov since he was dressed in his superior's overcoat with insignia of rank, even having a gold tooth similar to the descriptions of Vlasov. Vlasov was taken to *XXXVIII Korps* for interrogation by a *Hauptmann* von Schwerdtner, who then handed Vlasov over to the *18th Armee* commanded by Vlasov's opposition in Volkhov, *Generaloberst* Lindemann.[768] The history of the anti-partisan war and the *Freiwilligen* was to change forever.

The battles become synonymous with the brutal fighting that would characterize the Eastern Front, as trapped Axis troops fought to the death, often hand to hand in several sectors, surviving off of dead animals, plants, and sometimes each other, with reports of cannibalism adding to the horror. However, the suffering was not restricted to the Germans. The local population was also starving, with Germans, Red Army, and partisan troops stealing food, animals, and able bodied men in their respective struggles. The battles around Demyansk-Kholm were also crucial in the fact that this was the first major Soviet operation utilizing partisan components *en masse* in conjunction with the Red Army in a sustained, long term action. The struggle depleted the Soviet's meager resources and supplies and wreaked havoc upon their logistics, effectively illustrating the fact that untrained and ill equipped civilian irregulars were no match for a well trained, well supplied, and highly disciplined conventional enemy force in continuous action. From this point forward Soviet partisan groups operating without direct Red Army support and guidance would maintain the genuine tactics of "guerrillas," still relying upon the tried and true tactic of hit and run operations.

Although exact figures are not available it has been assessed that perhaps a full third of the Soviet casualties during the battle were partisans, either independent factions operating locally or consolidated and organized groups within the military auxiliary proper. By the time the Germans at Demyansk were relieved on 30 April 1942, Stalin had written off nearly a quarter of a million men and all of their equipment, regardless of their military or civilian component. In analyzing the Soviet handling of the Demyansk and Kholm operations, a broader picture emerges. Although the Soviet effort accomplished little regarding the region around Lake Ilmen and Demyansk, the stalling of the entire German *II Korps* and preventing their advance, retreat, or consolidation allowed great gains to be made further south. Hitler had received the combat reports and he was understandably concerned about the rising partisan problem. In issuing the elimination orders to supplement the liquidation of political commissars he unwittingly compounded the problem for all time.

Generaloberst Franz Halder would become a charter member in the Army's attempt at drafting a policy of containment in handling the partisan/guerrilla problem, which would have some merit, although his plan would eventually prove as futile as the previous efforts. The implementation of specific strategies regarding the insurgency problem occurred when Halder supervised certain activities during the *Abwehrschlachten*.[769] Unfortunately, his records do not reflect this activity in great detail, and only the interviews with particular officers who were involved such as Kumm, Falkenhahn, Degrelle, Hossfelder, and Wolff offer any substantial evidence of this.

Another commander plagued by partisan activity was Hans Doerr. During the battle for Uman (after being attached to the *17th Armee* under Heinrich von Stuelpnagel from June-July 1941[770]) in August 1941, Doerr resorted to the usual plan of action when partisans attacked his supply depots.[771] Doerr also initiated counterinsurgency operations during the Dnieper assault from 29 August-12 September 1941, using attached Romanian and additional *Waffen SS* units with marginal success.[772] Following Doerr's initiation *Generalleutnant* Helmuth Stieff also encountered partisan activity (much of it attributed to Vlasov) on the Moscow Front through November-3 December 1941 and again during the Soviet counteroffensive from 6-31 December 1941.[773] The intelligence reports compiled by Gehlen's office regarding further contacts with partisans by German forward units at Malojaroslawecs, Kaluga, and Medyn from 1-22 January 1942; south of Moscow from 22-27 January; at Juchow from 28 January-22 February 1942; along the retreat from 23 February-18 April 1942 and again from 24 May-22 June 1942. This activity stressed that more support was seriously needed in counterinsurgency operations, and *still nothing was done*.[774]

Regarding Doerr's problems with partisans, this would become a primary focal point in the High Command after his continued encounters at Voronezh, Kharkov, Isjun, Stalingrad, Rostov, the Crimea, Wotlschansk, and the Caucasus in 1942 while commanding *4th Panzer Armee*.[775] *Generalfeldmarschall* Gerd von Schweppenburg was another innovative field commander of the old school who decided to initiate anti-partisan missions before his soldiers became victims, operating without orders and proving fairly successful.[776] Schweppenburg was even successful in collecting guerrillas who operated as auxiliaries within his army with great success in gathering intelligence and performing invaluable forward reconnaissance missions.

The *12th Armee* under Wilhelm List, which included the *III Panzer Korps* nearly fell apart under heavy partisan and Red Army attacks in the area around Kharkov (of which

Otto Kumm was a member of *2nd SS "Das Reich"* at this time) and in the Caucasus and Samara regions between 25 March-16 May and 17-28 May 1942 with serious results.[777] The unit was heavily engaged south of Woltschansk beginning on 29 May and concluding on 16 June 1942, as the Red Army began using the irregular forces as combat auxiliaries on a massive scale, a tactic that would not become actual Soviet policy until later in the year.[778]

The additional partisan and Red Army pressure assisted in stalling *I Panzer Armee* as it was leaving the Caucasus to support the Stalingrad operation, thus maintaining a running battle from November 1942 to January 1943, facilitating the disaster that befell Paulus' *6ᵗʰ Armee*.[779] The heavy conventional and partisan assaults forced *I Panzer Armee* to retreat against Hitler's orders to salvage its lines of supply and communications.[780] This culminated in another lengthy engagement at Kupjansk from 17-26 June 1942. Rostov was the next phase of the concerted attacks between 27 June and 25 July 1942. *I Panzer Armee* was being bled white even as the next phase of the Soviet plan sprang to life at Maikop on 26 July-15 August; at Terek on 16-28 August; Baksan on 26 August-20 September; Terek-Basin again from 21 September-18 October; Naltshik from 19 October -12 November; Ordschanikidse from 13-21 November, and the Caucasus again from 1-21 November 1942.[781]

The story of the *15ᵗʰ Infanterie* Division under *Brigadegeneral* Wilhelm Willemer also illustrates the growing insurgency problem, as Willemer felt the sting of partisans at Smolensk on 15 July 1941, on the Dnieper-Vyazma front on 7 November 1941, and again at Moscow on 2 November 1941.[782] The unit almost ceased to exist after massive partisan attacks supported by Red Army tank units in the Donetz Basin shredded his defenses, with the greatest attack to date occurring on 2 September 1943.[783] Further engagements at Krivoy, Dnepropetrovsk, the Dniestr River, Jassy, Husi, and the southern Carpathian Mountains during the retreat in October 1944 eventually rendered the division virtually worthless.[784] Further operations in Mistok around the southern mountains would almost complete the destruction of the *15ᵗʰ Infanterie* Division by 26 November 1944.[785] It would be during the final retreat throughout April 1945 that the division would collapse in total during the fighting and eventually surrender in Slovakia on 1 May 1945. Willemer's experience with the partisans would continue, such as when the reconstituted *6ᵗʰ Armee* in Romania saw an intense struggle ensue between irregulars and the *306ᵗʰ Infanterie* Division from 20 August through 26 September 1944, with the battle of Tirasopol on 20-22 August bringing heavy casualties.[786]

The explosion of partisan activity in 1943 saw the German High Command rapidly increase its foreign recruiting, with the *Waffen SS* creating twenty new divisions by the end of the war (see *Appendix B*). This was especially true of the Ukraine; "In 1943 the German authorities calculated that sixty percent of the area of north-west Ukraine was under the control nationalist partisans."[787] This critical period saw Himmler lower the stringent racial purity requirements, as well as Hitler and Himmler both authorizing the formation of large units of indigenous forces. Part of this process included the expansion and eventual commitment of the reconstituted pro-German Free Russian Army in 1943, but still in limited numbers, and not being committed to full strength until 1944 under the direction of the *Kommandeur des Ostersatzregiments Mitte, Generalleutnant* Hellmich,[788] who was appointed to the post on 21 January 1944, and under *Generalfeldmarschall* Ernst Koestring.[789] Hellmich would function as overall commander of the *Ost Freiwilligen* until that department was taken over by Koestring personally on 1 January 1945.[790]

Koestring was the son of a bookseller and served in the Imperial German Army during the First World War, and his experience in both combat and the Russian language, in conjunction with his previous experience as Military Attaché to Moscow from 1927-30, then again from 1935 until the invasion of the Soviet Union made him the most experienced officer on the Soviet problem. Ironically, it was Koestring who first informed Hitler upon returning to Berlin via Istanbul in July 1941, that Germany could not win a sustained war of attrition against the Soviet Union, based upon his touring of the Soviet industrial centers.[791] Koestring also informed Hitler that Stalin and Molotov fully expected a German betrayal of the Non-Aggression Pact at some point, but not in 1941.[792] This opinion was based upon the fact that Hitler had committed vast forces to the Balkans, the invasion of Crete, as well as supporting the newly instituted Africa campaign. All of these activities apparently convinced Stalin that a German diversion into the Soviet Union was impossible. Koestring, who was opposed to the timing of the invasion and the additional commitment of Germany's already thinly stretched assets, was perhaps the most valuable component in Hitler's final decision to invade the Soviet Union. Hitler knew, that despite his lack of National Socialist zeal Koestring was an intelligent and astute officer who knew what he was talking about.

Despite falling from Hitler's grace with such disturbing news, Koestring was recalled to duty on 10 August 1942. Reporting to the *Fuehrer Hauptamt* at Vinnitza, Ukraine, the operating area for *Armee Gruppe A* (later designated *Armee Gruppe Sued*) Koestring was to begin a new career as an international auxiliary commander.[793] Koestring was also an intelligent man who did not waiver in explaining to Hitler the flaws in the liquidation program, since most of these forces being organized were auxiliary units from the regions affected by the pogrom, making recruiting difficult. Despite the obvious problems Koestring managed to collect tens of thousands of volunteers who were assigned to the counterinsurgency role throughout the Eastern Front. These forces were created to fight Stalin, following the National Socialist agenda, and believed they were fighting for their own autonomous nation states once Stalin was defeated. These multitudes would fight valiantly for the most part, only to be decimated as the Soviet steamroller advance crushed everything in its path from 1943 onwards.[794] Otto Kumm was one of these leaders who helped plan the counterinsurgency operations along with *Oberfuehrer* (later *Gruppenfuehrer*) Felix Steiner.[795] Kumm explains how the mission took place:

At this time I was serving with *2ⁿᵈ SS* Division *"Das Reich"* as a company commander and we were ordered to locate and destroy the partisan forces. The problem we had was that we were not accustomed to seeking out an enemy and giving chase, since the Soviet soldiers fought bravely, and usually until they were either killed, captured, or out of ammunition. The partisans operated as a hit and run unit, firing a few shots, dropping back, firing again, luring our men into ambushes and trying to penetrate our flanks. Some even carried radios to call artillery and air strikes against us. This was not what we were used to. Finally we decided on a tactic of probing forward with a squad, followed by a platoon, which would be flanked by a platoon on each side. Once the partisans fired the center squad would give chase, dropping to fire as the following center platoon rushed through under cover fire. The two flanking platoons were in radio contact with the rest, so depending upon which way the partisans ran the facing platoon would stand fast, while the entire formation would pivot around behind the enemy, chasing them into the line of fire of the stationary unit. This plan worked well, and once the enemy were engaged the platoons would call artillery fire behind the partisans preventing escape, forcing them to stand and fight. This is when the heavy weapons would take over and the artillery would be walked back into the partisan unit. It took a few practices to get this down to a proper format, but it proved to be quite effective.[796]

Kumm was once again involved in a massive anti-partisan effort at Kharkov in February 1943, when as a *Sturmbannfuehrer* he was commanding a reinforced company of *"Der Fuehrer"* Regiment[797] of *2nd SS "Das Reich."*[798] During the Soviet attack, launched by the 5th Guards Tank Army, the Soviet infantry and armor were channeled into the "bottleneck" by five German divisions.[799] The partisan pressure supporting the thrust became unbearable, so Kumm organized a group of men to follow the tracks left in the snow by the retreating partisans, and with the aid of a Fiesler *Storch* reconnaissance aircraft trapped approximately twenty irregulars in a small farm complex. The *SS* men entered the farm under withering fire and killed or captured the entire partisan force, while suffering a few light friendly casualties and no fatalities. Those captured were later executed by firing squad, although Kumm disagreed with the decision.[800] Kumm would eventually become one of the most experienced *SS* officers in the art of counterinsurgency warfare, winning the Knight's Cross, Oak Leaves and Swords for his efforts, and rising from major to major general in only two years.

Perhaps the best measure of how important the partisan/guerrilla problem had become arrived in the form of reports submitted by *Generalfeldmarschall* Erich von Manstein,[801] a man Hitler would listen to out of respect. Manstein related the ongoing difficulties with partisans at Stalino in August and Rostov in November 1941, and again in Sevastopol during the Crimean campaign the following year.[802] As the commander of *Heeresgruppe Suedukraine* and *Nordukraine* in 1944[803] Manstein's operational planning began to include counterinsurgency operations that were implemented extensively on 26 June-4 July 1944, although it was far too late to alter the coming disaster.[804] Further experience in the Baltic region[805] and Italy (especially on 25 May 1944)[806] would illustrate just how feeble the German counterinsurgency measures had been, and Russia would become the excepted rule for determining what would and would not work. Where the Germans had failed in using their own forces in a successful counterinsurgency role, their hope lay in the recruiting effort of the *Freiwilligen* to assist in combating the irregulars. However, despite the most fervent efforts and best intentions of the senior German officers involved, this damage control measure would also fall apart, primarily due to the field commanders worst enemy; the leadership in Berlin.

10

German Counterinsurgency Tactics

*We must thoroughly clear away all ideas among
our cadres of winning easy victories through good
luck, without hard and bitter struggle, without sweat
and blood.*

- Mao Tse Tung
28 December 1945.

Germany did create several forms of counterinsurgency tactics during the war, modifying various elements depending upon the operational situation and logistical circumstances. The necessity for such doctrine became apparent following the invasion of the Soviet Union on 22 June 1941 (as previously stated) when the first glimmer of a massive insurgency reaction began to appear later that year. It would be the vast fields and numerous towns and villages of Russia where the German tactic evolved, later to be exported to other regions of Europe, including the Balkans. As previously stated, the summer of 1942 saw the greatest increase of partisan/guerrilla activity since the start of the war nearly three years earlier. It would be the units blooded in the counterinsurgency war on the Eastern Front who would later commit the worst atrocities throughout occupied Europe, carrying their *modus operandi* as if a form of plague, decimating untold numbers of innocent victims who were unlucky enough to cross their path.

Where the Germans (and other militaries in the world) failed in their counterinsurgency activities was to properly understand the nature of the insurgent, whether he was a "partisan" or "guerrilla," Communist or nationalist, Eastern or Western European, potential ally or dedicated adversary. The primary method of operation for an irregular was to interdict supplies and communication, supplying himself with whatever he captured, reducing or eliminating enemy strength through assassination and sabotage, imposing an effective method of psychological warfare upon the enemy while simultaneously initiating delaying actions against a superior conventional force. The German responses, such as "passive" measures would only provide the insurgents with better opportunities to plan and provide greater targets to exploit, with few exceptions.

"Active" counterinsurgency methods would produce high body counts among both irregulars and civilians, while feeding the fuel for local resistance recruiters who advertised the atrocities perpetrated against villages. The irregulars knew this fact, and in many cases partisans and guerrillas would launch attacks against the Germans, then withdraw into the unsuspecting villages and towns to blend in with the local population. This tactic was superb in order to draw reprisals from the enemy, a guaranteed way to stiffen the resolve of the survivors in either supporting or joining the insurgents' cell network. They simply allowed the Germans to perform all the heavy lifting.[807]

As in the case of any military planning and operational preparation, intelligence gathering on enemy activity is paramount to launching an effective mission. It is considered that anything gathered within six to twelve hours may be useful intelligence, while anything over twelve hours is suspect and must be re-confirmed. Any tactical data collected over twenty-four hours old is considered nothing more than a rumor. Part of the planning in reducing an insurgent threat was the labeling and constant surveillance of all villages, usually with local support, collecting the names of all local residents for identification purposes. The problem with this procedure was that the locals recruited for such duties were not always reliable, and even if their political reliability was beyond question the potential for intimidation and retribution by irregular forces often reduced their morale and effectiveness.[808] Also, villages were difficult to readily identify in Russia from aerial observation or from a distance, "and often a church built on high ground or a church tower is the only visible sign of an inhabited place."[809] These deficiencies would force German units to detach groups for security and reconnaissance duty, isolating them from the main contingent and practically inviting a partisan/guerrilla attack.

Another problem was the need for security among German units and the use of surprise tactics to entrap irregular forces. However, due to the fact that German motorized units on the move, regardless of how small were difficult to conceal, and the irregulars could always use their greater flexibility, mobility, and smaller numbers to circumvent such tactics. Another problem was that conventional forces were usually encumbered with heavy gear and vehicles that limited their mobility, making them vulnerable to attacks. However, the advantage of the regular counterinsurgent (especially in the German case) was the availability of artillery and aircraft as support weapons.

In order to develop a realistic counterinsurgency campaign the target audience must be studied and analyzed. Their political, social, historical and cultural peculiarities must also be taken into consideration, and a valid picture of the population presented. However, what is most important is that the ideals and ambitions of the target population must also be examined. What positive factors do they respond to? What would provoke a negative response? With regard to adopting a strategy these considerations become all important. The initiator of counterinsurgency must *think* like the insurgent to understand him. In all cases the use of "death squad" tactics has always proved to be a complete failure in every conflict. The Germans did contemplate the use of troops to guard crops and starve out the irregulars in Greece during that country's occupation, but strategic planners ruled it out as being highly unfeasible, mainly due to the fact that active operations were the rule in the Balkans. Unlike the Balkans, the Germans in the Soviet Union used a combination of "passive" and "active" methods, which were also employed in Western Europe.[810]

With regard to formulating counterinsurgency tactical doctrine, the first lesson that must be learned is; much like in conventional warfare, the terrain and weather dictate actions in the field. What limits a conventional force will not always be a negative factor for the insurgent, just as a strength for the insurgent will not always be a weakness for his enemy, the counterinsurgent. The irregular operative will blend in with his surroundings to find safety or to gather intelligence, unlike the counterinsurgent, which in most cases happens to be a foreign component. The tactic of "weeding out" suspected insurgents and their sympathizers would become the greatest weapon available to the Germans (both for and against their interests) for the wholesale slaughter of civilians, since the German military was instructed to consider everyone a "potential enemy." Psychology as much as stealth must be applied, and in this area the Germans committed the greatest failures in the history of armed conflict. Regardless of the terrain and the culture these facts are always a reliable and universal constant. The German military was ill prepared for such an excursion and they critically ignored the warning signals regarding these problems, believing that the applied force of superior arms would defeat any enemy, and therefore they failed by fervently believing their own propaganda.

The planning phase of an anti-partisan mission would become the most detailed and intricate method devised by the German military for ground operations in any theater of the war. Part of the problem was that for intelligence to be valuable it had to be current and constantly updated from the raw data collected in the field, and the use of agents, prisoners and local informants was considered crucial, although this was not always successful.[811] The human intelligence collection method became problematic, especially in the case of the insurgents, due to the fact they were not always well informed or reliable. The electronic intelligence method so successful in the west was basically ineffective in the east, since the Soviet insurgents rarely communicated by use of radios with adjacent units or even higher authority. This was primarily due to the fact that they were less well equipped than their conventional brethren, therefore denying the Germans access to electronic intelligence through interception, decryption, and location.

Another problem was that, unlike conventional military forces, partisans and guerrillas did not often travel in vehicles, nor did they adhere to any standardized operational tactic or strategy that could be studied and thwarted. In fact, irregulars in wartime, especially in Eastern Europe and the Balkans rarely adhered to any set practice regarding conventional military conduct, just as conventional militaries rarely treated irregulars according to the accepted protocols of warfare. The inability to handle the insurgency problem in a standard fashion based upon a sensible policy proved to be the most difficult problem for the Germans, whose military doctrine was one of the most rigid in the world regarding operational planning. Also taken out of the equation was the human intelligence factor, which could be collected, either through a defector or a captured insurgent. This tactic was not utilized as well as it could have been since the Germans believed that irregulars, depending upon their ethnicity and classification under the racial policy tended to cloud the judgment of the interrogators. Most of the irregulars who defected to the Germans were considered in league with Jews and Communists, and therefore ignored based upon an illogical stereotype. The opportunities for their utilization were vast and would have increased the German potential for success. This failure must be added to the list of terminal blunders initiated by German policy in defiance of military necessity.

Human intelligence is the most faulty and least reliable of all intelligence gathering methods since it relies upon several factors: the reliability of the informant, the knowledge he may possess, the time line with regard to his acquisition of the knowledge, the method of interrogation, and the personal experiences, objectives, and political convictions of the interrogated subject. Also creating difficulty was the most academic problem of all; unlike conventional military forces who must halt the march to refuel and re-supply, insurgents must maintain constant movement to evade detection and capture, as well as constantly locate sources of shelter, supplies, and food. The highly mobile irregular units were rarely detected until they struck, and by then it was too late for an effective response plan. That was the case until the new method of irregular interdiction was introduced in 1943, as mentioned by Wolff and Kumm.

As we will see, the Germans developed two tactics for dealing with irregulars, and both were as marginally effective as they were simple in concept.

Passive Counterinsurgency Operations

The *Abwehr* and *SD Amt IV* worked in conjunction with field commanders in the rear and forward areas and front-line reconnaissance pilots to plot, follow and interdict partisan/guerrilla movements through accurate and constantly updated information collection. These successes were achieved through a variety of passive countermeasures, such as the placing of spies within partisan units (which was rarely successful in the east), random searches and sweeps, and collaborating local officials at the village, city, and even district levels. Special orders were issued to rear echelon units, particularly smaller support units and respite-depot areas that proved to be the favorite targets of irregulars.[812] Other measures included staking out watering areas, especially in the regions further south where potable water was scarce during the dry summer months. Irregulars, Red Army and Germans alike needed water, and this need became the necessary bait to locate, trap, and annihilate an opposing force.

Also instituted was a network of communications consisting of both landline and radiotelephone systems as a backup, since landlines could be cut and spliced allowing for electronic eavesdropping, just as radio communications could be intercepted. The introduction of special radio codes, call signs, and encrypted tables of reference were incorporated to increase communications security. This intricate array of communication devices allowed for the transmission of the ever-changing data being gathered as fast as it was received and analyzed. Once the intelligence was collated it could then be disseminated to the respective unit commanders for their planning purposes. This special staff was organized and directed by only the most trusted *SD* officers, who in turn issued orders to subordinate *SS* and Army detachment leaders, particularly those units under the classification of *Einsatzgruppen*.

With regard to local defense, indigenous personnel were regularly recruited without difficulty. Partisans, guerrillas, and the Red Army preyed upon their fellow countrymen, stealing crops, livestock, weapons, clothes, and farm machinery without compensation.[813] They even forcibly pressed young men, women, and even children into service at gunpoint, sometimes killing those who were uncooperative, further alienating the population. The Germans knew this and in certain sectors *Wehrmacht* and *SS* commanders went out of their way to avoid angering the population in order to secure their support against the common threat. These friendly persons would be hired as guards, or in some cases recruited into the Army or *SS*, while others joined the Germans in a guerrilla or anti-partisan capacity.

Security was consistently the greatest problem and specified roads and railways were always heavily guarded and patrolled by German troops or trusted auxiliaries, with all traffic halted after sunset. Even during hours of daylight convoys were initiated under strong guard and deployed at ever changing and staggered time intervals to avoid establishing a detectable pattern. Guards were placed on all bridges, trains, marshaling yards, airfields, and respite locations for front-line soldiers who were frequently targeted by irregulars.[814] Villages were regarded as areas requiring constant surveillance, which was conducted by Germans as well as local volunteers.[815] The extent to which German commands placed guards at the above locations is illustrated by *Generalmajor* Dietrich Hrabak, *Kommodore* of both *Jagdgeschwader (JG)* 52 and 54 on the Eastern Front at various times during the war:

> In Russia we were always aware of the possibility of partisan attacks against our airfields. We had *Luftwaffe* ground soldiers assigned to our fields; never trusting the volunteers, not with the aircraft. I never really had problems with partisans attacking my airfields in particular, and the only problem I remember having was when we were in the Kurland. The Red Army was attacking and we had to leave rather quickly, but I cannot say for certain if this involved partisans or not. I do know that we took every precaution against partisan sabotage.[816]

Fortifications were erected that included block houses, pill boxes, razor and electrified wire fencing, and mine fields specifically placed in conjunction with "tangle foot"[817] to channel the enemy into pre arranged "killing zones"[818] reaching to and from important areas within the defense system. Mobile patrols consisting of both German and foreign auxiliaries covered these protected areas, operating as the eyes and ears of the defensive plan.[819] Forests were cleared for several hundred meters to prevent large numbers of partisans from approaching unobserved. Special killing zones were established so that every heavy machine gun could support the others flanking with interlocking fields of fire, with each strong point connected to the next by trenches, wire communications, bunkers, and a specifically built and maintained road, all of which was heavily guarded and primarily built using slave labor.[820]

The guards were as heavily equipped as their front-line counterparts, and in some cases even better, with all of the weapons found in the infantry inventory including mortars, howitzers, and on call artillery, usually 88mm and 105mm flak guns, and in some cases self-propelled artillery specially detailed to support their missions.[821] Guard dogs were trained and deployed along with the well paid and well fed indigenous militiamen, whose responsibility was to patrol the outlying villages ahead of the German units proper. Another tactic was to employ the services of friendly indigenous personnel in the capacity of guides, guards, translators, and other crucial services. When German forces treated the locals with kindness and understanding, the dividends usually paid off. As cited in *Fighting in Hell*:

> Russian civilians living in the area where the reconnaissance was made, who had been treated well by the Germans billeted in their villages at an earlier date, were of great assistance. Local guides led the patrol around enemy and partisan strongholds, and provided shelter in farmhouses.[822]

With respect to rail traffic (a special target of irregulars) two gondola cars placed at either end of the locomotives protected them from heavy weapons fire, while machine gunners and even horse mounted cavalry and motorcycle reconnaissance troops routinely traveled in armored trail cars to pursue irregulars should they be engaged. The train escorts, numbering between forty and fifty men were augmented on occasion by *flakwierling* detachments using high angle, swivel mounted high rate of fire anti-aircraft guns of the 20mm, 37mm and 40mm variety. These weapons were placed on flat bed cars as an air defense as well as ground defense system. Occasionally, flat bed spacer cars would be used, placed between the troop carriers to facilitate troops in dismounting the rolling train, as well as providing additional light weapons platforms, such as MG 34 and MG 42 machine guns to provide high rate of fire support. This defense method allowed for fire superiority as well as offering a diverse array of weapons to contend with virtually any kind of enemy activity (see *Table 1*).

Active Counterinsurgency Operations

On combating irregular activity German units and commanders realized that swift, direct, and decisive action was needed. As stated in *Fighting in Hell:*

> Following the pattern of large-scale police raids, such anti-partisan actions must converge on a definitive objective, achieve complete surprise, and be executed with the utmost thoroughness. Merely combing through a vast forest and swamp area for partisans or trying to seal it off will require the use of inordinately large forces and perhaps, may have the effect of pacifying the area temporarily. But the result in the long run will hardly justify the means employed.[823]

German security forces in rear and adjacent areas by late 1942 were given massive regions to patrol, areas that were far too large to effectively control. Due to the great expanse that is Russia and the limited numbers of troops assigned to counterinsurgency operations, these forces nearly always required the assistance of front-line units, which were primarily *Waffen SS* and drained manpower from the ever critical combat front. One of these specially trained units was the *707th Sicherheit* Division, an *SD* unit whose base of operations was in the Minsk region of Belorussia, where the great expanse of the Baranovichi Forest (a region larger than Austria) provided a haven for the largest groups of partisans on the Eastern Front.[824] Protection of military supply routes, checkpoints, respite centers, fuel and ammunition depots were the primary objectives. The active pursuit of the partisans was a supplementary duty, usually requiring larger conventional support, especially when the Soviets began to actively support the irregulars with air operations, including parachutists and combat support personnel after 1942.

The German details organized staggered patrol intervals and sweeping grids within the forest proper, thereby maintaining pressure on the irregulars in order to prevent their organizing into larger groups and launching effective, coordinated raids or counter-attacks. Once these camps were detected the usual method of force deployment was to call artillery on the suspected positions. This would disrupt the irregulars, forcing them to break from cover and concealment and scatter into smaller groups for survival, running away from the "creeping fire."[825] A spotter in an aircraft or the commander on the ground would "walk" the artillery into their positions on the ground, leaving certain areas free of fire, ostensibly offering a safe route of evacuation for the irregulars. These free areas would be the "killing zones" where the Germans would be waiting with heavy weapons, eliminating those who survived the barrage. Once out in the open they could be pursued by highly mobile German units waiting two to five kilometers outside the impact zone ahead of the barrage, where the irregulars could be overrun and decimated. Those who survived the rain of steel and the ambush patrols would be rounded up later in the after action security sweeps. The German units flanking the perimeter would then sweep the shelled area searching for wounded and hiding partisans, taking prisoners for interrogation purposes, destroying any munitions, communications, combat equipment or bunkers detected (see *Table 2*).

Regular army units supported many of these operations, and sometimes specialized units of the *Wehrmacht* were specifically detailed for such duty, as related by Guy Sajer in his autobiography.[826] The regular Army contingents were supervised by *SS* and *SD* officers in the round ups, although they were usually kept uninformed as to the true nature of the mission or the finite details of the action to be undertaken. This security measure was maintained until the moment of deployment to further maintain security and prohibit any potential damage to morale. This high level of security was also maintained within the ranks of the actual counterinsurgency units themselves, with every piece of information being passed down through the ranks on a "need to know" basis only.[827] The active pursuit troops were only informed of their mission at the moment of arriving at the demarcation line, or in some cases only after entering the objective area proper, usually at a rally point within a day's march of the target area.[828]Nothing was to be written down; no diaries or journals (except for the operational unit war diary), and letters written by the troops were heavily censored.

As to the assembly of the counterinsurgency forces, the unit integrity and formation was accomplished at least a full day's march from the intended area of operation. This movement was timed throughout the planning stage to ensure that all participating units arrived on time at the proper location, thus maximizing the Germans' numbers with precision and discipline, if not superior firepower and greater mobility. The base of the assault force would be placed along natural obstacles that could be easily defended and traversed should the irregular force retreat in that direction. Rivers, open fields with a tree line to the rear, or carefully prepared hasty minefields prevented escape, while the forward units advanced, constantly pushing the irregulars into the well prepared defensive positions. Sentries positioned within sight of each other while maintaining radio and visual contact with adjacent sentries relayed all observed movements to higher command authority, thereby augmenting the outer line of the encirclement.

Behind this wall of sentries pursuit detachments waited to strike, as leaflets were dropped by air or specially designed artillery shells ordering the population within the trap to arrive at a designated point for inspection. The ring, which would sometimes span ten miles in width would begin to slowly close in upon the irregulars, with the Germans averaging two to three miles per day depending upon the terrain and weather conditions, and operating only in daylight. The troops were placed in their established positions before nightfall, usually in easily defended and secured natural obstacles such as rivers, hill tops and bluffs in order to prepare hasty defensive positions. Primary, secondary, and alternative fighting positions were also created as part of the planning, with fields of fire cleared by removing foliage and brush, with sector sketches made for the commander and the troops allowing them to become more familiar with the terrain before nightfall (see *Table 3*).

This prepatory action facilitated the placing of mines, aiming stakes, positioning of sentries and establishing landline communications between the command post and adjacent position to assist the commander in maintaining complete radio silence and command and control over the unit (see *Table 3*). Night procedures regarding security were rigidly dictated and enforced. Passwords, call signs, and identity badges were required to pass from one checkpoint to another, all of which required the explicit permission and signatures of the individual commanders of the respective groups. Many Germans were shot by their own comrades for failing to adhere to these basic principles of security.[829]

Once the units continued their advance the following day additional propaganda would be disseminated over the area in the familiar form of leaflets and loudspeaker broadcasts from villagers and persons suspected of having friends and relatives among the partisans, pleading for their surrender. While this was undertaken the ring grew smaller, until the partisans were virtually strangled, forcing either capitulation or a breakout, which usually resulted in costly fights to the death. Although these operations were highly complex and required large numbers of soldiers and material resources, this tactic was considered by all of the upper echelon commanders to bear the greatest fruit. According to Otto Kumm:

> It was like gathering ants by burning their perimeter, forcing them into the ever tightening circle. The few who attempt to leave get burned, while the rest would group together find some moral security in their closeness. This we exploited by bombing, artillery or machine gun fire, but it was always a costly tactic employed by the partisans. I would have to say that this tactic was definitely the best method of containment and liquidation we ever used.[830]

In order to appreciate the complexity of these operations one must analyze the requirements. All ranks, down to the lowest private had to be fully cognizant of not only his own specific duties, but also the duties of his comrades and the responsibilities of the men in the neighboring units, as well as their primary and supplemental positions. The force also had to maintain complete noise and light discipline while constantly maintaining vigilance and unit integrity. The smallest deviation from the operational plan or breach in security could disturb the continuity of movement, alerting the insurgents and thereby compromising the mission. In this type of warfare the weakest link could definitely break the strongest chain.

It is arguable that the most disciplined of Germany's soldiers served within the ranks of the counterinsurgency forces, where individual intelligence and training meant little without courage and strict obedience to orders. Another factor illustrating their discipline was the fact that anti-partisan units tended to spend more time in the field than other units, constantly on operations and without an established program of rest and rotation. Unlike forward combat forces, these units did not usually have a reserve component; operating for months at a time without even visiting a soft bed or having a hot meal. Only the toughest men were selected for this duty, which explains why the *Waffen SS* and Mountain troops were considered the best candidates.

However, the irregulars were equally if not more hard pressed, since their base of supply was usually dependent upon a foraging existence, and when they had little or nothing their ability to sustain operations fell apart. It was during the hard winters that the Germans sometimes gained ground in their ongoing war against the irregulars due to local food shortages. The Soviet soldier was a master of deception and the irregular was no less inclined regarding ingenuity. The accounts of major insurgency operations were studied by the German anti-partisan units, such as in the prevention of bridges and railroads being destroyed.

This was especially critical following Stalin's Rail Campaign, targeting German communications and rear areas.[831] The irregulars' method of securing a bridge destruction would be to herd civilians over a bridge with the German guards suspecting nothing, considering the people to be refugees. As soon as the head of the column reached the bridgehead diversion fire would be directed toward the Germans, and the clandestine "civilians" would allow the partisans to place demolition charges and secure the destruction.[832] The German method of preventing such a disaster would be to simply fire upon anyone crossing the bridge without proper written authorization.

The irregular method of attacking convoys also proved successful, and according to Richard Overy, 65,000 vehicles and 12,000 bridges fell victim to partisans and guerrillas, a figure considered reasonable given the testimonies of the German officers interviewed for this project. The irregular method of attacking a convoy would be to place felled trees behind the last vehicle, or in some cases park a blocking vehicle behind the last German vehicle to prevent escape. Hasty barricades would sometimes be erected to slow the convoy and weapons fire would saturate the vehicles and men, sometimes initiating fierce fire fights, since many German convoys carried heavy machine guns and accompanying infantry.[833]

The next section details how these operations were planned and executed in the face of the infamous Russian winter.

Operations in Winter

The fabled Russian winter wreaked havoc among the Germans during the first year of the war, and this hardship did not diminish over the next three years, notwithstanding the addition in 1942 of winter clothing and better equipment. It was during these periods that counterinsurgency operations reaped their greatest harvests due to the ease of tracking irregulars through the snow and the ability of the elite German ski commandos to pursue them with speed and lethality. Also, given the problems of foraging and re-supply partisan/guerrilla activities usually ceased altogether, preferring warmer weather until 1943, when the Red Army began supplying the irregulars *en masse*. Going "to ground" and waiting out the weather (the Red Army functioned on an opposite strategy, preferring to attack in such conditions)[834] would prove disastrous to many irregular groups, as the Germans would increase their activity as much as possible due to their having access to the roads and supplies that were not being attacked or impeded by weather. The irregulars often gave themselves away by burning fires that could be seen miles away by air or land, but the fires were necessary to prevent the resistance members from freezing to death. It is ironic that the only method for their survival was also the source of their destruction, for once they were located there was usually no escape.

In devising the winter operations, German field commanders found themselves in the same gray area as in the early days of the war. Their original winter doctrine was ad-hoc and based upon the same hit and miss methods as before. Partisans and guerrillas, once supported by the Red Army following Stalin's establishment of the Central Staff for Partisan Warfare on 30 May 1942 in Moscow under Belorussian Party Secretary Panteleymon Ponomorenko (becoming Chief of Staff for Partisan Warfare), with adequate equipment and training increased their operations in winter, thus becoming more effective as the war progressed, and eventually operating hundreds of units numbering between 3,000-5,000 personnel per group.[835] Red Army support was considered critical for re-supply and intelligence collection, since irregulars rarely had access to electronic intelligence gathering. Likewise, the Red Army also needed the mobile and highly effective irregulars blending into the general population to collect intelligence that was otherwise unavailable to conventional commanders.

The Soviet soldier was usually better adapted to the cold weather due to his lifestyle, training, specialized clothing, weapons lubricants and constant exposure to the elements. Over seventy percent of the Soviet military was comprised of farmers; peasants who had worked outdoors all their lives. The Germans were not so hearty, although many of the men staffing the ranks of the elite units were mountaineers, skiers, and athletes. German winter operations began slowly, but the progress was steady as the weapons were getting better and the inclusion of *SS* and Army *Edelweiss*[836] units, specially recruited, trained, and placed on special assignment began to make the difference. One unit to receive the complete package for combating irregulars in winter was *"Florian Geyer,"* explaining its unsurpassed record against partisans and guerrillas during the war.[837]

The *Edelweiss Gebirgsjaeger* were the ultimate practitioners of rough terrain fighting and cold weather warfare, able not just to survive but excel due to their specialized boots, clothing, weapons, training, skis, snowshoe equipment, and pioneer gear such as axes, picks, man-packed artillery, demolition, crew served weapons and mortars. Having served in Norway, the Caucasus, Alps (for training), the Balkans and Crete, their experience and discipline made them a dangerous foe to the irregulars. The success of the *Edelweiss* units and the rising approval of the counterinsurgency methods still did not rule out the one constant weapon still in effect; propaganda. The effect of propaganda, both positive and negative will be examined in the next section.

TABLE 1

GERMAN SECURITY TRAIN

↑
|
|
DIRECTION OF TRAVEL

1-LOCOMOTIVE
2-ARMED GONDOLOA CARS
3-FLAT BED CARS WITH AA GUNS
4-TROOP CARS
5-SPACER CARS

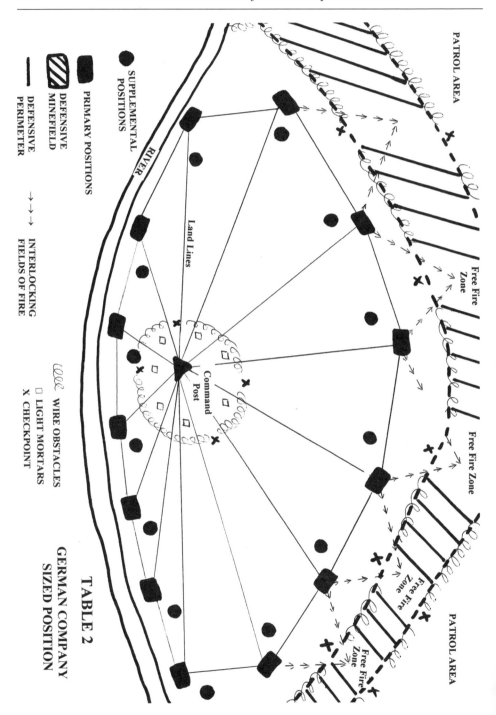

TABLE 2

GERMAN COMPANY
SIZED POSITION

TABLE 3

ANTI-PARTISAN OPERATION (POST 1942)

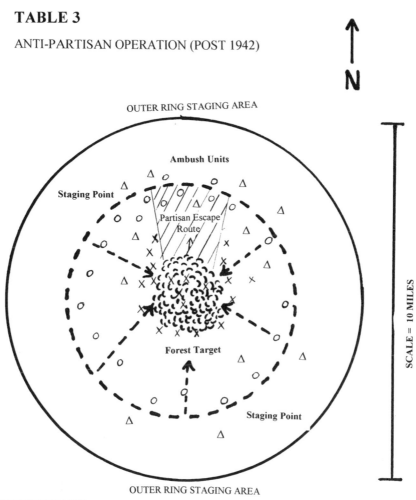

X ARTILLERY IMPACTS

O GERMAN TROOP LOCATIONS

Δ MOTORIZED UNITS

— —→ DIRECTIONS OF SECURITY SWEEP
FROM STAGING POINTS

 KILLING ZONE

11

Irregulars of the Third Reich

In times of difficulty we must not lose sight of our achievements, must see the bright future and must pluck up our courage.

- Mao Tse Tung
8 September 1944

Attempts at Conversion

The roots of the German campaign at recruiting and converting the European masses was a great part in the creation of the Greater Germany, if not converting them into the fascist camp then at least into an anti-Communist coalition. The concept stemmed from Hitler's belief that Communism was the ultimate evil, stripping away the dignity and freedoms from the subjugated masses. This theory from such a ruthless dictator sounds even more hypocritical given the tenants of National Socialism as practiced by the Third *Reich*, and outlined in Hitler's own book, *Mein Kampf*. Both Hitler and Himmler believed that, by raising the level of terror among Communist sympathizers and rewarding those who opposed Communist ideology, the propaganda effort would effectively support the massed auxiliary peasant army deemed necessary in achieving ultimate victory. This was especially true regarding the civilian irregular components in the occupied nations who were the greatest threat to German hegemony. As stated by Leon Degrelle during his interviews in 1984-85:

Partisans were the greatest nightmare we as soldiers faced during the war in the east. With the Red Army we knew their tactics, which were constantly evolving yet based on established procedure, and they adapted our method of *Blitzkrieg* later. However, the partisans were dangerous because they did not wear uniforms and didn't operate as a disciplined, traditional military force. Instead, they functioned as a random hit and run guerrilla group, striking anywhere and everywhere without warning. They did of course suffer from one great flaw; their inability to function outside their own areas of operation, mainly due to their inability to maintain a viable supply and communications network, as well as the fact that they were not fully supported by the Red Army until late in 1942-43. Another problem facing the partisans in the east, and not just Russia, was the fact that despite numbering in the hundreds of thousands, various partisan groups did not always share

156

the same political ideology or ultimate post-war objective, let alone share the same motivation for waging war. Many times partisans would fight each other over limited resources. Sometimes long standing hatreds would create a problem, igniting in-fighting as well, such as the conflict between the Georgians and Ukrainians. All of these we tried to use to our advantage. These were the problems we tried to exploit.[838]

Like the Soviets, the Germans began the practice of placing political officers in the ranks in order to "educate" and hopefully convert the population to the ideals of National Socialism. In some cases the program worked, although this was usually only true in the regions shattered by the Stalinist pogroms and heavy *NKVD* "recruitment." It was simply a matter of convincing the local populations to accept the lesser of two evils, a decision not easy to make depending upon which side of the ideological line one stood. Leon Degrelle explained the concept and how it was implemented:

> The political officers would do their best to bring these disaffected factions over to our side, and in many cases it worked. It worked very well with the Ukrainians, Bessarabians, Belorussians, and others, because many of these people had suffered under Stalin. However, due to the German method of handling the local populations our own applications for support of these groups were met with an understandable amount of skepticism. It was of course the senseless slaughter of civilians that actually created the partisan problem. We were only able to become successful against the partisans by being able to think like them, understand their motivations and desires; how, where, when, and why they functioned as they did, and try to mentally outmaneuver them.[839] This soon became the basis for our countermeasures. Unfortunately, Berlin did not see the utility in our cause, and even Gehlen became tired of trying to convince Hitler that there was a better way of dealing with the problem. It was not until Steiner, Wolff, and Gehlen came together with their new plan that we were able to completely take the fight to the partisans successfully. Most of our planning was initiated at the division level and filtered down to the company level, with regimental commanders having great flexibility in the execution of their operations. Still, despite all of the innovations we devised, there was still no substitute for treating the population gently, and this failure was the ultimate mistake.[840]

The Germans did manage to succeed in their attempts at converting certain partisan and guerrilla groups to join their cause, mostly due to the same long standing hatreds mentioned by Degrelle. Some successes were achieved through the simple application of humanitarian gestures, such as food, medical treatment, rebuilding churches and compassion for those who surrendered, although these were obviously isolated cases. As stated by Otto Kumm:

> The amazing part of the effort to convert the masses to our ideology hinged upon how they were treated. On the one hand, we could reduce a village and think that we had solved the problem in that area, only to realize that the problem had

just increased in severity. However, when we assisted in the rebuilding of towns, churches, or even allowed the local civil administration to maintain control over their people without a strong military presence, we yielded greater results. This fact was self-evident to those of us in the field. We could not convince our superiors in Berlin to agree to such a method. This was where we failed.[841]

The Ukrainian Nationalist Movement (UPA) was deemed acceptable for German assistance, and as the strongest guerrilla group in Eastern Europe their numbers would augment German losses, since they were eventually included within the ranks of the auxiliaries and later formed into their own independent *Waffen SS* divisions. The UPA qualified as "guerrillas" due to their long term plan to overthrow the existing Soviet regime in the Ukraine, where the coexistence between partisans and guerrillas was the most tenuous, and establish an independent Russian Orthodox state. They proposed a campaign against the Communist partisans to the Germans through *Oberkommando der Wehrmacht.*[842] The hierarchy in Berlin would not agree to such an arrangement at first, and so it fell upon the field commanders who understood the realities on the ground and knew what was necessary to secure their own agreements with the Ukrainians.[843] The effect was immediately felt as the UPA often combated the Communists without German support or prompting.[844]

However, all was not well within the tenuous arrangement between the German military and Ukrainian guerrillas. There were many clashes between the UPA and the *Polizei* and *Einsatzgruppen* units, although the regular front line units were usually left unmolested and they in turn did nothing to antagonize the UPA.[845] Despite the confusion as to when and whom to fight, the most obvious benefit to the Germans was the UPA's effectiveness at harassing and, in many cases, effectively reducing Soviet field assets, especially in raids behind Red Army lines.[846] Another factor that assisted the Germans, especially during the days of tactical withdrawal during late 1943 were the various uprisings by the Ukrainians, such as the revolts in Kiev in 1944. This created a situation that forced perhaps five front line Red Army divisions to be diverted as a reaction force to suppress the rebellion.[847]

Such was the case for recruiting Poles and White Russians in 1944 (of which the *"Kaminsky" Brigade* was a prime example) to support the German military, a propaganda program initiated by exploiting centuries of Russian subjugation of Poland; the fact that the Red Army offered no assistance, and the Germans reminding the Poles that the Russian Civil War had brought a Soviet invasion of Poland in 1920 assisted the conversion effort. This cataclysmic event was still fresh in the minds of many Poles, where many had suffered at the hands of the Bolshevik forces. The Poles were also reminded of their sufferings in 1772, 1793 and 1795 by Russia, although the Prussian and Austrian contributions during these partitions were omitted. The roots of discontent among the Poles towards the Russians ran deep, and in many cases this was the tool most successfully used in recruiting from the population. However, despite the relatively moderate success of this phase of the recruiting program, the German handling of the Polish population in general had already destroyed what little chance of reconciliation and trust that may have existed.

German propaganda was effectively using history, hatred, and psychology as weapons, a fact not lost upon the Soviets or the Western Allies. Hitler's disingenuous pledge to "salvage Poland from the Communist scourge" was only taken seriously by a select minority. Polish nationalism was infectious after the First World War, when Poland became a free and sovereign nation under Woodrow Wilson's Fourteen Points following the signing of the Treaty of Versailles.[848]

The Polish election of the fifty-one year old Marshal Jozef Klemens Pilsudski infuriated the Soviets, who loathed the thought of a western supported democracy on their European frontier. Pilsudski had ample reason to stimulate anti-Soviet sentiment, since he had suffered for five years in a Siberian labor camp for anti-Czarist sentiments, and was the ultimate Russophobe who had formed a partisan army under the Austrians during the First World War. This army became the Polish Legion and fought the entire war quite successfully on the Eastern Front. His image became an icon that appealed to the anti-Communist concepts of freedom, nationalism, and self-destiny. Hitler's and Stalin's simultaneous invasions of the country, and the decimation of the Jews and intellectuals were a difficult damage control problem to overcome. In trying to salvage something from the self-made debacle, Hitler and Goebbels appealed to the Pole's sense of pride, reminding them of their great victories over the Red Army during the Russian Civil War. The Polish capture of Kiev on 7 May 1919 by a combined Polish, Ukrainian and White Russian force, as well as the destruction of the Soviet force at Warsaw in 1920 by an ill equipped, ill-trained army of conscripted women (which had elevated Pilsudski's strength from 150,000 to a force of approximately 370,000) and partisans were symbolic of the Polish desire for freedom.[849] Hitler's overtures were as thinly veiled as they were insincere.

The same program was played out in other parts of Europe in the vain hope that the European community, solidified under the umbrella of German dominated National Socialism would rise against Communism and support Hitler in his "great crusade." When this plan failed Hitler finally ordered the conscription of suitable Europeans (including Poles and Slavs) into the military as foreign auxiliaries in the equally vain hope of stemming the Soviet avalanche. *Nazi* political officers were quite active in the recruiting and indoctrination of their target audience, and this effort lasted throughout the war. The only tangible successes were the *Freiwilligen* who volunteered for military service, and they were usually placed within the ranks of the conventional military. As we will see in the next chapter, the success of the German recruiting program did pay dividends. The regular and auxiliary forces numbered approximately 2,000,000, of which 1,400,000 would serve in uniform against the Soviets. Their activity would write a seldom-told page in the annals of military conflict.

In discussing the Europeans who fought in support of *Nazi* Germany, we have already seen many circumstances where non-Germans volunteered their services, risked their lives and betrayed their nations for a cause, whether this cause was personal or political is highly relevant. However, there were many groups that, although fighting alongside Germany against Stalin, were never assimilated within the National Socialist framework, even refusing to become part of the Greater German *Reich*. Many fought under the condition that they remain autonomous, creating new nations out of the former Soviet Union and maintaining a friendly yet distant relationship with Germany. During the course of the war no unit was as unique, controversial, and expansive as the Free Russian Army, also known as the Russian Liberation Army, or ROA (*Russkaya Osvoboditelnaya Armiya*) and the Russian National Army of Liberation, commanded by Lieutenant General Andrei Andreyevich Vlasov.[850]

Vlasov's military career was quite distinguished. He served as a commander in the Red Army's 2nd Don Division in the Ukraine and Crimean Peninsula, reaching command over a Turkestani unit at the regimental level before World War II. Vlasov witnessed Stalin's bloody purge of the ranks first hand while commander of the 72nd Infantry Division, himself surviving due to his lack of Imperial duty under the Czar. Vlasov later served as a military advisor to Chiang Kai-Shek in China, whom Stalin supported against the Japanese while simultaneously supporting Mao-Tse Tung and the Chinese Communists.[851]

Stalin's faith in Vlasov stemmed from his successful service as commander of the 4th Tank Corps in Finland during the costly Winter War of 1939-1940, a brutal campaign for which he was awarded the Order of Lenin. The failure of the Red Army to stem the German advance following *Barbarossa* saw Vlasov placed in command of the largest Soviet field force up to that time. This occurred following the disastrous collapse of the Bialystok-Minsk line, which in conjunction of the Smolensk debacle netted the Germans over 325,000 prisoners, 3,300 tanks, and 1,849 artillery pieces by 15 July 1941.[852] This massive defeat was not very well known among Soviet forces, and Stalin wanted it kept that way. According to Anna Nikolina:

> We knew what had happened, because rumors spread. We were told not to listen to these rumors, and anyone repeating them would be shot, I saw this happen. But what is difficult to understand is why so many of these soldiers became traitors. We were fighting for our homeland, and they betrayed our cause. Their actions are unforgivable.[853]

Captain Gregor Koronov's interpretation was more pragmatic:

> You must understand that when people speak of the Soviet Union and Russia, they are not speaking about the same country. Russia is just one of the many nations that created the Soviet Union. These soldiers who killed their officers and defected did so because they were forced to live under a system that they did not want, fighting in an army they did not volunteer for, and fighting for a man (Stalin) who had perhaps ordered the executions and deportations of people they probably knew. You must also look at the fact that these soldiers were White Russians, Belorussians, Ukrainians, and so on. What loyalty were they expected to have? I am not surprised that these incidents occurred. I am only surprised that more such incidents are not recorded. If this information were to have been released by the *Stavka* in Moscow the effect would have been widespread panic, and we may have lost the war.

Vlasov's capture near Demyansk on 12 July 1942 was a major turning point in the German war against the Soviet Union, both politically and militarily. Upon his capture, Vlasov was transferred to Vinnitza where he was quartered with General Vladimir Boyarski, the former commander of the 41st Guards Division who was also wounded and captured.[854] The two men spoke about their country, Stalin, and the Communist ideal, and further discussed the possibility of a future Russia without Stalin. Vlasov had always been an anti-

Communist, yet had served his nation faithfully and apolitically, just as most soldiers in the western democracies did, including the professionals of fascist Germany. When Vlasov was later involved in discussions with German officers interested in using him as a rallying point for a future Free Russian Army, the details were outlined and the plan put forward. The recruiting, equipping, and deploying of former Soviet soldiers already written off by their government was a possibility, especially since thousands of Soviet citizens had already joined the *Wehrmacht* in opposition to Stalin.

Vlasov was impressed with the German method of conversation, as officers could speak freely in each other's company about policy, tactics, and strategy without fear of informants and reprisals. Officers developing field policy to suit a given situation would send the proposals up through their chain of command and wait for a response. Regarding counterinsurgency operations, field commanders adapted their tactic to the situation using individual initiative, something that was impossible in the Red Army. Generals had been shot for even suggesting a change in a policy, tactic, or strategy, let alone volunteering information and making suggestions contradictory to the established policy or executing their own judgment.

Vlasov agreed to the *Freiwilligen* concept in principal, as long as there were certain assurances from Hitler. One concession was that the various Soviet republics would be granted their independence from German control once the war was over. Another point was that former Soviet citizens of the various national states would be allowed to vote for the government they wanted in free elections. The third point was the assurance that all Soviet POWs would be given the opportunity to leave the camps and fight in units created under their individual ethnic leaderships. All of these units would fall under the overall command of Vlasov, who would be subordinate to a higher German *Korps* command structure. Vlasov knew that millions of former Soviet soldiers turning on Stalin would create a nightmare for the Kremlin. He was also intelligent and knowledgeable regarding the various ethnic groups within the Soviet Union, and which groups would be the most likely to join an anti-Communist coalition.

Vlasov and Boyarski were transferred to Berlin, where they were united with General Vassily Feodorovich Malyshkin, the former Chief of Staff of the Soviet 19th Army.[855] Malyshkin had been tortured for months during the 1939 purge, and when released he taught at the Moscow Academy where he met Vlasov. These three officers were the nucleus of the future Vlasov Army of the new National Russian Government, and their proposals were approved all the way to *OKW* and were partially approved by *Generalfeldmarschall* Wilhelm Keitel.[856] Vlasov had contributed by writing several leaflets detailing Stalin's crimes, asking Soviet soldiers to rally behind the forces combating Stalin and his tyranny. This was the core of the recruiting effort recorded by Kasantsev and supported by Zykov, another victim of the purge who believed that a great alliance could be formed should Hitler seriously consider the prospect of overthrowing Stalin.[857] The result was impressive, even by Hitler's standards, and according to Karl Wolff:

Himmler was impressed with the concept of using Vlasov[858] as a propaganda tool, as was Josef Goebbels, the Propaganda Minister. The problem, as they saw it, was insuring the loyalty of these troops who had served in the Red Army. There were several German commanders who would like to have had these troops, and perhaps even more who wanted nothing to do with them. This was the problem. However, Stauffenberg,[859] Strikfeldt, Tresckow[860] and others knew that these soldiers had nothing to lose.[861] They were dead or worse if they were returned to the Soviets, so their loyalty was really less important than their desire to survive. The other problem was meeting all of Vlasov's terms, which Hitler would never do. There was never any chance of granting autonomy to the Soviet dominions, although the political officers we had captured would not be included in the Free Russian program. Only those we knew who were simple soldiers could be accepted, and we had millions of them working in the camps.[862]

The fact that so many Soviet soldiers turned against their former leader is one of the greatest enigmas in history, and this has never been mentioned in post-war Soviet textbooks and rarely touched upon in western texts. Even the efforts of the Ukrainian anti-Communist political writer Georg Leibbrandt, whose name was stricken from the roles of Russian writers were considered treasonous and banned by Stalin. Leibbrandt worked for the *Reichsleiter*, under Dr. Alfred Rosenberg in the Foreign Office as a Russian specialist. His function was to supervise the governing of the Ukraine after the war under *Gauleiter* of East Prussia Erich Koch, establishing a pro-German sentiment while inhibiting the rise of pro-nationalism that would hinder a successful German subjugation and exploitation of oil and grain production. Others working in the Department for General Policy included Dr. Gerhard von Mende, a lecturer who was chosen as administrator for Turkestan and the Caucasus for their rich oil reserves.[863] Each region under administration was designated as a *Reichskommissariat* and governed by hand picked experts in their respective fields.

One German officer who noticed the willingness of many Russians to abandon Stalin and the Red Army (to include civilians) was *Major* Heinz Danko Herre, a competent officer who had previously served in Poland, France, Yugoslavia, and the Ukraine between 1939-41.[864] At the time of *Barbarossa* he was the *1A* (General Staff Officer for Operations and Leadership, comparable in NATO to the G-3 at division level; below division level the term is S-3) for the *49th Gebirgsjaeger Korps* based at Stalino. Herre spoke fluent Russian and he was in demand as the victorious *Wehrmacht* was welcomed with open arms by multitudes of "delivered" people. Herre was also responsible for the arming and equipping of Russians and Ukrainians who volunteered as rear area security personnel, appointed duties at supply and ammunition depots as well as anti-partisan activities. Much of his success was due to the fact that he was supported by the Propaganda Ministry and allowed to distribute pamphlets, informing the populations that their land would be returned to them under German appointed administrators following their liberation.

Herre was one of the many officers who supported and believed the pretense that liberated regions would be allowed to operate as German allies in their new freedom, and this allowed officers like himself to make their offers in good faith. What was unknown to men like Herre and their indigenous clients were the actual plans coming from Berlin. Case in point was the arrival of the *SS Polizeiabteilung* in the vicinity of Stalino and the town of Olginskoye.[865] Herre had armed and issued directives to a recruited group of locals to function as police for rear area security, but the arrival of the *SS* death squads under the direction of *Gauleiter* Erich Koch, and the disarming and execution of these pro-German troops as "partisans" altered Herre's plan, and forever ruined the chance of a large scale Ukrainian support network.[866]

Herre was upset about these developments and believed that there had been some sort of misunderstanding that needed to be clarified in the future with written orders. During the retreat of the *49th Korps,* Herre learned of the condition of the prisoners back at Stalino, so he returned for an inspection. The people were being starved, worked to death and executed, as well as suffering from typhus, with the overseers being Ukrainians themselves. Herre learned after several interrogations that hundreds were dying every day. Herre reported the brutality to a *Generalleutnant* Conrad who apparently did not believe him, but said he would look into it and rectify any conditions he felt were inappropriate.

In January 1942 Herre wrote to his wife's uncle, *Oberst* Hasso von Wedel at *OKW* stating his concerns that such situations would hinder the acquisition of support from the locals, and may even become detrimental in terms of German morale and the recruitment of indigenous military support.[867] Herre saw things clearly, and long before he received the benign reply from von Wedel. Herre had witnessed the *Einsatzgruppen* at work and realized that his efforts and promises made in good faith had been hollow. Herre was summoned to the personnel department of the Army General Staff at *OKH* in April 1942 where he was transferred to the Department of Foreign Armies East under *Oberstleutnant* Reinhard Gehlen, who planned all the necessary logistical support for *Barbarossa* and was apparently unaware of the hidden agenda regarding the local populations.

In particular, the 17 May 1941 *Kommissariat Befehl* (Commissar Order) that all political leaders be handed over to the *SD* to be executed upon capture was challenged by such luminaries as future Field Marshals Gerd von Rundstedt, Fedor von Bock and Wilhelm von Leeb.[868] All voiced their dissent to the Chief of the Army Staff, *Generaloberst* (later *Generalfeldmarschall*) Walther von Brauchitsch.[869] When Gehlen became aware of these activities he joined Herre and the others in voicing his dissent. One of the chief persons responsible for performing what was once considered impossible, a pro-Soviet Ukraine, was *Reichskommisar* Erich Koch, *Gauleiter* of East Prussia. As cited by Richard Overy, Koch's inaugural address in Rovno left no doubts as to the long term aims of *Nazi* policy: "I am known as a brutal dog... Our job is to suck from the Ukraine all the goods we can get hold of...I am expecting from you the utmost severity towards the native populations."[870] Koch can be placed alone in the pantheon of ruthless and uncomprehending thugs who managed to eliminate the potential large-scale support from the almost exclusively anti-Communist population dedicated to the overthrow of Stalin. Gehlen apparently knew that Koch was a liability following his appointment in 1941, although his opinion meant nothing, as Koch was a Hitler favorite and had been personally appointed by the *Fuehrer.*

Brauchitsch supported the plans and detailed his own reason for the importance of the doctrine, yet he failed to convince Hitler in his position as Chief of the General Staff. It is widely believed (and supported by Wolff and Kumm) that he never even submitted the proposals in writing to Hitler for his opinion, sensing his own demise and eventual dismissal that followed the sacking of Fedor von Bock. These unfortunate events seriously damaged the recruiting effort from a legitimate standpoint, yet the "illegal" recruiting still took place, as most senior officers turned a blind eye to these events.

Events were still in motion and Gehlen informed Herre that a quarter of a million Russians were already serving in the German military, and that he was also aware of the conditions of the prisoners as witnessed by Herre.[871] Gehlen and von Brauchitsch tried in vain to change Hitler's mind, citing the fact that if German capture meant death, then Stalin would maintain the upper hand in numbers and political viability. This was the point at which the Germans lost the "hearts and minds" campaign before it ever had a chance.

Despite the exceptions, such as the Ukrainian, Free Russian and other *Wehrmacht, SS,* and *Freiwilligen,* Berlin labeled these groups as "illegal." The field commanders for the most part saw the reality on the ground and understood from their own perspective that the political dogma of the *Nazi* Party did not support this reality; the Russian volunteers swelling the German ranks were a "necessary evil." These ongoing developments were finally considered as an undeniable fact by late 1942, and the majority of the volunteers gave an outstanding account of themselves. Karl Wolff explained the dilemma:

> The Propaganda Ministry was already gearing up to take the credit for the recruiting and deployment of these international brigades by November 1941. Josef Goebbels and his disciples at 10 Viktoriastrasse were unaware of the activities regarding recruitment until Herre's letter to *OKW* and *OKH.* The Office of Eastern Languages, headed by Dr. Eberhardt Taubert (from 1937-41) and the secrecy was exposed on the day of *Barbarossa.* Most of what they accomplished was the creation of interesting propaganda catch phrases that would hopefully turn the population against Stalin. There was some success, yet overall, I would have to say that we failed dismally.[872]

During this period Stalin's forces had been decimated in the Ukraine, and 600,000 Red Army troops were captured or killed in a rapid pincer movement, forcing Vlasov and his 20th Army to retreat from his Dnieper defense as Kiev fell with high losses on both sides.[873] The months of constant campaigning saw Vlasov hospitalized for exhaustion in November 1941 in Moscow, just as generals Hermann Hoth and Heinz Guderian rolled within artillery range of the capitol.[874] Hastening from his sick bed he took command of the southern Moscow defense, initiating a series of successful counter attacks on 6 December 1941 against *Generalfeldmarschall* Fedor von Bock's Army Group Center.[875] Following this success Vlasov went to command forces on the Leningrad Front, pitting him against *Generalfeldmarschall* Wilhelm *Ritter* von Leeb and Army Group North.[876]

Vlasov's last command was still the 20th Soviet Army and 2nd Shock Army that had been part of the raging battles around Demyansk and Kholm from January to June 1942. His main opposition during this period was the *9th Armee.* It would be Vlasov's capture as he was wounded and hiding in a barn that would propel his new career. The holder of the "Hero of the Soviet Union," "Order of Lenin" and the "Red Banner Order," highly propagandized in the Soviet press for his outstanding combat leadership was now a German POW. Vlasov soon learned through his housekeeper, who arrived in February with a message written on a napkin that read "Guests have come," meaning that the *NKVD* had paid his wife and son a visit and executed them. Stalin's declaration that no Russian taken prisoner would be welcomed back into his homeland proved to be a critical flaw. Vlasov, his family removed and his life effectively over had little choice. However, he did have a new mission.

There were many German officers akin to Herre who had seen the value of recruiting and training the international volunteers, and White Russians were welcomed into the various commands as were the Ukrainians. *Generalfeldmarschall* Guenther von Kluge was one of the more vocal supporters, and he authorized the activities of *General Graf* von Schenckendorff [877] and *Major der Reserve* Hans Weiss (who had been secretly recruiting Russians for auxiliary service) from his staff at Army Group Center that had just weathered the first winter in Russia, as well as the battles at Kholm and Demyansk.

The auxiliaries had so impressed von Kluge during an inspection on 16 December 1942 that he authorized the award of Iron Crosses for heroism to former Red Army soldiers who had distinguished themselves above and beyond the call of duty, even for a German soldier. [878] It is not known if all of the requests were approved, although several non-Germans won high decorations for valor, such as Leonidas Maximciuc, who although was never a member of the Red Army, he was a Bessarabian Russian aristocrat decorated by Goering and praised by von Kluge. An interesting development occurred during one of these visits by von Kluge. During his later 1943 tour of the Free Russian Air Force, commanded by General V. Maltsev, he met Leonidas Damianov Maximciuc, who relate the event:

> We had been flying continuously for several weeks, and I was a new pilot in the unit, but we had flown many ground support and covering operations for Army Group Center. Kluge was very impressed by the fact that we flew in any kind of weather, when many *Luftwaffe* units did not. He later officially designated us as his combat air support, over the *Luftwaffe* units. That was quite an honor. [879]

Major Weiss had not only created the units themselves, but he also created the rank insignia the men wore along with an independent chain of command structure, with the ultimate authority residing with himself and Schenckenforff's adjutant, a *Major* von Kraewel, who had created *Abteilung 600,* led by Russian Major Ivan N. Kononov, a Finnish Winter War Veteran and recipient of the Order of the Red Banner. Kononov was the former commander of the 436th Infantry Regiment of the 155th Infantry Division who had deserted the Red Army, along with nearly his entire regiment from the Don region on 22 August 1941 after a sweep and purge operation by the *NKVD*. [880] Kononov's unit had operated as an anti-Cossack unit within the Red Army with *NKVD* support, and upon his defection he was appointed an *Oberstleutnant* in command of a cavalry regiment in the mounted counterinsurgency role protecting German rear areas.

Kononov's abilities soon saw him transferred to the *8th Waffen SS* Division *"Florian Geyer"* commanded by *SS Oberfuehrer* (later *Gruppenfuehrer*) Hermann Fegelein, serving directly under *Obersturmbannfuehrer* (later *Oberfuehrer*) Gustav Lombard. [881] Following this breaking in period he was promoted to *Obersturmbannfuehrer der SS* and authorized to create his own regiment, which he accomplished by recruiting Cossacks from the Mogilev prison camp, among others. This unit became the 120th Don Cossack Regiment, but was renamed the 600th Don Cossack Battalion due to a 27 January 1943 order that *Freiwilligen* units could not be organized in units above battalion level, despite the fact that the unit had

2,000 men with another 1,000 expected to join them soon. Bypassing the regulations the 17th Cossack Armored Battalion assigned to *3rd Armee* and was created to handle the additional men.[882]

Vlasov's capture meant two things for the Germans; a high profile war hero who could, by name recognition alone perhaps cause defections from the Red Army and rally anti-Stalin support, and a capable professional who was completely knowledgeable of the Soviet order of battle and intelligence related matters. The propaganda value to the Germans was a given. One of the most important members of the German High Command to actively pursue Vlasov was *Hauptmann* Wilfried Strik-Strikfeldt, a native of Danzig of Russo-German parentage, educated in St. Petersburg and a young veteran of the Czar's Army in the First World War. Strik-Strikfeldt served as a representative to a British firm in Riga, Latvia from 1920 until the German invasion of Poland in 1939. Strikfeldt left Posen and the Soviet sphere after witnessing the purge first hand during their occupation. His knowledge of the Russian language secured him a place as a top ranked translator for *Generaloberst* (later *Generalfeldmarschall*) Guenther von Kluge, commander of Army Group Center.[883]

In reference to the Russian *Freiwilligen*, the previously mentioned *"Kaminsky Brigade"* was reorganized as a *panzer* unit while assigned to the *Wehrmacht* prior to their transfer to the *Waffen SS*. *Generaloberst* Rudolf Schmidt, commander of the *2nd Panzer Armee* equipped the unit with captured T-34 tanks, artillery, well trained infantry and weapons. After witnessing a couple of their finer moments in the field Schmidt wrote a memorandum for increasing the size and legitimizing the unit, a request which was never taken seriously. Despite this setback Schmidt decided to work with the others in recruiting Russians and filed reports regarding his actions. Whatever happened to these reports remains a mystery, although Karl Wolff admitted to reading some of them before they were passed on to Himmler.[884]

Assembling this umbrella organization was *Oberst* Henning von Tresckow who had been under the command of Fedor von Bock during his tenure as C-in-C of Army Group Center. Tresckow (who became *1A* under von Kluge) was present when the Russian defenders of Smolensk had defected *en masse* and proclaimed the city the capitol of the new "Russian Republic." Smolensk would become the organizational headquarters for all Russians wishing to divest themselves of Stalin's rule and join the fight against Bolshevism for a Free Russia. Unfortunately for the nationalist Russians, von Bock had little interest and no experience in politics, which was the case with most of Germany's professional officer corps. However, von Bock did forward the permission requests to *OKW* and *OKH* in September 1941 for the forming of *Freiwilligen Ostruppen* units, and by November he still had not received a reply. He was sacked on 18 December 1941 and replaced by von Kluge, a situation that further delayed the paperwork.

Ironically the words *"ost"* and *"truppen"* were proving to be a problem in recruiting Russians, since *ost* (meaning "east" in German) was a term used in the deportment and transport of conquered persons to labor camps, and *truppen* (meaning "troops") sounded frighteningly familiar to the Russian word "trup," meaning "corpse." Despite this and other problems Tresckow managed to recruit 200,000 Russians while working with Stauffenberg, Strik-Strikfeldt, Gehlen, Herre, and others in optimizing these vast resources of manpower. Tresckow planned ahead, thinking that the requests were simply bogged down in the endless paper trail of bureaucracy. The Germans were still waiting several months for resupply and replacements since they had long ago overrun their supply lines. Receiving important communications from higher authority was less than perfect unless a military disaster loomed ahead or a new set of directives or a dismissal and appointment were issued.[885]

Tresckow and Strik-Strikfeldt were old friends, anti-Hitler in their personal and political beliefs, and certain that unless a mass support network for the *Wehrmacht* was obtained and maintained among the Russian population Germany could never win the war in the east. Strikfeldt adopted a policy plan that would allow the Russians to live in a Communist free non-Czarist state similar to National Socialism, yet without direct manipulation from Berlin. The plan worked in the representation to the forces they recruited, and their success rate was impressive. However, as hard as they tried to portray the Army as a liberation force their brethren in the *SD* sabotaged every gain with their murder and destruction, creating more problems than the recruiting effort could manage with even the best damage control.

Having dealt with this problem first hand while assigned to *"Das Reich"*, *Gruppenfuehrer* Otto Kumm summarized the situation faced by the two officers:

> If Berlin genuinely cared about winning the war in the east they would have completely supported the recruiting plans, and maintained a reign on the *Einsatzgruppen* activities. Hitler's dream was a united Europe that would eclipse and destroy Communism, yet the greatest potential weapon in his inventory was the massive Russian population. Had he taken the situation seriously and logically analyzed the realities, we would not be discussing this today. It was unbelievably stupid and was, in my opinion, the reason why we lost the war in total.[886]

Reinhard Gehlen also feared that a mass influx of former and potential German allies into labor and death camps would have a disastrous public relations result among the conquered civilian populations, and that rear area security units (including the *Gestapo*) would need to divert front-line combat units to handle the uprisings. The treatment of these people would come back to haunt the German military in the form of the two Warsaw Uprisings and the various civil disturbances throughout the *Reich*.

Many leaders within the *Waffen SS* felt the same way, understanding that the only effective way to relieve the pressure from insurgents was to make the population feel secure and inclusive. Assistance for the *Freiwilligen* and auxiliary concept would come from unexpected places, and this assistance would be used by Tresckow and Strikfeldt to execute the mission. Tresckow's rationale for recruiting was to remove from Stalin the potential partisan armies at his disposal and use them against him. This seemed to be more palatable to some in higher authority than using captured POWs, who were never completely trusted by most of the upper echelon commanders.

However, Tresckow found that von Kluge's lack of interest in the political arena regarding the *Freiwilligen* made von Bock seem like a staunch lobbyist. Kluge did see the military value of the internationals, as seen by his faith in Vlasov's forces and Leonidas Maximciuc's fighter squadron. In fact, von Kluge ordered von Schenckendorff to raid POW camps, hospitals, labor details and all areas for those Russians who "fit the bill."[887] The plan worked with intermittent success until the works of the *Einsatzgruppen* and *Sonderkommando* became known. These murderous groups even raided the *Freiwilligen* units for the forced labor industry of *Organization Todt*.[888] Many villages failing to supply their quota of able bodied men and women would be burned out as an example to others, while "churches and cinemas were raided and the people inside shipped off to Germany."[889] These counter-productive operations became frustrating and time consuming, so the Germans (under Kluge's direction) recruiting the eastern troops decided to keep their operation a secret to ensure success, taking the position that "what Berlin doesn't know can't hurt us."[890]

12

Selection & Deployment

*New things always have to experience difficulties
and setbacks as they grow. It is sheer fantasy to
imagine that the cause of socialism is all plain sail-
ing and easy success, without difficulties and setbacks or the exertion of tremendous efforts.*
- Mao Tse Tung
27 February 1957.

With regard to the selection process, perhaps one of the most important figures to become involved was *Sturmbannfuehrer* Dr. Fritz Rudolf Arlt, who had been briefed on the
current recruiting process and approached Vlasov.[891] Arlt was a seasoned combat officer and
a specialist in Russian nationalities who had been called upon to define the "true definition"
of Nordic types among these eastern peoples. Arlt believed that the racial criteria were
basically ridiculous, since bravery and intelligence had nothing to do with a man's nationality and was counter-productive to the overall mission. The setbacks experienced by Germany due to the "non-Aryans" seemed to support his belief.

There were many loopholes in the racial regulations, and Arlt informed Himmler (witnessed by Wolff) in 1943 that 3,000,000 men in the Ukraine qualified if the "restrictions
were lessened or redefined."[892] Arlt's personal history is also quite interesting, considering
the fact that, despite being a major in the *Waffen SS*, his personal views were openly anti-
National Socialist and he never joined the *Nazi* Party. Arlt found difficulty in publishing his
research since he opposed the National Socialist viewpoints on racial associations and politics.[893] He served in Poland in 1939 under *General* Johannes von Blaskowitz,[894] then was
reassigned to Governor General Hans Frank, *Gauleiter* of Poland, but his lack of enthusiasm with the relocation operations as overseen by Frank assured a short lived relationship.
Unlike Frank, Arlt's method of handling the population was through understanding and
courtesy, and he was barely tolerated by Frank and Himmler, despite the fact that he achieved
remarkable results during the relocation of the ghettos, being considered the "one humanitarian in a world of misery," according to Karl Wolff.[895] Arlt was also instrumental in the
creation of the *Roland* and *Nightingale* units; Ukrainian forces trained by the *Abwehr* to
fight the Communists according to the *Brandenburger* concept of deception. Wearing Soviet uniforms and speaking the language they wreaked havoc in Red Army rear areas, sev-
ering supply lines, assassinating officers, cutting lines of communication and even liberat-

ing German and fellow Ukrainians from temporary POW compounds prior to their being shipped to Siberia.

Arlt had been actively recruited into the *SS* in 1941 personally by *Obergruppenfuehrer* Reinhardt Heydrich, and due to his open minded approach to problems and the honesty with which he dealt with both superiors and subordinates alike he was appointed to Prague in a similar capacity as an aid to Heydrich. Upon Heydrich's death he was transferred at his own request to the *Waffen SS*, serving in *2nd Waffen SS Panzer* Division *"Das Reich,"* where he served under Otto Kumm for a time, and he was instrumental saving the command headquarters from a Soviet tank assault during the Kharkov action in February 1943. In February 1944 he was wounded by a direct hit from an artillery shell that killed seven men around him. After recuperating he was assigned to the *SS Hauptamt* in Berlin where he worked under Karl Wolff. Arlt, like Bittrich, Steiner, Falkenhahn, Kumm, and others was considered "too intelligent and humane" to serve in the *Allgemeine SS*, hence their assignment to front line duties in the *Waffen SS*.

Arlt was also a key player in the creation of the following *SS* divisions: *13th "Handschar," 14th "Galizische" Nr. 1* (Galician and Ukrainian), *15th "Lettische" Nr. 1* (Latvian), *19th "Lettische" Nr. 2, 21st Gebirgs "Skanderberg"*[896] *(Albanische Nr. 1* or Albanian*), 25th "Hunyadi"*[897] (Hungarian), *26th "Ungarische" Nr. 2* (Hungarian), *29th "Russische" Nr. 2* (Russian), *30th "Russische" Nr. 2* (White Russian), *33rd Kavallerie "Ungarische" Nr. 3* (Hungarian), and the *33rd "Charlemagne"*[898] *Nr. 1* (French/Alsatian).

Despite the apparent success with the creation of these *Freiwilligen* units Arlt learned that all was not well. The problem was the Ukrainians, who (according to Arlt) were fractional, disunited, and would be difficult to place within specific collective units. The Ukrainians would have to be placed under a command they all respected, and due to the experiences in the east this ruled out most Germans, especially within the *SS*.[899] There were many Ukrainians who had fled and joined the Polish Army before the war, setting up their own government in exile.[900] It would be from this Diaspora that Arlt would form the nucleus of his Ukrainian Legion.

Most of these men had been captured by Germans forces in 1939, or captured and executed by the Soviets following the partition of Poland, with many ending up in the Katyn Forest.[901] Ukrainians who had remained under Communist rule in the Soviet Union and changed their loyalties were not considered "true patriots," just as the former Polish recruits were considered "traitors." Thus the hostility against the Communists was intense. The answer to this problem came from General Pavlo Shandruk, himself a refugee from Stalin who suggested the Ukrainians serving in the *SS* be labeled *"Ukrainische"* instead of *"Galizische"* and remove German officers from command and replace them with fellow Ukrainians.[902] This logical recommendation went through Arlt, the *SS Hauptamt* and the *Abwehr,* circumventing policy and "reinterpreting" orders, allowing life to be breathed into the Free Russian and auxiliary *Freiwilligen*. However, Arlt defended his creation of the term *"Galizische",* stating that Berlin would never have approved a "Ukrainian" unit under their own ethnic name, since it would undermine the external German policy of complete and total control over all subject peoples, and may even foster nationalist concepts of independence from Germany. Shandruk stated that was precisely why the Ukrainian (if not the entire Free Russian coalition) would never amount to much. He flatly stated to Arlt; "You must give something to receive something," and this was quoted by Wolff:

Shandruk outlined specific conditions, much like Vlasov, that had to be met if Germany wanted another ally against Stalin in the Ukrainian Nationalist Party. These were self-control and command of all present and future units under Ukrainian officers, freedom for all Ukrainians from prison and concentration camps, and the creation of an independent Ukraine allied to, but not under the domination of Germany. Berlin was not about to agree openly, and this would prove difficult for us later.[903]

Arlt knew that these conditions were impossible to obtain, and he was no liar, offering to shake on the deal and promised to do his best to get Berlin to honor the requests. He even extended Shandruk the offer of the rank of *Gruppenfuehrer* in the *Waffen SS,* which Shandruk initially declined, but a week later agreed to conditionally. Vlasov was informed of these events as well as the formation of the two Caucasus *SS* divisions in Denmark and Italy.[904] Vlasov even mentioned to Zykov, Malyshkin, and Lieutenant Fedor Ivanovich Trukhin[905] the possible necessity of contacting the British and Americans through the Swiss (with whom they had a contact) to establish their goals and aims, which were clear and distinct from Hitler's. The understanding must be made clear to the west: the Free Russian forces would not combat the Western Allies,[906] but would possibly fight the Germans if assured the possibility of contesting Stalin later with Anglo-American support. Regardless of the eventual outcome, Vlasov did not want his men handed over to the Red Army at all costs.[907] One setback was the refusal of the Swiss *Charge d'Affaires* to grant visas to non-Communist Russians, due to their uncertain potential post-war relationship with the Soviet Union.[908] Strik-Strikfeldt was unaware of these talks, although he was well aware of Vlasov's and the other Russians' distrust of the Germans, as cited in his post-war memoirs, and he did not blame them. However, despite these obstacles the forming of the units continued.

Along with these auxiliary units created by Arlt came Himmler's permission to create and expand existing training camps and academies, even encouraging the best of the foreign officer material to attend the *SS* Officer's Academy at Bad Toelz.[909] Other developments witnessed Pannwitz incorporating his Cossacks into the *Waffen SS*, since they would be more reluctant to demobilize one of their own.[910] The *SS* inclusion would also assure the Cossacks of the best equipment and primary protection against the *Einsatzgruppen,* since the *Waffen SS* "protected their own." Pannwitz had witnessed the successes of other *SS Freiwilligen* units, such as the *"Estnische"* (Estonian) *Nr.1,* considered one of the best units fielded and even had seven men awarded the Knight's Cross, with one soldier winning the Oak Leaves before being decimated in the Kurland and disappearing into mass graves or Soviet labor camps in 1945. He was also impressed with the Walloon regiment and pressed for the unit to be increased officially to division status under Degrelle, who already wore the Knight's Cross and would be awarded the Oak Leaves by Hitler personally. The Belgians had already become legendary in war in Russia.

Another successful *Waffen SS* unit was *"Nederland,"* with an impressive combat record against the Red Army as well as against irregulars and itself had a series of heroes. One such luminary was Johannes Munk, who won the Iron Cross in both classes and an appointment to Bad Toelz for saving his company commander's life. Another luminary was eighteen year old Knight's Cross recipient Gerardes Mooyman, possibly the first non-German and the youngest soldier up to that time to win the award while serving as a Pak-40 75mm anti-tank gunner in the division's *14ᵗʰ Panzerknacker* (Anti-tank) *Kompanie*. Mooyman's single-handed destruction of eight T-34's after the rest of the gun crew had been killed, with a collective total of fifteen tanks destroyed within thirty minutes was impressive, effectively halting a minor Soviet offensive.

The other notable Dutch/Flemish unit was *"Langemarck"* with a Knight's Cross going to Remy Schrynen for his single-handed destruction of seven T-34's while being seriously wounded, saving an entire company from being overrun. These actions justified the recruiting effort and supported the belief in the European volunteers, and the propaganda value was immeasurable. These units had all served with distinction with Army Group Center, and Arlt thought these records would support his cause with von Kluge as well as Himmler, according to Karl Wolff. Arlt's other problems (similar to Tresckow's) were that while Kluge was a fierce, competent fighter and stellar commander of troops in the field, he displayed no such character when confronting Hitler or the High Command. His interests lay simply in victory and objectives, not political mechanics, and Tresckow altered his approach to von Kluge with a strictly military and apolitical standpoint, crunching the appropriate numbers and offering several operational studies from many of his supporters as to the feasibility of forming more Free Russian units.

Other problems included the fact that German soldiers (especially the *SS*) were reluctant to render traditional customs and courtesies to foreign superiors, especially Russian officers, which in turn reduced their legitimacy in the eyes of their own men.[911] The most glaring problem was just how to offer a proposal to these recruits, since their had never been an instituted doctrine regarding the Russian *Freiwilligen*; no official policy offering to extend any form of autonomy to the Free Russians once the war was won. There was simply a promise to free them from Stalin and allow them to return to their own lands.[912] For the majority of the recruits this was good enough, but to the better educated members of the Russian military elite they needed more, and any treaty or agreement on paper was at least something if not a binding contract. This savvy understanding of the world and the situation was displayed by Vlasov, when he had his officers and men agreed to sign the declaration stating that Free Russian forces would not engage the Western Allies in combat unless fired upon. The ROA units were allowed to fire in self-defense, but only if there was a clear and present danger.

Kluge's group of activists decided to instill trust among the Russians, or at the very least within Army Group Center. Kluge issued orders that any unit or group entering his area of command for the distinct purpose of gathering slave labor or executing "partisans" would be arrested and court-martialed on the spot, since it created tension between the Germans and the *Freiwilligen*, many of whom were ex-partisans or guerrillas themselves. This actually occurred on one occasion, proving that Kluge was a man of his word if nothing else. Other essential players in this drama, as well as the psychological warfare planning branch (a primary consideration in recruiting enemy forces) were *Hauptmann* Nikolaus von Grote, holding the new position of *Sonderfuehrer*.[913] Grote was born in Lithuania and served in the Russian Imperial Army during World War I, and afterward trained as a journalist and contract litigate at St. Petersburg University, Vilnius University, and the *Polytechnische* in Berlin. His skill at speaking Russian, German, English, French, and every Baltic dialect assured him of a prominent position, and von Grote was consulted by Tresckow regarding the best methods of recruiting the Russians for German service.

Grote understood that the peasantry was the root mass, and to effectively reach them their love of the land would be the best approach; satisfy their desire for private land ownership, offer freedom from collectivization and freedom of worship and the masses would follow. Regarding religion, Tresckow took the matter to heart, coming to the enlightened conclusion that had escaped his superiors. Offering the freedom to practice their Russian Orthodox faith secured for Germany many recruits, as this factor and the possibility of even that small freedom was enough to make them fight Stalin. There were many reasons for Stalin to fear his own people, not the least of which was over religion. As stated by Richard Overy:

> For years Russian Christians were forced to live a subterranean existence like the Christians of the ancient world. Churches and monasteries were closed down and their communities disbanded. Before the Revolution there 50,000 priests and 163 bishops in the Russian Church. By 1941 there were around one hundred priests and only seven bishops. Their lives were closely monitored by the regime. Thousands of practicing Christians received communion in secret masses, but the risks they ran were enormous. With the outbreak of war the attitude of the regime began to change...Stalin, the ex-seminarian, ...told the British ambassador that, in his own way, 'he too believed in God.' The word began to appear in *Pravda* with a capital letter.[914]

German construction crews began to rebuild the churches destroyed by Stalin during the purges and German forces during the war, and they began actively supporting the clergy. This approach was to open an entirely new door for the German war against Communism. All of this was Hitler's plan to "dull the senses of the local population and make German rule more tolerable."[915] Both Stalin and Hitler realized that religion would become one of the most important tools in fostering support for their own personal agendas.

Tresckow collated the data and stressed the importance, simplicity, and soundness of the information to his superiors, since the same tactic had worked for the Bolsheviks during the Revolution. The peasants were targeted specifically and offered food, shelter, work, and land. Since the basic ideal of the average Russian had always been the land and family, as well as their individual freedoms, the victory lay in the simplicity of the tactic. However, the introverted history and natural xenophobia of the average Russian would not be so easily overcome as long as the death squads operated with reckless abandon.

Tresckow and Grote knew that Hitler and the High Command had no intention of honoring any agreement with Russian peasants who were slated for a life of servitude to their future German overlords, a throwback to the feudal system supported by modern technology by a ruthlessly oppressive government. Tresckow's efforts did see some benefit in that a new branch was created on 14 March 1942; the *Wehrmacht Propaganda IV* (*WPr IV*) commanded by *Oberst* Hans Martin as a liaison between the Propaganda Ministry and *OKW*. Martin operated with the expert advice of von Grote and the Russian born *Leutnant* Eugen Duerksen.[916] Duerksen was responsible for Russian language propaganda leaflets and approved newspapers that were distributed by land, sea, air, and in some cases artillery. He also controlled the radio broadcasts to Soviet forces, parroting the Party line to solicit defectors, even using a mobile loudspeaker system that was utilized all along the front. So effective and impressive was the tactic it soon was adopted by Ilya Ehrenberg, the "Soviet Goebbels" and master manipulator for use against German troops, although with far less effectiveness. The Soviets first used the Duerksen method at Stalingrad in December 1942 when they offered warm food and medical attention to any German surrendering, and continued the method throughout the war.[917]

Grote and Duerksen would spend most of Vlasov's capture with the Russian general, analyzing him and making recommendations based upon their many interviews. Duerksen worked closely with the exiled Russian Alexander Stepanovich Kazantsev, a devout follower of the self-appointed leader of the *NTS (Nacionalo Trudovoi Soyus)*, or the National Labor Union, Viktor Baidalakov.[918] This organization was based in Belgrade, Yugoslavia with departments in Budapest, Bucharest, and staffed by Russian expatriates since the early 1920's. This was the original nucleus of the Russian "experts" and technicians who joined the ranks of the German military and propaganda machines. They were all willing to fight Stalin. Whether or not the High Command would listen was another matter.

Regarding Tresckow's innovation regarding religion, he was presented with no opposition from higher authority, so the active recruitment of Russians continued. This recruitment was even extended to the Orthodox priests, since their devotion to their faith and their masses of followers offered a justification for defying the Communists.[919] The active Tresckow even organized the previously mentioned details to rebuild churches destroyed by Stalin, and the people in the various regions were encouraged to practice their religion, since it made good propaganda as well as practical common sense.

One of the collective ironies of the Soviet Communist purge of the Orthodox Church is that this attack, by in large, was what alienated most of the people who would have otherwise supported Stalin, even with the economic and physical suffering they had endured. As related in the post-war interrogations of various German officers who actually worked within the framework of subversion and resistance among the Russian clergy, these priests and monks had always maintained their own intelligence and resistance network throughout Russia and the Balkans, to include Eastern and Central Europe.[920] The priests who were recruited as a method of increasing pro-German support among their flocks soon became more involved in the fight against Stalin. Reports regarding priests volunteering for sabotage, to include parachuting behind Soviet lines on what can best be described as suicide missions are well documented by the Germans who served on the program, including Otto Kumm, Karl Wolff, and documented in the autobiography of Hans-Ulrich Ruedel.[921] Many of these priests who had been tortured, imprisoned, and banished to Siberian labor camps during the early days of the Communist era volunteered for sapper, parachute, demolition, and assassination duties. Some were trained to infiltrate Red Army units and eliminate key individuals, as well as place time delay charges as diversions to support German attacks.[922] Their history under Stalin explains their attitude and motivation, and by 1942 hundreds of these holy men had performed their one way missions, never to be heard from again. Many others were recruited for the propaganda and psychological warfare campaign used extensively by Germany (and later adopted by the Soviets in 1944) under the direction of *Standartenfuehrer* Guenther d'Alquen.[923]

Guenther d'Alquen had tried to convince Himmler that the political and ideological war against the *untermenschen* had failed, reminding the *Reichsfuehrer* that these so-called "subhumans" had managed to destroy more than one German army, and that creating the auxiliary units made perfect sense, at least as a new psychological weapon against the Soviets.[924] Himmler had coldly received d'Alquen, perhaps due to the fact that the man was an intellectual superior who intimidated him and was a man who commanded the trust and loyalty of all his subordinates. Previous methods of psychological utility had been applied without success, such as the executions and destruction of homes and villages. In addition, the psychological program was not always intended to be directed against the Soviets, with German troops receiving a heavy dose of propaganda and psychological reinforcement to make the "necessary deeds" more palatable. Such programming included stating that Russian women were actually Jews "whose Jewish origin cannot be seen."[925] Other ridiculous applications included the statements that women and children were actually agents and spies and were a great threat to the German military, in order to make their liquidation less morally debilitating.[926]

The department headed by d'Alquen also handled the commando Russian Orthodox priests and the traveling loudspeaker units, as well as supporting the religious convictions of the people. Part of the psychological program was the wide distribution of leaflets by air and land, under the code name *"Wintermaechen,"* or "Winter Tale." Part of the information dispersed included methods of self-mutilation to avoid military service and the using of women's voices as sexual bait to lure the enemy through innuendo. Part of determining just what the tools of psychological victory should be was left up to von Grote and Martin, who interviewed the high ranking Russian prisoners kept in Berlin on an individual basis. The Russians were maintained in an exemplary fashion with rations equal to those of the Germans, including creature comforts, much to the disdain of the more conservative members of the General Staff and High Command. There were not even guards or barriers placed upon the high ranking prisoners to prevent escape, lending a sense of trust and comradeship to the POWs. This tactic was a passive psychological tool in order to extract the most positive results from the interrogations that were usually handled by von Grote.

However, another situation arose in the form of Soviet Major Nikolai Golovin, a defector who offered his services in recruiting many others, but only under specific and nonnegotiable conditions. First, Golovin wanted assurances that Russia would be *Russian* with a free and independent government after Stalin was defeated, and that all of the territories conquered by Germany would be returned after the peace was achieved, complete with trade agreements between the two nations. On the surface these were not extraordinary requests and were to be expected, especially since German propaganda had been alluding to these items for months, albeit without mentioning specific terms and conditions. Golovin was no fool and he wanted these promises in writing. All of this was facing von Grote when another turning point occurred on 20 April 1942; the attacks at Kholm and Demyansk by Vlasov's 20th Shock Army supporting Zhukov's defense of Moscow. On this day *Oberst* Martin was informed by *Oberstleutnant* Bernd Wessel von Freytag-Loringhoven, the *1C*[927] of Army Group South (just emerging after the heavy battles in the Don and Caucasus during the drive to Stalingrad) that he had a special prisoner needing protection from the *SS*.[928]

The prisoner was Soviet Major Militei Aleksandrovich Zykov, and he was not initially trusted due to his status as a defector. This attitude changed once Gehlen learned he was Jewish, although a devout Marxist, having served in the Youth Communist League and a former member of the Lenin Guard following his service in World War I. His wife was the daughter of Andrei Bubnov, the Soviet Commissar for Education who, along with Aleksei

Rykov and Nikolai Bukharin (the founder of *Izvestiia* to whom Zykov was an assistant) was "removed" by Stalin during the first Great Purge. Bukharin was replaced by *GRU* chief Nikolai Yeshov and deported to Siberia with Zykov. The war had brought Zykov from penal exile due to his special military skills and saved him from the mass purge of the old guard military elite from 1937-39. By the time of his defection he had been the political commissar of an entire Red Army Corps. All of this evidence tended to prove that not even the devious Stalin would send someone (especially a Jew) into Hitler's arms bearing gifts. These "gifts" would surpass even Martin's and Gehlen's wildest expectations.

Zykov knew very well the fate of the Soviet prisoners in German hands, since the word had spread through survivors and escapees,[929] and his assistance was conditional and dependent upon the same criteria as Golovin: assurances for a free and independent Russia. If he did not receive these assurances he would not assist the Germans in their recruiting campaign (which was well known within the Red Army), nor would he supply his knowledge of Red Army tactics, strategy, armaments, and assured his captors that he may "develop rapid amnesia." In response Zykov was assured of Germany's noble intentions, and in *quid pro quo* fashion he supplied a plethora of documentation on arms production, raw materials, transportation attributes and distribution, labor and work forces, and the locations of thousands of factories on both sides of the Urals. His greatest gift was the Soviet plan for the resurgence in the south, and he outlined in great detail Stalin's defensive plans for the oil fields in the Caucasus; Stalin planned to blow them up as soon as the first Germans were visible on the horizon. It was this information, according to Karl Wolff and Hans Hossfelder (who was on the mission) that forged the plan to send *Hauptsturmfuehrer* Adrian von Foelkersam and his *Brandenburgers* in disguise to capture the fields intact.

Zykov also offered von Grote and Martin a proposal to more effectively turn the population against Stalin, which paralleled the previous plans already mentioned, while supporting the organization attempting to "legitimize" the recruiting of Russians.[930] Zykov also proposed that a former Soviet officer of high rank and great reputation be chosen to lead the Free Russians. The man had to have an anti-Stalinist (if not anti-Communist) disposition with which to create the image of unquestionable legitimacy. It was Zykov who submitted the three names for overall command consideration; Malinovsky (who was not a prisoner),[931] Malenkov, and Vlasov. The most reliable division level commander according to Zykov was Major General Sergei Kuzmich Bunyachenko (promoted on 12 November 1944) who later commanded the 1st Vlasov Division.[932] However, despite the great promise this information offered it was all completely academic until proof could be offered that the concept was even feasible, which led Tresckow to make a suggestion; that the first Russian unit be a brigade in composition with its own distinctive uniforms and insignia, altered from their Red Army issue to both save money and offer a sense of individuality. He also suggested the issuance of captured Soviet weapons and the men placed under a Russian command structure with German liaison officers and advisors. This effort would see the creation of the first true German Russian Foreign Legion.

The nucleus of this force was taken from *Abwehrabteilung 203*, known as *Operation Grayhead* and consisted of ex-Soviet officers, such as Lieutenant Igor Zakharov (who was well known to Hitler personally) as well as members of the *Oberkommando des Heeres,* since he had fought with the fascists and Germans supporting Franco during the Spanish Civil War; Colonel Konstantin Kromiadi,[933] Major Uri Lovaliski, and Lieutenant Count

Grigory Lamsdorff,[934] most of whom had been in German custody since June 1941. Karl Wolff was working in Berlin under Himmler when all of this was occurring:

> The unit was in the forming stage in March 1942 but would not reach operational strength until August with 7,500 men. There was great concern regarding their reliability, and many officers in the field did not want them. Tresckow's recommendation for an independent command was frightening, even with German officers, since many of these men had executed their own Soviet leaders in order to defect in the first place. When the unit was finally deployed it contained artillery and infantry battalions and operated as a commando unit operating with success behind Soviet lines. They did suffer high casualties, but that was to be expected. The *Abwehr* finally lost interest in them and they stagnated until Vlasov was appointed the military leader of the Free Russian Army, which became known incorrectly as the Vlasov Army.[935]

Kromiadi carried a great amount of credibility with guerrilla leaders who made great efforts to locate and contact him, although these were "partisans" according to Sven Steenberg.[936] True, some of the "partisans" did offer to fight for the Free Russians, thereby altering their allegiance, although they could not completely trust the Germans. Those "partisans" who did come over were actually "guerrillas" fighting for a free Russia, and the Free Russian Army offered them a chance at fighting the Communists on their own terms. Tresckow and *Oberst Freiherr* von Gersdorff[937] were given permission to take control of the unit, now dysfunctional and leaderless, and they took great care to prevent von Kluge from meeting them due to their vocal political demands and apparent disdain of Germans in general. These men were at least able to reconcile their dual oaths to Hitler and Mother Russia; one as a liberator and the other the liberated.

On 16 December 1942 *Generalfeldmarschall* Guenther von Kluge came to inspect the new Russian Army after meeting the divisional commander, Russian General Georgy Nikolayevich Zhilenkov, complete in Russian uniform.[938] Kluge, apparently appalled at the sight immediately ordered the unit dispersed to German formations and issued German uniforms.[939] Tresckow attempted to dissuade Kluge from this decision, citing their previous combat history and the fact that Stalin had disowned them. He also outlined what the Russians were fighting for, and that they had far more to lose than a German if captured by the Red Army. Guenther von Kluge would not be convinced, although he had accepted and in fact *requested* the Free Russian Air Force as his personal close air support due to their fanatical devotion to the Germans and fellow Free Russians on the ground, and their tenacious skills against the Red Air Force, especially in the all weather and ground attack roles.

Zhilenkov was informed of Kluge's decision and could almost understand it, although his adjutant, Colonel Boyarski was less subtle, and he drafted his own response. Gersdorff carried the proposal through the proper channels and when it landed on Kluge's desk the situation came to a head. Kluge gave his reply to Zhilenkov personally; disband or be arrested. Zhilenkov assured Gersdorff the Free Russians would not be disarmed so easily, and Tresckow and Gersdorff were horrified at the possibility of a fight between the Germans and their tenuous allies. If Kluge pushed the issue the Russians would have nothing to lose. According to Karl Wolff, Hitler did have a moment of lucidity:

Hitler wanted an investigation done as to the numbers of *Freiwilligen* who had actually re-defected to the Soviets, and how many had actually defected as opposed to being recruited from prison camps. This was in January 1943. As far as I remember Gehlen headed this investigation (actually overseen by Herre) and the results were something like 1,300 documented defections, less than one point five percent of the entire volunteer force at that time. The numbers of those who actually defected from the Soviet ranks as opposed to those in camps was something like eighty percent. Hitler finally allowed the various field commanders to use these troops in the summer of 1943 in time for the Kursk offensive, but he wanted them under direct German command and at all times supervised. I do know that Army Group Center under von Kluge had the largest elements, and they apparently proved quite useful.[940]

These desertion rates mirrored German military desertions of the 12,000,000 men at arms during the war, including those executed for treason and cowardice. Herre gave these results to Zeitzler, who had just been rebuffed by Hitler via Keitel on the use of the volunteers. However Hitler in his moment of flexibility ordered that 50,000 of these soldiers be sent to labor duty in the Alsatian coal mines, and Gehlen argued that this would effect the morale and undermine the recruiting process. Zeitzler tried to remain noncommittal and sent the new information forward, and Hitler, after discussing the situation with *Generaloberst* (later *Generalfeldmarschall*) Alfred Jodl and Wilhelm Keitel "still wanted the Russians moved to the Western Front as an occupation force to relieve the Germans garrisoned there."[941] This deployment would allow hundreds of thousands of Germans to go east while removing the temptation from the Russians to "go home." However, the Free Russian doctrine of not combating Western Allied forces was to prove a problem, reinforcing Hitler's distrust of the Free Russian forces and other collaborators.[942]

The approximately 850,000 Eastern European volunteers comprised of seventy-two battalions were to be moved west in a rest and refit operation in January 1944. This was partially accomplished, although it proved to be a problem, since Vlasov and the Free Russians had placed an additional condition on their service; they would not fight against the British and Americans, only the Communists. Regardless of this condition the Free Russians were transported west and Zhilenkov traveled to France to check on the men. The trip was eye opening. Most of the German liaison officers had either never worked with eastern troops or served in Russia, and their inability to comprehend the situation, let alone verbally communicate with the men further exacerbated the problem.[943] It was at this time Trukhin visited the Free Russian units in Northern Italy along with a *Hauptmann* Dellinghausen and his adjutant, Romashkin, under Karl Wolff's guidance.[944] The situation there was even worse, considering that this was a fighting front and the men were ill equipped and improperly led.[945]

The relocation of the Russians west did not begin until May 1944, with units sent to France, Belgium, and Northern Italy. One unit receiving orders early was the *Kaminsky Brigade* that had been serving in the *2ⁿᵈ Panzer Armee*, receiving the order to move on 29 September 1943. There was some dissent when Kaminsky ordered 15,000 troops and 3,000 women and children, his T-34 tanks, artillery and herds of cattle across the Peritorgi Bridge over the Desna River then being protected from partisans. The partisans had the upper hand

and were masters of propaganda, inciting unrest and threats of defection among the men. Kaminsky took a Fiesler *Storch* to one of the headquarters that was suffering from morale problems, and in front of the assembled men strangled their commanding officer to death and shot a few others. This became a standard method for Kaminsky as he traveled to his various commands, and by the end of the week sent his report to the Army Group Commander, stating "everything was proper."[946]

Due to the *Kaminsky Brigade's* (and other units') service records (comitting atrocities) there were many who felt that the movement orders were a disservice to the units that had served so well. One of the supporters for keeping the units in the east was *Gruppenfuehrer* Curt von Gottberg, district commander for the Lakoty region. Gottberg offered Kaminsky an option: transfer to the west or assimilation into the *Waffen SS* with the rank of *Brigadefuehrer* and similar ranks conferred upon his men, including *SS* issued weapons, uniforms, and equipment. Kaminsky agreed to accept if his civilians would be cared for, and they were. Kaminsky's unit became the *29th der Waffen SS Panzergrenadier* Division *"Russische Nr. 2"* under the command of a *Gruppenfuehrer* Seidling. This unit was in support of *2nd Waffen SS Panzer* Division *"Das Reich"* during the march through France in June-August 1944 and handled anti-partisan operations against the *Resistance*. They were transferred again to the Eastern Front where they fought until "being removed from the roles" and disappearing in the fog of war. There are no known survivors.

As if the Germans were not already creating problems for themselves, *Reichsfuehrer* Heinrich Himmler issue an order on 14 October 1943 at Bad Schachen, stating his desire to "remove all good blood from the Russians and Czechs (in essence all Slavs) from the general mass," even if they had to kidnap the ethnically acceptable children from their parents. Himmler openly gave his blueprint for the slave labor force that would support the *Reich*, stating that he was unconcerned about how many millions died from work as long as that work served Germany. Even among the battle hardened combat leaders of the Army and *Waffen SS* these remarks were unsettling, but when word of this reached the Free Russians a tempest was in the making.

During Himmler's speech he mentioned Vlasov in detail, stating the error in giving him sanction to speak to Germans and supporting notions that he had something to offer the war effort. He also stated that Germany would rule the world from France to the Orient, enslaving the multitudes who were not Germanic. This speech had a tremendous effect upon those listening who had placed their faith in Germany in the fight against Communism. Vlasov had somehow acquired the entire speech translated in Russian, and it was perhaps at this point that he decided to make contact with the Western Allies as a security precaution, which was completely understandable.

Tresckow knew of the events via Herre and decided that the conscripted workers could not come from Army Group Center. Tresckow took operational command in Kluge's absence on 17 December 1942, and he tried to tackle the problem with Gehlen's assistance. Zhilenkov and Boyarski were transferred to Berlin and the Northern Front respectively, while the Russian Brigade fell under the command of a Major (later Colonel) Rily.[947] Due to these internal struggles and the uncertain futures of the men within the unit, over 300 soldiers deserted and became actively engaged in partisan warfare against the Germans, a condition that did not go unnoticed in Berlin.[948]

Meanwhile another Soviet officer, Brigadier General Krupyennikov, commander of the 3rd Guards Army had been captured at Stalingrad. Krupyennikov had considered working against Stalin after his personal experiences with the dictator. It was Krupyennikov who informed his interrogator (Herre) that they should seek out those men (including their collective families) who had been persecuted, imprisoned, or tortured by the *NKVD*. Herre asked him how many people did he estimate were qualified, and Krupyennikov's response was "about one in five above the rank of major, and fifty percent for generals."[949] The active recruitment of specific individuals, rather than from the general Russian military population seemed the best way to accomplish their task, and the Germans began combing the POW camps and interrogation files. Offering a second chance to men who had suffered under Stalin would be the new plan.

Another ally in the war against Stalin was former General Blagoveshchensky of the Soviet Marines, captured in 1941. His function was to speak with recent and long term Soviet POWs and attempt to convince them of their true enemy and cultivate defections. Blagoveshchensky also created the Russian Officer's Education Academy at Dabendorf, a re-education center for prospective volunteers operated by the Propaganda Ministry in conjunction with Gehlen and the *Abwehr*.[950] General Blagoveshchensky was appointed camp commandant, and his aid was *Graf* Georg von der Ropp who operated the training program.[951] This would become the first in a series of such academies established for ethnic volunteers, such as the School for Native Officers, Officer Candidates and Interpreters at Mariampol, Lithuania (later transferred to Conflans, France in May 1944); the school for Infantry Officers at Danzig, later expanded to handle dozens of nationalities from the eastern regions. There was also a training school attended by Cossacks in Tyrol, Italy and would be copied by the *SS* with various non-commissioned officers' schools established in the occupied countries.

The response from the former Soviet soldiers was overwhelming. The Don and Kuban Cossacks also responded well to this approach, joining the Germans in large numbers as evidenced by the service of Leonidas Maximciuc, himself a Don Cossack and member of the Romanov Imperial family by birth, whose family had been purged and his father murdered by the Communists. Gehlen and Tresckow witnessed the response upon Vlasov's return to Berlin on 10 March 1942, following his broadcast with the creation of several new anti-Communist units: the 601, 602 and 605 Eastern Battalions consisting of White Russians; the 700 and 701 Special Service Volunteer Regiments, and the Cossack Detachment 600 with Don and Kuban representation. The creation and deployment of these units still needed sanction from Berlin, just as 200,000 Russians were preparing to combat the Red Army as German allies. The greatest problem with this arrangement was that the volunteers had sworn loyalty to Vlasov and Free Russia, not Hitler and *Nazi* Germany, therefore making Vlasov crucial for any future success. It was an insurance policy Vlasov desperately needed since he was transferred to his old battleground in the sector of Army Group North, where he was to assist in the anti-partisan war and recruit POWs and deserters. His adjutant was a Captain Antonov who had deserted at Stalingrad after reading one of the many pamphlets dropped during the propaganda campaign.[952]

During this propaganda campaign Vlasov, Malyshkin, and *Generaloberst* Wedel spoke at every major Baltic and Russian city. Vlasov, standing over six feet tall was an imposing figure to many and his words of a better Russia without Stalin and the Communists carried the ring of truth and promise, which was sometimes enough to persuade a change in loyalty.[953] The program gained momentum until a letter was received by Wedel from Wilhelm Keitel on 17 April 1943 asking "… what the hell was going on, and why were Vlasov and Malyshkin giving speeches without Hitler's consent?" Karl Wolff explained the situation:

> Keitel went into a frenzy and demanded a word for word translation transcript of every word spoken. He also said that Wedel 'had better pray Vlasov did not promote himself as the future Russian leader.'[954] Himmler was even on Keitel's list, thinking the *Reichsfuehrer* had been involved. Himmler soon became quite incensed and joined the attack. It looked as if the great Free Russian experiment was about to end in firing squads for everyone. [955]

Keitel received the information he requested and he forwarded a memorandum to all concerned agencies and departments. Gehlen, Wedel, Kluge, Stauffenberg, and Tresckow, along with a host of others all received the following message:

> In view of the outrageous, impudent remarks made by the captive Russian General Vlasov on a visit to Army Group North, which was carried out without the *Fuehrer's* knowledge and without my knowledge, it is ordered that Vlasov be transferred immediately under special guard to a prisoner of war camp. The *Fuehrer* no longer wishes to hear the name Vlasov in any context except for pure propaganda activities which may require the name, but certainly not the person of General Vlasov. If General Vlasov should come forward personally once more he must be turned over to the *Gestapo* and rendered harmless.[956]

Gehlen and the field commanders were upset about this for more than the obvious reasons: the German counter-offensive against Kharkov was scheduled for 6 May 1943, but due to the inability to mass the necessary forces in time was postponed indefinitely. The main *Waffen SS* units being moved into the region according to the Steiner Plan were the *1st* *"Leibstandarte," 2nd "Das Reich," 5th "Wiking"* and *9th "Hohenstauffen"*[957] *Waffen SS Panzer* Divisions; the *"Wallonien"* Regiment, along with the *"Grossdeutschland"* and several other crack battle-hardened units. Vlasov's forces would have amply supported the anemic German ranks and allowed the attack to commence on schedule before the Red Army became aware of their intentions and reinforced the area. Hitler had effectively killed the painful gains made by the Vlasov supporters and ruined a chance to defeat an entire Soviet Army in the field. Otto Kumm summed up the situation:

> The idleness of 600,000 men prepared to fight against their former comrades with another 200,000 wasting away in prison camps exemplified the incompetence of the High Command. Felix Steiner was incensed that his plan had been shelved, as he was relying upon the Vlasov Army to support our forces in the offensive. By the time we actually launched the attack Soviet forces outnumbered us heavily and were prepared. It was such a waste.[958]

Himmler relented to some degree on the Vlasov issue, but he insisted that Vlasov be kept out of the Ukraine. The compromise ended with Zhilenkov and Zykov being escorted by d'Alquen, where they were to assume command of the troops assigned to Army Group South under *Generalfeldmarschall* Model. However, Zykov and his adjutant never arrived. They were last seen being approached by three civilians males while on their way to make a telephone call next door to their apartment, and were placed in a civilian automobile, never to be heard from again. [959] Only Zhilenkov would make the trip to Model with d'Alquen to the headquarters at Lvov to assume his role in *Operation Skorpion*.

The only flaw in the plan was the replacement of Vlasov with Zhilenkov, and the latter would not accept due to the legend and loyalty of Vlasov among the Free Russian troops. The failure to appoint Vlasov began to tell when over 4,500 men deserted. The German offensive of 11 July 1944 was still to be initiated and things seemed to be falling apart. However, the German propaganda machine was still purporting (although inaccurately) the great support Lieutenant General Andrei Vlasov[960] was giving the National Socialist cause, and by 14 July thousands of former Red Army soldiers and irregulars had deserted to German formations.

It was during this period that d'Alquen flew to speak with Himmler to convince the *Reichsfuehrer* to change his mind about Vlasov, or at the very least have Himmler speak with the man before issuing any final orders. Himmler stated that he would discuss this with Hitler and get back to him.[961] Meanwhile, d'Alquen went to meet with Vlasov in order to prepare him for the coming events, since everything hinged upon Vlasov convincing Himmler that the cause was worthy. D'Alquen was summoned to Himmler on 17 July 1944 in Rastenburg, East Prussia, and the *Reichsfuehrer* informed his visitor that Hitler had agreed to continue using Vlasov for propaganda purposes, and he wanted Vlasov brought to him on 21 July. Hitler was offering Vlasov the title of "Marshal of the Free Russia Liberation Army," according to Karl Wolff.[962]

However, events were to derail the planned meetings. Immediately upon his return to Army Group South on 20 July, d'Alquen was informed of the assassination attempt on Hitler, with Stauffenberg named as the main culprit. Since Stauffenberg had been an integral part of the planning with regard to the *Freiwilligen* units the situation was even more precarious. It was soon discovered that Tresckow was also implicated along with Freytag-Loringhoven, thus the meeting between Hitler and Vlasov was delayed. Vlasov, Strik-Strikfeldt and Sergei Froehlich went to a convalescent home in southern Germany on 27 July to await the meeting with Himmler, and Hitler tentatively rescheduled the event for 16 September. Upon their arrival Strik-Strikfeldt was not allowed in, only Vlasov, d'Alquen and a Dr. Kroeger.[963] Himmler immediately began to apologize for Vlasov's treatment and any mistakes that had been made, but he was certain that this was the time to bridge the gaps in their differences and make progress. Wolff was aware of the event:

> Vlasov opened up immediately, stating that he admired Himmler for his position of power, and that he (Vlasov) was the general who destroyed the German forces of Army Group Center, but that he hated the Stalinist system and would prefer that the Russian Liberation Army be equipped and treated as equals. If this were accomplished he believed that Stalin could be defeated, especially since Vlasov

and the other officers knew Stalin's and the Red Army's tactics and weak points. Vlasov also told us that Stalin never believed that Germany would attempt to win the war militarily, that no one could be that stupid. Stalin believed that Hitler would wage war with propaganda, psychological and political campaigns to weaken the morale of the Soviet people, reducing their faith in the Communist Party and their faith in Stalin. Vlasov also said that Stalin's greatest flaw was the widespread knowledge of his purges and the policy against Red Army soldiers who were captured, and these went against him. Vlasov also reminded Himmler that Russians could be more effective against other Russians than the Germans had been. Who knew Russians better than Russians?[964]

According to Strik-Strikfeldt's memoirs and Wolff's interviews, Himmler was mindful of the fact that if the 6,000,000 Russian laborers were released to fight at the front German war production would grind to a halt. He therefore authorized Vlasov to raise two divisions, with more to be created later, and he agreed in principle with all of Vlasov's comments. The existing Russian units would be diverted to Vlasov and re-equipped upon arrival. Once these details were ironed out the meeting ended six hours after it began. Himmler was still suspicious of the value of the eastern forces and scrutinized them in every detail.

As illustrated in the following chapter, the most successful Free Russian Legion during the Second World War would be created right under Hitler's nose. Even Himmler would only learn of its existence after it had secured a prominent place in history, and their role as a conventional counterinsurgency force would prove the value of utilizing foreign troops, although far too late to turn the tide in Germany's favor.

13

The Cossack Storm & Vlasov's Debut

In their social practice, men engage in various kinds
of struggle and gain rich experience, both from their
successes and their failures...
- Mao Tse Tung
May 1963

Friends and Brothers! Bolshevism is the enemy of the Russian people. It has brought countless disasters to our country. Enough blood has been spilled! There has been enough starvation, forced labor and suffering in the Bolshevik torture chambers! Arise and join the struggle for freedom! Long may peace with honor with Germany prevail!
Vlasov's broadcast to the Soviet Union at Smolensk, 27 December 1942[965]

The only unit to escape the scrutiny of Himmler and Berlin and effectively function without hindrance was the Cossack Division. The Cossacks had a long, ancient history of tribal alliances and nomadic warfare, and their loyalty was highly prized by the rulers of Imperial Russia. The dream of forging an independent Cossack nation, "Kazakia," propelled most of the Cossacks to continue their fight against the Soviets from the 1917 Revolution forward, and the German invasion provided a vehicle by which the Cossacks could continue their program of anti-Soviet behavior, and the Germans were more than pleased to have such an ally in their anti-partisan campaign.[966]

The Cossacks were placed under the command of an outstanding cavalry officer, *Oberst* Hellmuth von Pannwitz, a man regarded as a humanitarian who was not a favorite of either Hitler or Himmler, yet he was highly respected by his men. His friendly disposition towards the Cossacks he commanded and the Russians he captured, as well as his feared reputation in battle on the other side made him the most logical candidate. He also became the first non-Cossack in history to be nominated a field *ataman* of the Cossack military at the Field Congress held at Verovititsa on 29 March 1945.[967]

Pannwitz received the bulk of his troops from the pool of Central and Southern Army Cossacks at his headquarters in Milau, East Prussia. He was offered the command since he spoke some Polish and was quickly learning Russian, while having his speeches prepared in both languages. This attempt to speak their language impressed the Cossacks, and he often threw parties and riding tournaments for the troops, building *esprit de corps* and creating a bond that is essential between men in battle. It was considered a high honor to become a member of Pannwitz's bodyguard, and those who volunteered were chosen carefully and swore to defend their commander to the death. German officers and higher-ranking generals were sometimes unnerved to see the Cossacks quickly surround anyone coming to close to him, with sabers drawn. This was observed by several officers who related tales to Wolff and others, impressing upon the *Generalstabs* that the unit and its commander should be taken seriously.

During this period *Generaloberst* Koestring was summoned to Hitler for a complete numerical breakdown of the exact units and total numbers of Russian *Freiwilligen*, regardless of their regional origin. Himmler was informed that in the *Kriegsmarine* and *Luftwaffe* alone there were nearly 100,000 men serving, with another 1,000,000 within the ranks of the *Wehrmacht Heer* and 40,000 currently serving in the *Waffen SS*. According to Wolff, "Himmler had been unaware of these figures and the surprise was evident on his face."[968] Among these groups were thousands of Caucasians who felt no allegiance to Vlasov or his proposed government, and were unimpressed with his arrangements, since they had been fighting with the Germans against the Red Army since the fall of 1941.[969]

Over 100,000 Caucasians were serving Germany with 6,800 in the *Waffen SS*, 217 in the *Luftwaffe* and 25,000 in the Army with the balance operating as friendly guerrillas. These groups included Georgians, Armenians, Azerbaijanis, Turkmeni, Kazakhs, and other ethnic groups, and most served in the auxiliary reconnaissance role as anti-partisan cavalry in units such as *"Florian Geyer," "Maria Theresia"* and *"Prinz Eugen."* Their petition was signed by their greatest leaders, such as Alibegov, Chamalyan, Kantemir, and Misha Khedia. These men carried great weight with their people and therefore could not be ignored.

Koestring met with Guderian in Berlin, who ordered him to organize as many of these Russian divisions as soon as possible since Guderian was once again the *OKW* Chief of Staff. Guderian knew the situation for what it was; a debacle of unimaginable proportions. Koestring did not receive the necessary support from Keitel and Jodl and their deportment indicated that Hitler was unaware (or at least not supportive) of Himmler's plan. Koestring found himself virtually alone in his attempt to support Vlasov, since d'Alquen would be bed ridden with scarlet fever in February 1945, and the rest of the support network fell apart following the purge of the suspected participants in the bomb plot the previous July. Those who survived were reassigned, retired, eventually killed in action, or captured. Meanwhile, as the powers and egos in Berlin were becoming "wrapped around the axle" over political doctrine versus ideological dogma, Vlasov was quietly forming his government while his troops became fragmented and dispersed throughout the German armed forces.

The proclamation of the Free Russian Government was announced in Prague on 14 November 1944 in a well-orchestrated and quite sterile environment. Vlasov was warned by Strik-Strikfeldt to not completely trust the *SS* (which was seconded by Arlt) and watch his back at all times. This became evident once rumors surfaced of the *SD* arresting and executing members of Kaminsky's command, following Erich von dem Bach-Zelewski's ordering Kaminsky arrested following the Second Warsaw Uprising. Kaminsky himself was executed, although his men were informed that "partisans had killed him."[970] Vlasov

needed no encouragement where his paranoia was concerned and he detailed specific instructions to his command should anything happen to him.[971]
    The organizational headquarters was commanded by Malyshkin, now second in com-
mand under Vlasov. The civilian department for labor and support was entrusted to Sakutny,
while the Command Staff for the Vlasov Army was led by Trukhin. The *1A* of the Army was
Lieutenant Colonel Nikolayev and the 1ˢᵗ Division commander was the stalwart Bunyachenko.
The formation of the unit would be initiated by the collection of the survivors of the *Kaminsky
Brigade* and the *30ᵗʰ der Waffen SS* Division, both units being ground up in the Ukraine and
Croatia. Along with this arrangement came a familiar face assigned to Koestring's staff,
Oberst Danko Herre, who had just returned from the Italian Front as the *1A* of the *232ⁿᵈ
Infanterie* Division. Herre was ordered to begin an officer's training school at Muensingen
under Colonel Meandrov (captured in 1941) for the 1ˢᵗ Vlasov Division, and establish an-
other school at Heuberg for the 2ⁿᵈ Vlasov Division commanded by General Suvyev.
    In Russia the first full scale units (as well as replacements) had been assigned to Army
Group Center under the command of von Kluge and *Oberst* (later *Generalmajor*) Wilhelm
von Henning, the future commander of the *18ᵗʰ Armee*, while other volunteers went to
Generalleutnant Ullmer and *3ʳᵈ Panzer Armee*. The Cossacks under Pannwitz were to prove
the greatest challenge since their ranks included Czarist era veterans and young former
members of the Red Army, each with their own personal and political agendas. The Don
and Kuban Cossacks had often fought each other as well as the Germans, White Russians,
Ukrainians, Poles, and Soviets. Clan cliques often erupted, challenging German authority
and only Pannwitz was capable of handling these problems. His extraordinary abilities saw
the unit raised to 20,000 men and re-designated the *15ᵗʰ Kossack Korps* and placed under
Waffen SS command, although the men were never on the *SS* payroll.[972]
    However, the Kuban Cossacks under their *atamans* offered the Germans grain, sheep,
horses, and other livestock as their pledge to fight for their freedom from Communism.
Unfortunately, they were also to be betrayed. Perhaps the greatest Cossack group was that
of *Hetman* Kulakov, whose followers united at a meeting of the clans at Poltava.[973] News of
Kulakov joining the fight brought thousands of Red Army Cossacks, sometimes in division
strength to desert to the German side. So influential was Kulakov's image the few Cossacks
in German camps (they usually fought to the death) also volunteered. Soon Pannwitz's
force, commanded by General A.G. Shkuro, a former Czarist officer decorated by King
George V with the Order of the Bath grew by 300 percent, with over a quarter of a million
Cossacks fighting against Stalin, the largest single unit within the entire *Freiwilligen* inventory.[974]
    Kulakov was a Cossack legend who had led Cossack and White Russian units against
the Communists after World War I, fighting alongside the "Iron Division" made up of Polish and German volunteers. He was rumored to have been long dead, as such was stated by
Stalin. His reappearance was considered a miracle and divine intervention by many of the
older, more traditional Cossacks. Due to the differences in the various Cossack communities there were two camps of thought. Those who wanted to join the Germans and serve in
German uniforms would remain at Poltava, while those wishing to fight under their own
atamans in Cossack dress independently gathered at a Soviet factory in Voyenstroi Seleschina.
For the Cossacks a specific school of thought persisted: they would maintain as self-gov-

erning clans with their own political interests (which were anything but Communist) and harvest their own crops, and they would also form separate fighting groups taking all of the able bodied men for the war.

These Cossack units would prove to be the most formidable of all the *Freiwilligen* units, whose tenacious combat record, unyielding application of cavalry warfare and battle-field brutality against their hated Communist enemy would become legendary. One unit in particular was the *Kalmuck Squadron* that took to their task against the partisans and Red Army with such enthusiasm it horrified even the battle hardened *Waffen SS* units attached to them. Karl Wolff and Otto Kumm mentioned this fact unit during their respective inter-views:

Wolff;

There was a report from (Herman) Fegelein regarding a Cossack unit on anti-partisan duty that the Cossacks were butchering their prisoners, and that a unit from *"Florian Geyer"* had to intervene. This was becoming even more of a prob-lem later, especially in Yugoslavia and the Caucasus.[975]

Kumm;

Pannwitz's Cossacks had developed a reputation for combat effectiveness that garnered them respect, yet there had to be an established limit to the killing, espe-cially if Russians were to be recruited for the Vlasov Army. Decades of hatred was being unleashed, and the program was in serious jeopardy. The Cossacks were not a lighthearted people when it came to war; they were trained from the cradle to ride and fight. Their cavalry and marksmanship qualities were excellent by any standard, although their formation discipline was not quite to Red Army let alone German standards, and they bore no resemblance to disciplined conventional front-line units. Once they were German trained in anti-partisan warfare they were vir-tually unstoppable. I once told Fegelein, 'God help us if they ever learned that we were destined to sell them out.'[976]

Kumm respected the fighting quality of the Cossacks and had served with them in the east. The German Cossack recruiting effort in the Caucasus was spearheaded by Ernst Koestring in his campaign of "winning them over."[977] Koestring had immediate success with the local Kabardians, after informing them that Germany planned to return their lands and freedom to them, without great elaboration. These agrarian and nomadic peoples of-fered over a hundred of their best horses and warriors to join the fight against Stalin. Koestring met with similar success in the Balkans with the peoples there. The Kabardians threw a feast in Koestring's honor and gave him a magnificent gold embroidered horse bridle to present to Hitler as a token of friendship. The Germans present felt ashamed at their role in the deception, knowing full well that Hitler would never honor the agreements and that Stalin would persecute them for their taking Germany's side.

Pannwitz's Cossacks and their patriarch, the famous and highly respected General Pyotr Nikolayevich Krasnov arrived in Yugoslavia in December 1943 for anti-partisan and prepatory operations should the Allied forces invade the Balkans. They immediately began counterinsurgency operations against Tito's irregulars in a brutal campaign that lasted until

January 1945. The Cossacks proved very effective in the mountainous terrain and won praise from the High Command after their destruction of the Soviet bridgehead near Piomaka on 26 December 1944, killing thousands of Red Army troops and capturing a large number of prisoners.[978] Even the *13th der SS* Division *"Handschar"* was detached and ordered to support them, and they eventually fell under Pannwitz's command within two weeks of their arrival. However, this use of the Free Russian forces was not what Vlasov had in mind at all.

Finally, despite all of the obstacles, the 1st and 2nd Vlasov Divisions marched on parade as a cohesive and united combat unit, long after most of these men had already been fighting against Stalin for a couple of years and far too late to effect the outcome of the war. As Vlasov and his generals watched they saw the fleeting moment for what it was; the nucleus of a former partisan army supporting a doomed cause, despite the fact that the former Soviet soldiers still knowingly flocked to the Free Russian cause. Liberated Russians were soon collecting weapons and joining their former captors rather than face the wrath of their political officers for having been captured.

The German High Command maintained a stream of orders to the various Free Russian units and tried in vain to contact Pannwitz's Cossack Division, out of radio contact since the unit had begun fighting partisans, guerrillas, Red Army, and Bulgarian Army forces in February 1945 in the mountains of Yugoslavia. They had been fighting to maintain an open corridor to allow German forces an avenue of retreat from Greece through Macedonia to link up with the Free Russians. As units became embroiled in endless fighting and were decimated one after another communications, command, and control became a thing of the past.[979] Insurgency activity through Allied support had exploded in the Balkans and danger was everywhere, and many Free Russian or German uniforms contained impostors infiltrating the units. Sporadic killings created more tension, and reprisal killings became the order of the day.

Pannwitz demonstrated remarkable leadership by maintaining discipline and a cohesive, effective fighting force despite being cut off from his supply lines and communications, and the endless battles with regulars and irregulars alike. The *Freiwilligen* units were effectively on their own from that point forward, cut off from the ever dwindling support, while the Red Army and their new allies flooded in from the east. Meanwhile, other volunteer groups were being created and thrown into the grinder, with decimated units expanded by an ever younger crop of idealists and selected unfortunates, since conscription had become commonplace.[980]

General Komonov, leader of the Plastun Cossack Brigade met with Pannwitz and the *atamans* on 6 April 1945. They decided to set aside their differences and try to reach Vlasov's units in the north, although they were unaware of the developments regarding the 1st and 2nd Vlasov Divisions. The Cossacks were willing to join Vlasov and fall under his command, since he at least carried the aura of legitimacy necessary for negotiations with the Western Allies. The Cossacks led by Pannwitz chose a group of emissaries led by Prince Johannes von Schwarzenberg, an aristocrat who served with Pannwitz and was an artillery officer by trade. His mission was to contact the nearest British Expeditionary Force commander and negotiate; they were to offer themselves as a supporting force against the Communists, offering their unconditional allegiance for the unit's safe conduct through British lines. Sensing the end was near Vlasov also promoted Kononov to major general and placed him in charge of all Cossack formations once Germany capitulated. He then resumed his plans for a trip to the Oder Front.[981]

Vlasov, accompanied by *SS* liaison officer Dr. Erhard Kroger and *Sturmbannfuehrer* Friedrich Buchardt, the former head of *Amt IIIb*[982] returned to Berlin and met with *Obergruppenfuehrer* Karl Wolff, who had just returned to visit his family before heading back to Italy to meet with *Generalfeldmarschall* Albert Kesselring.[983] Part of this meeting had to deal with the Italian Communist guerrilla problem, irregulars who were mistakenly (albeit understandably) referred to as "partisans" by Kesselring and Wolff. Kesselring was not by nature a ruthless man, and he was in fact a reluctant practitioner of retaliatory measures. However, when the situation with the insurgents became intolerable following the Allied landings in Sicily, and later on the Italian mainland, the *Luftwaffe* Field Marshal made the following statement in 1943:

> In my appeal to the Italians, I announce that severe measures are to be taken against partisans. This announcement must not represent an empty threat. It is the duty of all troops and police in my command to adopt the severest measures. Every act of violence committed by partisans must be punished immediately. Reports submitted must also give details of countermeasures taken. Whenever there is evidence of considerable numbers of partisan groups, a proportion of the male population of the area will be arrested, and in the event of an act of violence, these men will be shot. The population must be informed of this. Should troops be fired at from any village, the village will be burnt down. Perpetrators or ringleaders will be hanged in public, and in such cases, the whole population of the village will be assembled to witness the execution. After the bodies have been left hanging for twelve hours the public will be ordered to bury them without ceremony and without the assistance of a priest.[984]

Through Wolff's influence and opportunity Vlasov was hoping to make contact with British Field Marshal Sir Harold Rupert Leofric George Alexander, C-in-C of the Allied Armed Forces.[985] Kroeger sent *Sturmbannfuehrer* von Sivers (who served with Alexander as a volunteer during the 1921 crisis in the Baltic) and a former Soviet officer, Captain *Graf* Luedinghausen-Wolf to Bozen with a letter signed by Vlasov. Unable to meet with Alexander personally both men spoke with a Colonel Lehman, a Canadian intelligence officer, and they were immediately interned.[986] Kromiadi and Malyshkin attempted similar overtures without success.[987]

The Free Russians found themselves heading southwest through Czechoslovakia to surrender to the advancing Allied forces, all the while combating partisans and guerrillas along the way. The sudden explosion of Czech activity made their progress slow and dangerous, although the Czech partisans spoke to Bunyachenko and asked him for his support against the Communists during the coming Czech Rising, since they expected the Americans to reach Prague.[988] It was believed that if a Czech national government were installed the Allies would not forcefully abolish it, and if the Free Russians assisted it would probably secure their position to remain in the west. The Czechs even offered asylum to the Vlasov members who desired to remain.[989] It was at this time that Bunyachenko made perhaps the greatest error in judgment imaginable, and it would prove costly. He decided to avoid committing his men to the agreement and wait for Vlasov to arrive, maintaining that he "did not have the authority to negotiate such terms."[990] The nationalist Czechs took this position as a "no" and considered the Free Russians unreliable and a potential threat.

On 8 May 1945 the three messengers lifted off in a Fiesler *Storch* in an attempt to reach American forces and were never heard from again; the same day Pannwitz learned from a radio broadcast by Tito's 8th Partisan Army that Germany had unconditionally surrendered, which was confirmed by another transmission from *"Handschar."* The terms were explicit: no further movement was allowed; all enemy forces were to remain stationary until contacted by higher Allied authority. Pannwitz knew that this order was a death sentence for himself and his men and that he could not obey such a demand. Pannwitz ordered the unit to march towards the British Eighth Army of Field Marshal Sir Bernard Law Montgomery, which was reported to be somewhere in Austria. The 2nd Cossack Division fought partisan and guerrilla units along the way, losing troops as they were continually cut off and fighting to escape.

On 9 May a forward Cossack unit led by Pannwitz came across the British 11th Armored Division, and he requested to speak with the commanding officer. Pannwitz ordered his units of the 1st Cossack Division to form up in parade fashion in order to surrender just as they had fought; a well-disciplined and cohesive military organization.[991] The proud Cossacks were now interned by the British who held their fate in their hands. On 23 May 1945 an agreement was signed in Vienna between British Field Marshal Alexander of the Allied Balkan Command and the Headquarters of the Red Army; all Cossack units were to be surrendered to the Soviets by 28 May. The Soviets had labeled Pannwitz's unit the *15th SS Cossack Kavallerie Korps* (a unit that never existed) in order to convince the British into agreeing to the arrangement. The word came down to an *Oberst* Wagner and Pannwitz that the unit was to be surrendered in separate formations: Germans and Cossacks were not to be intermixed. Being no fool Wagner informed his men of the situation, and since no one thought that the Soviets would take great care in distinguishing punishments between Germans and Free Russians the word spread; breakout anyway they could, every man for himself.[992]

Pannwitz was taken by the Soviets while Wagner and many of his men were assisted by a British lieutenant in escaping through holes in the yet incomplete wire fencing, fleeing into the mountains. Pannwitz's fate was unfortunate, given his role as a true military combatant. Even as a uniformed German officer he was still publicly hanged in Moscow after a kangaroo court in January 1947. The civilians left behind suffered a fate at the hands of the Red Army that appalled even the most battle hardened British soldiers who witnessed the atrocities, although they had explicit orders not to interfere as the rapes and murders began in earnest. Executions began immediately, with British soldiers hearing the repeated chatter of Soviet machine guns and rifles for six hours straight, while many of those handed over proceeded to commit suicide by whatever means was available. Vlasov was yet to meet his fate.

Further north, due to Himmler's incompetence as the newly ordained commander of Army Group Vistula and the bureaucratic entanglements that denied the Free Russians weapons, uniforms, vehicles, ammunition, helmets and fuel, the 1st Vlasov Division did not see action as a complete unit until 6 March 1945.[993] On that day the Reconnaissance Company moved out with *Oberst* Danko Herre in front. As they passed through the various villages their ranks swelled immensely, as forced laborers and farmers abandoned their work, hearing of the Vlasov Army. Overpowering their guards and taking their weapons they joined the 1ˢᵗ Division as it headed east to board trains for Lieberose, joining the command of *Generaloberst* Gotthard Heinrici.[994] Most of these men would fight and die supporting the German defense of the Seelow Heights in April 1945, dispersed throughout the *9ᵗʰ Army* under *Generaloberst* Theodor Busse in the center facing Marshals Zhukov and Koniev and *3ʳᵈ Panzer* Army under *Generaloberst* Hasso von Manteuffel facing primarily Rokossovsky to the north.[995]

Like a plague of locusts the unit grew from 13,000 to 20,000 personnel within a week, living off the land and leaving a barren wasteland in their wake after stripping the countryside of crops, animals, and food stockpiles. It was not until 13 April 1945 that the newly, yet partially, reorganized Free Russian Army under Vlasov actually saw sporadic combat, despite the fact that many of the members were battle hardened veterans fighting with the Germans since 1941. Bunyachenko led the 1ˢᵗ Division into the breach over the scattered bodies of their German and Free Russian predecessors, supported by an artillery barrage but lacking adequate air support. Bunyachenko saw that no further progress could be made without reinforcements and a flanking maneuver by the available German units. The German commander, *Generaloberst* Theodor Busse had no air support to offer since their primary air support unit, *STG-2 "Immelmann"* was grounded due to a fuel shortage.[996]

The 2ⁿᵈ Vlasov Division was still moving forward to its objectives at Muensingen from their base at Heuberg (with Trukhin remaining behind with the staff) and was too far away to lend credible support to Bunyachenko. The Free Russians had two major problems; the wire and fixed fortifications in the Soviet defenses could not be breached without armor and air support, and Bunyachenko understood Busse's method of attack; he was going to use up the remaining Free Russians as cannon fodder to support his drive. Bunyachenko countered by ordering his troops back to their starting positions in order to consolidate and reorganize the remaining 17,000 men. By the time they started again Bunyachenko hoped to have the materiel and air support he was promised, and he was still dealing with the growing insurgency problem that met him everywhere.

The Germans were less interested in the Russian infantry as their artillery, which was ordered to remain behind by the *275ᵗʰ Infanterie* Division until Bunyachenko countermanded the order and brought the guns along with his division to Cottbus, East Prussia. He had recently received orders from *Generalfeldmarschall* Ferdinand Schoerner to place his division in the rear area security position to act as a springboard, ready to launch into the Red Army units that may penetrate German lines. This arrangement suited Bunyachenko (who was nursing a broken leg) to some degree, as it would allow him to personally control his artillery and direct his fire to support his advance. However, Bunyachenko had also assumed control of the Ukrainians, and he made it clear that he would answer only to Vlasov, and no one else. The German *9ᵗʰ Armee,* formerly under the command of *Generalfeldmarschall* Walther Model had always maintained a level of high respect for and cordiality with the Free Russians, especially the 2ⁿᵈ Ukrainian Division ever since the Demyansk operation. Bunyachenko hoped that this benevolent feeling had not been lost.

The 1st Vlasov Division reached Hoyerswerda, where Bunyachenko received a radio message from Schoerner to take his unit to Kosel, six kilometers northwest of Niesky, but Bunyachenko ignored the directive. Instead, he took the division to Kamenz, due west of their present position where they received the order to embark by rail to Czechoslovakia. Fearing deception and possible annihilation, rather than board the train, Bunyachenko decided to force march his men to their next destination to give them a fighting chance.[997] On 22 April they reached Bad Schandau and received another order from Schoerner delivered in person by a *Major* Neuner, ordering Bunyachenko to meet the Field Marshal at Haida on 24 April at 1700 hours. Bunyachenko was unable to make the appointment, instead sending Captain Kostyenko of the Reconnaissance Company, who informed Schoerner that his general had been in an auto accident, which was probably a ruse since the leg had been broken for perhaps three weeks.

Schoerner sent his emissary, *Brigadegeneral* von Natzmer to persuade (if not order) Bunyachenko into the fight, abandoning his provisions and relying upon food and ammunition from German units along the way. Bunyachenko knew better, as he had played that game before and he knew that German soldiers were unable to receive even the bare essentials for themselves, let alone supply his division. Germans and Free Russians soon clashed over stockpiles and a group of Germans were found shot. Upon receiving this information Schoerner had finally had enough, and he went to meet Bunyachenko on the march into Czechoslovakia bearing vodka and cigars. Schoerner left after being totally frustrated with the Russian general and receiving no firm commitment. It may be assumed that Bunyachenko did not want his force drawn into a lengthy protracted battle with the Soviets, since it would upset his chances of surrendering to either the Americans (closing on Muensingen) or the British, with whom they wanted to establish their claims of a new Russian government friendly to the Western Allied cause. However, Schoerner still had the 2nd Ukrainian Division in his pocket.

As the situation deteriorated the 2nd Ukrainian Division (*Wehrmacht Heer* and not *SS* comprised of converted guerrillas for the most part) fought as an isolated unit without support, weapons, and ammunition resupply, and the men captured by the Soviets were immediately executed. The commander of the division, a Colonel Diachenko along with his unit eventually ceased to exist. The 1st Ukrainian Division (*Heer*) under General Shandruk proved more fortunate, since it was shifted south to fill the gaps left by the deserting Hungarian units, eventually standing alone to stem the advance of an entire Red Army Corps. They defended with tenacity and courage, buying time for their German comrades to fall back and establish a strong defensive position in the defense of Budapest from December 1944 until the city fell on 14 February 1945.[998] The units included elements of *1st Waffen SS Panzer* Division *"Leibstandarte"* and *2nd Waffen SS* Division *"Das Reich"* that were part of Josef "Sepp" Dietrich's *6th SS Panzer Armee*. They fought to exhaustion against Soviet and partisan forces in some of the toughest fighting since Stalingrad and Kursk, and many of Germany's best perished on the road to Budapest. One of the survivors was a Knight's Cross and Oak Leaves recipient, *Oberfeldwebel* Albert Kerscher, a veteran *Tiger* tank commander of Kursk with *Panzerabteilung 502 "Schwere"* who was present at the Budapest defense:

> The fighting was intense and the casualties were high. My unit had the *Koenigstiger*[999] and we were constantly engaged with superior Soviet armored forces. We destroyed over sixty enemy tanks, just my four tank platoon, and were out of ammunition. I remember the Russian allies who supported us, and they

fought with great courage. I had served with *"Das Reich"* all along and could compare the Russians and Ukrainians with our own troops. There was no appreciable difference in their overall fighting quality. When it came to combating partisans the Ukrainians were perhaps the best and most ready to commit their forces, especially when fighting with a German unit that they felt appreciated them. I am glad that we did not have to fight against them.[1000]

Shandruk's 1st Ukrainian Division fought even as it was trying to establish contact with the British and Americans, where Shandruk convinced them that his unit was actually Polish since it still bore the name *"Galizische,"*[1001] which prevented their being handed over to the Soviets. This ruse worked, since the Western Allies through Churchill and Roosevelt had a special fondness for Poland and had made the stipulation during the Yalta Conference that the country was to have free elections once the war ended, and Galicians were Poles of Russian origin who had been Polish citizens until 1939 when they fell under the Soviet partition of Poland. This fact gave them refugee status as internees instead of POWs and deportees, and the Soviet demand that they be handed over was refused based upon the Geneva and Hague Conventions and the tenants of Yalta.

Events were developing around the Free Russian units that were to force their hand, since on 18 April 1945 orders were issued for the 2nd Vlasov Division to defend Linz, Austria. The unit marched on three separate routes to the railhead in order to arrive quickly, with the remaining brigades and auxiliaries to support either Schoerner or *Generaloberst* Lothar Rendulic, who was holding the Red Army back on the frontiers of Austria while outnumbered twelve to one. During the march the 2nd Vlasov Division came across an *SS* detachment force marching Russian POWs across a field. The prisoners broke ranks to join their fellow Russians and were fired upon by the *SS*, who were in turn gunned down by Vlasov's men. The scene was apparently one of Dantean proportions, and a total battle of annihilation was prevented by the arrival of Vlasov and Herre who diffused the situation.

On 1 May Trukhin and the forward units of the 2nd Division arrived at Linz with the remainder still moving through central Czechoslovakia. Unknown to them until a few days later Schoerner had issued orders to his forces under Hermann Hoth to locate, surround, and disarm or destroy the Vlasov units the day before Trukhin arrived in Linz. This prompted Vlasov to meet with Schoerner, and he convinced the zealot to rescind the order, stating that the Western Allies may see a future in fighting the Soviets if there was an intact and viable Free Russian Army in the field ready to support a drive against the Red Army. Schoerner bought into the thinking and rescinded the order.[1002]

Trukhin and his men remained in place until 4 May, when they learned from an American unit commander arriving under a white flag that their fate was being decided. Trukhin returned to Budweis and awaited the decision, which came on 6 May; the Free Russians would cross into the American zone into captivity. Trukhin, who was suspicious and would not commit himself until Vlasov gave the word waited a full day before deciding to drive to Prague with Romashkin and Shapovalov to meet with Vlasov, yet a Soviet road guard apprehended them. They learned that Boyarkin had been captured and hanged just as Shopovalov was taken from the vehicle and shot, while Trukhin was sent to Moscow.[1003] Romashkin was later liberated by the 1st Vlasov Division as it passed through the town during the retreat. During this period the men in Budweis waited for Trukhin to return, and when he did not arrive chaos erupted, since most of the men in the chain of command were either swinging from trees or shot in the back of the neck. Only two men survived from Sveryev's command staff, and of the two a Captain Tvardiyevich reported to Vlasov what had happened to the 2ⁿᵈ Division.

Of the Free Russian forces in Italy, the 162ⁿᵈ Turkic Division under *Generalleutnant* Rolf von Heygendorff and their German allies had been fighting delaying actions around Padua, facing off with the American forces under Lieutenant General Mark Clark[1004] and former Italian soldiers allied with partisans that had been hammering away at the German *10ᵗʰ Armee*, successfully penetrating the Gustav Line. Heygendorff's men understood their pending fate after one of their soldiers returned from an extended leave of absence as a Soviet prisoner. The man was an Azerbaijani who was captured near Rome by an American unit and subsequently handed over to the Soviets, and instead of being shot he was sent to a labor camp in Siberia. The fortunate man was then conscripted and sent back to the front in the Red Army in November 1944, fighting in the Kurland where he escaped again, somehow managing to make his way to Italy and rejoining his unit. With this news spreading like small pox the Free Russians decided that the Americans could not be trusted, and this explains their final fanatical stand at Padua that had been typically restricted to *Waffen SS* and *Fallschirmjaeger* units.

Heygendorff was a thinker, and he issued civilian clothes and documents to all of the troops, stating in writing that they had been part of a labor detail and not a fighting unit, just in case they should end up in Soviet hands. He also requested through Army Group South that the men be considered in any negotiations with the British and Americans, since they were part of a German Army, not an independent Russian force such as Vlasov's. The German officers were separated from their men after capture by the Americans, and as the Soviets arrived to take custody of their "traitors" many of the men committed suicide, with some of the *mullahs* resorting to self-immolation in protest. Those who were captured and failed to jump train or from the ships at Odessa disappeared forever.

Vlasov, Zhilenkov, Malyshkin, Boyarski, and German *General* Heinrich Aschenbrenner had previously met with Strik-Strikfeldt in Pomerania, where it was decided that Vlasov would surrender to the Americans or British as soon as possible before the Germans turned their guns on them again. Strik-Strikfeldt (who spoke English, French, Russian as well as German) decided to escort the Free Russians, accompanied by Malyshkin to the Americans, whom he believed would be more receptive to the arrangement. Had the German officer known of the Yalta Conference and the deal made between the three major allies he would have thought quite differently.

Meanwhile, Vlasov had located Bunyachenko, who told him of the meeting he had with the senior Czech officers attacking German units. Bunyachenko was told and given a signed document, stating that any Russian residing with them would find a safe homeland in the new Czech Republic, if the Czech nationalists secured the country before the Red Army arrived to link up with the Czech Communist guerrillas. Vlasov could not support the decision, but he allowed Bunyachenko to strike whatever deal he could for his men. Bunyachenko took his men to Prague and captured dozens of German aircraft as well as the main airport, often fighting partisans and *Waffen SS* formations alike while losing 300 men in the process.[1005] However, this dream would never materialize, since Eisenhower agreed to halt his forces at the Karlsbad-Pils-Budweis line at the request of Stalin on 4 May 1945, sealing the fate of every Russian, German, and Czech nationalist in the country. As soon as the firing subsided the Czech Communists proclaimed a Communist state allied with the Soviet Union, and again fighting broke out between Czech nationalists and Communists, with the retreating Germans and Free Russians caught in the cross-fire.

The new Czech government was declared following a vote that surprised no one, given the fact that eight out of the twelve presiding members were Communists, and Bunyachenko was informed that Jodl had signed the Unconditional Surrender on 7 May, effective immediately.[1006] He was also informed by a Soviet political commissar that Stalin was waiting to welcome him and his men back into the Red Army, so could they wait one more day? The over burdened Bunyachenko was then informed by the Czech nationalists that his deal was null and void since the Americans discontinued their advance. Bunyachenko finally replied to the political commissar (who arrived by parachute), telling him to "go to hell" and ordering a mass evacuation westward, every man for himself.

Later that day the 1st Vlasov Division found itself marching (or running) alongside *Wehrmacht Heer* and *Waffen SS* formations with whom they had just been fighting with *and against*, all of them headed west. The Czechs who had supported the Free Russians turned against them, guiding Soviet forces to intercept them en-route. On 10 May 1945 the marathon to freedom came to an end when the columns came across an American reconnaissance unit. The Americans, upon seeing Vlasov's Army thought they were a Red Army unit that had traveled too far west or had become lost, and the commanding officer asked the Russian officers to dinner.[1007]

Strik-Strikfeldt and Malyshkin surrendered to an American armored unit of the U.S. VII Army. The two men were blindfolded and taken to division headquarters where they were interviewed by a Lieutenant Colonel Snyder, who had "never heard of Vlasov or his army." They were brought to General Alexander Patch,[1008] U.S. VII Army commander who was accompanied by an interpreter named Artamanov.[1009] Through the dialogue Malyshkin had to explain why thousands of Russians in German uniforms were captured fighting in the west. He told patch that they were not part of Vlasov's forces and he was supported by Strik-Strikfeldt. Malyshkin brought up the League of Nations Charter on political asylum and recited history in which Americans had fought against tyranny and even supported anti-Communist actions. Patch listened with genuine interest, and citing the proviso of protocol told the men he would pass their request through to General Eisenhower.

The next day Patch looked at the men and told them that Eisenhower had no authority in the mater; it would be decided by Washington.[1010] He offered condolences as a fellow soldier and told them that he personally supported them and would do whatever he could. During this period the commander of the 2nd U.S. Armored Corps, General Kennedy stated that "he was prepared to cover Maltsev's (aviation) group and would not hand them over to the Soviets...he would do so on his own responsibility and would not report it to his superiors."[1011] This promise could not be kept. By 8 May 1945 Germany had officially surrendered and all of the Vlasov soldiers surviving the war and in retreat were interned in British and American POW camps. One war was over, but another and more dangerous contest was just beginning for the Free Russians. During this period Vlasov had been personally referred by Aschenbrenner to American General George S. Patton, Jr.,[1012] commander of the 3rd U.S. Army. Patton initially agreed to take the Vlasov men and protect them from the

Soviets, but the next day word came that Patton had rescinded; situations beyond his control and an order from Eisenhower prevented him from honoring the request.

With all of the focus being placed upon the ground units of the Free Russian Government, historians and the wartime belligerents tend to overlook the role of the Free Russian Air Force, a separate entity under the direction of Colonel Maltsev. On 4 May a *Leutnant* Buschmann of the air division landed in a Fiesler *Storch* and met with Vlasov. The debate was over the fate of the air service as well as the ground personnel, where Vlasov had offered to allow himself to be handed over to the Soviets if his men were spared extradition. Maltsev was consulted, and the colonel said that Vlasov should do what he could to support the cause. Vlasov spoke with one of his pilots, Captain Antilevski, who had defected some time before.[1013] Antilevski had the airplane, fuel, and flight plan to take Vlasov to Spain if he wished, but Vlasov would not abandon his men when they needed him most. Another meeting between Vlasov and the squadron leader of the Free Russian fighters, Lieutenant Colonel Leonidas Maximciuc clarified the options:

> When I met with Vlasov he said that the options were simple; the men who were Romanian or had been living in Romania could either destroy their uniforms and just assimilate into the population, or they could come west and surrender to the British and Americans, as he was doing. I returned to the unit, destroyed all of the records and gave the men their options. Then we disbanded the unit.[1014]

Vlasov continued to move west with the men of the 1ˢᵗ Division, and on 19 May he met with General Patch personally. Vlasov offered himself as a sacrifice to the Red Army if his men could remain in American captivity, and Patch understood and respected the Russian leader's concern for his men. Patch made Vlasov the same promise he made to Malyshkin, that we would do his best. Vlasov learned that Bunyachenko and about 15,000 of the survivors were in Schluesselburg (Trukhin had 20,000 in Czechoslovakia) where Soviet partisans had been parachuted as a forward reconnaissance force to support the Red Army advance, so an American Captain named "Donahue" escorted the general through the town.[1015] There was a lengthy interrogation (the details of which are unknown) in which Donahue reported that the Russian general was quite comfortable with his position as long as his men were cared for. The captain promised to protect Vlasov, who was quartered in the medieval castle until higher authority had a chance to meet with him. The next morning saw Donahue being tested at his word as Red Army trucks and troops poured into the streets.[1016]

Vlasov was offered assistance to escape in disguise due to his detailed knowledge of the Soviet military and its tactics and strategies, not unlike so many German officers with similar experience. Vlasov continued to refuse these gestures or abandon his men, instead requesting that in the light of international law he and his men should stand before an international tribunal to explain their actions. Donahue radioed Vlasov and gave him the grave news; the United States would not allow the "Vlasov Legion" into the American zone of occupation, and the transporting of prisoners to Pilsen and Plattling in Bavaria eventually saw over 4,000 of Vlasov's troops deposited there.[1017]

The end result was that most of the men of both the 1ˢᵗ and 2ⁿᵈ Vlasov Divisions were interned by the Americans and British and then turned over to the Red Army, and those who did not escape the transport were tried and executed. Vlasov was handed over on 12 May 1945 along with thousands of his men. Of these, Pannwitz and 30,000 Cossacks were also turned over, since the Soviet argument that they were an *SS* unit paid off, which was not legally true. Pannwitz was even on the same aircraft to Moscow via Vienna with Ferdinand Schoerner and his wife, and was amazingly well treated.[1018] However, the Western Allies also complied with an illegal request offered by Stalin. The Soviet dictator wanted all former Russian and Soviet citizens who had emigrated to other nations or been captured during the war as POWs or for forced labor returned as traitors, especially those whom had fought as German allies, such as the Cossack leaders Kulakov and Peter Krasnow, both former White Russian anti-Bolshevik leaders during the Civil War. All of the senior leaders were tortured, tried, and executed. Potentially millions of people who had fled the Bolshevik Revolution were threatened to be returned, although this was not part of the compulsory repatriation agreement reached at the Yalta Conference.[1019] An interesting chronicle regarding the treatment of a Soviet lieutenant, wounded severely with three fingers on one hand missing and captured at Orel in October 1941 and repatriated, proves how ruthless Stalin could be towards his own people. As cited by Overy:

How it happened that I, an officer, a candidate for Party membership, failed to shoot myself as instructed and how I let myself be taken prisoner, I cannot explain. Perhaps the acute pain in my hand held me back, or maybe the utter exhaustion after eleven days of uninterrupted fighting had rendered me completely apathetic...[1020]

This officer escaped to the west, following a demeaning return, forced labor, and threatened with execution. According to Overy's research:

Between 1945 and 1947, when the program was completed, some 2,272,000 Soviet citizens were returned by the Western Allies to their homeland, many of them from as far afield as prisoner of war camps on the American west coast. Altogether, 5,457,856 were repatriated by 1953. Those found guilty of collaboration with the enemy, real or imagined, were sent to the revolutionary Tribunal in Frankfurt an der Oder, where they were sentenced to be shot or to periods of forced labor. It has been estimated by Soviet historians that around one-fifth of all those who returned were executed or sentenced to the maximum twenty-five years in the Gulag. Others were sent to work with forced labor units rebuilding the Soviet infrastructure or to exile in Siberia. Around three million men and women were sentenced to terms in the camps.[1021]

Thousands of brave men dedicated to fighting not for Hitler and National Socialism, but against what they perceived to be as an illegal and tyrannical regime in their homelands were allowed to be forcibly repatriated against their will. This occurred in many countries throughout Europe, including neutral Sweden and the United States. These decisions witnessed these soldiers facing certain hardship if not death, in clear violation of both international law and even the most loosely interpreted tenants of the Yalta Agreement of 11 February 1945. The integrity of the Western Allies would be forever questioned when the subject of honoring asylum was granted by those fleeing Communist tyranny.

The end result of the German efforts were the creation of a Free Russian Army, complete with its own air force, artillery, cavalry, anti-partisan and reconnaissance units. The final wartime numbers appear to be thus: 600,000 former Soviets serving in uniform with the *Wehrmacht* and *Waffen SS*, nearly 60,000 with the *Luftwaffe*, and 15,000 serving in the *Kriegsmarine*. These figures do not include the tens of thousands more who served as civilian guerrillas and scouts, or those serving in non-combat oriented support fields such as garrison, guard, and sentry duties.[1022] Unfortunately for the hundreds of thousands of men who risked their lives for a greater cause, Hitler and his associates never intended to honor any of the agreements, effectively throwing away a golden opportunity. Hitler's plans for the future of Europe did not include the establishment of any independent governments, including the Free Russians or any of the non-Aryan races represented in the following matrix:

1-*Reichkommissariats*-formerly occupied areas governed from Berlin by a regional *Reichskommissar* and supported by military garrisons. These regions included all of the Soviet Union and the Baltic States.

2-Greater German *Reich*-nations occupied and absorbed into the Third *Reich* as proper parts of Germany such as France, Norway, Morocco, Algeria, Tunisia and Denmark.

3-Satellite States-primarily those nations allied to Germany through convenience such as Romania, Hungary, Finland and Bulgaria.

4-Annexed/Subjugated States-these include Austria, Yugoslavia, Croatia, Crete, Moravia, Bohemia, Sudetenland Poland (including Danzig-West Prussia/ Wartheland), Belgium (Wallonia/Flanders and Alsace-Lorraine), Luxembourg, Crimea and Greece.

5-Independent Neutral States- including Spain, Slovakia, Portugal, Switzerland and Sweden.

6-Ideologically Acceptable States-nations of Germanic origin. Holland was the only candidate.

7-States Under Guidance-This refers mainly to nations to immense or too far away to effectively govern properly, but would assist in the maintenance of the Greater *Reich* proper, such as Great Britain, Italy, Libya, Cyprus and other smaller islands in the Mediterranean formerly under British control.

8-Unassigned Border States-designed as buffer states no worth the time and expense of governing properly, such as eastern Finland and Lapland.

It was this overall land distribution plan that assisted Hitler in accepting the recruitment of the *Freiwilligen* within the German ranks, with the *SS* receiving the best if not the majority of the international representation. Men from Russia, Ukraine, Georgia, the Caucasus, Moldavia, Romania, Hungary, Italy, Finland, Norway,[1023] Holland,[1024] Belgium,[1025] Latvia, Lithuania, Greece, Denmark,[1026] Spain, Estonia, Croatia, Serbia, Albania, Galicia, Iceland, Switzerland, France, and even fifty-one British soldiers would serve within the ranks of the *Waffen SS*. Had Hitler been less prejudiced, more intelligent, and more enlightened he would have more than likely achieved his united Europe, a dream that seems to only become feasible in the last decade.

In a similar method of conformity, Himmler understood that in order to increase the ranks of the *Waffen SS* there would have to be an attitude adjustment among the Germans towards the target audiences. The same treatment meted out in Poland and Russia would not have had a positive result in Holland and Denmark. However, most of Himmler's concerns regarding his issuing orders to his recruiters and administrators were not well founded; the entire German attitude among the military reflected the opinion of German society as a whole: Western Europeans were placed in a different social and racial category from Eastern Europeans, and this was reflected in their treatment of the respective populations. As stated by Karl Wolff:

> During the early days it was important to place a humane and very caring face on the recruiting effort. I spoke with Himmler about the eventual expansion of the *SS* in general, and he stated that: "we will concern ourselves with the *Waffen SS*," as this was 1941, "and fill out the ranks with those men we know to be suitable. I would prefer to keep the *SD* and *Gestapo* completely German, for security, you understand." Himmler was dedicated to creating a greater Germanic Community, with the *SS* being seen as the pinnacle of this new order. As you well know, there was some measure of success.[1027]

This attitude revision was also quite evident in the handling of the partisan and guerrilla problem in the west as opposed to the east. Himmler even went so far as to issue orders that there was to be no theft, public drunkenness, or rude behavior in general during the occupation of the targeted Western European nations, stating that they "had come as 'protectors' rather than as 'conquerors.'"[1028] They were also ordered to "respect the lives, property, political and religious opinions of the people." *SS* men were advised to "speak slowly and clearly" in German, not to "shout or order people about," and to be patient with the expected "slow and reserved" responses.[1029] Such considerations were almost unknown in the east.

The appeal of the *SS* has been explained quite eloquently by Mark P. Gingerich. He states in his article that the pro-fascist segments, as well as the average man in the occupied nations saw in the *SS* the elite of Germany, and therefore the best in Europe as early as 1940, very early in the days of the *Waffen SS*.[1030] Association with the *SS* was a certain way out of a possible future as a common laborer, as well as a way of earning a living and having a chance at a career. With German victories electrifying Europe and the smart appearance of the troops, the young men of Europe were easily seduced. It is ironic that due to a combination of language barriers and simple misunderstandings, as well as misrepresentations by recruiters, many of the men who joined the *Waffen SS* were unaware that they were joining for a long-term hitch in a "German Foreign Legion." Those who clarified their positions with the *SS* administration were allowed to serve a few months and return home. This benevolent atmosphere would become part of the distant past by 1943.

Another problem arising was that all branches of the German military (with exception to the *Luftwaffe*) stated their rights and requirements to certain percentages of the qualifying populations for induction. Considering the population density of the various nations, as well as the strict racial purity requirements at the time, Gottlob Berger "...believed the *Waffen SS* would not be able to obtain 18,000 men yearly (the number Himmler believed necessary following *Operation Barbarossa*), even if the 1939 ratios were not changed because of the limited pool of manpower."[1031] The same problem that plagued the German counterinsurgency recruiting effort throughout Europe had its origins in the Western European recruiting drive; the constant conflict over which branch of service had the authority and jurisdiction to function and recruit within the various territories placed the *SD, Waffen SS*, and *Wehrmacht* at constant odds with each other. Army and *Waffen SS* commanders and recruiters would often be at odds over which department had authority within a specific region, and the tensions mounted as the closing dates for quotas neared. It was common for the German equivalent of Royal Navy press gangs to simply take the men they needed later in the war, as stated by Hans Hossfelder:

> I remember in 1940 when I joined; the difference from that time, to say 1943, or even later. I remember men being in the unit (*"Das Reich"*) who could not only not speak German, but often thought they were being taken for forced labor. There was one man in particular whom we grabbed in Luxembourg in 1944 who was astonished that, instead of shooting him we gave him a uniform and a rifle. He immediately began fumbling with the weapon and accidentally shot another man who was standing nearby. The wounded man was all right, only slightly wounded. This was indicative of how low we had sunk; we were not the same *Waffen SS* of legend. I believe that this situation was symptomatic of the eventual destruction of Germany and the best Germany had. It was just our time.[1032]

According to Gingerich, the inaccuracies in record keeping and the constant political in fighting between the various military branches, as well as the irregular treatment of *Freiwilligen* troops constituted a tenuous situation at best. Gingerich states quite accurately that, "it is clear that in terms of manpower goals, the recruitment of Germanic volunteers in the period before *Barbarossa* was a failure."[1033] This is in spite of the fact that, also according to Gingerich:

> The overall racial quality of the Germanic volunteers inducted into the *Waffen SS*...(that) according to Berger, with the sole exception of the Flemish, on average 25-30% of the Germanic applicants were determined to be racially and physically suitable for service in the *Waffen SS*, a higher figure than that reached in Germany itself."[1034]

As also stated by Gingerich, the political and military appeal of the *Waffen SS* cannot be underestimated, and it was perhaps this initial attempt at inducement that witnessed the recruiting drive mushroom into the eventual enlistment of over 600,000 non-Germans within the ranks; an expansion that fueled the concept of an ever expanding auxiliary force within the *Wehrmacht* proper. The Germans had the opportunity, through the humane and just treatment of all the subject peoples to defeat Communism and offer better terms to the Western Allies. Had the success of the *SS* recruiting program after 1941 been extended to the target populations in the Soviet Union and Balkans this would have been undeniable. The fact that this was not even seriously considered until 1942, and then only by a few officers is beyond any doubt the greatest contributing factor to the loss of the *Wehrmacht's* (and Germany's) perceived legitimacy as a liberation force as opposed to an oppressive occupation force.

In this simple abandonment of logic *Nazi* Germany threw away its best and last chance for victory in the east. The fact that Hitler knew the score was stated in a meeting in the *Wolfschanze* in 1944, where he stated that "including anti-Bolshevik Russians of Aryan ethnicity will prove crucial in undermining support for Stalin and the Red Army."[1035] Adoption of a more lucid policy would have at the very least offered a better bargaining position for a negotiated peace later. The Soviets were well aware of the German methods of recruiting their countrymen. The next chapter will evaluate how the Soviets attempted to reduce the German efforts and establish a new doctrine for partisan support, a move that would define irregular warfare for the rest of this century.

14

The Soviet Response

*It is well known that when you do anything, unless
you understand its actual circumstances, its nature
and its relations to other things, You will not know
the laws governing it, or be able to do it well.*
- Mao Tse Tung
December 1936.

During the period 1942-43 Soviet counter-propaganda stated that Vlasov had obviously been killed, and his supposed collaboration with the Germans were outright lies by Hitler and Goebbels. Many Russians believed this, and according to Captain Koronov:

> People could not believe that a man such as Vlasov could become a traitor to Russia. However, this reality became known after Vlasov, as well as *General* Gersdorff and others broadcast a speech. He spoke about Stalin, the crimes he had committed, the failures of the Communists to keep their promises to the people, and that Russians should all consider themselves only "Russians" and not "Soviets." It had a tremendous effect on those already tired of the system, and probably contributed to the defections experienced in many units.[1036]

The broadcast mentioned was coordinated through Stauffenberg and Tresckow and occurred on 26 February 1943 at Smolensk over German short wave radio and delivered in Russian. Vlasov dismissed the possibility that Germany could enslave the Russian people due to the sheer size of the country. He also outlined every act of domestic terror Stalin and his deputies had committed against the people, and mentioned the prospect of free independent states under German rule, without promising what he could not deliver. Stalin's response is not recorded in the documents to date.

The Soviets were also highly active in the recruiting of foreign nationals in the fight against Germany. The Poles were also targeted by the Soviets for indoctrination, as were the peoples of the Baltic States and the Balkans. These operations fell under the direct command of a General Kubalov, military assistant to Levrenti Beria, the paranoid sadistic head of the *NKVD*. Kubalov's troops entered the various regions with a two fold mission; recruit and support anti-German groups into the Soviet system, and locate and exterminate all anti-Communist factions whether they were pro-German or not. Others involved in this methodical operation were Merkulov, who headed the *NKGB* and was succeeded by Viktor Abakumov, the former head of *Smersh* in 1946; Serov (Kubalov's adjutant, and Naum Etingon (alias General Kotov), the planner behind the Leon Trotsky assassination in Mexico. These men would rise to prominence under Stalin's successors in the post-war world with exception of Beria, who would be executed for treason shortly after Stalin's death.

The counter-guerrilla division of the *NKVD* was marginally effective and it eventually turned out to counterproductive, due to their acts of brutality against the people they intended to convert. Their actions alone drove thousands of Eastern Europeans into the German camp, including large numbers of Don and Kuban Cossacks. In many cases the first Soviet representative a foreign village saw was the *NKVD* performing their not so delicate rituals, incensing the population and convincing them that perhaps the Germans were in fact a liberation force. The *NKVD* infiltration within partisan units was not always appreciated, since many of the irregulars were not Communist supporters, or were fighting for a cause separate from Moscow's agenda, and deplored the rigid conformity and strict authority.[1037] The Germans managed to exploit these facts successfully on many occasions, and the mass refugee problems from 1944-45 were in many cases created by the fear of a Soviet presence.[1038]

Soviet partisan recruitment efforts were a well-constructed and highly structured organization by late 1942, complete with a Central Staff overseen by the Supreme Soviet High Command (*Stavka*). Under the High Command was the Partisan Directorate commanded by General P.K. Ponomarenko from 1942-44 that controlled the subordinate units and their operations, both politically and militarily, under the *NKVD-NKGB* and *GRU*. Under this direction the partisans would advance ahead of the Red Army following the Battle of Kursk in August 1943.[1039] Their missions would be to penetrate behind German lines by various methods of insertion, including parachutes, link up with other friendly resistance forces and attempt to control their operations by offering the Red Army logistical and material support. This method became highly effective throughout Eastern Europe and laid the groundwork for the brush fires of local resistance that had been dormant for several years during the German occupation.

Following these advance partisan units were the extermination squads similar to the *Einsatzgruppe* method, specially detailed to eliminate "liberated" Soviet prisoners who had been in German captivity, supported by Stalin's order No. 270 in 1941, as well as German stragglers and POWs, collaborators, and others deemed a "security risk" or "traitors."[1040] The greatest collective entity of partisans were the Special Assault Divisions under Kubalov, which were specially detailed to combat anti-Communist and nationalist partisans and guerrillas. These actions often divided the partisan camps, since several partisans may have been fighting in the same unit, but for different reasons. Mass defections to the German cause were common, as seen in the swelling of the ranks of Vlasov's Free Russian Army once these terror units entered specific areas.

Vlasov had substantial support from the German officer corps for the creation of his unit for political and propaganda value, if not for the potential military benefits. Such support came from Oskar Niedermayer in September 1943.[1041] Niedermayer, a colleague and supporter of the Lettow-Vorbeck concept from the First World War[1042] had responded to the partisan uprisings by issuing order Nr. 325 on 16 October 1942, regarding dealing with partisans, guerrillas, and Communist Party members. The order was issued to the *Verteitigung*

Kommissariat (Defense Commissars) near Moscow. Niedermayer was instrumental in forming the Persian *Freiwilligen* (in Iran)[1043] from 17 January-16 April 1942 and the *"Turkisches" Freiwilligen* Division *Nr. 162* in Neuhammer on 31 May-27-September 1943. [1044] The Turkish unit was transferred to Udine on 29 September 1943 and was in action through 15 November of that year at the battles of Manfacone, Planina, Laibach, Sesana, and Lubliana-Triest in Italy through 14 January 1944.[1045]

The Baltic States were highly targeted by the Soviets, and the Lithuanian, Estonian and Latvian experience under both German and Soviet domination is crucial in the overall analysis. The Lithuanians had celebrated the lifting of the Soviet yoke following the German invasion of June 1941, and Hitler did little to interfere with the established local governments that had been at least neutral if not supportive of German policy. Germany exploited the hatred of Communism by the Lithuanians, creating an impressive military and guerrilla force to supplement their Army Group North by 1943. Of all the nations that supplied *Freiwilligen* to the *Wehrmacht* and *Waffen SS,* the Lithuanians, Estonians and Latvians proved to be some of the most overall resilient, combat effective, politically reliable and proficient troops, although they were also some of the most ruthless in dealing with their local Jewish populations. The soldiers within their ranks were trained as anti-Soviet partisan hunters and were organized into their own independent *SS* formations, such as the two Latvian units; the *15ᵗʰ Waffen Grenadier* Division *der SS "Lettische" Nr. 1,* and *19ᵗʰ Waffen Grenadier* Division *der SS "Lettische" Nr. 2.* The Estonians were formed into the *20ᵗʰ Waffen Grenadier* Division *der SS "Estnische Nr. 1,"* which had an impressive combat record. These units were highly respected by the Red Army and were held in high regard along with *"Wiking"* and *"Wallonien"* as some the best foreign *SS* units, which speaks volumes about their capabilities. All of these Baltic units were eventually thrown into the meat grinder of the Kurland defense in the attempt to stop the Red Army from encircling an entire army in late 1944 to May 1945 under *Generalfeldmarschall* Ferdinand Schoerner, and they were completely decimated. The Soviets executed every man captured (and in some reports their entire families) for fighting in German uniforms.

The Soviets were gaining valuable experience in the realm of unconventional warfare and irregular command and control capabilities, eventually eclipsing the Germans in their methodology and success rates despite the obvious flaws in their system. This experience would become the nucleus for the exporting of insurgency forces and actively supporting left-wing guerrillas throughout the Third World for decades to come, primarily through Moscow supported proxy client states. The Cold War would be made possible as much by this experience in clandestine warfare as the nuclear arms race, since small wars and insurgencies would become the hallmark of the struggle between eastern and western global domination. The Western Allies were well aware of the Soviet methods regarding the utilization of partisans and guerrillas, and the fledgling special operations forces of the British and Americans carved out of the World War II experience would come into their own during the post-war era, by studying the German and Soviet methods, and analyzing the cause and effect of direct, indirect, clandestine military and psychological operations.

It is amazing to realize that, despite the cornucopia of information supplied by the Germans and Communist defectors that created the study (of which one, KGB defector Igor Orlov[1046] is specifically mentioned in the work and is the subject of several books on Cold War espionage), the American military establishment, entrenched in the same myopic tunnel vision that handicapped the Germans were the slowest to respond in a positive and effective nature to the insurgencies which erupted around the globe on their watch. Part of this study will examine the myopia of the conventional theorists; self appointed intellectuals and gifted strategists who were opposed to the creation of special warfare units, even after certain crises had presented themselves, such as the Chinese Revolution, Korean War, Suez Crisis, Congo Crisis, Malay Emergency, the Cuban Revolution and the rise of Fidel Castro, the unstable Central and South American governments and the Iranian Revolutions replacing Mosadeq and later overthrowing the Shah.

The creation of these units have their history in the Office of Strategic Services, much in the way that the Special Air Service had its roots in the Western Desert campaign in North Africa under David Stirling, although not originally created as a counterinsurgency support branch. It may be far reaching to posture (although the risk will be taken) that, had the Germans adopted a similar doctrine regarding counterinsurgency between the world wars and abandoned the irrational racial policy based upon "social Darwinism" and other "scientific" rhetoric espoused by Chamberlain, Gobineau, de Lapouge, Grant, Gumplowicz and Lenz, all of which formed the basis for Hitler's racial beliefs published in *Mein Kampf*,[1047] Hitler would have had more than a good chance of winning the war against Stalin. If one were to theorize even further, it could even be stated that the possibility of a separate peace being negotiated with Stalin would have not been unlikely, due to the potential for massive revolts and defections within the Soviet Union. This would have forced the Western Allies to re-evaluate their commitment to the war effort, analyze the costs and estimate the overall feasibility of continuing the war against not only an increased German force coming from the east, but the potential infusion of millions of Russians and Eastern European allies swelling the German ranks.

It would seem feasible that, once the Western Allies abandoned the attempt to defeat Germany in Europe, Hitler would have either successfully captured the Suez Canal and driven on to the Persian oil fields, or removed his forces from Africa under a mutually satisfactory agreement. At the very least this agreement would have allowed the British and Americans to shift the weight of their military and economic power to the Pacific Theater of Operations. Had this been accomplished, Japan would have been inundated by sheer weight of numbers, and the dropping of the two atomic bombs on Hiroshima and Nagasaki may have never occurred. At the very least there would have never been a Cold War as we have come to understand it.

Hitler's warped agenda is beyond question the greatest detriment to the potential German military victory in Europe. The greatest mistakes by Hitler and the German military included many factors. The most glaring abandonment of logic was of course the self-destructive and counterproductive genocide program. If this pogrom had been halted (let alone never implemented) it is highly probable that the war could have been won by the Germans in Europe, given the millions of potential pro-German (or at the very least anti-Communist) insurgents at Germany's disposal. This would have been feasible, of course, until the advent of atomic weapons by the United States, which would have more than likely been used against *Festung Europa* had the Soviet Union collapsed under the weight of a German military and anti-Communist guerrilla supported onslaught. However, had Germany managed to negotiate a peace with Stalin prior to the Casablanca Conference of

14-24 January 1943, and had Britain acquiesced, the possibility of a German dominated Europe grows exponentially.

The next phase is to examine the individual German units involved in the controversial counterinsurgency role and their military activities, including the actual (although varied) applications of counterinsurgency policy as dictated by unit commanders at the division level down to the brigade. These leaders were given basic operational guidelines to follow, although they usually allowed their subordinate commanders complete freedom of move- ment with regard to exactly how these tactics were to be implemented. Such freedom was not enjoyed by any other units in either the *Waffen SS* or *Wehrmacht Heer* during the war. Another facet of the German application of the counterinsurgency policy are the differences between regular Army and *Waffen SS* units, both of which were initially quite different in their application of counterinsurgency doctrine until 1943, when the policy was amended to enjoin these units into collective, cohesive, and hopefully more effective organizations.

The new collective application regarding operational coordination was not always met favorably by either Army or *Waffen SS* commanders. The research has shown that internal friction between Army and *SS* (to include *SD*) leaders almost led to open revolt among the troops themselves, hindering any possibility of an effective, cooperative effort. The pri- mary problem regarding friction came from specific unit commanders, such as *Generaloberst* Hasso von Manteuffel, who in 1942-43 commanded the elite *Panzer* Division *"Grossdeutschland."*[1048] During 1943-1944, when his division was the spearhead of several armored assaults on the Eastern Front, *"Grossdeutschland"* was supplemented by various *Waffen SS* motorized infantry and adjacent *panzer* units such as *"Das Reich"* and *"Leibstandarte."*

Given the titled status of the Army's *"Grossdeutschland"* Division (all *Luftwaffe,* elite Army and *SS* units wore cuff titles on their sleeves, along with special cuff titles for signifi- cant battles)[1049] and its heavy *Waffen SS* support contingent, it was assumed by the *SD, Waffen SS, Einsatzgruppen* and even the *Sonderkommando* that these army units would assist in the pursuit, collection, and liquidation of "suspected" partisans, which usually meant the liquidation of Jews, Orthodox Christians, Roman Catholics, Gypsies, and Com- munist political commissars. In many cases there was actually little (if any) partisan activ- ity along the portion of the front under von Manteuffel's control, primarily due to his hands off policy regarding civilians. However, this did not prevent the *SD* and *SS* from attempting to collect men from various battalion and company commands to support their own activi- ties. This occurred several times during the war, until von Manteuffel became aware of it in December 1943. Manteuffel refused to allow his junior commanders to detach their troops for *SS* and *SD* use, creating friction that was to reach Himmler in Berlin.[1050] Manteuffel issued an order threatening court-martial of any officer in his command who detached sol- diers without permission from the divisional intelligence officer, and counter-signed by the general himself. Although this continued to occur sporadically it never became a policy under Manteuffel's command. Karl Wolff described Himmler's reaction to this order:

> I do not remember exactly how this information came to be known by the *Reichsfuehrer,* although I can tell you that I had never seen him so upset about anything personally. Once Manteuffel's statement had been confirmed, I was or-

dered to draft a letter to the general, asking him to clarify his position on this matter. Within two weeks Manteuffel had responded, and his blunt method of dealing with our office only made the problem worse. Himmler finally had a meeting with Hitler, and most of us on the Staff were present except Goering. Himmler wanted to know what should be done about Manteuffel and his disregard for the field orders. Hitler simply said, "I would not concern myself with Baron Manteuffel. He seems to have his house in order." I don't believe that Himmler thought this a satisfactory answer, and he never forgave Manteuffel for threatening his field commanders.[1051]

Due to the interviews and the research conducted, it would appear that the methodology of counterinsurgency as practiced by the Germans was an evolutionary trial by error process, with the policy being amended as deemed necessary, at least until the proper formula was considered achieved in a touch and go *modus operandi*. Unfortunately for the Germans, their forces never achieved ultimate success in what the Americans would later call the "hearts and minds" campaign in Vietnam. German forces were hardly allowed the discretion of selectively choosing which collective body of suspected irregulars would be separated, incorporated, or interrogated on a large scale in order to sift through the populations, segregating potential supporters from the actual threats, unlike in the west.

In addition, the German ground force commanders found themselves in an ever increasing and expanding situation due to the fluid, progressive nature of the war in the east. The mounting burdens of command were accentuated by the rise of the numbers of partisans and guerrillas. However, this initial confrontation was fairly minimal and did little to inhibit the forward momentum of Army Groups North, Center, and South until the debacle of Moscow in December 1941, which completely stalled the advance, and the following disaster at Stalingrad in 1943. By the time of the Kursk-Orel offensive in July 1943 the irregular threat had not reached beyond a manageable level had certain precautions and considerations been taken.

Perhaps the final blow to German military hegemony and their perceived legitimacy among many within the pro-fascist ranks came after the reversal at Kursk-Orel in 1943; any possibility of actually creating a friendly indigenous anti-Communist partisan corps was destroyed after these reversals, hammering home the fact that a fully operational, viable, and sensible policy towards actively recruiting friendly insurgents and *Freiwilligen* was never properly adopted. This was true, at least in the east and Balkans, despite the success of Vlasov's recruits. This lack of foresight in addition to the existing racial policies created a recipe for disaster. The policy of complete liquidation of all suspects without even the remotest hint of humane justice with regard to operational necessity violated common sense, and mirrored the Stalinist pogrom. This was proven to be the "Achilles Heel" of the German occupation and counterinsurgency effort. It is this primary area of political, social, and psychological perception and a cogent practical application that is the axis upon which operational success revolves.

With regard to Hitler's and Himmler's plans to create a pro-German insurgency corps from the indigenous personnel under their yoke, the collective recruitment effort after 1942 for non-Germans to join the fight against Communism proved reasonably successful, at least numerically. A prime example as previously illustrated were the hundreds of thousands of Europeans who joined the *Waffen SS* during the course of the war, given that they met the stringent yet constantly amended racial purity requirements initiated by Himmler in 1934. Ironically, this strict standard would decrease every year following 1943, when combat attrition forced the active recruitment and eventual conscription of more non-Germans. By the end of the war approximately 940,000 men had served within the ranks of the forty-five (thirty-eight active) *Waffen SS* divisions, although most units never reached full division strength. The numbers represented over a dozen nationalities, while approximately only 250,000 members at the most were actual Germans (excluding the *Reichsdeutsche*) forming the nucleus of the original units. Some were even Masurians, a group of predominantly Polish speaking Protestants who had voted to remain under German rule following World War I.[1052]

The Germans pressed nearly every operational unit into an anti-partisan role at one time or another depending upon the military and political necessities at the time. Although specialized detachments were created in most of the infantry units for specifically handling counterinsurgency operations, certain units were specifically created, trained and detailed for their collective counterinsurgency attributes and capabilities. These were traditional units containing elements prepared for counterinsurgency operations: *1st Waffen SS Panzer* Division *"Leibstandarte,"* *2nd Waffen SS Panzer* Division *"Das Reich,"* *3rd Waffen SS Panzer* Division *"Totenkopf,"* *4th Waffen SS* Division *"Polizei,"* *5th Waffen SS Panzer* Division *"Wiking,"* *6th Waffen SS* Division *"Germania,"* *7th der Waffen SS* Division *"Nordland,"* *9th SS Panzer* Division *"Hohenstauffen,"* *10th SS Panzer* Division *"Freundsberg,"* and *12th Waffen SS Panzer* Division *"Hitlerjuegend,"* [1053] *17th Waffen SS Panzer* Division *"Goetz von Berlichingen,"* *28th der Waffen SS* Division *"Wallonien,"* and the *7th der Waffen SS* Division *"Prinz Eugen."* The *8th Waffen SS Kavallerie* Division *"Florian Geyer,"* *13th der Waffen SS* Division *"Handschar,"31st der SS* Division *"Boehmen-Mahren"* and the Free Russian Cossack units under Pannwitz were specifically designed in their entirety for the counterinsurgency role.

The foreign units were primarily staffed by German officers and commanded by Germans in most cases, carrying the designation *"der SS,"* or "of the *SS*" to distinguish the *Freiwilligen* from the German units. It has been conclusively proven that the greatest bulk of atrocities, including the ghetto deportations, death camp operations and round ups were committed by these *Freiwilligen* troops of the *SS*, such as at Warsaw, Riga, Vilnius, Kharkov and Kiev. The foreign units were also highly valued in field operations against irregulars, such as at Kholm, Demyansk, and Cherkassy, the latter engagements being brutal fights to the death involving seventy to a hundred straight days of constant partisan and Red Army attacks and counter-attacks, with nearly every battle involving hand to hand combat.[1054] This continued exposure to battle was a logical approach, given the fact that Himmler felt that the *Waffen SS* units should be maintained as a field combat force, and rightly so. The use of foreigners allowed the Germans to maintain a strong field presence while also maintaining the *Auslanderdienst* (Foreign Service) behind the lines where they could be observed and managed.

Although *Waffen SS* units such as *"Totenkopf,"* *"Das Reich"* and *"Leibstandarte"* received the bulk of post-war attention with regard to their individual atrocities, the most active and effective of the predominantly German *SS* units in the counterinsurgency role was without doubt the *8th Waffen SS Kavallerie* Division *"Florian Geyer."* One of the division's earliest commanders was the gentlemanly and humane Wilhelm Bittrich, later of Arnhem fame in 1944. The ruthlessly efficient and quite capable *Gruppenfuehrer* Herman Fegelein replaced him in 1943.[1055] *"Florian Geyer"* was created for two distinct purposes: to operate as an armored and mounted cavalry reconnaissance force supplying real time information to higher Army units, and as a premier counterinsurgency location and strike force first operating in southern Russia. The unit saw action on the Eastern Front until the last day of the war.

The *8th Waffen SS* also differed from other divisions in that the men who staffed its ranks were already experienced in combating partisans, including former *Brandenburgers* or aristocrats from the old German nobility. Several prominent and highly decorated men served with the unit in this role and excelled at their work. One such man was Gustav Lombard, commander of the *1st Kavallerie* Regiment who received the Knight's Cross for his efficient and ruthlessly effective operations and personal exploits.[1056] Lombard's close association with Andrei Vlasov[1057] made his *Sturmbattalion* the most effective counterinsurgency unit in the German military, and during the period March 1943 to October 1944 (just before Vlasov was finally given the command of the entire expatriate force, and before his promotion to *Oberfuehrer* and transfer) Lombard served as a company, battalion, and regimental commander, hand-picking his own men for operations. The exact numbers of partisans killed by his efforts will never be known, but it has been estimated that over 4,000 were hunted down by Lombard's units alone, with *"Florian Geyer"* accounting for over 16,000 partisans division wide.[1058]

Despite some misconceptions, the *Waffen SS* was not the only military organization to fill out its ranks with non-Germans, although in fact it recruited the bulk of the foreign volunteers in comparison to the other branches of the military per capita.[1059] The Army and *Luftwaffe* also incorporated many multi-nationals within their ranks. The *Luftwaffe* fighter force auxiliary was especially heavy with Croatian, Italian, Slovak, Free Russian, Romanian, Bulgarian, Hungarian, Finnish, and even Danish and Norwegian representation, with 3,700 foreigners dying in aerial combat for the Third *Reich*,[1060] flying as independent units yet often assigned to the various *Jagdgeschwader* in the *Staffel* capacity. With regard to the *Luftwaffe*, the Free Russian Fighter Squadron at various times numbered between sixty to seventy personnel, and although independent and never under direct German command was equipped with German built *Messerschmitt* Me-109 fighters after 1943.

The last commander of this unique squadron, comprised of a collection of various ethnic Russian anti-Communist expatriates was Lieutenant Colonel Leonid Damianov Maximciuc, who at age sixteen was the youngest fighter pilot in history.[1061] A lieutenant colonel at age nineteen with fifty-two victories, he was discussing the fate of his unit with Lieutenant General André A. Vlasov as the war ground to a halt in April 1945.[1062] Vlasov had apparently believed the rumors of disaffection with Hitler that had been rumored since the early days of the war, believing that an internal collapse was possible, although he was reluctant to immediately join the ranks of his former enemy.[1063] Knowing that the war was lost Vlasov allowed his subordinate commanders to decide the fates of their units.

The most energetic and exhaustively engaged *Freiwilligen* unit during the war was perhaps the *28th der Waffen SS* Division *"Wallonien"* commanded by the energetic former lawyer and intellectual from Belgium, *Oberfuehrer* Leon Degrelle. Degrelle's hatred for Communism was manifested by his enlistment in the German Army in 1940 as a private, turning down a direct commission as a *leutnant*. He was joined by other Belgians, many of whom were personal friends and they were eventually placed in their own company, which was then expanded to an infantry battalion attached to *5ᵗʰ Waffen SS Panzer* Division *"Wiking."* The Walloon unit grew into a brigade element by the time of the Moscow offensive and Degrelle rose rapidly through the ranks, his courage and daring earning him almost every German decoration for valor, including the Oak Leaves. His reward was an officer's commission and command of a company. By the time of the Demyansk operation in January 1942 he commanded a company of engineers, quickly converted into an ad-hoc counterinsurgency unit due to the pressures placed upon them by the irregulars assisting the Red Army. Although not specifically assigned anti-partisan duties, the unit fought large bands of partisans on the Caucasus and again in Hungary in 1945.[1064]

Demyansk was one of the few major battles that saw large numbers of partisans actively engaged in open combat operations, which was rather unique, since Stalin did not order Red Army assistance for the irregulars until late in 1942, and most of the assistance rendered was not in effect until 1943.[1065] These partisans were fighting with the bare minimum in weaponry and ammunition, relying upon battlefield finds and captured stocks. By the time the Germans were prepared for a push forward they discovered that they were encircled. The *3ʳᵈ* and *5ᵗʰ* SS Divisions, along with the *9ᵗʰ Armee* fought for nearly three months without reinforcements with only airdrops as a method of re-supply. The divisions managed to fight their way out, but of the 40,000 *SS* men in the pocket less than 11,000 survived, and most of these were wounded. During the course of the battle the Red Army lost over 300,000 soldiers, and thousands of partisans were also killed, although their casualties do not appear in the Soviet records. Without doubt the partisan contribution proved the greatest threat to the Germans during this operation, since the irregular forces were as much a psychological threat as a viable offensive military entity. Degrelle summed up the partisan war and the doctrine they used during his interview in 1985:

> The one thing my men and I knew was that however large and present the threat presented by the Soviet army, the partisans were the worst enemy to fight. Since they did not wear uniforms, unless they were in German clothing sometimes, and they blended in well with the local population, which created a problem in choosing who was and who was not a partisan. Unless you caught one with a weapon, or were actively engaged against them, it was impossible. Later during the war they were absorbed into Red Army infantry and tank units, and sometimes they were given uniforms. I would say the most disturbing aspect of fighting the partisans was that unlike the Soviet military, the partisans adhered to no set doctrine, used no set order of battle that we could study, and basically struck where it was the most opportune. In this method they excelled, yet they could not engage in a prolonged fire fight. If we caught and cornered them they were dead, and they knew it. That is why they fought like fanatics.

Degrelle and three other men would survive the war and the post-war captivity out of the nearly 22,500 men who served within the ranks of the Belgian volunteers.[1066] Their losses are one of the highest recorded from an active foreign division, although they were one of the few counterinsurgency units not engaged in the partisan war full time.

The German attempts to stamp out the fires of partisan and guerrilla resistance in Russia were not usually very well planned or even well executed operations. The greatest problem with their program was the basic concept of elimination of all resistance and suspected resistance without discretion. This policy infuriated the local populations, quite understandably swelling the partisan ranks immensely. The Germans would in theory have been better served by a policy that incorporated most of the population that had suffered under Stalin's pogroms, such as the ultra-nationalist Ukrainians, who numbered some 4,000,000 and incorporated them immediately into armed auxiliaries on a large scale. Although two Ukrainian *SS* divisions *were* created from volunteers, with thousands more joining Vlasov's and Pannwitz' growing forces, the bulk of the population that had welcomed the Germans as liberators justifiably turned against them *en masse* within the first year. The reliability of the Ukrainians (or any of the former Soviet troops) were always in question, and this was openly stated by *Obergruppenfuehrer* Paul Hausser, who commanded the *II SS Panzer Korps* during *Operation Zitadelle* (Citadel), the Kursk-Orel offensive in 1943. However, Hausser later amended his opinion after the two Ukrainian *SS* units distinguished themselves in both counterinsurgency and open combat roles against superior Red Army and partisan forces.

Despite the reservations many German officers held regarding the *Freiwilligen* and the varying methods employed in combating insurgents, the fact remained that in most cases the international volunteers were the most capable in dealing with the problem. German commanders in the field on many occasions preferred to have auxiliaries or *Freiwilligen* either supporting their units during counterinsurgency operations or actively leading such missions. Of all the interviews conducted with *Wehrmacht Heer, Luftwaffe Fallschirmjaeger* and *Waffen SS* personnel engaged in such activities who operated with foreign troops there were few exceptions.

15

Background of Dissent

*In this world, many things are complicated and are
decided by many factors. We should look at problems from different aspects, not from just one.*
                                    - Mao Tse Tung
                                    17 October 1945.

It is the considered opinion of this thesis that the liquidation policy against Jews, commissars, and other target populations precipitated not only the rise of partisan and guerrilla
resistance, but of the already existent (if subdued) anti-*Nazi* feeling within the German
military.[1067] Much of this resentment already existed, and came to a head in 1938, yet was
extinguished by the events following the Munich Agreement of 29 September 1938, allowing Hitler to enter the Sudetenland in Czechoslovakia following his successful entry into
the Rhineland.[1068] Hitler ostensibly undertook the invasion in order to reunite and pacify the
region following the riots and mayhem that occurred under the administration of President
Dr. Eduard Benes.[1069] These actions, as well as the *Anschluss* of Austria, legitimized Hitler,
tempering any covert movement against him.[1070] The tacit approvals by Neville Chamberlain and Edouard Deladier would witness Hitler invading the rest of Czechoslovakia the
following March. A.J.P. Taylor as states that these unregulated and seemingly rewarded acts
of overt aggression only secured the legitimacy of Hitler in the eyes of the world, as well as
stroked his ego and supporting his plans for future aggression in 1939.[1071] It may be stated
with confidence that the gains Germany made through both diplomacy and war laid the
groundwork for the overwhelming anti-Communist sympathies that arose, a fact that would
manifest itself in the success of the *Freiwilligen* within the military.

It must also be stated that the German Army (even under the *Reichswehr* limited by the
Versailles Treaty to 100,000 men[1072]) was, for the most part, fairly apolitical by nature, stemming from the Army's rigid policy of *Uberparteilichkeit*, or "total abstention from politics," which was also incorporated into the Defense Law. This was still the rule even after
the 2 August 1934 enforcement of the oath of allegiance sworn to Hitler by the military
personally.[1073] Much of the internal opposition within the officer corps stemmed from Hitler's
policies towards the churches, and especially the Catholic dominated *Zentrumpartei*[1074] during the 1930s, which displayed his attitude towards the Catholic Church in general.[1075] Even
upon signing the Concordat with the Vatican guaranteeing the independence of the Catholic

Church, Hitler continued to destroy the Church from within.[1076] However, Hitler's attacks included the Protestant faiths as well, continually eroding support for the *NSDAP* in many areas, since perhaps ninety-five percent of all voting Germans maintained loyalty to one of the Christian denominations.[1077]

However, both Catholic and Protestant factions among the officer corps were not totally refusing to embrace the concept of *Nazism*, and were actually united in their dependence upon the government and the *NSDAP*.[1078] The fear and complete opposition to Communism which Hitler, through which his distorted sense of history and altered reality also managed to equate with Judaism, was apparently not taken seriously by the more cogent within the officer corps, despite the tacit acceptance and implementation of national policies. Also, the history of the Catholic Church remaining indifferent to (if not actively working against) the Jews of Europe in some cases probably assisted Hitler and his supporters in the relocation and eventual genocide program, without fear of open reprisal from that segment of the population.

It has also been noted by Julie M. Baxter that "the Prussian Confessional Church was the only religious body in the entire twelve years of the Third *Reich* to publicly protest (referring to the Declaration by the Consistory of the Confessing Church of the Old Prussian Union) against the atrocities done to the Jews."[1079] This opposition was extended to the euthanasia policy, which witnessed thousands of clergymen being placed into concentration camps for voicing their discontent.[1080] Such anti-Socialist luminaries included Dietrich Bonhoeffer,[1081] Reverend Martin Niemoeller (head of the Confessional Church), *Pater* Alfred Delp, Pastor Grueber, Father Lichtenbergand, and *Graf* Galen, the Bishop of Muenster, who criticized the *Gestapo* and the *SS* as well as the euthanasia policy quite openly. Galen's activities actually forced a cessation to the euthanasia policy in Muenster, as well as a halt to the confiscation of Church property.[1082] The Vatican and Pope Pius XII, who were actively assisting the *Nazi's* in Italy during the war did not openly support all of these victories by their constituents, maintaining a silent and hands off approach.

These situations would lead to a series of events focused upon the eventual removal of Hitler by a selected cadre of military officers and civilians, despite the fact that the anti-Hitler movement in Germany never flourished into being as in the nations occupied by Germany.[1083] Nonetheless, these resistance factions must be analyzed as to not only their effectiveness (or rather their lack of influence) but their mere existence as an internal "guerrilla" movement. One example was the pacifist *Weisse Rosen* (White Rose) movement of German students, primarily located in Munich betwenen1942-43 in conjunction with the international anti-*Nazi* movements.[1084]

Despite the post-war belief that the entire German military was indeed behind the horrors of the Holocaust and fervently supported the genocide policy, which became the main reason for the continental anti-German insurgency, a few interesting facts must be examined. First, despite the racial propaganda instilled within German society and the military, there were several influential and successful German officers, even from the *SS*, who openly disapproved of the Party polemic and resisted the rhetoric emanating from Berlin.

A prime example occurred during a meeting in 1941 of ranking *Waffen SS* field commanders, when *Oberfuehrer* (later *Gruppenfuehrer*) Wilhelm Bittrich openly opposed Himmler's policies on racial cleansing in the east, stating: "The things Heinrich says are sheer nonsense! Things will go badly if we don't change our ways," and he called Himmler "a fool" in front of fifteen high ranking officers, and no one turned him in to the *Gestapo*. Among those present were fellow generals Felix Steiner, Karl Wolff, Paul Hausser, Josef Dietrich, Theodor Eicke, and F.W. Krueger, who openly supported Bittrich.[1085] It is truly a shame that these influential officers did not carry more weight with Hitler and Himmler, and in some fashion assist in averting the catastrophe that would become a lasting legacy to the defeat of German arms, and forever tarnish German honor.

16

Loyal Legionnaires

In seeking victory, those who direct a war cannot overstep the limitations imposed by the objective conditions; within these limitations, however, they can and must play a dynamic role in striving for victory.
- Mao Tse Tung
May 1938.

Lieutenant General Andrei Vlasov and his deputy, Lieutenant General Bunyachenko were quite successful in recruiting hundreds of thousands of soldiers and senior officers disillusioned by Stalin's treatment and the Red Army's attitudes towards their POW status, as well as the recent memory of the Great Purges. This cataclysmic debacle cost the nation eighty percent of its colonels and another twenty-five percent of the junior officer ranks for a total of 30,000 trained and combat experienced soldiers.[1086] Vlasov had survived the purge, wounds, and constant combat, only to be later handed over to the Red Army by his British and American captors and executed.[1087] There is no greater irony.

Certain historians erroneously state that there "was never an organized resistance to Stalin during his reign."[1088] If the 1,400,000 former Soviet soldiers and 600,000 civilians who defected to the Germans due to Stalin's excesses and served under Andrei Vlasov, as well as the post-war Romanian, Polish, Hungarian, Czech, and Cossack revolts under Soviet occupation do not count as "organized resistance," then nothing does. These historians forgot or were honestly unaware of the massive guerrilla wars fought against the Red Army in the Ukraine, Caucasus, Mongolia, and Eastern Europe before, during and following World War II; internal conflicts lasting through the 1950s by many who apparently were less than satisfied with the government in Moscow.

A prime example of a resistance fighter who had fought in uniform during the war against the Communists is Leonid Maximciuc, previously mentioned as a fighter pilot and squadron leader. Following the war Maximciuc was arrested, tortured, and slated for deportation to Moscow. Only his convoy being ambushed by partisans, allowing him to escape spared his life, and he joined their ranks as an anti-Communist partisan in Romania. This arrangement lasted until the government placed a price on his head that was so exorbitant it forced him to leave the country in 1948.[1089] The numbers of disaffected Soviet citizens who wished to be free and fought for that freedom and died in the process may never be known for certain.

Interviews with many of these expatriates show that another (and perhaps the most common) cause for their volunteering for German military service were primarily economic, as opposed to simply political ideologies. The enforced collectivization and labor, as well as the random and senseless purges and deportations alienated a large segment of the population against Stalin. Hitler could have provided a better economic and political environment, thus solidifying his chosen position as the "liberator" of Europe, while establishing some form of political legitimacy for the Third *Reich*. However, when faced with working in a coal mine, munitions plant or a collective farm, the lure of better pay and the youthful enthusiasm for adventure usually assisted in the decision to enter uniform. Having collaborated with the enemy and being discovered by their fellow countrymen was also a strong incentive to leave home in most cases. The same must be said for the insurgents who initially rallied to the German cause.[1090]

Few people could blame the average European layman for becoming confused over the years, such as the open British and French stand against Germany being tempered by the fact that both nations had acquiesced to Hitler and scolded the Soviet Union for attacking Finland; even planning for a material assistance package to the nation in defiance of Stalin.[1091] This position perhaps further complicated British and French positions regarding political affairs to the Europeans, since it is ironic that neither country had a vested interest in the future of Spain during the Civil War, when Hitler and Mussolini supported Franco and the Soviets assisted the Republican government.[1092] German Foreign Minister Joachim von Ribbentrop[1093] even consulted Hitler on 7 December 1939, and issued a Foreign Ministry Circular.[1094] The concern toward Finland was commendable yet illustrated a selective application of foreign policy, a rather flawed and empty gesture since there had been no serious discussion regarding assistance to other nations such as Albania, which had been annexed and invaded by Italy in 1939, or Ethiopia and Libya, both of which were also invaded by Mussolini's forces. Also known to many of the more educated and literate members of the European community was the fact that Admiral Sir Roger Keyes of the Royal Navy had stated flatly that he believed "Britain should declare war on both Germany and the Soviet Union," primarily due to the Non-Aggression Pact signed between both nations following the partition of Poland in September 1939.[1095]

This prospect was not welcomed by most of his contemporaries, although the list of nations falling into either the National Socialist or Communist sphere of influence was unnerving to both the British and French governments to say the least. The greatest measure of activity occurred when the League of Nations expelled the Soviet Union from its membership (of which it had only been a member since September 1934),[1096] in essence offering lip service without any substantial program of military and economic sanctions. Just as many irregular forces supported the Germans throughout the war, it is also critical to remember that many nations' militaries had succumbed to international events with their collective professional corps of soldiers becoming unemployed. Men who have trained and lived for a particular way of life and have failed to assimilate into civilian life tend to fall back upon what they know best; the German experience alone should be an indicator. The professional bearers of national arms were a major component in the creation of the *Freiwilligen*, such as the Latvian and Estonian contingents who were also incorporated into their own *Waffen SS* units by 1944, with the Latvians having two divisions of volunteers totaling nearly 30,000 men.[1097]

Another group given little in the way of historical exposure are the Bosnian-Serbs who operated as anti-Tito partisans, to include the *Chetniks*. So effective, resourceful, and energetic in their own policy of killing Communists, Jews, prisoners of war, and others who were not considered worthy of residence in Yugoslavia that Heinrich Himmler ordered the creation of the *13th der SS* Division *"Handschar"* (literally *Scimitar*). As part of their uniforms they wore the traditional *fez* of their culture and were even allowed to practice Islam, which was incorporated into their National Socialist training regimen with a special handbook created for their indoctrination, courtesy of the Propaganda Ministry. It is the story of the *"Handschar"* and their role as active counterinsurgents in support of the German occupation that opens one of the bloodiest chapters in the annals of counterinsurgency warfare in history, and is therefore a critical component of this project.

Although interviews were conducted with two surviving members of the *13th der Waffen SS "Handschar"* from Belgrade and Sarajevo, the documentation on the unit is at last notice primarily restricted to the German archives at Freiburg, the British Public Records Office in London, and minimal information being available at the United States National Archives in College Park, Maryland. Both members declined to be quoted or identified for this project, and their wishes were honored. The fact that the few survivors of the unit surrendered to British forces in May 1945 as opposed to the Soviets (with little wonder, they were turned over to the Red Army and Tito anyway) is possibly the only reason for any information to exist at all. The British supplied most of the surviving unit documentation to Germany during the 1950s and 1960s as the Cold War progressed, when President for life Josip "Broz" Tito's precarious position as the only Communist leader in Europe not on Moscow's leash was an uncertain condition at best.

Other partisan factions throughout Europe were worthy of both German and Allied attention, such as the partisans and guerrillas in Greece, both nationalist and Communist in political orientation, as well as the Albanians, both of whom were able to thwart Italian ambitions from 1939-41[1098] and seriously hinder German attempts at complete occupation, although Greece fell shortly after Yugoslavia when Belgrade capitulated on 12 April 1941.[1099] So effective were the Albanians, Hitler decided that large-scale occupation was an expensive and unproductive avenue, deciding to allow the Italians and a few token German units to manage the problem. The Albanians had formed their own Communist political structure before the war and were successful after the war without the influence of the Soviet occupation forces, much like Yugoslavia.[1100] Hitler abandoned the nation to its fate, cutting it off from all economic aid and assistance, hoping the small nation would "wither on the vine."[1101] However, several thousand Albanians did volunteer to fight Communism, as evidenced by the creation of their own *"Skanderberg"* Division.

The Dutch Resistance, which grew rapidly to over 30,000 active members by the end of 1944 and with a total strength being approximately 76,000 for the entire war (and almost as mythical in proportion to the *Maquisard* in post war memory) was in fact much more effective than the French in several areas.[1102] The most predominant factors were the active hiding of Jews (which proved more difficult than hiding the resistance fighters, due to the flat terrain[1103]) from the Germans during the great sweeps of 1943-44;[1104] the collaboration between politically opposed factions for the common good,[1105] as well as the collection and safe return of Allied airmen, although not on the scale nor with the success of the French and Belgians, or of the Danes with regard to salvaging the Jews. Despite the shortcomings and successes of the various partisan and guerrilla movements, each nation performed a role that was crucial to the overall success of the Allied victory in Europe. The ability to foster good will and win the support of the people is all-important, as stated by Aaron Bank:

> By the time I had parachuted into France with the Jedburgh Teams, the European resistance movements were well underway. Much of this had been due to the SOE efforts, especially in France, Holland, Belgium and the Balkans. When we look back upon the severity and overall complexity of the German occupation, it is amazing to think that the resistance movements could have been successful at all, even with massive Allied support. However, as I have always believed, and maintained as doctrine for the Special Forces, as you know, is that any resistance movement that has the support of the people, is supported and maintained by an external ally for material and political assistance will almost always succeed over the occupier and aggressor. Guerrilla warfare is the one tried and true method of achieving victory at relatively low cost, and we must never forget that.[1106]

As stated by Colonel Aaron Bank and demonstrated throughout this book, the failure of the Germans to effectively secure the confidence of the people, and obtain their support proved their greatest error in judgment. The Allies who were successful in their attempt to support and foster underground activities were more fortunate; they were operating in an environment conducive to intervention and were perceived as legitimate by nearly every indigenous faction. As seen in the following and final chapter, the credibility factor became all-important. In the final analysis, the endeavor is supported by an avalanche of archive documentation and hindsight, the veneer of ambiguity is peeled away from the surface of reality, exposing all for the world to view.

Conclusion:
Supportive Considerations

All through the course of the research regarding partisan and guerrilla activities, the questions as to "what exactly initiated insurgency warfare" and "what is the difference between the partisan and the guerrilla" have been examined. The answers offered may be considered subjective with regard to the remarks obtained from the respective soldiers, operatives, agents, partisans, and guerrillas interviewed. What is perhaps a more factual common denominator than simply the taking up of arms against an aggressor for individual reason, such as nationalism, is simply economics and the desire to survive.

Many pro-German Europeans may label one particular motivation as their conscious belief in (and support of) an ultimate German victory. Since Hitler's military had established itself as the premier force on the continent from the Spanish Civil War through the conquest of Western Europe, the "sunshine patriot" syndrome, or the wish to be on a "winning team" for personal gain must also be considered.[1107] Also, given the fact that Europe in general had been severely influenced by the global depression of 1929 may have also raised interest in the Hitlerian promise of a united Europe for the common good. What is glaringly obvious is that approximately 2,000,000 persons throughout German occupied Europe (including 55 Britons under the traitor John Avery) joined the German cause, whatever their motivation, and this fact cannot go unnoticed when evaluating the perceived legitimacy of National Socialism as a viable political and social entity.

Also of importance with regard to international public perception was Britain's policy early in the war to bombard Germany with leaflets instead of bombs during the first months of hostilities.[1108] This perceived military and political impotence could only have enhanced Germany's position and increased Hitler's resolve. However, the German handling of the Jews and the local populations under domination were definitely the most lethal of Germany's self-inflicted wounds. Rather than capitalize upon their successes and exploit their few positive advantages among many of their potential supporters in Europe, the unnecessary programs of brutality and exploitation practiced by the Germans and the Soviets proved just as flawed for Communism in the long run as well. The Western Allies, who studied the counterinsurgency operations of Germany and chose the opposite political and psychological direction proved more successful during the post-war years, thus the final balance sheet in the post Cold War world illustrates.

Had Hitler harnessed the immense manpower at his disposal and utilized this asset as a cohesive and supportive military or paramilitary force, the history of the Second World War may have been quite different. This is due to the fact that with the people come the economic benefits and political support necessary to sustain a long term conflict. It was the loss of legitimacy and the resources such as grain, oil, iron, precious metals and other commodities that forced Germany into a defensive posture after 1943. Given these facts, it is also logical to assume that, had Hitler been successful in obtaining this massive support network the war in the east would have had either one of two results: it would have been a much longer, protracted and bloody affair that would have inflicted far more damage in material and economic areas than was actually experienced, or the Germans would have forced a separate peace from Stalin and turned their full attention westward. The failure of Germany to achieve its primary objectives is the responsibility of Hitler and the High Command of the Armed Forces, and *not* the individual soldier who fought a remarkable war in the field against overwhelming odds. The failed application of doctrine and propaganda simply backfired with tragic results.

The root of all wars and political insurgencies are tied to the land, crops, and the potential for profit or sustenance. Once the land is threatened the population will in every case resort to the use of unconventional methods to prevent its destruction or possible confiscation. This attitude towards economics could also include the firm belief by many in the European blue-collar sector that Hitler and the National Socialist Workers Party offered an opportunity unavailable to them by their individual governments. Had Hitler not brought Germany out of the global depression? Had the National Socialists not provided jobs and expanded their internal economic dynamics, virtually eliminating unemployment?[1109] Were the British not suffering from massive unemployment during the same period, even after the war had ensued?[1110] These factors were vividly apparent to Germany's neighbors, especially the Soviet Union, prompting Stalin to openly state his desire to remain completely non-confrontational with Hitler.[1111] It has also been deduced from several of the interviews conducted with former *Freiwilligen* members, that inclusion within the illusory *Volksgemeinschaft*[1112] as an ally of Germany and the accompanying income earning potential was preferable to an uncertain existence under Stalinist Communism or exploitative western capitalism.

Other factors that supported not only the widespread belief in many of the volunteers in an eventual German victory, but also prompted Hitler to believe that the British government would never unite as a collective body to effectively hinder his ambitions were the numerous anti-war and "No Conscription League" rallies held throughout the United Kingdom.[1113] Other factors included the newspaper attacks against the British government for waging a "phony war" of its own, while subjecting the population to martial law, high taxation and rationing.[1114] Some of these attacks were made in open forum, such as the 31 October 1939 debate in the House of Commons, when Mr. Dingle Foot, Liberal M.P., accused the British government of fascist policies towards the public interest.[1115] Another attack came from Mr. Kingsley Griffith who:

> ...warned the House that the terms of the Emergency Powers (Defense) Act effectively meant the complete abolition of *Habeas Corpus* and implied that if the government continued on the same tack, conditions would soon be right for the creation of the first British concentration camps.[1116]

These public displays of disunity by the working class public against what they called an "Imperialist" war was misinterpreted by many in the German High Command as being a major weakness within the British political and social fabric. This was stated by *Luftwaffe* ace *Generalleutnant* Guenther Rall, who cited his January 1944 meeting with Hitler, one of his many during the war:

> We had lunch him (Hitler), and as usual he started to talk. Everybody expected the invasion all along the Channel Coast, wondering when it was coming and how they were coming and so on. At that time he developed his ideas, and you could see that Hitler was hopping around, very uncertain. Also, you know, one thing that was very typical of him was his stating how the British were always having problems with their opposition parties, the Labor Party, the labor unions and so on. It was clear to me that this man was a little out of his mind. Hitler did not have a clear, serious concept of the situation. Whatever their problems, the British people come together during war; they are one nation.[1117]

It was this exact premise of a disjointed international community that Hitler (according to those persons interviewed who knew him) believed would rally the multitudes of the east and west to his cause; a united Europe free of Communism following years of failed Stalinist Five Year Plans determined to bring the Soviet Union into industrial and agricultural independence,[1118] gross land mismanagement and the Communist Party's Draconian policies towards former landholders. This was particularly true of the population in the Ukraine. True, Hitler envisioned a German land reform conglomerate that would supply the *Reich* with the necessary agricultural produce and slave labor to continue the planting and harvesting.[1119] However, his failure to take into account the fact that the peoples of the east may not readily exchange one tyranny for another, let alone take up arms in support of his invasion *en masse* proved disastrous. The same could be said of several collective groups within Britain, when the anti-government political left, seeing the apparent conflict between their admiration for the Soviet system and the realities of the Soviet invasions of Poland and Finland eventually brought them into line.[1120] This renewed unity helped create the Coalition Government in May 1940, as stated by Gunther Rall. This failure by Hitler to comprehend the overall international political situation is summed up by *Generalleutnant* Hans Baur:

> I remember during the "Hitler Over Germany" campaign when he was running for the *NSDAP* to be elected, he would often discuss the problems in Britain and France. This was accentuated later during the war when the British put up

such stiff resistance during the summer of 1940. Hitler knew that there were socialist factions within the British working community.[1121] He firmly believed that the public pressure placed upon the government would alter the official British policy towards Germany, and favor us over the Soviet Union. The anti-Communist feeling in Britain was well known. I believe that this anti-Communist sentiment that swept through Europe was the single greatest factor in his deciding to launch *Barbarossa* when he did.[1122]

When analyzing the failure of the German foreign policies towards a conquered group of nations, the senior officers interviewed were in majority (if not unanimity) convinced of the following: the German government should have planned a program of wider assimilation among the various peoples, incorporating them into the *Reich* proper and offering a better lifestyle under National Socialism that encouraged profit along capitalist lines (as practiced in German industry), yet still maintaining firm government control over the execution of that commerce and industry. This program would have perhaps appealed to the large majority of the populations, encouraging them to work the land for themselves, in essence sharecropping for profit instead of mere subsistence while assisting and being supported by the German government.

Several German industrialists and planners, as related by the late *Generalleutnant* Hans Baur (a former World War I fighter ace and *Lufthansa* airline pilot between the wars) actually envisioned this type of program. Hans Baur was the personal pilot, or *Fliegerchef* (*Flugfuehrer*) *der Fuehrer* to Adolf Hitler. Baur's interviews over the years proved insightful as to Hitler's personal beliefs regarding the conduct of the war, and as Hitler's closest confidant from 1932-1945, Baur's recollections and written memoranda eventually became a book, a highly recommended autobiography published in both Germany and the United States.[1123] The many conversations with Baur proved enlightening as to the perceptions and lack of action regarding the insurgency problems as perceived in Berlin.

The analysis with regard to the potential threat of irregulars behind and flanking German units on the defense, as well as on the retreat, became especially important once the *Abwehr* intelligence estimates came into effect. Baur was present along with *Sturmbannfuehrer* Rudolf von Falkenhahn and *Generalleutnant* Adolf Galland when Hitler allowed Reinhard Gehlen to give his estimates of Soviet forces in November 1942. The intelligence officer, at this time only a captain and a junior in the department offered the *Fuehrer* numbers that included projected Red Army support of partisans and the exponential rise of hostile paramilitary units throughout the occupied territories. Gehlen offered an honest and educated opinion, and this dedication to duty almost saw him committed to an insane asylum, according to Hans Baur.[1124]

Hitler would not hear of such large figures, not after the previous eighteen months of combat resulting in the killing or capturing over 7,000,000 Soviet soldiers.[1125] Anyone supporting such "nonsense" in the future would keep such information to himself, and this wall of silence regarding the very real and ever growing threat of irregular activity did not help the Germans in the field combat the problems that plagued them and were completely ignored in their capital. Few people would overtly attempt to persuade Hitler of this folly, although notable exceptions were Felix Steiner, Hasso von Manteuffel, Heinz Guderian, Fedor von Bock, Kurt Zeitzler, and on different matters *General der Jagdflieger* Adolf

Galland.[1126] In order to offer some perspective as to the range of this spineless incompetence, after his capture in 1945 Hermann Goering was asked about any personnel he knew of personally who had openly stood up to Hitler with regard to his various racial policies. Goering simply stated, "no one standing vertical."

The Germans realized only too late their mistakes and failed to take corrective action in many spheres, especially with regard to the power and value of irregulars and the need to respect their capabilities at the highest levels. This flaw in perception was not the always case among the commanders in the field, who were subjected to partisan and guerrilla attacks, and later became responsible for the counterinsurgency campaigns to follow. Commanders such as Kumm, Steiner, Degrelle, Stroop, Bittrich, Fegelein and Bach-Zelewski understood only too well what was occurring. The war against the insurgents became a tangled web, complete with all of the traditional nightmares related to modern large scale military operations, such as logistics, intelligence, manpower, arms and the need for realistic short term as well as long-term political considerations.

The most unexplored region with regard to the prosecution of the counterinsurgency war is the psychological implication of these prolonged operations upon both the German and irregular alike. This concern was reflected by Bartov in *Hitler's Army*, and the argument makes sense. He states that, "while the generals had little scruples about issuing orders to shoot men and uproot whole populations, they feared that executing women and children might cause disciplinary problems among the troops, and normally preferred the *SS* and *SD* to carry out such unsavory tasks."[1127] The morale of the Germans following extended combat is also mentioned: "The discipline of the troops has deteriorated during the winter. This is shown also by the increasing number of trials. Guard duty has particularly been neglected, spelling danger for the troops."[1128]

The Germans found that their troops needed to be rotated very few months from these duties due to combat fatigue, stress, depression, moral conflict and of course wounds and injuries. Much of this stress stemmed from the obvious problems of fighting in a foreign and hostile land far from home, with the fear of death superseded only by the fear of capture, and the fact that the harsh discipline found in the German military exacted the best as well as the worst from its men.[1129] The brutal treatment of subordinates for even minor errors of judgment easily created a resentment to authority, allowing the German soldier, and especially the *Freiwilligen* to feel that the average enemy civilian, as well as opposing soldiers were the reason for his being in the situation in general. Hitler's decree of 25 February 1943 stated:

> I have found out that during the retreats and evacuations ordered in the last few weeks, there have been some unpleasant and unruly scenes...This is unbearable...The reason for this is that commanders do not make use of all (disciplinary) measures...The harder the times, all the tougher should be the measures by which the commander enforces his will. I therefore demand that every commanding officer and NCO, or in extraordinary situations every courageous man, will enforce the execution of orders, if necessary by the force of arms, and will immediately open fire in case of insubordination. This is not only his right, but also his duty.[1130]

This counterproductive attitude was to seal Germany's fate as a military power and effective colonial administrator, since the allowance of such barbarity even among their own troops portended the attitude the men developed against those deemed unworthy of kind consideration. As stated by Bartov: "Indeed, one can say that the typical *Landser* was a very frightened man, scared of his commanders, terrified of the enemy; this is probably why he seems to have enjoyed so much watching others suffer."[1131] This sadistic attitude was also reflected within the ranks of the Imperial Japanese Army, where the discipline was even more brutal, and the harshness meted out can be attributed to most of the horrific acts committed by these otherwise decent young men who would have never given a moment's thought to such actions in civilian life.

However, it can also be stated that the men who survived and even thrived in this environment were beyond doubt among the most brutally effective soldiers to fight in the Second World War, and in war the most intelligent and brutally efficient usually survive. This fact is lost upon those who read and critique the actions of soldiers who have not worn a uniform themselves, served their country, or faced an enemy in armed conflict. The term "armchair quarterback" is most appropriate.

The challenge is open to any man to walk a year in the boots of the average combat infantryman of any nation during wartime; suffer the pain, fear, hunger, cold, lice, disease, trench foot, pneumonia, exposure, living on bad if any food, and little if any sleep, then state with a clear mind and absolved conscience that he knew for certain that every decision he personally made, and every order he followed or issued was well thought out, planned and executed. Then, compound these experiences with an apathetic High Command, a faulty political leadership, death and destruction all around while fighting an enemy, sometimes operating as civilians intent upon your death in an unaccustomed fashion, and with no other agenda to divert his attention, and you may have some idea as to why the German soldier was unsuccessful in the counterinsurgency role.

Beyond doubt the greatest debilitating factor with regard to morale was the witnessing and participation in combat, but even more pointedly the killing of civilians who were obviously non-combatants. These acts must have preyed upon the minds of many soldiers, despite the thinly veiled justification for such activity by their superiors. The brutality so common to the Eastern Front that enhanced the ranks of the partisans and guerrillas was also a detriment to the morale and good order within the German military. Despite the commonly accepted caricature of the average bloodthirsty German killing anything and everything non-German, there were great concerns from some commanders in the field regarding the morale of their troops, with many of these commanders rejecting the policies of extermination and prevented their troops from participating, often at risk to their careers and even their lives.[1132]

Maintaining the battlefield capability of each soldier, both medically and logistically had always been understood as a prime consideration for success, yet it was the psychological well being of the men that was a new phenomenon. Erich von dem Bach-Zelewski's nervous breakdown during the 1944 Warsaw Uprising is a prime example of the stress and the toll it took upon the participants, and the resulting rest and refit periods were instituted following the campaigns in Russia. The partisans and guerrillas of the Russian steppe and forests were unlike any enemy ever encountered by German forces, perhaps equaled only by the Yugoslav irregulars. This appreciation of the partisan threat, especially in the east can be summed up by Robert L. O'Connell:

> They became a nation at arms. In their reliance on snipers,[1133] and in the partisan campaigns, they did not so much fight the Germans as hunt them. At times they advanced under orders to take no prisoners. As this is characteristic of such struggles, women became involved in the fighting, though on a larger scale than ever before, even flying combat missions, acting as snipers, and participating in human wave assaults. In short, the Russians fought with the desperation of those preyed upon.[1134]

It is understandable that nearly every German commander in the field could justify the liquidation of captured partisans and guerrillas, since civilians bearing arms without any outward distinction as to their organizational loyalty, such as a uniform, were not protected under the Geneva and Hague Conventions, despite the constant reference to these articles and their being misquoted on·occasion. The soldier involved was a human being, and if a young man had been exposed to National Socialist doctrine all of his formative life, then served in a rigid military structure, a rubric that demanded immediate and decisive action and unhesitating loyalty and reaction, in lieu of analytical thought to resolve an issue, then he is definitely a product of his environment, as any sociologist or psychoanalyst can support.

The linear method of operational thinking has always been the case with traditional militaries, and the political branch supporting this type of thinking simply presented a hand in glove situation. This fact was demonstrated during the post-war trial of *Generaloberst* Kurt Student,[1135] commander of Germany's elite *Fallschirmjaeger*. Student was initially convicted of war crimes for the killings of civilians in Crete by a British tribunal in 1946, but this adjudication was later overturned on appeal due to the literal interpretation of the previous Laws of Land Warfare, and the fact that the civilians had armed themselves and therefore forfeited their protective status. Student authorized the executions of suspected partisans during *Operation Mercury*, the May 1941 invasion of Crete, when the civilians emerged with farm and kitchen tools, attacking, killing and mutilating several dozen paratroops as they struggled to get free of their parachute harnesses, or while hanging in the trees of the olive grove near the Tavronitis River bed. The Germans later found their comrades with their eyes gouged out, chests ripped open, limbs severed and throats cut. Those who survived described the event and helped locate and identify the villagers responsible, and over a hundred were executed via radio command from Student at his headquarters in Greece.

One event was captured on film by Franz-Peter Weixler during the retaliation at Kondomari village on 2 June 1941. Student stated clearly how the procedure was to occur: "All operations are to be carried out with great speed, leaving aside all formalities and certainly dispensing with special courts… These are not meant for beasts and murderers."[1136] Following the event leaflets were dropped by aircraft stating: "Ten Cretans would be shot for every soldier killed by civilians."[1137] However, on the other side of the dilemma is the case of Erich Priebke. The former *SS Hauptsturmfuehrer* who was located in Argentina in 1994 and arrested, extradited, and tried for war crimes in Italy in 1996 for the execution of

335 Italian civilians in the Ardeatin Caves near Rome in 1944. The civilians had been involved in attacks upon German soldiers, killing several and wreaking havoc as the Allies advanced toward the capitol. Priebke's defense was that his orders were clear; eliminate the partisans which was standard procedure, and Priebke understood the Geneva and Hague Conventions regarding armed civilians. His acquittal in the Italian court and the following conviction in a German court in July 1997 made world headlines.[1138]

Other documented atrocities that later altered the perceptions of legitimacy regarding many German units (and the *Waffen SS* in particular) were events such as the murders of fifty-five Canadian and British troops by *Unterscharfuehrer* Fritz Knochlein of *2ⁿᵈ Waffen SS Division "Das Reich"* during the invasion of France in 1940. Knochlein was later tried and executed for war crimes after the war, and rightly so. The "infamous" *Obersturmbannfuehrer* Joachim Peiper, the former adjutant to Himmler who blazed a trail through Russia and earned the sobriquet "Blowtorch" was implicated in the Malmedy Massacre of December 1944, while commanding *Kampfgruppe Peiper,* spearheading the *1ˢᵗ Waffen SS Panzer* Division *"Leibstandarte"* during the ill fated Winter Offensive.[1139] Other events, such as the newly uncovered evidence regarding the 17 December 1944 massacre of eleven African-American soldiers at the Belgian village of Wereth are also worth noting.[1140] The killings had been originally attributed to Peiper, although his unit never passed through the area, and are now proven to have been committed by *Obersturmbannfuehrer* Gustav Knittel of the *1st SS Panzergrenadier* Regiment, commanded by *Standartenfuehrer* Max Hansen. These acts support the lack of insight and brutal nature of men in a remorseless war of attrition.[1141]

The Allies also had their share of atrocities, with the most obvious and often overlooked events occurring in Italy following the Allied invasion. The Free French Army supporting the Allied force of British, Canadian, American, Free Polish, and ANZAC forces usually maintained a decent level of treatment towards the civilian population and the Axis prisoners taken. However, the actions of the Moroccan colonial troops fighting with the Free French must be examined. In order to convince these men to fight, certain "incentives" were offered, not the least of which was the *legal authority* to loot and rape without fear punishment, courtesy of the de Gaulle government in exile. This occurred with such frequency the Italian government eventually offered these victims of rape compensation pensions after the war.[1142]

The activities previously mentioned regarding the *Freiwilligen* units and the multitude of atrocities too numerous to list illustrate the German inability to rationalize the proper and improper use of violence, further undermining their legitimacy in the eyes of the target populations. Their actions definitely created the problems they were forced to contend with, exacerbating a festering situation to the point of political and military anarchy.

As confusing as the differences between defining partisans and guerrillas may be to comprehend, the confusion over the legitimacy and illegitimacy of combating civilians sometimes becomes even more ambiguous for the soldiers involved, hence the committing of what are sometimes deemed "atrocities" by opposing governments in a hypocritical evaluation often conducted by non-combatant military and civilian adjudicators. This ambiguity illustrates the conflict in fully understanding the rules of war. The laws of war place civilians, their homes, and property off limits, just as POWs are given special protection status since they become non-combatants once they have been captured. Once civilians take up arms, especially under the banner of a government that has capitulated they immediately lose their special protection status, since this involves them in offensive military operations supporting a government at war. Depending upon how the laws are perceived they may be treated as POWs or executed as participants in espionage.

Adolf Hitler issued over 200 *Fuehrer Befehle (Fuehrer* Directives or Orders) during the war, and the order issued regarding the treatment of captured partisans and guerrillas (without making any distinction between the two factions) did not fall outside the provision of the existing Geneva Convention, although his 18 October 1942 *"Kommando Befehl"* ordering the execution of Allied commandos behind German lines was an outright violation of international law.[1143] Although condemned after the war for these acts, by law the irregulars were legitimate targets of selective treatment as defined by the laws of land warfare, hence no war crimes could legitimately be drawn up against field commanders who exercised these actions, as witnessed by Student's acquittal for the executions on Crete. The difference between Student and Priebke was that Student had eyewitnesses who could actually identify persons involved, and many were captured soon after the acts with the incriminating evidence. The Italian situation was that of random murder; a quota system that was being enforced without regard to proving the guilt of those rounded up for retribution. It is true that many persons were executed as "suspected" partisans, and these would definitely be war crimes by any interpretation.[1144]

This was illustrated by the capture of several German commandos during the Battle of the Bulge in the Ardennes during Hitler's Winter Offensive, launched on 16 December 1944. *Obergefreiter* Manfred Pernass was just one of several men executed by an American military tribunal for wearing an American uniform and posing as an enemy soldier. This qualified him for execution under the Geneva accords, even if he had been wearing civilian clothing. The same application practiced by the Germans brought many courts-martial and prison sentences for German commanders after the war. The fact that the victor always dictates the rules and metes out the punishment after the termination of a conflict means that the interpretation of the rules regarding land warfare needed to be clarified, and this was nearly accomplished in the Geneva Convention of 1949.

However, where the Germans, Soviets and British (with the "de-housing" program initiated by Sir Arthur Harris) deviated from the understandable and acceptable norms of modern warfare was the actual, conscious, and direct application of force against a targeted civilian population. The war against the partisans and guerrillas in the east was without doubt a brutal and systematic eradication of irregulars and non-combatants alike. Events such as the "de-housing" policy of RAF Bomber Command was deemed necessary to win the war, although there were no recriminations for the acts once the war was won. However, one of the charges against Hermann Goering at his trial was for bombing civilian centers and causing non-combatant deaths in a "war of aggression." The selective application of "justice," while not undeserved in the case of most of the German defendants, illustrates the lack of credibility with such tribunals, as demonstrated by the presence of Soviet general grade officers on the panel at Nuremberg. No mention of the their genocide policies, starvation, and the illegal reinterpretation of international law regarding German POWs was ever acknowledged.

The lessons learned from the German experience were displayed throughout the world in the second half of this century, and with mixed results, but always with the intent of winning the confidence of the target audience and gaining their support. Depending upon individual perspectives, it could be debated that, despite the lessons of the past only the results have hopefully changed, if not the methods. Given the constant reminders of modern day insurgencies, especially given the Balkans and the troubled regions of Russia, it would appear that here is much to learn, and little time in which to do it. Only time will tell.

Appendix A:
Waffen SS Combat Formations, Both German & *Freiwilligen** Including Their Regimental Compositions

1ˢᵗ Waffen SS Panzer Division *"Leibstandarte"* Adolf Hitler (LSSAH); *1ˢᵗ, 2ⁿᵈ* and *3ʳᵈ* SS *Panzergrenadier* Regiments. This unit fought in France, Russia, the Ardennes, Hungary. Most of the unit that survived the Eastern Front were destroyed in the defense of Budapest in 1945.

2ⁿᵈ Waffen SS Panzer Division *"Das Reich;" 2ⁿᵈ SS Panzer* Regiment, *3ʳᵈ SS Panzer-grenadier* Regiment *"Deutschland," 4ᵗʰ Panzergrenadier* Regiment *"Der Fuehrer."* This division was destroyed and rebuilt several times, and was finally surrendered to the US Army after the collapse of Hungary and Austria.

3ʳᵈ Waffen SS Panzer Division *"Totenkopf;" 3ʳᵈ SS Panzer* Regiment, *5ᵗʰ SS Panzer-grenadier* Regiment *"Thule," 6ᵗʰ SS Panzergrenadier* Regiment *"Theodor Eicke."*

4ᵗʰ Waffen SS Panzergrenadier Division *"Polizei;".4ᵗʰ Panzerabteilung.*

5ᵗʰ Waffen SS Panzer Division *"Wiking;" 5ᵗʰ SS Panzer* Regiment, *9ᵗʰ SS Panzer-grenadier* Regiment *"Germania," 10ᵗʰ SS Panzergrenadier* Regiment "Westland."[1146]

6ᵗʰ SS Gebirgs Division *"Nord."*

7ᵗʰ Gebirgs Division *der SS "Prinz Eugen."*[1147]

8ᵗʰ Waffen SS Kavallerie Division *"Florian Geyer."*[1148]

9ᵗʰ Waffen SS Panzer Division *"Hohenstauffen;" 9ᵗʰ SS Panzer* Regiment, *19ᵗʰ* & *20ᵗʰ SS Panzergrenadier* Regiments.

10ᵗʰ Waffen SS Panzer Division *"Freundsberg;" 10ᵗʰ SS Panzer* Regiment, *21ˢᵗ* & *22ⁿᵈ Panzergrenadier* Regiments.

11ᵗʰ Panzergrenadier Division *der SS "Nordland;" 11ᵗʰ Panzerabteilung "Herrmann von Salza."*

---

*noted as *der SS*

12th Waffen SS Panzer Division *"Hitlerjuegend;" 12th SS Panzer* Regiment, *25th & 26th Panzergrenadier* Regiments.[1149]
13th Gebirgs Division *der SS "Handschar."*[1150]
14th Grenadier Division *der SS "Galizische-Ukrainische Nr. 1."*[1151]
15th Grenadier Division *der SS "Lettische Nr.1."*[1152]
16th Waffen SS Panzergrenadier Division *"Reichsfuehrer-SS;" 16th Panzerabteilung.*
17th Waffen SS Panzergrenadier Division *"Goetz von Berlichingen."*[1153]
18th Panzergrenadier Division *der SS "Horst Wessel;" 18th Panzerabteilung.*
19th Grenadier Division *der SS "Lettisische Nr.1."*[1154]
20th Grenadier Division *der SS "Estnische Nr.1."*[1155]
21st Grenadier Division *der SS "Skanderberg."*[1156]
22nd Cavalries Division *der SS "Maria Theresia."*[1157]
23rd Gebirgs Division *"Kama."*[1158]
23rd Panzergrenadier Division *"Nederland."*[1159]
24th Gebirgs Division *der SS "Karstjaeger."*
25th Grenadier Division *("Ungarische") Nr. 1 "Hunyadi."*[1160]
26th Grenadier Division *"Ungarische Nr.2."*
27th Grenadier Division *"Langemarck."*
28th SS Panzergrenadier Division *der SS "Wallonien."*[1161]
29th Grenadier Division *der SS "Russische Nr. 1."*[1162]
30th Grenadier Division *der SS "Russische Nr.2."*
31st Panzergrenadier Division *der SS "Boehmen-Mahren."*[1163]
32nd Panzergrenadier Division *"30 Januar."*[1164]
33rd Kavallerie Division *der SS "Ungarische Nr. 3."*[1165]
34th Grenadier Division *der SS "Landstorm-Nederland."*
35th Panzergrenadier Division *der SS "Polizei."*
36th Grenadier Division *der SS "Dirlewanger."*[1166]
37th Kavallerie Division *"Luetzow."*
38th Grenadier Division *"Niebelungen."*
39th Gebirgs Division *der SS "Andreas Hoefer."*
40th Panzergrenadier Division *"Feldhernhalle."*
41st Grenadier Division *der SS "Kalevala."*
42nd Grenadier Division *"Niederschen."*
43rd Division *der SS "Reichsmarschall."*
44th Panzergrenadier Division *der SS "Wallenstein."*
45th Division *der SS "Warager."*[1167]

Appendix B:
Maps of Germany Army Locations and Strengths

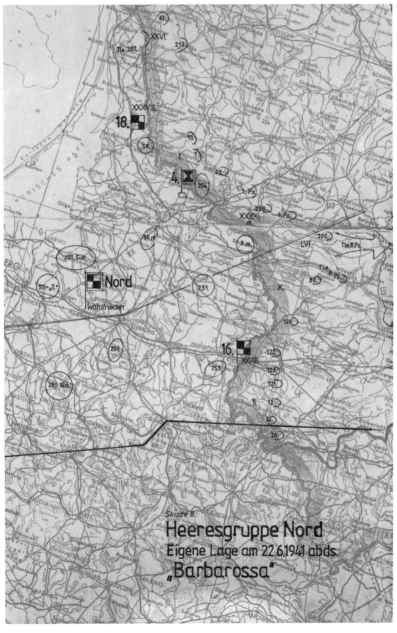

Army Group North unit deployments as of 22 June 194 1.

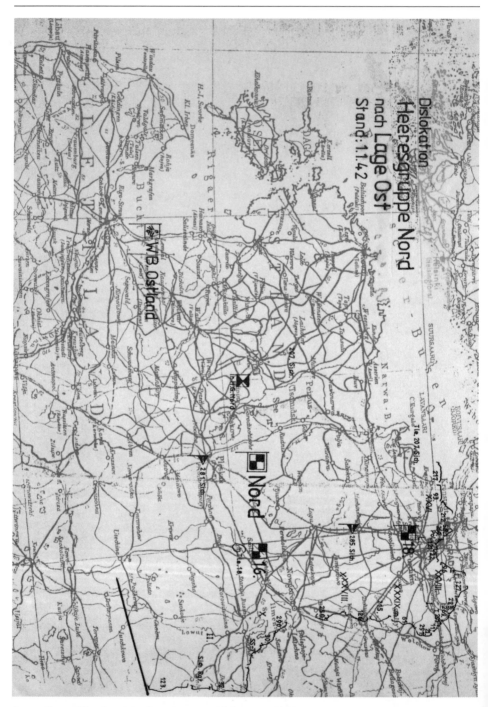

Army Group North unit re-locations as of I January 1942.

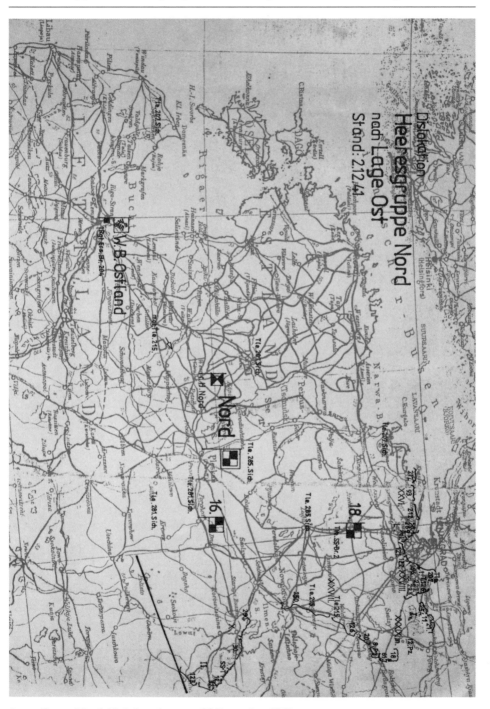

Army Group North Unit locations as of 2 December 1941.

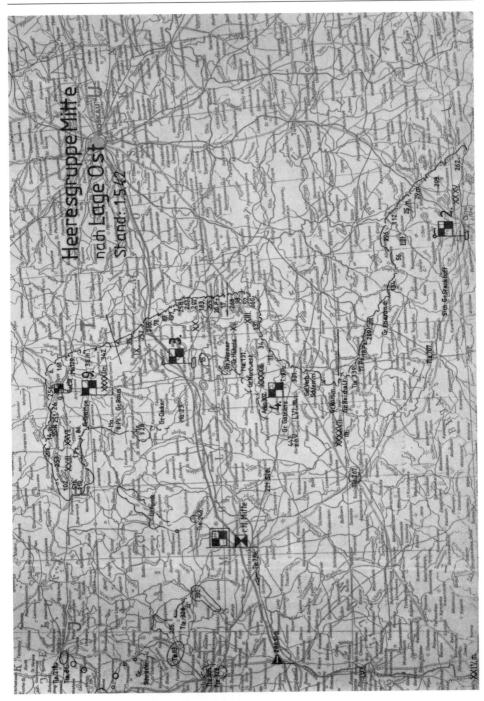

Army Group Center unit locations as of I May 1942.

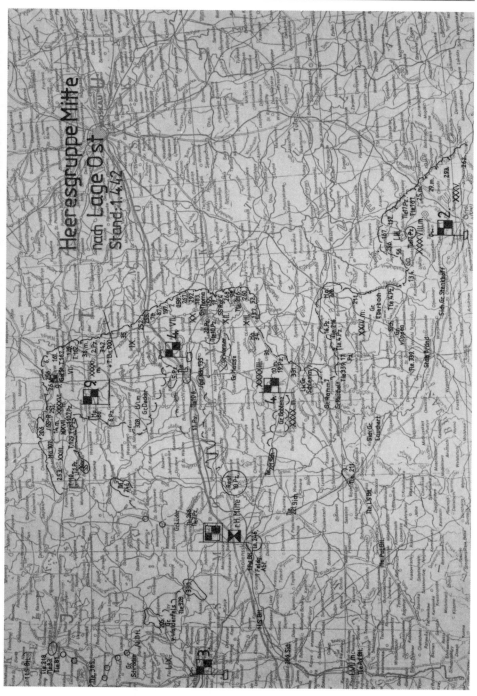

Army Group Center unit locations as of I April 1942.

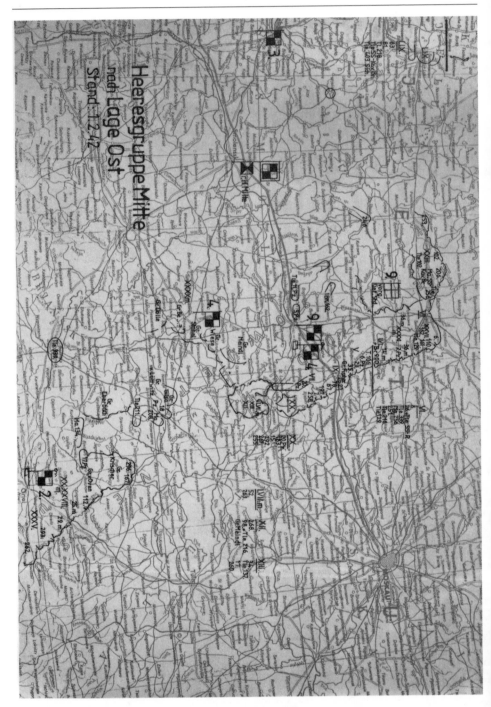

Army Group Center unit locations as of I February 1942.

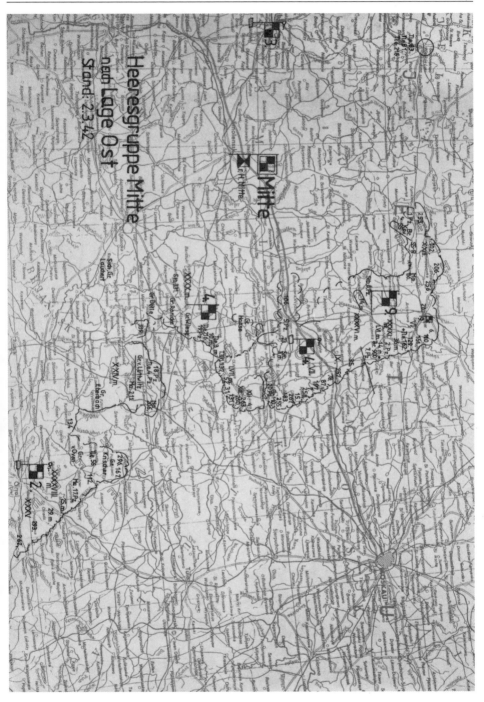

Army Group Center unit locations as of 2 March 1942.

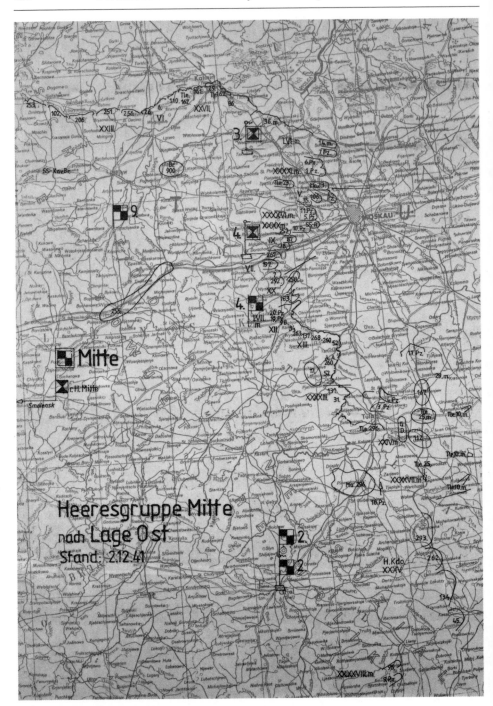

Army Group Center unit locations as of 2 December 1941.

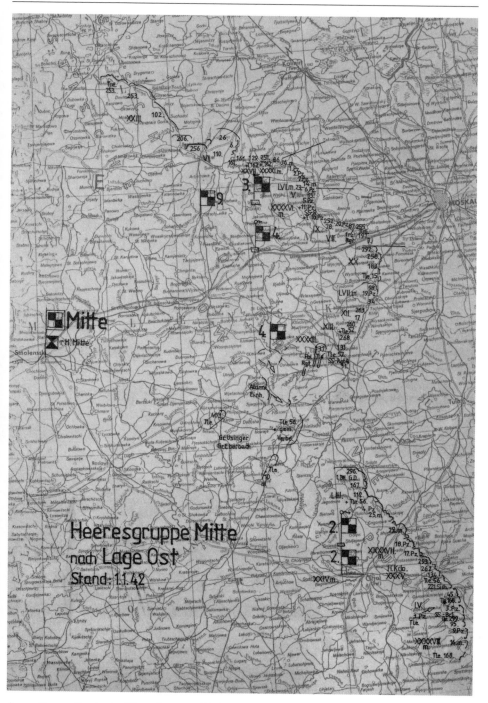

Army Group Center unit locations as of I January 1942.

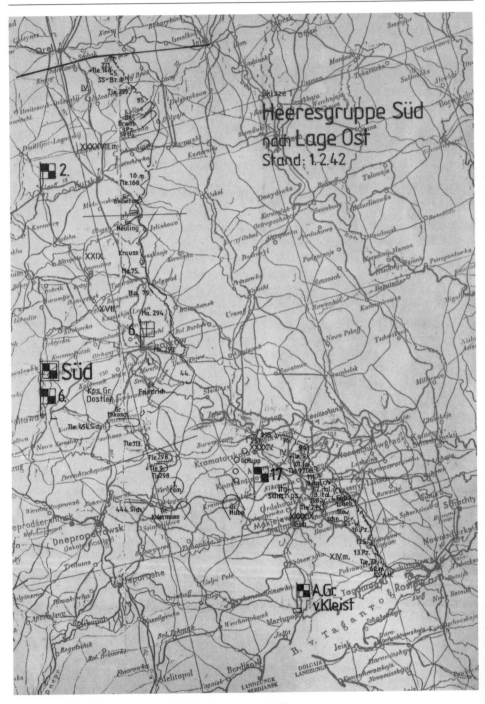

Army Group South unit locations as of I February 1942.

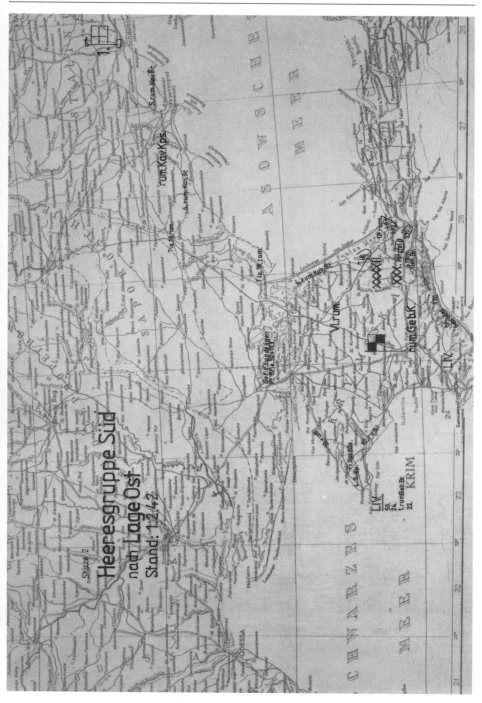

Army Group South unit locations (Crimea) as of I February 1942.

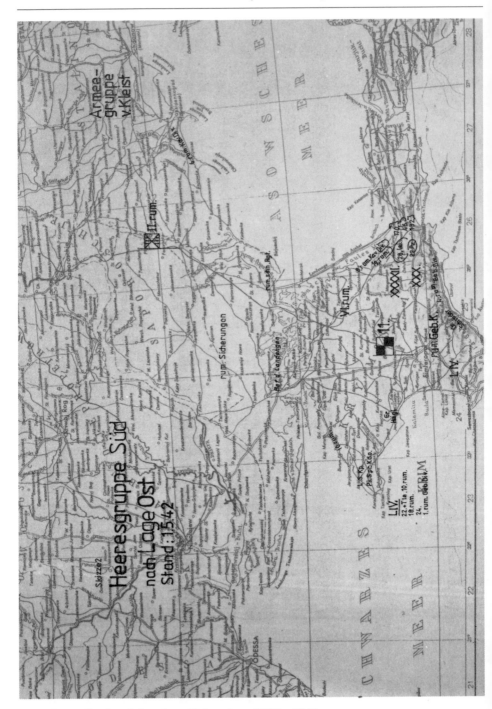

Anny Group South unit locations (Crimea) as of I May 1942.

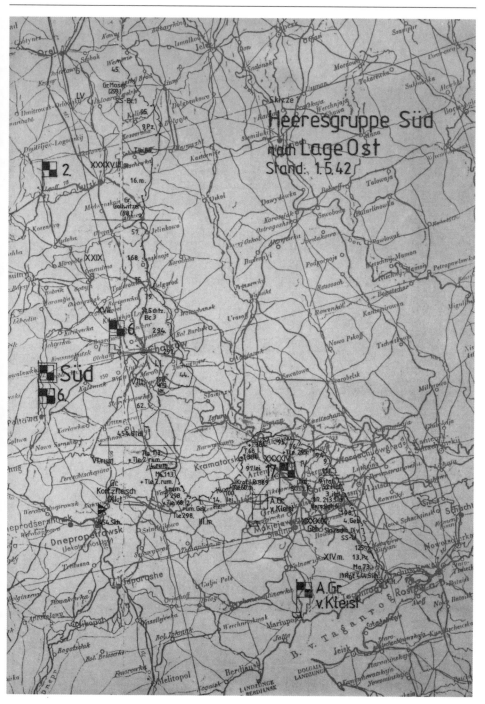

Army Group South unit locations as of I May 1942.

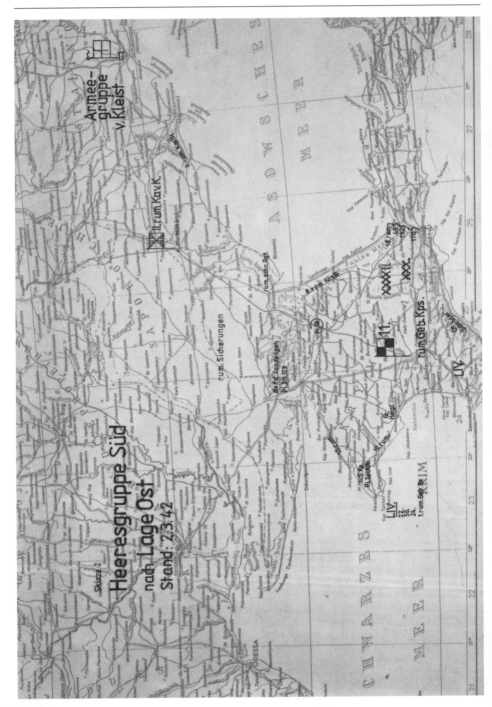

Army Group South unit locations (Crimea) as of 2 March 1942.

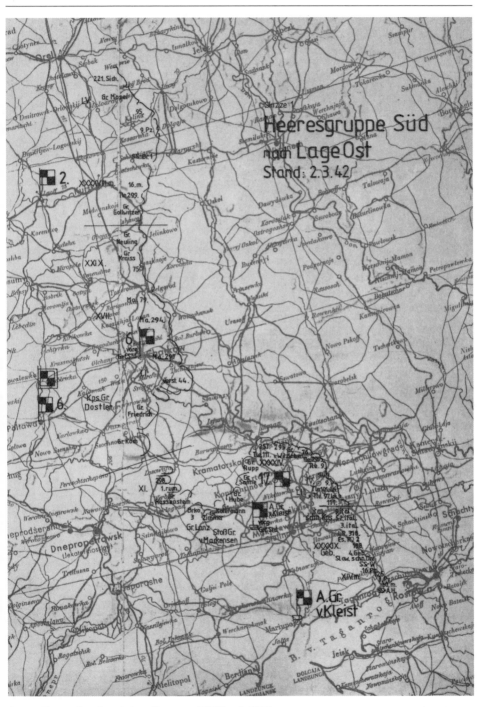

Army Group South unit locations as of 2 March 1942.

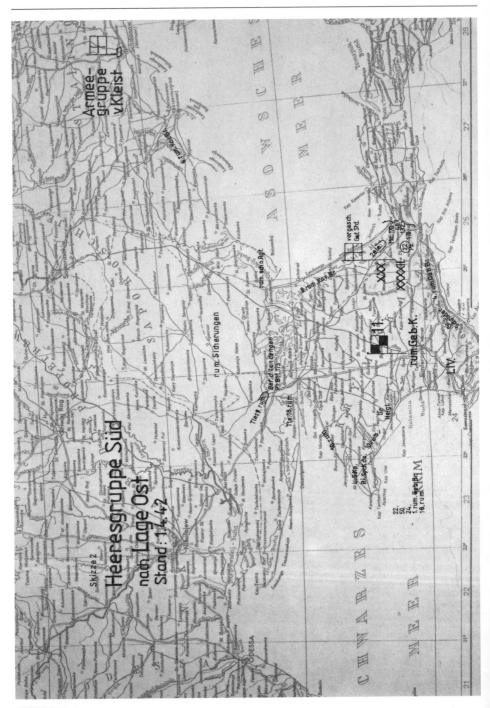

Army Group South unit locations (Crimea) as of I April 1942.

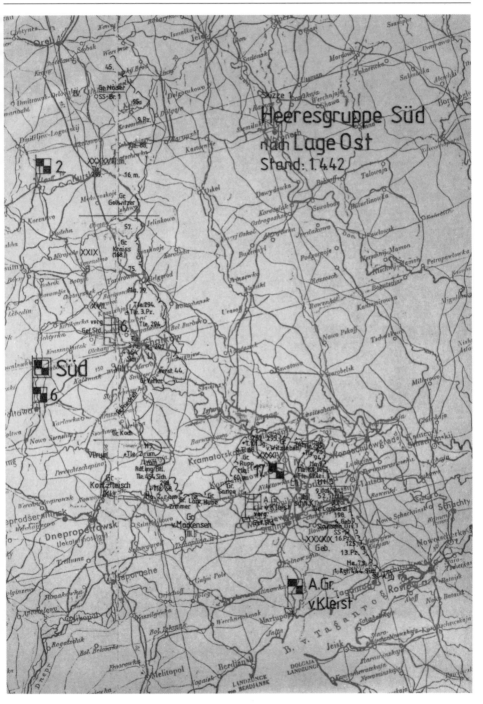

Army Group South unit locations as of I April 1942.

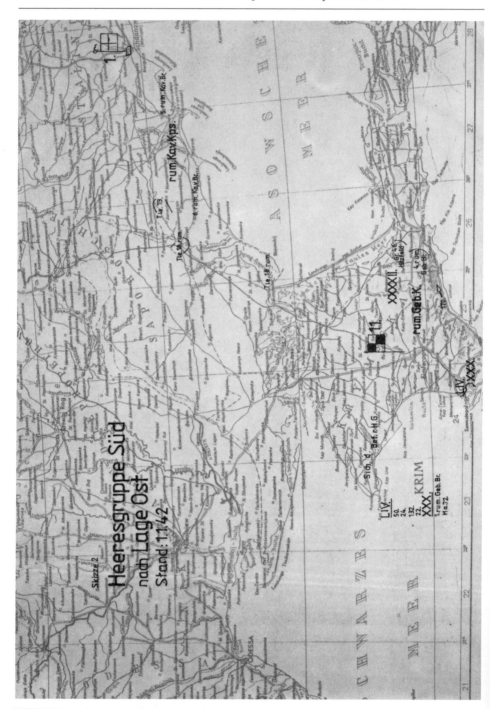

Army Group South unit locations (Crimea) as of I January 1942.

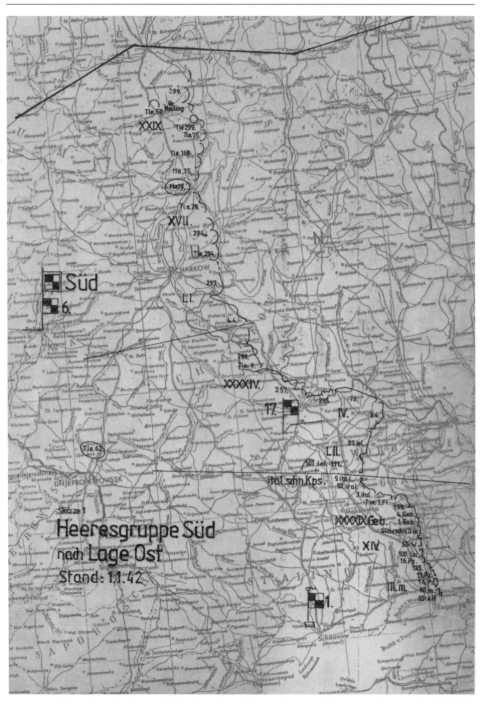

Army Group South unit locations as of I January 1942.

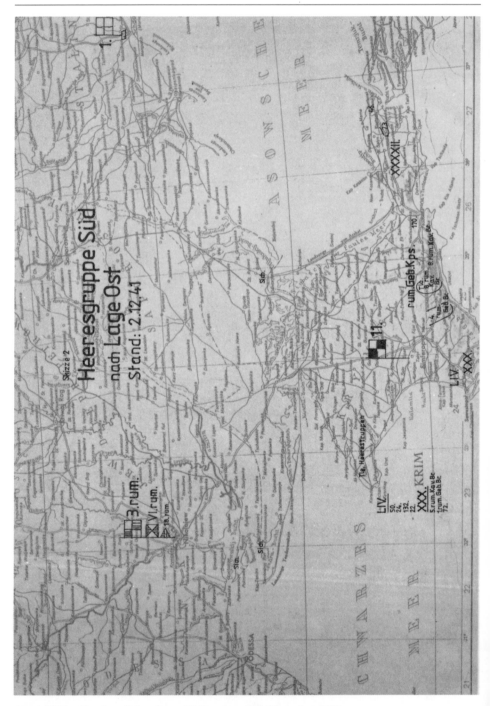

Army Group South unit locations (Crimea) as of 2 December 1941.

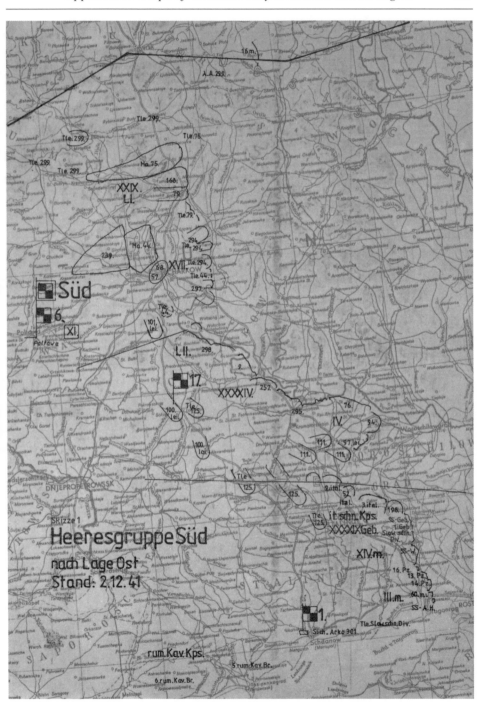

Army Group South unit locations as of 2 December 1941.

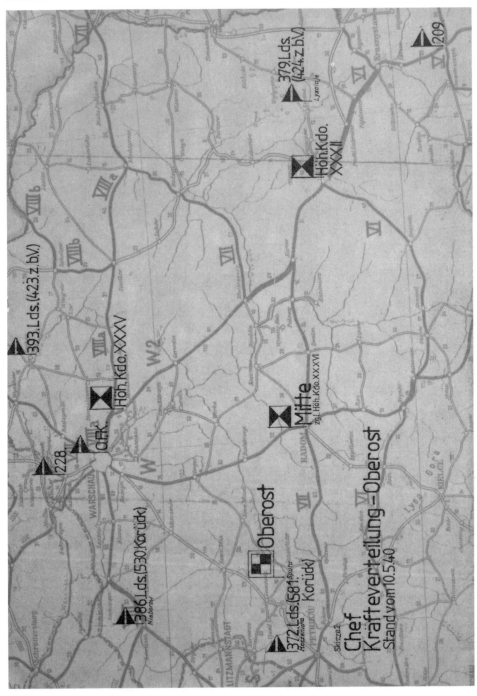

German unit strengths and locations in Poland as of 10 May 1940.

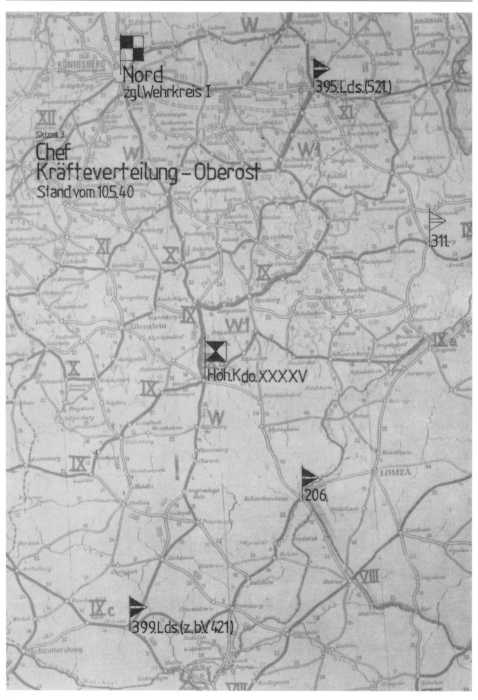

German unit strengths and locations in East Prussia as of 10 May 1940.

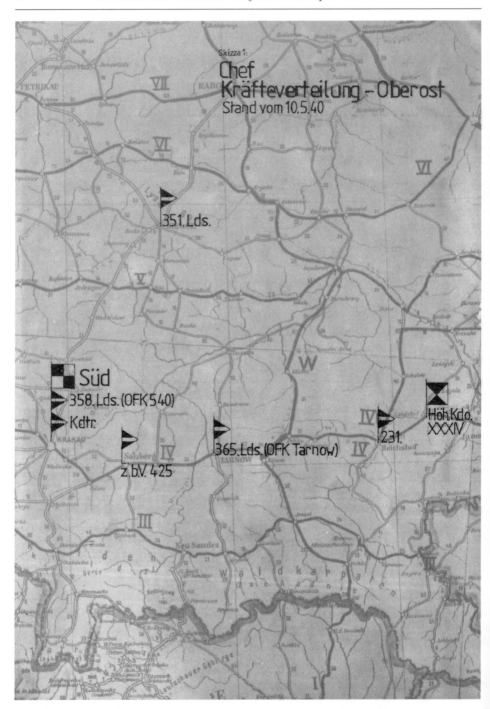

German unit strengths and locations in the south-east Austria/Poland/North Romania as of 10 May 1940.

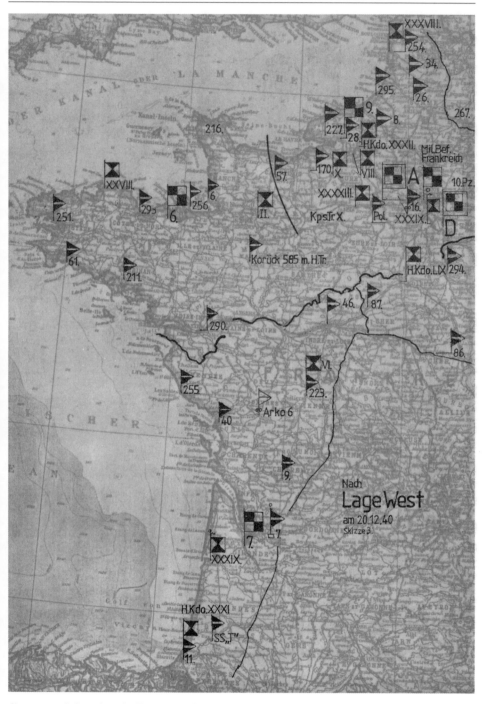

German unit locations in France as of 20 December 1940.

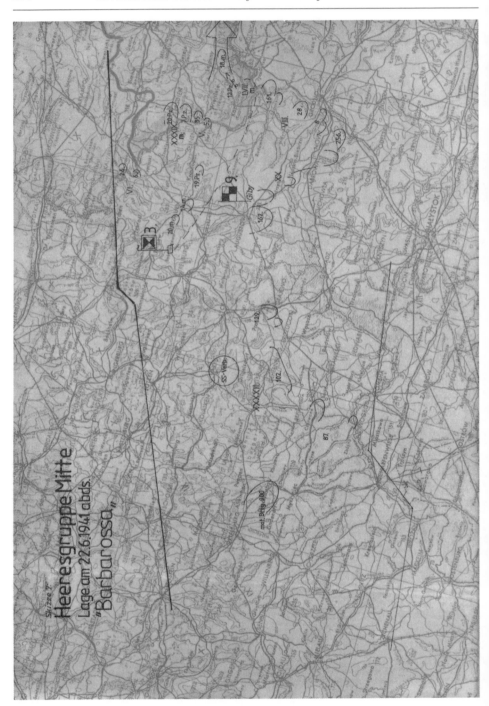

Army Group Center unit locations in East Prussia/Poland as of 22 June 194 1.

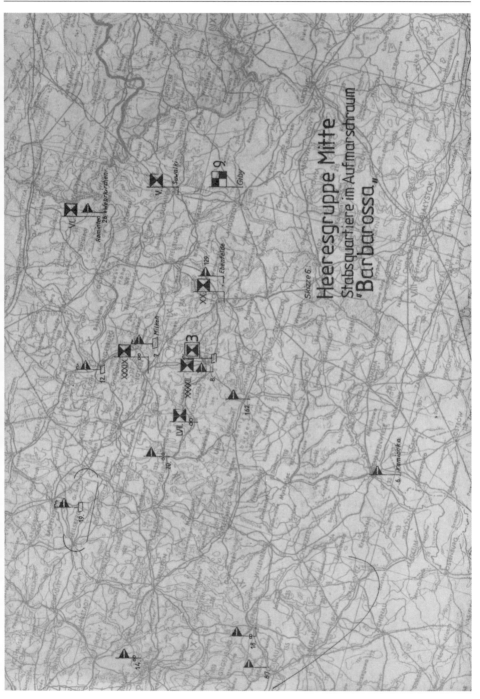

Army Group Center units in order of march during Barbarossa, 22 June 194 1.

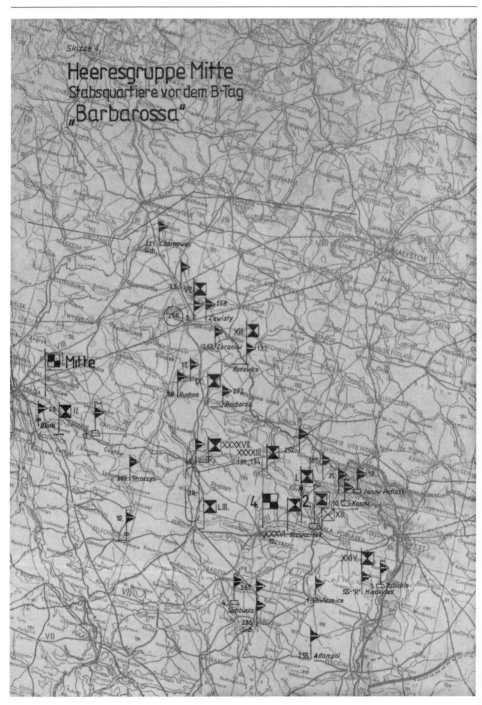

Army group Center staff unit locations for Barbarossa.

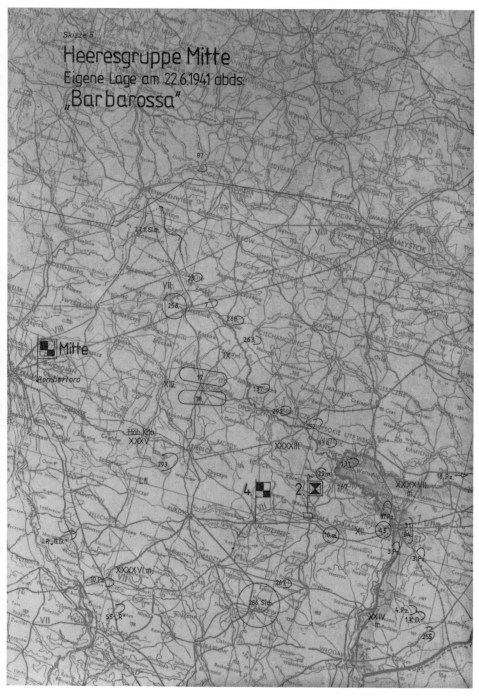

Army Group Center unit locations and staging plans as of 22 June 194 1.

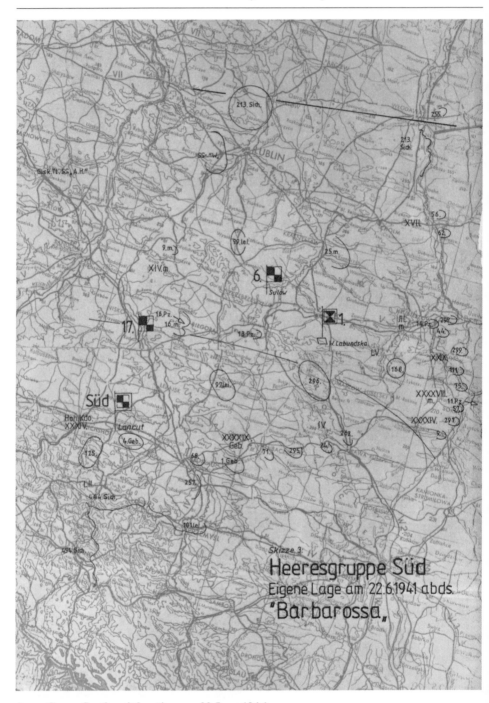

Army Group South unit locations on 22 June 194 1.

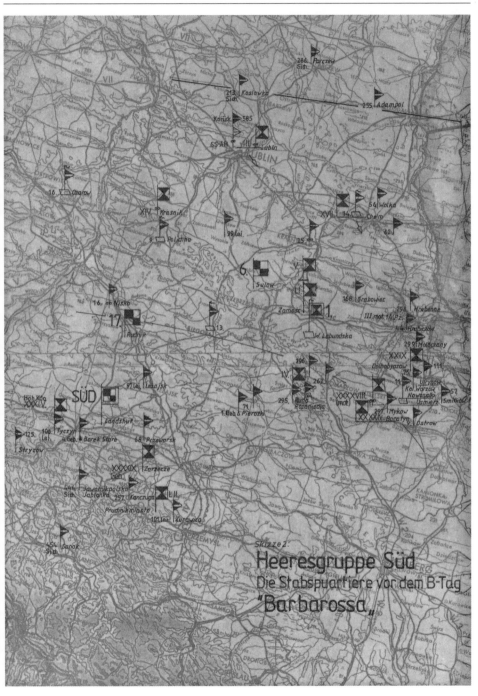

Army Group South Staff locations on 22 June 1941.

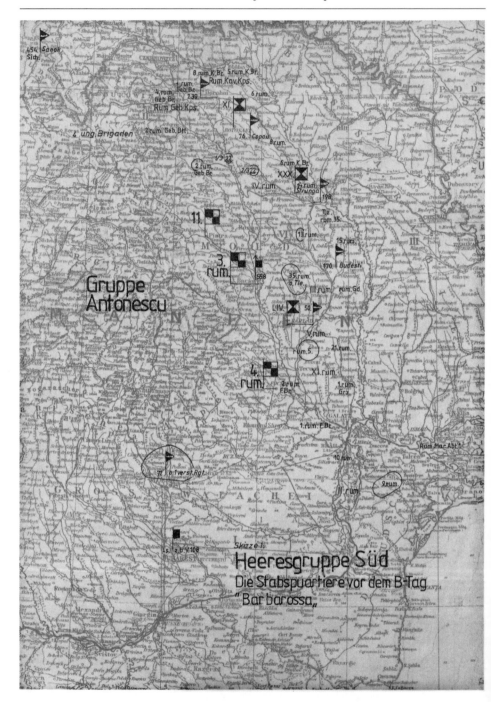

Army Group South staff locations with Romanian support during Barbarossa.

Geheim!

Einsatzgliederung vom 15. Mai 1941.

Bezirkschef Bordeaux
Bordeaux

Unmittelbar unterstellte Einheiten:
1. Geheime Feldpolizei
   Leitender Feldpol.Direktor Bordeaux und B.
2. Feldgendarmerie
   Feld-Ers.Kp.7,Bordeaux

	Charente Inférieure	Charente	Gironde	Landes	Basses Pyrénées
Geh.Feldpolizei	Gruppe 1/2 Bordeaux	Gruppe 1/2 Komm. Bordeaux	Gruppe 1/2 Komm. Bordeaux	Gruppe 1/2 Komm. Biarritz	Gruppe 1/2 Komm. Biarritz
Trn.Übungsplatz-Kdtrn.	La Bracanne	La Bracanne	Souge		
Heeres-Verpflgs.Stellen	Angoulême	Angoulême	Bordeaux	Mont de Marsan	Bayonne
Heeres-Unterkfts.Verw.	La Rochelle	Angoulême	Bordeaux Souge	Mont de Marsan	Bayonne
Lds.Regt.Stäbe	5/6	5/6	5/6 Bordeaux	5/6	5/6
Kgf.Bez.Kommandant			H Bordeaux		
Stalag-Kdtrn.		Angoulême	St Medard	Onesse et Laharie	Bayonne
Lds.Batle. der Stalags		527 Angoulême	961 Andernos-les-Bains	690 Onesse	
Departements:	La Rochelle	Angoulême	Bordeaux	Mont de Marsan	Bayonne
Feld-Kommandanturen	640 La Rochelle	527 Angoulême	529 Bordeaux	541 Mont de Marsan	
Kreis-Kommandanturen	730 Royan, 734 Saintes, 886 Jonzac	777 Cognac, 779 Angoulême, 887 La Rochefoucauld	796 Blaye, 796 Langon, 798 Libourne, 885 Bordeaux	667 Mont de Marsan, 766 Dax	649 Bayonne, 732 St Jean-de-Luz
Lds.Batle. der Departements	640 Saintes	640 Angoulême	792 Bordeaux, 9?1 Bordeaux	320 Mont de Marsan	800***, 359 Biarritz, Bayonne (Anglet) I.T.Gef.Bewachung

German unit allocations to Bordeaux as of 15 May 194 1.

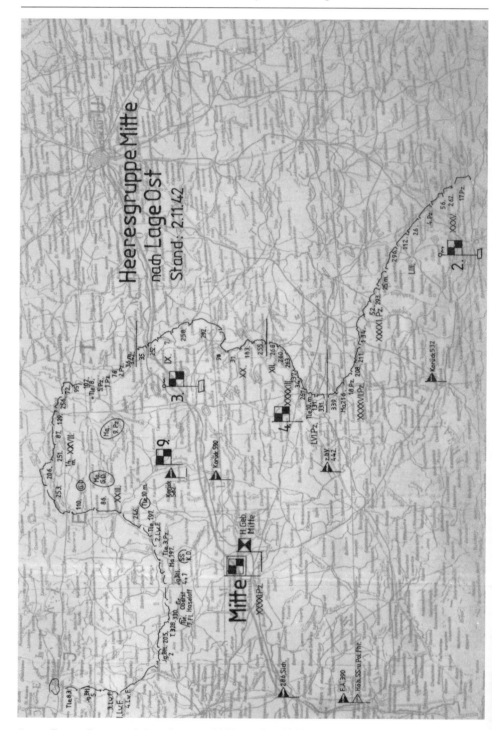

Army Group Center unit locations as of 2 November 1942.

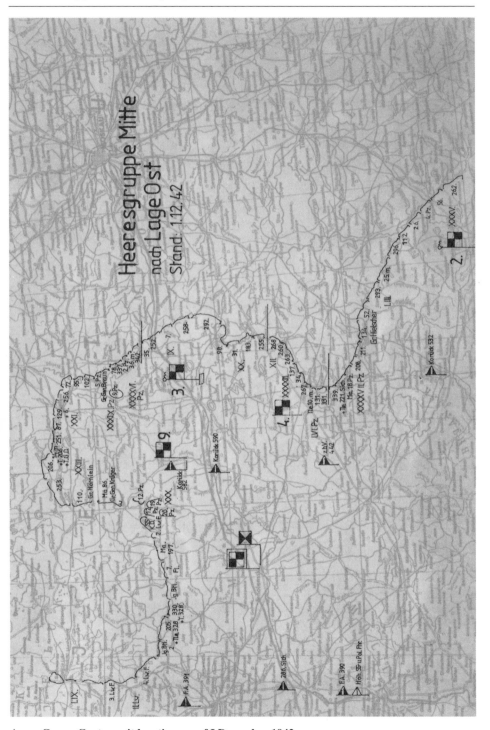

Army Group Center unit locations as of I December 1942.

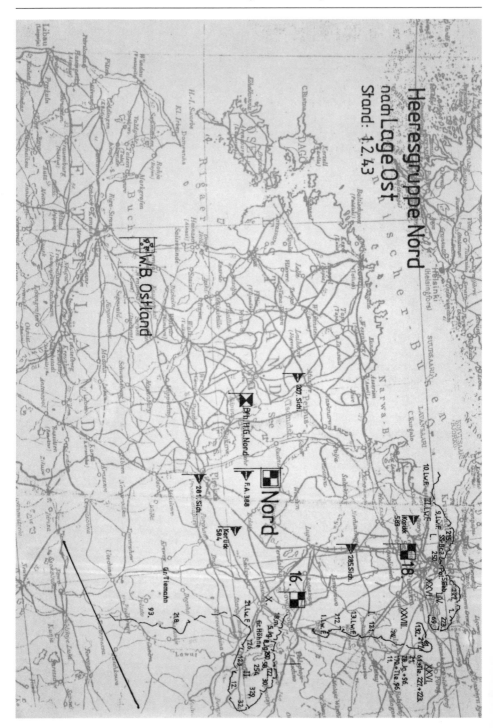

Army Group North unit locations as of I February 1943.

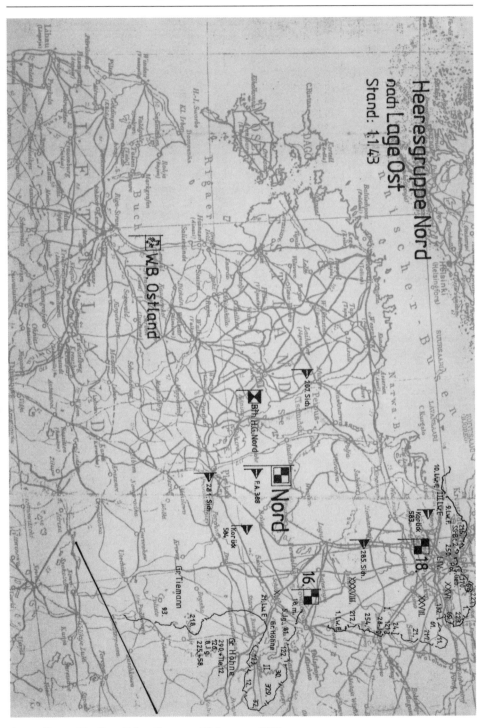

Army Group North unit locations as of I January 1943.

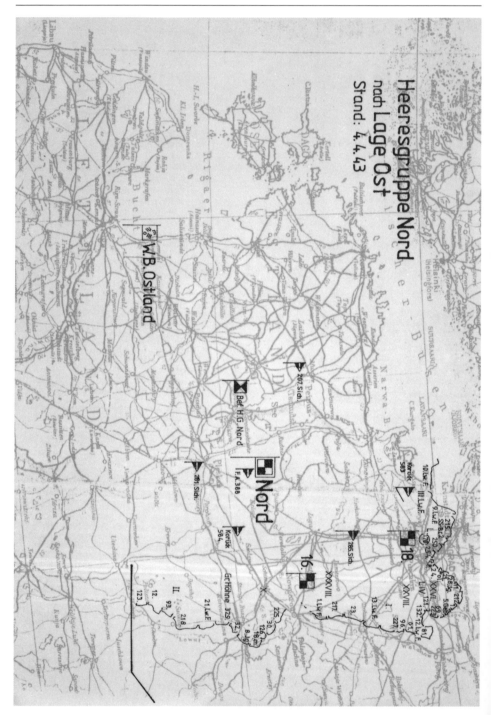

Army Group North unit locations as of 4 April 1943.

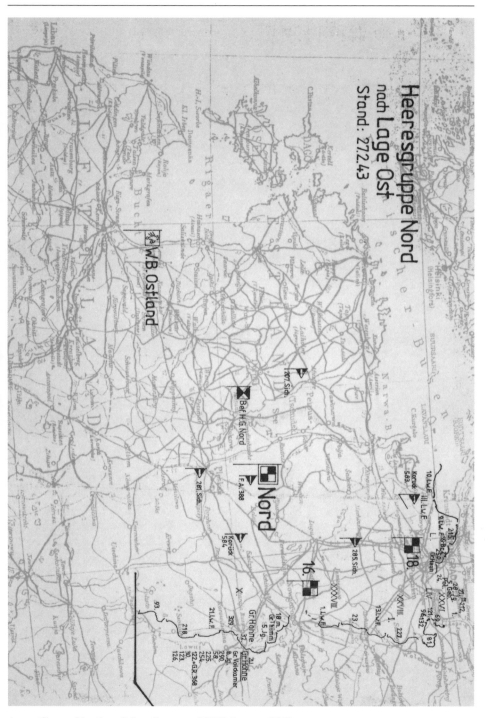

Army Group North unit locations as of 27 February 1943.

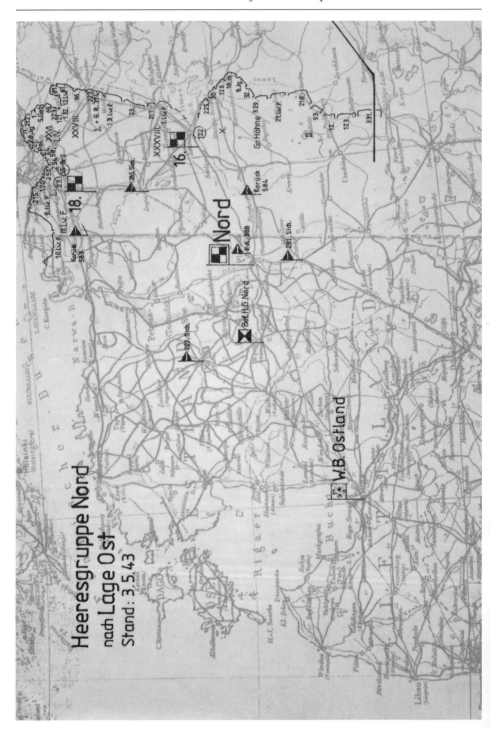

Army Group North unit locations as of 3 May 1943.

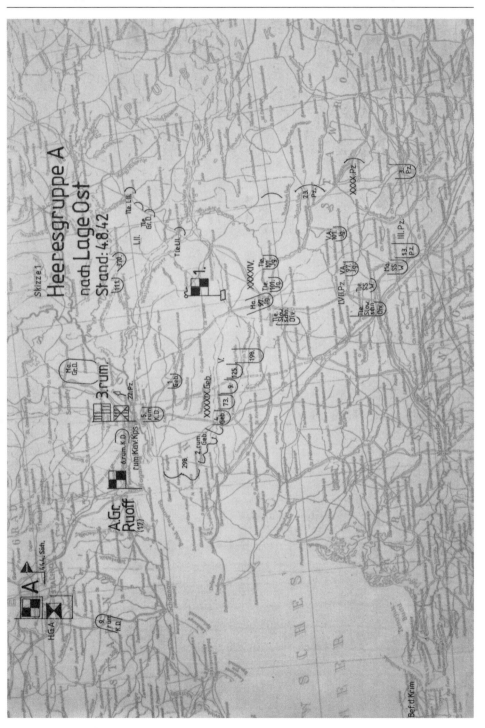

Army Group A (Caucasus) unit locations as of 4 August 1942.

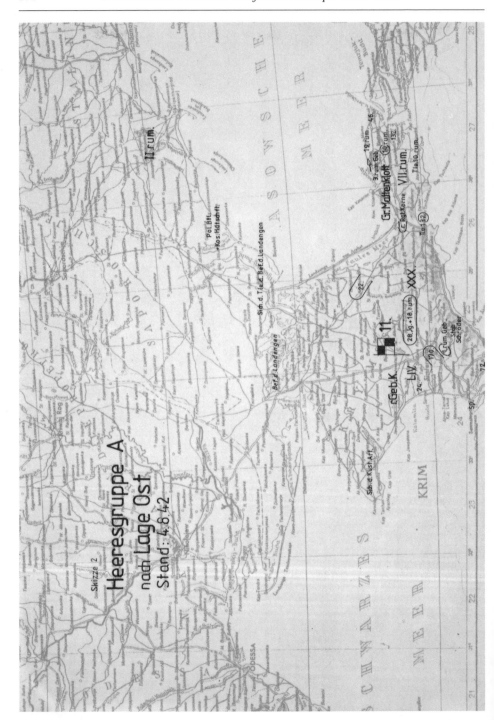

Army Group A (Crimea) unit locations as of 4 August 1942.

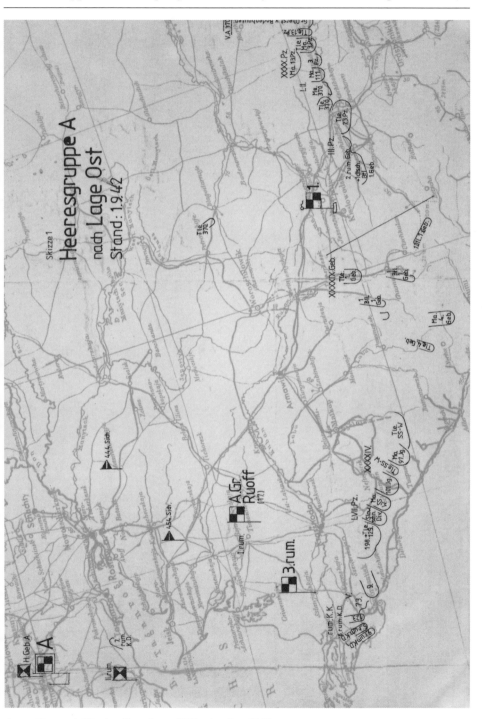

Army Group A (Rostov Front) as of I September 1942.

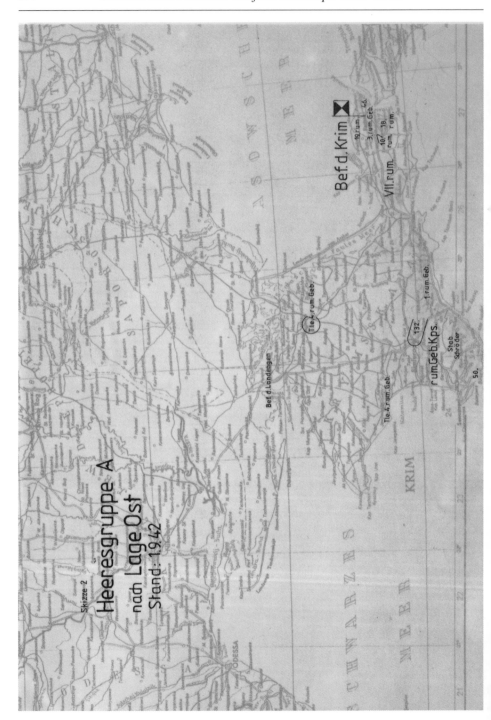

Army Group A (Crimea) unit locations as of I September 1942.

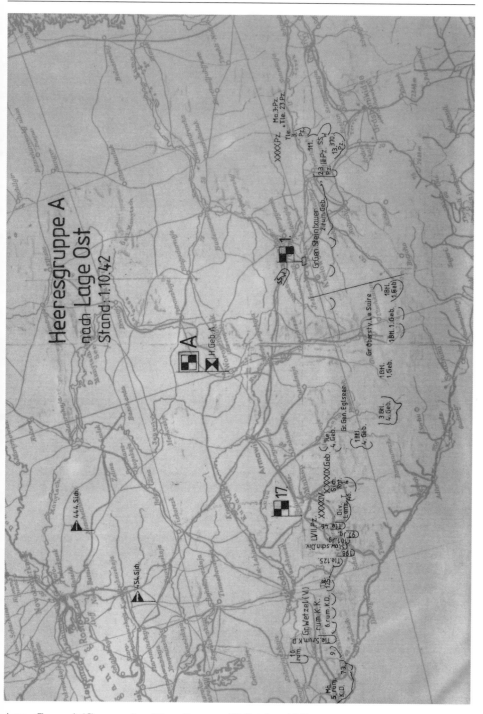

Army Group A (Caucasus) unit locations as of I October 1942.

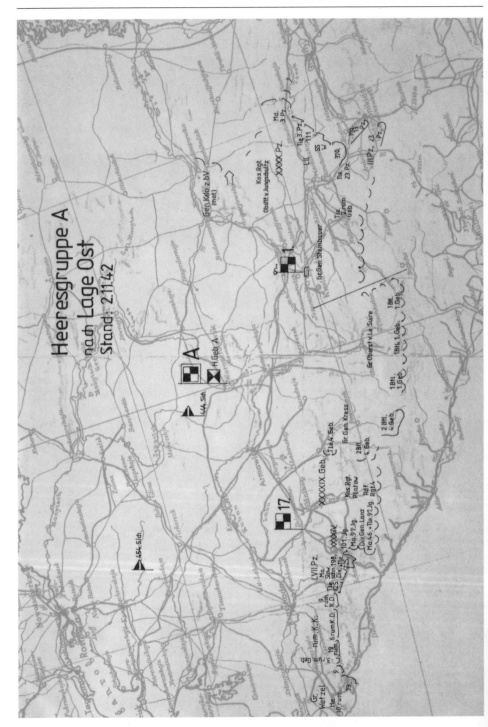

Army Group A (Caucasus) unit locations as of 2 November 1942.

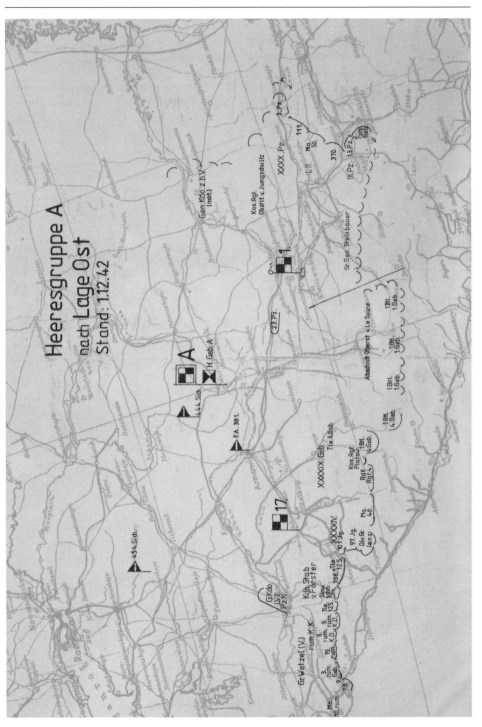

Army Group A (Caucasus) unit locations as of I December 1942.

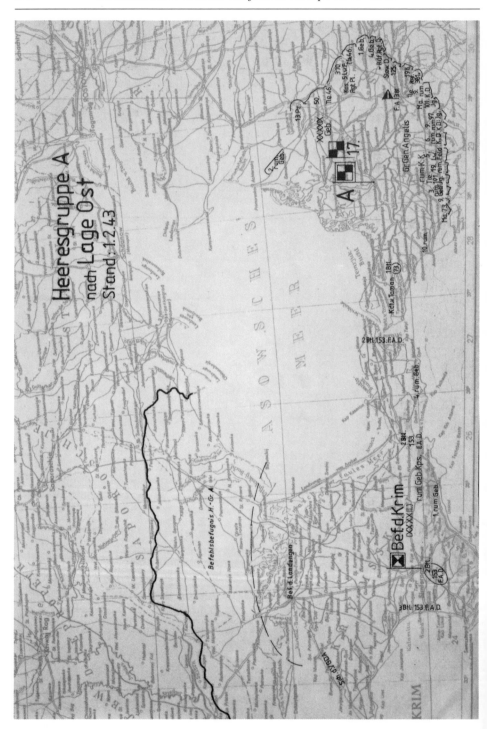

Army Group A (Sea of Azov Front) unit locations as of I February 1943.

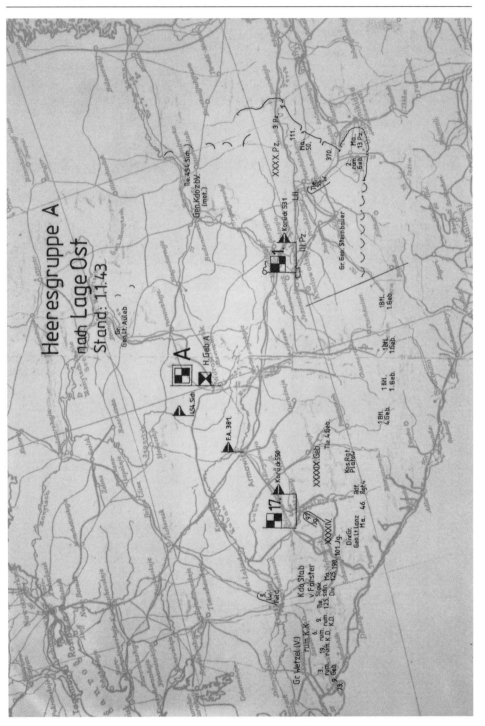

Army Group A (Caucasus) unit locations as of I January 1943.

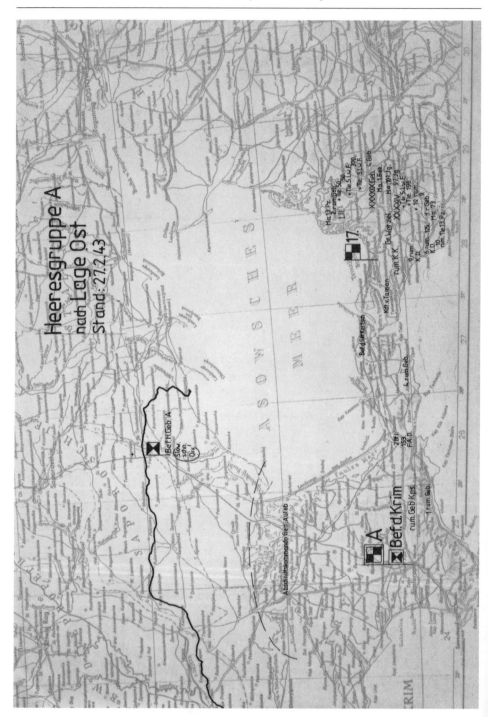

Army Group (Crimea/Taman Peninsula) unit locations as of 27 February 1943.

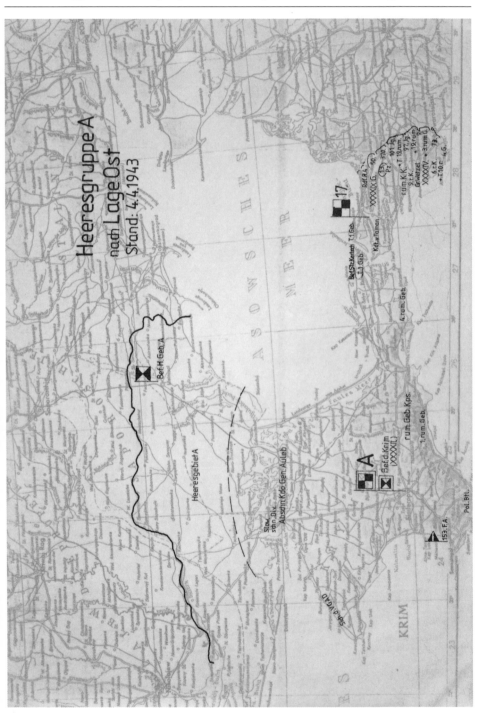

Army Group A (Crimea/Taman Peninsula) unit locations as of 4 April 1943.

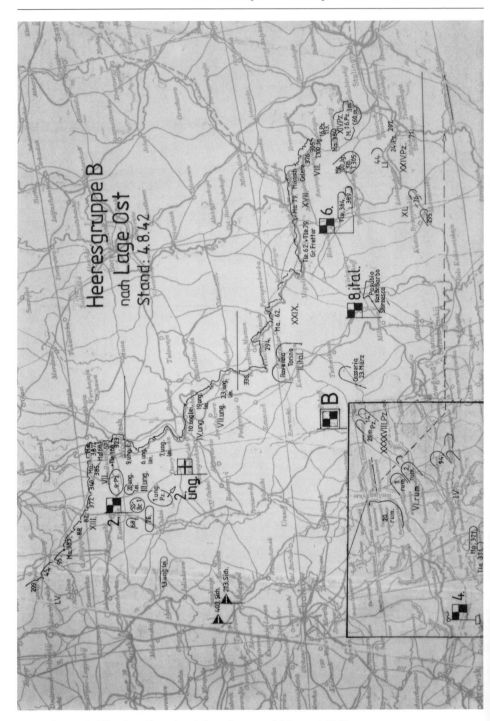

Army Group B (Kharkov Front) unit locations as of 4 August 1942.

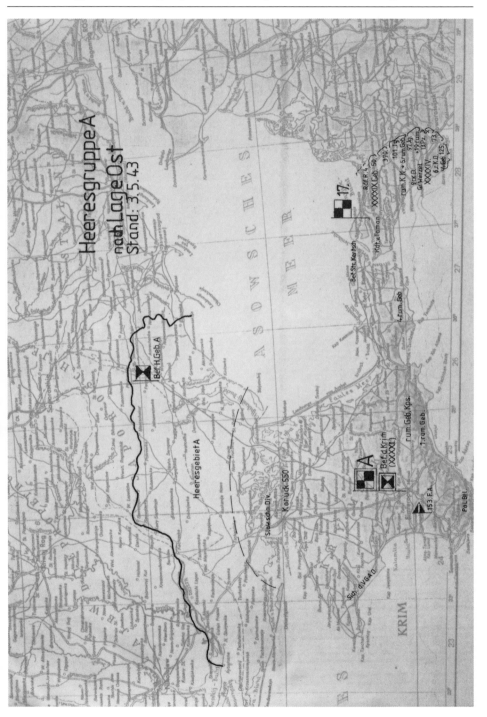

Army Group A (Crimea/Taman Peninsula) unit locations as of 3 May 1943.

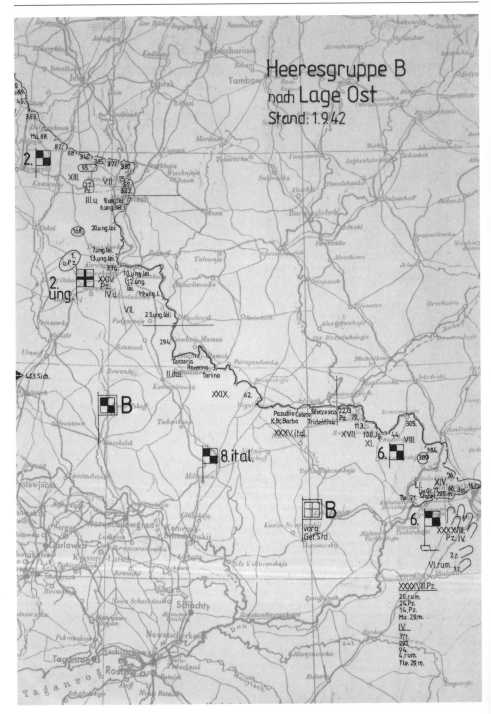

Army Group B (North-East Caucasus Front) unit locations as of I September 1942.

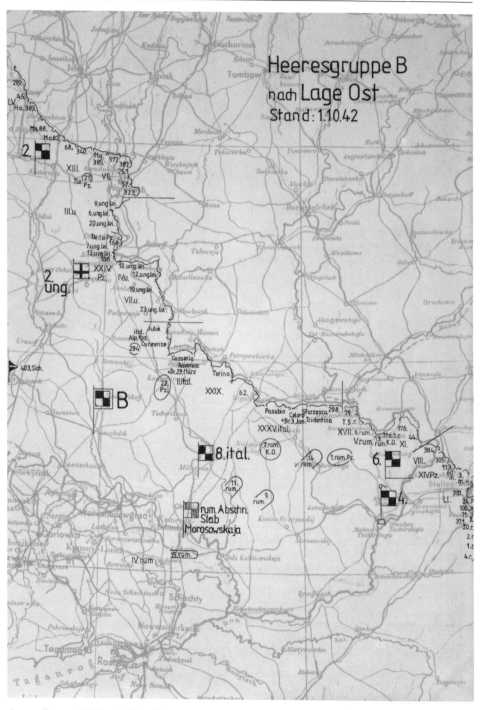

Army Group B (North-East Caucasus) with Italian and Hungarian unit locations as of I October 1942.

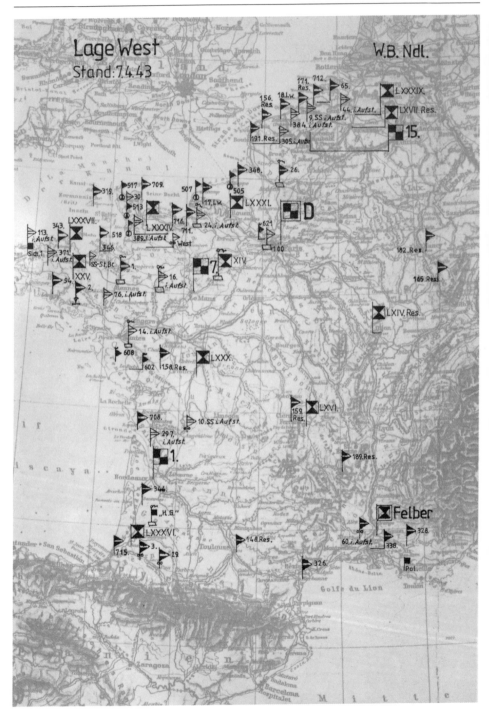

German unit locations in France and Belgium as of 7 April 1943.

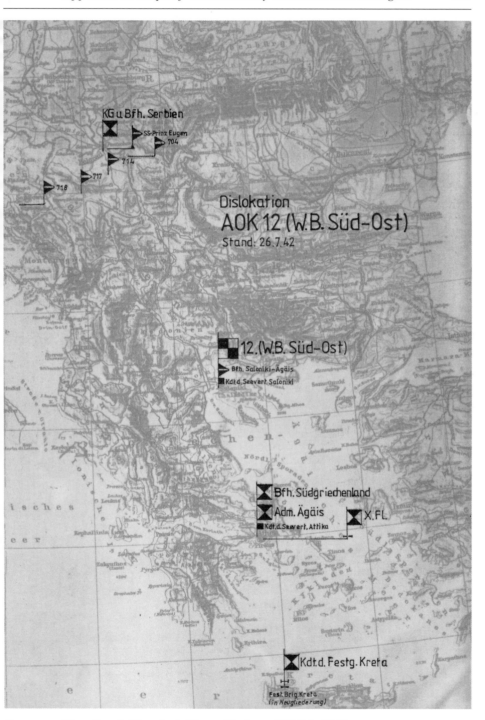

German unit locations in Yugoslavia/Greece/Crete as of 26 July 1942.

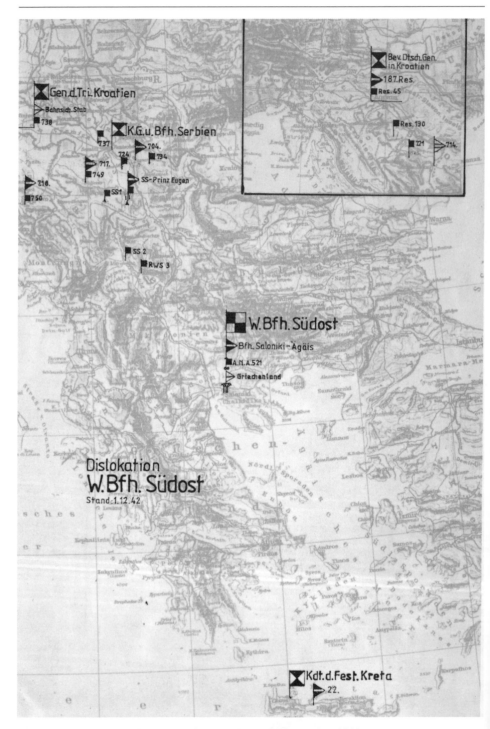

German unit locations (South-east Command) as of I December 1942.

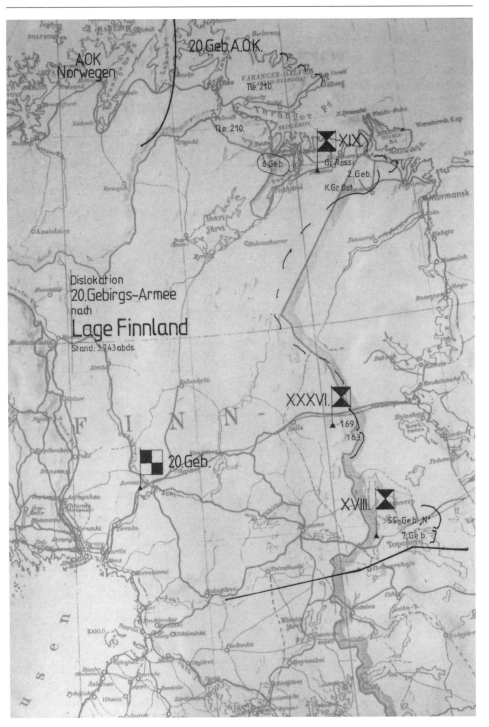

German unit locations in Norway/Finland as of 3 July 1943.

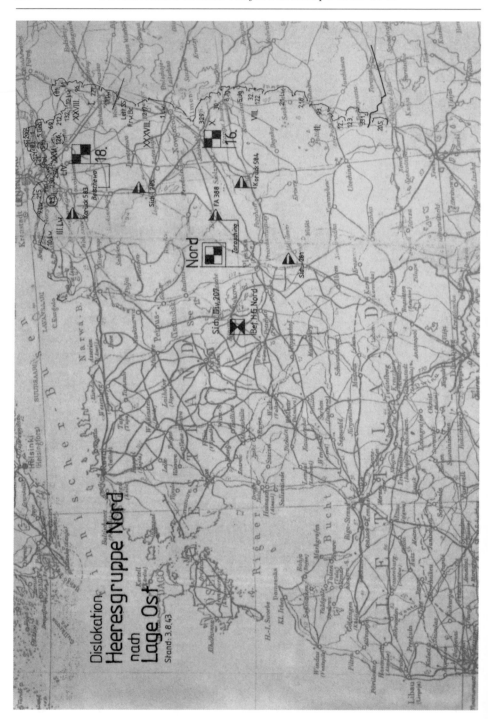

Army Group North (Leningrad Front) unit locations as of 3 August 1943.

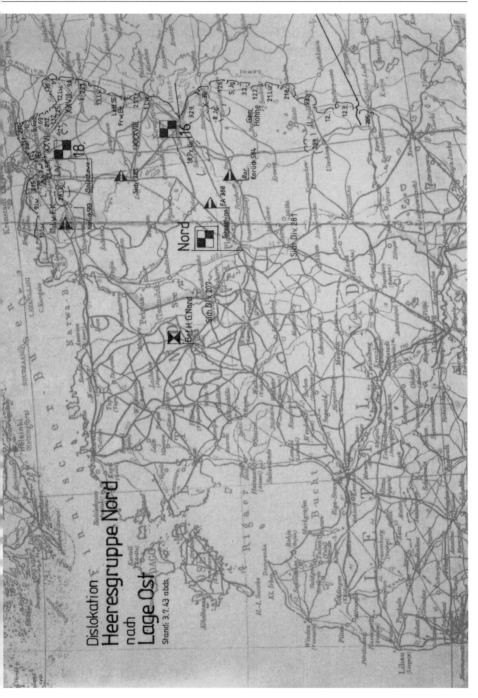

Army GroupNorth (Leningrad Front) unit locations as of 3 July 1943.

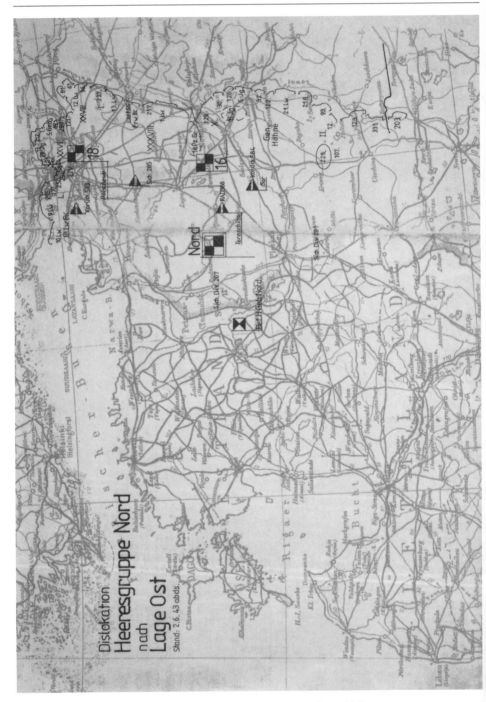

Army Group North (Leningrad Front) unit locations as of 2 June 1943.

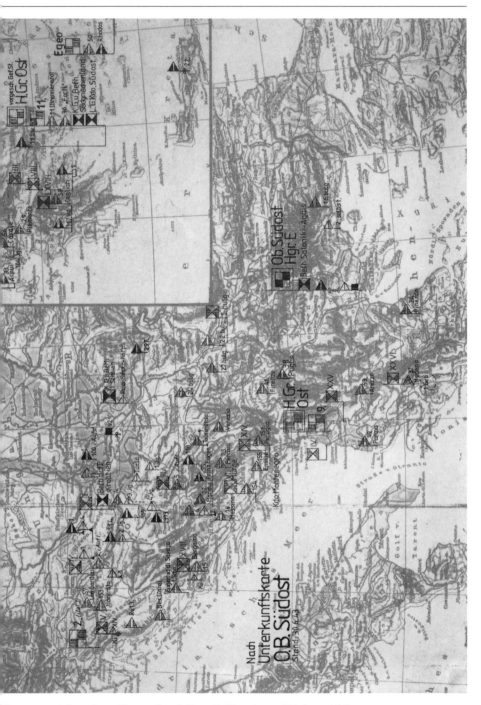

German unit locations (Group South-East-Balkans) as of 30 June 1943.

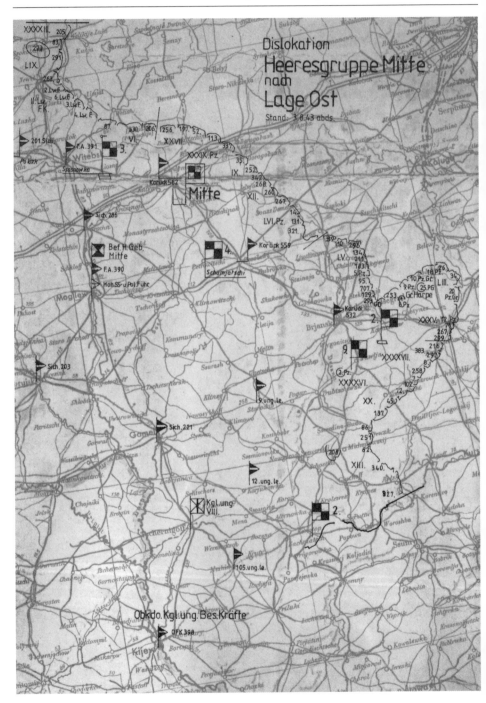

Army Group Center unit locations as of 3 August 1943.

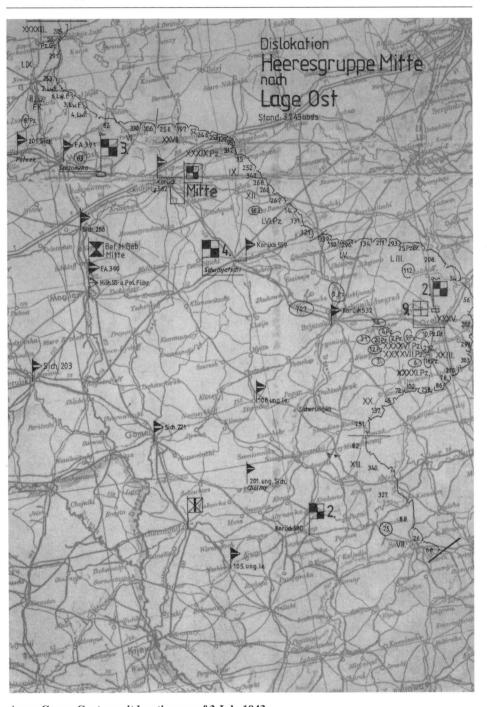

Army Group Center unit locations as of 3 July 1943.

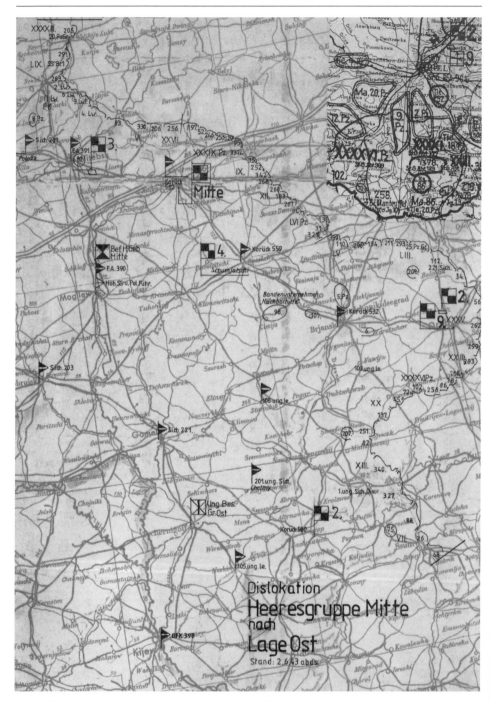

Army Group Center unit locations as of 2 June 1943.

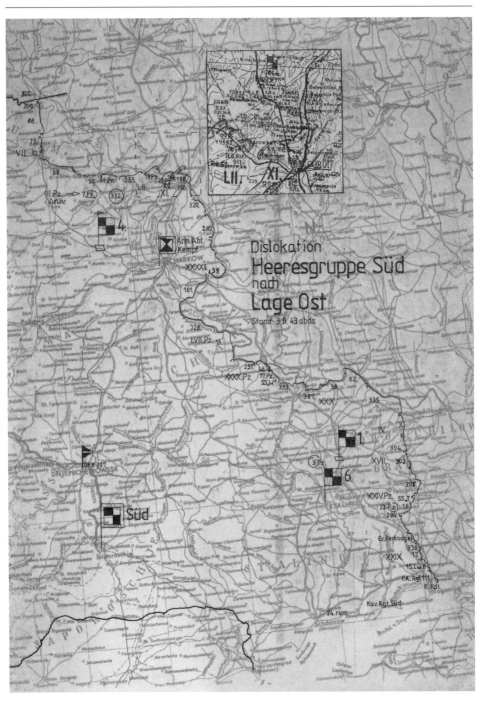

Army Group South (Kharkov/Stalino Front) unit locations as of 3 August 1943.

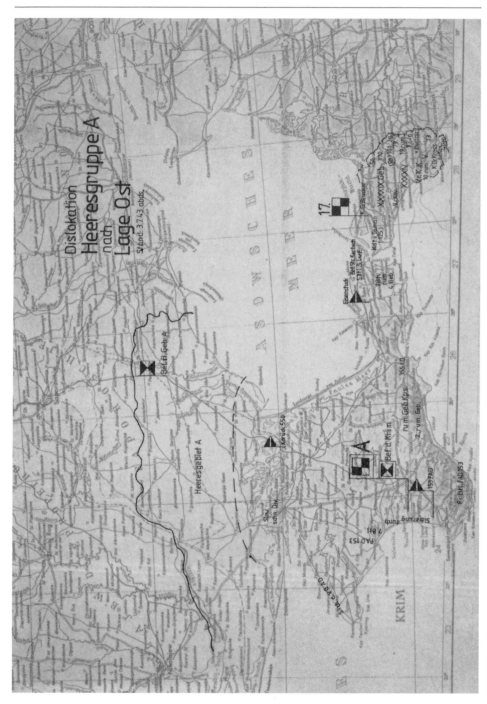

Army Group A (Caucasus/Taman Peninsula) unit locations as of 3 July 1943.

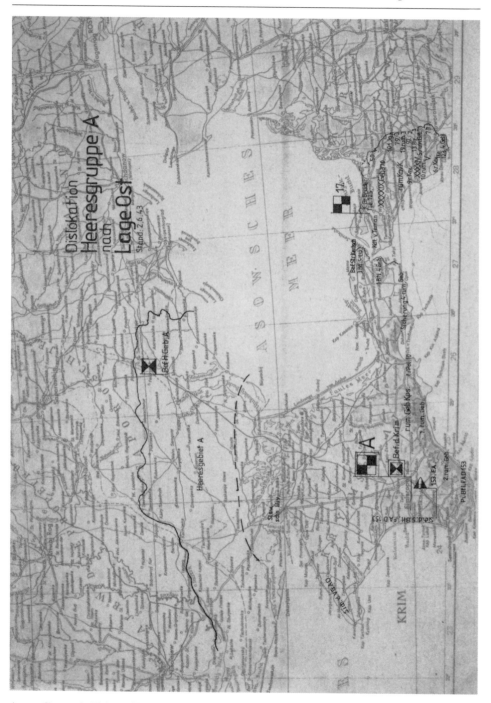

Army Group A (Crimea/Taman Peninsula) unit locations as of 2 June 1943.

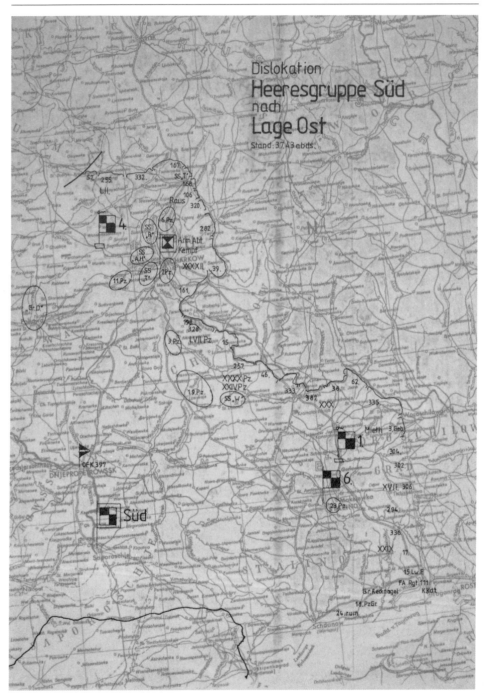

Army Group South (Kharkov/Stalino Front) unit locations as of 3 July 1943.

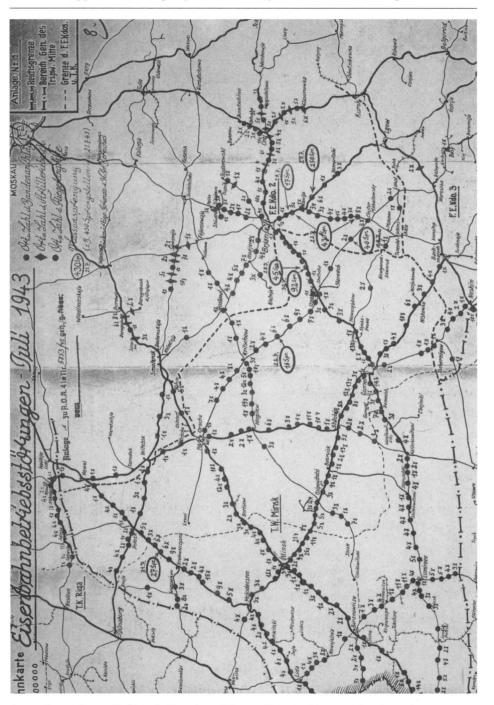

Army Group Center Railroad allocations (Moscow Front) with operational matrix.

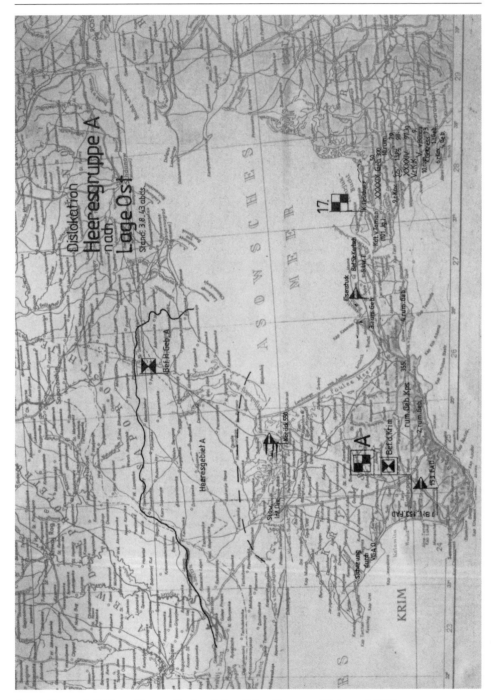

Army Group A (Crimea/Taman Peninsula) unit locations as of 3 August 1943.

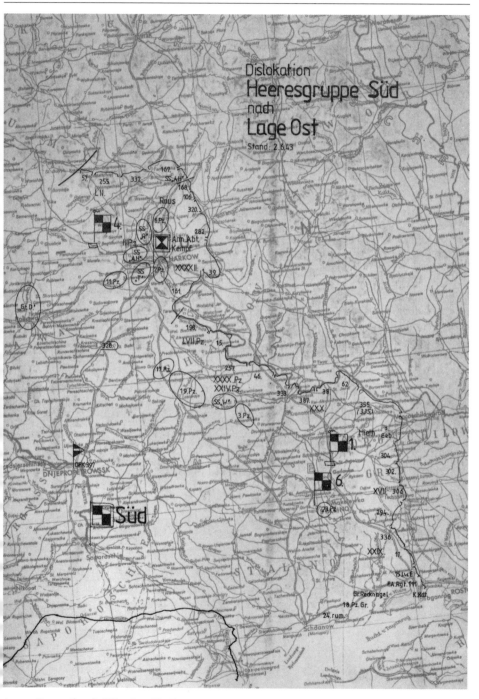

Army Group South (Kharkov/Stalino Front) unit locations as of 2 June 1943.

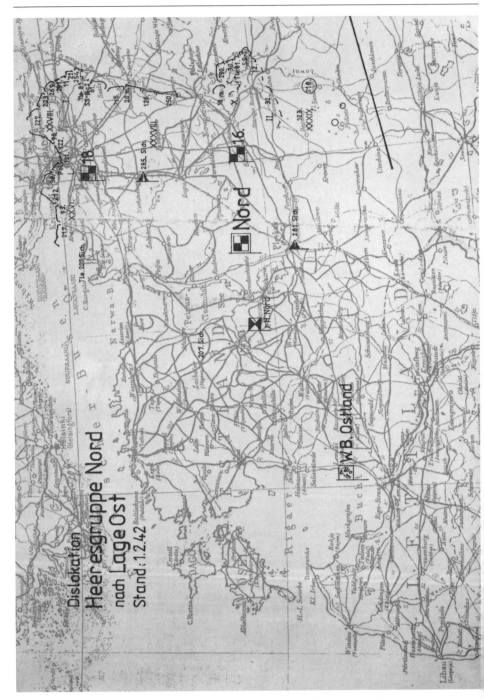

Army Group North (Leningrad Front) unit locations as of I February 1942.

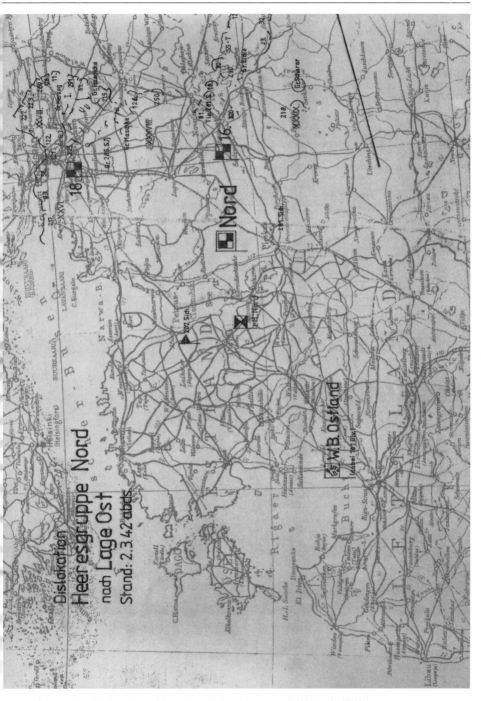

Army Group North (Leningrad Front) unit locations as of 2 March 1942.

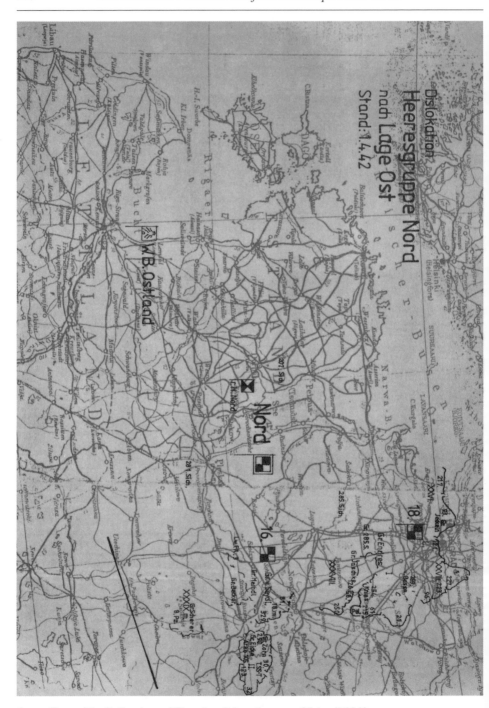

Army Group North (Leningrad Front) unit locations as of I April 1942.

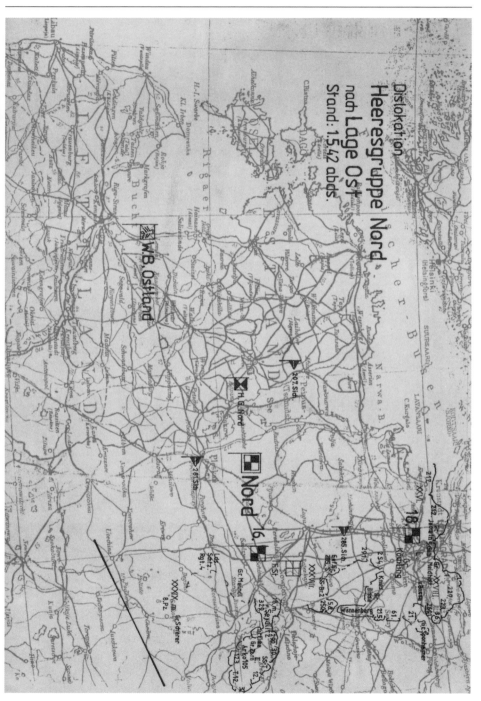

Army Group North (Leningrad Front) unit locations as of I May 1942.

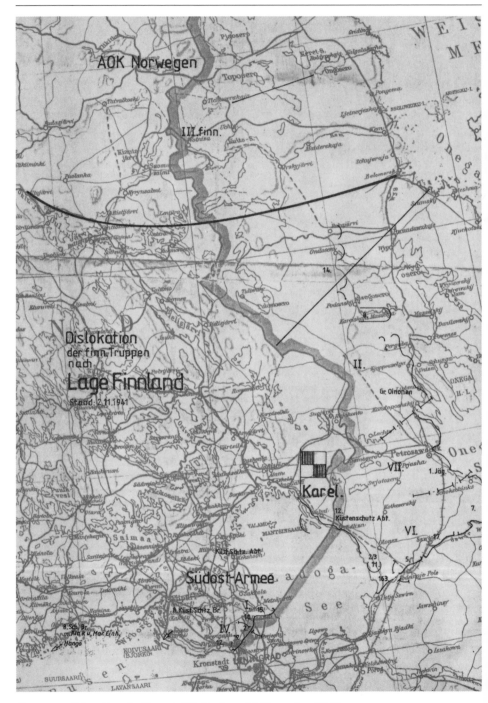

German unit locations in Norway/Finland as of 2 November 1941.

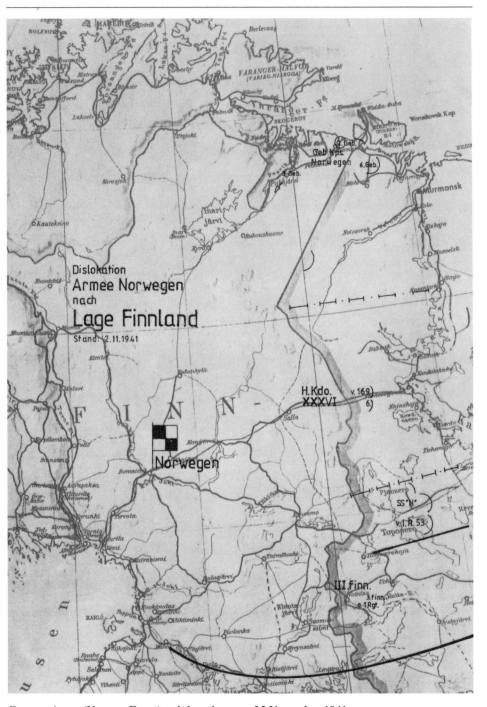

German Army (Norway Front) unit locations as of 2 November 1941.

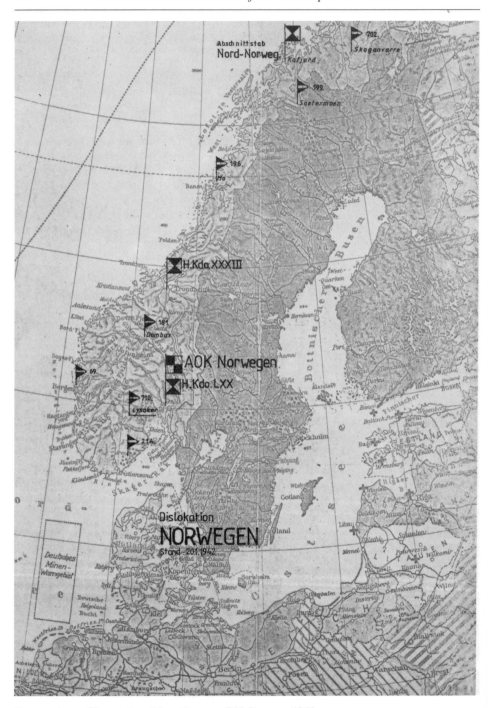

German Army (Norway) unit locations as of 20 January 1942.

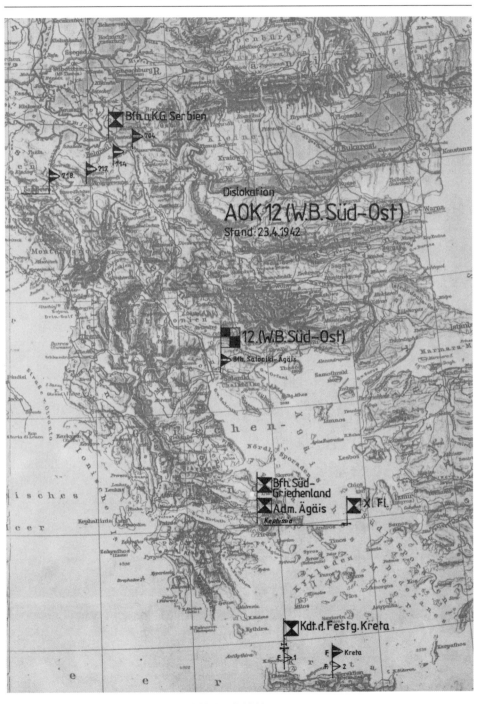

German unit locations (Balkans) as of 23 April 1942.

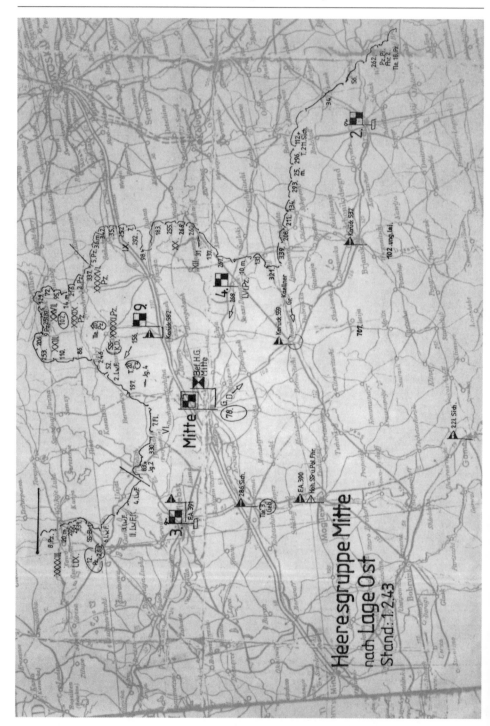

Army Group Center (Vitebsk Front) unit locations as of I February 1943.

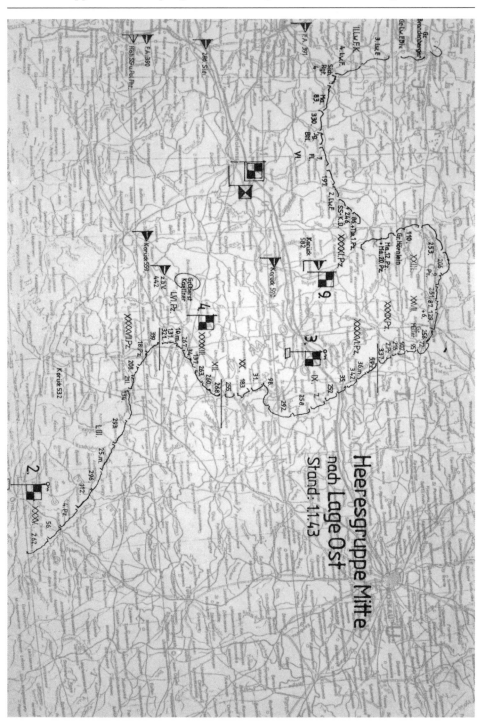

Army group Center (Briansk Front) unit locations as of I January 1943.

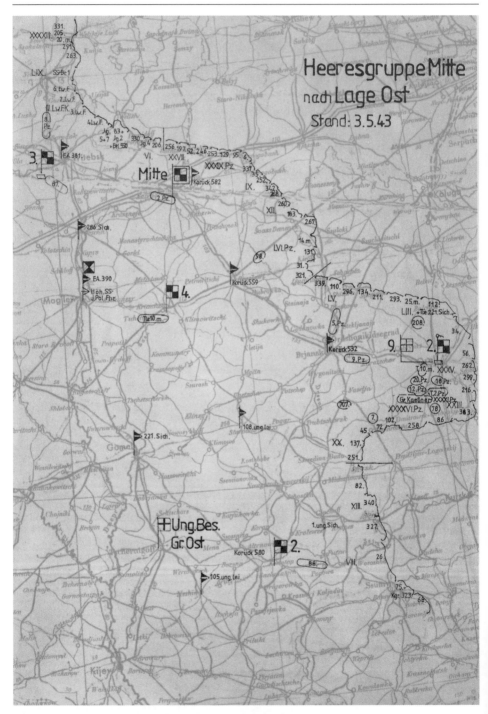

Army Group Center (Briansk Front) unit locations as of 3 May 1943.

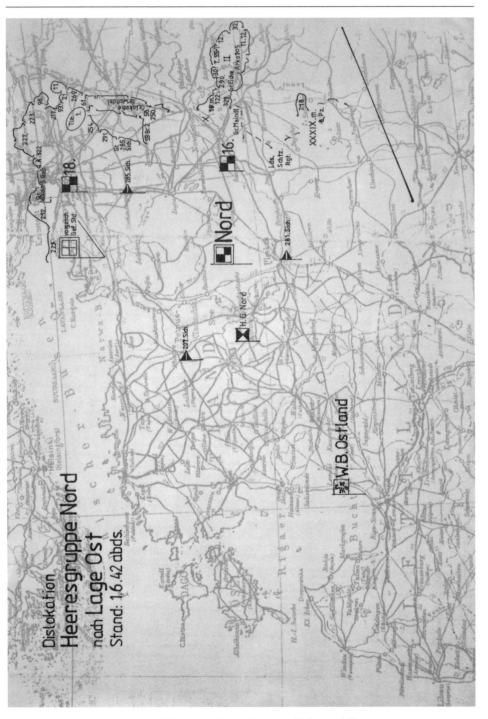

Army Group North (Leningrad Front) unit locations as of I June 1942.

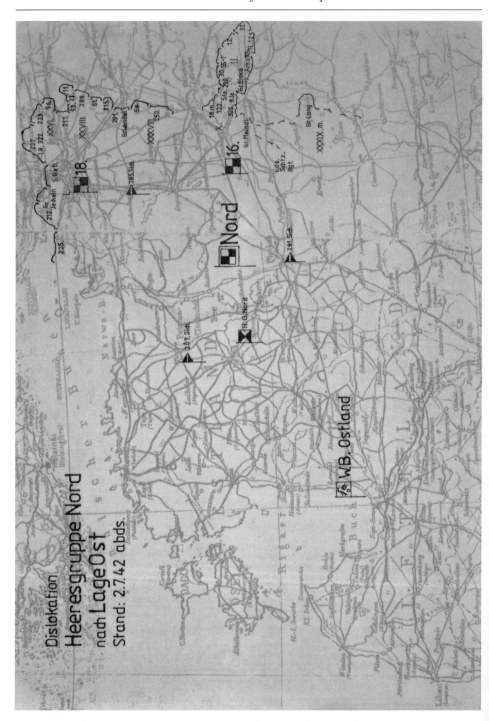

Army Group North (Leningrad Front) unit locations as of 2 July 1942.

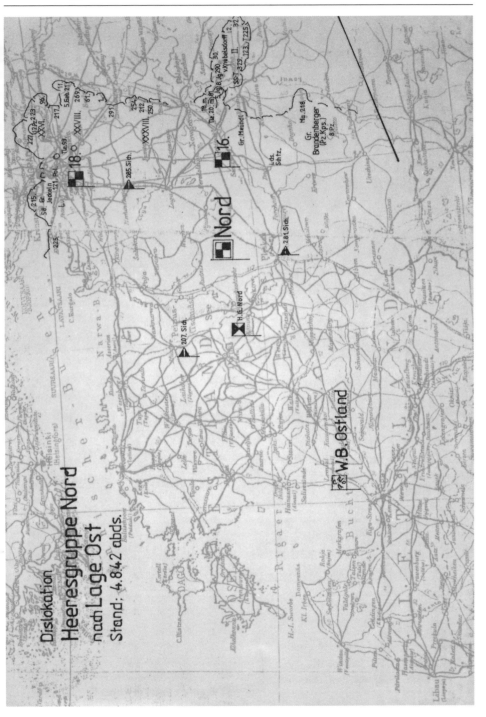

Army Group North (Leningrad Front) unit locations as of 4 August 1942.

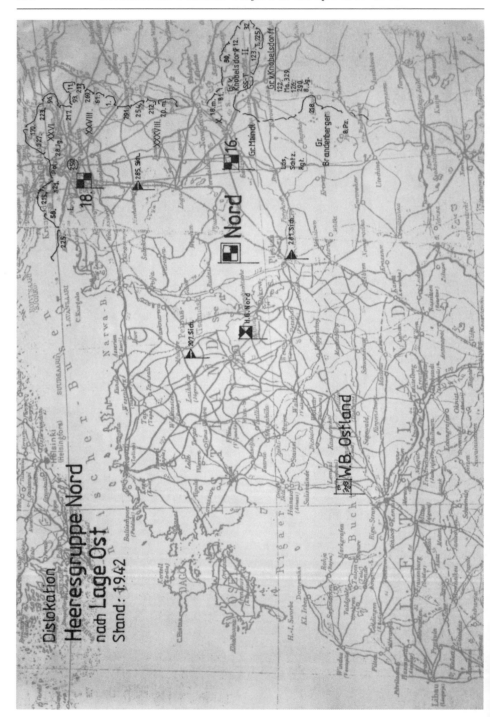

Army Group north (Leningrad Front) unit locations as of I September 1942.

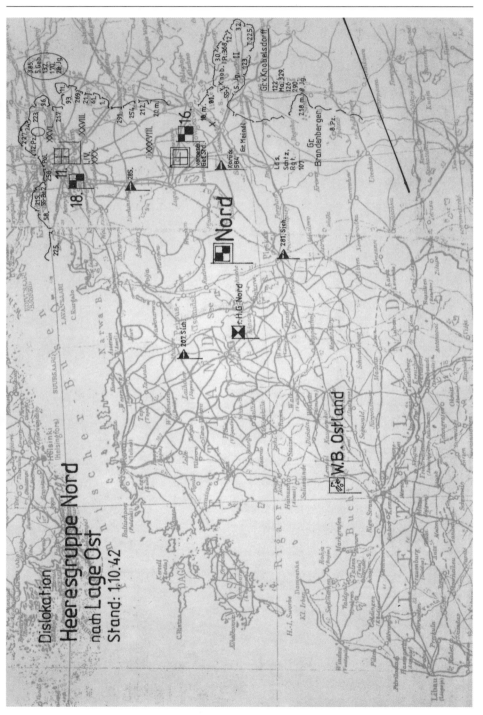

Army Group North (Leningrad Front) unit locations as of I October 1942.

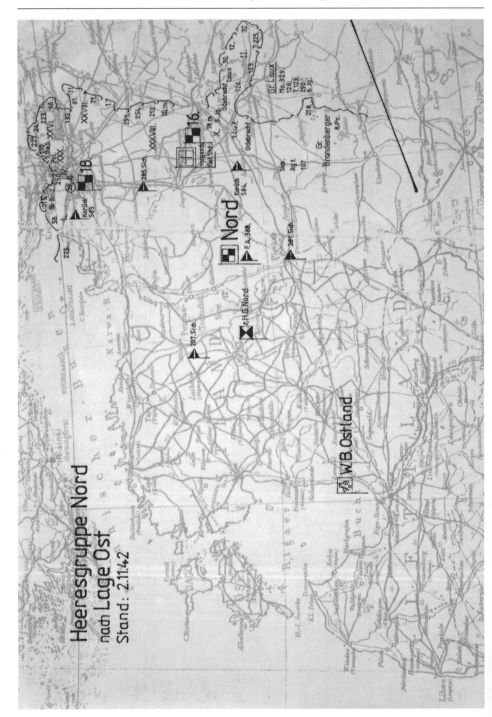

Army Group North (Leningrad Front) unit locations as of 2 February 1942.

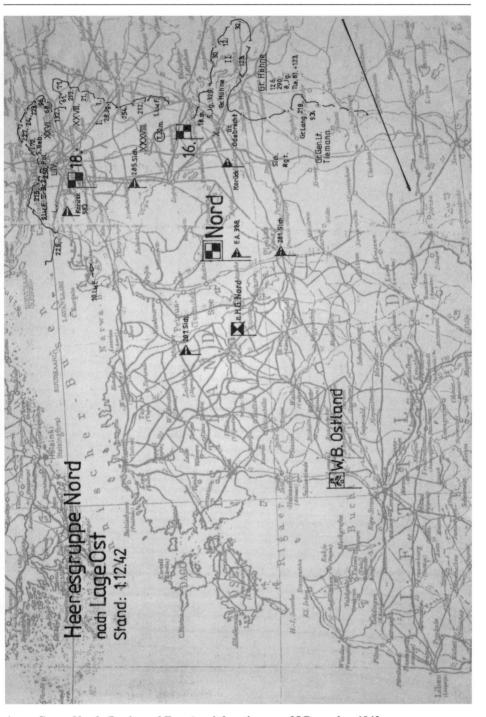

Army Group North (Leningrad Front) unit locations as of I December 1942.

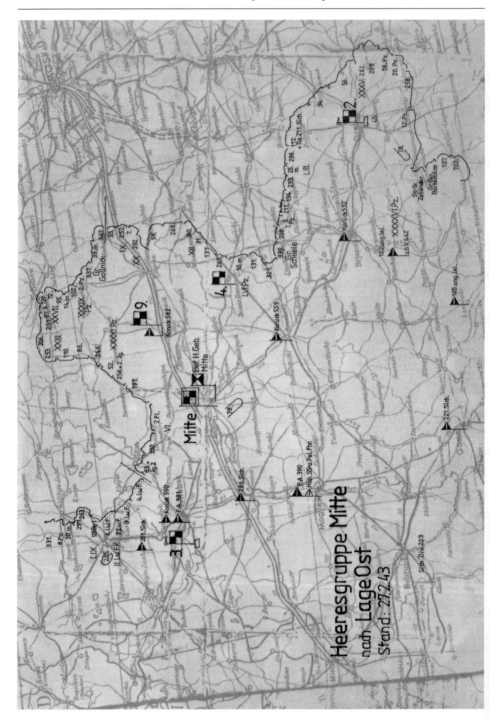

Army Group Center (Rzhev Nyazma Front) unit locations as of 27 February 1943.

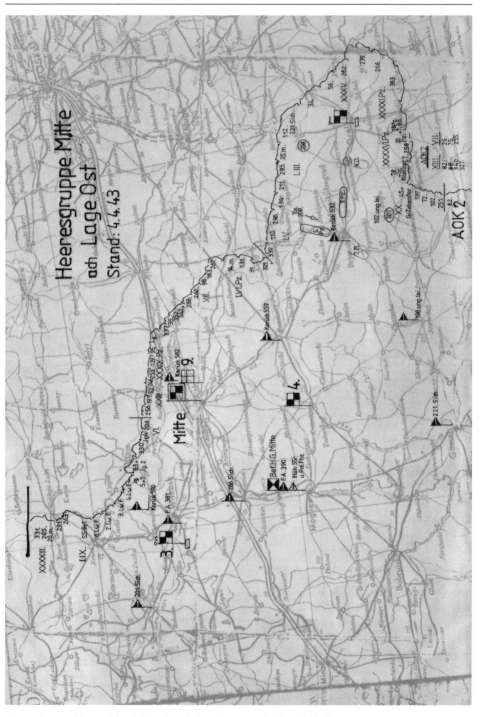

Army Group Center (Orel Front) unit locations as of 4 April 1943.

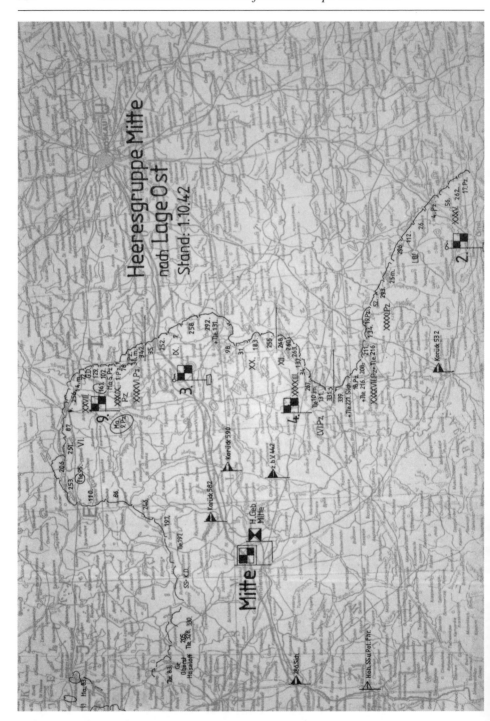

Army Group Center (Smolensk Front) unit locations as of I October 1942.

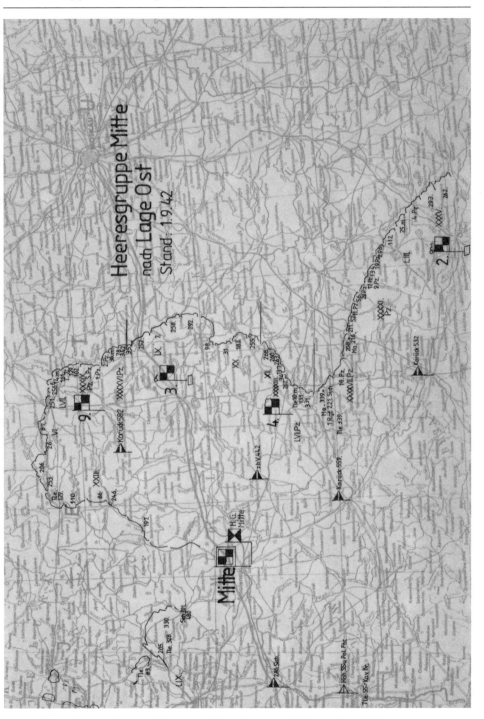

Army Group Center (Smolensk Front) unit locations as of 1 September 1942.

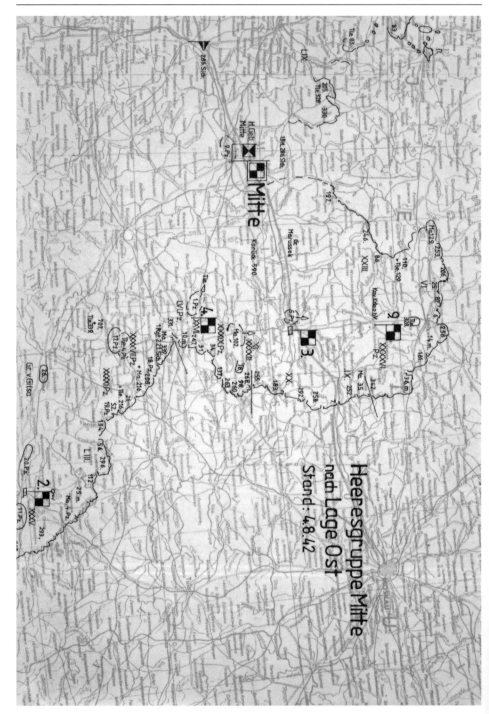

Army Group Center (Smolensk Front) unit locations as of 4 August 1942.

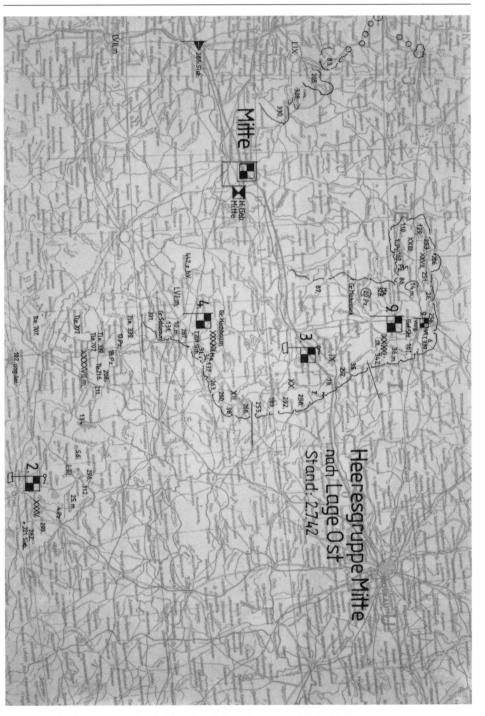

Army Group Center (Smolensk Front) unit locations as of 2 July 1942.

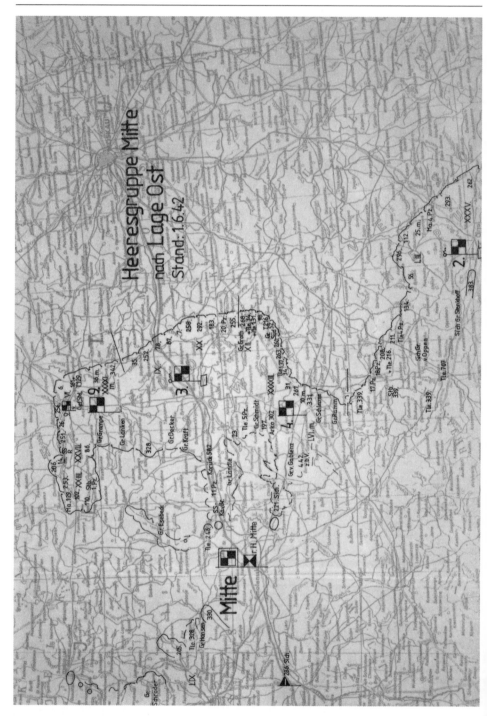

Army Group Center (Smolensk Front) unit locations as of I June 1942.

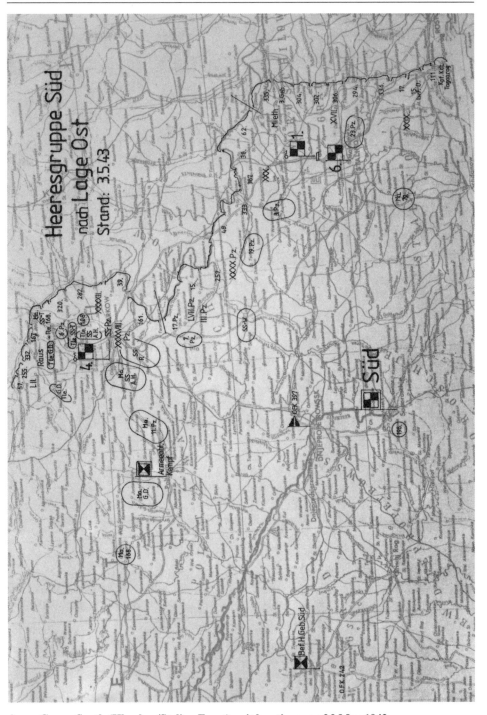

Army Group South (Kharkov/Stalino Front) unit locations as of 3 May 1943.

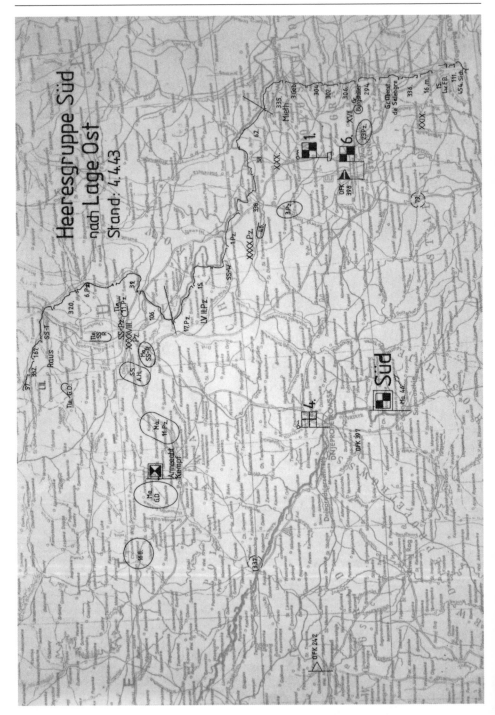

Army Group South (Kharkov/Stalino Front) unit locations as of 4 April 1943.

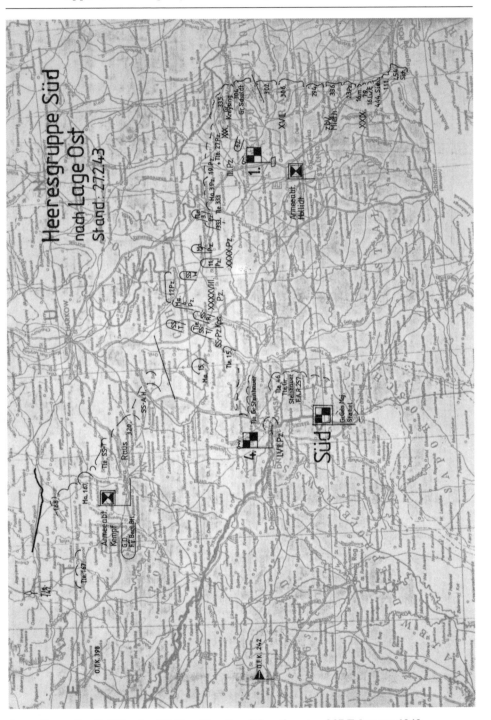

Army Group South (Kharkov/Stalino, Front) unit locations as of 27 February 1943.

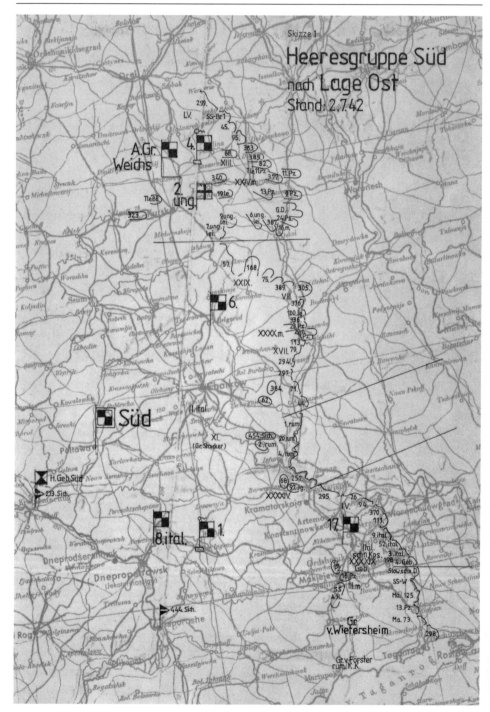

Army Group South (Kursk/Kharkov/Stalino Front) unit locations as of 2 July 1942.

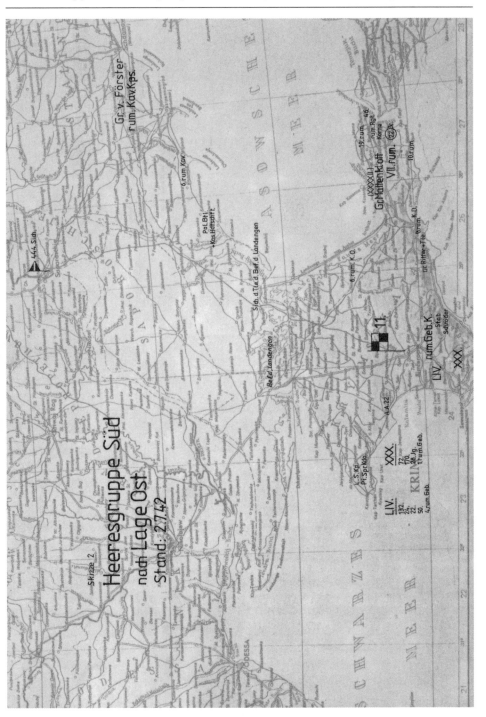

Army Group South (Crimea/Taman Peninsula) unit locations as of 2 July 1942.

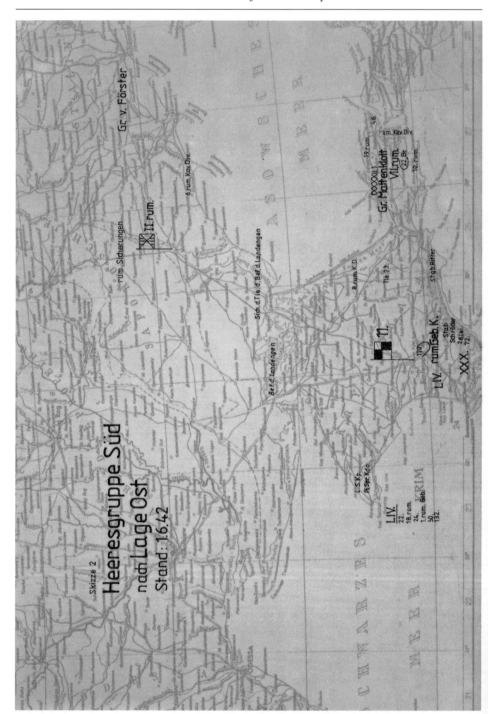

Army Group South (Crimea/Taman Peninsula Front) unit locations as of I June 1942.

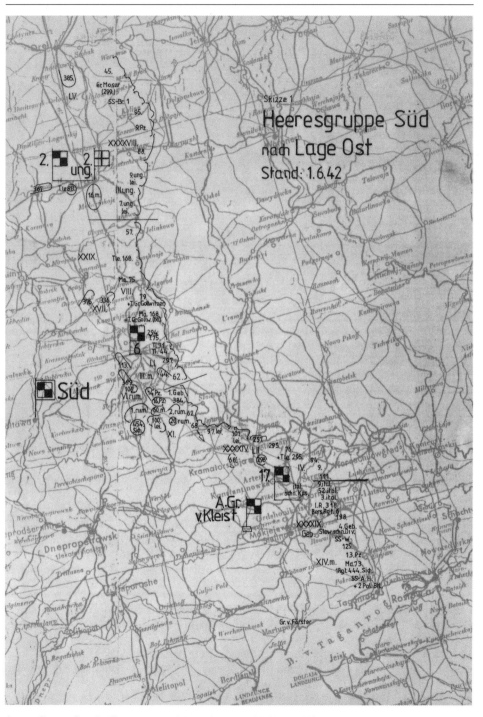

Army Group South (Caucasus) unit locations as of I June 1942.

Notes

[1] Joseph Stalin (1879-1953) was born Joseph Vissarionovich Djugashvili. He had been a member of the October Revolution Committee in 1917; Secretary General of the Communist Party in 1922. He and Trotsky were locked in a power struggle following Lenin's death.

[2] Translated, *justice of war* and *justice in war*, as stated by Walzer, *Just and Unjust Wars: A Moral Argument with Historical Illustrations* (New York: Basic Books, Inc., 1977) p. 21. Walzer states "A legitimate act of war is one that does not violate the rights of the people against whom it is directed," p. 135.

[3] See Sven Steenberg, *Vlasov*, trans. by Abe Farbstein (New York: Alfred A. Knopf, 1970) pp. 8-9. Also on Vlasov see Albert L. Weeks, "Personality," *World War II*, Vol. 12, No. 4 (November 1997) Leesburg, VA: Cowles History Group, pp. 8-10, 78.

[4] Josef Goebbels (1897-1945), *Die Tagebucher von Josef Goebbels*, Vol. 2, p. 743, entry dated 2 December 1936. *Generalleutnant* Hans Baur corroborated this testimony, since he was apparently at the reception dinner being held during his 1985 interview. See also Ian Kershaw, *The Nazi Dictatorship: Problems and Perspective of Interpretation*, 3rd ed. (New York: Routledge, Chapman & Hall, 1993) p. 125. Goebbels joined the *NSDAP* in 1924 . See record at *Bundesarchiv* Koblenz, N-1118.

[5] See record at *Bundesarchiv* Koblenz, N-1128.

[6] See Richard Overy, *Russia's War* (London, UK, New York: Penguin Books, 1997) p. 23.

[7] Ibid.

[8] Gehlen (3 April 1902-1979) was the son of a former Silesian artillery officer turned book publisher. Gehlen joined the *Reichswehr* in 1919, becoming a *Hauptmann* in 1935. Gehlen, who was aide to Franz Halder from July-November 1940, would rise from *Hauptmann* (1934, *Major* in 1939, *Oberstleutnant* July 1941, *Oberst*, December 1942) to *Generalmajor* (December 1944) becoming of Chief of Foreign Armies East (April 1942-April 1945) and command the *Abwehr* following the arrest of Admiral Wilhelm Canaris (1887-9 April 1945). Canaris was a U-boat commander during WW I, and *Abwehr* Chief in 1935. He was executed at Flossenburg. Gehlen, as a member of the *Generalstabs* and head of Foreign Armies East was a vocal opponent of Hitler's and Himmler's methods in the east, and he offered proof positive as to how their policies would become counterproductive. The Gehlen interrogation files are located on microfilm at US National Archives, College Park, Maryland Roll M-

1270/24/0395. The *Abwehr* was absorbed into the *RSHA* in June and incorporated within the *SS* in September 1944. The *RSHA*'s counter-espionage section was *Amt IV*.

⁹ On Willi Fey, see Gregory T. Jones, "Personality," *World War II,* Vol. 6, No. 2 (July 1991) Leesburg, VA: Empire Press, Inc. pp. 20, 78-82.

¹⁰ Kershaw, *The Nazi Dictatorship*, p. 73.

¹¹ Ibid.

¹² Himmler's *SS* was a vast and complex machine, incorporating the *Ordnungspolizei* (*Orpo*) responsible for civil police duties within Germany; *Sicherheitspolizei* (*Sipo*) responsible for police duties throughout the extending *Reich,* and divided into the *Geheimstaatspolizei* (*Gestapo*), an extension of the original *Nazi* political police of Prussia in Section *IV*, which overlapped with the *Sicherheitsdienst* (*SD*) or Party Security Service of Section *III*, and the *Kriminalpolizei* (*Kripo*). See Herbert Walther, *Waffen SS* (Atglen, PA: Schiffer Publishing, Ltd. 1989) for a detailed analysis of the fighting branch. See also Walther's *The 1ˢᵗ SS Panzer Division* (Atglen: Schiffer Publishing, Ltd. 1989) and *Twelfth SS Armored Division* (Atglen, PA: Schiffer Publishing, Ltd.) dealing with the 12ᵗʰ *SS "Hitlerjuegend"* Division. See also Bernd Wegner, *The Waffen SS,* trans. Ronald Webster (Oxford, UK: Basil Blackwell, Ltd. 1990). See also Mark C. Yerger, *Waffen SS Commanders: The Army, Corps and Divisional Leaders of a Legend: Augsberger to Kreuts* (Atglen, PA: Schiffer Publishing, Ltd. 1997).

¹³ *Waffen SS Gruppenfuehrer* Otto Kumm interview, January 1984.

¹⁴ The first *Einsatzgruppe* was formed in 1938 by *Brigadefuehrer* Walter Schellenberg (1911-1952). He joined the *SD* in 1934, created a special branch for kidnapping, such as the British agents in Holland in 1939. Following Canaris' downfall he took over Combined Intelligence and was involved with Himmler through Sweden in negotiating a German surrender. He escaped to Sweden, surrendered to the Allies and drew a six year sentence in 1949.

¹⁵ Karl Wolff (1900-1984), record located at *Bundesarchiv* Koblenz, N-1465, interview, December 1983. This policy was followed after Hitler issued the *"Kommissar Befehl"* in 1941 and was disseminated throughout the *SD* by Ernst Kaltenbrunner. This policy had nothing to do with the eventual "Final Solution," according to Kershaw, *The Nazi Dictatorship*, pp. 85, 100. Wolff was functioning in Northern Italy towards the end of the war in the delayed withdrawal of German forces, while also preparing the negotiated surrender of *SS* forces, and was therefore not able to personally direct the destruction of all the documents (see Laska, *Women in the Resistance and the Holocaust: Voices of Eyewitnesses. Contributions to Women's Studies* No. 37 (Westport, CT: Greenwood Press, 1983) p. 150). Wolff did have occasion to become involved during an April 1945 visit to Berlin to see his family and check of the situation. The most effective and brutal *Sonderkommando* leaders in the various regions were as follows: Ukraine in total-*SS/SD Gruppenfuehrer* Dr. Thomas (who replaced Dr. Rasch), a physician by profession, and his adjutant was *Oberfuehrer* Ehrlinger; *Abteilung Leiter III* was commanded by *Obersturmbannfuehrer* Bendt and *Sturmbannfuehrer* Schimmrohn; *Abteilung Leiter IV* was commanded by *Obersturmbannfuehrer* Dr. Knab and *Sturmbannfuehrer* Vollmer; the Kovno commander was *Obersturmbannfuehrer* Puetz, a highly esteemed anti-partisan fighter and supporter of the use of local anti-Semites in the killing of Jews. See Richard Overy, *Russia's War* (London, UK, New York: Penguin Books, 1997) p. 140. The Kiev *SD* commander was *Oberfuehrer* Ehringer, a veteran of reprisal activity in Norway, Prague, Warsaw and Minsk, decorated with the Iron Cross 1ˢᵗ Class for his counterinsurgency efforts. The Kremenchug commander was *Sturmbannfuehrer* Plath; Chernigov was commanded by *Obersturmbannfuehrer* Christensen; Dnepropetrovsk was *Sturmbannfuehrer* Link (replaced for being too lenient by *Sturmbannfuehrer* Mulde); Kharkov was commanded initially by a *Standartenfuehrer* Blobel (previously in Kiev who claimed he had ordered 60,000 killed that were placed in an anti-tank ditch and 30,000 in another location) and later by *Obersturmbannfuehrer* Dr. Linmann. It is interesting that with regard to the *SS/SD* operations in Kiev, all new arrivals were invited to participate in executions, feeling "it was their honor bound duty" which were scheduled one day per week, and that no one was forced to participate. Ironically, the men

who participated were plied with large amounts of vodka after every execution. See NA M-1270/24/ 0838-0840. For more on the roundup and killings of Jews in the opening phase of Barbarossa, see Overy, *Russia's War*, p. 139.

[16] Record of Olbricht (4 October 1888-20 July 1944), *Militaerarchiv* Freiburg, no file number to date. Olbricht was executed with *Oberst* Claus August Schenk *Graf* von Stauffenberg, Ludwig Beck and others following the failed bomb plot to kill Hitler.

[17] Christopher Browning, *Ordinary Men: Reserve Police Battalion 101 and the Final Solution in Poland* (New York: Harper Collins, 1992).

[18] Guy Sajer, *The Forgotten Soldier.* 2nd printing (Baltimore, MD: The Nautical and Aviation Company of America, 1988). Sajer was an Alsatian volunteer in *Panzer* Division *"Grossdeutschland."*

[19] Overy, *Russia's War*, pp. 233-34.

[20] Stalin ordered that all German prisoners be categorized as common criminals to prevent their appealing to the International Red Cross and relying upon the Geneva Conventions articles related to the treatment of prisoners of war.

[21] Walzer, *Just and Unjust Wars*, p. 182.

[22] Overy, *Russia's War*, p. 151.

[23] The U.S. support for the *Contras* in Nicaragua and the Duarte government in El Salvador are just two examples of how successful insurgency and counterinsurgency operations respectively can be maintained and victory assured.

[24] See reference in R.D. Foot, *SOE in France: An Account of the Work of British Special Operations Executive in France, 1940-1944* (Baltimore, MD: University Publications of America, 1984) p. 187.

[25] John S. Mosby, *Mosby's War Reminiscences: Stuart's Cavalry Campaigns* (Camden, SC: John Culler & Sons, 1996). Also on the mounted guerrilla war see Richard S. Brownless, *Gray Ghosts of the Confederacy: Guerrilla Warfare in the West, 1861-1865* (Baton Rouge: Louisiana State University Press, 1984). See also Edward E. Leslie, *The Devil Knows How to Ride: The True Story of William Clark Quantrill and His Confederate Raiders* (New York: Da Capo Press, 1998), and Duane P. Schultz, *Quantrill's War: The Life and Times of William Clark Quantrill, 1837-1865* (New York: St. Martin's Press, 1996).

[26] Mosby, pp. 29, 39, 44, 66, 85 (official dispatch from W.W. Taylor, A.A.G. to Col. John S. Mosby, C.S.A., and Maj. Gen. J.E.B. Stuart, C.S.A., dated 23 March, 1863) pp. 86, 110, 112 (official dispatch from Gen. Robert E. Lee, C. S.A. to Confederate President Jefferson Davis dated 4 April 1863) pp. 119, 130, 152, 156, 159 (official dispatch from Mosby to Maj. Gen. J.E.B. Stuart dated 10 June 1863 (fn)) pp.170, 218, 241, 261.

[27] Ibid. pp. 113-14 (official dispatch from Maj. Gen. Jubel. Stahel, USA to Maj. Gen. Heintzelman, USA, dated 2 April 1963) p. 115 (referencing Washington D.C. newspapers using the term "guerrilla,") pp. 116, 122, 154 *(fn)* p. 171 (official dispatch from Lt. Gen. Hooker, USA to Maj. Gen. Hancock, USA, regarding orders to Maj. Gen. Stahel dated 23 June 1863 *(fn)*).

[28] George Stewart, *The White Armies of Russia: A Chronicle of Counter-Revolution and Allied Intervention* (New York: Russell & Russell, 1970) reprint of the1933 edition, pp. 279, 299, 324-25, 352, 382-83, 387, 393-95. See also David L. Bullock, "Reds Versus Whites," *Military History*, Vol. 9, No. 2 (June 1992) Leesburg, VA: Cowles History Group, pp. 42-49.

[29] John B. McKenna, "Hitler and *Nazi* Germany: Imperialistic Legacy or Revolutionary Dictatorship?" Unpublished Dissertation. Glasgow, UK: University of Strathclyde Department of History, 1991, p. 39; and McKie, "Was Hitler's Extermination of the Jews Inevitable?" Unpublished Dissertation. Glasgow, UK: University of Strathclyde, Department of History, 1990, p. 1.

[30] The reality of women fighting as irregulars, such as hurling stones down upon an enemy was illustrated in *The Peloponnesian Wars*, p. 238.

[31] Balchen (23 October 1899-23 October 1973) was a Polar explorer who flew over both poles. During the war he flew for the Royal Norwegian Air Force, then later with the United States Army Air Force.

His work with the partisans with his 801st/492nd "Carpetbaggers" Bomb Group was one of the most memorable scenarios of the war, where he returned over 3,000 Allied personnel and a crashed V-2 to Britain. Balchen also flew OSS and SOE agents into Norway. His establishment of *Operation Sepal* was to drop saboteurs into Norway, Denmark and Sweden. His last major wartime mission was *Operation Where and When*, moving 1,400 Norwegian troops and 1,100 tons of supplies into the country. Just after the he organized the relief flight for 70,000 Soviet and Serb POW's in Norway until the International Red Cross could handle the problem. See C.V. Glines, "The Amazing Bernt Balchen," *Aviation History*, Vol. 8, No. 6 (July 1998) Leesburg, VA: Primedia Publications, Inc. pp. 34-40, 74. See also Bernt Balchen, *Come North With Me: An Autobiography* (New York: E.P. Dutton & Co., 1954). See also George A. Reynolds, "Undercover," *World War II*, Vol. 5 No. 5 (January 1991) Leesburg, VA: Empire Press, Inc. pp. 16, 62-67.

[32] Donnelly, "The *Nazi*-Soviet Pact of 23rd August 1939 and the Relations Between the Two Countries Until the German Invasion of Russia on 22nd June 1941." Unpublished Dissertation. Glasgow, UK: University of Strathclyde, Dept. of History, 1983, p. 48. The Soviet mastermind of the armored offensive was Marshal Andrei Yeremenko (1892-1970) who commanded a mechanized cavalry corps. Afterward he commanded Red Banner Army E in Siberia. He was severely wounded at Bryansk in 1941, and was appointed commander of the Stalingrad Front in August 1942. Yeremenko later commanded the Baltic Front then moved to the Crimea as commander of the Independent Coastal Army, a collection of partisans and Soviet sailors, marines and soldiers. He returned to the Baltic taking Latvia, and later commanded the 4th Ukrainian Front that invaded Czechoslovakia and destroyed Army Group Center in 1945.

[33] Churchill (1874-1965) was twice Prime Minister from 1940-45 and 1951-55. During WW I he was First Lord of the Admiralty and was responsible for some the greatest blunders and disasters during both world wars.

[34] Ibid.

[35] Donnelly, pp. 48-49; Liddell-Hart, *History of the Second World War* (New York: Pan, 1982) p. 49; and Max Beloff, *The Foreign Policy of Soviet Russia*, Vol. 2 (London: O.U.P., 1947) p. 309.

[36] McKie, p. 34; Laura Doran, "The *Nazi* Economic Persecution of the Jews: An Interpretation." Unpublished Dissertation. Glasgow, UK: University of Strathclyde, Department of History, 1996, p. 31; Paley, "The Deficiencies of 'Itentionalism' and 'Functionalism:' An Examination of *Nazi* Jewish Policy and the Origins of the 'Final Solution." Unpublished Dissertation. Glasgow, UK: University of Strathclyde, Department of History, 1997, pp. 5, 49, 51-53; Christopher R. Browning, "Beyond 'Intentionalism' and 'Functionalism:' *A Reassessment of Nazi Jewish Policy from 1939-1941";* Thomas Childers and Jane Caplan (eds.) *Reevaluating the Third Reich* (New York: Holmes & Meier, 1993) p. 219.

[37] The SS originally started out as the *Schutzkommando* in April 1925, commanded by Julius Schreck. The unit became the *Schuetzstaffel* on 9 November 1925 when 800 men staffed its ranks, later increasing their numbers to 1000 men the following July under Josef Berchthold, editor of the *Volkischer Beobachter*. Membership dropped by 1929, when only 280 men remained. The purpose of the unit was complete loyalty to Hitler and to perform as his bodyguard. See Pauline Russell, "The Rise of the SS: Historical Accident or Astute Planning?" Unpublished Dissertation. Glasgow, UK: University of Strathclyde, Department of History, 1994, p. 4; and Claudia Hand, "The Origins and Genesis of *Nazi* Racial Policy" Unpublished Dissertation. Glasgow, UK: University of Strathclyde, Department of History, 1996, pp. 17, 26-28. See also Osborne, "National Socialism: A Coherent, Relevant Ideology?" Unpublished Dissertation. Glasgow, UK: University of Strathclyde, Department of History, 1996, p. 17; and Paley, pp. 23, 30-31, 33, 37.

[38] On 7 October 1939 *Reichsfuehrer SS* Heinrich Himmler (so appointed on 6 January 1929, record located at *Bundesarchiv* Koblenz, N-1126) was appointed *Reich* Commissioner for the "Strengthening of Germanism;" on 15 October 1941, and issued a report that stated the objective of the

Einsatzgruppen was "the total elimination of all Jews." See William Carr, *Hitler: A Study in Person- ality and Politics* (London: Edward Arnold, 1978) pp. 70, 81; on this and Heydrich's ghetto orders and deportations of Jews to Poland see McKie, pp. 32-34. *SS Obergruppenfuehrer* Karl Wolff inter- view, January 1984. Wolff fell into American hands from 1945-46, and worked with U.S. intelligence on Soviet affairs.

[39] This was contrary to the original plan of the *SS*, which was to force Jews from public life and eventually have them emigrate. Other plans were the Protection of German Blood and Honor, pre- venting "interracial" marriages between Jews and Aryans, the Nuremberg Laws legalizing anti- Semitism, and the *Reich* Citizenship Act in lieu of the Civil Service Act of 7 April 1933 regarding Jews in civil service. See McKie, pp. 12-18, 20-21 (on approximately 30,000 Jews placed in concen- tration camps to force emigration; also on ghettos and Reinhardt Heydrich) pp. 22, 25-28; on geno- cide plans pp. 30-33; on death squads pp. 30, 38; see also Ridley, "The Disintegration of the Weimar Republic and the Rise of National Socialism." Unpublished Dissertation. Glasgow, UK: University of Strathclyde, Dept. of History, pp. 49-51; Martin Broszat and Krausnick, *The Anatomy of the SS State* (Cambridge: Cambridge University Press, 1968) pp. 49, 59 (on memorandum circulated to all Diplo- matic Missions and Consulates on 5 January 1939) p. 63. See also Ian Kershaw, *The Nazi Dictator- ship,* which is also worthwhile reading on the topic. See also Omer Bartov, *Hitler's Army: Soldiers, Nazi's and War in the Third Reich* (New York: Oxford University Press, 1992) p. 83.

[40] Gunn, "German Foreign Policy, 1933-39: The Intentionalist-Functionalist Debate in German His- tory." Unpublished Dissertation. Glasgow: University of Strathclyde, Department of History, no date. p. 14. See also M.M. Lee, and Michlka, p. 156; and McKie, p. 14, (on Hitler's indecision on what to do with the Jews) pp. 38-39; Broszat and Krausnick, p. 32. See also Hand, pp. 1-2, 31; on Jewish fatalities of 5,271,000, see Jeremy Noakes, and Pridham, *Nazism, 1919-1945: A Documentary Reader, Vol. 3: Foreign Policy, War and Racial Extermination* (Devon, UK: University of Exeter Press, 1991) p. 1048. See also Mills, "The Dutch Experience in World War Two." Unpublished Dissertation. Glasgow, UK: University of Strathclyde, Dept. of History, 1997, pp. 37-38, regarding Dutch camps such as Vught, Ommen, Westerbork and Amersfort.

[41] *Oberkommando des Heeres (OKH) Ostamt* (East Office) and *Oberkommando der Wehrmacht (OKW)* reports and the Albert Speer documentation regarding replacement components. *Obergruppenfuehrer* Felix Steiner was also involved in the study of the report, which was completed for Hitler by March 1945. Courtesy of *Bundesarchiv* Koblenz via Robert G. Ridgeway, and interview with Karl Wolff, January 1984. Speer (19 March 1905-1 September 1981, record located at *Bundesarchiv* Koblenz, N- 1340) had been Hitler's architect and was promoted to Minister of Armaments and Munitions follow- ing the death of Fritz Todt. He was sentenced to twenty years at Nuremberg for using slave labor. For more detail see N-1340, *Bundesarchiv* Koblenz. Following the war Speer wrote his memoirs. See *Inside the Third Reich* (New York: Bantam Books, 1976).

[42] McKenna, p. 41; Mills, p. 45. See also Vladimir Belyakov, "Stunned by War's Outbreak," *World War II*, Vol. 6, No. 2 (July 1991) Leesburg, VA: Empire Press, Inc. pp. 34-41.

[43] Romania ceded Northern Bukovina region to the Soviet Union after Germany applied pressure to avoid a Romanian-Soviet conflict. The deal was signed on 23 January 1940. See Donnelly in total.

[44] Overy, *Russia's War*, p. 150.

[45] Lithuanian Jews had large numbers emigrate abroad, and were considered better educated than most other eastern European Jews. Maureen Cowan, "Immigration of European Jews into Glasgow: 1889-1939." Unpublished Dissertation (Glasgow, UK: University of Strathclyde, Department of His- tory, 1993) p. 3.

[46] June Carruthers, *Civilian and Military Prisoners in Britain During the Second World War*. Unpub- lished Dissertation. Glasgow, UK: University of Strathclyde, Department of History, date unknown. p. 54. The Geneva Conventions were first held in 1884 with the intent of protecting captured and

wounded soldiers during wartime. These rules were expanded and ratified at the subsequent Conventions of 1906 and 1929, with the Convention of 1929 declaring prisoners off limits to reprisal. The Convention of 1949 finally declaring international protection for civilians equal to that of combatants, as well as protection to shipwrecked persons, the wounded and sick. *Article 2* of the 1929 draft covered World War II and was revised as *Article 12* in 1949. This Article strictly forbade the killing of military prisoners, the forced labor of officers in all cases, and forbade the use of POW's as human shields or war production labor for an enemy. The Article also states that pilots and aircrews parachuting to safety could not be fired upon, since their method of waging war was not in effect. Alternately, paratroopers were legitimate targets while in the air, since vertical envelopment was their method of waging war. It also states that POW's must be protected from harm using the 5 "S" method: SEARCH for weapons and documents; SEGREGATE by rank, gender and nationality; SAFEGUARD from mistreatment; SILENCE POW's to eliminate communication; SPEED the POW's to the rear for proper interrogation, processing and placement in an approved POW camp.

[47] The Soviets had perfected this method during the Spanish Civil War, while assisting in the indoctrination and recruitment of soldiers into Communist militias, which later became the regular army. See Killen, "The Communists and the Popular Front: Spain 1936-1939." Unpublished Dissertation. Glasgow, UK: University of Strathclyde, Department of History, 1994, p. 32.

[48] US National Archives microfilm, Roll M-1270/24/0508. This roll contains interrogation files on dozens of captured officers and enlisted men from all branches of service. Included the interrogation of Reinhard Gehlen, Hermann Goering, and his brother Albert Goering.

[49] Ibid.

[50] Karl Wolff also mentioned this in January 1984, although there was no hard evidence to support this statement before this microfilm was purchased and reviewed.

[51] This occurred in Spain also, and the pattern was established for internal cannibalization of these fighting assets. See Killen, pp. 39-40; and Victor Alba, *The Communist Party in Spain*. (Princeton, NJ: Princeton University Press, 1983) p. 257.

[52] See reference by Steenberg, *Vlasov*, p. 33.

[53] Warsaw had been turned into the largest ghetto in Europe. Over 5,000,000 people were forced to deport for relocation east and eventual extermination following the Wansee Conference of January 1942. McKie, p. 35; Carr, *Hitler*, p. 75; *Encyclopedia Judaica*, Vol. 5 (Tel Aviv: 1971) p. 1429; and Laura Doran, p. 33. On Konev (1888-1973), see Jonathan M. House, "Personality," *World War II*, Vol. 4, No. 5 (January 1990) Leesburg, VA: Empire Press, Inc. pp. 12, 16, 54.

[54] Grant, "The British Attitude to the Expulsion of the German Population from Those German Territories East of the Oder-Neisse Line That Formed Part of the Polish State After 1945." Unpublished Dissertation. Glasgow, UK: University of Strathclyde, Department of History, 1986, pp. 2, 14, 16.

[55] Ehrenberg was Stalin's "Goebbels," and his rhetoric has been blamed for much of the horror inflicted upon the European victims of Stalin's forces. See Grant, pp. 31, 40-41, 45; also PRO N11630/96/55/ FO 371/4760, and PRO C2919/12/18/FO 371/55392. See reference in Overy, *Russia's War*, p. 163 regarding Ehrenberg's propaganda.

[56] McIntyre, "The Emergence of Soviet Dominance in Central Europe, 1945-1948." Unpublished Dissertation. Glasgow, UK: University of Strathclyde, Dept. of History, 1986, p. 33; this is the main point of Zbigniew A. Brzezinski in *The Soviet Bloc in Unity and Conflict*. (Cambridge: Harvard University Press, 1967). Industrialization, censorship, collectivization and peasant control through local "cominterns" were to become the economic standard, with reduction of suspected persons and the constant reminder of war debts included in the political aspects of rule, minus the conscription service. Ibid. pp. 36-37. This was considered similar to the German method of occupation to many, forcing their resistance. However, given the industrial increase with the Soviet Union supplying raw materials, reparations were reduced. Romania's reparations were reduced by 50% for supplying the Soviet Union. Ibid. p. 36.

[57] Romania had thirty infantry divisions and two aircraft squadrons fighting with the Germans in Russia until they switched alliances in 1944. McIntyre, p. vi. Also, Romania was not considered very important by Hitler, although he did have Bishop Wilhelm Staedel (12 January 1890-1971) head the *Landeskulturamtes der deutschen Volksgruppe Rumaniens in Hermannstadt* in 1940. See Staedel records at *Bundesarchiv* Koblenz, N-1252 (NL-252) *Bundesarchiv* Koblenz.

[58] See Overy, *Russia's War*, p. 284.

[59] McIntyre, p. 35.

[60] Ibid. p. 7.

[61] Ibid. p. 8.

[62] Ibid. p. 18.

[63] Ibid. pp. 20, 24. This occurred throughout every Soviet occupied nation, with repression, condemnation and elimination becoming the order of the day.

[64] Harry S. Truman (1884-1972) was the 33rd President of the United States, following Roosevelt (1882-1945) as his Vice President. A WW I veteran and anti-Communist he attended the Potsdam Conference, and he never trusted Stalin.

[65] McIntyre, p. 25.

[66] Ibid. pp. 26-27.

[67] Ibid. p. 27; and Charles S. Maier (ed.), *The Origins of the Cold War and Contemporary Europe.* (New York: Houghton Mifflin, 1978) p. 118.

[68] McIntyre, pp. 4-6. The Bulgarian government was elected by a 86% majority, with the struggle between the Social Democrats and the factions of Obbov of the left and G.M. Dimitriov (later forced to resign by the Soviets, disappearing in favor of Nikola Petkov, the right-wing Agrarian Party leader) of the right. Petkov was executed on 16 August 1947. King had little choice when Stalin had Petru Groza placed in power in Romania in February 1945, which sparked greater partisan activity against the occupation forces. The government was not recognized by the west, although Groza, with the help of Gheorghiu-Dej was lenient towards nationalists, liberals, and socialists, who were all integrated into the government. Ibid. pp. 18-19. Hungary and Admiral Horthy surrendered to the Red Army on 15 October 1944 with General Miklos who became head of the National Council. This provisional government signed an armistice with the Western Allies, while German forces invaded en masse to prevent a complete Soviet avalanche.

[69] Ibid. p. 21.

[70] Interviews with several former partisans such as Leonidas Damianov Maximciuc, Stan Foltyn, and other former partisans explain the rationale behind the anti-Soviet movement after "liberation." See also Roslyn A McIntyre, pp. 3, 17.

[71] See Ed McCaul, "Hungarian Freedom Fighter," *Military History*, Vol. 15, No. 4 (October 1998) Leesburg, VA: Primedia Publications, Inc. pp. 38-44.

[72] Mills, pp. 2, 51. The Soviets actually sent agents to support the Communist underground after they rose up against Germany following *Operation Barbarossa*. Approximately one-third of the 10,000 members of SOE were women, with fifty being parachuted into occupied Europe; fifteen were captured, with ten being executed by firing squad (four at Dachau) or lethal injections, one died in Bergen-Belsen, one in Ravensbrueck, and three surviving. One of those executed at Dachau was Noor Inayat Khan, a wireless operator born in Moscow to an Indian prince, and a cousin of Mary Baker Eddy. See Laska, p. 8. On Khan see also Foot, *SOE in France*, pp. 324, 334, 337, 428-29; on SOE's creation on 16 July 1940 by Churchill see p. 8.

[73] Jill Carruthers, *The Post-War American Public and Communism-The Means Through Which They Learned to Fear.* Unpublished Dissertation. Glasgow, UK: University of Strathclyde, Department of History, 1996. p. 4.

[74] Franklin Delano Roosevelt (1882-1945) was the 32nd President of the United States. During WW I he was the Secretary of the Navy, and had been Governor of New York.

[75] Carruthers, p. 21. See also R.J. Donovan, *Tumultuous Years,* Vol. 2, p. 123.
[76] Interviews with such USAAF luminaries as Generals Curtis E. LeMay (1989), James H. Doolittle (1991) and Colonel Donald S. Blakeslee (1990) explain this trepidation. Blakeslee flew the first P-51 *Mustang* escort shuttle mission to Russia in 1944, and the tensions were obvious.
[77] Joyce, "Anti-Communism in the USA." Unpublished Dissertation. Glasgow, UK: University of Strathclyde, Department of History, 1997, p. 3.
[78] Ibid. See also Allan William Tait, "Influence or Significance? A Critical Assessment of the Importance of Domestic Factors in the Timing of *Nazi* Foreign Policy." Unpublished Dissertation. Glasgow, UK: University of Strathclyde, Department of History, no date, p. 46.
[79] James Joll, *Europe Since 1870: An International History* (New York, San Francisco: Harper & Row, 1973) p. 406.
[80] See Roll M-1270/24/0485 on the *Chetnik* and DRINA civil war.
[81] See James Hutchison, "British Food Supply and Distribution Problems During the Second World War." Unpublished Dissertation. Glasgow, UK: University of Strathclyde, Department of History, 1968. For brevity, see "Introduction," pp. 1-5, "Conclusion," pp. 66- 68. This work covers the British domestic food problem, requiring large amount of imported goods, especially from Canada and the United States. This thesis offers insight regarding the situation as outlined. See *Table I:* "Foodstuff Product/Annual Average 1934-38," p. 2; *Table II:* "Food Supplies per Head in 1944 Expressed as Percentage of Supplies in Britain," p. 4, *Table III*, p. 11; *Table IV:* "Crop Acreage's and Livestock Numbers on Agricultural Holdings in Great Britain," p. 12; *Table V:* "Livestock Numbers in British Farms," p. 13; *Table VI:* "Earned Net Income per Farm in England and Wales and Scotland," p. 16; *Table VII,* p. 22, *Table VIII:* "Annual Average," p. 24, *Table IX,* p. 25, *Table X:* "Home Produced Meat," p. 27, *Table XI:* "Annual Average 1944," p. 30, table XII, pp. 30-31, *Table XIII:* "Total Imports," p. 32, (Cont.) 34, *Table XIV,* 37, *Table XV,* p. 38, *Table XVI,* p. 40, *Table XVII:* "Cattle," p. 42, *Table XVIII,* p. 44, *Table XIX,* p. 54, *Table XX,* p. 56, *Table XXI;* "Civil Defense Region," p. 59, *Table XXII;* "Food Commodity," p. 61; See also *Ministry of Food: How Britain Was Fed in War Time* (London: HMSO) pp. 1, 5, 8-9, 11-14, 17-19, 25, 28-29, 34-36; and K.A.H. Murray, *History of the Second World War-Agriculture* (London: Her Majesty's Stationary Office, Longman, 1955) pp. 255, 260-63, 266, 279, 293-94, 296, 371, *Table II;* pp. 275-76, 382, *Table XII;* Central Statistical Office, *Monthly Digest of Statistics* (London: HMSO, January 1946) pp. 53, 67-69. J.R. Borchert, "The Agriculture of England and Wales, 1939-1946," *Agricultural History,* Vol. 22 (January 1948) 56-62.
[82] McKie, p. 1. On the Dutch relocation, including the deportation east of non-Jews, see Mills, pp. 7, 22; J.H. Posthumus, "The Structure of the Occupational Government," *The Annals of the American Academy of Social and Political Science,* Vol. 245 (May 1946) 1-2; Kollewijn, R.D. "The Dutch Universities Under *Nazi* Domination," *The Annals of the American Academy of Social and Political Science,* Vol. 245 (1946) 118; and Dr. Felix Kersten, *The Memoirs of Dr. Felix Kersten* (New York: Macmillan, 1974) pp. 81-93.
[83] Thucydides, *The Peloponnesian Wars.* Betty Radice (ed.), Trans. by Rex Warner, introduction by M.I. Finlay (New York: Penguin Books, 1982).
[84] See Brenda Ralph Lewis, "Caesar's Battle for Britannia," *Military History,* Vol. 12, No. 6 (February 1996) Leesburg, VA: Cowles History Group, pp. 46-53.
[85] *The Hutchinson Dictionary of Ancient and Medieval Warfare* (Oxford: Helicon Publishing, 1998) p. 56.
[86] Ibid. p. 44. Governor of Rome from AD 58-61, and Consul in AD 69.
[87] Ibid. pp. 312-13.
[88] Ibid. pp. 139-40. See also Greg Yocherer, "Classic Battle Joined," *Military History* (February 1992) Leesburg, VA: Empire Press, Inc. pp. 26-32; and Daniel A. Fournie, "Intrigue," *Military History,* Vol. 14, No. 7 (March 1998) pp. 12, 65.

[89] Ibid. pp. 286-287. See also D. Kent Fonner, "Personality," *Military History*, Vol. 12, No. 7 (March 1996) Leesburg, VA: Cowles History Group, pp. 10-12, 16.

[90] Mosby. p. 43.

[91] Overy, *Russia's War*, p. 143.

[92] Mosby, pp. 124, 331. These Legions were led by Vespasian (AD 9-79) himself, although he had to depart and leave his son Titus to finish the Jewish Wars. He also participated in the invasion of Britain under Emperor Claudius in AD 43. For more on Jotopata, see Mark Wayne Biggs, "Forty Days at Jotopata," *Military History*, Vol. 16, No. 1 (April 1999) Leesburg, VA: Primedia Publications, Inc. pp. 27-33. On a reference to Masada see Laska, p. 9.

[93] *The Hutchinson Dictionary of Ancient and Medieval Warfare*, pp. 206-07, 124-25. See also Donald O'Reilly, "Besiegers Besieged," *Military History*, Vol. 9, No. 6 (February 1993) Leesburg, VA: Empire Press, Inc. pp. 58-65, 94-96.

[94] Ibid. p. 86.

[95] Ibid. p. 42.

[96] Primarily at *Militaerarchiv* Freiburg im Breisgau and *Bundesarchiv* Koblenz, Germany.

[97] Interrogation files of Kumm, Dietrich and Wolff are courtesy of the U.S. National Archives, College Park, Maryland. Wolff's service record is located at the *Bundesarchiv* Koblenz, N-1465.

[98] Heinrich Himmler, *NSDAP* No. 42404 (7 December 1900-May 1945) was second of three sons in a Bavarian Catholic family, whose personality was difficult to ascertain. See Russell, pp. 7-11, and Joachim Fest, *The Face of the Third Reich*, 3rd ed. Trans. Bullock (London: Weidenfeld & Nicolson, 1970) pp. 111, 172. For more on Himmler, see Breitman, *Architect of Genocide* in total; Doran, pp. 2, 24, 28-29, 33-34; Osborne, p. 17; Paley, pp. 53, 55, 63; and for further information, see F. Smith, *Heinrich Himmler: A Nazi in the Making* in total and Peter Padfield, *Himmler: Reichsfuehrer-SS* (New York: Macmillan, 1990) in total.

[99] Dietrich (1892-1966) was a WW I sergeant major who joined the *NSDAP* and became the commander of Hitler's bodyguard elite, winning the Diamonds to the Knight's Cross. He was convicted of war crimes regarding Malmedy in particular and served ten years, although a German court gave him eighteen months in addition for the "Knight of the Long Knives." For an authoritative biography see Charles Messenger, *Hitler's Gladiator: The Life and Times of Oberstgruppenfuehrer and Panzergeneral-Oberst Der Waffen SS Sepp Dietrich* (London: Brassey's, 1988) in total.

[100] For more on this topic see Peter R. Black, *Ernst Kaltenbrunner: Ideological Soldier of the Third Reich* (Princeton, NJ: Princeton University Press, 1984) p. 125. See also Degrelle, *Campaign in Russia: The Waffen SS on the Eastern Front* (Torrence, CA: Institute for Historical Review, 1985) in total.

[101] Perhaps one of Degrelle's motivations in joining the *Wehrmacht* and leaving Belgium was that a *Luftwaffe* officer, Helmuth Pess, who had been having an affair with Degrelle's wife was found dead, shot through the heart. Degrelle called the *Gestapo* and stated that Pess had "wished to commit suicide." See Black, *Ernst Kaltenbrunner*, p. 125.

[102] See Bruce Quarrie, *Hitler's Samurai: The Waffen SS in Action,* 2nd ed. (Wellingborough, UK, New York: Patrick Stephens, 1984) pp. 33, 156; also Davis, *Waffen SS,* 2nd ed. (New York, Sydney: Blandford Press, 1987) pp. 185, 195, and K. Williamson, *The SS: Hitler's Instrument of Terror-From Street Fighters to the Waffen SS.* (Osceola, WI: Motorbooks International & Wholesalers, 1994) p. 132.

[103] Major of the *SS*.

[104] Heaton. "Taking Belgrade by Bluff," *Military History,* Vol. 12, No. 5 (January 1998) Leesburg, VA: Cowles History Group, pp. 30-36.

[105] Deshayes operated under the code-names *Mussel* and *Rod*. Interviews of 1993-94.

[106] For more information on this topic, see H.R. Kedward and Roger Austin, *Vichy France and the Resistance: Culture and Identity* (London: Croom & Helm, 1985); also by Kedward and Austin, *Resistance in Vichy France: A Study of Ideas and Motivations in the Southern Zone, 1940-1944* (New

York: Oxford University Press, 1978). See also Kedward, *In Search of the Maquis: Rural Resistance in Southern France, 1942-1944* (New York: Oxford University Press, 1978).
[107] Supplied by Karl Wolff during his first interview, December 1983.
[108] On *Torch*, see Pierre Comtois, "First Fire of Operation Torch," *World War II*, Vol. 11, No. 4 (November 1996) Leesburg, VA: Cowles History Group, pp. 54-60, 82.
[109] Darlan (1881-24 December 1942) was recognized by Roosevelt, but Churchill elected to support de Gaulle.
[110] Kelly Bell, "Darlan Assassination: Death of a Double Dealer," *World War II*, Vol. 13, No. 3 (September 1998) Leesburg, VA: Primedia Publications, Inc. pp. 50-56. See also Alfred J. Rieber, *Stalin and the French Communist Party, 1941-1947* (New York, London: Studies of the Russian Institute, Columbia University Press, 1962) p. 19; and Foot, *SOE in France*, p. 220.
[111] General Charles Joseph André Marie de Gaulle (1890-1970) led the Free French movement from his office in London. Other than for propaganda value, his net worth is debatable.
[112] Henri Giraud (1879-1949) commanded both the 7th and 9th French Armies in 1940, captured 19 May 1940. He escaped to Algiers and succeeded Darlan following his death in December 1942. Pressure from de Gaulle who hated being upstaged saw Giraud resign and withdraw from the war effort, despite his competence and success in Corsica in September 1943, and his popularity with Roosevelt and Churchill.
[113] Ibid. p. 50.
[114] Rieber, p. 9.
[115] Ibid. p. 54.
[116] Foot, *SOE in France*, p. 136.
[117] Rieber, p. 14.
[118] Ibid. p. 8.
[119] Foot, *SOE in France*, p. 141.
[120] Ibid. p. 231, citing M to AD/S on 22 January 1942.
[121] Rieber, p. 56.
[122] Pierre Laval (1883-1945) was Prime Minister and Foreign Secretary from 1931-32 and 1935-36. Was Vice Premier under Petain (1856-1951) in June 1940, was dismissed in December 1941 and reinstated on Hitler's order as Foreign Minister in 1942. His treasonous activities made him a marked man, and he was captured and shot in 1943 while trying to take poison.
[123] See Robert J. Brown, "Britain's Bold Strike on the French Fleet," *World War II*, Vol. 12, No. 3 (September 1997) Leesburg, VA: Cowles History Group, pp. 50-56. See also Foot, *SOE in France*, p. 134.
[124] Kelly Bell, *World War II* (September 1998) pp. 50-56. Also on Darlan, see Black, *Ernst Kaltenbrunner*, p. 256.
[125] PRO HS-5/150, Most Secret and Personal Report from the Defense Committee Special Operations in the Balkans: Coordination of OSS and SOE. Note by Ambassador to Yugoslavia dated 1 December 1943. Donovan was fortunate to have many friends within SOE, and his reputation served him well. See Foot, *SOE in France*, p. 31.
[126] Waddell, "Resistance to National Socialism Within the *Wehrmacht.*" Unpublished Dissertation. Glasgow, UK: University of Strathclyde, Department of History, 1978; on Canaris see pp. 28, 38, 49. See also R. F. Fraenkel and Manvel. *The Canaris Conspiracy: The Secret Resistance to Hitler and the German Army* (London: Heinemann, 1969) and W.C. Waddell (on the secret negotiations) p. 45. On Canaris' plan to arrest Hitler upon invading Czechoslovakia see McGrath, "German Political Opposition to National Socialism? 1933-1939." Unpublished Dissertation. Glasgow, UK: University of Strathclyde, Department of History, 1984, pp. 74-75; and Jeremy Noakes and Pridham (eds.), *Documents of Nazism, 1919-1945, Vol. 1* (London: Oxford University Press, 1974) p. 304. See also R.

Murray Chastain, "Undercover," *World War II*, Vol. 8, No. 3 (September 1993) Leesburg, VA: Empire Press, Inc., pp. 14-20, 72-74.

[127] The *Abwehr* would be incorporated into the *RSHA* on 1 June 1944, allowing Himmler the right to exert some modicum of control over what intelligence went up the chain to Hitler. Gehlen usually ignored the *Reichsfuehrer* and went directly to Hitler on numerous occasions.

[128] See Steenberg, *Vlasov*, p. 35. For a detailed account of the training program established by the Germans at Krasnigorsk, see NA M-1270/24/1054-1055.

[129] Overy, *Russia's War*, p. 135.

[130] Ibid. pp. 163-4.

[131] Steenberg, p. 36.

[132] *RNNA* (*Russkaya Natsionalnaya Narodnaya Armiya*) published its own newspaper, *Rodina* for the troops. Ibid. p. 57.

[133] Ibid. p. 78.

[134] Ibid. p. 37. See also Overy, *Russia's War*, p. 130.

[135] Grant, pp. 27-28; Mills, p. 41; E. Ringleblum, *Notes from the Warsaw Ghetto* (New York: Shocker, 1974) p. 2; and Alfred M. De Zayas, *Nemesis at Potsdam: The Anglo-Americans and the Expulsion of the Germans: Background, Execution, Consequence*. Forward, Robert Murphy 2nd ed. (London: Routledge & Keegan Paul, 1979) pp. 103, 171.

[136] Richard Schultz, Jr., Robert L. Pfaltzgraf, Jr., Uri Ra'anan, William J. Olson, and Igor Lukes (eds.), *Guerrilla Warfare and Counterinsurgency: US-Soviet Foreign Relations in the Third World* (Lexington, MA; Toronto, CA: Lexington Books/DC Heath and Co., 1989) p. 227.

[137] Vidkun Quisling (1887-1945) led the Norwegian Fascist Party from 1933. He assisted the Germans during the invasion of 1940 by delaying troop movements and Hitler appointed him premier. He was shot for treason.

[138] Foot, *SOE in France*, p. xviii. The department responsible for selection into SOE was F Section, who hurriedly tried to collect as many French for screening as possible before they were lost to de Gaulle's "army." Ibid. p. 53.

[139] Author's parentheses.

[140] Bartov, *Hitler's Army*, p. 150 (*en 120*) citing H.F. Richardson, *Sieg Heil! War Letters of Tank Gunner Karl Fuchs 1937-1941* (London: Hamden, 1987) p. 69.

[141] Author's parentheses.

[142] Bartov, *Hitler's Army*, p. 153 (*en 132*). Karl Fuchs letter dated 28 June 1941.

[143] Also known as *La France Combatante*. See Kirk, "To What Extent Can the French Resistance be Described as a Popular Movement?" Unpublished Dissertation. Glasgow, UK: University of Strathclyde, Department of History, 1996, pp. 3, 21; on de Gaulle's BBC announcement for a resistance movement, p. 9. See also Alexander Werth, *France 1940-1945* (London: R. Hale 1956) p. 134, and Alan S. Milward, "French Labor and the German Economy, 1942-1945: An Essay on the Nature of the Fascist New Order," *The Economic History Review*, 2nd series, Vol. 23, No. 2 (August 1970) 343. See also Fritz Hines, "Undercover," *World War II*, Vol. 8, No. 6 (March 1994) Leesburg, VA: Empire Press, Inc. pp. 12-16.

[144] By November 1941, of this group six were shot, six decapitated and several deported to Germany for forced labor or concentration camps. See Kirk, pp. 11-12, 18; John F. Sweetes, *Choices in Vichy France: The French Under Nazi Occupation* (New York: Oxford University Press, 1986) p. 160.

[145] The most successful sabotage component was code-named ARMADA and consisted a group of great diversity, led by a former fireman and a mechanic. See Foot, *SOE in France*, p. 50.

[146] The *11th Panzer* Division took a week to reach the Rhine River from Russia, but three weeks to continue west to Caen due to rail disruption. See Foot, *SOE in France*, p. 411.

[147] Kirk, pp. 18, 21, 60. The town of Royan was forced to pay 3,000,000 francs for the shooting of a German, while Nantes was fined 7,000,000 francs for damage resulting from sabotage. On the "Spe-

cial Income from Abroad" extortion, which covered every country under German occupation, 42% was taken from France. See Kirk, p. 30.

[148] This is when everyone in France became a member of the *Resistance*, no matter how true the statements.

[149] Rieber, pp. 24, 32.

[150] Kirk, pp. 43, 61; and Werth, *France 1940-1955*, p. 167.

[151] Such papers as *La Releve* were widely distributed. The most provocative was *Defense de la France,* which ran a special editorial featuring photographs from concentration camps, with the phrase: "So That No Frenchman Can Say 'I did not know.'" See Kirk, p. 30; also *Musee de la Resistance et de la Deportation*. On French *Resistance* aid to downed airmen, see Thomas Fleming, "Espionage," *Military History*, Vol. 11, No. 1 (April 1994) Leesburg, VA: Cowles History Group, pp. 26-28, 84-86.

[152] Deshayes interview by letter and telephone, 1994. Much of the problem stemmed from the 600,000 unemployed that needed to provide for their families, since only work permits issued by the Germans ensured work. See Kirk, p. 17.

[153] Lynsey E.K Kirk, pp. 8, 19.

[154] Karl Wolff and Otto Kumm, both of whom served in France during the war during their respective interviews supported this statement.

[155] Charles de Gaulle, *The Army of the Future* (London, Melbourne: Hutchison & Co. Publishers, 1938) p. 75.

[156] Deshayes interview, March 1994. Supreme Headquarters Allied Expeditionary Forces (SHEAF) estimated the strength of the *Resistance* at 350,000 serving in the *Maquis, Liberte, Humanite, Armee Secrete* and *FTP* (*Francs-tireurs et partisans*) with another 3,000,000 serving in various areas of the *Resistance*. Also factored in were approximately 2,000,000 Trade Unionists who would start strikes, crippling transportation and manufacturing. Despite these numbers, the total active *Resistance* membership during the war was approximately 2% of the French population. See Kirk, p. 60; and *Musee de la Resistance et de la Deportation*. For more on Deshayes see Foot, *SOE in France*, pp. 247, 384. On Moulin, see also Foot, *SOE in France*, p. 166 and p. 541 (index) for various references; on his successor Parodi see p. 414.

[157] John M. Glenn, "Father of the Green Berets," *Military History* (February 1998) p. 53. Bank took the capabilities and experience of the OSS to new heights, and was the one primary factor in creating the United States Army Special Forces, of which this author was a selected member in 1984. Much of this information was also secured through interviews by this author with Aaron Bank in 1990 and 1991.

[158] Simon Wiesenthal, introduction to Laska, pp. xi-xii.

[159] Kirk, p. 40.

[160] Groups such as *Liberation Nord, defense de la France, Organisation Civilie et Militaire, Ceux de la resistance, Movement Nationale Revolutionaire, Front National*, etc. See Kirk, p. 20 and p. 21 on Marcel Simon's four man resistance team that later joined a larger force.

[161] Ibid. p. 2. This dissertation offers valuable insights regarding the difference between active and passive resistance.

[162] Ibid. p. 18. Pierre Deshayes supported this during his interviews.

[163] Ibid. p. 12.

[164] Bank interview, 1986.

[165] Kirk, pp. 8, 17. See also Foot, *SOE in France*, p. xxi.

[166] Ibid. p. 31.

[167] Ibid. p. 31.

[168] Kirk, p. 48.

[169] See Foot, *SOE in France*, p. 134. The decree was named for Edouard Deladier (1884-1970) French Prime Minister from April 1938-March 1940 and signed the Munich Agreement with Ribbentrop and

Arthur Neville Chamberlain (1869-1940). He worked for the Germans following his arrest, and after the war was elected to the Chamber of Deputies from 1946-1958.

[170] Charles A. Jones, "Perspectives," *World War II,* Vol. 12, No. 1 (May 1997) Leesburg: Cowles History Group, pp. 16-18, 70. See also Laska, p. 3. See also Foot, *SOE in France,* p. 399. See also the reference in Max Hastings, *Das Reich: The March of the 2ⁿᵈ SS Panzer Division Through France* (New York: Holt, Rinehart and Winston, 1981) for excellent photos and narrative on the massacre.

[171] Foot states "About 700 people were killed, but of course a few did get out alive." This probably stems from the French civilian report that exaggerated the number of dead, which may have been intentional. See *SOE in France,* p. 399.

[172] Russell Miller, et al. *The Resistance* (Alexandria, VA: Time-Life Books, Inc., 1979) p. 185. See also Laska, p. 3.

[173] Karl Wolff interview, January 1984. French volunteers were so numerous several units were created to accommodate them, such as the *33ʳᵈ der Waffen SS-Grenadier* Division *(Franzoesische Nr. 1) "Charlemagne,"* which achieved an enviable combat record in the east, yet never reached full division strength. Most of the French were believed to have fought due to anti-Communist (if not pro-fascist) political convictions. See Williamson, p. 244; also Quarrie, *Hitler's Samurai,* pp. 32-33, 48, 81, 157.

[174] Quarrie, p. 42. See also C. Tillon, *On Chantait Rouge* (Paris: Les FTP, 1977) p. 15. Courtesy of Pierre Deshayes.

[175] Kirk, p. 9. See also Alan S. Milward, *The Economic History Review* (August 1970) 337; Werth, *France 1940-1945,* p. 142. The Vichy Commissariat for Jewish Affairs was led by Xavier Vallat, who was responsible for the identification, location and deportation of French Jews in the Vichy region, working closely with the *Gestapo,* including the "Butcher of Lyon," Klaus Barbie, who was convicted of war crimes in 1985, and died in prison in 1991. On 6 May 1942 Vallat appointed Louis Darquier Commissioner of Jewish Affairs, and on 29 May he ordered the wearing of the yellow Star of David. Petain issued the Statute of the Jews on 3 October 1942, banning Jews from professional life. This would lead to a full third of French Jews (of the 75,000 Jews deported less than 2,500 survived) perishing through the assistance of the Petain government. See Kirk, p. 32, and *Musee de la Resistance et de la Deportation.* Maurice Papon, a collaborator and frequent visitor to Hitler was responsible for the deportation and murder of 1,690 French Jews between 1942-1944, while serving as a police supervisor in Bordeaux, although he denied the allegations which surfaced in January 1997, when he was 86 years old. Papon went on French national television, attacking the charges, denying several historical facts such as the Holocaust, infuriating Jews and non-Jews alike. He was convicted in June 1998. See *Wilmington Star News* (UPI) "Ex-Vichy Official to Stand Trial," 27 January 1997, Sec. A-1, p. 2; and 30 January 1997 sec. A-1, p. 1.

[176] Kirk, p. 34. A total of 805 POW's were from the North and 223 from Vichy. The *Gestapo* cleared every prisoner returning to France from German POW camps. Laval followed the directions of Fritz Sauckel (1894-1946), who was responsible for the collection of foreign labor and hanged at Nuremberg. See Foot, *SOE in France,* p. 283.

[177] Kirk. pp. 34-35.

[178] Ibid. p. 8.

[179] Darnand (1897- 3 October 1945) took a commission in the *SS* and swore allegiance to Hitler. He escaped to Germany after the war, but was captured, tried and executed by the French.

[180] Kirk. pp. 18, 33. Marcel Drossier, known as the "Mechanic of Rennes" was captured and executed on 17 September 1940 for destroying telephone lines in the South. See also Foot, *SOE in France,* p. 120.

[181] Ibid. p. 33; and *Musee de la Resistance et de la Deportation.* Also supported by Pierre Deshayes.

[182] Sweetes, pp. 155-160.

[183] The code-name for the invasion of France through Holland and Belgium in 1940.

[184] Kirk, p. 21.

[185] Ibid. pp. 3, 10. See also Sweetes, pp. 134, 157. This position was supported Otto Kumm and Karl Wolff during their respective interviews.

[186] For further information regarding Frenay's relationship with the Germans (including Pierre Boissier), especially regarding his importance in the counterinsurgency planning of *Generalfeldmarschall* Maximilian *Freiherr* von Weichs, see records at *Militaerarchiv* Freiburg, N-19/13. See also Foot, *SOE in France*, pp. 145, 226. See Frenay's book, *La Nuit Finira* (Paris: Laffont, 1973).

[187] Kirk, p. 23.

[188] Ibid. p. 22, and Pierre Deshayes interview, March 1994.

[189] Kirk, p. 42. This decision did not please the Soviets who had begun supporting the *Maquis* covertly.

[190] Ibid. p. 24; also H. Gough and J. Horne, *De Gaulle and Twentieth Century France* (New York: Edward Arnold, 1994) p. 25.

[191] Kirk, p. 41; Gough and Horne, p. 25. Frenay did agree that de Gaulle was crucial for the political and military unification of the *Resistance*. Frenay did not think de Gaulle should have had operational control, hence the mission of sending Jean Moulin.

[192] Rieber, p. 47, citing *Foreign Relations of the United States, Diplomatic Papers: Conferences of Cairo and Tehran (fn 32)* p. 484.

[193] Kirk, p. 56; and Ehrlich, *The French Resistance* (London: Weidenfeld & Nicolson, 1966) p. 57.

[194] Kirk, pp. 23-24; on his conversation with Jean Moulin regarding de Gaulle, see p. 41. See also Werth, *France, 1940-1955*, p. 169.

[195] Kirk, p. 26.

[196] Deshayes interview, March 1994.

[197] A good article on Stalingrad is Vladimir Belyakov, "No Retreats Allowed," *World War II*, Vol. 7, No. 3 (September 1992) Leesburg, VA: Empire Press, Inc. pp. 23-29, 70-71.

[198] On the American Airborne drop into Sicily, see Martin F. Graham, "Terrible Lessons Learned," *World War II*, Vol. 8, No. 2 (July 1993) Leesburg, VA: Cowles History Group, pp. 22-28, 70.

[199] See Pat McTaggart, "War's Greatest Tank Duel," *World War II*, Vol. 8 No. 2 (July 1993) Leesburg, VA: Cowles History Group, pp. 30-37.

[200] Kirk, p. 37, Miller, *The Resistance*, pp. 85-86; and Werth, *France 1940-1955*, p. 137.

[201] Kirk, p. 37.

[202] Ibid.

[203] Ibid.

[204] Ibid. pp. 37, 50; see also *Musse de la Resistance et de la Deportations*; and Henri Michel, *Les Courants de Pensee de la Resistance*, trans. by Richard Barry (New York: Harper & Row, 1972) p. 6. Maquis were not exclusively Communist, as nationalism and patriotism brought many political and religious backgrounds into the collective. See also Michel, *The Shadow War: European Resistance, 1939-1945*, trans. Richard Barry (New York: Harper & Row, 1972). See also Michel, "Shadow States: Émigré Governments in London, 1940-42," *History of the Second World War*, Vol. 3 (1966) pp. 1118-1120.

[205] Pierre Deshayes also related this concern, as he was knowledgeable of the meeting between Roosevelt and Churchill, where the occupation was considered necessary. See Kirk, p. 38; Gough and Horne, p. 31.

[206] This includes pilots in the RAF, the *Normandie-Nieman* Squadron assisting the Red Air Force in the Soviet Union, and the French Foreign Legion. On the ground forces, see Kirk, and Gough and Horne, p. 19.

[207] Deshayes interview, March 1994.

[208] Ibid. pp. 10-11 (on Frenay) p. 23. See also *Musee de la Resistance et de la Deportation*.

[209] Lynsey E.J. Kirk, p. 31 and Sweetes, p. 165.

[210] See Lynsey E.J. Kirk, p. 21 and Gough and Horne, p. 21.

[211] Chuck Yeager interview by Jeffrey L. Ethell, 1994. Courtesy of Jeffrey L. Ethell.

[212] Paul Bodot, "American Airmen Saved," *World War II*, Vol. 7, No. 6 (March 1993) Leesburg, VA: Empire Press, Inc. pp. 38-44.

[213] Madame Fourcade would receive the *Legion d' Honneur* and the Order of the British Empire for her service to the Allies. She also became an author and a member of the European Parliament.

[214] Laska, p. 137.

[215] Ibid. p. 138.

[216] Frank Perkins, "Perspectives," *World War II*, Vol. 13, No. 3 (September 1998) Leesburg, VA: Primedia Publications, Inc. pp. 60-64. The survivors of the mission from the 383rd Squadron, 364th Fighter Group embarked on a mission to raise $200,000 to replace the windows of the 13th Century church damaged that day where Braly's body lay.

[217] Founded on 26 April 1933 with Hermann Goering as its leader. See Pauline Russell, p. 20; Hans Buccheim, "Instrument of Domination," Broszat and Krausnick, *Anatomy of the SS State*, p. 147.

[218] Kirk, p. 10;

[219] See Laska, p. 6.

[220] Steven J. Legge, "Personality," *World War II*, Vol. 13, No. 2 (July 1998) Leesburg, VA: Primedia Publications, Inc. pp. 8-14, 68-70. See also Foot, *SOE in France*, p. 357. Ortiz was a sergeant at age 20, one of the youngest in the Legion. After serving his five years as a parachutist, worked in the film industry in California, rejoined the Legion with a commission, was wounded in France and captured. He finally escaped after sixteen months and several foiled attempts, made it to Portugal, joined the Marines as a 2nd lieutenant, promoted to captain in 1942. He joined the OSS after being wounded again in North Africa.

[221] Ibid. p. 8. Union was primarily an OSS Jedburgh Team mission with some SOE support and commenced on, to assess the status of the *Maquis* and support them with weapons.

[222] Ibid. *Union II* commenced on 1 August 1944 as a joint OSS-SOE Operation to assess the *Maquis* reliability in the Savoie, Drome and Isere regions.

[223] Ibid. p. 14.

[224] Ibid. p. 68. Ortiz would receive a second Navy Cross after the war for his successes with the partisans. Two films based upon his exploits were *13 Rue Madeleine* (1946) starring James Cagney and *Operation Secret* (1952) starring Cornel Wilde. He became good friends with director John Ford, who in turn became the godfather of Ortiz' son, Pierre Julien Ortiz, Jr., who became a Marine officer, graduating from the U.S. Naval Academy in 1975. "Pete" Ortiz died in 1988 aged seventy-five of cancer, and is buried in Arlington National Cemetary. According to a member of the *Union* missions under Ortiz, Jack Risler, "All of the seemingly incredible stories about him are true. *Union II* is really a story about Pete Ortiz. The rest of us were just along for the ride." Ibid. p. 70.

[225] Kirk, p. 9; Werth, *France 1940-1955*, p. 142.

[226] Kirk, p. 35; on de Gaulle's appointment, p. 50.

[227] Werth, p. 36. On D-Day and the liberation of Paris on 25 August 1944, see p. 38.

[228] Ibid. p. 22, and *Musee de la Resistance et de la Deportation*.

[229] Fritz Hines, *World War II* (March 1994) pp. 12-16. Ibid.

[230] De Gaulle, *Army of the Future*, p. 121.

[231] For additional on Morel see Foot, *SOE in France*, p. 541 (index) for relevant entries.

[232] The *157th Alpen* Division was a regular army unit that utilized *Waffen SS Gebirgsjaeger* contingents. See Foot, *SOE in France*, p. 394.

[233] Deshayes interview, March 1994.

[234] Deshayes interview, 1993; see also *Military History* (February 1998) p. 53.

[235] Foot, *SOE in France*, p. 356, citing a 10 October 1945 memorandum in the Foreign Office files. Karl Rudolf Gerd von Rundstedt (1875-1953) was a soldier of the old school and WW I veteran. His tactical skill assisted in the planning for nearly every German invasion. He was key to the invasion of France, although his concerns regarding the over extended German lines of communication and support prompted Hitler to halt any land drive towards Dunkirk, allowing for the evacuation. Rundstedt later served as C-in-C West, dismissed on occasion and later brought back. He was charged with war crimes at Nuremberg, but these were later dismissed.

[236] The German atomic research project would be destroyed by a mission led by Knut Haukelid and eight other SOE trained and supplied partisans. See Foot, *SOE in France*, p. 147.

[237] Laska, p. 121.

[238] Ibid. pp. 110, 121.

[239] This was the *National Socialistische Bewegung* under Anton Mussert. See Laska, p. 91.

[240] John C. Breen, "Attitude and Opinion During the Phony War: September 1939-April 1940." Unpublished Dissertation. Glasgow, UK: University of Strathclyde, Department of History, 1974. pp. 17, 23-24. See also the *Daily Record & Mail*, 4 January 1940 and the *Manchester Guardian*, 5 January 1940. See also John R. Bittner, "Undercover," *World War II*, Vol. 5, No. 1 (May 1990) Leesburg: Empire Press, Inc. pp. 8, 64-66.

[241] Mills, pp. 30-31, 46; C.H.J. Marliepaard, "The Dutch Agricultural Situation," *Annals of the American Academy of Social and Political Science*, pp. 48-50;

[242] Mills, pp. 56-58, 60; Henri van der Zee, *The Hunger Winter: Occupied Holland, 1944-45* (London: Jill Norman & Hobhouse, 1982) p. 71. Swedish Red Cross overtures to alleviate the starvation was finally supported by the Allies on 29 October 1944, yet was rebuked and delayed by Germany for months, with the first aid arriving on 27 February 1945. At least 18,000 people starved to death. See H. van der Zee, p. 37. The Dutch population lost 219,300 civilians of which 6,000 were soldiers fighting against Germany, and with 3,700 killed as *Freiwilligen*.

[243] Mills, p. 37; Warmbrunn, p. 110.

[244] See table on *German Military Unit Dispositions*, 10 May 1940, taken from Major General R.H. Barry, "Military Balance Within Western Europe, May 1940," *History of the Second World War: An International History*, Vol. 1 (London: Methuen, 1966) p. 172; also cited in Mills, p. 63.

[245] Mills, pp. 27-29; R.D. Kollewijn, 118-120.

[246] Mills, pp. 20, 22, 46-47, 58, photos-pp. 77, 79; Warmbrunn, p. 35; H.L. Mason, "Testing Human Bonds Within Nations: Jews in the Occupied Netherlands," *Political Science Quarterly*, Vol. 99 (1984) 324. *Operation Market-Garden* was intended to capture the major bridges spanning the Rhine at Eindhoven Nijmegan, Arnhem and other locations, allowing Allied armor to strike the industrial Ruhr, ending the war by Christmas 1944. For further on Seyss-Inquart (1892-1946) who was hanged at Nuremberg, see record at *Bundesarchiv* Koblenz, N-1180.

[247] Mills, p. 46; Richard Overy, "Hitler's War and the German Economy: A Reinterpretation," *Economic History Review*, Vol. 35 (1982) 290.

[248] Mills, pp. 50, 58; H. van der Zee, p. 111.

[249] K. Vonk, "The Transportation System in the Netherlands," *Annal of the American Academy of Social and Political Science*, Vol. 245 (1946) 77; Mills, pp. 46-47, 50; H. van der Zee, p. 29.

[250] See Rebecca Gray, "Perspectives," *World War II*, Vol. 13, No. 5 (January 1999) Leesburg, VA: Primedia Publications, Inc. pp. 18-24.

[251] Mills, p. 52.

[252] Roberta Donovan, "Undercover," *World War II*, Vol. 7, No. 4 (November 1992) Leesburg, VA: Empire Press, Inc. pp. 10-12, 77-80.

[253] Ibid.

[254] This was supported by interviews with Karl Wolff (1984) and Hans Baur (1985).

[255] See Jodl records at *Militaerarchiv* Freiburg Document N-69/28. Jodl (10 May 1890-16 October 1946) signed the German surrender at Reims on 8 May 1945 and would be hanged for crimes against humanity following his conviction in Nuremberg. He drew up the plans for Greece and Yugoslavia and was instrumental in the planing for *Barbarossa*.

[256] Ibid. N-69/28.

[257] Laska, p. 6.

[258] Montgomery (1887-1976), 1st Viscount of Alamein, commanded troops in France, Africa and the occupation of Germany, promoted Field Marshal in 1944

[259] Laska, p. 57.

[260] Fleming, *Military History* (April 1994) p. 26.

[261] Ibid. See also Laska, pp. 128-29. Andree de Jongh would receive the George Medal from the British government, the highest non-combat civilian award for bravery. After the war she served as a nurse in the Belgian Congo, and a leper hospital in Addis Ababa, and in Senegal.

[262] Ibid. 84.

[263] Laska, p. 272.

[264] See Black, *Ernst Kaltenbrunner*, p. 177. Heydrich (1904-1942) was thrown out of the Navy following a scandal involving an admiral's daughter. He joined the SS, then helped create the SD. Heydrich was appointed deputy to Himmler and masterminded the Gliewicz scenario in 1939 as Germany's pretext to invade Poland, as well as the *Einsatzgruppen* concept in 1941. Heydrich was also the charter participant in the Wansee Conference.

[265] M-1270/24/0827.

[266] Ibid. The Krakow Ghetto would be the site of the first major Jewish resistance group in Poland, formed during 1942 and patterned on the Vilnius, Lithuania Ghetto's Jewish Fighters' Organization the winter of 1941. See Laska, p. 99.

[267] The Passover morning saw the remaining 60,000 Jews (300,000 were already gone and perishing mostly in Treblinka) initiate combat for survival. The two uprisings destroyed the myth that the Jews did not fight back, and were willing to trust in the support expected from the Western Allies. See Laska, p. 9.

[268] Ibid. p. 4.

[269] Fiona Mitchell, pp. 5, 16-18, 33-36; J.A.S. Grenville, *The Major International Treaties, 1914-1973*, pp. 57-58. The Treaty of Versailles was in the international press on 26 April 1920, although the Minorities Treaty was not included. Poland abrogated the Treaty on 15 September 1934, in which the minorities issue was ratified by a clause in the Treaty of Riga in 1921, which Poland signed. In 1922 the Polish government granted autonomy to Galicia on 26 September 1922 which was a result of both previous treaties. During the Conference of Ambassadors in March 1923 Poland secured legal occupation of Eastern Galicia, and enforcing a "Polonization" policy in education, government and society in general, which angered majority nationalist Ukrainians, as well as Lithuanians, White Russians (Belorussian) and others. Atrocities occurred during this period, further enraging the non-Polish population on grounds of "terrorist activity", and solidifying Hitler's propaganda platform on the elimination of Poland. These ethnic groups would form some of the most anti-Polish and fanatical *Freiwilligen* units within the *Waffen SS*. See Fiona Mitchell, pp. 23-25, 27-33; and Hans Roos, *A Modern History of Poland*, p. 133.

[270] See chart in Fiona Mitchell, p. 12.

[271] The Soviet Union lost parts of Ukraine and Beylorussia to Poland, which Stalin never forgave. The Poles were still unimpressed, even when Molotov negotiated the Polish-Soviet Non-Aggression Pact of 1934, which was reaffirmed on 26 November 1938 and was probably due to the Franco-German Agreement signed the same day. See Donnelly, pp. 15, 22, 29; Tait, p. 24; R.J. Sonntag and J.S. Beddie (eds.), *Nazi-Soviet Relations: 1939-1941: Documents From the Archives of the German For-*

eign Office (Westport, CT: Greenwood Press, 1974) p. 85; Kaiser, *Economic Diplomacy*, p. 279; and Max Beloff, *The Foreign Policy of Soviet Russia, 1929-1941*, Vol. I pp. 139-140.
²⁷² Donnelly, p.16, and Beloff, pp. 143-148. Poland was also at odds with Germany over the rights to Memel, further exacerbating the problem. See also Grant, pp. 18-29; and PRO file listings in *bibliography*. The British or Americans would never champion the Polish claims due to the Soviet influence. See Grant, pp. 38-39; Hansake Persson, "German Refugees: A British Dilemma? The British Policy on German Refugees at the End of the Second World War." *Workshop on European and Middle East Refugees in the 20ᵗʰ Century* (Oxford: Oxford University Press, August 1985) p. 13; and PRO C5753/ 95/18, FO 371/46812.
²⁷³ McGrath, pp. 25, 27. This apparent cooperation between Stalin and Hitler would become a major problem in creating an effective Communist underground movement within Germany during the war. Also, much of the distrust stemmed from the ideological conflict in Spain during the Spanish Civil War. On this factor and the Spanish Communists, see Killen on the *Falange Espanola*, p. 10. The *Nazis* and Communists became involved in a street fight in the Altona district of Hamburg on 17 July 1932, which became known *Blutsonntag*, or Bloody Sunday.
²⁷⁴ See Catriona Adams, "Stalin: A Popular Leader?" Unpublished Dissertation. Glasgow, UK: University of Strathclyde, Department of History, no date, pp. 9, 13-15, 18-19, 21, 23-25; McGrath, p. 26, and Killen, p. 40. For more on the purges see Robert Conquest, *Stalin: Breaker of Nations* (New York: Viking Press, 1991), Alan B. Ulam, *Stalin: The Man and His Era* (New York: Viking Press, 1973); N. Mandlestram, *Hope Against Hope* (London: Collins & Harvill Press, 1989), M. McAuley, *Politics in the Soviet Union* (New York, NY and London: Penguin, 1977); Leon Trotsky, *Stalin* (New York: Hollis & Carter, 1947); Wilson, pp. 1-5, 17-25, 44, on the 5,000,000 peasant deaths in Ukraine, see p. 22; R. Conquest, *The Harvest of Sorrow* (New York: Oxford University Press, 1986) p. 303, on Ukrainian and Caucasus, see also Robert Conquest, *The Great Terror: A Reassessment* (New York: Oxford University Press, 1990) Ch. 16 in total; on the Georgians, see also Wilson, *The Nationalities Question in the Soviet Union 1917-1938*, Unpublished Dissertation. Glasgow, UK: University of Strathclyde, Department of History, 1996, pp. 28-35; on the purges see R.A. Medvedev, *Let History Judge* (New York, NY and London: Oxford University Press, 1989). On the Chinese, Armenians, Greeks, Latvians and Koreans, see George Wilson, p. 45. On the French *Maquis* see Kirk, pp. 47, 48. The *Maquis* were self-labeled as anti-Capitalists, until the Soviet Union became a Western ally, then they were "anti-fascists" to suit the current agenda.
²⁷⁵ See Mark Mazower, *Inside Hitler's Greece: The Experience of Occupation, 1941-44* (London, UK and New Haven, CT: Yale University Press, 1993) p. 220 (photo p. 223). Schimana was a counterinsurgency specialist and assisted in creating the working doctrine in Russia.
²⁷⁶ Stroop was an egomaniac who wrote an after action report; "Report Concerning the Uprising in the Ghetto of Warsaw and the Liquidation of the Jewish Residential District," that was later published as a book titled; *There is No Longer a Jewish Quarter in Warsaw* (Berlin: Volk und *Reich* Verlag, 1944) and he later served as the *SS* and political leader in Greece, responsible for commanding the anti-partisan units and continuing the transport of Greek Jews to death camps. He was fired due to his boss Ernst Kaltenbrunner (Himmler's deputy) fearing he may make matters worse, due to his ruthless nature and complete lack of political and social skills. Stroop was convicted of war crimes by an American tribunal and handed over to the Polish government after the war, and was hanged within sight of his former headquarters on 8 September 1951. Ironically, it was his own book that was used in evidence against him, securing the conviction. See Jon Guttman, "Genocide Delayed," *World War II*, Vol. 8, No. 1 (May 1993) Leesburg, VA: Empire Press, Inc., pp. 44-52; also Time-Life, *The Apparatus of Death* (Alexandria, VA: Time-Life Books, Inc., 1991) p. 139. On his service in Greece, see Mazower, *Inside Hitler's Greece*, pp. 220-22 (photo p. 221).
²⁷⁷ Guttman, *World War II* (May 1993) p. 44.

[278] Overy, *Russia's War*, p. 246.

[279] Wilfred P. Deac, "City Streets Contested," *World War II*, Vol. 9, No. 3 (September 1994) Leesburg, VA: Cowles History Group, pp. 32-44, 66; see p. 38. Rokossovsky (1896-1968) commanded the 16th Army during Moscow in 1941; Don Front in 1942 against the German *6th Armee* at Stalingrad; the Central Front at Kursk in 1943, and the 1st Belorussian Front in 1944. He met the British at Wismar on 5 May 1945, and after the war was C-in-C of Soviet forces in Poland.

[280] Overy, *Russia's War*, p. 247.

[281] *Brigadefuehrer* Bronislav Kaminsky had been a mayor in Lokoty District and was a professional engineer, until falling into disfavor with the *NKVD*. He was sent to a penal camp; was later exonerated and banished to his old district. He later commanded one of the two most notorious groups of *SS* men, and other battle hardened *SS* men avoided them fearing guilt by association. Rape, murder, and looting were their primary activities, and most of the ethnically diverse men, compromising perhaps the most international collection representing over a dozen nations, and were recruited from prisons, labor and POW camps, or Russian deserters who joined up for food. They were a tough bunch against unarmed civilians, yet their combat record was less than stellar until their appointment in the anti-partisan role. Kaminsky was killed by his own men as they deserted in 1945, possibly on Himmler's orders. None are known to have survived, or rather admit their association. See also reference on Kaminsky at Warsaw in Overy, *Russia's War,* p. 129.

[282] Wolff interview, January 1984. According to Wolff, Degrelle and Kumm, Hans Frank never hid disdain of the use of *Ostruppen*.

[283] Zelewski was the overall commander of anti-partisan forces from October 1942, and was captured in May 1945 and placed under indictment for war crimes for the Warsaw Uprising of August-October 1943, although his activities in Russia had been deemed "appropriate under the circumstances" under the Geneva Accords. He offered testimony against other officers whom he felt had exceeded the operational requirements, including murdering women and children. He died in 1972. See Quarrie, *Hitler's Samurai*, p. 150; Williamson, *The SS: Hitler's Instrument of Terror*, pp. 134, 191.

[284] Overy, *Russia's War*, p. 140.

[285] Ibid. p. 145.

[286] The unit was listed as the *29th der Waffen SS* Division *RONA* on paper, which would have given it a compliment of 17,000 men at least. However, the unit never reached a peak average strength of approximately 8,500. See Steenberg, *Vlasov*, p. 170.

[287] Supported by Karl Wolff and Otto Kumm during their respective interviews.

[288] Dirlewanger was a convicted child molester and rapist who was given a reprieve to command another collection of criminals in a penal unit, including murderers, rapists, pedophiles, reprieved homosexuals (those in concentration camps who agreed to castration to be released) many of whom were serving in other German units when they committed their offenses, and formed *Brigade Dirlewanger*, which never grew larger than this size despite his unit receiving divisional recognition in 1944.

[289] Wilfred P. Deac, *World War II* (September 1994) pp. 32-44, 66; see also Time-Life, *The Apparatus of Death*, pp. 136, 138-3.

[290] For more details on Hans Frank, see Black, *Ernst Kaltenbrunner*, pp. 3, 140 *(fn. 17)* p. 150. Frank (1900-16 October 1946) was one of the most ruthless anti-Semites and fled as the Soviet military pushed through Poland. He was tried, sentenced and executed at Nuremberg. See Frank records at *Bundesarchiv* Koblenz, N-1110.

[291] SOE and the Foreign Office's desire to reinstate Benes to power under the agreement negotiated with Seton-Watson in 1918 was sometimes a point of contention. See Foot, *SOE in France*, p. 129. Benes (1884-1948) was President from 1935-1939, and headed the Czech government in exile in London. The Communist coup in 1948 forced him to resign a second time.

[292] PRO HS-4/1 Most Secret memorandum, "Meeting with General Ingr on 8ᵗʰ December," no year on document. See also PRO HS-4/1 Most Secret memorandum dated 30 December 1942 with handwritten addendum dated 1 January 1943. Regarding taking "a strong line with Benes should get us what we want." See also PRO HS-4/1 "Record of a Meeting with Moravec on 11ᵗʰ January 1943."

[293] Karl Wolff interview, January 1984.

[294] PRO HS-4/7 Cipher Telegram dated 8 October 1944.

[295] PRO HS-4/16. Most Secret memorandum, no date.

[296] SOE believed that the best operatives came from outside the military, preferably natives of the target nations due to their familiarity with the language, customs and their ability to expand the network by gaining trust and support. See Foot, *SOE in France*, p. 42.

[297] Heydrich's successor as *Reichsprotektor von Boehmen und Maehren* was Konstantin *Freiherr* von Neurath (2 February 1873-14 August 1956, record located at *Bundesarchiv* Koblenz, N-1310) a WW I veteran officer and skilled diplomat, serving in several European capitols between 1903-32. Neurath served as Protector from May 1941-25 August 1943 and was involved in the round up of Jews in the Protectorate. He was captured in May 1945, tried at Nuremberg, and on 1 October 1946 was sentenced to fifteen years. See N-1310. See also British Document Book No. 12B (German language) *Bundesarchiv* Koblenz. See also Laska, p. 32. It would be the decisions reached at the Wansee Conference that would bring the likes of *Obersturmbannfuehrer* Adolf Eichmann (1906-1962) and *Hauptsturmfuehrer* Dr. Josef Mengele to the forefront after the war. See also Overy, *Russia's War*, p. 139.

[298] The reprisals were ordered by Hitler and Himmler and carried out by Karl Hermann Frank (1898-1946), Secretary of State for Bohemia and Moravia in 1939. He was personally responsible for the mass murders at Lidice on 10 July 1942. He was captured and hanged in Prague.

[299] Ibid. On the training and preparation requirements, see PRO HS-4/16 Most Secret-*A Summary of the Memorandum of Principles of Training for Special Purposes Submitted by General Ingr,* no date.

[300] For information regarding SOE trained Czech operatives, see PRO HS-4/78, a Most Secret document on a Captain Gajdos. This personnel file and operational record offers interesting data.

[301] PRO HS-4/7 memorandum from A/D.H. to C.D. dated 8 January 1945 (MEDCOS 227) paragraph No. 2.

[302] PRO HS-4/1. This was a Most Secret letter detailing the meeting. See also letter to 12ᵗʰ Army Group from SHAEF authenticated by Maj. Gen. H.R. Bull, no date. Regarding the support to 3ʳᵈ Army, see Top Secret Cipher Telegram from SHAEF Forward to The War Office, dated 25 April 1945, signed by Eisenhower (1890-1969).

[303] PRO HS-4/79 memorandum from MY to MP dated 18 September 1943.

[304] Ibid.

[305] PRO HS-4/7 Report dated 16 May 1945.

[306] HS-4/1 Top-Secret Priority message dated 27 April 1945 from 12ᵗʰ Army Group (Bradley) to SHAEF for distribution to OSS.

[307] PRO HS-4/7 memorandum from A/DH to CD dated 8 January 1945, paragraph No. 5.

[308] Ibid.

[309] On cursory information regarding Dietrich's capture and interrogation, see David Irving, *Hitler's War*, Vols. 1 & 2 (New York: Viking Press, 1977) p. xiv. See also Truman R. Strobridge, "Personality," *World War II*, Vol. 7, No. 5 (January 1993) Leesburg, VA: Empire Press, Inc. pp. 8, 69-72.

[310] PRO HS-4/1 Most Secret Record of a luncheon given by SO for President Benes. Also present were General Ingr, Colonel Moravec, D/CD (CD being the designation of the executive director) & MX on 24 September 1942; report dated 25 September 1942.

[311] PRO HS-4/1. On deployment planning within the Protectorate, especially Slovakia and Bohemia see PRO HS-4/1 Copy 1, "Record of a Meeting with General Moravec on 11 January 1943," dated 12 January 1943.

[312] PRO HS-4/1 Report on a Discussion with General Golian at Tri Duby, Slovakia on October 7th, 1944. On OSS support to the Slovak's through Colonel Threlfall see PRO HS-4/1 document dated 23 October 1944, regarding Threfall's report dated 7 October.

[313] PRO HS-4/7 Top Secret Cipher outward telegram from the Foreign Office to Moscow, dated 12 March, 1945.

[314] PRO HS/7 letter dated 30 August 1944 from Philip Nichols to Sir Anthony Eden.

[315] PRO HS-4/1 Top Secret Cipher Telegram dated 25 April 1945 from SHAEF to AMSSO regarding War Office for internal distribution.

[316] PRO HS-4/1 Most Secret memorandum "Czech Affairs" dated 16 January 1943.

[317] PRO HS-4/56 Top Secret memorandum from the Central Department dated 1 September 1944 and received on 5 September.

[318] PRO HS-4/1.

[319] Ibid.

[320] Ibid.

[321] PRO HS-4/82.

[322] PRO HS-4/92.

[323] PRO HS-4/1 memo dated 21 April 1945 regarding C.O.S. dated 9 November 1944 and 18 January 1945.

[324] Allied Expeditionary Forces.

[325] PRO HS-4/1 Internal Distribution memorandum.

[326] PRO HS-4/1 from Chiefs of Staff.

[327] PRO HS-4/1 Secret Cipher Telegram dated 8 May 1945 from AMSSO to SHAEF Forward.

[328] PRO HS-4/7 Top Secret telegram from Foreign Office to Moscow dated 3 April 1945, paragraph 1.

[329] Ibid. Paragraph No. 2.

[330] PRO HS-4/7 General Situation report by SOE, no date.

[331] Ibid.

[332] These teams were ROTHMAN, CHURCHMAN, FOURSQUARE, and PIGOTITE. See PRO HS-4/7. On WOLFRAM see PRO HS-4/44.

[333] Ibid.

[334] Ibid.

[335] Ibid.

[336] Ibid.

[337] Thomas H. Wolf, "Perspectives," *World War II*, Vol. 10, No. 3 (September 1995) Leesburg, VA: Cowles History Group, pp. 66-72.

[338] PRO HS-4/44.

[339] PRO HS-4/7 Report dated 16 May 1945.

[340] Ibid.

[341] Ibid.

[342] PRO HS-4/7 letter from M.P. to C.D. dated 16 May 1945, p. 3. See also PRO HS-4/92 Account of EPIGRAM Mission from Captain E.A. Howe and Lieutenant T.E. Byron of Force 399 to various departments, dated 7 November 1944. This report discusses the condition, activities and attitude of the Red Army while in Czechoslovakia as observed by SOE operatives. See also HS-4/7 Report dated 16 May 1945 on Soviet conduct towards civilians.

[343] PRO HS-4/11 Top-Secret AAA XXX report from the Northern Department, titled "The Russians in Ruthenia," dated 12 January 1945 and received on 16 January. Classification: "This report must in no circumstance get back to the Czechs, or the Russians, and should be handled with special care."

[344] Ibid. Top Secret AAA XXX letter from Northern Department dated 21 January 1943 titled "Relations with Czechs: Carpatho-Ukraine, etc."

[345] PRO HS-4/7 Report dated 16 May 1945.

[346] See PRO HS-4/1 dated 3 June 1942 on Heydrich and the fact that Benes was kept in the dark on the matter. Heydrich was succeeded by *Obergruppenfuehrer* Dr. Ernst Kaltenbrunner (1902-October 1946).

[347] Ibid. Future Planning-Czechoslovakia, no date.

[348] PRO HS-4/7 letter from Philip Nichols to Sir Anthony Eden dated 30 August 1944.

[349] *Kneaz* is a Prince in Cossack culture. Maximciuc is a descendant of the Romanov dynasty.

[350] On Maniu and Antonescu (1886-1946) see National Archives Roll M-1270/24/0456, hereafter M-1270/24/with relevant frame numbers.

[351] McIntyre, p. vi. See also Seton-Watson, pp. 85-86. On the correspondence between *Generalfeldmarschall* Ewald von Kleist (8 August 1881-October 1954) and Marshal Antonescu (1886-1946) where Kleist thanked the Marshal for providing of Romanian troops in a letter dated 21 March 1942 see N-354/19. Kleist died in Soviet captivity. On Kleist's involvement in the 20 July plot, see National Archives M-1270/24/0430.

[352] Hans Doerr (14 September 1897-9 September 1960) had previously held the position of *Kommissar fuer das Kriegstransportwesen (Heimat)* from 1939-42. See records at *Militaerarchiv* Freiburg, N-29/1.

[353] Ibid. N-29/2. Ambrosio (1897-1958) commanded the 2nd Italian Army in Yugoslavia in 1942, became Chief of Staff of the Italian Army in January 1942, and Chief of the Italian General Staff in February 1943. His opposition to Mussolini and the German occupation of Italy shortened his career.

[354] Ibid. N-29/3, 4.

[355] McIntyre, p. 24.

[356] Ibid. p. vii; and Seton-Watson, p. 88.

[357] McIntyre, p. vii; and Martin McCauley (ed.) *Communist Power in Europe, 1944-1949* (London: Macmillan & School of Slavonic and East European Studies, University of London, 1977) p. 112.

[358] McIntyre, p. viii; and Seton-Watson, p. 83. On the fall of the Antonescus, see National Archives Roll M-1270/24/0456.

[359] Ibid. p. viii; and McCauley, p. 201.

[360] McIntyre, p. ix. See also Seton-Watson, p. 97.

[361] McIntyre, p. ix.

[362] Ibid. p. viii.

[363] Nicholas de Nagybanya Horthy (1868-1957) was a Austro-Hungarian naval officer in WWI; leader of the counterrevolutionary "White Movement" overthrowing Bela Kun, and became regent in 1920. He ordered Hungarian forces to support Germany's invasion of Yugoslavia in 1941. By 1943 Horthy tried to gain greater independence from Hitler, prompting the Skorzeny intervention.

[364] On an example of an SOE mission, see PRO HS-4/92 Secret report from Captain E.A. Howe to H.Q. Force 399 C.M.F. on "EPIGRAM" mission of dated 15 November 1944 and received on 28 November 1944.

[365] McIntyre, p. ix.

[366] See Heaton, *World War II* (January 1998) pp. 30-36. See also Roslyn A McIntyre, p. ix.

[367] McIntyre, pp. ix-x.

[368] Ibid. p. x.

[369] Ibid.

[370] Ibid.

[371] Ibid. xi. See also McCauley, p. xiii. The Yalta Conference of February 1945 was to decide the fate of post-war Europe between the Western Democracies and the Soviet Union. The nations involved were never consulted as to their wishes. Yugoslavia was to be divided, with Britain obtaining Greece, while Romania, Hungary and Bulgaria fell to Stalin singly. Poland was to have free elections, and the fate of the Baltic States were still in question, due to the tentative nature of the agreement and due to

the American presence; although in meetings between Anthony Eden and Molotov in October 1944, it seemed certain they would also fall to the Soviets, until the inception of the Declaration on Liberated Europe, which all Allies signed, the Stalin remained "...open on the subject of Poland and Eastern Europe." However, the expulsion and forced detainment of ethnic Germans was never discussed, and Poland's claims were deemed unrealistic, with exception to Danzig, Oppeln, Silesia (which Poland gained after WW I) and East Prussia. See PRO C14985/231/55 -FO 371/34562. See also Grant, pp. 3, 22, 24-25; also PRO C910/258/55, PRO C849/231/55 FO 371/34560, PRO C12169/464/55, FO 371/ 31091. For Sir Anthony Eden's reactions see PRO CC11657 FO 371/34562, and Grant, p. 23. See also PRO C11657/231/55 FO 37134562. On Eden's agreement with Stalin handing over Eastern Europe, see Overy, *Russia's War*, p. 120. See also John Gardner, "Could the *NSDAP* Have Attained Power Without the Personality and Politics of Adolf Hitler?" Unpublished Dissertation. Glasgow, UK: University of Strathclyde, Department of History, 1992. p. 11. For Churchill's comments in the House of Commons on 15 December, 1944 see Grant, pp. 26-27; see A.M. de Zayas, *Nemesis at Potsdam: The Anglo-Americans and the Expulsion of the Germans* in total. Stalin's plan was similar to that of the Greek and Turkish divisions of their ethnic peoples in the Balkans during the 1920s, supervised by the League of Nations. This was an attempt at curbing possible guerrilla warfare that would lead to open hostilities between the major powers. See Grant, pp. 4, 17. Ironically the British and Americans refused to allow refugees into their respective zones, fearing disease and the inability to feed and control such numbers, consigning hundreds of thousands to a fate at the hands of the Soviets. See Grant, pp. 34-35; and PRO FO 46812. President Harry S. Truman took severe criticism from his republican opponents, who stated that "...pro-Communists had negotiated at Yalta and given Eastern Europe to the Soviets." See Joyce, p. 7.

[372] McIntyre, pp. x-xi. This was the first scenario, which helped establish the conditions for the Cold War. Ironically, Churchill's knowledge of the very Europe he wanted to dominate proved wanting, when at the conference he displayed his ignorance of the fact that there were two Neisse Rivers; the Western (or Lusatian) and the Eastern (or Glatzer), which join at the Oder-Neisse. See Grant, p. 19, and Wiskemann, p. 76.

[373] Kerscher interview, 1985.

[374] PRO HS-4/115. This letter is preserved in both Hungarian and English versions.

[375] Ibid.

[376] PRO HS-4/92.

[377] Overy, *Russia's War*, p. 143.

[378] Ibid. p. 151.

[379] Mazower. See his spelling as *"Andartes,"* the word for "Guerrilla," p. 125

[380] PRO HS-5/151. This was clearly an understatement regarding the Communist loyalties of the guerrillas.

[381] Benito Mussolini (1883-1945) was Prime Minister from 1922-25 and dictator from 1925-43.

[382] Mazower, *Inside Hitler's Greece*, p. xiii. See also Laska, pp. 114-20.

[383] Mazower, p. 67.

[384] Mazower, p. xv.

[385] Velouchiotis (*aka* Thansis Klaras, 1905-1945) was a former KKE member and a trained agricultural specialist and a cofounder of ELAS. He was a brutally violent man, bordering on sadism towards both Germans and his own people, and he never trusted the Western Allies. He was also a staunch anti-monarchist. Churchill never trusted him and even Tito and Stalin even agreed he would have to go after the war, due to his brutality and the lack of trust and faith in him among his followers. He was killed after being surrounded by British supported Government troops at the village of Mesounda.

[386] See Mazower, *Inside Hitler's Greece*, p. 98.

[387] Ibid. p. 137.

388 Zervas (1891-1957) became the leader of EDES in Espiros. He founded the right-wing National Party, serving as Minister of Public Order in 1947. His shadowy past and speculations that he had been a German collaborator forced his resignation. He returned to public life as Minister of Public Works from 1950-51.

389 Yugoslav Communists of the *CPY* assisted the ELAS during their Civil War, shortly after winning their own revolution. See Tim Pott, "The Yugoslav National Question." Unpublished Dissertation. Glasgow, UK: University of Strathclyde, Dept. of History, p. 26, and Joyce, p. 6. Both Stalin and Tito agreed that after the war Velouchiotis would "have to go, but not before," due to his operational effectiveness. The Greek Communist partisan had managed to alienate himself from all active support, and was well known to execute prisoners and suspected collaborators without trial or approval from higher authority. Ronald Bailey, *Partisans and Guerrillas* (Alexandria, VA: Time-Life Books, 1978) p. 158. See also Harry J. Karapalides, "Militiaman in the Greek Civil War," *Military History*, Vol. 16, No. 1 (April 1999) pp. 51-56. Although Stalin did not openly or actively support the Greek Communists, Yugoslavia's Tito, Albania's Enver Hoxha (who had replaced King Zog living in exile) and even Bulgaria, recipients of massive Soviet aid did assist. British Intelligence was led by Alan Hare, although Harold Adrian Russell "Kim" Philby who ran the Intelligence Section undermined their activities, and defected to the USSR in 1963.

390 By late 1943 only 11,000 workers out of 5, 400,000 were Greek. See Mazower, *Inside Hitler's Greece*, p. 77.

391 Ibid. p. 1.

392 Ibid. p. 16.

393 On Crete and Lieutenant General Sir Bernard Cyril Baron Freyberg VC, DSO (1889-1963) see David T. Zabecki, "Personality," *World War II*, Vol. 12, No. 1 (May 1997) Leesburg, VA: Primedia Publications, pp. 8-12, 69.

394 Panay interview, 1992. Freyberg won the Victoria Cross, three Distinguished Service Orders and was wounded nine times. He was governor general of New Zealand from 1946-52. One interesting note was the British commando and partisan kidnapping of German *General* Karl Heinrich Georg Kreipe in April 1944. Kreipe commanded a division at Leningrad and was the occupation commander on Crete. He spent the rest of the war as a POW.

395 Mazower, *Inside Hitler's Greece*, p. 2.

396 Chief of the General Staff.

397 Mackensen (24 September 1889-19 May 1969) was also *Kommandeur III Panzer Korps*, Chief of Staff *12ᵗʰ Armee*, and later *Oberbefehlshaber der I Panzer Armee* from 1941-43. He also served in Italy as commander of the *14ᵗʰ Armee*, where he stymied the Allied landing at Anzio. After the war he was tried and sentenced to death, but this was commuted to life and he was released in 1952. See records at *Militaerarchiv* Freiburg, N-581/8-11. *III Armee* and *II Panzer Korps* would move to their staging areas in Poland for *Operation Barbarossa*. N-581/16.

398 This was when 100,000 Greek farmers were forced out of Macedonia and Western Thrace by Bulgarian forces and replaced by Bulgarian settlers. Other regions were affected by German and Italian military considerations, since both nations divided Greece into zones of occupation. See Mazower, *Inside Hitler's Greece*, pp. 20-22.

399 Ibid. p. 26.

400 Ibid. p. 9. Goering (1893-1946) was a WWI ace and *Pour le Merite* recipient who joined the *NSDAP* in 1922. Be commanded the *SS* until handing this responsibility over to Himmler, when he became Commander in Chief of the *Luftwaffe*. Goering committed suicide prior to his execution following his conviction at Nuremberg.

401 Ibid. p. 89.

402 Mazower, *Inside Hitler's Greece*, pp. 48-49.

403 Ibid. p. 88.

[404] Ibid. p. 87 citing Hondros, *Occupation and Resistance: The Greek Agony, 1941-44* (New York: Pantheon, 1983) pp. 97-100.

[405] Ibid.

[406] Ibid.

[407] This division was headquartered in Jannina, and the unit concerned was the *98th* Regiment commanded by *Oberst* Josef Salminger. See Mazower, *Inside Hitler's Greece*, p. 193. Salminger was killed in his staff car during an ambush in September 1943. See p. 170.

[408] Kershaw, *The Nazi Dictatorship*, pp. 163-64. See also Mazower, *Inside Hitler's Greece*, pp. 191-200 for an in depth report on the Komeno massacre from both the German and Greek perspectives. This particular situation came to haunt the future Austrian President Kurt Waldheim, since he was the young *leutnant* handling the intelligence summary while working in the planning office of the General Staff in Athens while recovering from wounds sustained on the Eastern Front.

[409] Mazower, *Inside Hitler's Greece*, pp. 191-92.

[410] Ibid. p. 195. See p. 196, photo plate No. 35 for a 1988 photograph of Mallios near the river where he escaped with his sister during the massacre.

[411] Kershaw, *The Nazi Dictatorship*, p. 164.

[412] Ibid.

[413] Ibid. (*en 194*) citing Mark Mazower, "Military Violence and National Socialist Values," *Past & Present*, No. 134 (1992), 129-58.

[414] Ibid. p. 166.

[415] Mazower, *Inside Hitler's Greece*, p. 197.

[416] Ibid.

[417] Ibid. The commanding officer of the *1st Gebirgsjaeger* Division was *Generalleutnant* von Stettner. See p. 177.

[418] Ibid. p. 199.

[419] Ibid. p. 153.

[420] The partisans of both factions were the forces primarily responsible for Mussolini's casualties in 1940. Unfortunately, this reality forced Hitler to invade the Balkans to attack Greece and relieve the beleaguered Italian forces.

[421] Mazower, *Inside Hitler's Greece*, p. 138. This was Group HARLING commanded by Brigadier General Edmund Meyers, leading the British Military Mission. Meyers would be at odds with the Foreign Office over the handling of the irregulars, opting to keep SOE free to operate unencumbered. Meyers' second in command was Lieutenant Chris Woodhouse, who managed to make contact with Zervas, after Velouchiotis was deemed unreliable.

[422] PRO HS-5/151, report titled "Guerrilla Activities in Greece," no date.

[423] Mazower, *Inside Hitler's Greece*, p. 131.

[424] On incident occurred near Banja Luka, when Colonel Luboric of *Ustascha* (commanding 10,000 men of the Jasenovic Brigade) ordered sixty Serbian volunteers taken from a German train and shot, with no punishment meted out. NA M-1270/24/0488.

[425] NA M-1270/24/0489. Glaise von Horstenau probably wanted to establish greater distance from these groups, which would not assist in negotiating a separate peace with the Western Allies later, should this become necessary. Part of the proposal was that "independent Austria" would possibly secede from the German union, with Kaltenbrunner as its new leader for peace. Ironically, Gottlob Berger was considering approaching the Soviets with the same idea in 1944, in order to stabilize the Western Front against the Americans and British. See Black, *Ernst Kaltenbrunner*, pp. 223-24.

[426] Ibid. Ibid.

[427] PRO HS-5/150, Secret Memorandum for Brigadier General John R. Deane: "Subversive Reforms in the Balkans," dated 20 August 1943 and signed by OSS Director Brigadier General William J. Donovan (1883-1959). This memo also stipulates to resistance support and operator in Bulgaria,

Romania and Hungary, with special continued support for Yugoslavia, naming Tito and Draza Mihailovic. On Mihailovic and the Greek connection, see Mazower, *Inside Hitler's Greece*, p. 88.

[428] PRO HS-5/151.

[429] See Mazower, *Inside Hitler's Greece*, p. 101.

[430] Ibid. p. 102.

[431] Ibid. p. 142.

[432] Ibid. p. 109. The greatest problem was making other Communists and their supporters understand why EAM/ELAS had decided to work with the "bourgeois" forces. This mission was carried out by Kostas Gambetas in Athens early in 1942.

[433] Ibid. p. 116.

[434] Ibid. p. 121.

[435] Ibid. p. 109.

[436] Mark Mazower, *Inside Hitler's Greece*, p. 85.

[437] Ibid.

[438] Ibid. p. 86. In Crete the locals began forging passes utilizing actual blank documents to escaping British and Commonwealth troops following the German occupation. If caught the penalty was death. See Mazower, *Inside Hitler's Greece*, p. 87.

[439] PRO HS-5/151.

[440] Mazower, *Inside Hitler's Greece*, p. 103. This coalition agreement was decided at the 6th Plenum, and saw the formation of EEAM-the National Workers' Liberation Front. It would be the 7th Plenum that witnessed the formation of EAM in September 1941 due to low support from mainstream politicians. This would be the first attempt at creating a coalition network organized with a solid structure, the first time in the history of Greek politics. It was also during this time that EDES (the National Republican League) was formed in response. See pp. 104-06.

[441] Ibid. p. 87.

[442] PRO HS-5/150 letter to Donovan signed by Brigadier General John R. Dean, dated 7 September 1945.

[443] Mazower, *Inside Hitler's Greece*, p. 113. This was part of *Operation Mincemeat*, the strategic bluff regarding the Allied "12th Army" planning to invade the Balkans from Egypt during 1943. See p. 144.

[444] Ibid. This period saw the *Wehrmacht* and civil defense forces build up Greece for a defensive war in case of Allied incursion. During Hitler's 20 May directive named *Operation Konstantin* (revised following the Allied landing in Sicily, code named *Operation Husky*) even badly needed troops were pulled from the Eastern Front and Yugoslavia, to include the *Luftwaffe's 11th Feld* (Field) Division placed at Corinth, the *117th Jaeger* Division diverted from Yugoslavia, and reinforcements from the *104th Jaeger* Division, *164th Infanterie* Division, *1st Gebirgsjaeger* Division (transferred from the Caucasus) commanded by the ruthless racist *General* Karl Le Suire (operating in the Pelopponese), the *4th Waffen SS Panzergrenadier* Division *"Polizei"* commanded by *Brigadefuehrer* Fritz Schmedes, and the *1st Panzer* Division. See p. 144.

[445] Ibid. See pp. 208-210.

[446] Ibid. p. 177.

[447] Ibid. p. 178.

[448] Ibid. p. 158 (*en 6*) citing Lanz, NA RG 338; "Partisan Warfare in the Balkans," MS. P-0551, p. 56.

[449] See also the reference in Daniel Jonah Goldhagen, *Hitler's Willing Executioners: Ordinary Germans and the Holocaust* (New York: Vintage Books, 1997) p. 18. See also Laska, p. 4.

[450] Overy, *Russia's War*, p. 149.

[451] Hossfelder interview, 1985.

[452] Mazower, *Inside Hitler's Greece*, p. 147. Loehr had stated earlier that an Italian armistice "was only a matter of time." See p. 148.

[453] Ibid. p. 149.

[454] Ibid. p. 152.
[455] Ibid. p. 162.
[456] Ibid. p. 159.
[457] Ibid. pp. 159-60.
[458] Ibid. p. 148.
[459] See Mazower's reference to this menagerie, pp. 163-64.
[460] Antranig Chalabian, "Personality," *Military History*, Vol. 12, No. 2 (June 1995) Leesburg, VA: Cowles History Group, pp. 10-12, 16.
[461] See Stout, "Undercover," *World War II*, Vol. 5, No. 6 (March 1991) Leesburg, VA: Empire Press, Inc. pp. 12-16.
[462] Ibid. 14.
[463] One specialized *Sonderkommando* (*Sonderkommando Lange* of *Abwehr II*) company was commanded by a *Hauptmann* Lange of the *Wehrmacht*, who won the Knight's Cross for commando raids behind Russian lines on the Eastern Front. He was assigned to Greece with a detachment of *"Skanderberg"* (assigned to Army Group F) until injured in a hunting accident on Lake Ohrid, when the unit was renamed *"Albanien"*, and maintained its counterinsurgency activities. His successor was a former Hitler Youth leader, *Hauptmann* Moriz, court-martialed for fraud and brutality towards enlisted men. See NA M-1270/24/0075-0076.
[464] See Quarrie, *Hitler's Samurai*, pp. 32, 45, 47, 81, 156; see also Davis, *Waffen SS*, p. ii.
[465] Stout, *World War II* (March 1991) p. 13.
[466] Ibid. 14.
[467] Ibid. 15.
[468] Ibid.
[469] Ibid. Erwin Rommel (1891-1944) was a WW I *Pour le Merite* holder for his actions at Caporetto, and commanded troops in Belgium, France and won fame in North Africa. He was appointed by Hitler to prepare the Atlantic Wall prior to the Allied invasion. His complicity in the bomb plot was minimal, but it did warrant a one way visit from the *Gestapo*. He committed suicide in order to save his family.
[470] Wolff interview, January 1984.
[471] Ibid.
[472] Ibid. 15-16.
[473] Ibid. 16.
[474] Ibid.
[475] Ibid. See also Jozo Tomasevich, *The Chetniks: War and Revolution in Yugoslavia, 1941-1945* (Stanford, CA: Stanford University Press, 1975) p. 62.
[476] Ibid.
[477] Ibid.
[478] Tomasevich, *The Chetniks*, p. 64, referencing DGFP, Series D, Vol. 12, pp. 395-96.
[479] See Heaton, *World War II* (January 1998) pp. 30-36; see also Time-Life Books, *The SS* (Alexandria, VA: Time-Life Books, Inc., 1989) pp. 157, 163; and Quarrie, *Hitler's Samurai*, pp. 19, 27, 98-99, 101, 122. German losses during the invasion were 151 killed, 392 wounded with fifteen missing in action. The Germans captured approximately 254,000 prisoners excluding those persons non-Serbian origin. See Tomasevich, p. 74.
[480] Formed in 1940 as *Cetnicka komanda* in April 1940 under the Yugoslav military it was organized around a strength of seven battalions, six full strength and one partial. See Tomasevich, *The Chetniks*, pp. 58, 121. The Yugoslav Army had drafted a special report on modern guerrilla warfare and the use of *Chetniks* supplemental to the 1929 draft in 1938. See p. 121.
[481] PRO HS-5/151. See also Joll, p. 406.
[482] Tomasevich, p. 120.

483 Ibid.

484 Ibid. p. 137, citing NA T-314/1457/1322. Draza Mihailovic (1873-1946) would discover that infighting with Tito as well as the Germans was an expensive error. He was shot for treason.

485 Ibid. p. 82. This section covers the author's interview with Tito on 4 August 1965.

486 Stalin's reaction to Tito's independent position during the war was well known. See Rieber, p. 21.

487 On Alexander I see Wil Deac, "Undercover," *World War II*, Vol. 13, No. 3 (September 1998) Leesburg, VA: Primedia Publications, Inc. pp. 18-24, 70-72.

488 NA M-1270/24/0481. Horstenau would not be popular with the *SS* commanders, and following the 20 July bomb plot, although there is no evidence that he was informed, let alone involved, rumors were spread about him to remove him from the problem. See NA M-1270/24/0489. The German police units would not arrive in Croatia until the spring of 1943 at the request of Pavelic, when the resistance activity exploded. The German police had no executive powers in Croatia, since it was treated as an independent state. See NA M-1270/24/0115. This was also when *"Handschar"* was created. See also Tomasevich, p. 99.

489 Ibid. It is Horstenau's integrity that during his interrogation he never claimed innocence, although he did state that he resisted the efforts of the *SS* and his superiors (in effect Hitler) to wage a campaign of terror. He also stated that anyone connected to the Yugoslav campaign shared some guilt, and should "therefore expect punishment."

490 Model (24 January 1891-7 May 1945) was to reach the zenith of his career as the commander of the *9th Armee* and *2nd Panzer Armee* on the Eastern Front, winning the *Brillanten,* or Diamonds to the Knight's Cross. Model commanded Army Group B in Holland; commanded Army Group Center as of 29 June 1944 upon his transfer, foiling *Operation Market-Garden* in September 1944, and organized the push into the Ardennes in December 1945. Model committed suicide rather than become a POW following his defeat in the Ruhr. See Model records at *Militaerarchiv* Freiburg, N-6, and references in Overy, *Russia's War*, pp. 10, 203-6, 243.

491 Ibid. N-6/3.

492 Re-designated Commander-in-Chief of German Troops in the Balkans from Commander-in-Chief of the *12th Armee* on 17 May 1941. Hitler's Directive No. 31a would order List to crush the Serb uprising on 16 September 1941. This latest Directive would also place *General* Franz Boehme, commander of *XVIII Armee Korps* in Greece, relocated to Serbia, replacing *General* Danckelmann (who was relived of his post) while simultaneously ordering the reduction of the "Communist Armed Resistance Movements in the Occupied Areas." Boehme would successfully carry out the orders and his *Korps* would relocate to Finland by December 1941. See Tomasevich, pp. 96-98.

493 List (14 May 1880-16 August 1971) was one of the more seasoned and competent conventional military thinkers. See his record at *Militaerarchiv* Freiburg, N-33 in total.

494 N-33/34.

495 Weichs (12 November 1881-27 September 1954) was a WW I veteran who served with distinction and obtained great experience in the counterinsurgency struggle on every front. He won the Oak Leaves to the Knight's Cross for his efforts.

496 N-19/6-9, 12, 16, 21.

497 Mazower, *Inside Hitler's Greece*, p. 173.

498 Tomasevich, p. 145.

499 *Militaerarchiv* Freiburg, N-19/12-16. Reference to *Kriegstagebuch* (War Diary) at N-19/15.

500 Ibid. N-19/15.

501 Hermann von Witzleben (b. 19 March 1892) was cousin to *Generalfeldmarschall* Erwin von Witzleben (1881-1944) who was executed at Ploetzensee for his role in the 20 July Bomb Plot. See N-223/2. Erwin von Witzleben (4 December 1881-8 August 1944) would become disillusioned by the atrocities committed and join the resistance against Hitler. He was hanged in Ploetzensee due to his collaboration with *Oberst* von Stauffenberg (record located at *Militaerarchiv* Freiburg, N- 2292),

General Henna von Tresckow and others. Hermann von Witzleben would escape the gallows. On Erwin von Witzleben see records at *Militaerarchiv* Freiburg, N-231. *As Oberkommando des Heeres (Gruppe IIa)* and *Stabsbefehle* (Staff Orders) on 17 March 1941; *Generalstabs Heeresgruppe* (General Staff Army Group) *D* on 22 March 1941 and *Oberbefehlshaber der Wehrmacht* on 20 July 1944; see Hermann von Witzleben records at *Militaerarchiv* Freiburg, N-23/6.

[502] N-223/3. This section also deals with the *Altenstadts Plan* with Gersdorf and Tresckow.

[503] NA M-1270/24/0488.

[504] Ibid.

[505] Ibid.

[506] Ibid.

[507] Ibid.

[508] This was a unit assigned to the Russian Army of Liberation under Vlasov.

[509] NA M-1270/24/0489.

[510] Captain.

[511] Regarding the Italian occupation forces and their dealing with the *Chetniks* and Germans, see Tomasevich, pp. 101-04. The primary source documentation as footnoted is also worth examination. See also Black, *Ernst Kaltenbrunner*, p. 193; also Rudy A. D'Angelo, "Perspectives," *World War II,* Vol. 3, No. 3 (September 1999) Leesburg, VA: Primedia Publications, Inc., p. 18. Marshal Pietro Badoglio (1871-1950) was WW I general and Chief of Staff from 1919-1921. He commanded the 1935 Abyssinian invasion force, then was again appointed Chief of Staff in 1940. Following Mussolini's arrest in July 1943 he became Prime Minister and signed the Surrender Act on 3 September 1943. He resigned and retired in 1944.

[512] Antonucci interview, 1990.

[513] May ethnic Germans living in various parts of Eastern Europe (in 1907 approximately 760,000 lived in Posen, along with 900,000 Poles) were Hitler's excuse for expansion, as well as the rallying cry for the *Freiwilligen* to join the German military. Grant, pp. 6, 9. See also Norman Stone, *Europe Transformed, 1878-1919* (London: Hadder & Stoughton, 1980) p. 172.

[514] *Ustascha* became a viable political organization in 1930. *Ustascha* was a Catholic dominated group dedicated to the elimination of the Serbian Orthodox Christian influence and control of Yugoslavia.

[515] Pavelic, a former unsuccessful lawyer had apparently made a secret agreement with Mussolini, signed on 18 May 1941, stating that the Prince from the House of Savoy would assume the title King of Croatia. This is according to the post-war interrogation of *General der Infantry* Glaise von Horstenau by US Army intelligence attached to 7th Army Interrogation Center. See NA M-1270/24/0482. On the Italian involvement see Tomasevich, pp. 101-02.

[516] Jonathan Gumz, "German Counterinsurgency Policy in Independent Croatia, 1941-1944," *The Historian*, Vol. 61, No. 1 (Fall 1998) p. 38.

[517] NA M-1270/24/0489. See also Tomasevich, p. 105.

[518] Tomasevich, p. 106.

[519] Gumz, pp. 34-5.

[520] Ibid. 38.

[521] NA M-1270/24/0485.

[522] Gumz, p. 38.

[523] Ibid.

[524] Ibid.

[525] Ibid.

[526] Ibid.

[527] Ibid.

[528] Ibid.

[529] Ibid. See also Tomasevich, p. 149. This evidence offers conclusive proof of *Chetnik* collaboration with German forces, and Mihailovic's fluctuating position, as supported by Wolff, Kumm and the various SOE reports.

[530] NA M-1270/24/0485

[531] The first SOE mission was dispatched on 14 September 1941 to Mihailovic was headed by Captain Duane T. "Bill" Hudson, *aka* "Marko" who was British military liaison to Mihailovic. It took Hudson until 25 October to locate the *Chetnik* leader. Hudson's reports on the *Chetnik* and Communist rivalry was the first such information to reach the Foreign Office. See Tomasevich, pp. 138-39, 143, 283. On the first arms deliveries to the resistance on 9 November 1941 see p. 149. Hudson was in contact with both Tito and Mihailovic, yet discovered and reported to London that the *Chetniks* had actively cooperated with the Germans. This may explain why Hudson had great difficulty in obtaining cooperation and coordinating operations.

[532] Gumz, p. 38.

[533] Many of these priests joined the Communists due to their being purged by *Ustascha*. See Tomasevich, p. 177.

[534] See Paul S. Burdett, Jr., "Personality: Evelyn Waugh," *World War II*, Vol. 14, No. 1 (May 1999) Leesburg, VA: Primedia Publications History Group, pp. 16-20, 74-6, 80. Waugh was a successful novelist before the war, and later published his classic *Brideshead Revisited*. He died in 1966 at age 63.

[535] Ibid. p. 80.

[536] Ibid.

[537] NA M-1270/24/0832.

[538] Burdett, Jr., p. 80.

[539] Tomasevich, p. 298.

[540] One of the premier *Wehrmacht* units that recruited its own replacements from the population was the *399th Infanterie* Division, known as the "Devil Division." See NA M-1270/24/0115.

[541] John Clearwater, "Undercover," *World War II*, Vol. 13, No. 6 (February 1999) Leesburg, VA: Primedia Publications, Inc. pp. 60-64. See also Tomasevich, pp. 212, 236.

[542] Tomasevich, p. 250. See also T-78/332/6,290,062-63 as cited by Tomasevich.

[543] Ibid. pp. 252-3.

[544] Ibid. p. 254.

[545] Ibid. *"Prinz Eugen"* managed to secure the surrender and disarmament of only 120 *Chetniks,* with the rest fleeing into the mountains. See p. 256.

[546] Ibid. p. 62.

[547] Hans Baur interview, 1991. Otto Skorzeny (1908-1975) was an advocate and practitioner of irregular and counterinsurgent warfare. His activities prompted Churchill to call him "the most dangerous man in Europe" following his mission regarding Tito, Mussolini and Horthy, as well as his activities in recruiting English speaking troops dressed in American uniforms during the 1944 Ardennes offensive. Skorzeny was tried and acquitted of war crimes, with his greatest supporter ironically being Yeo-Thomas of SOE, the "White Rabbit."

[548] Tito (1892-4 May 1980) had been Josip Broz to a Slovene mother and Croatian father. Tito served as a NCO in the Austrian Army during WW I. He was wounded, taken prisoner by the Russians, and converted to Bolshevism. He returned to Croatia as an illegal Communist Party organizer, serving a prison term from 1928-1934, adopting "Tito" as an alias. He returned to Moscow, worked in the Comintern (later Cominform) and returned to Yugoslavia, becoming Secretary General of the Communist Party. His ability to maintain the collection of volatile anti-fascist groups challenging the Serb domination of Yugoslavia was crucial to his ability to unite resistance under a single partisan framework, guided by the CPY, which was nothing short of impressive. The Allies began to actively support Tito in early 1943, and gave complete legitimacy to him in 1944. They recognized him as Prime

Minister in March 1945, which he relinquished in 1963, although he was named President for Life in 1974. Tito's position of non-aggression, détente, and condemnation of Soviet policy (such as Hungary in 1956, Czechoslovakia in 1968, and Afghanistan in 1979) was a benchmark for other Communist nations to challenge Soviet dogma and become more independent.

[549] The formation of *"Handschar"* is mentioned in NA M-1270/24/0115, offering the number of 16,000 men who served. The last effective commander was Karl von Krempler. See Tomasevich, p. 331. For the list of German assets see NA T-313/488/350 which lists Krempler's announcement regarding mobilization of Serb forces.

[550] See Heaton, *World War II* (January 1998) pp. 30-36.

[551] Stavic interviews of 1985 and 1995. He considered himself and his comrades "partisans" and not "guerrillas," although this project offers a different point of view.

[552] Pankosk interviews of 1984, 1998.

[553] Steenberg, *Vlasov*, p. 117. This was a unit exclusively of émigrés who volunteered to fight against Stalin but were diverted to the Balkans.

[554] Gumz, p. 39, citing *General der Infanterie (Generaloberst)* Edmund Glaise von Horstenau (b. 28 February 1882) *Ein General in Zwielicht: Die erinnerungen Edmund Glaise von Horstenau*, Vol. 3, Peter Broucek (ed.) (Vienna: Hoffmann, 1988) p. 321. See also National Archives Roll M-1270/24/0480-0481 for his personal history and Allied interrogation; also NA T-501/264/522 and RG 226, OSS File No. XL13599.

[555] Wolff interview of January 1984.

[556] Gumz, p. 39.

[557] Ibid. This was confirmed by *Obergruppenfuehrer* Karl Wolff during a brief conversation in December 1983. See also Tomasevich, p. 99. who would not tow the German line.

[558] Tomasevich, pp. 99-100. Lueters would also issue the order of 28 March 1943 disarming the *Chetniks* who would not tow the German line. See p. 230.

[559] Tomasevich, p. 235.

[560] Gumz, p. 40.

[561] Ibid.

[562] Named for Prinz Eugen of Savoy, allied to the English cause during the War of the Spanish Succession, and the primary ally of the Sir John Churchill, the 1st Duke of Marlborough.

[563] NA M-1270/24/0488.

[564] See Tomasevich, p. 258.

[565] Ibid.

[566] Gumz, pp. 48-9.

[567] NA T-501/249/61, 142, 524.

[568] The Croats had 62,020 troops in German uniform, with 36,000 independent troops supplied and trained by the Germans, and 62,760 independent Croats placed under German command as auxiliaries as of 1 September 1943. The Croatian Army were a rather ineffective rabble when compared to the *Chetniks* and especially their primary adversaries, the Titoist guerrillas. See Tomasevich, pp. 107-08. On *Chetnik* strengths as of 15 May 1942 (13,400 placed in seventy-eight detachments, and German reports of seventy-two *Chetnik* officers, 7,963 men being maintained) see Tomasevich, p. 111 and p. 127 respectively. The authorized peak strength was 8,745. See NA T-501/247/757.

[569] On the *Chetniks* turning against the Germans see Tomasevich, p. 111. On Mihailovic's pre-war career, see pp. 122-24, 130-33.

[570] See reference in Rieber, p. 28. On Mihailovic and the establishment of a United Yugoslav Front see NA M-1270/24/0489. On Mihailovic's rivalry with *Chetnik* leader Kosta Milovanovic Pecanac see Tomasevich, p. 110. Pecanac wanted to control all *Chetnik* units in Serbia, and issued a statement to the population, addressing "illegal" and "illegitimate" *Chetnik* forces, referencing Mihailovic's units. Mihailovic later had him executed.

571 Karl Gaisser (17 March 1880-29 April 1958) served in the police forces under Lettow-Vorbeck from 1907-1917. See Gaisser records at *Militaerarchiv* Freiburg, N-279/2-8 and on his membership in the *Schuetztruppen* in Africa N-279/26, 31k-32k.

572 N-279/29-30. Gaisser published a book on his WW II service, titled *Partisanen Kaempfe in Kroatien* in 1950. See reference in N-279/12.

573 Gumz, p. 41. See also NA M-1270/24/0482.

574 M-1270/24/0485.

575 Gumz, 41. Baader had also managed to secure an agreement between Major Dangic, representative of Mihailovic and Nedic regarding cessation of hostilities against Axis forces in return for support against the Communists. The new Armed Forces Commander Southeast Europe, *Generaloberst* Walter Kuntze and the Croatian authorities could not agree on terms and specifics. See Tomasevich, p. 160. On 9 September 1942 Baader issued the order to combat the *Chetniks*. This would bring *7th SS* Division *"Prinz Eugen"* and the *Brandenburg* Division into the picture.

576 Gumz, p. 41. This thesis states that Tito's forces were actually "guerrillas," not "partisans."

577 Tomasevich, p. 209.

578 Zeitzler (9 June 1895-25 September 1963) served in Poland, France, the Balkans and Russia; appointed as Chief of Staff to *I Panzer Armee* during *Barbarossa*, and operated extensively in both the conventional and counterinsurgency combat roles, and was especially effective in command of *Freiwilligen* units, paratroops, tank units, cavalry, and was heavily active in Russia using volunteers against partisans from 21 April-7 July 1942, code named *Blau 2* (Blue 2) and *Fredericus 2*. See records at *Militaerarchiv* Freiburg, N-63/26-27, 34, 35. Zeitzler, who played a role in the debate regarding the leadership of the *6th Armee* at Stalingrad and supported von Paulus' (1890-1957) request to withdraw which Hitler forbade. See Irving, *Hitler's War*, Vol. 1, p. 483. Zeitzler served as von Rundstedt's Chief of Staff during 1942; the planning staff for *Operation Zitadelle,* and became *Generalstabs des Heeres* in July 1944 until replaced by Guderian. He openly disagreed with Hitler, stating the *6th Armee* should retreat from Stalingrad to shorten their supply lines, to no avail. He was retired on 31 January 1945 and was interrogated as a POW by American General Lucius D. Clay and Brigadier General Telford Taylor. See N-63/1. On the Vlasov situation see Steenberg, p. 95. On Zeitzler and the Stalingrad issue, see Overy, *Russia's War*, p. 178.

579 N-63/27.

580 Hess (1896-1987) was deputy *Fuehrer* who defected to Britain on 10 May 1941. He died under mysterious circumstances in Spandau prison in Berlin, and was the last prisoner held there.

581 Wolff information supplied in 1979 to Jeffrey L. Ethell, who supplied this information in 1996.

582 See N-63/40.

583 Ibid. *Freiwilligen* units carried out nearly all of these operations.

584 This increase in activity would see an exponential increase in *Freiwilligen* counterinsurgency units. The summer of 1943 would become the benchmark of German occupation and activity.

585 Gumz, p. 37.

586 Ibid.

587 See Black, *Ernst Kaltenbrunner*, p. 176.

588 Ibid. pp. 46-7. See cite for *369th* Division War Diary, entries of 14 and 15 January 1943, NA Nr. 1, T-315/2154/116-18. Between 20 January and March the unit suffered 110 killed, 288 wounded, 44 missing with a body count of 1,937 "enemy" dead. Many of these were undoubtedly civilians killed in reprisal for partisan activity.

589 Ibid. See also report of *Hauptmann* Artur Haeffner to *Generalleutnant* Edmund Glaise von Horstenau dated 27 September 1942. Records of German Field Commanders: Rear Areas, Occupied Territories and Others. NA T-501/265/224-26.

590 Gumz, pp. 42-3.

591 Ibid. p. 43.

[592] Wolff interview, January 1984.

[593] See PRO HS-5/151 (Plans/180/1436, *Appendix A*) detailing the strengths of *Chetnik* forces fighting against the Germans and Bulgarians.

[594] Gumz, p. 45. Supporting these operations was *Sonderkommando Lange* comprised of Albanians, and coordinated by *Obersturmbannfuehrer* Anton Fest, Head of *Einsatzkommando Sipo (Sicherheitspolizei)* in Sarajevo from September 1943-April 1945. Fest was captured following his retreat with German troops from Zagreb, when he went to visit his family in Weissenbach. See NA M-1270/24/0110; covering his interrogation and arrest handled by the U.S. 7ᵗʰ Army Counterintelligence Sections.

[595] David L. Bullock, *Military History* (June 1992) p. 42. This article concerns an interview with Nikolai Vladimirovich Volkov, a participant in the war fighting for the White Russians.

[596] Steiner was a Rhodes Scholar, historian, and perhaps the best tactician in the ranks of the *SS*. He helped plan the pincer movement and the capture of Kharkov in 1942 and supported the use of Russian forces to buttress German forces. Steiner (who won the Knight's Cross with Oak Leaves) was also instrumental in the planning of *Barbarossa*. Like Kumm, Wolff, Degrelle, Kurt *"Panzer"* Meyer, and other *SS* generals he was opposed to the open murder of civilians. Steiner would die in Berlin in the last stand against the Red Army in May 1945.

[597] Karl Wolff interview, January 1984.

[598] On the efforts to unite the two factions, see Tomasevich, p. 139.

[599] Ibid. pp. 140-1.

[600] Ibid. Women played a major role in every facet of Communist resistance activities, including combat arms, whereas the *Chetniks* were vehemently opposed to their inclusion for a variety of reasons.

[601] Ibid.

[602] Tomasevich, p. 195.

[603] Pankosk interview. For a British SOE perspective on the Soviets in the region, see PRO HS-4/92.

[604] PRO HS-4/92 report dated 7 November 1944 by Captain E.A. Howe and Lieutenant T.E. Byron. All spelling variations are reproduced as stated in the document.

[605] See PRO HS-4/92.

[606] See PRO HS-5/151.

[607] Overy, *Russia's War*, p. 149.

[608] See Pat T. McTaggart, "Winter Tempest in Stalingrad," *World War II,* Vol. 12, No. 4 (November 1997) Leesburg, VA: Primedia Publications, Inc. pp. 30-36.

[609] See Charles W. Thayer, *Guerrilla* (New York: Harper & Row, 1963) p. 65, and Steenberg, *Vlasov*, p. 32.

[610] Most of these were gone by 1943. See Steenberg, p. 32.

[611] Ibid. p. 114.

[612] Ibid. pp. 115-6.

[613] On trained dogs, see Raymond A. Denkhaus, "Armament," *World War II,* Vol. 8, No. 2 (July 1993) Leesburg, VA: Cowles History Group, pp. 14, 68-9.

[614] Koronov interview, 1985, 1993. See also Peter A. Huchthausen, "Perspectives," *World War II* (November 1997) p. 70. Included is a reunion with German and Soviet veterans of the ordeal.

[615] Overy, *Russia's War*, p. xvii.

[616] Ibid.

[617] Ibid. p. 143.

[618] Donnelly, p. 10. See also Issac Deutscher, *Stalin* (London: O.U.P, 1967) pp. 403-404, Peter D. Swan, "How Influential Were the Economic Considerations in the Formation of German Foreign Policy Towards the Soviet Union?" Unpublished Dissertation. Glasgow, UK: University of Strathclyde,

Dept. of History, 1995, pp. 17-19, 23; and McKenna, p. 21. See reference in Karl Wever file, *Militaerarchiv* Freiburg, N-1203/3 in total or *Bundesarchiv* Koblenz, NL-203/3.

[619] Overy, *Russia's War,* p. 10.

[620] McGrath, p. 21, and H.P. von Strandmann, "Industrial Primacy in German Foreign Policy? Myths and Realities in German-Russian Relations at the end of the Weimar Republic." Richard Bessel and E.J. Feuchtwanger (eds.) *Social Change and Political Development in Weimar Germany* (London: Croom Helm, 1981) pp. 241-67.

[621] Donnelly, p. 16, and L. Schapiro, *The Communist Party of the Soviet Union,* 6ᵗʰ ed. (London: Methuen, 1978) p. 483.

[622] McKenna, p. 21.

[623] Donnelly, p. 11. See also J.W. Hiden, "The Weimar Republic." *Seminar Studies in History,* pp. 27, 31; Mills, p. 11; Tait, pp. 2, 36, 39; K.D. Bracher, *The German Dictatorship: The Origins, Structure and Consequences of National Socialism* (London, New York: Penguin, 1970) p. 68; Adolf Hitler, *The Second Book,* pp. 27, 96; Swan, pp. 4, 23, 29; Tom Devaney, Ch. 6 in total, p. 2; Ridley, pp. 20, 25, 56, 59; Carr,. *Arms, Autarky and Aggression,* p. 7; Hildebrand, *Foreign Policy,* p. 32; Paley, p. 12; Mitchell, p. 9; and Osborne, pp. 2, 5, 10.

[624] J. Reid, "Why the *Nazi* Party Came to Power." Unpublished Dissertation. Glasgow, UK: University of Strathclyde, Dept. of History, pp. 72-3.

[625] Ibid. 76. See also James and Suzanne Pool, *Who Financed Hitler? The Secret Funding of Hitler's Rise to Power, 1919-1933* (New York: Pocket Books, 1997) pp. 111, 298-300, 311.

[626] Donnelly, pp. 23, 32, 57. See also Gunn, pp. 3, 15; A. Bullock, *Hitler: A Study in Tyranny* (London: Penguin, 1984) p. 370; and Adolf Hitler, *Mein Kampf,* D. Watt (ed.), (London: Hutchinson, 1977) p. 156. Regarding France, see Adolf Hitler, *Secret Book* (New York: Grove Press, 1961) p. 141; Osborne, pp. 1, 34; Gunn, p. 16, Paley, pp. 9, 11, and Bobby Chaudry, "Factionalism in the NSDAP 1925-1933: A History and Evaluation." Unpublished Dissertation. Glasgow, UK: University of Strathclyde, Department of History, 1994, p. 34.

[627] Much support came from Spanish Communists and the *Comintern* in general. See Killen, p. 5.

[628] Donnelly, p. 14. See also Schapiro, p. 483. Regarding Posen and the free city of Danzig (the Polish Corridor of West Prussia) see Grant, pp. 10-11; Gunn, p. 31; A. Bullock, *Hitler,* p. 497; Mark Devaney, "The Road to Munich." Unpublished Dissertation . Glasgow, UK: University of Strathclyde, Department of History, no date. Ch. 1, pp. 1-2, 6-8, Ch. 6, pp. 1-6; and Anthony Konjathy and Rebecca Stockwell, *German Minorities and the Third Reich: Ethnic Germans of East Central Europe Between the Wars* (New York: 1980) p. 6; and Fiona Mitchell, p. 9.

[629] See records of the Moscow born *General der Kavallerie* Ernst Koestring (20 June 1876-20 November 1953) located at *Militaerarchiv* Freiburg, N-123/15 and Bd. 3 (8 August 1940).

[630] Donnelly, p. 45; and Issac Deutscher, "Stalin." *Political Leaders of the Twentieth Century.* (New York: Penguin, 1979) p. 432. See also Overy, *Russia's War,* p. 150.

[631] This was especially true of Romania, Bulgaria and Hungary.

[632] Hans von Seeckt (22 April 18-27 December 1936) was a *Pour le Merite* with Oak Leaves recipient in WW I *and Chef des Generalstabs* in 1915. Seeckt devised a plan titled *"Die Teilung Polens"* for *Generaloberst* Erich von Falkenhayn in 1915 and briefed *Generaloberst* Erich Ludendorff in August that year. Seeckt foresaw the use of combined arms in a modern warfare role. Seeckt devised the Army Organization Planning in 1917 and was advisor to King Ferdinand of Bulgaria In 1916. He was advisor to the Turkish Army under Enver Pasha in 1917, serving in Mesopotamia. He later became *Chef der Heeresleitung* on 17 March 1920-1926, when he was replaced by *Generalleutnant* Heye. Seeckt's treatise on modern warfare was required reading in German academies. See *Militaerarchiv* N-247/23, 27-28, 32, 38-52, 57; also references in W.C. Waddell, pp. 16-18. See also Herbert Rosinski, Intro. & ed. by A. Craig. *The German Army* (London: Pall Mall, 1966) pp. 165, 173; McKenna, p. 17,

and Karl Demeter, *The German Officer Corps in Society and State: 1650-1945*, intro. Howard (London: Weidenfeld & Nicolson, 1965) pp. 54-5.

[633] Foot, *SOE in France*, p. 13, citing Liddell Hart's *Defence of the West* (1950) chapter VII.

[634] Donnelly, p. 1. This policy was written on 22 September 1920. See also J.C.G. Roehl, "From Bismarck to Hitler." *Problems and Perspectives in History* (1981) pp. 107-8.

[635] *Militaerarchiv* N-247/58. Seeckt also drafted a proposal on 21 August 1917 regarding the United States' entry into the war with grim foreboding. See N-247/60. On Seeckt's proposals for the new army, as well as the handling of Russian military and civilian prisoners in a future conflict in 1919-20 for the *Truppenamt* titled "*Germany and Russia*" see N-247/67, 72, 92 respectively. Seeckt later went to China as advisor to Chiang Kai Shek. See N-247/133-35.

[636] Laska, p. 51.

[637] N-247/204.

[638] John Gardner, pp. 18, 22, 27; Gunn, p. 13; McKenna, pp. 18-22, and John W. Hiden, *Germany and Europe* (New York: Longman, 1977) p. 59. See also Bobby Chaudry, p. 30; Peter D. Swan, pp. 11, 32, 36.

[639] Donnelly, p. 2. See also Waldemar Gurian, "From Lenin Through Stalin." *Soviet Society: A Book of Readings.* Alex Inkeles and Kent Geiger (eds.). (London: Constable & Co., Ltd. 1961) pp. 32-33, and Kelly J. Reid, "Why the *Nazi* Party Came to Power." Unpublished Dissertation. Glasgow, UK: University of Strathclyde, Department of History, 1985) p. 16.

[640] Jaqueline Davidson, "The Formation and Social Structure of the *NSDAP's* Constituency, 1928-1932." Unpublished Dissertation. Glasgow, UK: University of Strathclyde, Dept. of History, 1996, p. 1; Ridley, p. 13; Conan Fischer, "The Appeal of *Nazism*," *History Teaching Review Year Book*, Vol. 9 (1995) p. 8.

[641] Jaqueline Davidson, p. 4; Ridley, pp. 32, 52-3; Paley, pp. 13-14; and Osborne, pp. 1, 4, 9, 20, 26, 32, 35.

[642] Rosenberg's book, *Future Roads For German Policy* (Berlin: Volks Verlag, 1932) is interesting reading. Rosenberg (1893-1946) was hanged at Nuremberg. See also John Gardner, pp. 9-10; Paley, p. 61, and Bobby Chaudry, pp. 4-5, 33.

[643] Currently renamed Tallin, Estonia.

[644] Gunn, p. 4; E. Jaeckel, *Hitler's World View: A Blue Print for Power* (Washington, DC: Howard University Press 1981). See also Steenberg, *Vlasov*, p. 34.

[645] Ridley, p. 46; Ian Kershaw, *Profiles in Power: Hitler* (New York: Longman, 1991) p. 29.

[646] See Black, *Ernst Kaltenbrunner*, pp. 173-4.

[647] Kelly J. Reid, p. 11. See also Gardner, p. 8; and on unemployed in the *SA* see Osborne, p. 25; Z.A.B. Zeman, *Nazi Propaganda*, 2nd ed. (London: Oxford University Press, 1973) pp. 23-4.

[648] Pauline Russell, p. 3 and Robin Lumsden, *The Black Corps* (New York: Ian Allan Publishing, 1992) p. 12.

[649] *Sturmabteilung*, or "Storm Detail" (Detachment). These were the notorious "Brown Shirts" who originally supported Hitler and the *NSDAP* as a collective group of thugs from the early days (including the Beer Hall Putsch in the *Burgerbraukeller* on 8 November 1923 in Munich) and was commanded by *Hauptmann* (Captain) Ernst Roehm, a decorated WW I hero and homosexual. Hitler ordered him killed via Theodor Eicke during the "Night of the Long Knives" on 30 June 1934, when the *SS* removed the *SA* from prominence, securing the support of the Army who felt the *SA* was a threat to their security and validity, and altering the face of the military structure of the Third *Reich* forever. See Gardner, pp. 11-13, 15, 18, 24-26, 31, 38-40, 43; Joachim Fest, *Hitler* (London: Weidenfeld & Nicolson, 1974) p. 169; Ian Kershaw, "Ideology, Propaganda and the Rise of the *Nazi* Party," Peter Stachura (ed.),*The Nazi Machtergreifung* (London: George Allen & Unwin , 1983) p. 174; Kershaw, *The Nazi Dictatorship*, p. 72; Toland, *Adolf Hitler*, pp. 182, 249; Bullock, *Hitler*, p. 103; and McKie, pp. 9, 22, 25. See also Chaudry, pp. 2-3, 8-9, 11, 28, 39-44; Russell, pp. 2, 12-19,25; Doran, pp. 15,

22; Davidson, pp. 27, 42, 46, 48; Carr, *Hitler,* pp. 61-69; Ridley, pp. 31, 51; Childers, *The Formation of the Nazi Constituency* (London: 1986) p. 132; Osborne, pp. 20, 23, 25-26, 35; Tait, pp. 10-11; Paley, pp. 23-4, 27-8, 33-4, 37, 62-3; and Fischer, *The Rise of the Nazis* (Manchester, UK and New York: Manchester University Press, 1995) pp. 57-58, 145.

[650] See Waddell, p. 15.

[651] Membership would include *Obergruppenfuehrer* Reinhardt Heydrich (future *Obergruppenfuehrer* and Protector of Czechoslovakia), *Reichsfuehrer-SS* Heinrich Himmler, Josef "Sepp" Dietrich (future *Oberstgruppenfuehrer* and commander of Hitler's bodyguard unit and *1ˢᵗ Waffen SS Panzer* Division *"Leibstandarte"*), Kurt Daluege (Chief of the Regular police Branch of the *Gestapo*), Friedrich Wilhelm Krueger, Theodore Eicke (future C.O. of the *3ʳᵈ Waffen SS Panzer* Division *"Totenkopf"*) and many others. See Pauline Russell, p. 3, and Robin Lumsden, *The Black Corps* for more information. On Daluege see Black, *Ernst Kaltenbrunner*, pp. 107-8, 110, 112.

[652] McGrath, pp. 23, 25, and J.J. Ward, "Smash the Fascists?: The German Communist Efforts to Counter the *Nazis*, 1930-1931." *Central European History*, Vol. 14 (1981) 61; Rona Dickie, "Were the Western Powers Correct in Insisting Upon Unconditional Surrender or, in the Light of Opposition in Germany to Hitler, did it Prolong the War?" Unpublished Dissertation. Glasgow, UK: University of Strathclyde, Dept. of History, 1995, p. 28; von Hassell, *The Von Hassell Diaries 1938-44: The Story of the Forces Against Hitler Inside Germany* (New York: Doubleday, 1947) p. 333, and Doran, p. 5.

[653] This was *Hauptsturmfuehrer* Fritz Klingenberg's capture of the city with a half dozen men on 12 April 1941. See Heaton, *World War II* (January 1998) pp. 30-6.

[654] The German defenders at the small pocket in Kholm (not including nearby Demyansk also under attack) in the Lake Ilmen region numbered 5,200 and were attacked by three Soviet Divisions commanded by Vlasov, holding on till 5 May 1942. Only 1,234 Germans survived, making the *Kholmschild* one of the rarest German decorations. The Soviets lost three times that number, of which many were partisans.

[655] See *Generaloberst* Erhard Rauss, *General der Infanterie* Hans von Greiffenberg, *General der Infanterie* Dr. Waldemar Erfurth, Tsouras (ed.), *Fighting in Hell: The German Ordeal on the Eastern Front* (London: Greenhill Books, 1995) p. 55. See also Erhard Rauss, *The Anvil of War* (London: Greenhill Books, 1994) in total.

[656] Named for a 15ᵗʰ Century Teutonic Knight.

[657] For an account on Latvian participation in the *Waffen SS*, see Jason Lewis, "The Picture That Finally Proves Konrad Kalejs was a *Nazi* Killer," *The Scottish Mail on Sunday* (9 January 2000) pp. 8-9. The article on Konrad Kalejs, an *SS* volunteer with the Arajs Commandos (named for Viktor Arajs, the commanding officer), accompanied by documentation and interviews with former Latvian *SS* members Viktors Ennitis, Georgijs Pimanis, Karlis Strazds, and Karlis Rozkalns.

[658] Bronislav Kaminsky became legendary for the ruthlessness of his command. During the Second Warsaw Uprising of 1944, his troops were allowed free reign to rape and murder, as long as they cleared the ghetto. Even *Obergruppenfuehrer* Erich von dem Bach-Zelewski was shocked at the reports that fell on his desk, prompting his nervous breakdown.

[659] Supported by the interviews with Karl Wolff, January 1984 and Otto Kumm, 1984. On *"Totenkopf"* see Mark C. Yerger, *Knights of Steel: The Structure, Development, and Personalities of the 2. SS-Panzer* (Atglen, PA: Schiffer Publishing, Ltd., 1994) in total.

[660] Walther Reinhardt (24 March 1872-8 August 1930) record at *Militaerarchiv* Freiburg, N-86/14.

[661] Ibid. N-86/16. One of the catalysts for the proposal was to secure a more stable officer corps following the November 1918 Revolution in Germany.

[662] Ibid. N-86/16.

[663] Ibid. N-86/18. The *Eberhardt Plan* was presented on 8 November 1919. Involved in the planning were *General* Gustav *Graf* von Goltz, *Generaloberst* von Beseler, and *General* Groener. It must be stated that the White Russians were the first group to called "partisan" by the British during the

Russian Civil War. They were also labeled "Socialist-Revolutionaries." See George Stewart, *The White Armies of Russia*, p. 279.

[664] Ibid. N-86/23.

[665] N-86/20.

[666] *Generalleutnant* Paul von Lettow-Vorbeck (20 March 1870-9 March 1964) served in China during the Boxer Rebellion of 1900-01; was *Kommandeur der Schuetztruppen fuer Sued West Afrika* from 1905-06, based at Dar es Salaam, Tanzania, and *Kommandeur der Truppen Ost Afrika* (*Schuetztruppen*, numbering 1,500) from 1914-18, appointed as advisor to the *Reich* Colonial Office on 11 December 1917. See records at *Militaerarchiv* Freiburg, N-103/19, 63, 65, 113. He was later *Kommandeur der Freiwilligen* Division *"von Lettow-Vorbeck"* during the war in charge of German and foreign troops on 22 January 1918. See N-103/19, 21-28, 33, 36, 45-46; Bd. 3, 4, 6, 8. Lettow-Vorbeck also commanded *Reichswehr Brigade 9* from 9 March 1919 during the Kapp Putsch. See N-103/1-7, 54, 56. On the troop movements and operational deployment reports of 29 October 1916 regarding Nyakisku, Kangulio, Beobeo, Kiderngua and Mgeta see N-103/86. Regarding the Marnes see N-103/86, 91. Regarding correspondence with Jan Smuts in South Africa on developing joint cooperation see N-103/106. On Lettow-Vorbeck's campaigns in Africa see Barry Taylor, "Personality," *Military History*, Vol. 8, No. 2 (August 1991) Leesburg, VA: Empire Press , Inc. pp. 8, 12-6; also Frank A. Contey, "British Debacle in German East Africa," *Military History*, Vol. 13, No. 5 (December 1996) Leesburg, VA: Cowles History Group, pp. 58-65, 86-7.

[667] Smuts left the Africa campaign on 11 July 1917 for the Imperial Conference in London, where he met with Prime Minister David Lloyd George, where he was asked to stay on as a member of the War Cabinet, provided he would not engage in political activities. Smuts accepted. See David Divine, *The Broken Wing: A Study in the British Exercise of Air Power* (London: Hutchinson & Co., Ltd., 1966) pp. 107-08. For further information, see John Davenport, "Bloody Finale to 'Black Week'," *Military History*, Vol. 12, No. 6 (February 1996) Leesburg, VA: Cowles History Group, pp. 30-36.

[668] Pieter Krueler (10 April 1885-1986) interview, 1984. See also Jeffrey A. Murphy, "Personality," *Military History*, Vol.12, No. 4 (October 1995) pp. 20, 24, 28, 80, 81.

[669] Mackensen (6 December 1849-8 November 1945) commanded foreign troops in Finland, Italy, and Russia. See records at *Militaerarchiv* Freiburg, N-39 in total. On Finland see N-39/85. Also on German command of foreign troops, see records of *Generaloberst* Franz Halder (30 June, 1884-2 April 1972) who served in Finland from 24 June-3 July 1939. See record at *Militaerarchiv* Freiburg, N-220. Halder testified for the prosecution at Nuremberg, following his arrest and incarceration at Dachau after the 20 July bomb plot.

[670] Ibid. On reference to letters to an *Oberstleutnant* Ritgen regarding arrangements, see N-39/85.

[671] Yitzhak Arad, Krakowski and Shmuel (eds.) *The Einsatzgruppen Reports* (New York: Holocaust Library and Yad Veshem Martyr's Remembrance Authority, 1989). The reports on *"Florian Geyer"* and the *Sonderkommando* operations are quite revealing.

[672] Although the report does not identify the commander, it is known that *Gruppenfuehrer* Theodor Eicke, division commander of *3rd SS "Totenkopf"* was operating out of Minsk at this time and that the *Einsatzgruppe* reported to him directly.

[673] See reference to *Einsatzgruppen* in the Ukraine in Overy, *Russia's War*, p. 133.

[674] Bartov, *Hitler's Army*, p. 161 (*en 180*) citing *Deutsche Soldaten sehen die Sowjetunion* (Berlin: Volk und Reich Verlag, 1941) pp. 44-5. This collection was published under the direction of the Propaganda Ministry and Dr. Josef Goebbels. These letters were of course collected selected for their demonstrative propaganda value.

[675] Irving, *Hitler's War*, Vol. 1, p. xv.

[676] Tsouras, citing *General der Infanterie* Hans von Greiffenberg, p. 285.

[677] Overy, *Russia's War*, p. 135.

[678] Bartov, *Hitler's Army*, p. 162 (*en 188*) citing O. Buchbender and R. Stertz, *Das andere Geschicht des Krieges* (Munich: 1982) letter 351.

[679] Black, *Ernst Kaltenbrunner*, p. 136.

[680] Goldhagen, p. 5.

[681] See Davis, *Waffen SS*, pp. 13-4. There were other *SS* academies for officers and NCO's established throughout occupied Europe as the *SS* grew. Locations such as Arnhem, Lauernberg, Radolfzell, Laibach, Lublinitz, Posen-Taskau, and Bruansberg. See Quarrie, *Hitler's Samurai*, p. 32; also Time-Life, *The SS*, pp. 135, 145-6.

[682] Overy, *Russia's War*, p. 135.

[683] Tsouras, p. 116.

[684] Otto Kumm interview, 1984. Unfortunately the literature on this topic is minimal and nothing has been published from anyone on the German side from a leadership viewpoint regarding partisan warfare.

[685] See Christopher Lew, "Undercover," *World War II*, Vol. 11, No. 2 (July 1996) Leesburg, VA: Cowles History Group, pp. 8, 20.

[686] Special Duty and Construction Company No. 800. See *World War II* (July 1996) p. 8; also Foot, *SOE in France*, p. 390.

[687] Soviet Secret Police, originally the *Cheka* in 1917, then later re-designated as the *OGPU* in 1922, becoming the *NKVD* in 1934, and reorganized in 1946 as *MGB*, later known as the *KGB (Komitet Gosudarstvennoy Bezopasnosti)* in 1954. The Secret Police operated the state mental hospitals, gulags (labor camps) prisons, and handled the investigations, arrests and purges of suspected "enemies of the state."

[688] Lew, *World War II* (July 1996) p. 8.

[689] This was similar to Fritz Klingenberg's capture of Belgrade in April 1941. See Heaton, *World War II* (January 1998) pp. 30-36. See also Quarrie, *Hitler's Samurai*, pp. 19, 27, 98-9, 101, 122.

[690] Clearwater, *World War II* (February 1999) pp. 60-4.

[691] Pat McTaggart, "Desperate *Panzer* Counterattack at Debreccen," *World War II*, Vol. 11, No. 7 (March 1997) Leesburg, VA: Cowles History Group, p. 46.

[692] Meaning *Voyska Spetsial' nogo Naznacheniya*. In the post-war configuration *Spetsnaz* units included four naval brigades equal to four Soviet fleets. The numbers of how many personnel were involved on active duty at any one time range from the U.S. Defense Intelligence Agency study reflecting 12,500 (500 men in each of the twenty-four brigades) to the report delivered by a *GRU* defector who stated that 30,000 (1,300 per brigade) was the actual average. This would become the platform upon which the Soviet Union would lunch its global extraterritorial special operations missions, fostering and training pro-Communist guerrillas around the world, based upon the SOE, SAS and Special Forces standard.

[693] See Professor Dr. Rolf Himze (b. 5 February 1922). Himze states the problems with partisans attacking trains and railway lines, and the experienced partisan warfare at Kholm, Demyansk, Velikye-Luki, and the retreat from Moscow in 1941-42. Himze was captured by American forces and handed over to the Soviets, where he was interned at the POW camp in Budweiss, Czechoslovakia and later transferred to Szigett, Constanza, Romania, then to Sevastopol. He was released in 1955 by the Soviets and received a doctorate in physics. During the war as a partisan fighter he received the *Verwundetabzeichen in Gold* (Wound Badge in Gold) for three wounds, the *Sturmabzeichen* in Silver, the Iron Cross both 1st and 2nd Class, and the *Ostfrontmedaille* (East Front Medal). See Himze records at *Militaerarchiv* Freiburg, N-331/1-2. On the Soviet cavalry detachments referenced by *Generaloberst* Erhard Rauss see Tsouras, pp. 39-40.

[694] N-63/49-50. On Kiev see N-63/63, 66-67, 74. Zeitzler was openly against the terror policy despite his great success in combating irregulars, although he hoped to convert as many over from Commu-

nism as possible. This worked tactic worked many times due to his humane treatment of those who surrendered. Zeitzler would later be instrumental in gathering support for the Vlasov Army within the *Wehrmacht* and *SS*, although Heinrich Mueller of the *Gestapo* wanted them all killed, as supported by Karl Wolff's interview. See Steenberg, *Vlasov*, pp. 100-01. Mueller was Head of *Amt IV* and disappeared in the final days of the war and has not been seen since.

[695] Ibid. N-63/32. On Rostov see N-63/120, which also includes Zeitzler's handwritten notes on Sevastopol.

[696] Ibid. N-63/29.

[697] Ibid. N-63/28.

[698] Ibid. N-63/61, 63/52, 67, 77. Many of the defectors were anti-Communists who had suffered under Stalin, especially in the regions concerned. These personnel would become the basis for the Vlasov Army of 1944-45.

[699] Ibid. N-63/54-55, 60, 62, 64, 69, 74. On Tagenrog see N-63/77. The furthest point east into Russia was Ordzhonikidze, 400 km/250 miles northwest of Baku, taken in August 1942, but recaptured the following December.

[700] Ibid. N-63/31.

[701] Ibid. N-63/56.

[702] Ibid. N-63/12. On Kursk see also Tsouras, pp. 82-83, 112.

[703] N-63/78. Gehlen's intelligence reports on the Leningrad Front stated that large numbers of red Army and partisan troops were amassed southeast of Leningrad, threatening the Demyansk-Kholm region. The *OKH* and *OKW* received these reports on Vlasov's forces, which Hitler called "fantasies" to Gehlen's face. *Sturmbannfuehrer* Rudolf von Falkenhahn and *General der Jagdflieger Generalleutnant* Adolf Galland were witnesses to this. Hitler's failure to heed these warnings would result in the near disasters just south of Lake Ilmen. See also reference to Korsun-Cherkassy in Overy, *Russia's War*, p. 235.

[704] See Overy, *Russia's War*, p. 235.

[705] Schoerner (12 June 1892-2 June 1973) was a lower class Bavarian who studied philosophy and languages at the University of Munich, WW I veteran of Verdun, winning the *Pour le Merite* from Kaiser Wilhelm II. After WW I he joined the *Reichswehr* and joined the *19th Gebirgs* Regiment. Schoerner joined the *Nazi* Party in 1923 and served in combat from the first day of the war to the last. Schoerner commanded the *6th Gebirgsjaeger* Division during the 6 April 1941 Balkans invasion, and along with *2nd Panzer* Division captured Athens, which brought Schoerner the Knight's Cross. He was appointed commander of the *XIX Gebirgsjaeger Korps* on 15 January 1942 that included the *3rd Gebirgs* Division of *Generalleutnant* (later *Generaloberst*) Wilhelm Dietl (1890-1944) and *5th Gebirgs* Division during the occupation of Norway in 1941-42 (promoted to *Generalmajor* on 15 January 1942) and later *Kommandeur Gebirgstruppen* on 1 June 1942 prior to *Operation Barbarossa*. Schoerner later commanded the *XXXX Panzer Korps* in the Ukraine 1943; replaced *Generaloberst* Ewald von Kleist as C-in-C *Army Group A* in February 1944 (later called Army Group South Ukraine), then appointed C-in-C *Army Group North* on 23 July 1944. Schoerner would become the twenty-fourth of twenty-seven soldiers to the *Brillanten* to the Knight's Cross on 1 January 1945, when he was appointed C-in-C of *Army Group Center*. The next day *Luftwaffe Oberst* Hans Ulrich Ruedel would be so decorated with the highest Germany award, the Golden Oak Leaves, Swords and Diamonds to the Knight's Cross, the only man to be awarded the distinction. He was promoted to Field Marshal on 5 April 1945 before being captured along with his wife as the commander of *Armee Gruppe Kurland* by U.S. forces after his plane crashed in Austria on 18 May 1945. The Americans handed him over to the Soviets, who imposed a twenty-five year sentence on him. After just under a decade in Russia, Schoerner returned to West Germany, and was again convicted of manslaughter for executing his own troops without trial, where he served another four and a half years in prison. See Schoerner records at *Militaerarchiv* Freiburg, N-60 in total; also Brian Lindsey, "Personality," *World War II*, Vol. 14, No. 2

(July 1999) Leesburg, VA: Primedia Publications, Inc. pp. 68-76. Lindsey states that Schoerner's death was on 6 July 1973, although the *Nachlasse* states he died on 2 June 1973. I have preferred to use the German records for the date in question.

[706] See N-60/97.

[707] N-60/99. On correspondence with Hasso von Manteuffel see N-60/100.

[708] N-63/78.

[709] Bartov, *Hitler's Army*, p. 85. According to Browning, Lemelsen's sentiments simply indicated that he was a more enlightened *Nazi*, believing that the necessity for a labor force outweighed the rationale of murder. However, regardless of Lemelsen's true motives regarding lenient treatment to soldiers, this did not extend to political leaders.

[710] Ibid. p. 87.

[711] Ibid. (*fn 104*) Citing BA-MA/RH26-1005/42, 19/9/42.

[712] Ibid. Citing BA-MA/RH 26-1005/47, 26/4/43. The division was under the command of *Generalleutnant* Hermann Balck (1893-1972), a WW I infantry officer who commanded a rifle regiment of *1st Panzer* Division during France and Poland, later commanding a *Panzer* regiment and then promoted to command *11th Panzer* Division in May 1942, promoted to *Generalleutnant* August 1942, *Generalmajor* January 1943 commanding *"Grossdeutschland."* Commanded Army Group G in France in 1944 then commanded the *6th Armee* in Hungary through the capitulation.

[713] Ibid. p. 90.

[714] Ibid. p. 91, citing BA-MA/RH26-12/245, 17/11/41, 20/11/41, 2/12/41, 11/12/41.

[715] Ibid. p. 90, citing BA-MA/RH 26-12/244, 22/6/41.

[716] Detlev Peukert, "Alltag und Barberei," p. 61 as cited by Kershaw in *The Nazi Dictatorship*, p. 195.

[717] Ibid. pp. 146-7 (*en 113*) citing Hans Mommsen, *"Kriegsfahrungen," Uber Leen im Krieg.* U. Borsdorf (ed.), and M. Jamin (Hamburg: Reinbeck 1989).

[718] Hans Hossfelder interview, 1985.

[719] Bartov, *Hitler's Army*, p. 92.

[720] Ibid. p. 91 (*en. 135*) citing BA-MA/RH26-12-246, 31/1/42.

[721] Ibid. p. 93.

[722] Kumm interview, 1985.

[723] Bartov, *Hitler's Army*, p. 129.

[724] Walther von Reichenau (1884-1942) commanded the *10th Armee* during Poland, *6th Armee* in Belgium, France and Russia. He was rewarded for his efforts at Kiev with the command of Army Group South, and died of a heart attack soon after.

[725] Ibid. pp. 129-30 (*en 59*) citing Christian Streit, *Keine Kameraden* (Stuttgart: 1978) p. 115.

[726] Overy, *Russia's War*, p. 84.

[727] Kumm interview, 1985.

[728] Wolff interview, January 1984.

[729] Kumm interview, April 1985.

[730] These facts are referenced in *Fighting in Hell: The German Ordeal on the Eastern Front.*

[731] Gehlen interrogation records on microfilm, NA M-1270/24/0395.

[732] U.S. NA M-1019/39.

[733] Ibid. NA M-1019/80 in total.

[734] Ibid. NA M-1270/23.

[735] Tsouras, p. 31.

[736] On Halder and the *Freiwilligen* see Steenberg, *Vlasov*, p. 35.

[737] Overy, *Russia's War*, p. 153.

[738] Tsouras, p. 284.

[739] Ibid. Introduction, Chapter 2, p. 146.

[740] Overy, *Russia's War*, p. 152.

[741] Tsouras, p. 284.

[742] Ibid.

[743] Robert Barr Smith, "Nuremberg: Final Chapter for the Thousand Year *Reich*," *World War II*, Vol. 10 No. 4 (November 1995) Leesburg, VA: Cowles History Group, p. 38. See also by Robert Barr Smith, "Final Verdict at Nuremberg," *World War II*, Vol. 11, No. 4 (November 1996) Leesburg, VA: Cowles History Group, pp. 38-44, 83, 88.

[744] See reference in Overy, *Russia's War*, pp. 84-5.

[745] Quote from Kumm interview, 1984.

[746] Ibid.

[747] See record of Dr. Rolf Himze, N-331/1 *Militaerarchiv* Freiburg.

[748] Russell H.S. Stolfi, *"10ᵗʰ Panzer's* Lightning Eastern Front Offensive," *World War II*, Vol. 12, No. 3 (September 1997) Leesburg, VA: Cowles History Group, pp. 34-40. Sadly, less than 60,000 of these prisoners would ever to return home at war's end, and many of those would be executed or placed in labor camps for having surrendered. The ambiguity of the total number of prisoners is yet to be resolved. German records state that 633,000 were taken, while Soviet records stated that 463,000 men were lost. Given the confusion within the Soviet ranks, the German figure would probably be the more accurate.

[749] Laska, p. 13; Overy, *Russia's War*, p. 140.

[750] Overy, *Russia's War*, p. 141. See also Overy's accounts of other mass murder sites in the Soviet Union.

[751] See N-39/317. Most of these units would be deployed to Sicily and be actively engaged there following the Allied invasion (*Operation Husky*) in 1943 between October 1942-September 1943. See N-39/456. On the overall command of *Freiwilligen* units, see record of *General der Kavallerie* Ernst Koestring, N-123/1, 2. Koestring was appointed *Kommandeur der Freiwilligen Verbaende OKH* on 1 January 1944. He was also *Inspekteur fuer Tuerkvoelkische* (Turkish People's) *Verbaende.*

[752] Fedor von Bock (3 December 1880- May 1945) was appointed *Oberbefehlshaber des Heeres* on 21 June 1941 and *Oberbefehlshaber der Wehrmacht* on 13 July 1942. He was killed in an air raid following his dismissal after disputing with Hitler over strategy and the *Freiwilligen* situation. See records at *Militaerarchiv* Freiburg, N-22/7, 9.

[753] See N-220/2. On his role as *Generalstabs des Heeres* in 1944 see also N-220/2.

[754] On the 2ⁿᵈ Shock Army see Overy, *Russia's War*, p. 130.

[755] Leeb (1876-1956, record located at *Militaerarchiv* Freiburg, N-145) had been pulled from retirement and commanded Army Group C during France, and Army Group North during *Barbarossa*. In January 1942 Leeb requested a retreat to the Lovat River to protect his right (north) flank, and Hitler refused. Leeb requested that Hitler either assume personal responsibility or relive him of command. He became a civilian within a matter of days.

[756] Keller, the former commander of the air and civil transport school ordered his aircraft to land at the small unimproved airstrip and drop supplies while rolling for landing and take-off, never stopping. They managed to do this only a few times, as the Soviets destroyed four of his seven Ju-52's. Most of the drops were made by parachute canisters, converted medium bombers (Do-17 and Ju-88 types) and DSF-230 gliders of *Kampfgeschwader (KG)-4 "General Wever."* Keller knew that Demyansk required 300 tons of supplies per day including food, medical supplies and ammunition. Following the first setbacks, Hitler ordered 337 Ju-52's deployed under *Generalfeldmarschall* Hans Jeschonnek who appointed *Oberst* Fritz Morzik, *Kommandeur* of *Luftflotte I* consisting of sixteen transport groups. Operational responsibility fell upon *Generalleutnant* Wolfram *Freiherr* von Richthofen who sent over a hundred flights per day into the cauldron. By the first week of April, over 65,000 tons had been delivered and 35,000 wounded troops evacuated with replacements flown in. The Germans lost 262 transports during the long relief, effectively destroying the transportation corps that had never fully recovered from the 271 losses at Crete in May 1941. Despite the later resurgence of industrial output

under Albert Speer, Germany would never fully replace these losses. The failure to supply Stalingrad was a direct result of these previous losses.

[757] It would be Kluge who requested and received Free Russian fighter-bomber support for his command in 1942. The last commander of the fighter squadron was *Oberstleutnant Kneaz* (Prince) Leonidas Damianov Maximciuc. Kluge (1882-August 1944) commanded the *4th Armee* in Poland and Russia, promoted to *Generalfeldmarschall* in July 1940. After a stellar career in the east he succeeded Gerd von Rundstedt as C-in-C West in 1944, but was relieved after the Falaise Gap disaster and replaced by Model. He was implicated (although not charged) in the bomb plot, and like Rommel he was invited to commit suicide.

[758] Falkenhahn interviews, 1984-85. Falkenhahn also knew Schoerner, spending time in Soviet custody with him and his wife. Falkenhahn was the *SS* officer responsible for locating Model during the Allied invasion of Holland in September 1944, yet never found him.

[759] On Belov see Steenberg, *Vlasov*, p. 58.

[760] Georgy Konstantinovich Zhukov (2 December 1896-18 June 1974) was arguably the best Soviet general of the war and awarded "Hero of the Soviet Union" on four occasions (the only man so honored), as well as the Order of Lenin and every Soviet medal for bravery. He joined the Communist Party in 1919, became Chief of Staff of the Red Army in 1941, becoming a Marshal in 1943. Zhukov was instrumental in every major Soviet victory and was Soviet commander of Soviet forces in East Germany after the war. Stalin became jealous of his popularity, and his friendship with Nikita Khrushchev kept him alive. After Stalin's death in 1953, Khrushchev also became wary of Zhukov, forcing him into retirement in 1957. Zhukov returned to public life and wrote his memoirs regarding the war, Stalin's purges, and the treatment of Soviet citizens that was suppressed and edited without his permission.

[761] Degrelle's comments regarding this are interesting.

[762] On 16 January 1942 Hitler issued the first "Stand Fast Order" to Army Group Center as it reeled from the 6 December 1941 Soviet counter-attacks around Moscow. Hitler later upgraded this type of order to a *Festungbefehl*, which was another way of informing his soldiers and commanders that they were expendable. Hitler would issue a total of eighteen Fortress Orders during the war.

[763] Eicke (KIA 26 February 1943) was the first commandant of Dachau concentration camp and was Inspector of Camps when it was built for political prisoners in the 1930's. He won the Knight's Cross with Oak Leaves and commanded *3rd SS* until his death, when his courier plane was shot down by a Soviet fighter. For more on Eicke see Black, *Ernst Kaltenbrunner*, pp. 86, 143.

[764] *"Wiking"* would just reach the region when it would be diverted to the Ukraine, where Degrelle's unit would be attached as auxiliaries.

[765] The *"Wallonien"* would be reduced to less than 400 men by 7 March 1945 and disbanded by Degrelle on 30 April. They would reconstituted in 1943 as an *SS* auxiliary unit, and designated as the *28th SS* Division in 1944.

[766] Olivier Thoring (12 February 1921-29 December 1944) would later join the *" Wallonien"* as a liaison officer, since he spoke Flemish. Thoring was born in Antwerp to a German father and Belgian mother. He served in *"Leibstandarte"* during the Balkans campaign, then was assigned to the *Freiwilligen "Wallonien"* since he spoke French, Flemish and English. Thoring won the Knight's Cross in 1943 at Kursk supporting a tank assault, but was later killed in January 1945 in the counterinsurgency fighting around Breslau, Silesia. His other awards included the Iron Cross in both classes, the German Cross in Gold, Close Combat Bar in Silver, Anti-Partisan Badge in Silver, and four *Panzerknackerabzeichen in Gold* (Tank Destruction Badges) for the single handed destruction of twenty Soviet tanks. Information courtesy of Leon Degrelle. See also Pat McTaggart, "City's Death Throes," *World War II*, Vol. 5, No. 5 (January 1991) Leesburg, VA: Empire Press, Inc. pp. 22-8.

[767] Steenberg, *Vlasov*, pp. 26-7.

[768] Ibid. p. 28.

[769] See N-220/127. The *Abwehrschlachten* (Counterintelligence battle) picked up momentum following the appointment of Reinhard Gehlen as *Abwehr Chef* for field operations. The actual term given was *"Abwehrschlachten in Russland nach dem werdepunkt im Krieg,"* or the *Counterintelligence Battle Getting to the Point in War.* It would be these duties that would prompt a response from the *Daily Telegraph and Morning Post* on 7 July 1947 while Halder was in Allied custody, titled: "Germans Still Untried-General Halder and Hitler." See also N-220/159. On his *Verabschiedung* (farewell from active duty) on 31 January 1945 and placement in the *Fuehrerreserve* see N-220/2. The *Fuehrerreserve* was the pool where older, severely wounded and "dismissed" officers were placed, and were able to be recalled if needed. Several prominent German officers found themselves recalled, such as Gerd von Rundstedt, Heinz Guderian, Walter von Brauchitsch (1881-1948), Gotthard Heinrici and *Oberst* Claus von Stauffenberg.

[770] *17ᵗʰ Armee* would later be commanded by *Generaloberst* Erwin Jaenecke, until Schoerner sided with Hitler on refusing to evacuate the division from Sevastopol, sacking Jaenecke on 27 April 1944. See Lindsey, *World War II* (July 1999) p. 72.

[771] See N-29/8.

[772] Ibid. N-29/10. Doerr exchanged letters with *Generalmajor* Otto Jacobsen concerning these events, especially at Medyka, with copies forwarded to *General* E. Marcks and *Generalleutnant* von Briesen in June 1941. N-29/11.

[773] See Himze, N-331/1.

[774] Stieff (6 June 1901-8 August 1944) would be executed following the 22 July 1944 assassination attempt against Hitler due to his contacts with Henna von Tresckow. On partisan activity see N-114/28-30, and NA M-1270/24/0430.

[775] N-29/14.

[776] Schweppenburg's (2 March 1886-27 January 1974) model was used until later doctrine could be applied in 1943. See *Militaerarchiv* N-254/51. On the Kharkov Cauldron on 17-25 August 1942 see also Mackensen, N-39/318.

[777] Ibid. N-581/16, 60. *Generalfeldmarschall* Ewald von Kleist also remarked on the Kharkov operation. See N-354/17-19.

[778] Ibid. N-581/60. On the fighting at Woltschansk south of the Donets Basin from 29 May-16 June 1942 and Kupyansk from 17-26 June, 1942 see von Mackensen, N-39/318. For the list of units involved: *3ʳᵈ, 13ᵗʰ, 14ᵗʰ, 16ᵗʰ , 22ⁿᵈ-23ʳᵈ, 44ᵗʰ, 60ᵗʰ* (Motorized*), 62ⁿᵈ, 71ˢᵗ, 73ʳᵈ, 76ᵗʰ*, and *113ᵗʰ Infanterie* Divisions; *100ᵗʰ, 125ᵗʰ, 295ᵗʰ, 297ᵗʰ, 298ᵗʰ, 370ᵗʰ, 384ᵗʰ, 389ᵗʰ* (Light) *Infanterie* Divisions; *Panzer* Division *"Grossdeutschland"*, *1ˢᵗ* & *5ᵗʰ Waffen SS* Divisions, *1ˢᵗ Gebirgsjaeger* Division, 1ˢᵗ Romanian *Infanterie* Division, 2ⁿᵈ Romanian *Gebirgs* Division (*Gruppe Mackensen*) see also N-39/318.

[779] Ibid. N-581/18-19. This section also covers the activity of the *I Panzer Armee* in the Donetz region from February-March 1943.

[780] Ibid. N-581/20.

[781] Ibid. N-581/60-62.

[782] Wilhelm Willemer (13 January 1905-27 January 1967) was said to have ordered every suspected partisan shot regardless of gender and age. See records at *Militaerarchiv* Freiburg, N-342/6-7. Willemer's command would be so decimated at Kronstadt between October-November 1944 it was later reconstituted as a *Volksgrenadier* Division under the status *"Kampfgruppe Winkler,"* specifically organized to combat partisans. See N-342/9.

[783] Ibid. N-342/8.

[784] Ibid. N-342/10.

[785] Ibid. N-342/13.

[786] Ibid. N-342/8.

[787] Overy, *Russia's War*, p. 150.

[788] Steenberg, *Vlasov*, p. 103.

[789] N-123/17. See reference to Koestring's book, *Ghost of the Vlasov Army* in N-123/11; and Steenberg, *Vlasov*, pp. 122, 151-2, 168, 171, 177, 179, 196, 212-3.

[790] Steenberg, p. 122.

[791] This was supported by the Gehlen Reports, although Gehlen was referring to numbers of troops, while Koestring was referring to the industrial capacity of the Soviet Union.

[792] For a worthwhile revisionist theory regarding Hitler's invasion of the Soviet Union and Molotov's potential contribution, see Albert L. Weeks, "Perspectives," *World War II* Vol. 13, No. 4 (November 1999) pp. 12-24. Ian Kershaw also mentions the lack of substance regarding the Non-Aggression Pact in *The Hitler Myth: Image and Reality in the Third Reich* (New York: Oxford University Press, 1987) p. 173. See also Albert L. Weeks, "Undercover," *World War II*, Vol. 10, No. 3 (September 1994) Leesburg, VA: Cowles History Group, pp. 8-10, 14-6.

[793] *Generalfeldmarschall* Wilhelm List commanded Army Group A until he was sacked and replaced by Ewald von Kleist as German forces attacked the Caucasus Mountains. At this time Army Group South was organized as follows: *I Panzergruppe* under *Generaloberst* Ewald von Kleist; *6ᵗʰ Armee* under *Generalfeldmarschall* Walter von Reichenau; *11ᵗʰ Armee* under *Generaloberst* Eugen Ritter von Schobert; *17ᵗʰ Armee* under *Generaloberst* Heinrich von Stuelpnagel. The foreign units under the command were as follows: 3ʳᵈ Romanian Army under General Dumitrescu; 4ᵗʰ Romanian Army under General Ciupera. There were many Free Russian and White Russian units that do not carry unit designations until 1942-43. It was not until June 1942 that the Hungarian units would form part of Army Group South, and the Italian units would operate in the Caucasus. During Koestring's visit to Vinnitza, another officer was headed there to receive the Oak Leaves to the Knight's Cross, *Luftwaffe Hauptmann* (later a post-war *Generalmajor*) Dietrich Hrabak, who scored 125 victories during the war. See Hrabak interviews of 1993-94, University of Strathclyde, Department of Oral History, Glasgow, UK, and Temple University, Philadelphia, PA. This interview is both taped and transcribed by Colin D. Heaton.

[794] See list of *Waffen SS* units at *Appendix B*

[795] Quarrie, *Hitler's Samurai*, pp. 27, 25 with photo captions.

[796] Kumm interview, 1985.

[797] This was the *No. 4 regiment*, since each regiment was ordained with a separate title.

[798] *"Das Reich"* was part of *XI Korps* and under the command of *Generaloberst* Erhard Rauss, who wrote *The Anvil of War* (London: Greenhill Books, 1994).

[799] Tsouras, pp. 68-69. Supporting *"Das Reich"* was the *Wehrmacht's 3ʳᵈ Panzer* Division.

[800] Kumm interview.

[801] Erich von Manstein (1887-1973) was Chief of Staff to von Rundstedt during the Polish and French campaigns, and commanded a *Panzer Korps* of Army Group North during *Barbarossa*. Later he commanded the *11ᵗʰ Armee* in the Crimea, and upon capturing Sevastopol was promoted to *Generalfeldmarschall*. His exploits included trying to assist the *6ᵗʰ Armee* at Stalingrad, and his withdrawal of Army Group South following Kursk. He was dismissed and later fell into obscurity. See record at *Militaerarchiv* Freiburg, N-507.

[802] *Militaerarchiv* N-507/84, 82, 83 respectively.

[803] Ibid. N-507/80, 36, 39 respectively.

[804] Ibid. N-507/26-29, 85. On execution of the plans, see N-507/86-89. This delay was called the *Planpausen*, and Manstein would never recover from its failure.

[805] Ibid. N-507/35.

[806] Ibid. N-507/32.

[807] The Viet Cong in Vietnam would perform the same actions, provoking a response from American units.

[808] Tsouras, citing *General der Infanterie* Hans von Greiffenberg, Chief of Staff to Army Groups Center and A, p. 285.

[809] Ibid. Citing *Generaloberst* Erhard Rauss, p. 148.

[810] Mazower, *Inside Hitler's Greece*, p. 172.

[811] Tsouras, p. 285.

[812] The Germans established a network of hotels where front-line soldiers could take a break and relax from combat, having a bath, delousing, shave, haircut, hot meals, medical treatment, issue of new gear, etc. This was of particular importance during the winter when frostbite, snow blindness, hypothermia and exhaustion were the primary concerns.

[813] See reference in Tsouras, p. 120.

[814] Ibid. pp. 120-21.

[815] Ibid. p. 285.

[816] Hrabak interview, 1993.

[817] This is a low placed series of wires from ankle to knee high, making walking difficult, and in limited visibility it could be deadly. Many times they were attached to bells or other devices to warn on intrusion, as well as rigged to grenades and explosives.

[818] Killing zones are narrow channels that allow the defender to determine where the attacker can move with the least difficulty, much like electricity taking the path of least resistance. Once enemy forces found the "easier way" they would be engaged and annihilated.

[819] Tsouras, citing von Greiffenberg, p. 285.

[820] *Organization Todt* was responsible for much of this work until 1942, as well as building roads, airfields and temporary structures.

[821] These assets were usually reserved for *SS* units, who handled most of the activity.

[822] Tsouras, p. 155.

[823] Ibid. Comments from *General der Infanterie* Hans von Greiffenberg, p. 285.

[824] Ibid. p. 121. See also Overy, *Russia's War*, p. 145.

[825] Artillery rounds "walked in" slowly to cover a dense area, saturating the ground in a forward motion.

[826] Sajer, *Forgotten Soldier*.

[827] Tsouras, p. 121.

[828] Ibid.

[829] This situation occurred in 1943 when *Major* (later a post-war *Oberst*) Erich Hartmann, 352 victory *Luftwaffe* ace had been shot down and escaped from his Soviet captors. Hartmann managed to feign injury, slipped away and reached German lines. He just happened to come across one of these sentries at night, and despite speaking German and identifying himself was shot at. The bullet passed harmlessly through his trousers leg. Hartmann interview of 1984. Hartmann would later receive the Swords and Diamonds as well. See Heaton, "The Count: *Luftwaffe* Ace Walter Krupinski," *Military History*, Vol. 15 No. 2 (June 1998) Leesburg, VA: Primedia Publishing Group, Inc., pp. 61-68; interview with Hartmann 1991.

[830] Kumm interview, 1985.

[831] Overy, *Russia's War*, p. 150.

[832] Tsouras, p. 118.

[833] See reference in Overy, *Russia's War*, pp. 150-51.

[834] Tsouras, p. 55.

[835] Ibid. pp. 116-7. See also Overy, *Russia's War*, p. 145.

[836] Named for the small white mountain flower found in the Alps. These were the elite of the Alpine troops, and both the Army and *SS* had their own detachments. Leon Degrelle volunteered for the elite *Edelweiss* qualification, perhaps the toughest training in the world.

[837] See Quarrie, *Hitler's Samurai*, pp. 30-2, 34, 39, 45, 47, 81, 97, 105-6, 118, 139. On winter as a factor on German forces and their abilities, see Tsouras citing *Generaloberst* Erhard Rauss, Commander of the 4th and 3rd *Panzer Armee* on the Eastern Front, pp. 145-67.

[838] Degrelle interviews, 1984-85.

[839] Ibid. April 1985.

[840] Ibid.

[841] Kumm interview by letter dated 1988.

[842] Tsouras, p. 124.

[843] Ibid. Kumm and Wolff concurred in their respective interviews, as did Leon Degrelle. Koronov offered is own perspective, having fought the UPA on occasion.

[844] Tsouras, p. 124.

[845] Ibid.

[846] Ibid. Supported by Kumm, who stated that friendly guerrillas assisted in several operations in which he participated.

[847] Ibid.

[848] Robert Szymzack, "Bolshevik Wave Breaks at Warsaw," *Military History,* Vol. 11, No. 6 (February 1995) Leesburg, VA: Cowles History Group, pp. 54-61, 90.

[849] Ibid. On the Civil War, see also Alexander Dubrovolsky as told to Nicholas Dodge, "Revolutionary Upheaval Survived," *Military History*, Vol. 11, No. 5 (December 1994) Leesburg, VA: Cowles History Group, pp. 54-61.

[850] On the ROA see Steenberg, *Vlasov*, p. 66. Most of Bronislav Kaminsky's men would join the ROA following his execution; see p. 169.

[851] It was during this period that Soviet forces clashed with Japanese units in Mongolia and eastern Siberia.

[852] This was the same day that Hitler appointed Dr. Alfred Rosenberg as Minister for the Occupied Eastern Territories. He traveled on Himmler's staff train to meet with Dr. Otto Braeutigam, Chief of Departmental Policy in the Ministry and liaison with *Oberkommando des Heeres*.

[853] Nikolina interview, 1984.

[854] On Boyarski see Steenberg, *Vlasov*, pp. 30-1, 55, 60-2, 153, 175, 190, 202.

[855] Steenberg, p. 47. Malyshkin was the son of a bookkeeper from Novocherkassk, joined the Communist Party as a young NCO and graduated from the Military Academy, where he also taught after receiving his doctorate. He was severely tortured following the purge, when his division commander, Velikanov was shot, and hated Stalin and the system he had believed in. When the war started he was Chief of Staff to the Soviet 19th Army.

[856] Keitel (22 September 1882-16 October 1946) was the Chief of the High Command throughout the war and was Hitler's most trusted military advisor. Keitel had dictated the terms of the French surrender in June 1940. He was convicted of war crimes at Nuremberg and hanged. See record at *Militaerarchiv* Freiburg and *Bundesarchiv* Koblenz, N-54.

[857] See Steenberg, *Vlasov*, pp. 45-6. Zykov spent three years in Siberian exile.

[858] Vlasov refused to wear a German uniform and he could not wear a Soviet one, so for public appearances he wore black trousers with General's piping, a dark brown jacket without tabs or epaulettes, and a brown coat with lapels with gold buttons. Ibid. See p. 69.

[859] Ibid. p. 35. Claus August Schenck *Graf* von Stauffenberg (1907-1944) was seriously wounded in North Africa, and while working in Russia became disillusioned with the genocide policy and the failure to incorporate the human resources to support Germany's efforts. He was a long time member of the conspiracy to kill Hitler, and he planted the bomb on 20 July 1944. He and over 200 others were shot soon afterward, although more than 5,000 people would be killed and many more placed into concentration camps due to suspicion.

[860] Ibid. pp. 39-40. It was Strikfeldt who approached Vlasov regarding the leadership of the Free Russian forces. For a full account of his activities, see Strik-Strikfeldt, *Against Stalin and Hitler: Memoir of the Russian Liberation Movement, 1941-45* (New York: Macmillan, 1970).

[861] This would include a co-conspirator in the bomb plot, Frits-Dietlof *Graf* von der Schulenburg (5 September 1902-10 August 1944). Schulenburg was born in London, well educated and joined the

NSDAP in 1932, becoming the President of the Berlin Police in 1937. He first met Beck (record located at *Militaerarchiv* Freiburg, N-28) and Stauffenberg in 1938, and the following year became *Oberpraesident in Breslau.* He was hanged in Ploetzensee. See records at *Militaerarchiv* Freiburg, N-1301, and *Bundesarchiv* Koblenz, NL-301.

[862] Wolff interview, December 1983 and supplemental in January 1984. This attitude towards his own countrymen was Stalin's greatest error. Stalin's son was captured and allowed to die in a camp, although Hitler offered to make a deal for his return.

[863] These were put into effect to support Hermann Goering's Four-Year Plan, which was actually supervised by Goering's adjutant, Undersecretary Hans-Joachim Riecke. This attempt to maintain control over the Caucasus oil would become the primary reason for the Russian invasion under Boris Yeltsin and subsequent war in Chechnya during the 1990s.

[864] On Herre see Steenberg, *Vlasov*, p. 168.

[865] "SS Police Detachments." These were auxiliary SS units that would be incorporated into the *Einsatzgruppen*, and were actually *SD* in disguise for the most part. These units were later incorporated into the *Waffen SS*, such as the *4th SS* Division *"Polizei"* in 1942. Few historians make the clear distinction between these units and the combat formations of the *Waffen SS*, although the veterans themselves do.

[866] Herre report to *Oberst* Claus von Stauffenberg, provided by Wolff.

[867] Steenberg, *Vlasov*, p. 49.

[868] Tsouras, p. 32.

[869] Brauchitsch (1881-1948) was a WW I staff officer and rose to command the General Staff in 1938, until suffering a heart attack, forcing him to resign. His failure to halt the Soviet forces at Moscow and his clashes with Hitler saw him relieved of command.

[870] Overy, *Russia's War,* p. 133.

[871] Many of these were of the ethnic White Russian Diaspora recruited from Croatia and Serbia and given German liaison officers. The Russian Defense Corps of Serbia numbered 12-15,000 men under General Staifon, who broke it up into five separate infantry regiments. They operated as an anti-partisan unit along with *13th der Waffen SS* Division *"Handschar"* in Yugoslavia. Other units, such as Pannwitz's Cossacks would also serve in this campaign.

[872] Wolff interview, January 1984.

[873] Many of the Soviet troops reportedly shot their officers and political commissars and defected to the German ranks, which would explain the high number of Ukrainian volunteers during this period.

[874] Guderian (17 June 1888-15 May 1954) was one of the best known and respected tank generals on either side of the war, serving in both World Wars and developing the armored spearhead tactic. By 1938 he commanded all German tank units. Hitler "retired" him until 1944 when he was appointed Chief of the General Staff from July 1944-March 1945. His books *Panzer Leader,* 8th ed. (London: MacDonald & Co., 1982) and *With Panzers in the East and West* (*Mit Panzern in Ost und West*) are classics. The Allied capture and interrogation of Guderian dated 31 May 1945 by the U.S. 7th Army is located at NA M-1270/24/0655-0660.

[875] Army Group Center at this time was organized as follows: *9th Armee* under *Generaloberst* Alfred Strauss; *2nd Panzergruppe* under *Generaloberst* Heinz Guderian; *3rd Panzergruppe* under *Generaloberst* Hermann Hoth. Hoth (1895-1971, record located at *Militaerarchiv* Freiburg, N-503) was another WW I era cavalry officer who also commanded *3rd Panzer Armee* and captured 300,000 Soviet prisoners in 1941, ending up 19 km from Moscow. He commanded *4th Panzer Armee* at Kursk and was later relieved and retired.

[876] Army Group North at this time was organized as follows: *18th Armee* under *Generaloberst* Georg von Kuechler; *4th Panzergruppe* under *Generaloberst* Erich Hoeppner (1886-8 August 1944); *16th Armee* under *Generaloberst* (later *Generalfeldmarschall*) Ernst Busch (1885-1945). Eventually 100,000 Free Russians would be serving in Army Group Center by 1943. See Steenberg, *Vlasov*, p. 73; on

Busch <u>see</u> Overy, *Russia's War*, p. 237. Leeb commanded Army Group North from June –December 1941. He was charged with war crimes stemming from his 18 September 1941 order to shell civilians fleeing Leningrad while under siege. Given the articles covering the rules of war, and the fact that the population was offered terms of surrender he was acquitted. See Walzer, *Just and Unjust Wars*, p. 166. Hoeppner was executed at Ploetzensee for his involvement in the bomb attempt on Hitler's life.

[877] <u>See</u> Steenberg, *Vlasov*, p. 64.

[878] On Kluge's inspection <u>see</u> Steenberg, *Vlasov,* p. 61. One of these men decorated was Leonidas Maximciuc.

[879] Maximciuc interviews, 1994-1999.

[880] On Kononov, <u>see</u> Steenberg, *Vlasov*, pp. 73-6, 116, 124, 182-3, 203.

[881] For "*Florian Geyer's*" activity in Hungary in late 1944, <u>see</u> Pat McTaggart, *World War II* (March 1997) p. 47.

[882] Steenberg, *Vlasov,* p. 75.

[883] Strikfeldt published his memoirs, <u>see</u> *fn 813*. On Strikfeldt, <u>see</u> Steenberg, *Vlasov*, p. 33.

[884] Wolf interview, 1984.

[885] Otto Kumm stated that this was standard operating procedure; interview 1985.

[886] Ibid.

[887] <u>See</u> reference in Overy, *Russia's War*, p. 134 in slave labor in the Ukraine, which supplied four-fifths of all eastern labor..

[888] Dr. Fritz Todt (1891-1942) was Hitler's expert on arms and munitions production, as well as the designated foreman for the Greater *Reich* expansion program. He was responsible for the *autobahn* system, the Siegfried Line and Atlantic Wall fortifications. Todt's crew collected slave labor from all of the occupied countries and built or repaired roads, railways, operated coal mines, blast furnaces, and aircraft factories. Todt died in a mysterious plane crash in 1942 following his strong recommendation to Hitler that he terminate the war with the Soviets, and was replaced by Albert Speer.

[889] Overy, *Russia's War*, p. 134.

[890] Tresckow's remarks to Stauffenberg, recorded by *Hauptmann* Adrian von Schlabrendorff.

[891] Arlt (b. 1912) attended the University of Leipzig, studying the classics, languages, mathematics, statistics, philosophy, theory, genetics, psychology, social, biological and medical sciences. He also attended various universities in an exchange program in Poland, Czechoslovakia (Prague University), Hungary, Austria (University of Vienna) and became a professor of population statistics at the University of Breslau, Silesia in 1936 at age twenty-four.

[892] Wolff interview, January 1984.

[893] On Arlt <u>see</u> Steenberg, *Vlasov*, p. 141 (*fn 5*).

[894] Johannes von Blaskowitz (1883-1946) argued against the treatment of Jews in Poland, and was relieved by Himmler of his command. He later commanded troops during *Barbarossa* and during the Eastern Front campaign until placed in command of Army Group G in southern France. He fought the American advance in the Rhone Valley following *Operation Dragoon*. Despite being relieved of command by Hitler for failing to destroy the city of Nancy, he later commanded Army Group H defending Holland. Captured by Canadian forces, he committed suicide while awaiting trial at Nuremberg. For an article on Blaskowitz on the Western Front, <u>see</u> Lawrence M. Greenberg, "Rolling Advance Stymied," *World War II*, Vol. 6, No. 2 (July 1991) Leesburg, VA: Empire Press, Inc. pp. 26-33.

[895] Wolff interviews along with Rudolf von Falkenhahn in January 1984.

[896] Named for George Kastrioti "*Skanderberg*" (1405-68), Serb Albanian leader captured by the Ottomans as a boy and served as commander for Murad II (1404-51) who named him Alexander and made him governor, or "bey". He joined Hunyadi against the Turks, survived the defeat at Kosovo, and later defeated Turks at Albulena in 1457.

[897] Named for Janos Corvinus Hunyadi (c. 1387-1456), regent of Hungary from 1446-52 who forced the Turks from Transylvania in 1442 and prevented Belgrade from capture in 1456. He was finally defeated by Murad II at Kosovo, Serbia in 1448.

[898] Named for the first Holy Roman Emperor Charlemagne (742-814), King of the Franks.

[899] *SS Oberstgruppenfuehrer* Paul Hausser, commander of *II SS Panzer Korps* was an exception to the rule and he was highly regarded, and he welcomed the Free Russians and Ukrainians.

[900] This was the UNR, or Ukrainian National Republic under the leadership of Colonel Simon Petlyura, who was later assassinated after the failed 1921 Ukrainian fight for independence. Petlyura's successor was a shadowy figure know only as Levicki, who was in Lodz under the scrutiny of the *SD*. Arlt was consulted with Levicki, who in turn recommended General Pavlo Shandruk who had always stood for a united independent Ukraine as the best candidate for Ukrainian leadership.

[901] The Katyn Forest was where the Red Army murdered perhaps 11,000 Polish officers (although 4,000 bodies were recovered by the Germans) and buried them in mass graves, then placed the blame on the Germans. It was only through forensic investigation several years ago that the truth was conclusively proven. This event was the primary catalyst for the souring of relations between the Poles and Soviets, and General Wladislaw Sikorski (1881-4 July 1943), the former Polish Prime Minister (1922-23) and head of the Polish government in exile from 1939-43 had to be urged by Churchill to maintain even the coolest of relations with Stalin. He was killed in a plane crash near Gibraltar under mysterious circumstances. See references in Overy, *Russia's War*, pp. 53, 82-3, 295-6, 297.

[902] Wolff interview, January 1984.

[903] Ibid.

[904] The unit being formed in Denmark was an infantry battalion being built up, while the Italian effort was a Cossack unit that would be attached to *"Florian Geyer."*

[905] Steenberg, *Vlasov*, p. 85. Trukhin was a Russian aristocrat and Chief of Staff of the Baltic region when he was wounded and captured.

[906] See reference in Overy, *Russia's War*, p. 131.

[907] Steenberg, p. 181. Overtures were even made through the Russian wife of the American ambassador to Madrid, Spain, Norman Armour via ambassador Marzhan.

[908] Ibid.

[909] This was spearheaded by Arlt's commanding officer, *Obersturmbannfuehrer* Ludwig Wolff, no relation to *Obergruppenfuehrer* Karl Wolff.

[910] There was also discussion in the spring of 1944 between Shkuro and Vlasov about placing Pannwitz's unit under Vlasov's control. See Steenberg, *Vlasov*, p. 124.

[911] This problem began to be resolved by Koestring as he gained more authority and assumed responsibility of the Free Russian *Luftwaffe* auxiliary units in 1943, which had so far escaped the attention of Hitler, Jodl and Keitel. Koestring also managed to establish field hospitals and recruited medical staffs, increasing the *Freiwilligen* units' operational survivability.

[912] This is revealed by the Stauffenberg reports, Tresckow journals and the surviving communiqués issued from Himmler through Gehlen. These memoranda all state the same phrase without clarification. The intended ambiguity was not lost upon Vlasov and the other ranking Russians.

[913] "Special Leader," equivalent to a Warrant Officer, although a "leader" could technically be of any rank. The job descriptions were dependent upon special skills such as languages, university education, technical specialties like communications, ordinance, political science, geography, etc. Grote, like Strikfeldt, was of Baltic origin and a true diplomat. See Steenberg, *Vlasov*, p. 42.

[914] Overy, *Russia's War*, p. 162.

[915] Ibid. p. 163.

[916] Steenberg, p. 42. Duerksen and Martin worked closely with Strikfeldt, when Martin was head of Eastern Propaganda.

⁹¹⁷ This plan was devised by Marshal Fedor Ivanovitch Tolbukhin (1894-1949) who was previously dismissed for failing to relieve Sevastopol with two armies. After proving the failure was not his fault he was placed in command of the 57ᵗʰ Army at Stalingrad and coordinated the encirclement with Vasilevsky (1895-1977). In March 1943 he was in command of the Southern Front in the Crimea, capturing 67,000 prisoners. Following this success he commanded the 3ʳᵈ Ukrainian Front through the end of the war, liberating Belgrade, Budapest, and occupying Vienna. Marshal Alexander M. Vasilevsky (1895-1977) was appointed Chief of Staff in 1942 and worked on the planning of all the major Soviet operations, including Kursk, with Zhukov. In May 1945 he was appointed as Commander Far East and planned and executed the invasions of Mongolia, Korea, Manchuria, and the Kurile and Sakhalin Islands of Japan. Also involved with the Stalingrad encirclement was General Nikolai A. Vatutin (1901-1944) who was defeated by Manstein, liberated Kiev and was killed in an ambush by Ukrainian Nationalist partisans near Rovno in February 1945.

⁹¹⁸ Steenberg, *Vlasov*, pp. 42-4.

⁹¹⁹ NA M-1270/24/0430.

⁹²⁰ NA M-1270/24/083, regarding p. 51 of CI-FIR/123, Secret Report.

⁹²¹ Hans-Ulrich Ruedel, *Stuka Pilot*, 3ʳᵈ ed. (New York: Bantam Books, 1956). Forward by Group Captain Sir Douglas Baader (New York: Bantam Books, 1956). Also on Ruedel, see Pat McTaggart, "Personality," *World War II*, Vol. 7, No. 2 (July 1992) Leesburg, VA: Cowles History Group, pp. 10, 67-70. See also Ken Kotik, "Eagle of the Eastern Front," *Second World War,* Vol.5, No. 2 (September 1996) Canoga Park, CA: Challenge Publications, Inc., pp. 65-68. Stalin was so distraught over Ruedel's accomplishments (519 tanks, the battleship *Marat,* eleven fighters and twelve locomotives destroyed) that he placed a 100,000 ruble price on his head. No one collected the bounty. Regarding assessments on Ruedel's character, see Heaton, "Luftwaffe Ace Guenther Rall Remembers," *World War II*, Vol. 9, No. 6 (March 1995) Leesburg, VA: Cowles History Group, pp. 34-40, 77-78. Rall and other prominent fighter pilots from the Eastern Front knew and flew cover for Ruedel's *Stukageschwader 2 "Immelman,"* and *Generalleutnant* Guenther Rall's comments on Ruedel are quite enlightening. See also report CI-FIR/123 at NA M-1270/24/0831. On Rall's comments during his interview see Heaton, *World War II* (March 1995) p. 38.

⁹²² Many of these "priests" and "monks" were actually working as Soviet double agents, sent to gather intelligence on the Germans and infiltrate the German intelligence community. Their leader was Patriarch Sergius of Moscow, who joined the Bolsheviks in order to save his life and the church offices. See M-1270/24/0831-0832.

⁹²³ Guenther d'Alquen (b. 1910) was the son of an Essen wool merchant, who joined the *SA* in 1926 and was wounded in a fight against Communists at a factory. His father disowned him and he went to work as a journalist in Munich and Berlin as a founding editor for *Die Schwarz Korps*, the journal of the *SS*. He joined the Army and was recruited into the *SS* as a *Kriegsberichter* (war correspondent) and made a recruiter. D'Alquen, one of the youngest colonels in the *SS* collected the best men available to begin their work during the French Campaign of 1940. Their bravery under fire to get the perfect camera shot or newsreel footage created high casualties, and many were decorated for bravery. Their techniques, enhanced by the fact that the *SS* were always in front and involved in the thickest fighting, and were always afforded transportation. Their successes have been considered the benchmark for all modern combat correspondents and journalists.

⁹²⁴ See reference in Steenberg, *Vlasov*, p. 138.

⁹²⁵ Bartov, *Hitler's Army* (*en 149*) p. 94, citing BA-MA/RH26-12-245, 13/10/41.

⁹²⁶ Ibid.

⁹²⁷ Intelligence at the division level and higher. The NATO equivalent is G-2; below division level the position is S-2. *Oberstleutnant* Bernd *Freiherr* Freytag von Loringhoven (record located at *Bundesarchiv* Freiurg, N-525) devised the *Manual 5000*, grouping the auxiliaries under an estab-

lished guideline. His successor Herre renamed it *Regulation 5000*, which gained support from several German generals, including Kurt Zeitzler. Zeitzler's endorsement forced Hitler to take a second look at the inclusion, and Vlasov was eventually given command under von Kluge. See Steenberg, *Vlasov*, p. 44.

[928] Loringhoven interview, 1985.

[929] Overy, *Russia's War*, p. 147.

[930] Supported by Karl Wolff in January 1984, who handled the information in conjunction with Reinhard Gehlen, both of whom apparently "neglected" to inform Himmler.

[931] On Marshal Rodion Yakolevich Malinovsky (1898-1967) and his command of the 2nd Ukrainian Front in 1944, see Pat McTaggart, *World War II* (March 1997) pp. 42-8.

[932] Bunyachenko, a Ukrainian was neither a supporter of Hitler or Stalin, although he had commanded the Far-East Division in Vladivostok in 1939, served on Marshal Semyon Timoshenko's (1895-1970) staff, and commanded the 1st Vlasov Division. He had defected early in the war. See Steenberg, *Vlasov*, p. 171. Timoshenko was an old friend of Stalin who survived the purges. He was defeated in 1942 when the *6th Armee* drove toward Stalingrad and other German units invaded the Caucasus. He was sent to Moscow where he spent the remainder of the war preparing offensive plans for Soviet strategy, in which he excelled. See reference to Bunyachenko in Overy, *Russia's War*, p. 129.

[933] Ibid. p. 56.

[934] Ibid. p. 58.

[935] Wolff interview, January 1984.

[936] Steenberg, *Vlasov*, p. 57.

[937] Ibid. On Gersdorff see p. 58. On Gersdorff and the 20 July bomb plot see NA M-1270/24/0430.

[938] On Zhilenkov, see Steenberg, *Vlasov*, pp. 53-5.

[939] Ibid. p. 81.

[940] Wolff interviews, December 1983 and January 1984.

[941] Ibid.

[942] See reference in Overy, *Russia's War*, p. 132.

[943] Steenberg, *Vlasov*, p. 125.

[944] Wolff interview.

[945] Ibid. p. 126.

[946] Wolff recounted this story, since he stated that it even shocked Himmler. Interview, January 1984.

[947] Ibid.

[948] Ibid.

[949] Herre's post-war memoirs based upon his wartime diaries of 1941-45, courtesy of Johannes Steinhoff. This was also corroborated by Wolff.

[950] Steenberg, *Vlasov*, p. 83.

[951] Ibid. p. 84.

[952] Gehlen reports.

[953] J. Epstein, "Die Ausflerung der Wlassow-Truppen," *New Yorker Staatszeitung und Herold* (12 March 1955).

[954] See also George Fischer, "Vlasov and Hitler," *Journal of Modern History*, No. 23 (March 1951) and "General Vlasov's Official Biography," *Russian Review*, No. 8 (October 1949).

[955] Karl Wolff interview, January 1984. Wolff stated that Keitel complained that Hitler went into a rage when he heard about Vlasov, since he had not personally authorized the tour.

[956] *OKW* communiqué dated 18 April 1943.

[957] Named for the dynasty that ruled Prussia until their defeat by the Hohenzollern confederacy.

[958] Kumm interview, 1985.

[959] See reference to this in Steenberg, *Vlasov*, p. 137. To this day the mystery has never been solved.

[960] Andrei Andreyevich Vlasov (1 September 1900-2 August 1946) was born in the village of Lomakino

near Nishni Novgorod, the eighth child and youngest son of a tailor, he graduated from the Russian Orthodox seminary, yet joined the Red Army in March 1919, assigned to China in November 1938, promoted to Major General 4 June 1940, Lieutenant General on 24 January 1942; 6 March 1942 he was deputy Commander of the Northwest Front, captured after Battle of Volkhov on 12 July 1942. He was a Cossack leader of great skill and was a favorite of Stalin's, decorated with the Hero of the Soviet Union and commander of several Red Army units, such as the 2nd Division, 99th Division, 4th Armored Corps (Lvov), 20th Army and 37th Army. He was a key defender of Moscow in 1941 at the Rzhev Gap, yet was executed after the British and Americans surrendered his staff to the Red Army. See Steenberg, *Vlasov*, pp. 5-6, 14, 22, 229-30.

[961] This was witnessed by Himmler's adjutant, Karl Wolff and related during this January 1984 interview.

[962] Ibid.

[963] See reference in Steenberg, *Vlasov*, pp. 147-9.

[964] Wolff interview, January 1984.

[965] As cited by Overy, *Russia's War*, p. 125.

[966] Ibid. p. 127.

[967] Steenberg, *Vlasov*, p. 182.

[968] Wolff interview, January 1984.

[969] Arlt managed to have Stefan Bandera released from prison and have the Galician *SS* Division renamed *1st Ukrainian* Division *der Waffen SS*, later commanded by a *Standartenfuehrer* Diachenko to appease the senior Russian generals.

[970] Steenberg, *Vlasov*, pp. 168-71.

[971] Part of these instructions went to the Free Russian Air Force supporting Army Group Center, when Maximciuc was the commanding officer of the fighter squadron.

[972] Steenberg, *Vlasov*, p. 124. This fact would be ignored after the unit surrendered to the British in April 1945. Stalin convinced his ally that the unit was indeed the *15th der SS* Division, and the men were handed over. No one is known to have survived.

[973] Overy, *Russia's War*, p. 128

[974] Steenberg, p. 117.

[975] Wolff interview, January 1984.

[976] Kumm interview, February 1984.

[977] Comment made to Koestring by Ewald von Kleist upon his arrival in Vinnitsa on 13 August 1942.

[978] Steenberg, *Vlasov*, p. 175.

[979] Wolff was transferred to Northern Italy at this time and was well aware of the Cossack efforts, and many of them would survive, and as stragglers enter his area of responsibility.

[980] According to Wolff, Bunyachenko was so alarmed at the state the men were in when he received them, he shot some of the officers and "detained" the rest "Cossack style." There is no record as to what this meant exactly, but he did manage to restore order and discipline within a few days.

[981] Steenberg, *Vlasov*, p. 183.

[982] Ibid. p. 130.

[983] Ibid. p. 190. This was also stated by Wolff in 1984. Albrecht "Smiling Albert" Kesselring (1885-1960) was replaced by *Generaloberst* Heinrich von Vietinghoff as Army Group Commander in Northern Italy. Kesselring was sentenced to death at Nuremberg, but the sentence was commuted to life, and he was released in 1952. He joined the *Bundesluftwaffe* before his death.

[984] Rudy A. D'Angelo, *World War II* (September 1999) p. 16.

[985] Alexander (1891-1969), 1st Earl Alexander of Tunis commanded the British 1st Division in France in 1939-40; C-in-C Burma in 1942, reassigned to North Africa August 1942, becoming deputy to Eisenhower in 1943 in Tunisia. He became a Field Marshal in command of Allied Forces MTO in 1944.

[986] Rudy D'Angelo, pp. 190-91.

[987] Ibid. p. 191.

[988] Ibid. p. 195.

[989] Ibid. p. 196.

[990] Ibid.

[991] These included the Mounted Artillery Battery, 1st Don Cossack Regiment, 2nd Siberian Cossack Regiment, 4th Kuban Cossack Regiment, and a myriad of other units thrown together as their ranks were decimated.

[992] This was similar to the order Leonidas Maximciuc received from Vlasov regarding the fighter squadron, where the men had to choose to return to Romania anonymously or surrender to the British with Vlasov.

[993] For the primary source records of Army Group Vistula during this period see U.S. National Archives microfilm series T311, Rolls 167-70.

[994] Heinrici was the commander of Army Group Vistula, but he had been replaced and given defensive responsibilities during the Seelow Heights campaign in April 1945.

[995] Manteuffel, Heinrici, and Busse were interviewed by Cornelius Ryan after the war for his book *The Last Battle*. This interview is located in the Cornelius Ryan papers, Ohio State University, Box 67, Folder 16. Courtesy of Timothy A. Wray.

[996] *Stukageschwader-2* named for WW I ace Maximilian Immelman, inventor of the combat maneuver known as the "Immelman Turn" and holder of the *Pour le Merite*, which received its nickname "Blue Max" from him. The unit was commanded by *Oberst* Hans-Ulrich Ruedel. On Ruedel's unit in action, see Pat McTaggart, *World War II* (July 1993) pp. 30-7.

[997] See references to Bunyachenko, Schoerner and Busse in Steenberg, *Vlasov*, pp. 186-90.

[998] Kerscher, Kumm, and Wolff interviews. See also Overy, *Russia's War*, p. 250.

[999] King Tiger, or Tiger II models.

[1000] Kerscher interview, 1992.

[1001] See reference in Steenberg, *Vlasov,* p. 163. The Galician division was decimated in July 1944 at Brody, and was never able to be completely rejuvenated.

[1002] Wolff interview.

[1003] Steenberg, *Vlasov*, pp. 202-4.

[1004] Mark Wayne Clark (1896-1984), WW I veteran and deputy to Eisenhower in 1942; commanded 5th U.S. Army in Italy, and later commanded the occupation forces in Austria. He was also C-in-C of UN forces in Korea from 1952-53.

[1005] Wolff interview.

[1006] On the participants and peculiarities regarding this signing, see Overy, *Russia's War*, p. 278.

[1007] Steenberg, p. 203.

[1008] Alexander McCarrell Patch (1889-1945) commanded the U.S. XIV Corps on Guadalcanal in 1942; in 1944 he commanded 7th Army during *Dragoon* and fought to Alsace. His army crossed the Rhine on 26 March 1945.

[1009] Steenberg, *Vlasov,* p. 211.

[1010] Ibid.

[1011] Ibid.

[1012] George Smith Patton (1885-1945) was a WW I veteran and commanded the 2nd Armored Division in 1940 and the 1st Armored Corps in 1941. His force landed at Casablanca during *Torch*; he commanded the 7th Army in Sicily (*Husky*) and 3rd Army across France into Germany and Czechoslovakia in 1944-45. His last command was the 15th Army, a paper command writing the history of the war. He died following a traffic accident.

[1013] Antilevski was awarded "Hero of the Soviet Union" for destroying over thirty German aircraft and a dozen German tanks while assigned to a Red Banner Squadron, the elite of the Red Air Force. See reference in Steenberg, *Vlasov*, p. 124.

[1014] Interview with Maximciuc in 1996.

[1015] Steenberg, *Vlasov*, pp. 205-7.

[1016] Ibid.

[1017] Plattling would prove to be one of the most blatant examples of American deception, since all of these men were handed over to the Soviets. Hundreds committed suicide, while the rest vanished without a trace. See also Steenberg, *Vlasov*, pp. 205-10 regarding Captain Donahue's meeting with Vlasov.

[1018] Ibid. p. 217.

[1019] See Overy, *Russia's War*, p. 299.

[1020] Ibid. p. 302.

[1021] Ibid. p. 303.

[1022] Steenberg, p. 225. These figures seemed accurate to Karl Wolff, who was the first person to present them to me when he showed me this very book, which I located again years later.

[1023] Norway and Denmark were the first two nations to receive the attentions of Himmler's chief recruiter, Gottlob Berger, following Hitler's approval on 17 April 1940, although active induction did not occur until 1941. This became the nucleus of the *"Nordland"* Regiment, later to become the *Waffen SS* Division *"Nordland."* See Mark P. Gingerich, *"Waffen SS* Recruitment in the Germanic Lands, 1940-41," *The Historian*, Vol. 59, No. 4 (Summer 1997), 818. For more on Berger see Black, *Ernst Kaltenbrunner*, pp. 142, 173, 224-5. Vidkun Quisling, leader of *Nasjonal Samling* (National Unity) Party. It is ironic that, upon Britain and France declaring war upon Germany, King Haakon VII formally announced Norway's neutrality, and Britain was the first nation to violate it, despite the fact that most of Norway's commerce was with the newly formed Allies. Hitler had no intention of invading Norway to maintain his control over the rail transport of Swedish iron ore, since neutrals may engage in commerce with any and all belligerents. Churchill actually violated the neutrality, forcing Hitler to launch his invasion.

[1024] Himmler ordered a recruiting office established in The Hague on 25 May 1940, with the assistance of Anton Muscal, fascist leader of *Nationaal Socialistische Beweging* (National Socialist Movement). Hitler followed up two days later and formally authorized the formation of the *"Westland"* Regiment that consisted of primarily Flemish and Dutch *Freiwilligen*. Ibid. p. 819.

[1025] Flemish and Walloon Belgians were the next major group to be considered, primarily through the energies of Leon Degrelle and Gustav de Cleq, leader of *Vlaamsch Nationaal Verbond* (Flemish National Union). Ibid.

[1026] Ibid. p. 821. The meeting of 20 May 1940 between Cecil von Renthe-Vink, the German ambassador to Denmark and Himmler's appointed representatives outlined the recruiting of Danes. Recruiting and screening would occur in Hamburg, not Denmark. Many of these men were Danish volunteers who had served during the Winter War with Finland, scheduled to return early in July 1940, and would be placed in the *"Nordland"* Regiment. It would ironically be *"Nordland"* that would be the last combat strength *SS* Division to support Felix Steiner during the final days in Berlin. The same recruiting effort went into staffing the ranks of the newly organized *"Westland"* Regiment.

[1027] Karl Wolff interview, January 1984. The *Allgemeine SS* would receive many non-Germans within its ranks, although as the war progressed the *Waffen SS* demanded the most attention due to high casualty rates.

[1028] Gingerich, pp. 820-1.

[1029] Ibid. p. 821.

[1030] Ibid.

[1031] Ibid. p. 825. Hitler ordered the *Wehrmacht* to attain 180 divisions by 1 May 1941, and part of this program was the creation of the new 5th *Waffen SS* Division *"Wiking"* in September 1940, on Hitler's orders. Felix Steiner, formerly commanding the *"Nordland"* Regiment would become the first division commander of what would grow into a *SS Panzer* Division. This was the first *SS Freiwilligen* division, comprised of Danes, Dutch and Norwegians.

[1032] Hossfelder interview, 1985.

[1033] Gingerich, p. 830.

[1034] Ibid. Citing Berger's speech at Magdeburg on 27-30 April 1942, BA/NS19/2456, *Militaerarchiv* Freiburg.

[1035] *Generalleutnant* Adolf Galland interview of 1995. Galland was present during this meeting, long with *Generalleutnant* (then *Oberstleutnant*) Johannes Steinhoff.

[1036] Koronov interview, 1993.

[1037] See reference in Overy, *Russia's War*, pp. 145-6.

[1038] *Guerrilla Warfare and Counterinsurgency: US-Soviet Policy in the Third World*, pp. 216-17. Most of the partisan and anti-partisan activity was conducted by the *GRU*, although the *NKVD-NKGB* under General Mamsurov (who was successful in Finland and Spain) operated independently.

[1039] Ibid. pp. 214-5.

[1040] Ibid.

[1041] Niedermayer (8 November 1885-25 September 1948) was *Kommandeur der Ostruppen z.b.V. 703* and later *Oberkommando West* on 21 May 1944, and was a Soviet POW after the war. See records at *Militaerarchiv* Freiburg, N-122 in total. On Vlasov see N-122/3.

[1042] See N-122/2.

[1043] This was a curious footnote in history. The Allied entry into Iran 1941 saw the Shah Pahlavi ousted and his son Rezan placed on the Peacock Throne. Due to the possibility that the new Shah would not be pro-German, a group of brothers from the Ghasaghai clan planned an assassination of Rezan. Nothing came of it. See NA M-1270/24/0532.

[1044] On the Iranians and the correspondence with Malek Mansour Solat Ghasahghai and Mohammed Hussein Solat-Ghasahghai on 16 April 1942 see N-122/ 9 and on the Turks see N-122/3-4, 6-7.

[1045] See N-122/6-7.

[1046] Orlov's widow, Eleanore is a German national living in the United States, and she was instrumental in translating and supplying documents for this book.

[1047] Gunn, p. 16; Carr, *Arms, Autarky and Aggression*, p. 20; and McKie, pp. 3-5. See also the works of Georges Vacher de Lapouge, Madison Grant, Ludwig Glumplowicz; Hitler, *Mein Kampf*, pp. 270, 286-7, 620; Kershaw, *Hitler*, "Hubris," p. 24; Paley, p. 24; T. Taylor (ed.), *Hitler's Secret Book* (New York: Grove Press, 1961) p. 22; Tait, p. 2; John W. Hiden and John E. Farquharson, *Explaining Hitler's Germany: Historians and the Third Reich* (London: Batsford, Academic and Educational, Ltd.) pp. 10-151; Jill Stephenson, p. 181; Hand, pp. 4-5, 12; Mills, p. 8; H.A. van der Zee, p. 100; and Laura Doran, pp. 5-9, 11, 36.

[1048] Manteuffel was the 25th of only 27 men to win the *Brillanten* (Diamonds) to the Knight's Cross, Oak Leaves and Swords. Currently there is no official record at either Koblenz or Freiburg.

[1049] The *Luftwaffe Fallschirmjaeger* (parachute hunters) units won cuff titles for various battles, such as Narvik (Norway), Eban Emael, and Crete. Army and *SS* units won sleeve shield titles for *Demyansk*, *Kholm, Kuban, Krim* (Crimea), as well as *Kurland* cuff titles issued when the war was almost over, just to name a few. Individual soldiers were awarded the Anti-Partisan Badge, a decoration in Bronze, Silver and Gold levels, depicting a sword intertwined by two serpents surrounded by a wreath.

[1050] Wolff interview, January 1984.

[1051] Ibid.

[1052] These were East Prussians and Kashubians. See Grant, p. 16, and Elizabeth Wiskemann, *Germany's Eastern Neighbors: Problems Relating to the Oder-Neisse Line and the Czech Frontier Regions* (London: Batsford, 1956) p. 96.

[1053] *12ᵗʰ SS "Hitlerjuegend"* (Hitler Youth) was created in 1944 with *Standartenfuehrer* (later *Gruppenfuehrer*) Kurt *"Panzer"* Meyer (1910-23 December 1961) as its first commander as an auxiliary *panzer* division. See Patrick Brode, "Personality: Kurt *"Panzer"* Meyer," *World War II*, Vol. 12, No. 6 (February 1998) Leesburg, VA: Primedia Publications, Inc. pp. 18-24, 74-5. The unit took its name from the Hitler Youth that had replaced all other youth organizations by invoking the Hitler Youth Law on 1 December 1936, including the Boy Scouts and religious organizations. This was followed by a ban on religious activities, including Nativity plays and scenes. Crucifixes were removed schools and hospitals later during the war, although the Bavarians rebelled against this and they were reinstated. See McGrath, p. 4; Julie M. Baxter, "Church and State in *Nazi* Germany." Unpublished Dissertation. Glasgow, UK: University of Strathclyde, Department of History, no date, p. 33; and Richard A. Gruenberger, *Twelve Year Reich: Social History of the Third Reich* (London: Weidenfeld & Nicolson, 1971) p. 443.

[1054] Special awards would be struck to commemorate the German victories, which occurred at high cost. The *Kholmschild* and *Demyanskschild* were worn proudly by the men who earned them, and their numbers were few indeed.

[1055] Fegelein was wounded several times and earned the Knight's Cross with Oak Leaves for personal gallantry, and was married to Eva Braun's sister. Fegelein's special status did not prevent him from being shot for cowardice in the last days of the war, a charge that was apparently unfounded.

[1056] Lombard later commanded the *31ˢᵗ SS Freiwilligen* Division *"Boehmen-Maehren"* when it was formed in October 1944. The unit ceased to exist by March 1945 and Lombard was captured by the Soviets. Lombard miraculously survived captivity and was released in 1955 along with Hans Baur, Hajo Herrmann, Erich Hartmann and thousands of other German POWs in amazingly good health. *Sturmbannfuehrer* Rudolf von Falkenhahn served in the Lubianka Prison in Moscow and again with Lombard in a labor camp in Siberia. See Quarrie, *Hitler's Samurai*, pp. 33, 139 (photo).

[1057] Albert L. Weeks, *World War Two* (November 1997) p. 8.

[1058] These estimates come from Karl Wolff and Otto Kumm. Leon Degrelle thought the number was more like 18,000 during his interview.

[1059] The only other contingent with greater numbers was the Vlasov Army, and this was placed into its own separate command.

[1060] See Mills, p. 61; R.A.C. Parker, *Struggle for Survival: History of the Second World War* (Oxford, UK: Oxford University Press, 1989) p. 284.

[1061] Masajiro Kawato of the Imperial Japanese Navy was also a sixteen-year-old fighter pilot, yet was three months older than Maximciuc. Kawato claimed eighteen kills, Maximciuc confirmed fifty-two kills. Maximciuc came to the University of North Carolina at Wilmington, where I was teaching in the History Department during the summer of 1999 and spoke at a seminar for students and the general public, discussing his family and career in Romanian, Free Russian and U.S. militaries over career spanning six decades.

[1062] Grant, p. 20.

[1063] *Daily Record & Mail.* 6, 8, 12 September 1939. See also John C. Breen, pp. 15-6. David Dilks (ed.), *Diaries of Alexander Caldogan.* 1ˢᵗ ed. (London: Cassell, 1971) p. 226. Much of this feeling by Vlasov may stem from the fact that Goering had maintained secret communications (although the *Abwehr* was aware of them) with the British throughout the war, although the nature of these contacts is unknown. See Robert Rhodes James (ed.), *CHIPS: The Diaries of Sir Henry Channon*, 1ˢᵗ ed. (London: Weidenfeld & Nicolson, 1967) pp. 210, 230, 261, and John C. Breen, pp. 16-7, 23-5.

[1064] James Kleinwald, "No Relief for Stubborn Volunteers," *World War II*, Vol.7, No. 1 (May 1992) Leesburg, VA: Empire Press, Inc. pp. 30-6.

[1065] Supported by Nikolina and Koronov interviews.

[1066] Most of the men who survived the Russian Campaign died alongside Felix Steiner in the last ditch stand in Berlin in May 1945.

[1067] See such works as K.D. Bracher, *The German Dictatorship*; H.C. Deutsch, *The Conspiracy Against Hitler in the Twilight War* (Minneapolis, MN: University of Minnesota Press, 1968); Wolfgang Foerster, *Generaloberst Ludwig Beck* (Munich: 1953); Foot, *Resistance: European Resistance to Nazism, 1940-45*, 2nd ed. (London, UK and New York: McGraw Hill, 1977); Fraenkel and Manvel, *The Canaris Conspiracy* and also *Der 20 Juli* (Berlin: 1964); Robert J. O'Neill, *The German Army and the Nazi Party, 1933-1939* (London: Cassell, 1966); T. Prittie, *Germans Against Hitler* (London: Hutchinson, 1964); Gerhard Ritter, *The German Resistance: Carl Goerdeler's Struggle Against Tyranny* (Glasgow, UK: 1958); H. Rothfels, *The German Opposition to Hitler* (London: Oswald Wolff, 1961); and Fabien von Schlabrendorff, *The Secret War Against Hitler* (London: Hodder & Stoughton, 1966). For specific references on the pre-war opposition see Rona Dickie, p. 28; McGrath, pp. 66-76, Hans-Joachim Reichhardt and H. Graml and Hans Mommsen, *The German Resistance to Hitler* (London: Batsford, 1970) p. 146; Allan William Tait, p. 14; Carr, *Arms, Autarky and Aggression*, p. 172; Jacobson, *July 20, 1944*, p. 23; Hildebrand, *Foreign Policy*, p. 75.

[1068] McKie, p. 30. See also Killen, p. 32, Osborne, p. 6; Tait, pp. 1, 3, 11, 14; Carr, *Arms*, pp. 33, 172; Jacobson, *July 20, 1944*, p. 23; W.R. Keylor, pp. 80-1, 86; Tait, pp. 14, 39, 41; Bullock, *Hitler*, p. 467; and Devaney, ch.5, pp. 3-4; Ch. 6, pp. 4-5.

[1069] Ethnic Germans had been attacked and killed in anti-German protests, offering Hitler the justification to invade. See R.A. McIntyre, introduction, pp. v. See also Gunn, pp. 17, 37; H.W. Koch, "Hitler's Programme and the Genesis of Operation Barbarossa," *The Historical Journal*, Vol. 26 (1983) p. 143; G. Stoakes, *Hitler and the Quest for World Domination* (London, New York: Berg, 1986) p. 227; McKenna, p. 40; Ian Kershaw, *Hitler*, "Hubris," p. 145; Allan William Tait, p. 14; and A.J.P. Taylor, *Origins of the Second World War* (London: Hamish Hamilton, Ltd. 1961) p. 229.

[1070] McGrath, p. 73, and K.D. Bracher, *The German Dictatorship*. p. 395. See also Gunn, pp. 25-6, 37; E. Eyck, *A History of the Weimar Republic* (Cambridge, MA: Harvard University Press, 1964) p. 306; and W. Carr, *Arms*, p. 161. See also McKenna, p. 35; Richard Overy, *War and Economy in the Third Reich* (London: Oxford University Press, 1994) pp. 148-55; Mommsen, *Reflections*, p. 93; Bullock, *Hitler*, pp. 429-30; Tait, pp. 1, 10, 12-13, 15, 22-23, 29, 35, 40, 45; Swan, pp. 29-33, 37; Hiden, *Germany and Europe, 1919-1939*, p. 144; and McKie, p. 30.

[1071] See Gunn, p. 30; and A.J.P. Taylor, *The Origins of the Second World War*, p. 301.

[1072] See John Garner, p. 17.

[1073] *Generaloberst* Ludwig Beck called 2 August 1934 the "blackest day of my life," although he also took the oath. See Gunn, p. 25; Matthew Cooper, *The German Army 1933-1945: Its Political and Military Failure* (London: MacDonald & James, 1978) pp. 7, 37; and O'Neill, *The German Army*, p. 161. See also McGrath, pp. 66, 69; and D.C. Watt, *Too Serious a Business: European Armed Forces and the Approach to the Second World War* (London: Temple Smith, 1975). p. 40. Hitler's securing the loyalty of the German officer corps was solidified by his policy of ignoring the Versailles Treaty, and on 30 June 1934 after the "Knight of the Long Knives." The removal of the *SA* as a contender to the Army solved several issues for Hitler, and allowed his own *SS* to rise to numerically small yet great political prominence. McGrath, pp. 69, 71. See also Cooper, *The German Army*, p. 20.

[1074] "Center Party," a predominantly Catholic political group, basically opposed to the ideals of racism and the rhetoric of the *NSDAP*, which Hitler found incompatible within his version of the *Volksgemeinschaft* (People's, or National Community). Hitler included the Protestant and Catholic religious orders within his plan for complete *Gleischaltung* (Cooperation) among the various groups within Germany upon coming to power, including the Army, because he knew that he still needed mass support, and attacking the churches would not be in his best interest until he had consolidated his power. McGrath, pp. 5, 6, 9, 10, 33-6, 42, 67-9. See also Baxter, pp. 6, 8, 38; on *Gleischaltung* see pp. 24-5, 43.

[1075] Julie M. Baxter, pp. 2-4. See also Bracher, *The German Dictatorship*, p. 473.

[1076] McGrath, pp. 42-4, 57. See also G.O. Kent, "Pope Pius XII and Germany: Some Aspects of German-Vatican relations, 1933-1943," *American History Review*, No. 70 (1964-65) 59-68; Julie M. Baxter, pp. 6, 18-22, 34, 40, 43; and Bracher, *The German Dictatorship*, p. 480.

[1077] McGrath, pp. 39-54. See also J.S. Conway, *The Nazi Persecution of the Churches, 1933-1945* (London: Weidenfeld & Nicolson, 1968) p. xiii; J.R.C. Wright, *"Above Parties": the Political Attitudes of the German Protestant Church Leadership, 1918-1933* (London: Oxford University Press, 1974) p. vi; Baxter, pp. 3-4.

[1078] See Baxter, p. 36 and K.D. Bracher, *The German Dictatorship*, p. 461.

[1079] Julie M. Baxter, p. 37.

[1080] Some 5,000 clergymen were incarcerated, with approximately 2,000 perishing. Ibid. pp. 38-9. See also Bracher, *The German Dictatorship*, p. 477. Regarding Jews in the camps, see Laura Doran, pp. 27-34; and Hand, pp. 8-13. Also on euthanasia see Laska, p. 14.

[1081] Bonhoeffer's record is located at *Bundesarchiv* Koblenz, N-1308.

[1082] Baxter, pp. 39, 43. See also Kershaw, *The Nazi Dictatorship*, p. 174.

[1083] In particular: McGrath, p. 1; Waddell, pp. 9, 28-9, 31-50; Ritter, p. 104; O'Neill, p. 169; Wolfgang Foerster, p. 97; Fabien von Schlabrendorf, p. 252; Fraenkel and Manvel, *Der 20 Juli*. pp. 71, 147.

[1084] The "White Rose" leadership, including its legendary leader, twenty-two year old Sophie Scholl were arrested and Scholl beheaded on 22 February 1943. See Baxter, p. 40; and H. Siefken (ed.),*Die WeiBe Rose: Student Resistance to National Socialism, 1942-43* (London: University of Nottingham Press, 1991) p. 23. See also Kershaw, *The Nazi Dictatorship,* pp. 152, 155; Laska, p. 153. During this sweep over 400 nuns are known to have perished as well. Other groups included "Red Orchestra" and "Harro Schulze-Boysen," led by Libertas Schulze-Boysen.

[1085] Steenberg, *Vlasov,* p. 134. This was collected by Steenberg during his interview with Guenther d'Alquen, and was corroborated by both Hans Baur and Karl Wolff, who stated that this information had in fact reached Himmler and Hitler, but that "it was not considered important."

[1086] Donnelly, p .21, and Deutscher, *Stalin*, p. 377.

[1087] Grant, p. 20.

[1088] Adams, p. 1.

[1089] Maximciuc came and addressed a class I was teaching at the University of North Carolina in July 1999, offering his personal account of fighting against Stalin and his life as a Cossack.

[1090] Part of this pro-fascist and anti-Communist feeling throughout Europe may be explained in that the British were even divided in their own outlook on Germany in the early years of the war. Comments from Sir Henry Channon during the Spanish Civil War in September 1939 regarding Germany as "the west's best hope of destroying Communism" could have been tacitly viewed as British support for Hitler. See John C. Breen, p. 28 and Robert R. James, p. 114.

[1091] Breen, pp. 37-41. Breen also cites Lord Beaverbrook's concerns that an Allied stand against the Soviets would possibly force Stalin to join Hitler in an alliance. These concerns were mirrored in the *Daily Express* and *London Evening Standard,* p. 40; *Daily Record & Mail*, 2 January 1940 and Douglas Clark, *Three Days to Catastrophe* (London: Hammond, 1966) p. 15. See also Hadley Cantril (ed.),*Public Opinion 1935-1946*, 1ˢᵗ ed. (Princeton, NJ: Princeton University Press, 1951) p. 276. See also Donnelly, p. 47; Beloff, *The Foreign Policy of Soviet Russia*. Vol. 2. pp. 307-8, and Liddell-Hart, *History of the Second World War*, pp. 47-8. See also Grant, p. 19, and Killen, p. 9.

[1092] Killen, p. 22. This failure to support Spain forced Stalin to increase aid to the republicans in order to counter the German-Italian contributions, thus widening the gulf between fascist and Communist groups in Europe. This also included soldiers and airmen who participated in the fighting.

[1093] For more on Ribbentrop (1893-1946) who was hanged at Nuremberg see *Militaerarchiv* Freiburg and *Bundesarchiv* Koblenz N-1163

[1094] E. Bauer, *The History of World War II,* Vol. 1 (London: Orbis, 1983) p. 7, and Donnelly, p. 47. The circular stated that Italy and Belgium could not ship weapons, aircraft and ammunition across Germany to support Finland. This order was issued due to the Germans wishing exclusive rights to supply their potential ally currently fighting a future belligerent nation. Ribbentrop's interests also concerned the Czechoslovakian and Polish problems, and his foreign policy was ideologically married to Hitler's personal will, shared by the ultimate desires of the armed forces and big business alike. See Gunn, p. 27; and Hildebrand, *Foreign Policy of the Third Reich*, pp. 28, 49.

[1095] Breen, p. 41. See also *Forward*, 6 January 1940. Keyes was supported by General Gough who wanted to blockade Murmansk as well as the German ports. See also Grant, pp. 13, 27-8 regarding resettlement plans. See also Anna Bramwell, "The Resettlement of the Ethnic Germans, 1939-41," Unpublished Thesis, *Workshop on European and Middle East Refugees in the Twentieth Century*, Oxford University: August 1985; see also Gunn, pp. 19, 32 and McKenna, pp. 36, 38.

[1096] Killen, p. 8; and Alba, p. 167.

[1097] These men fell under the command of *Generalfeldmarschall* Ferdinand Schoerner, who eventually surrendered *Army Group Kurland* four days after the fall of Berlin.

[1098] Donnelly, p. 52.

[1099] Heaton, *World War II* (January 1998) pp. 30-6.

[1100] McIntyre, *Introduction*, p. iv. Czechoslovakia was occupied primarily by Western Allied forces, in particular the U.S. Army. It later fell into the Soviet sphere after the war due to the terms discussed at the Tehran Conference.

[1101] Comment from Karl Wolff, who temporarily functioned as Balkans Chief in Berlin under Himmler, before assuming his duties as *Persoenlich Stabs des Reichsfuehrers SS, Rohstoffamt* in March 1944, during his interview in January 1984. See also N-1465/8.

[1102] The distribution was as follows: 5,000 assigned to fighting units, 4, 000 spies, 25,000 working in clandestine/sabotage, publishing, and assisting Allied airmen, and 40,000 functioning as assistants in hiding, feeding and supporting the partisans. See Mills, pp. 1, 40, 49, 51; *Report on the First International Conference on the History of the Resistance Movements: Anti-Nazi Resistance in the Netherlands*, p. 147; van der Zee, p. 109; and H.C. Trouw, "The Resistance of the Netherlands Churches," *Annals of the American Academy*, Vol. 245 (1946) 159.

[1103] Mills, p. 51; Wright, *The Ordeal of Total War*, p. 149.

[1104] Mills, pp. 36-40; Lord Russell of Liverpool, *Scourge of the Swastika* (London: 1954) pp. 246-248; Warmbrunn, p. 35; H.L. Mason, 324. The Dutch were also far less active in supporting German atrocities against Jews, although collaboration did occur; see Mills, pp. 38-9, H.A. van der Zee, p. 128; Mason, "Testing Human Bonds," pp. 322-3; A.M. Meerloo, *Total War and the Human Mind: A Psychologist's Experience in Occupied Holland* (London: G. Allen & Unwin, 1944) p. 65; and W.B. Mass, *The Netherlands at War: 1940-45* (London: 1970) p. 13.

[1105] Mills, p. 50; Wright, *The Ordeal of Total War*, p. 148.

[1106] Aaron Bank interview, 1986.

[1107] Tait, pp. 20-1.

[1108] Breen, pp. 77-78 *(fn.5)*. See also the *Daily Record and Mail*, 5 September 1939.

[1109] John Gardner, pp. 22-3, 27; Gunn, p. 33. This was due to the four-year rearmament plan. See also Richard J. Overy, *The Nazi Economic Recovery 1932-39* (London: Macmillan, 1982) p. 53, and D. Kaiser, Tim Mason and Richard J. Overy, "Debate Germany: 'Domestic Crisis' and War in 1939," *Past and Present*, vol. 122 (1989) pp. 200-40. All three of the historians do not agree on every aspect of the *Nazi* recovery plans and the validity of the economic structure. All do agree that Germany needed wars of expansion to retain access to raw materials, since treaties were not always secure on their own. However, the war had to be short and immediately successful to avert material, political, and economic disaster. See also Bullock, *Hitler*, p. 357; and McKenna on unemployment figures, p. 34. Germany suffered approximately 6,000,000 persons unemployed between 1930-1932. Near Full employment was reached by 1936, including women's work in factories for domestic production, thus the beginning of Goering's "Four Year Plan," formed in conjunction with Dr. Hjalmar Schacht's

"New Plan." See Paley, p. 32; Ridley, p. 10; Alan S. Milward, *The Economic History Review*, Vol. 23, No. 2 (August 1970) p. 337; Tait, p. 12; and Koonz, *Mothers in the Fatherland: Women, the Family and Nazi Politics* (New York: St. Martin's Press, 1987) p. 394. This would increase exponentially as the war carried on. See Koonz, p. 394; Avraham Barkai, *Nazi Economics: Ideology, Theory, and Policy,* Ruth Hadass-Vashitz, Trans. (Oxford, UK: Berg, 1990) p. 226; Hiden and Farquharson, *Explaining Hitler's Germany,* pp. 143, 148; Leila J. Rupp, *Mobilizing Women for War: German and American Propaganda, 1939-1945* (Princeton, NJ: Princeton University Press, 1978) p. 74; Tait, pp. 20, 38; Ian Kershaw, *Popular Opinion and Political Dissent in the Third Reich: Bavaria 1933-1945* (Oxford, UK: Clarendon Press, 1983) pp. 90-1; Noakes and Pridham, *Documents on Nazism*, Vol. 1, p. 408; Jaqueline Davidson, p. 2; and David Schoenbaum, *Hitler's Social Revolution: Class and Status in Nazi Germany, 1933-1939* (New York: Norton, 1980) pp. 184-85. On Schacht's New Plan, see Larry Neal, "The Economics and Finance of Bilateral Clearing Agreements: Germany, 1934-8," *The Economic History Review*, Vol. 32, No. 3 (August 1979) 392-404.

[1110] John C. Breen, pp. 86-7 (fn.15). The unemployment figure stated here is 1,330,928. See *Daily Record and Mail,* 3 October 1939. 1932 estimates ran approximately 15.6% and 22.5% unemployed. See also Louise McElhone, "British Society During the Second World War: United or Divided?" Unpublished Dissertation. Glasgow, UK: University of Strathclyde, Dept. of History, 1986, pp. 2-7. This work cites the Hugh Dalton reports, which offer glaring evidence of the problem. See also Hugh Dalton, *The Fateful Years: Memoirs, 1931-45* Vol. 2 of 3 (London:, 1957). See Overy's reference to Dalton's perceptions of the Soviet military collapse in Overy, *Russia's War*, p. 76.

[1111] Killen, p. 7.

[1112] McKie, p. 7; David Welch, "Propaganda and Indoctrination in the Third *Reich*: Success or Failure?" *History Quarterly*, Vol. 17, No. 4 (1987) p. 404; Detlev Peukert, *Inside Nazi Germany: Conformity, Opposition, and Racism in Everyday Life,* Trans. Richard Deveson (New Haven, CT: Yale University Press, 1987) pp. 176-7, Rupp, *Mobilizing Women for War*, pp. 40, 47; Tim Mason, "Women in Germany, 1925-1940: Family, Welfare and Work," Jane Caplan, (ed.), *Nazism, Fascism, and the Working Class* (New York: Cambridge University Press, 1995) pp. 131-211; Jill Stephenson, "Middle Class Women and National Socialist 'Service,' " *History*, Vol. 67, No. 229 (1982) 8; David Schoenbaum, p. 178; Guenther Mai, "National Socialist Factory Cell Organization and German Labor Front: National Socialist Labor Policy and Organizations," Conan Fischer (ed.), *The Rise of National Socialism and the Working Classes in Weimar Germany* (Oxford, UK: Berghahn, 1996) pp. 124-125; Hand, pp. 7, 20; Tait, pp. 35, 37; Ridley, p. 14; and Chaudry, p. 6.

[1113] Breen, pp. 48-50. The largest of these meetings were held in Glasgow on 24 September 1939 and was attended by approximately 2,000 people. See also *Forward*, 16 September 1939. Conscription was authorized on 26 April 1939 by the Military Training Act, later followed on 24 August of the Emergency Powers Act, becoming law by a passage through parliament, and exercised on 28 August. This gave the government unprecedented powers over the civilian population, which was opposed by various political factions, including the Welsh and Scottish nationalists. The ages for conscription were to include men between ages eighteen and twenty-seven, with approximately 2,000,000 men drafted. See Breen, p. 55 (citing *Keesings Contemporary Archives*, p. 2671) p. 75 *(fn3)* p. 76, on Communist factions had constantly "called for a war on two fronts-against Hitler and against British capitalism," p .84. This attitude by Hitler was mentioned by *Generalleutnant* Guenther Rall during his interview. Refer to Heaton, *World War II* (March 1995) p. 39.

[1114] Breen, pp. 78-83, 92-4. See also the *Daily Record and Mail* (September 1939), pp. 2, 8, 13, 15; *Forward*, 16 September 1939 and 9, 16 March 1940.

[1115] Breen, pp. 84-5; also *fn.14.*

[1116] Ibid. p. 85. The British did in fact create the first concentration camps during the Boer War, in which thousands of civilians died of hunger and disease.

[1117] This was a meeting where *Oberleutnant* (later *Generalleutnant*) Rall (275 victories) received the Oak Leaves (later receiving the Swords). He was accompanied by *Luftwaffe Hauptmann* (later *Generalleutnant*) Johannes Steinhoff (176 victories) and several other airmen and soldiers. See Heaton, *World War II* (March 1995) p. 37. See also McElhone, pp. 8, 22, 33-40, 46; and Foot, *Aneurin Bevan: A Biography, Vol.1, 1897-1945* (London: Macgibbon & Kee, 1963) pp. 318, 330; Angus Calder, *The People's War: Britain 1939-1945* (London: Jonathan Cape, 1969) pp. 34, 96,178, 182, 212-15 (on class differences see pp. 166, 186). Regarding class differences in British society and welfare provisions, Louise McElhone, pp. 18-21, 42-45, 47-49; B. Bond and I. Roy (eds.) *War and Society* (Leicester, UK: 1984) p. 261; and J.B. Dillon, "An Investigation into the Working-Class Housing in Scotland Between 1920-1039 with Particular Analysis of the Springburn Ward of Glasgow." Unpublished Dissertation. Glasgow, UK: University of Strathclyde, Department of History, 1974, pp. 45-46. See also Derek Fraser, *The Evolution of the British Welfare State: A History of Social Policy Since the Industrial Revolution* (London: Macmillan, 1973) pp. 193, 195; M. Bruce, *The Coming of the Welfare State* (London: Methuen, 1961) p. 261; and Martin Gilbert, *Finest Hour: Winston S. Churchill 1941-1945,* 2nd ed. (London: Heinemann/Minerva, 1983) pp. 143, 298. See also A. Marwick, *The Home Front* (London: Thomas Hudson, 1976) p. 68. Angus Calder and Dorothy Sheridan, *Speak for Yourself: A Mass Observation Anthology 1937-1949* (London: Cape, 1984) p. 89. See also *Daily Record*, 14 September 1939, as cited by Louis McElhone, p. 44 regarding the children's evacuation.

[1118] Stalin's first two plans held little in the way of military expenditure. However, the third Five-Year Plan in 1937 was considerably different, and a full quarter of the work force was slave labor. See Catriona Adams, pp. 6-7; Donnelly, p. 56; Roger Munting, *The Economic Development of the USSR* (London: Croom Helm, 1982) p. 112. See also Killen, pp. 6-7.

[1119] The concentration camp complex management was overseen by the *SS* Executive Office for the Economy and Administration *(WVHA)* whose chief was *Obergruppenfuehrer* Pohl. See Laura Doran, pp. 27-34 and on Pohl p. 30; on slave labor and wages see pp. 32-3. *Operation Barbarossa* was to resolve the labor shortage for Germany; see Allan William Tait, pp. 28-9; U. Herbert, "Labor and Extermination: Economic Interest and the Primacy of *Weltanschauung* in National Socialism," *Past and Present*, No. 138 (February 1993), p. 167; Alan Milward, *War, Economy and Society: 1939-1945* (London: Allen Lane, 1977) p. 225.

[1120] Breen, pp. 96-7.

[1121] Ibid. p. 54. In addition to the socialists and Communists there were independent factions, such as Mosely's fascists and the Welsh and Scottish Nationalists, who sponsored anti-conscription and a service avoidance policy. See Breen, pp. 57-59; also the *Daily Record and Mail*, 23 September 1939.

[1122] Baur interview, 1985. For an article on Baur, see Paul E. Riley, "Personality," *World War II*, Vol. 8, No. 1 (May 1993) Leesburg, VA: Empire Press, Inc., pp. 8, 68-72.

[1123] Hans Baur (1897-1993), *Hitler at My Side* (Houston, TX: Eichorn Publishing, 1986). Baur, a nine victory WW I ace and the last surviving member of Hitler's inner circle autographed a copy for this author after one of the many interviews conducted with him.

[1124] Baur interview, August 1984.

[1125] Recalled by Galland and Falkenhahn, and also related by Wolff. Part of Hitler's disbelief was von Brauchitsch's reports from the summer of 1941 stating the "Red Army had 'no large reserve formations'; it was a spent force." See Overy, *Russia's War*, p. 117.

[1126] Galland's many battles with Goering and Hitler eventually saw him fired as General of Fighters in January 1945. Galland was "too honest and open for his own good," claimed *Generalmajor* Hannes Trautloft, Inspector of Day Fighters for the *Luftwaffe* during an interview in 1995.

[1127] Bartov, *Hitler's Army*, p. 93.

[1128] Ibid. p. 98. On the courts-martial and death sentences, see pp. 98-105.

[1129] See Bartov also for the 13,000-15,000 German soldiers executed by their own military for various infractions, as compared to forty British, 100 French, and one American (Eddie Slovik). One can only speculate how many Red Army soldiers found a similar fate. On a specific incident regarding a Lance Corporal Franz Aigner who was shot for cowardice, see p. 97 (*en 157*) citing BA-MA/RH27-18/74, 30/12/41. Several soldiers were also sentenced to lengthy prison sentences for sleeping on duty.

[1130] Bartov, *Hitler's Army*, p. 100, citing BA-MA/RH27-18/131, 25/2/43.

[1131] Ibid. p. 104.

[1132] G.K. Williamson, p. 191; see also Quarrie, *Hitler's Samurai*, pp. 27, 100, 105, 150.

[1133] On Russian snipers, see Vladimir Belyakov, *World War II* (September 1992) p. 28, and Pat McTaggart, "Soviet Encirclement Thwarted," *World War II*, Vol. 8, No. 5 (January 1994) Leesburg, VA: Empire Press, Inc., p. 36.

[1134] Robert L. O'Connell, *Of Arms and Men: A History of War, Weapons and Aggression* (New York: Oxford University Press, 1989) p. 286. Quoted from S.L. Meyer, (ed.), *The Russian War Machine 1917-1945* (London: Cape, 1977) pp. 44, 195. See also Tsouras, p. 33 regarding the first person assessment written by *Generaloberst* Erhard Rauss regarding women partisans.

[1135] Kurt Student (1890-1958) was a WW I reconnaissance pilot and was chosen to create the German airborne force. He was wounded in Holland in 1940, but later served as commander of the *Luftwaffe Fallschirmjaeger.*

[1136] Mazower, *Inside Hitler's Greece*, p. 173 (*en 36*) citing BA-MA, RH 28-5/4b, "*Vergeltungs massnahmen*, 31 May 1941.

[1137] Time-Life Books, *Conquest of the Balkans* (Alexandria, VA: Time-Life Books, Inc., 1990) p. 160; also Kelly Bell, "Costly Capture of Crete," *World War II*, Vol. 14, No. 1 (May 1999) Leesburg, VA: Primedia Publications, Inc. pp. 50-6. The village of Alikianos was also paid a similar visit. See Mazower, *Inside Hitler's Greece*, p. 173.

[1138] Wilmington, North Carolina. (UPI), "Ex-*Nazi* Officer Gets 5 years," *Wilmington Star News*, 25 July 1997, Sec. A-1, p. 2. Priebke was originally sentenced to fifteen years, but this was reduced to five years due to his age and the fact that he never tried to conceal his identity, even while living in Argentine for almost fifty years.

[1139] See Al Hemingway, "Ghost Front Attack," *Military History,* Vol. 9, No. 3 (August 1992) Leesburg, VA: Cowles History Group, pp. 50-7. See also John F. Murphy, Jr., "Endless Chain of Battle," *World War II*, Vol. 6, No. 6 (March 1992) Leesburg, VA: Cowles History Group, pp. 38-45.

[1140] Cindy Hayostek, "Undercover," *World War II*, Vol. 14, No. 1 (May 1999) Leesburg: Primedia Publications Inc. pp. 8-10.

[1141] The actual units that passed through were *Fallschirmjaeger* of the 3rd Parachute Division commanded by *Oberst* Friedrich August *Graf* von der Heydte on 18 December 1944; the 9th *Waffen SS Panzer* Division "*Hohenstauffen*" commanded by *Gruppenfuehrer* Sylvester Stadler on 19 December; and the records proving that elements of 1st *Waffen SS Panzer* Division passed by on the day in question. On von der Heydte's operations afterward, see Danny S. Parker, "Ten Percent Chance of Victory," *World War II*, Vol. 7, No. 2 (July 1992) Leesburg, VA: Cowles History Group, pp. 46-52, 62. Von der Heydte surrendered to the US 9th Division on 22 December 1944. The author is a direct relation.

[1142] See Walzer, *Just and Unjust Wars*, pp. 133-4, citing the following: Ignazio Salone, "Reflections on the Welfare State," *Dissent* Vol. 8, No. 189 (1961).

[1143] The commander of the *Afrika Korps*, Erwin Rommel tore up the order upon receiving it, not believing that such conduct was worthy of professional soldiers. See Walzer, *Just and Unjust Wars*, p. 38.

[1144] Hitler's personal secretaries, Gerda Christian and Traudl Junge were interviewed regarding this and other subjects. Junge (who lived in Berlin) and Hans Baur were very forthcoming with regard to the orders being issued, especially the partisan edicts. Gerda Christian (who lived and was interviewed in Duesseldorf) was less forthcoming, and she passed away in 1997. Baur died in 1993. See also Davis, *Waffen SS*, pp. 13-4.

[1145] Major General R.H. Barry, "Military Balance Within Western Europe, May 10 1940," *History of the Second World War: An International History,* Vol. 1, p. 172; and Mills, p. 63.

[1146] Although this unit originated as a *Freiwilligen* regiment, it was designated *Panzer* and therefore regarded as a German unit. Only German units and the *"Wiking"* Division carried the designation *"Panzer."*

[1147] A specialized counterinsurgency unit that operated primarily in the Balkans. They were ruthlessly effective.

[1148] This division had thousands of foreigners pass through its ranks, although was still maintained as a German *SS* combat division.

[1149] "Hitler Youth" created in April 1944. The first commander was *Gruppenfuehrer* Kurt Meyer (1910-23 December 1961).

[1150] Bosnian Muslims were the majority of the force, with a few Albanians.

[1151] Polish Galician and Ukrainian expatriates. They had a rather good combat record.

[1152] Latvian *Freiwilligen,* a ruthless group when it came to combating the Soviets and partisans. Most died in the Kurland or in Soviet captivity.

[1153] The last commander was Fritz Klingenberg of Belgrade fame, who died on the Western Front in April 1945.

[1154] Latvian *Freiwilligen,* active in counterinsurgency warfare. Most would suffer the same fate as their comrades.

[1155] Estonians; same destiny as the Latvians.

[1156] This unit was almost unique in its counterinsurgency, almost equaling *"Handschar"* for their level of effectiveness and brutality against insurgents.

[1157] An outstanding counterinsurgency unit, often compared with *"Florian Geyer"* for their capabilities.

[1158] Croatian *Freiwilligen,* a rather ineffective unit that operated an extermination campaign against Serbs for a short time under Army direction. The unit never reached beyond battalion level, and the concept was abandoned. See NA M-1270/24/0115.

[1159] This unit carries the unit designator *23rd* which seems confusing, although this was organized along separate lines as an Army unit that was transferred to the *SS,* thus the numerical designation remained.

[1160] This was a hastily gathered group of volunteers thrown together to fight in the Carpathian Mountains.

[1161] Man for man perhaps the best foreign *Waffen SS* unit to be fielded, along with *"Wiking."* Less than 400 men survived by March 1945, and three (including Degrelle) were known to have been alive following the surrender.

[1162] Originally a brigade under Kaminsky, it became a division following the Warsaw Uprising of 1944.

[1163] *"Boehmen-Mahren"* (Bohemia-Moravia) was a unit created from anti-Benes pro-fascists and conscripts. It was a worthless unit.

[1164] Like so many other late war volunteer units, it was a division on paper only.

[1165] This unit was so completely destroyed there are no records of it even existing, only being mentioned in a couple of dispatches.

[1166] This was a penal unit, and quite a murderous group at that.

[1167] Dissolved and incorporated into *"Nordland."*

Bibliography

Abel, Theodore. *Why Hitler Came to Power.* Cambridge, Mass: Harvard University Press, 1938.

Abraham, David. *The Collapse of the Weimar Republic.* Princeton: Princeton University Press, 1981.

Abramsky C. and B.J. Williams. *Essays in Honour of E.H. Carr.* London: Macmillan, 1974.

Adamthwaite, A. *The Making of the Second World War.* London: George Allen & Unwin, 1979.

Ailsby, Christopher. *SS: Hell on the Eastern Front: The Waffen SS War in Russia, 1941-1945.* Osceola: Motorbooks International, 1998.

Ainsztein, Reuben. *Jewish resistance in Nazi Occupied Eastern Europe: With a Historical Survey of the Jew as a Fighter and Soldier in the Diaspora.* London: Elek Books, 1974

Alba, Victor. *The Communist Party in Spain.* Translated by Vincent G. Smith. New Brunswick, London: Transaction Publications, 1983.

Aldcroft, D.H. *The European Economy, 1914-1980.* London: Croom Helm, 1980.

Alexander, E. *Holding the Line: The Eisenhower Era.* Bloomington: Indiana University Press, 1975.

Alexiyevich, Svetlana. *War's Unwomanly Face.* Translation by Keith Hammond and Lyudmila Lezhneva. Moscow: Progress Publishers, 1988.

Allen, William Sheridan. *The Nazi Seizure of Power: The Experience of a Single German Town, 1930-1935.* London: Eyre & Spottiswoode, 1966.

Andreyev, Catherine. *Vlasov and the Russian Liberation Movement: Soviet Reality and Émigré Theories.* Cambridge, UK: Cambridge University Press, 1987.

Angebert, Jean and Michael. *The Occult and the Third Reich.* New York: Macmillan, 1974.

Angress, Werner T. *Stillborn Revolution: The Communist Bid for Power in Germany, 1921-1923.* Princeton: Princeton University Press, 1963.

Arad, Yitzhak, Shmuel Krakowski and Spector (eds.). *The Einsatzgruppen Reports.* New York: Holocaust Library and Yad Veshem Martyr's Remembrance Authority, 1989.

Armstrong, John. *Ukrainian Nationalism.* 3rd (ed.). Englewood, CA: Ukrainian Academic Press, 1990.

_____. (ed.) *The Soviet Partisans in World War II.* Madison: University of Wisconsin Press, 1964.

_____. *The Politics of Totalitarianism: The Communist Party of the Soviet Union from 1934 to the Present.* New York: Random House, 1961.

Armstrong, William, (ed.). *With Malice Toward None: A War Diary by Cecil H. King.* London: Sidgwick & Jackson, 1970.

Arnold-Foster, M. *The World at War.* Thames TV presentation, London: Methuen, 1983.

_____. *1939: The Making of the Second World War.* London: Andre Deutch, 1973.

Aster, S. *Anthony Eden*. Introduction by A.J.P. Taylor. London: Weidenfeld & Nicolson, 1976.

Avrich, Paul. *Russian Rebels, 1600-1800*. New York: W.W. Norton & Co., 1972.

Bailes, Kendall. *Technology and Society under Lenin and Stalin: Origins of the Soviet Technical Intelligentsia, 1917-1941*. Princeton: Princeton University Press, 1978.

Bailey, Ronald. *Partisans and Guerrillas*. Alexandria, VA: Time-Life Books, 1978.

Balchen, Bernt. *Come North With Me*. New York: E.P. Dutton, 1970.

Balfour, Michael, Leonard Graham and Julian Frisby. *Helmuth von Moltke: A Leader Against Hitler*. London: Macmillan, 1972.

Balfour, Michael Leonard Graham. *Germany: The Tides of Power*. London, New York: Routledge, 1992.

_____. *The Adversaries: America, Russia and the Open World 1941-62*. London: Routledge & Keegan Paul, 1981.

Banac, Ivo, (ed.). *Eastern Europe in Revolution*. Ithaca, New York: Cornell University Press, 1992.

_____. *The National Question in Yugoslavia*. Paperback reprint. Ithaca, NY: Cornell University Press, 1989.

Barber, John and Mark Harrison. *The Soviet Home Front: A Social and Economic History of the USSR in World War II*. London: Longman, 1991.

Barkai, Avraham. *Nazi Economics, Ideology, Theory and Policy*. New York: Oxford University/Berg Press, 1990.

Baron, Salo W. *The Russian Jew under the Tsars and the Soviets*. 2nd ed. New York, Munich: Schocken Books, 1987.

Bartov, Omer. *Hitler's Army: Soldiers, Nazis and War in the Third Reich*. New York: Oxford University Press, 1992.

_____. *The Eastern Front, 1941-1945: German Troops and the Barbarization of Warfare*. New York: St. Martin's Press, 1986.

Baturina, K.S. (ed.). *Pravda Stavshaia Legendoi*. Moscow: Alma Alta, 1964.

Bauer, E. *The History of World War II*. 3 vols. London: Orbis, 1983.

Baur, Hans. *Hitler at My Side*. Houston, Texas: Eichorn Publishing, 1987.

Bayer, Hans, Ray, Jr. Miller and John Toothman. *A Dog's Life*. New York: University Press of America, 1993.

Baynes, N.H., (ed.). *Documents on German Foreign Policy, 1918-1945, Series C (1933-1937) The Third Reich: First Phase*. 5 vols. London: British Foreign Office; Her Majesty's Stationary Office, 1957.

_____. *Documents on German Foreign Policy, 1918-1945, Series D (1937-1945), The Third Reich: First Phase*, 9 vols. Vols. 3-9. London: British Foreign Office; Her Majesty's Stationary Office, 1957.

Beloff, Max. *The Foreign Policy of Soviet Russia*. 2 vols. London: O.U.P. 1947.

Berghahn, V.R. *Modern Germany: Society, Economy and Politics in the Twentieth Century*. Cambridge, UK; New York: Cambridge University Press, 1982.

Bessel, Richard. *Political Violence and the Rise of Nazism*. New Haven, CT: Yale University Press, 1984.

Bessel, Richard and E.J. Feuchtwanger, (eds.). *Social Change and Political Development in Weimar Germany*. London: Croom Helm, 1981.

Best, Geoffrey. *Humanity in Warfare*. London: Weidenfeld & Nicolson, 1980.

Bethell, Nicholas. *The Great Betrayal: The Untold Story of Kim Philby's Biggest Coup*. London: Hodder & Stoughton, 1984.

_____. *The War Hitler Won, September 1939*. London: Allen Lane/Penguin, 1972.

Bettelheim, Charles. *Class Struggles in the USSR*. Sussex, UK: Harvester Press, 1976.

Bialer, Seweryn (ed.). *Stalin and His Generals: Soviet Military Memoirs of World War II*. New York: Pegasus, 1969.

Black, Peter R. *Ernst Kaltenbrunner: Ideological Soldier of the Third Reich*. Princeton: Princeton University Press, 1984.

Blum, John Morton. *From the Morgenthau Diaries. Years of Crisis, 1928-1938; Years of Urgency, 1938-1941; Years of War, 1941-1945*. Boston, Mass: Houghton Mifflin, 1959-1967.

Blythe, Ronald. *The Age of Illusion: England in the Twenties & Thirties.* London: Hamish Hamilton, 1963.
Bond, Brian and Ian Roy (eds.). *War and Society: A Yearbook of Military History.* London: Croom Helm, 1975.
Bond, B. *War and Society in Europe, 1870-1970.* Leicester, UK: Fontana, 1984.
Borowiec, Andrew. *Yugoslavia After Tito.* New York: Praeger, 1977.
Boyce, R. and E.M. Robertson (eds.). *Paths to War: New Essays on the Origins of the Second World War.* London: Macmillan, 1989.
Bracher, Karl Dietrich. *The German Dictatorship: The Origins, Structure and Consequences of National Socialism.* London: New York: Penguin, 1970.
Bramsted, Ernest K. *Goebbels and National Socialist Propaganda, 1925-1945.* Ann Arbor: University of Michigan Press, 1965.
Braun, Hans-Joachim. *The German Economy in the Twentieth Century.* London: Routledge, 1990.
Breitman, Richard. *German Socialism and Weimar Democracy.* Chapel Hill: University of North Carolina Press, 1981.
Branson, N. *Britain in the 1920s.* London: Weidenfeld & Nicolson, 1975.
_____. *Britain in the 1930s.* London: Weidenfeld & Nicolson, 1971.
Brenan, Gerald. *The Spanish Labyrinth: An Account of the Social and Political Background of the Civil War.* 2ⁿᵈ ed. New York: Cambridge University Press, 1969.
Briggs, A. (ed.). *They Saw it Happen: An Anthology of Eye-Witness Accounts of Events in British History, 1897-1940.* London: Blackwell, 1960.
Broadwater, J. *Eisenhower and the Anti-Communist Crusade.* Chapel Hill: University of North Carolina Press, 1992.
Brooks, Jeffrey. *When Russia Learned to Read: Literacy and Popular Literature, 1861-1917.* Princeton: Princeton University Press, 1985.
Broszat, Martin. *Hitler and the Collapse of Weimar Germany.* New York: Berg, 1987.
_____. *The Hitler State: The Foundation and Development of the Internal Structure of the Third Reich.* Translated by John W. Hiden. London: New York: Longman, 1981.
_____. *German National Socialism, 1919-1945* New York: Clio Press: 1966.
Broszat, Martin and Krausnick. *The Anatomy of the S.S. State.* Cambridge, UK: Cambridge University Press, 1968.
Brown, Archie (ed.). *Political Culture and Communist Studies.* New York: M.E. Sharpe, 1985.
Browning, Christopher. *Ordinary Men: Reserve Police Battalion 101 and the Final Solution in Poland.* New York: Harper Collins, 1992.
_____. *The Final Solution and the German Foreign Office: A Study of Referat D III of Abteilung Deutschland, 1940-43.* New York: Holmes & Meier, 1978.
Brownlee, Richard S. *Gray Ghosts of the Confederacy: Guerrilla Warfare in the West, 1861-1865.* Baton Rouge: Louisiana State University Press, 1984.
Broszat, Martin. *Hitler and the Collapse of Weimar Germany.* Translation and forward by V.R. Berghan. Leamington Spa, New York: Berg/St. Martin's Press, 1987.
_____. *The Hitler State: The Foundation and Development of the Internal Structure of the Third Reich.* Translation by John W. Hiden. London: Longman, 1981.
_____. *German National Socialism 1919-1945.* New York: Clio Press, 1966.
Browder, George. *Foundations of the Nazi Police State.* New York: London: Peter Lang, 1988.
Bry, Gerhard. *Wages in Germany.* Princeton: Princeton University Press, 1960.
Brzezinski, Zbigniew K. *The Soviet Bloc in Unity and Conflict.* Cambridge, Mass: Harvard University Press, 1967.
Bukharin, N.I. *The Politics and Economics of the Transition Period.* London: Routledge & Keegan Paul, 1979.
Bullock, Alan. *Hitler and Stalin: Parallel Lives.* London: New York: Vintage Books, 1991.
_____. *Hitler: A Study in Tyranny.* 2ⁿᵈ ed. London: Penguin, 1962.
Burleigh, Michael & Wolfgang Wipperman. *The Racial State: Germany 1933-1945.* Cambridge, UK: Cambridge University Press, 1991.

Burleigh, Michael. *Death and Deliverance: Euthanasia in Germany, C. 1900-1945*. Cambridge, UK: Cambridge University Press, 1994.

Butler, Rupert. *The Black Angels: A History of the Waffen SS*. New York: St. Martin's Press, 1979.

Calder, Angus. *The People's War: Britain 1939-1945*. London: Jonathan Cape, 1969.

Calder, Angus and D. Sheridan. *Speak for Yourself: A Mass Observation Anthology, 1937-1949*. London: Jonathan Cape, 1984.

Calleo, D. *The German Problem Reconsidered*. Cambridge, UK: Cambridge University Press, 1978.

Caminada, Jerome. *My Purpose Holds*. London: Jonathan Cape, 1952.

Cantril, Hadley (ed.). *Public Opinion, 1935-1946*. Princeton: Princeton University Press, 1951.

Caplan, Jane and Thomas Childers. *Reevaluating the Third Reich*. New York: Holmes & Meier, 1993.

Carr, Edward Hallett. *International Relations Between the Two World Wars, 1919-1939*. London: Macmillan, 1965.

————. *The Comintern and the Spanish Civil War*. Tamara Deutscher (ed.). London: Macmillan, 1984.

————. *The Twilight of the Comintern, 1930-1935*. London: Macmillan, 1982.

————. *German Soviet Relations Between the Two World Wars, 1919-1939*. New York: Harper & Row, 1966.

————. *The Interregnum: 1923-1924*. London: Macmillan, 1960.

Carr, William M. "National Socialism: Foreign Policy and the Wehrmacht." *Fascism*. W. Laqueur (ed.). London, New York: Penguin, 1979.

————. *Hitler: A Study in Personality and Politics*. London: Edward Arnold 1978.

————. *Arms, Autarky and Aggression: A Study in German Foreign Policy, 1933-1939*. London: Edward Arnold, 1972.

————. *A History of Germany, 1815-1945*. New York, London: Edward Arnold, 1969.

Carrere d' Encausse, H. *Lenin: Revolution and Power*. London: New York: Longman, 1982.

Carsten, Francis Ludwig. *The German Workers and the Nazis*. Aldershot, Hants, UK; Brookfield, Vermont: Ashgate Publishing Co., 1995.

————. *Fascist Movements in Austria: From Schonerer to Hitler*. London: Sage Publications, 1977.

————. *Revolution in Central Europe, 1918-1919*. London: Temple Smith, 1972.

————. *The Rise of Fascism*. London: Methuen, 1970.

————. *The Reichswehr and Politics, 1918-1933*. Oxford, UK: Clarendon, 1966.

Carter, Stephen K. *Russian Nationalism*. London: John Speirs, 1990.

Chalou, George C. (ed.). *The Secrets War: The Office of Strategic Services in World War II*. Washington, D.C. National Archives and Records Administration, 1992.

Chamberlain, E.R. *Life in Wartime Britain*. London: Batsford, 1972.

Cecil R. *The Myth of the Master Race: Alfred Rosenberg and Nazi Ideology*. London: Batsford, 1972.

Chevrillon, Claire. *Code Name Christine Clouet: A Woman in the French Resistance*. College Station: Texas A&M University Press, 1995.

Childers, Thomas. *The Formation of the Nazi Constituency, 1919-1933*. London: Croom Helm, 1986.

————. *The Nazi Voter: The Social Foundations of Fascism in Germany, 1919-1933*. Chapel Hill; London: University of North Carolina Press, 1983.

Christman, Henry (ed.). *The Essential Tito*. London: David and Charles, 1971.

Churchill, Sir Winston. *Great Contemporaries*. 2nd ed. London: Macmillan, 1941.

————. *The Second World War*. 5 vols. London: Cassell, 1948-1954.

Clark, Douglas. *Three Days to Catastrophe*. London: Hammond, 1966.

Clark, Katerina. *The Soviet Novel: History as Ritual*. Chicago: University of Chicago Press, 1985.

Claudin, Fernando. *The Communist Movement: from Comintern to Cominform*. Harmondsworth, UK: Penguin, 1975.

Clutterbuck, Richard L. *Terrorism in an Unstable World*. London: Routledge, 1994.

————. *Terrorism and Guerrilla Warfare: Forecasts and Remedies*. London: Routledge, 1990.

————. *The Future of Political Violence: Destabilization, Disorder, and Terrorism*. New York: St. Martin's Press, 1986.

_____. *Guerrillas and Terrorists*. Columbus: Ohio State University Press, 1980.

Cobb, R. *French and Germans, Germans and French: A Personal Account of France under Two Occupations, 1914-1918/1940-1944*, 2nd ed. London: Hanover, 1984.

Cockett, R. *Twilight of Truth: Chamberlain, Appeasement and the Manipulation of the Press*. London: Weidenfeld & Nicolson, 1989.

Cohen, Stephen F. *Rethinking the Soviet Experience: Politics and History Since 1917*. New York: Oxford University Press, 1985.

_____. *Bukharin and the Bolshevik Revolution*. London: New York: Knopf, 1973.

Colton, Timothy. *Commissars, Commanders and Civilian Authority: The Structure of Soviet Military Politics*. Cambridge, Mass: Harvard University Press, 1979.

Combs, William L. *The Voice of the SS: A History of the SS Journal, "Das Schwarze Korps."* New York: Peter Lang, 1986.

Conquest, Robert. *Stalin: Breaker of Nations*. New York: Viking Press, 1991.

_____. *The Great Terror: A Reassessment*. New York: Oxford University Press, 1990.

_____. *The Harvest of Sorrow: Soviet Collectivization and the Terror*. New York: Oxford University Press, 1986.

_____. *The Nation Killers: the Soviet Deportation of Nationalities*. London: Macmillan, 1970.

_____. *Soviet Nationalities Policy in Practice*. London: Bodley Head, 1967.

Conway, J.S. *The Nazi Persecution of the Churches, 1933-1945*. London: Weidenfeld & Nicolson, 1968.

Conway, Martin. *Collaboration in Belgium: Leon Degrelle and the Rexist Movement, 1940-1944*. New Haven, CT: Yale University Press, 1994.

Cooper, Matthew. *The Phantom War: The German Struggle Against the Soviet Partisans, 1941-1944*. London: Macdonald & James, 1979.

_____. *The German Army 1933-1945: Its Political and Military Failure*. London: Scarborough House, 1978.

Craig, G.A. *The Germans*. New York: London: Penguin, 1982.

_____. *Germany 1866-1945*. New York: Oxford University Press, 1978.

_____. *The Politics of the Prussian Army*. New York: London: Clarendon Press, 1964.

Crew, David F. *Germans on Welfare: from Weimar to Hitler*. New York: Oxford University Press, 1998.

_____. *Nazism and German Society 1933-1945*. London: Routledge, 1994.

Crozier, Andrew J. *The Causes of the Second World War*. Oxford, UK: Blackwell Publishers, 1997.

_____. *Appeasement and Germany's Last Bid for Colonies*. Basingstoke, UK: Macmillan, 1988.

Dahrendorf, Ralf. *Society and Democracy in Germany*. London: Weidenfeld & Nicolson, 1967.

Dallin, Alexander and Ralph Mavrogordato. *German Rule in Russia, 1941-1945: A Case Study in Occupation Policies*. 2nd ed. Boulder, CO: Westview Press, 1981.

Dalton, Hugh. *The Fateful Years: Memoirs, 1931-45*. London: Croom Helm, 1957.

Dank, M. *The French Against the French: Collaboration and Resistance*. Southampton, UK: Caswell, 1978.

Davidowicz, L.S. *The War Against the Jews, 1933-45*. London: Weidenfeld & Nicolson, 1975.

Davies, Norman. *God's Playground: A History of Poland, Vol. II- 1795 to the Present*. New York: Oxford University Press, 1981.

Davies, R.H., M. Harrison and S.G. Wheatcroft (eds.). *The Economic Transformation of the Soviet Union, 1913-1945*. New York: Cambridge University Press, 1994.

Davis, Brian L. *Waffen SS*, 2nd ed. New York: Blandford Press, 1987.

Dedijer, Vladimir. *Tito Speaks: His Self Portrait and Struggle with Stalin*. London: Weidenfeld & Nicolson, 1953.

Degrelle, Leon. *Campaign in Russia*. London: Crecy, 1985.

Dehio, Ludwig. *German and World Politics in the Twentieth Century*. London: Chatto & Windus, 1959.

Demeter, Karl. *The German Officer Corps in Society and State: 1650-1945*. London: Weidenfeld & Nicolson, 1965.

Deutsch, H.C. *Hitler and His Generals: The Hidden Crisis January-June, 1938.* Minneapolis: University of Minnesota Press, 1974.

_____. *The Conspiracy Against Hitler in the Twilight War.* Minneapolis: University of Minnesota Press, 1968.

Deutscher, Isaac. *The Prophet Unarmed-Trotsky, 1921-1929.* New York: Oxford University Press, 1989.

_____. *Stalin: A Political Biography.* London: O.U.P., 1967.

Dicks, Henry V. *Licensed Mass Murderers: A Socio-Psychological Study of Some SS Killers.* Sussex, UK: Sussex University Press & Chatto-Heinemann, 1972.

Dilks, David (ed.). *Retreat from Power. Vol. 1: Studies in Britain's Foreign Policy, 1906-39.* London: Macmillan, 1981.

_____. *Retreat from Power,* Vol. 2: *Studies in Britain's Foreign Policy of the Twentieth Century After 1939.* London: Macmillan, 1981.

_____. *The Diaries of Sir Alexander Cadogan.* London: Cassell, 1971.

Divine, David. *The Broken Wing: A Study in the British Exercise of Air Power.* London: Hutchinson & Co., Ltd. 1966.

Dixon, C. Aubrey and Otto Heilbrunn. *Communist Guerrilla Warfare.* London: George Allen & Unwin, 1954.

Djalis, Aleska. *The Contested Country.* Cambridge, Mass: Harvard University Press, 1991.

Djilas, Milovan. *Tito: The Story from Inside.* London: Weidenfeld & Nicolson, 1981.

Djordjevic, Dimitrije. *The Creation of Yugoslavia 1914-1918.* Santa Barbara, CA: University of California Press, 1980.

Domarus, Max. *Hitler: Speeches and Proclamations, 1932-1945: The Chronicle of a Dictatorship: The Years 1939 to 1940.* 3 vols. New York: Bolchazi Carducci, 1992.

Dorpalen, Andreas. *German History in Marxist Perspective: The East German Approach.* London: I.B. Taurus, 1985.

Duignan, Peter and Lewis Gann. *The Cold War: End of the Aftermath (Hoover Essays, No. 16).* Hoover Institute Press, 1996.

Duke, A.C. and C.A. Tamse. *War and Society.* The Hague: Nijhoff, 1977

Dukes, P. *A History of Russia.* 2nd ed. New York: London: Macmillan, 1990.

Eckman, Lester and Chaim Lazar. *The Jewish Resistance: The History of the Jewish Partisans in Lithuania and White Russia During the Nazi Occupation, 1940-1945.* New York: Sheingold Publishers, 1977.

Edinger, L.J. *German Exile Politics: The Social Democratic Executive Committee in the Nazi Era.* New York: Berkeley, 1956.

Ehrlich, B. *The French Resistance.* London: Macmillan, 1966.

Eley, Geoff. *From Unification to Nazism: Reinterpreting the German Past.* London, Boston, MA: Allen & Unwin, 1986.

Ellwood, David W. *Rebuilding Europe: Western Europe, America and Post War Reconstruction.* New York, London: Longman, 1992.

Emsley, Clive, et al. *World War Two and its Consequences.* Buckingham, UK: Bristol, PA: Open University Press, 1990.

Encyclopedia Judaica. Vol. 13 of 16. Jerusalem: Keter Publishing House, 1972.

Erickson, John. *The Soviet High Command: A Military-Political History, 1918-1941.* London: Macmillan, 1962.

_____. *The Road to Berlin: Continuing the History of Stalin's War with Germany.* Boulder, Colo.: Westview Press, 1983.

_____. *The Road to Stalingrad: Stalin's War with Germany.* 2 vols. New York: Harper & Row, 1975.

Erlich, A. *The Soviet Industrialization Debate 1924-1928.* Cambridge, Mass: Harvard University Press, 1967.

Eschenberg, T. *The Road to Dictatorship: Germany, 1918-1933,* 2nd ed. London: Wolff, 1964.

Evans, Richard J. *In Hitler's Shadow: West German Historians and the Attempt to Escape from the*

Nazi Past. New York: London: Taurus, 1989.
_____. *Rethinking German History.* London: Allen & Unwin, 1987.
Evans, Richard J. and Geary, D. (eds.). *The German Unemployed.* London: Croom Helm, 1987.
Ewald, Johann. *Treatise on Partisan Warfare.* Translated and introduced by Robert A. Selig and David Curtis Skaggs. Westport, Conn.: Greenwood Press, 1991.
Eyck, E. *A History of the Weimar Republic.* Cambridge, Mass: Harvard University Press, 1964.
Fainsod, Merle. *Smolensk Under Soviet Rule.* Boston: Unwin Hyman, 1989.
Farber, S. *Before Stalinism.* New York: Oxford University Press, 1990.
Farquharson, John E. *The Plough and the Swastika: The NSDAP and Agriculture in Germany, 1928-45.* Beverly Hills, CA: Sage, 1976.
Farquharson, John E. and John Hiden. *Explaining Hitler's Germany: Historians and the Third Reich.* London: Batsford, Academic and Educational, Ltd., 1983.
Fein, H. *Accounting for Genocide: National Responses and Jewish Victimization during the Holocaust.* London: New York: Free Press, 1979.
Feis, Herbert. *Churchill, Roosevelt, Stalin: The War They Waged and the Peace They Sought.* Princeton: Princeton University Press, 1967.
Fest, Joachim C. *Hitler.* London: Weidenfeld & Nicolson, 1974.
_____. *The Face of the Third Reich.* 3rd (ed.). Translation by Michael Bullock. London: Weidenfeld & Nicolson, 1970.
Feuchtwanger, E.J. *From Weimar to Hitler.* London, New York: Macmillan, 1995.
Finer, S.E. *Comparative Government.* London: New York: Penguin, 1980.
Fischer, Conan. *The Rise of National Socialism and the Working Class in Weimar Germany.* Oxford, UK & Providence, RI: Berghahn, 1996.
_____. *The Rise of the Nazis.* Manchester, UK; New York: Manchester University Press, 1995.
_____. *The German Communists and the Rise of the Nazis.* Basingstoke, UK: Macmillan, 1991.
_____. *Stormtroopers: A Social, Economic and Ideological Analysis 1929-35.* London: Allen & Unwin, 1983.
Fischer, Fritz. *From Kaiserreich to Third Reich: Elements of Continuity in German History, 1871-1945.* London, New York: Unwin-Hyman, 1979.
_____. *World Power or Decline.* London: Weidenfeld & Nicolson, 1975.
Fischer-Galati, Stephen. *Twentieth Century Rumania.* New York: London: Columbia University Press, 1970.
Fischer, George. *Soviet Opposition to Stalin: A Case Study in World War II.* Cambridge, MA: Harvard University Press, 1952.
Fitzpatrick, Sheila. *The Russian Revolution, 1917-1932.* New York: Oxford University Press, 1982.
Flenley, Ralph. *Modern German History,* 3rd (ed.). London: Dent, 1964.
Foot, Michael R.D. *SOE in France: An Account of the Work of British Special Operations Executive in France, 1940-1944.* Reprint of 1966 (ed.). Baltimore: University Publications of America, 1984.
_____. *Resistance.* London: Paladin, 1978.
_____. *Resistance: An Analysis of European Resistance to Nazism, 1940-1945.* 2nd ed. London: Eyre Methuen, 1976.
_____. *Aneuran Bevan: A Biography, 1897-1945.* Vol I., 2nd ed. London: Granada, 1984.
Footman, David. *Civil War in Russia.* London: Faber, 1961.
Fraenkel and Manvel. *The Canaris Conspiracy: The Secret Resistance to Hitler in the German Army.* New York: McKay, 1969.
_____. *Der 20 Juli.* Berlin, West Germany: Press and Information Office of the Federal Government, 1964.
Frank, Anne. *The Diary of Anne Frank.* London: Pan Books, 1954.
Frenay, Henri. *La Nuit Finira.* Paris: Laffont, 1973.
Fuchser, Larry William. *Neville Chamberlain and Appeasement: A Study in the Politics of History.* New York: London: Norton, 1982.
Furmanov, Dmitri. *Chapaev.* Translation by George Kittel and J. Kittell. Moscow: Foreign Language Publishing House, 1959.

Fussell, Paul. Wartime: *Understanding and Behavior in the Second World War.* New York: Oxford University Press, 1989.

_____. *The Great War and Modern Memory.* New York: Oxford University Press, 1975.

Fyodorov, A.F. *The Underground Committee Carries On* . Translation by L. Stolitsky. Moscow: Foreign Language Publishing House, 1952.

Gallagher, Matthew. *The Soviet History of World War II: Myths, Memories, and Realities.* New York: Frederic A. Praeger, 1963.

Gann, Lewis. *The Defence of Western Europe.* London: Routledge, Keegan & Paul, 1987.

de Gaulle, Charles. *Memoires de Guerre L'appel, 1940-1942.* Paris: Laffont, 1954.

_____.*Memoires de Guerre L'unite, 1942-1944.* Paris: Laffont, 1954.

_____. *The Army of the Future.* London: Hutchinson &. Co., 1938.

Geary, D. *Hitler and Nazism.* London: New York: Routledge, 1993.

Gellately, Robert. *The Gestapo and German Society: Enforcing Racial Policy.* New York: London: Clarendon, 1990.

Gellner, E. *Nations and Nationalism.* London: Basil Blackwell, 1983.

George, M. *The Hollow Men: An Examination of British Foreign Policy Between the Years 1933 and 1939.* London: Frewin, 1967.

Gersdorf, Ursula von (ed.). *Frauen im Kriegsdienst, 1914-1945.* Stuttgart, West Germany: Deutsche Verlag, 1969.

Gertin, H.H. and Wright-Mills, C. (eds.). *From Max Weber: Essays in Sociology.* London: Routledge & Keegan Paul, 1948.

Getty, J. Arch. *Origins of the Great Purges: The Soviet Communist Party Reconsidered, 1933-1938.* Cambridge, UK: Cambridge University Press, 1985.

Getty, J. Arch and R. Manning. *Stalinist Terror.* Cambridge, UK: Cambridge University Press, 1993.

Geyer, Michael and J.W. Boyer (eds.). *Resistance Against the Third Reich, 1933-1990.* Chicago, London: University of Chicago Press, 1994.

Gilbert, Martin. *Finest Hour: Winston S. Churchill 1941-45.* 2ⁿᵈ ed. London: Heinemann/Minerva, 1989.

_____. *Second World War.* London: Weidenfeld & Nicolson, 1989.

_____.*The Holocaust: The Jewish Tragedy.* London: Collins, 1986.

_____. *Road to Victory: Winston Churchill 1941-45.* London: Heinemann, 1986.

_____. *The Final Journey: The Fate of the Jews in Nazi Europe.* London: Allen & Unwin, 1979.

Gilbert, Martin and R. Gott. *The Appeasers.* London: Weidenfeld & Nicolson, 1967.

Gill, Graeme. *The Origins of the Stalinist Political System.* Cambridge, UK: Cambridge University Press, 1990.

_____. *Stalinism.* Basingstoke, UK; New York: Macmillan Press, 1989.

Gillingham, J. *Industry and Politics in the Third Reich: Ruhr Coal, Hitler, and Europe.* London: Methuen, 1985.

Gisevius, Hans Bernd. *To the Bitter End.* Translation by Richard and Clara Winston. Westport, CT: Greenwood Press, 1947.

Glenny, Misha. *The Fall of Yugoslavia.* London: New York: Penguin Books, 1992.

Goebbels, Josef. *The Goebbels Diaries: The Last Days.* Translation by Hugh Trevor Roper. London: Secker and Warburg, 1962.

Goldhagen, Daniel Jonah. *Hitler's Willing Executioners: Ordinary Germans and the Holocaust.* New York: Vintage Books, 1997.

Gough, Hugh and John Horne. *De Gaulle and Twentieth Century France.* New York: Edward Arnold, 1994.

Goure, Leon. *The Siege of Leningrad.* Stanford, CA Stanford University Press 1962.

Graml, Hermann, Hans Mommsen, et al. *The German Resistance to Hitler.* Translation by Peter and Betty Ross. London: Batsford, 1970.

Grenville, J.A.S. *The Collins World History of the Twentieth Century.* New York: London: Harper Collins, 1984.

_____. *The Major International Treaties, 1914-1973.* London: Methuen, 1974.

Gross, Jan T. *Revolution from Abroad: The Soviet Conquest of Poland's Western Ukraine and Western Belorussia.* Princeton: Princeton University Press, 1988.

Grossman, Vasily. *Life and Fate.* Translation by Robert Chandler. New York: Harper & Row, 1987.

Gruenberger, Richard. *The Twelve Year Reich: A Social History of the Third Reich.* London: Weidenfeld & Nicolson; New York: Holt, Rinehart and Winston, 1971.

Guderian, Heinz. *Panzer Leader.* 8ᵗʰ (ed.). London: Macdonald & Co., 1982.

Gunther, H. *The Culture of the Stalin Period.* London: Macmillan, 1990.

Guttsman, W.L. *The German Social Democratic Party, 1875-1933: From Ghetto to Government.* London: Allen & Unwin, 1981.

Gvozdenovic, Dusan. *The Great Patriotic War of the Soviet Union, 1941-1945: A General Outline.* Moscow: Progress Publishers, 1974.

von Hagen, Mark. *Soldiers in the Proletarian Dictatorship: The Red Army and the Soviet Socialist State, 1917-1930.* Ithaca, NY: Cornell University Press, 1990.

Hale, Oren J. *The Captive Press in the Third Reich.* Princeton: Princeton University Press, 1964.

Hamilton, Richard F. *Who Voted for Hitler?* Princeton: Princeton University Press, 1982.

Hancock, W.K. and M.H. Gowing. *History of the Second World War-The British Economy.* London: Her Majesty's Stationary Office, Longman, 1949.

Hanfstaengl, Ernst. *Hitler: The Missing Years.* London: Eyre & Spottiswoode, 1957.

Hanson, Joanna K.M. *The Civilian Population and the Warsaw Uprising of 1944.* New York: Cambridge University Press, 1982.

Harrison, Mark. *Soviet Planning in Peace and War: 1938-1945.* New York: Cambridge University Press, 1985.

Haslam, Jonathan. *The Soviet Union and the Struggle for Collective Security in Europe, 1933-1939.* London: Macmillan, 1984.

_____. *Soviet Foreign Policy, 1930-33: The Impact of Depression.* London: Macmillan, 1983.

von Hassell. *The Von Hassell Diaries, 1938-44: The Story of the Forces Against Hitler Inside Germany.* New York: Doubleday, 1947.

Hastings, Max. *Das Reich: The March of the 2ⁿᵈ SS Panzer Division Through France.* New York: Holt, Rinehart and Winston, 1981.

Haupt, G.M. and J.J. Marie. *Makers of the Russian Revolution.* London: Allen & Unwin, 1974.

Hawes, Stephen and Ralph White (eds.), *Resistance in Europe: 1941-1945.* London: Allen Lane, 1975.

Heiber, Helmut. *Adolph Hitler: A Short Biography.* London: Oswald Wolff, 1961.

Heilbrunn, Otto. *Partisan Warfare.* New York: Frederic A. Praeger, 1967.

Heller, Mikhail and Aleksandr Nekrich. *Utopia in Power: The History of the Soviet Union from 1917 to the Present.* Translation by Phyllis B. Carlos. New York: Summit Books, 1986.

Herzmann, Lewis. *DNVP: Right Wing Opposition in the Weimar Republic.* Lincoln: University of Nebraska Press, 1963.

Herzstein, Robert Edwin, et al. *The Nazis.* Alexandria, VA: Time-Life, Inc., 1980.

Hiden, John W. *Germany and Europe, 1919-1939.* New York: Longman, 1977.

_____. *The Weimar Republic.* New York: Longman-Harlow 1974.

Hiden, John W. and John. Farquharson. *Explaining Hitler's Germany: Historians and the Third Reich.* London: Batsford Academic and Educational, Ltd., 1983.

Higham, Charles. *Trading with the Enemy: An Expose of the Nazi-American Money Plot, 1933-1949.* New York: Dell Publishing, 1983.

Hildebrand, Klaus. *Reich, Nation State, Great Power: Reflections on German Foreign Policy, 1871-1945.* London: German Historical Institute, 1995.

_____. *German Foreign Policy from Bismarck to Adenaur: The Limits of Statecraft.* London: Unwin-Hyman, 1989.

_____. *The Third Reich.* Translation by P.S. Falla. London: Boston: Allen & Unwin, 1984.

_____. *The Foreign Policy of the Third Reich.* Los Angeles: London: University of California Press/B.T. Batsford, 1973.

Hillgruber, Andreas. *Germany and the Two World Wars.* London: Cambridge, Mass: Harvard University Press, 1981.

Hirszowicz, Lukasz. *The Third Reich and the Arab East*. London: Routledge and Kegan Paul, 1966.

Hitler, Adolf. *Mein Kampf*. Translation by Ralph Manheim. Introduction by D.C. Watt. London: Hutchinson, 1974.

_____. *Hitler's Table Talk, 1941-1944*. Introduction by H.T. Roper. London: Weidenfeld & Nicolson, 1973.

_____. *Hitler's Secret Book*. Introduction by Hugh Trevor Roper. New York: Grove Press, 1961.

Hobsbawm, Eric. *The Age of Extremes: The Short Twentieth Century*. London: Michael Joseph, 1994.

_____. *Bandits*. London: New York: Penguin Books, 1969.

Hoffman, George W. *The Balkans in Transition*. Princeton: Van Nostrand, 1963.

Hoffmann, Peter. *Hitler's Personal Security*. London: Macmillan, 1979.

Holborn, H. *A History of Modern Germany, 1840-1945*. London: Eyre & Spottiswoode, 1969.

Homze, Edward L. *Foreign Labour in Nazi Germany*. Princeton: Princeton University Press, 1967.

Hondros, Ernest Demetrious. *Occupation and Resistance: The Greek Agony, 1941-44*. New York: Pantheon, 1983.

Howard, Michael. *Restraints on War*. London: New York: Oxford University Press, 1980.

Howell, Edgar. *The Soviet Partisan Movement, 1941-1944*. Washington D.C.: Department of the Army, 1956.

Hunt, Richard N. *German Social Democracy, 1918-1933*. 3rd (ed.). Chicago: Quadrangle, 1970.

Huntington, S.P. *The Soldier and the State*. Cambridge, Mass: Harvard University Press, 1957.

Huttenbach, H.R. *Soviet Nationality Policies: Ruling Ethnic Groups in the USSR*. London: New York: Mansell, 1990.

Iggers, G. (ed.). *The Social History of Politics*. Leamington Spa, UK: Berg Publishers, 1985.

Ignatov, P.K. *Partisans of the Kuban*. Translation by J. Fineberg. London: Hutchinson & Co., 1945.

Infield, Glenn B. *Hitler's Secret Life*. Feltham, Middlesex, UK: The Hamlyn Publishing Group, 1980.

Irving, David. *The War Path: Hitler's Germany, 1933-9*. London: Joseph, 1978.

_____. *Hitler's War*. 2 vols. London: New York: The Viking Press/Hoddard & Stoughton, 1977.

Jaeckel, Eberhard. *Hitler's World View: A Blue Print for Power*. Washington, DC: Howard University Press; Cambridge, Mass: Harvard University Press, 1981.

Jacobsen, Hans Adolf (ed.). *July 20, 1944: The German Opposition to Hitler as Viewed by Foreign Historians, an Anthology*. Bonn, W. Germany: Press and Information Office of the Federal Government, 1969.

James, Robert Rhodes. *Anthony Eden*. London: Weidenfeld & Nicolson, 1986.

_____. *The Czechoslovak Crisis*. London: Weidenfeld & Nicolson, 1969.

_____. (ed.). *CHIPS: The Diaries of Sir Henry Channon*. London: Weidenfeld & Nicolson, 1967.

Jelavich, Barbara Brightfield. *History of the Balkans*. 2 vols. Cambridge, UK; New York: Cambridge University Press, 1983.

Joes, Anthony James. *Guerrilla Warfare: A Historical, Biographical, and Bibliographical Sourcebook*. Westport, CT: Greenwood Publishing Group, 1996.

_____. *Guerrilla Conflict Before the Cold War*. New York: Praeger Publishing, 1996.

_____. *Modern Guerrilla Insurgency*. New York: Praeger Publishing, 1992.

Johnson, Paul. *A History of the Jews*. London: Weidenfeld & Nicolson, 1987.

Joll, James. *Europe Since 1870: An International History*. New York: Harper & Row, 1973.

Jones, Virgil Carrington. *Ranger Mosby*. MacLean, VA: EPM Publications, 1987.

Judt, Tony (ed.). *Resistance and Revolution in Mediterranean Europe, 1939-1948*. New York: Routledge, 1989.

Kagan, Jack and Dov Cohen. *Surviving the Holocaust With the Russian Jewish Partisans*. New York: London: Valentine Mitchell, 1998.

Kaiser, D. *Economic Diplomacy and the Origins of the Second World War: Germany, Britain, France, and Eastern Europe, 1933-1939*. Princeton: Princeton University Press, 1980.

Karov, D. *The Partisan Movement in the USSR, 1941-1945*. Munich: Institute for the Study of the History and Culture of the USSR, 1954.

Karski, Jan. *Story of a Secret State*. Boston: Houghton Mifflin, 1944.

Kater, M.H. *The Nazi Party: A Social Profile of Members and Leaders*. Cambridge, Mass; London: Harvard University Press, 1983.

Kedward, H.R. and Roger Austin. *Vichy France and the Resistance: Culture and Identity.* London: Croom & Helm, 1985.

_____. *Resistance in Vichy France: A Study of Ideas and Motivations in the Southern Zone, 1940-1944.* New York: Oxford University Press, 1978.

Kedward, H.R. *In Search of the Maquis: Rural Resistance in Southern France, 1942-1944.* New York: Oxford University Press, 1978.

Kele, Max H. *Nazism and Workers: National Socialist Appeals to German Labor. 1919-1933.* Chapel Hill: University of North Carolina Press, 1972.

Kellas, James. *The Politics of Nationalism and Ethnicity.* 2nd ed. New York: St. Martin's Press, 1998.

Kenez, Peter. *The Birth of the Propaganda State: Soviet Methods of Mass Mobilization, 1917-1929.* New York: Cambridge University Press, 1985.

Kershaw, Ian. *The Nazi Dictatorship: Problems and Perspectives of Interpretation.* New York: Routledge, Chapman & Hall, 1993.

_____. *Profiles in Power: Hitler.* New York: Longman, 1991.

_____. *Weimar: Why did Germany Fail?* London: Weidenfeld & Nicolson, 1990.

_____. *Popular Opinion and Political Dissent in the Third Reich, Bavaria 1933-1945.* Oxford, UK: Clarendon Press, 1983.

Kershaw, Ian and Moshe Lewin (eds.). *Stalinism and Nazism: Dictatorships in Comparison.* Cambridge, UK: Cambridge University Press, 1997.

Keylor, William. *The Twentieth Century World: An International History.* 2nd ed. New York: Oxford University Press, 1992.

Khrushchev, Nikita. *Khrushchev Remembers.* Translation and (ed.). by Strobe Talbott. Boston: Little, Brown & Company, 1970.

Klemperer von, Klemens. *German Resistance against Hitler: The Search for Allies Abroad, 1938-1945.* New York: Oxford University Press, 1992.

_____.*Mandate for Resistance: The Case of the German Opposition to Hitler.* Baltimore: Johns Hopkins University Press, 1969.

Klinksiek, Dorothea. *Die Frau im NS-Staat.* Stuttgart: Deutsche Verlag, 1982.

Knight, Amy. *Beria: Stalin's First Lieutenant.* Princeton: Princeton University Press, 1993.

Knight, F. *The French Resistance, 1940-1044.* London: Lawrence & Wishart, 1975.

Koch, H.W. (ed.). *Aspects of the Third Reich.* Basingstoke, UK: Macmillan, 1985.

Kochan, Lionel and Richard Abraham. *The Making of Modern Russia.* New York: Penguin, 1983.

Kochan, Mirriam. *Britain's Internees in the Second World War.* London: The Macmillan Press, Ltd., 1983.

Koenker, Diane P., William G. Rosenberg and Ronald G. Suny (eds.). *Party, State, and Society in the Russian Civil War.* Bloomington: Indiana University Press, 1989.

Kolarz, W. *Russia and Her Colonies.* Hamden, CT: Archon Books, 1967.

Kolko, Gabriel. *The Politics of War: Allied Diplomacy and the World Crisis of 1943-1945.* London: Weidenfeld & Nicolson, 1969.

Kolkowitz, Roman. *The Soviet Military and the Communist Party.* Boulder: Westview Press, 1985.

Koontz, Claudia. *Mothers in the Fatherland: Women, the Family and Nazi Politics.* New York: St. Martin's Press, 1987.

Kovrig, Bennett. *Communism in Hungary: From Kun to Kadar.* Stanford, CA: Stanford University Press, 1979.

Krausnick, Helmut and Martin Broszat, et al. *Anatomy of the SS State.* Translation by Dorrian Long and Marian Jackson. London: New York: Paladin Press, 1970.

Kuczynski, J. *Germany: Economic and Labour Conditions under Fascism.* Westport, CT: Greenwood Press, 1976.

Lacouture, Jean. *De Gaulle.* London: Hutchinson, 1970.

Lane, Barbara Miller and Leila J. Rupp (eds.). *Nazi Ideology Before 1933: A Documentation.* Manchester, UK: Manchester University Press,1978.

Laqueur, Walter. *A Terrible Secret: An Investigation into the Suppression of Information about Hitler's Final Solution.* London: Weidenfeld & Nicolson, 1980.

_____. *The Terrorism Reader: A Historical Anthology.* London: Wildwood House, 1979.

_____. *Fascism: A Reader's Guide*. 2ⁿᵈ ed. New York: Penguin, 1979.
_____. *Terrorism*. London: Abacus, 1978.
_____. *Weimar: A Cultural History, 1918-1933*. London: Weidenfeld & Nicolson, 1974.
Laska, Vera. *Women in the Resistance and the Holocaust: Voices of Eyewitnesses. Contributions to Women's Studies No. 37*. Westport, CT: Greenwood Press, 1983.
Latham, Earl. *The Communist Controversy in Washington: From the New Deal to McCarthy*. Cambridge, Mass: Harvard University Press, 1966.
Laurent, Livia. *A Tale of Internment*. London: Allen & Unwin, 1942.
Lee, M. and Michalka, W. *German Foreign Policy, 1917-1933*. New York: Berg Publishers, 1987.
Lentin, Antony. *Guilt at Versailles: Lloyd George and the Pre-History of Appeasement*. London: Methuen, 1985.
Lepre, George. *Himmler's Bosnian Division: The Waffen SS Handschar Division, 1943-1945*. Atglen, Penn: Schiffer Publishing, Ltd., 1997.
Leslie, Edward E. *The Devil Knows How to Ride: The True Story of William Clark Quantrill and His Confederate Raiders*. New York: Da Capo Press, 1998.
Levi, Primo. *The Drowned and the Saved*. London: Joseph, 1988.
_____. *If Not Now, When?* Translation by William Weaver. New York: Summit Books, 1985.
Levine-Meyer. *Inside German Communism: Memoirs of Party Life in the Weimar Republic*. London: Pluto Press, 1977.
Lewin, Moshe. *The Making of the Soviet System: Essays in the Social History of Interwar Russia*. New York: Pantheon Books, 1985.
_____. *Russian Peasants and Soviet Power: A Study of Collectivization*. Translation by Irene Nove. New York: W.W. Norton & Co., 1975.
Liddell-Hart, B.H. *History of the Second World War*. New York: Pan, 1982.
Loewenheim, F.L. et al (eds.). *Churchill and Roosevelt: Their Secret Wartime Correspondence*, vol. 3: November 1942-December 1943. London: Barrie & Jenkins, 1975.
Lindsay, Franklin and John Kenneth Galbraith. *Beacons in the Night: With the OSS and Tito's Partisans in Wartime Yugoslavia*. Stanford, CA: Stanford University Press, 1993.
Linz, Susan J. (ed.). *The Impact of World War II on the Soviet Union*. Ottawa, Ontario: Rowman & Allanheld, 1985.
Littlejohn, David. *The Patriotic Traitors: A History of Collaboration in German Occupied Europe, 1940-45*. London: Heinemann, 1972.
Lumins, Valdis O. *Himmler's Auxiliaries*. Chapel Hill: The University of North Carolina Press, 1991.
Lumsden, Robin. *The Black Corps*. London: Ian Allan Publishing, 1992.
Lydall, Harold. *Yugoslavia in Crisis*. New York: Oxford University Press, 1989.
Lynch, M. *Stalin and Khrushchev: The USSR 1924-64*. London: Hodder & Stoughton, 1990.
MacDonald, C.A. *The United States, Britain and Appeasement, 1936-1939*. London: Macmillan, 1981.
Maclean, Fitzroy. *Josip Broz Tito-A Pictorial Biography*. London: Macmillan, 1980.
Maier, Charles S. (ed.). *The Origins of the Cold War and Contemporary Europe*. New York: View Points, 1978.
Mangini, Shirley. *Memories of Resistance: Women's Voices from the Spanish Civil War*. New Haven, CT: Yale University Press, 1995.
Mann, Golo. *The History of Germany Since 1789*. New York: London: Penguin, 1985.
Marsh, P. *Collaboration in France: Politics and Culture, 1940-1944*. New York: London: Oxford University Press, 1989.
Marshall, S.L.A. *Bringing up the Rear*. Novato, CA Presidio Press, 1979.
_____. *Men Against Fire*. New York: William Morrow & Co., 1947.
Martin, Hugh, Douglas Newton, H.M. Waddams and R.R. Williams. *Christian Counter-Attack: Europe's Churches Against Nazism*. London: Student Christian Movement Press, 1943.
Martin, James Stewart. *All Honorable Men*. Boston: Little, Brown & Co., 1950.
Marwick, Arthur. *The Home Front*. London: Thames & Hudson, 1976.
Maser, Werner (ed.). *Hitler's Letters and Notes*. London: Heinemann, 1974.
_____. *Hitler's Mein Kampf: An Analysis*. New York: Faber & Faber, 1970.
Mastny, Vojtech. *Russia's Road to the Cold War*. New York: Columbia University Press, 1979.

_____. *The Czechs Under Nazi Rule.* New York: Columbia University Press, 1971.
Matthiessen, Peter. *Partisans.* New York: Vintage Books, 1987.
Mazower, Mark. *Inside Hitler's Greece: The Experience of Occupation, 1941-44.* New Haven, CT; London: Yale University Press, 1993.
McCauley, Martin. *Soviet Politics 1917-1991.* Oxford, UK: Oxford University Press, 1992.
_____. *Stalin and Stalinism.* London: Longman, 1983.
_____. *The Origins of the Cold War.* London: New York: Longman, 1983.
_____. *The Soviet Union Since 1917.* London: New York: Longman, 1981.
_____. (ed.). *Communist Power in Europe, 1944-1949,* London: Macmillan, 1977.
_____. *Politics in the Soviet Union.* London, New York: Penguin, 1977.
McClelland, J.S. *The French Right: From De Maistre to Maurras.* London: Jonathan Cape, 1970.
McKenzie, J.R.P. *Weimar Germany 1918-1933.* London: Blandford Press, 1971.
McMillan, J.F. *Twentieth Century France: Politics and Society 1898-1991.* London: New York: Edward Arnold, 1992.
Mednicki, Bernard. *Never Be Afraid: A Jew in the Maquis.* New York: Azenphony Press, 1996.
Medvedev, R.A. *Let History Judge.* New York: London: Macmillan, 1972.
Meerloo, Joost Abraham Mauritz. *Total War and the Human Mind: A Psychologist's Experiences in Occupied Holland.* London: Allen & Unwin, 1944.
Meinecke, F. *The German Catastrophe.* Boston: Beacon Press, 1963.
Merkl, Peter H. *The Making of a Stormtrooper.* Princeton: Princeton University Press, 1980.
Messenger, Charles. *Hitler's Gladiator: The Life and Times of Obergruppenfuehrer and Panzergeneral-Oberst Der Waffen SS Sepp Dietrich.* London: Brassey's, Inc., 1988.
Michel, Henri. *The Shadow War: European Resistance, 1939-1945.* Translation by Richard Barry. New York: Harper & Row, 1972.
Middlemas, K. *Diplomacy of Illusion: the British Government and Germany, 1937-1939.* London: Weidenfeld & Nicolson, 1972.
Miller, Barbara Lane and Leila J. Rupp. *Nazi Ideology Before 1933: A Documentation.* Manchester, UK: Manchester University Press, 1978.
Miller, Russell, et al. *The Resistance.* Alexandria, VA: Time-Life Books, Inc., 1979.
Milward, Alan S. *War, Economy and Society, 1939-45.* London: Allen Lane, 1977.
_____. *The New Order and the French Economy.* London: Clarendon Press, 1970.
_____.*The German Economy at War.* London: University of London/Athlone Press, 1965.
Mitcham, Samuel W., Jr and Gene Mueller. *Hitler's Commanders.* Lanham, Maryland: Scarborough House, 1992.
Mitchell, Otis C. *The Years of Dictatorial Rule.* New York, London: Peter Lang, 1981.
Mollow, Andrew. *Pictorial History of the SS.* London: Macdonald & James, 1976.
Mommsen, Hans. *From Weimar to Auschwitz.* Princeton: Princeton University Press, 1991.
_____. (ed.). *Fascism.* 2nd ed. London: New York: Penguin, 1979.
Mommsen, Wolfgang and Lothar Kettenacker. *The Fascist Challenge and Appeasement.* London: Allen & Unwin, 1983.
Montgomery, Hyde H. *Stalin: The History of a Dictator.* London: Rupert Hart Davis, 1971.
Morris, Alan. *Collaboration and Resistance Reviewed: Writers and the Mode Retro in Post-Gaullist France.* New York: Berg Publishers, 1992.
Morris, Eric and Alan Hoe. *Terrorism: Threat and Response.* New York: St. Martin's Press, 1988.
Mosby, John S. *Mosby's War Reminiscences: Stuart's Cavalry Campaigns.* Camden, South Carolina: John Culler & Sons, 1996.
Moskoff, William. *The Bread of Affliction: The Food Supply in the USSR during World War II.* New York: Cambridge University Press, 1990.
Mosse, George Lachmann. *Toward the Final Solution: A History of European Racism.* London: Dent, 1978.
_____. *Germans and Jews.* London: Orbach & Chambers, 1971.
_____. *Nazi Culture: Intellectual, Cultural and Social Life in the Third Reich.* London: Allen, 1966.

_____. *The Crisis of German Ideology: Intellectual Origins of the Third Reich.* London; New York: Grosset and Dunlap, 1964.

Mowat R.C. *Ruin and Resurgence, 1939-1965.* London: Blandford Press, 1966.

Muehlberger, Detlef. *Hitler's Followers: Studies in the Sociology of the Nazi Movement.* London, New York: Routledge, 1991.

Mulligan, Timothy. *The Politics of Illusion and Empire: German Occupation Policy in the Soviet Union, 1942-1943.* New York: Praeger Publishers, 1988.

Munting, Roger. *The Economic Development of the USSR.* London: Croom Helm, 1982.

Munoz, Antonio J. *Forgotten Legions: Obscure Combat Formations of the Waffen SS.* New York: Paladin Press, 1991.

Murray, Philomena and Paul B. Rich (eds.). *Visions of European Unity.* Boulder, CO: Westview Press, 1996.

Murray, K.A.H. *History of the Second World War-Agriculture.* London: Her Majesty's Stationary Office, Longman, 1955.

Newman, Bob. *Guerrillas in the Mist: A Battlefield Guide to Clandestine Warfare.* New York: Paladin Press, 1997.

Newman, W.J. *The Balance of Power in the Interwar Years, 1919-1939.* New York: Random House, 1968.

Nicholls, Anthony James. *Weimar and the Rise of Hitler.* London: Macmillan Press, 1979.

Noakes, Jeremy. *Government, Party and People in Nazi Germany.* Exeter, UK: Books Britain, 1980.

_____. *The Nazi Party in Lower Saxony, 1921-1933.* London: New York: Oxford University Press, 1971.

Noakes, Jeremy and Geoffrey Pridham (eds.). *Nazism: 1919-1945: Foreign Policy, War and Racial Extermination: A Documentary Reader.* 3 vols. Devon, UK: University of Exeter Press, 1991.

_____. *Documents of Nazism, 1919-1945.* London: New York: Oxford University Press, 1974.

Noblecourt, J. *Hitler's Last Gamble: The Battle of the Ardennes.* London: Chatto & Windus, 1969.

Nolte, E. *Three Faces of Fascism.* London: Weidenfeld & Nicolson, 1965.

Northedge, F.S. (ed.). *The Foreign Policies of the Powers.* London: Faber and Faber, 1974.

_____. *Descent from Power: British Foreign Policy, 1945-1973.* London: Allen & Unwin, 1974.

_____. *A Hundred Years of International Relations.* London: Duckworth, 1971.

_____. *The Troubled Giant: Britain Among the Great Powers.* London: LSE Bell, 1966.

Nove, Alec. *An Economic History of the USSR.* 5th (ed.). New York: Penguin Books, 1982.

_____. *Stalinism and After.* London: Allen & Unwin, 1979.

Novik, P. *The Resistance versus Vichy: The Purge of Collaborators in Liberated France.* London: Chatto & Windus, 1968.

Nyomarka, Joseph. *Charisma and Factionalism in the Nazi Party.* Minneapolis: University of Minnesota Press, 1967.

O' Connell, Robert L. *Of Arms and Men: A History of War, Weapons and Aggression.* New York: Oxford University Press, 1989.

Odom, William. *The Soviet Volunteers: Modernization and Bureaucracy in a Mass Public Organization.* Princeton: Princeton University Press, 1974.

Ojala, E.M. *Agriculture and Economic Progress.* New York: London: Oxford University Press, 1951.

Okey, Robin. *Eastern Europe, 1740-1980: Feudalism to Communism.* London: Hutchinson, 1982.

Orlow, Dietrich. *The History of the Nazi Party, Vol. II, 1919-1933.* London: Newton Abbot, 1971.

Osanka, Franklin Mark (ed.). *Modern Guerrilla Warfare: Fighting Communist Guerrilla Movements.* New York: The Free Press, 1962.

Ovendale, Ritchie. *'Appeasement' and the English Speaking World: Britain, the United States, the Dominions, and the Policy of 'Appeasement', 1937-1939.* Swansea: University of Wales Press, 1975.

Overy, Richard James. *Russia's War.* London: New York: Penguin Books/Allen Lane, 1997.

_____. *Why the Allies Won.* London: Jonathan Cape, 1995.

_____. *War and Economy in the Third Reich.* New York; Oxford, UK: Oxford University Press, 1994.

_____. *The Nazi Economic Recovery, 1932-1938*. London: Macmillan, 1982.

_____. *The Air War, 1939-1945*. London: Europa, 1980.

Padfield, Peter. *Himmler: Reichsfuehrer-SS*. New York, London: Macmillan, 1990.

Paret, Peter (ed.). *The Makers of Modern Strategy from Machiavelli to the Nuclear Age*. Princeton: Princeton University Press, 1986.

Parker, R.A.C. *Chamberlain and Appeasement: British Policy and the Coming of the Second World War*. London: New York: Macmillan, 1993.

_____. *Struggle for Survival: History of the Second World War*. Oxford, UK: Oxford University Press, 1989.

_____. *Europe, 1919-45*. London: Weidenfeld & Nicolson, 1969.

Paul, Gerhard. *Aufstand der Bilder: Die NS-Propaganda vor 1933*. Bonn, West Germany: J.H.W. Dietz, 1990.

Pavlowitch, Stevan Kosta. *The Improbable Survivor: Yugoslavia and its Problems, 1918-1988*. London: Hurst, 1988.

Paxton, Robert O. and Michael R. Marrus. *Vichy France: Old Guard and New Order, 1940-1944*. New York: Columbia University Press, 1972.

Peterson, E.N. *The Limits of Hitler's Power*. Princeton: Princeton University Press, 1969.

Pethybridge, Roger. *The Social Prelude to Stalinism*. London: Macmillan, 1974.

_____. *The Spread of the Russian Revolution: Essays on 1917*. London: Macmillan, 1972.

_____. *A History of Postwar Russia*. London: Allen & Unwin, 1966.

_____. *Witnesses to the Russian Revolution*. London: Allen & Unwin, 1964.

Peukert, Detlev. *The Weimar Republic: The Crisis of Classical Modernity*. London: Penguin Books, 1993.

_____. *Inside Nazi Germany: Conformity, Opposition and Racism in Everyday Life*. Translation by Richard Deveson. New Haven, CT: Yale University Press, & London: Batsford, 1987.

Pipes, R. *The Formation of the Soviet Union*. Cambridge, Mass: Harvard University Press, 1964.

Pool, James and Suzanne. *Who Financed Hitler? The Secret Funding of Hitler's Rise to Power, 1919-1933*. Revised (ed.). New York: Pocket Books, 1997.

Peterson, Edward Norman. *Hjalmar Schacht*. Boston: Christopher Publishing House, 1954.

Preston, A. (ed.). *General Staffs and Diplomacy Before the Second World War*. London: Croom Helm, 1978.

Prittie, T. *Germans Against Hitler*. London: Hutchinson, 1964.

Proudfoot, Malcolm Jarvis. *European Refugees 1939-1952: A Study in Forced Population Movement*. London: Faber & Faber, 1957.

Quarrie, Bruce. *Lightning Death: The Story of the Waffen SS*. London: Patrick Stephens, Ltd., 1991.

_____. *Waffen SS in Russia*. 2nd Reprint trade paper. New York: Harper Collins, 1988.

_____. *Hitler's Teutonic Knights*. Wellingborough: Patrick Stephen, Ltd., 1986.

_____. *Hitler's Samurai: The Waffen SS in Action*. Wellingborough: Patrick Stephens, Ltd., 1984.

Quigley, Carroll. *Tragedy and Hope*. New York: Macmillan, 1966.

von Rauch, G. *A History of Soviet Russia*. 2nd ed. New York: Praeger, 1958.

Rauss, Erhard. *The Anvil of War*. London: Greenhill Books, 1994.

Remak, Joachim. *The Origins of the Second World War*. New Jersey: Prentice Hall, 1976.

_____. *The Nazi Years: A Documentary Reader*. New York: Prentice Hall, 1969.

Reiss, Kurt. *The Nazis Go Underground*. New York: Doubleday, 1944.

Reitlinger, Gerald. *The Final Solution: The Attempt to Exterminate the Jews of Europe, 1939-45*. 2nd (ed.). 1968. London: Valentine & Mitchell.

Reitlinger, Robert. *The SS: Alibi of a Nation*. London: Arms & Armour Press, 1981.

_____.*The House Built on Sand: The Conflicts of German Policy in Russia, 1939-1945*. London: Weidenfeld & Nicolson, 1960.

Rhodes, James M. *The Hitler Movement: The Modern Millenarian Revolution*. Stanford, CA Hoover Institution Press, 1980.

Rich, Norman. *Hitler's War Aims: Ideology, the Nazi State, and the Course of Expansion*. 2 vols. London: Deutsch, 1973-1974.

Rich, Paul B. and Richard Stubbs (eds.), 1997. *The Counter-Insurgent State: Guerrilla Warfare and State Building in the Twentieth Century*. New York: St. Martin's Press.

Richardson, H.F. *Sieg Heil! War Letters of Tank Gunner Karl Fuchs, 1937-1941*. London: Hamden, 1987.

Richardson, P. *Britain, Europe and the Modern World*. London: New York: Cambridge University Press, 1970.

Rieber, Alfred J. *Stalin and the French Communist Party, 1941-1947*. New York, London: Studies of the Russian Institute, Columbia University Press, 1962.

von Riekoff, H. *German-Polish Relations, 1918-1933*. Baltimore: Johns Hopkins University Press, 1971.

Rigby, Thomas Henry, Archie Brown and Peter Reddaway (eds.). *Authority, Power and Policy in the USSR: Essays Dedicated to Leonard Shapiro*. London: Macmillan Press, 1980.

Rigby, Thomas Henry and Bohdan Harasymiw (eds.). *Leadership Selection and Patron-Client Relations in the USSR and Yugoslavia*. London: George Allen & Unwin, 1983.

Rigby, Thomas Henry. *Communist Party Membership in the USSR, 1917-1967*. Princeton: Princeton University Press, 1968.

Ringer, Fritz K. *The German Inflation of 1923*. New York: Oxford University Press, 1969.

Ringleblum, Emmanuel. Translation and (ed.). by J. Sloan. *Notes from the Warsaw Ghetto: The Journal of Emmanuel Ringleblum.*. New York: Schocken, 1974.

Rings, Werner. *Life With the Enemy: Collaboration and Resistance in Hitler's Europe, 1939-1945*. Translation by J. Maxwell Brownjohn. London: Weidenfeld & Nicolson, 1982.

Ritter, Gerhard. *Sword and Sceptre: The Problem of Militarism in Germany*. 3 vols. London: Penguin Books, 1973.

_____. *The German Resistance: Carl Goerdeler's Struggle Against Tyranny*. London: Croom Helm, 1958.

Robertson, E.M. (ed.). *The Origins of the Second World War*. London: Macmillan Co., 1971.

_____. *Hitler's Pre-War Policy and Military Plans, 1933-39*. London: Longman, 1963.

Rock, W.R. *British Appeasement in the Nineteen Thirties*. London: Edward Arnold, 1977.

Roos, Hans. *A Modern History of Poland: From the Foundation of the State in the First World War to the Present Day*. London: Eyre & Spottiswoode, 1966.

Root, Waverley. *The Secret History of the War*. 3 vols. New York: Scribner's & Sons, 1945.

Rosenhaft, Eve. *Beating the Fascists? The German Communists and Political Violence, 1929-1933*. Cambridge, Mass: Harvard University Press, 1983.

Rosinski, Herbert. *The German Army*. Introduction & (ed.). by Gordon Craig. London: Pall Mall, 1966.

Rossiter, Margaret. *Women in the Resistance*. New York: Praeger, 1986.

Rothfels, Hans. Translation by Lawrence Wilson. *The German Opposition to Hitler: An Assessment*. London: Oswald Wolff, 1970.

Rowbotham, Sheila. *Women, Resistance, and Revolution*. London: Penguin Books, 1972.

Ruedel, Hans-Ulrich. *Stuka Pilot*. Forward by Group Captain Sir Douglas Bader. New York: Bantam Books, 1956.

Runciman, Walter Garrison (ed.), *A Critique of Max Weber's Philosophy of Social Science*. New York: Cambridge University Press, 1972.

Rupp, Leila. *Mobilizing Women for War: German and American Propaganda, 1939-1945*. Princeton: Princeton University Press, 1978.

Rusinow, Dennison. *The Yugoslav Experiment, 1948-1974*. London: C. Hurst for the Royal Institute of International Affairs, 1977.

Russell, Francis, et al. *The Secret War*. Alexandria, VA: Time-Life, Inc., 1981.

Russell, Edward, Baron Lord of Liverpool. *The Scourge of the Swastika: a Short History of Nazi War Crimes*. London: Cassell, 1954.

Ryan, Cornelius. *A Bridge Too Far*. London: Hamish Hamilton, 1974.

_____. *The Last Battle*. London: Collins, 1966.

_____. *The Longest Day*. London: New English Library, 1959.

Rybakov, Anatolii. *Heavy Sand*. Translation by Harold Shukman. New York: Viking Press, 1981.
Sajer, Guy. *Forgotten Soldier*, 2ⁿᵈ ed. Baltimore: The Nautical and Aviation Company of America, 1988.
Salmaggi, Cesare, et al. *2194 Days of War: An Illustrated Chronology of the Second World War*. New York: Windward, 1979.
Schapiro, L. *The Communist Party of the Soviet Union*. 6ᵗʰ (ed.). London: Methuen, 1978.
Shennan, Andrew. *Rethinking France: Plans for Renewal, 1940-1946*. London: New York: Oxford University Press, 1989.
Schlabrendorff, Fabien Graf von. *The Secret War Against Hitler*. London: Hodder & Stoughton, 1966.
Schmidt, G. *The Politics and Economics of Appeasement: British Foreign Policy in the 1930's*. Translation by Jackie Bennett-Ruete. New York: St. Martin's Press, 1987.
Schmit, P. *Hitler's Interpreter*. London: Heinemann, 1951.
Schoenbaum, David. *Hitler's Social Revolution: Class and Status in Nazi Germany, 1933-1939*. New York: Norton, 1980.
Schoenberg, Hans W. *Germans from the East: A Study of Their Migrations, Resettlement and Subsequent Group History Since 1945*. The Hague: Nijhoff, 1970.
Scholtz-Klink, Gertrude. *Die Frau im Dritten Reich*. Tuebingen, West Germany: Grabert, 1978.
Schulte, Theo J. *The German Army and Nazi Policies in Occupied Russia*. New York: Berg Publishers, 1989.
Schultz, Duane P. *Quantrill's War: The Life and Times of William Clarke Quantrill, 1837-1865*. New York: St. Martin's Press, 1996.
Schultz, Richard, Jr., Robert L. Pfaltzgraf, Jr., Uri Ra'anan, William J. Olson and Igor Lukes (eds.). *Guerrilla Warfare and Counterinsurgency: US-Soviet Foreign Relations in the Third World*. Lexington, Kentucky; Toronto: Lexington Books/DC Heath & Co., 1989.
Schweitzer, A. *Big Business in the Third Reich*. Bloomington: Indiana University Press, 1964.
Scott, Joan Wallach. *Gender and the Politics of History*. New York: Columbia University Press, 1988.
Scriven, Michael and Peter Wagstaff (eds.). *War and Society in Twentieth Century France*. New York: Berg, 1991.
Seaton, Albert. *The German Army, 1933-45*. London: Weidenfeld & Nicolson, 1982.
_____. *Stalin as Warlord*. London: Batsford, 1976.
_____. *The Russo-German War*. London: Barker, 1971.
Seton-Watson, Hugh. *The East European Revolution*. London: Methuen, 1956.
Service, Robert. *Lenin: A Political Life*. London: Macmillan: 1985.
Sherwood, Robert Emmet. *The White House Papers of Harry L. Hopkins: an Intimate History*. 2 vols. Vol. 2: *January 1942-July 1945*. London: Eyre & Spottiswoode, 1949.
Shirer, William L. *The Rise and Fall of the Third Reich*. New York: Simon & Schuster, 1960.
Shoup, Paul. *Communism and the Yugoslav National Question*. New York: Columbia University Press, 1968.
Shub, Anatole. *An Empire Loses Hope: The Return of Stalin's Ghost*. London: Jonathan Cape, 1971.
Siefken, Hans. (ed.). *Die Weiße Rosen: Student Resistance to National Socialism, 1942-43*. Nottingham, UK: University of Nottingham Press, 1991.
Singleton, Fred. *A Short History of the Yugoslav Peoples*. London: Croom Helm, 1985.
_____. *Twentieth Century Yugoslavia*. London: Macmillan, 1976.
Slaughter, Jane. *Women and the Italian Resistance, 1943-45*. Denver, Colorado: Arden Press, 1997.
_____. "Soviet Women as Partisans." *Military Women Worldwide: A Biographical Dictionary*. Reina Pennington (ed.), Westport, CT: Greenwood Press, in press.
Smelser, Ronald. and Rainer Zitelmann (eds.). *The Nazi Elite*. London: New York: Macmillan, 1993.
Smith, A.L. *Churchill's German Army: Wartime Strategy and Cold War Politics*. London: Sage, 1977.
Smith, Bradley F. *Himmler: A Nazi in the Making*. Stanford, CA Stanford University Press, 1971.
Smith, David. *Left and Right in Twentieth Century Europe*. London: Longman, 1979.
Smith, Graham (ed.), *The Nationalities Question in the Soviet Union*. London: New York: Longman, 1990.
Smolar, Hersh. *The Minsk Ghetto: Soviet-Jewish Partisans Against the Nazis*. Washington, D.C: The U.S. Holocaust Memorial Museum Shop Memorial, 1989.

Sohn-Rethel, A. *Economy and Class Structure of German Fascism.* London: C.S.E. Books, 1978.
Sonntag, R.J. an J.S. Beddie (eds.). *Nazi-Soviet Relations 1939-1941: Documents from the Archives of the German Foreign Office.* Westport, CT: Greenwood Press, 1974.
Speer, Albert. *Inside the Third Reich.* London: New York: Cardinal/Bantam, 1975.
Stachura, Peter D. *Poland in the Twentieth Century.* Basingstoke, UK: Macmillan, 1999.
_____. *Unemployment and the Great Depression in Weimar Germany.* Basingstoke, UK: Macmillan, 1986.
_____. *Gregor Strasser and the Rise of Fascism.* London: Allen & Unwin, 1983.
_____. (ed.). *The Nazi Machtergreifung.* London: George Allen & Unwin, 1983.
_____. *The Shaping of the Nazi State.* London: Croom Helm, 1978.
Stalin, Joseph. *Problems of Leninism.* Moscow: Foreign Languages Publishing House, 1953.
_____. *The Great Patriotic War of the Soviet Union.* New York: International Publishers, 1945.
Steenberg, Sven. *Vlasov.* Translation by Abe Farbtsein. New York: Alfred A. Knopf, 1970.
Stein, George H. *The Waffen SS: Hitler's Elite Guard at War, 1939-45.* Cornell: Cornell University Press, 1984.
Steinhoff, Johannes and Peter Pechel, Dennis Showalter and Helmut D. Schmidt. *Voices from the Third Reich: An Oral History.* New York: Da Capo Press, 1994.
Stephenson, Jill. *The Nazi Organization of Women.* London: Croom Helm, 1981.
_____. *Women in Nazi Society.* London: Croom Helm, 1975.
Sternhell, Zeev. *The Birth of Fascist Ideology.* Princeton: Princeton University Press, 1994.
_____. *Neither Right nor Left: Fascist Ideology in France.* Reprint (ed.). Translation by David Maisel. Princeton: Princeton University Press, 1986.
Stewart, George. *The White Armies of Russia: A Chronicle of Counter-Revolution and Allied Intervention.* Reprint of 1933 edition. New York: Russell & Russell, 1970.
Stites, Richard. *The Women's Liberation Movement in Russia: Feminism, Nihilism and Bolshevism, 1860-1930.* Princeton: Princeton University Press, 1978.
Stoakes, Geoffrey. *Hitler and the Quest for World Domination.* London: New York: Berg, 1986.
Stolper, G. *The German Economy, 1870 to the Present.* London: Weidenfeld & Nicolson, 1967.
Stone, Norman. *Europe Transformed, 1878-1919.* London: Fontana Paperbacks, 1983.
_____. *Hitler.* London: Hodder and Stoughton, 1980.
Strik-Strikfeldt, Wilfried. *Against Stalin and Hitler: Memoir of the Russian Liberation Movement, 1941-45.* New York: London: Macmillan, 1970.
Sudoplatov, Pavel, Anatoli Sudoplatov, Jerrold L. and Leona P. Schecter. *Special tasks: The Memoir of an Unwanted Witness-A Soviet Spymaster.* Boston: Little, Brown & Co., 1994.
Sugar, Peter F. (ed.). *Ethnic Diversity and Conflict in Eastern Europe.* Santa Barbara, CA Oxford-ABC Clio, 1980.
Suny, Ronald Grigor. *The Revenge of the Past.* Stanford: Stanford University Press, 1993.
_____. *The Revenge of the Past: Nationalism, Revolution and the Collapse of the Soviet Union.* Stanford: Stanford University Press, 1993.
Sutherland, Christine. *Monica.* Paris: Farrar, Straus & Giroux, 1990.
Sutin, Jack and Rochelle, Lawrence Sutin (ed.). *Jack and Rochelle: A Holocaust Story of Love and Resistance.* St. Paul, Minn.: Graywolf Press, 1995.
Suval, Stanley. *The Anschluss Question in the Weimar Era.* Baltimore: Johns Hopkins University Press, 1974.
Sweets, John. *Choices in Vichy France: The French Under Nazi Occupation.* New York: Oxford University Press, 1986.
_____. *The Politics of Resistance in France, 1940-1944: A History of the Movements Unis De La Resistance.* Dekalb: Northern Illinois University Press, 1976.
Sydnor, Charles W. *Soldiers of Destruction: The SS Death's Head Division, 1933-1945.* Princeton University Press, 1990.
Taylor, Alan John Percivale. *How Wars Begin.* London: Hamish Hamilton, Ltd., 1979.
_____. *The War Lords.* London: Hamish Hamilton, Ltd., 1976.
_____. *Beaverbrook.* London: Hamish Hamilton, Ltd., 1972.
_____. *The Course of German History.* London: Methuen, 1961.

_____. *The Origins of the Second World War*. London: Hamish Hamilton, Ltd. 1961.

Tec, Nechama. *Defiance: The Bielski Partisans*. New York: Oxford University Press, 1993.

Teicova, A. *An Economic Background to Munich: International Business and Czechoslovakia, 1918-1938*. London: New York: Cambridge University Press, 1974.

Terry, S.M. *Poland's Place in Europe: General Sikorsky and The Origin of the Oder-Niesse Line, 1939-1943*. Princeton: Princeton University Press, 1983.

Thayer, Charles W. *Guerrilla*. New York: Harper & Row, 1963.

The Hutchinson Dictionary of Ancient and Medieval Warfare. Oxford, UK: Helicon Publishing, 1998.

Thompson, Mark. *A Paper House: The Ending of Yugoslavia*. New York: Pantheon, 1992.

Thornton, M.J. *Nazism, 1918-1945*. London: Permagon Press, 1966.

Thucydides. *The Peloponnesian Wars*. Betty Radice (ed.). Translation by Rex Warner, introduction by M.I. Finlay. New York: Penguin Books, 1982.

Tiemann, Ralf. *Chronicle of the 7. Panzer-Kompanie, I. SS Panzer Division: 'Leibstandarte.'* Atglen, Penn: Schiffer Publishing, Ltd., 1998.

Tillon, C. *On Chantait Rouge*. Paris: Les FTP, 1977.

Time-Life Publications, et al. *Scorched Earth*. Alexandria, VA: Time-Life Books, Inc., 1991.

_____. *The Apparatus of Death*. Alexandria, VA: Time-Life Books, Inc., 1991.

_____. *Conquest of the Balkans*. Alexandria, VA: Time-Life Books, Inc., 1990.

_____. *The Center of the Web*. Alexandria, VA: Time-Life Books, Inc., 1990.

_____. *The SS*. Alexandria, VA: Time-Life Books Inc., 1989.

_____. *The New Order*. Alexandria, VA: Time-Life Books, Inc., 1989.

Toland, John. *Adolf Hitler*. New York: Doubleday, 1976.

Toliver, Raymond F. and Trevor Constable. *The Blonde Knight of Germany*. 8th (ed.). New York: Tab Books, 1986.

Tolstoy, Nikolai. *Stalin's Secret War*. London: Jonathan Cape: New York: Pan, 1981.

_____. *Victims of Yalta*. London: Hodder & Stoughton, Ltd. 1977.

Tomasevich, Jozo. *The Chetniks: War and Revolution in Yugoslavia, 1941-1945*. Stanford, CA: Stanford University Press, 1975.

Trevor-Roper, H.R (ed.). *Hitler's War Directives, 1939-1945*. London: Pan, 1966.

Trotsky, Leon. *The Revolution Betrayed: What is the Soviet Union and Where is it Going?* New York: Merit, 1965.

_____. *Stalin*. London: Hollis & Carter, 1947.

_____. *The New Course*. New York: New International, 1943.

Trunk, Isaiah. *Judenrat: The Jewish Councils in Eastern Europe under Nazi Occupation*. New York: Macmillan, 1972.

Tsouras, Peter G. (ed.). *Fighting in Hell: The German Ordeal on the Eastern Front*. London; Mechanicsburg, Penn: Greenhill Books & Stackpole Books, 1995.

Turner, H.A. Jr. *German Big Business and the Rise of Hitler*. 2nd ed. New York: Oxford University Press, 1987.

_____. (ed.). *Reappraisals of Fascism*. New York: New Viewpoints, 1975.

_____. (ed.). *Nazism and the Third Reich*. New York: Quadrangle Books, 1972.

Ulam, Alan B. *Expansion and Coexistence: Soviet Foreign Policy, 1917-1973*. 2nd ed. New York: London: Praeger, 1974.

_____. *Stalin: The Man and His Era*. 2nd ed. New York: Viking Press, 1973.

Urwin, Derek. *Western Europe Since 1945: A Political History*. 4th (ed.). London: Longman Group, 1989.

Vakar, Nicholas. *Belorussia: The Making of a Nation: A Case Study*. Cambridge, Mass: Harvard University Press, 1956.

Verba, Sidney and Lucien Pye (eds.). *Political Culture and Political Development*. Princeton: Princeton University Press, 1965.

Vermeil, Edmond. *Germany's Three Reichs: Their History and Culture*. London: A. Dakers, 1945.

Viola, Lynne. *Russian Peasant Women*. New York: Oxford University Press, 1992.

Viola, Lynee and Beatrice Farnsworth (eds.). *The Best Sons of the Fatherland: Workers in the Vanguard of Soviet Collectivization*. New York: Oxford University Press, 1987.

Volokogonov, Dmitrii. *Stalin: Triumph and Tragedy.* Translation by Harold Shukman. Rocklin, CA Prima Publishing, 1992.

Vucinich, Wayne S. *Contemporary Yugoslavia: Twenty Years of Socialist Experiment.* Los Angeles: University of California Press, 1969.

Walliman, Isidor and Michael N. Dokowski (eds.). *The Coming Age of Scarcity: Preventing Mass Death and Genocide in the Twenty-First Century.* Syracuse, New York: Syracuse University Press, 1998.

_____. *Genocide and the Modern Age.* Westport, CT: Greenwood Press, 1987.

_____. *Towards the Holocaust: The Social and Economic Collapse.* Westport, CT: Greenwood Press, 1983.

Ward, Chris. *Stalin's Russia.* London: Edward Arnold, 1993.

Warlimont, Walter. *Inside Hitler's Headquarters, 1939-45.* London: Weidenfeld & Nicolson, 1964.

Wasserstein, Bernard, *Britain and the Jews of Europe, 1939-1945.* New York: London: Institute of Jewish Affairs: Oxford University Press, 1988.

Walther, Herbert. *Waffen SS.* Atglen, Penn: Schiffer Publishing, 1989.

_____. *Twelfth SS Armored Division.* Atglen, Penn: Schiffer Publishing, Ltd., 1989.

_____. *The 1ˢᵗ SS Panzer Division.* Atglen, Penn: Schiffer Publishing, Ltd., 1989.

Walzer, Michael. *Just and Unjust Wars: A Moral Argument with Historical Illustrations.* New York: Basic Books, Inc. 1977.

Watt, D.C. *Too Serious a Business: European Armed Forces and the Approach to the Second World War.* London: Temple Smith, 1975.

_____. *Contemporary History in Europe.* London: Allen & Unwin, 1966.

_____. *Personalities and Policies: Studies in the Formulation of British Foreign Policy in the 20ᵗʰ Century.* London: Longman, 1965.

Wegner, Bernd. *The Waffen SS.* Translation by Ronald Webster. Oxford, UK: Basil Blackwell, Ltd., 1990.

Weinberg, Gerhard L. *The Foreign Policy of Hitler's Germany: Diplomatic Revolution in Europe, 1933-1936* (revised paperback). Chicago: University of Chicago Press, 1983.

_____. "The German Generals and the Outbreak of War, 1938-1939." Adrian Preston (ed.). *General Staffs and Diplomacy Before the Second World War.* London: Croom Helm, 1978.

Weitz, Margaret C. *Sisters in the Resistance: How Women Fought to Free France, 1940-1945.* New York: John Wiley, 1995.

Welch, David. *The Third Reich: Politics and Propaganda.* London: Routledge, 1995.

_____. *Nazi Propaganda: The Power and the Limitations.* London: Croom Helm, 1983.

Wells, Mark K. *Courage and Air Warfare: The Allied Aircrew Experience in the Second World War.* London: Frank Cass, 1995.

Wellsted, Ian. *SAS With the Maquis: In Action With the French Resistance, June-September 1944.* Mechanicsburg, Penn: Stackpole Books, 1997.

Werth, Alexander. *De Gaulle: A Political Biography.* New York: London: Penguin Books, 1965.

_____. *Russia at War, 1941-1945.* New York: Avon Books, 1964.

_____. *The De Gaulle Revolution.* London: R. Hale, 1960.

_____. *France 1940-1955.* London: R. Hale, 1956.

_____. *Leningrad.* London: Hamish Hamilton, Ltd., 1944.

_____. *Moscow '41.* London: Hamish Hamilton, Ltd., 1942.

West, Richard. *Tito and the Rise and Fall of Yugoslavia.* New York: Carrol and Graf Publishers, Inc., 1995.

Wheeler-Bennett, J.W. *Nemesis of Power: The German Army in Politics, 1918-1945.* London: Macmillan, 1961.

White, Dmitri Fedotoff. *The Growth of the Red Army.* Westport, CT: Hyperion Press, 1981.

White, Stephen (ed.), *New Directions in Soviet History.* Cambridge, UK: Cambridge University Press, 1992.

_____. *Political Culture and Soviet Politics.* New York: St. Martin's Press, 1979.

Wilkinson, James D. *The Intellectual Resistance in Europe.* Cambridge, Mass: Harvard University Press, 1981.

Williamson, D.G. *The Third Reich.* (ed.). Reprint of 1982. Harlow, Essex, UK: Longman House. 1993.
Williamson, Gordon K. *Loyalty Is My Honor.* Osceola, WI: Motorbooks International, 1995.
_____. *SS: The Bloodsoaked Soil.* Osceola, WI: Motorbooks International, 1995.
_____. *The SS: Hitler's Instrument of Terror: The Full Story from Street Fighters to the Waffen SS.* Osceola, WI: Motorbooks International & Wholesalers, 1994.
Wilson, Sir Duncan. *Tito's Yugoslavia.* Cambridge, UK; New York: Cambridge University Press, 1979.
Wilson, Lawrence. *The Road to Dictatorship.* London: Oswald Wolff, 1964.
Wiskemann, Elizabeth. *Czechs and Germans: A Study of the Struggle in the Historic Provinces of Bohemia and Moravia.* London: Macmillan, 1967.
_____. *Europe of the Dictators, 1919-1945.* London: Collins, 1966.
_____. *The Rome-Berlin Axis: A Study of the Relations between Hitler and Mussolini.* London: Collins, 1966.
Wolfe, Thomas W. *Soviet Power and Europe, 1945-1970.* Baltimore: Johns Hopkins University Press, 1970.
_____. *Soviet Strategy at the Crossroads.* Cambridge, Mass: Harvard University Press, 1965.
Wolff, Robert Lee. *The Balkans in Our Time.* Cambridge, Mass: Harvard University Press, 1956.
Woodruff, J.H. *Relations Between the Netherlands Government in Exile and Occupied Holland During World War Two.* Lansing: University of Michigan Press, 1961.
Wright, Gordon. *The Rise of Modern Europe: The Ordeal of Total War, 1939-45.* New York: London: Harper & Row, 1968.
Yedlin, Tova (ed.). *Women in Eastern Europe and the Soviet Union.* New York: Praeger, 1980.
Yerger, Mark C. *Waffen SS Commanders: The Army, Corps and Divisional Leaders of a Legend: Augsberger to Kreutz.* Atglen, Penn: Schiffer Publishing, Ltd., 1997.
_____. *SS Sturmbannfuehrer Ernst August Krag: Trager Des Ritterkreuz Mit Eichenlaub, Kommandeur SS Sturmgeschutzabteilung 2.* Atglen, Penn: Schiffer Publishing, Ltd., 1996.
_____. *Knights of Steel: The Structure, Development, and Personalities of the 2. SS-Panzer.* Mark C. Yerger, 1994.
Young, Peter, et al. *Atlas of the Second World War.* London: Weidenfeld & Nicolson, 1973.
Zadka, Saul. *Blood in Zion: How the Jewish Guerrillas Drove the British Out of Palestine.* London: Brassey's, Inc., 1995.
Zee, Henri A. van der. *The Hunger Winter: Occupied Holland, 1944-45.* London: Jill Norman & Hobhouse, 1982.
Zeman, Z.A.B. *Nazi Propaganda.* 2nd ed. London: New York: Oxford University Press, 1973.
Ziemke, Earl and Magna Bauer. *Moscow to Stalingrad: Decision in the East.* United States Army Historical Series, Washington D.C.: Center of Military History, United States Army, 1987.

Primary Sources
Public Records Office, Kew, London: British Archives
PRO FO 371/24078/233 (W 14035/45/480) Home Office Memorandum of 20 Sept. 1939, on Jews not allowed to immigrate to Britain due to fund shortages, and unrest in Palestine. No interest in the British government to help.
PRO CAB 98/1/262- Home Secretary Memorandum for Cabinet Committee on Refugee Problem, Dec. 1939. Much of this was due to financial assistance to Jews in Britain now unemployed; 3,000 domestic servants. Cites "Germans and Austrians in this country, being nationals of a state with which His Majesty is at war, are liable to be interned as 'enemy aliens,' but most of the Germans and Austrians now here are refugees from the regime against which this country is fighting, and many of them are anxious to help the country which has given them asylum(It would therefore be wrong to treat all Germans and Austrians as through they were 'enemies.' Cites Home Office Memorandum for the Guidance of Persons Appointed by the Secretary of State to Examine Cases of Germans and Austrians, September 1939, ISA 2D/38/41.
PRO FO 371/24078/233 ff. (W 14035/45/48). Home Office Memorandum, 20 September 1939-Certain foreigners were placed in either restrictive or non-restrictive categories. Also Jewish Chronicle,

13 Oct., and 10 Nov. 1939. Rumor of a German 'fifth column' in Holland that assisted the German invasion, written by the British Minister at The Hague, Sir Neville Bland, and disseminated throughout Whitehall. He advocated the internment of all Germans and Austrians without distinction. PRO FO 371/25189/462 (W 7984/7941/49). Minute of 14 May 1940. The criticism of interning only males in Britain from Sir Robert Vansittart, Chief Diplomatic Advisor to the Foreign Office. PRO FO 371/25189/425 (W 7984/7941/49) Minute of 20 May 1940.

PRO FO 371/24388/210 (C 2578/6/18) -British Consul General in Zurich warned about persons in Britain being used through their relatives still in Germany, providing cases to support this. Cites Memorandum by J.E. Bell, 6 February 1940.

PRO FO 371/25189/421 (W 7958/7941/49). Yencken to Foreign Office, 21 May 1940. Additional 'fifth column' information emerged from the British Embassy in Madrid regarding Jewish refugees in Spain and other places, who were promised the release of their relatives and safe return to Germany. Jews were being blamed for undercover support of the Germans.

PRO FO 371/25248/366 (W 8972/7848/48).-Italians interned also despite the fact that many had been in Britain for decades, fought in the last war for Britain, and were British citizens. Cites V. Cavendish-Bentinck minute, 29 July 1940.

PRO FO 371/25240/1 ff. (W 2812/38/48). Prejudice against Jews in Britain, mention of emigration to Palestine. Cites Minutes by R.T. E. Latham, 4 April 1940, and J.E.M. Carvell, 8 April 1940.

PRO FO 371/25253//140 (W 8686/8686/48). Latham was against anti-Semitism and alien male round-ups. Criticized British policy. Cites Latham minute, 27 June 1940.

PRO FO 371/25252/198 (W 10429/8261//48). United States permitted temporary emigration of Jews as long as Britain agreed to take them back six months after the war was over. MI5 refused fearing espionage and the return of agents.

PRO FO 371/25252/192 (W 10429/8261/48). Cites Minutes of Overseas Travel Committee, 28 October 1940, and Lothian to Foreign Office, 1 September 1940.

PRO FO 371/39092-July 1944 report by the Inter-Departmental Committee on the Transfer of German Population.

PRO FO 371/55831-Remarks on decreased German populations; demographic changes from September 1945 (30,000 Poles to 180,000-200-000 Germans) to September 1946 (100,000 Poles to 20,000 Germans) in Breslau, capitol of Silesia.

PRO C910/258/55 FO 371/34563-Response of J. Roberts in the Foreign Office on the Polish government's claim via General Sikorski's visit to the United States in 1942 on the Riga region. Roberts understood the Polish concern, since the once the Soviets were firmly on Polish soil, they would not be removed. Roberts also replied that it would serve the Poles no purpose, that it was "no good trying to mobilize us and the Americans against the Russians."

PRO C1089/258/55 FO 371/34563-Regarding minutes of the discussion on Polish complaints on the Soviet failure to recognize Polish expatriates living outside the Soviet controlled zone.

PRO C1286/12/18 FO 371/55391-Remarks of George Bell, Bishop of Chichester regarding statements in the House of Lords. His statement was that atrocities under Nazis were being reenacted at the current time, challenging the morality of trying war criminals at Nuremberg while civilians were being starved to death.

PRO C2269/12/18 FO 371/55392-Polish handling of Germans; forcing civilians to wear white arm bands, much like Jews with Stars of David under Nazism; German refugees given less food than Poles; risk of starvation.

PRO C2919/12/18 FO 371/55392-Regarding article published in the *Manchester Guardian* supporting reports of refugee women being raped, reported deaths to exposure, thefts of personal belongings by Poles, people under fifty kept as forced labour.

PRO C4301/4216/9 FO 371/46961-Regarding Stalin's comments during the Potsdam Conference over the ethnic Germans in the Oder-Neisse region. Stalin claimed they had departed, which was not true. Since an estimated 10,000,000 lived in the region and 5,000,000 had become refugees, the claim could not be taken seriously.

PRO C5243/95/18 FO 371/46812-Foreign Office and intelligence estimate in August 1945 that 900,000 refugees had received one night's shelter in Berlin. This memorandum was concerned with the immense population growth and the potential for disease. Also of concern was the need for the American and British zones to be opened to receive refugees; the local German government ordering 4,000,000 refugees out of Saxony in August 1945, and the failure of the Allies to assist in any way.

PRO C5257/95/18 FO 371/46812-Concern over public opinion to press reports, such as *The Times* and *The Economist*.

PRO C5753/95/18 FO 371/46812-Admission by J. Troutbeck, head of the Committee in July 1944 investigating problem of transfers and expulsions of ethnic Germans. His statement supported the government's position that nothing could be done. Cites the British plan to disclaim responsibility for disaster in Central Europe and blame Soviets. Clement Atlee made the statement on 13 September 1945 to a church delegation at No. 10 Downing Street.

PRO C6110/220/18 FO 371/39092-Suggestion on Britain not becoming deeply involved (e.g. troops in the region of Polish accessions) due to the potential psychological and political fall out of such an experience.

PRO C6546/95/18 FO 371/46813-Author Victor Gollancz (Our Threatened Values, 1946) letter to *The Times*, stating concern over British opinion regarding occupation of Germany becoming a burden, and the need to feed Europe as well in the coming winter.

PRO C6993/95/18 FO 371/46813-Request to Poland to suspend German expulsions.

PRO C7038/95/18 FO 371/46814-Letters from Germans in Silesia, mostly Evangelical Church members routed through George Bell, Bishop of Chichester, stating conditions under the Poles. Cites concern over British inspectors in Stettin due to crime.

PRO C849/231/55 FO 371/34560-Concerns over Poland's claims and the potential relocation of German civilians.

PRO C11469/3520/18 FO 371/55853-Confict regarding refugee problem; British plan to obtain German support by blaming the Soviets; Schumacher of the SPD in Cologne on 12 November 1945 stated that "…the frontiers of the east are frontiers with which a Social Democrat cannot agree." Konrad Adenauer demanded that all refugees should be returned to the eastern provinces, which should be returned to Germany.

PRO C11657/231/55 FO 371/34562-British reaction to the position of the Polish government in exile in London, as well as the Polish population in general in October 1943. This followed the break between Poland and the Soviet Union over the Katyn Forest incident. Anthony Eden's reaction and response to the Polish concerns are cited.

PRO C12169/464/55 FO 371/31091-Polish government memorandum regarding territorial claims to Oppeln district of Silesia, Danzig, East Prussia and bases on the Baltic Sea, without reference to Soviet territories, placing the Polish border with Germany at the Oder River.

PRO C13234/352/18 FO 371/55853-Report by L.G. Holliday on the population of Pomerania and East Prussia; the report considered it "…unwise to have handed over so much territory to the Poles…"

PRO C13266/2555/18 FO 371/47651-Report by L.G. Holliday of October 1946; Poles had achieved 60% of pre-war population and 40% of agricultural production.

PRO C14985/231/55 FO 371/34562-Concerns over Poland's ability to mandate and control large portions of previous German territory, as well as population relocation.

PRO HS-4/1-Most Secret Record of luncheon with President Benes dated 25 September 1942 regarding the assassination of Heydrich and the resistance in Czechoslovakia; another meeting with General Ingr on 8 December 1942 dated 11 December 1942 regarding possible rising in Czechoslovakia. Also Most Secret record from D/CD (O) to CD via Colonel Threlfall regarding record of meeting between MX and Colonel Moravec, dated 30 December 1942. Report on meeting with General Golian at Tri Duby, Slovakia on 7 October 1944, dated 23 October 1944. Memorandum from Major General H.R. Bull 5086 SHAEF to 12th Army Group regarding resistance in Czechoslovakia and UK base for OSS. Memorandum by SOE on Czechoslovakia dated 21 April 1945 regarding previous references dated 9 November 1944 and 18 January 1945. Top Secret cipher telegram from SHAEF to War Office dated 251610 April 1945. Top Secret cipher telegram dated 251640 April 1945 received 26 April 1945 from SHAEF Forward to 12th Army Group, War Office, UK Base (OSS) signed by Eisenhower regarding Czech resistance. Top Secret cipher telegram dated 26 April 1945 received on 27 April 1945 from AMSSO to SHAEF Forward regarding SOE control of resistance operations in Czechoslovakia. Letter from General Ingr relinquishing command of Czech forces dated 25 April 1945 with copies to Major General Gubbins, Horse Guards, Whitehall. Top Secret Priority Message from 12th

Army Group to SHAEF regarding OSS, SOE dated 271230B April 1945 received 272350B April 1945. Secret cipher telegram from AMSSO to SHAEF dated 8 May 1945 received 10 May 1945.
PRO HS-4/7-Cipher telegram dated 10 August 1944 regarding Czech deserters in Northern Italy and resistance potential. Immediate letter dated 30 August 1944 from British Embassy to the Czechoslovak Republic and Anthony Eden. Message from A/DH to CD regarding Yugoslavian resistance dated 8 January 1945. Outward telegram from Foreign Office to Moscow No. 1222 dated 12 March 1945 regarding SOE support of Czech resistance. Top Secret outward telegram from Foreign Office to Moscow dated 3 April 1945 regarding SOE position in Czechoslovakia. Letter dated 16 May 1945 regarding SOE and Russian attitude towards Czechs. Handwritten letter from M.P. to C.D. dated 16 May 1945 regarding German Army movement west and condition of troops. Report dated 16 May 1945 regarding the Czech rising, History of events from 30 April to 9 May 1945.
PRO HS-4/11-Top Secret report on Soviet Activity in Czechoslovakia dated 12 January 1945.
PRO HS-4/16-Most Secret Memorandum of Principles of Training for Special Purposes from General Ingr, no date.
PRO HS-4/44-Post Operational Report of Team Wolfram regarding partisan support operations in Czechoslovakia on 13 September 1944.
PRO HS-4/56-Top Secret report on Political and Partisan Activities in Slovakia from Central Department, No. 290 dated 1 September 1944.
PRO HS-4/68-Personal History Record of Frank Slepan, Slovak SOE volunteer with service file photographs. Personal History record of Michael Zipay, Czech SOE volunteer with photo-graphs.
PRO HS-4/78-Letter from MP to AD/E; "Project: Lone Parachute Agent for Protectorate" dated 25 January 1944. Most Secret memorandum from The Director of Training to the Commandant, Group A dated 28 January 1944 regarding Captain Gajdos' operation and logistics. Most Secret copy of letter from Commandant, Group A routed from MT regarding Gajdos' training and possible deployment.
PRO HS-4/79-Czech Brigade and SOE recruiting dated 18 September 1943.
PRO HS-4/82-58507-Black List of Gestapo Agents and Informers in Brno dated January 1944. List of agents and collaborators with their addresses for liquidation operations.
PRO HS-4/89-Top Secret map of Yugoslav Special Operations Executive mission assignments.
PRO HS-4/92-Letter from MPH2 to MP dated 4 October 1944 regarding declining role of SOE due to Russian advance; inability to monitor/control underground activities. Also Secret Report from Force 399 Account of Epigram Mission by Captain E.A. Howe and Lieutenant T.E. Byron regarding Hungary and Yugoslavia operations in support and evaluation of partisans and meeting with Red Army, assessment of situation; Appendix A regarding Gestapo atrocities against Serbs by "Spieler" in concentration camp.
PRO HS-4/115-Letter to "Aladar" from Gyorgy Paoloczi Horvath (alias George Peter Howard) dated 7 January 1942 (both English and Hungarian language documents) regarding Hungarian occupation by German Forces and potential for Hungary to join Allies, outlining potential dangers.
PRO HS-4/133 Supplemental operations assessment.
PRO HS-5/146-Top Level Planning-Istanbul HQ Policy, Planning & Organization of SOE Activities General. SOE Policy in South-Eastern Europe; Future of the Balkan States; Plan of Action for the Balkans; Suggestion on Policy for Yugoslavia; Notes on Policy for Romania; Hungary-Considerations of Policy.
PRO HS-5/148-Balkans-Top Level Planning, Policy & Planning of SOE Activities in General. Top Secret Cipher Telegram from AMSSO to AFHQ Algiers repeated JSM Washington, dated 28 June 1944 regarding Balkan Air Force and no change in SOE operations in Rumania and Bulgaria.
-Most Secret Cipher Telegram dated 20 May 1944 from AFHQ to AMSSO regarding Balkan Air Force supporting Soviet air operations from Italian bases, support for Tito's partisans and the evacuation of their wounded, continuing operations in Balkans.
-Most Secret memorandum by SOE dated 14 February 1944 regarding supplies to resistance groups.
-Most Secret cipher telegram from Air Ministry to Mideast dated 26 October 1943; concerns over Hungary and Rumania troubles over Transylvania. Concerns that SOE sponsored unrest would prove detrimental in enemy propaganda.
-Most Secret message from Algiers to "Etousa" dated 21 October 1943 regarding aid to partisans in Balkans with special airfield in Italy being prepared.

-Most Secret message from AGWAR to USFOR (ACTION) & ALGIERS 432 (ACTION) dated 19 October 1943 regarding guerrilla strengths at 230,000 in Balkans aided by SOE working in organized groups. These units were containing 17 German and 8 Bulgarian divisions in Yugoslavia, Albania and Greece. Organizing of supplies, munitions and captured Italian equipment to guerrillas on Dalmatian coast.

-Most Secret cipher telegram from Air Ministry to Britman in Washington dated 17 October 1943; impact of guerrilla operations in Yugoslavia, Albania and Greece, stating same numbers and information regarding partisans. Importance of maintaining pressure on German forces in Balkans in order to facilitate Italian campaign.

-Most Secret cipher telegram from Mideast to Air Ministry dated 15 October 1943; plan to create hostilities between Hungary and Rumania by firing on border guards to divert German divisions to quell any disturbance.

-Copy No. 14 of Most Secret & Personal memorandum dated 17 October 1943 regarding minutes of 22nd meeting and policy towards resistance groups in Greece. Concern over Evritana ELAS bands that attacked British Liaison Mission at Trikklinos, killing Lt. Hubbard, a New Zealander, as well as "submitting another British officer and a British other rank and a Greek interpreter under their protection to gross indignities."

-Most Secret memorandum preceding 15 October proposal to ignite hostilities between Hungary and Rumania, no date

-Most Secret cipher telegram from Mideast to Air Ministry dated 3 October 1943 regarding arming and supplying left-wing guerrilla forces, and the bleak prospect of the monarchy surviving in Greece and Yugoslavia, wishes to limit the assistance given to Communist guerrillas.

-Report dated 1 June 1943 regarding SOE Activities in Yugoslavia; cites racial enmities between Croats, Slovenes and Serbs, making build up of General Mihailovic as resistance leader in all Yugoslavia impossible, and his plans for a civil war once the war was over.

-Report dated 31 May 1943 on SOE Activities in Yugoslavia, attempt to build Mihailovic up as resistance leader nationwide; denouncing his Montenegrin leaders over the BBC.

-Memorandum dated 5.6.43 from CD to SO regarding support of the guerrilla war in Albania; belief that the Communists in Greece will support the monarchy with British and USA support, although Yugoslavia is unclear.

-Most Secret letter to Sir Anthony Eden from unknown source regarding concern over SOE developments in the Balkans, especially Yugoslavia and Greece.

-Secret memorandum by SOE dated 8 December 1942 regarding policy towards Rumania; German oil production, establishing sabotage parties.

-DPA Paper No. 2-SOE Policy for South Eastern Europe; fostering subversion against puppet governments and German allies, arming, assisting in all methods.

PRO HS-5/150-Balkans: OSS/SOE Coordination in the Balkans, May-December 1943.

-Copy No. 19 of Most Secret & Personal memorandum dated 23 December 1943 regarding Force 133 operations in Greece and Serbia.

-Copy No. 12 of Most Secret & Personal Memorandum from defense Committee, Special Operations in the Balkans: Coordination of OSS & SOE, note by H.M. Ambassador to Yugoslavia, dated 1 December 1943.

-Copy No. 12 of Most Secret & Personal Memorandum from Special Operations Committee, SOE/OSS Relations, note by Secretary, dated 21 November 1943.

-Secret letter dated 7 September 1943 from Brig. Gen. John R. Deane to Brig. Gen. William J. Donovan, Director, OSS.

-Secret memorandum dated 20 August 1943 from OSS, Washington, DC to Brig. Gen. John R. Deane from Brig. Gen. William J. Donovan.

-Most Secret Memorandum dated 20 October 1943 from The Hon. Sir Alexander Cadogan, Foreign Office.

-Secret memorandum dated 13 October 1943 from Sir Alexander Cadogan for circulation.

-Most Secret letter dated 4 October 1943 to Sir Alexander Cadogan to from C.D. regarding meeting with Donovan on OSS/SOE relations.

-Most Secret memorandum from C.D. to Cadogan dated 29 September 1943 regarding OSS in Bulgaria, Hungary, Rumania, also discussion with Donovan.
-Most Secret letter regarding OSS In Bulgaria, Rumania, and Hungary dated 25 September 1943 from C.D. to Cadogan.
-Minutes of meeting dated 29 September 1943 between Maj. Gen. Gubbins, Brig. Gen. Mockler Ferryman, Col. G.F. Taylor, Lt. Col. L. Franck, Lt. Col. B. Pleydell-Bouverie of SOE; Brig. Gen. W.J. Donovan and Col. David K.E. Bruce of OSS.
-Letter dated 11 August 1943 from A/D1 to V/CD regarding OSS/SOE Middle East Command, Southern France and Balkans operations.-Most Secret telegram from the Foreign Minister to the Minister of State, Cairo concerning American use of Heliopolis.
-Most Secret letter dated 28 July 1943 titled SOE/OSS COLLABORATION IN THE MIDDLE EAST.
PRO HS-5/151-Balkans: Resistance Movements & Partisan Forces/Assessment of Efficiency, December 1942.
-Memo dated 13 December 1942-Guerrilla activities in the Balkans, lack of transport being greatest failing in supporting movements.
-List of supplies and materiel sent to Yugoslavia, Albania, Greece.
-Copy No. 13 of Most Secret Memorandum by SOE dated October 1943 regarding support of guerrilla forces in Yugoslavia, Albania, and Greece.
-Report dated 16 December 1942-SOE Activities in the Balkans and their possible Allied Operations in the spring of 1943.
PRO HS-5/152-Balkans-Cairo HQ: Resistance Movements & Partisan Forces/International Relations Between Resistance Movements-Greece/Bulgaria.
-Memorandum on "Recent Military and Political Developments in Eastern Macedonia and Western Thrace" by Captain Riddle; citing difficulties between factions; Communists throwing people in jail without trials; unrest in general; Soviet Col. Zeitzoff's arrival and greeting provoked hostile reaction from EAM towards SOE; breakdown of political sympathies by region; offers military assessment of capabilities and weaponry; ELAS disarming SOE and other partisan groups.
-Memorandum dated 11 October 1944-Greece: Political. EAM-ELAS cooperation with Bulgarians; Sofia government instructed army to support "partisans," SOE concerns regarding separation of Macedonia from Greece through Bulgarian influence with Communist partisans.
PRO HS-5/153-Balkans: BARI SOM HQ-Resistance Movements & Partisan Forces: SOE Responsibility to Groups After the Liberation.
-Top Secret letter dated 29 August 1944 from HQ SOM CMF to BAF, BMM to JANL regarding SOM Obligations Post Resistance. While enemy is in occupation of Yugoslavia, provisions and supplies for 300,000 partisans will be maintained; upon withdrawal or collapse of enemy forces "even partial the measure of supplies should be immediately reviewed; provision only for resistance groups in enemy territory, not liberated areas; upon armistice all support should cease."
PRO HS-5/154-Balkans-SOE/Soviet NKVD Relations in Balkans: January 1944-June 1945 Part I.
-Most Secret cipher telegram No. 336: reports from Brinckman 30 Military Mission to War Office on Soviet attitudes; rapes, murders of civilians, his personal incarceration for six weeks, statement by Soviet commander that "Budapest would be ravaged." Disorderly conduct of Soviets, shooting of own officer trying to intervene in a rape, etc.
-Cipher telegram dated 3.11.44 of Soviets dismantling Ploesti refinery, requesting the return of all components.
-Most Secret cipher telegram dated 15 October 1944 from British Military Liaison Bucharest to War Office regarding Soviet acquisition of Rumanian naval assets taken to Odessa from Coustanza.
-Secret cipher telegram dated 15 October 1944 from Allied Control Commission Bulgaria to War Office regarding Tito's aspirations with Slav federation and Bulgarian mission to his headquarters.
-Cipher telegram from "Rocket" to "Glean" regarding Bulgarian atrocities against US airmen. Stating Bulgarians much worse than Rumanians; suspicion that OSS mission is to locate those guilty of atrocities.
-Cipher telegram to Moscow from MP dated 11.9.44 regarding Czech request for 10,000 units of anti-tetanus serum and 20,000 field dressings to supplement aid given by Soviets.

-Cipher telegram dated 16.8.44 from Force 133 to London stating no evidence of Soviet support for ELAS. Zervas uncommunicative when asked about the future.
-Cipher telegram dated 10.8.44 from Moscow regarding German High Command; POW Colonel stating High Command knows war is lost; ordered halt to deportations and village burnings, fear of reprisals by Soviets.
-Cipher telegram from Force 133 dated 8.8.44 regarding Soviet mission to Greece in violation of agreement.
-Most Secret cipher telegram from SAM via Moscow dated 27.4.44 and received 28.4.44 regarding continued distrust between NKVD and SOE.
-Most secret cipher telegram dated 21.4.44 from SAM referencing Moscow to War Office regarding Bulgarian partisan army of 7,000 and their status, most without arms.
-Most Secret cipher telegram from Moscow/SAM dated 19.4.44 regarding partisan activity listing infantry and artillery units in Bulgaria using captured stockpiles.
PRO HS-5/155-Balkans:SOE/Soviet NKVD Relations in the Balkans Part II.
-Most Secret cipher telegram from War Office to Military Mission Moscow dated 22 October 1943 regarding partisan success and continued operations in Yugoslavia and Greece. EDES (Moderate Republican-strength 5-6,000) extensively sabotaged communications in west; ELAS (Communist strength at 15,000) murdered British liaison officer. ELAS disarming EDES and Italian partisans.
-Cipher telegram to Moscow detailing Soviet drop of two men and one woman agent into Yugoslavia, despite NKVD/Soviet claims of no contact or interest.
-Letter dated 18 May 1944 from D/HT to AD/H1 citing 300,000 Russians fighting with Germans against resistance movements.
-Top Secret cipher telegram dated 17 April 1944 from Air Ministry to Britman in Washington regarding citing Soviet grievance over lack of support that would undermine Pointblank Directives. This includes support for Tito.
-Cipher telegram to Moscow dated 10.5.44 mentioning all Balkan countries, specifically clashes between ELAS and Zervas, rise of new anti-Communist pro-German EASAD in reign of terror.
-Cipher telegram dated 5.4.44 regarding report of both Antonescus returning from a meeting with Hitler; *100th Jaeger* Division pulled from Albania and withdrawn to Hungary.
-Cipher telegram to Moscow dated 24.3.44; Balkan background No. 10 stating ELAS, Zervas and Archbishop in Athens agree to cooperate with Cairo government if a) the King did not to return to Greece before general election: b) Liberal leader becomes Prime Minister upon German withdrawal. King unwilling to sign provisional act.
-Cipher telegram dated 7.3.44, Balkan Background No. 8 regarding Rumanian forces not willing to surrender to Soviets alone, but want British intervention; also agreement between Zervas and ELAS to stop civil war and unite against the Germans.-Letter from DP to AD-Cooperation with NKVD in Balkans dated 18 January 1944. Questions regarding feasibility and utilizing Soviet resources.
-Cipher telegram to Moscow dated 29.2.44, Balkans Background No. 7-High level conference between Zervas, EKKA, EAM, ELAS derailed German troops train, 200 officers drowned.
-Cipher telegram dated 18.1.44 states Albanians more interested in Left vs. Right Wing internal struggle than fighting Germans; EDES/Zervas and ELAS struggle continues, but there is hope; 17 German divisions remain in Yugoslavia, partisans having successes.
PRO HS-5/156-Balkans: SOE/Soviet NKVD Relations in the Balkans Part III.
-Cipher telegram dated 1.1.44 regarding Donovan's trip to Moscow, citing Soviet indifference to agreements; OSS management of re-supply fleet from Italy.
-Most Secret Cipher telegram from SAM regarding supplies and boots for partisans in Yugoslavia.
-Cipher telegram No. 865 to Moscow from "Rocket" dated 22.12.43 regarding Donovan's tours and his belief that OSS is viable and needs no tutelage from SOE, does not feel obligated to former agreements, OSS willing to coordinate with SOE on higher level.
-Cipher telegram No. 866 dated 22.12.43 from Rocket regarding Donovan's desire for independence in Balkans is considered dangerous, yet manageable.
-Most Secret Cipher telegram dated 19.12.43 regarding key codes to telegrams and personnel identification.

PRO HS-5/166-Balkans Report.
-Report dated 8.4.41: Small Scale Day to Day Sabotage in the Balkans Reported From 1st March to Date. Lists of sabotage through the Balkans by various groups supported by SOE.
-Letter to the Prime Minister dated March 1941 regarding Danube blocking planning to deprive Germans of materiel movement, especially oil; great hope pinned upon Maniu, Leader of the Rumanian Peasant Party; plans on cement filled barges to be used.
-Draft minute to Prime Minister dated 7 March 1941 regarding iron ore mines destroyed reducing Axis supply by 20% at Loznica, 100 km south-west of Belgrade; 154 wagon loads of coal destroyed between 27 December-18 January; limpet mine sank Italian steamer *Senio* (1,400 tons) loading meal near Split on 26 February; leading members but not top figures arrested.
PRO HS-5/167-Balkans: Possible Personnel. Recruitment, selection, interviews and service records of SOE personnel.
PRO HS-5/171-Foreign personnel: Security, Recruitment and Miscellaneous inquiries M-V.
PRO FO 916/90/19 War Office to Foreign Office, 31 July 1941.
PRO FO 371/25248/331 (W 8962/7848/48) Mrs. Theresa Steuer to H.W. Butcher, MP, 8 July, 1940.
PRO FO 371/25248/330 ff. (W 8962/7848/48) R.A. Butler minute of 12 July 1940 and R.T.E. Latham minutes of 10 and 16 July 1940.
PRO FO 371/25248/369 ff. (W 8972/7848/48) Aliens Policy memorandum by R.T.E. Latham, 19 July 1940.
PRO FO 371/25248/365 (W 8972/7848/48) J.G. Ward memo regarding Latham's denunciation of MI5 empowerment, 25 July 1940.
PRO FO 371/25248/366 (W 8972/7848/48) Minute of 29 July 1940.
PRO FO 371/25248/367 (W 8972/7848/48) Minute of 1 August 1940.
45/23515 (GEN 200/117/163) Home Office papers of 11 August 1941, 45/23514 (GEN 29/3/438).
PRO FO 371/25249/58, Minutes of Alien Advisory Committee, 22 November 1940.
PRO FO 371/25243/593 (W 12102/761/48) T.M. Snow minute, 11 December 1940.
PRO FO 371/25254/490 (W 12667/12667/48) Luxembourg Foreign Minister to British *Charge d' Affaires*, 16 December 1940.
PRO FO 371/25254/489 (W 12667/12667/48) Haveling to Lord Halifax, 17 December, 1940.
PRO FO 371/25254/487 (W 12667/12667/48) Latham minute 24 December 1940.
PRO FO 371/32683 (W 12276/4993/48) Millard (Foreign Office) to Thornley (Colonial Office), 4 September 1942.
PRO FO 371/25254/496 (W 12667/12667/48). Letter from Snow to Haveling, 13 January 1941.
PRO PREM 3/42/2/2. E.F. Jacob to Prime Minister Churchill, 13 January 1941.
PRO PREM 3/42/2/3. Churchill minute, 3 January 1941.
PRO FO 371/32683 (W 11681/4993/48) Minute by A.W.G. Randall, 7 September 1942 and minutes by F.K. Roberts, A.W.G. Randall, and R.L. Speight.
PRO FO 371/32681 (W 14673/4555/48) Minutes of meeting, 28 October 1942.
PRO FO 371/42725/14 (W 6380) Minutes of meeting at Foreign Office, 12 April 1944.
PRO PREM 4/39/3 Churchill minutes, 25 January 1941.
PRO FO 371/24481/40 (C 5143/5143/55) Pritt to Butler, 2 April 1940.
PRO FO 371/24461/57 (C 6231/5143/55). Letter from Savery to Maikens, 25 April 1940.
PRO FO 371/24481/60 (C 6231/5143/55). Letter from Wilkinson to Maikens, 6 May 1940.
PRO FO 371/24481/48 (C 5143/5143/55). Memorandum from Butler to Pritt, 27 July 1940.
PRO FO 371/24481/62 (C 8802/5143/55). Memorandum from Savery to Roberts, 19 August 1940.
PRO FO 371/24481/72 (C 10125/5143/55). Letter from Sir H. Kennard to Lord Halifax, 20 September 1940.
PRO FO 371/26769 (C 4878/4655/55) Minutes by F.K. Roberts, 13 May 1941.
PRO FO 371/24481/64 (C 8923/5143/55) Charles Bridge to F. Savery, 21 August 1940.
PRO FO 371/26769 (C 4878/4655/55) Minute by K.K. Roberts, 13 May 1941.
PRO FO 371/26737/35 (C 3836/815/55) Minute by C.W. Baxter, 22 April 1941.
PRO FO 371/26769 (C 4878/4655/55) Minute on meeting between R.A. Butler, Anthony Eden, Sidney Silverman, MP and Lady Reading, 26 May 1941.

PRO FO 371/26737/34 (C 3836/815/55) Minute by F.K. Roberts, 19 April 1941 and A.W.G. Randall minute, 21 April 1941.
PRO FO 371/39480 (C 1906/918/55) D. Allen minute, 15 February 1944.
PRO FO 371/39480 (C 2243/918/55) Tom Driberg, MP to R. Law, 12 February 1944.
PRO FO 371/26440 (C 12454/125/62) R.R. Stokes, MP to Sir Anthony Eden, 7 February 1941.
PRO FO 371/26640 (C 12778/125/62) Eleanore Rathbone, MP to R. Law, 1 November 1941.
PRO FO 371/26640 (C 12454/125/62) R.R. Stokes, MP to Eden 25 November 1941.
PRO N11630/96/55 FO 371/47650-Warning that Soviet soldiers were robbing everyone, including British inspectors and medical personnel.
PRO N12628/96/55 FO 371/47650-Report on the diminished Polish population in the East Prussian region under Soviet occupation. Also reports of poles changing German names of cities, reducing monuments, and the complete transition of Gdansk (formerly Danzig).

Her Majesty's Stationary Office London
Ministry of Food. *How Britain Was Fed in War Time.* Central Statistical Office; Monthly Digest of Statistics, January 1946.

Primary Sources and Locations
France
Musee des Invalides
Musee de la Resistance et de la Deportation.

Germany
Freiburg im Bresgau; Koblenz/Wartime Publications/Memoranda
Gehlen, Reinhard. *Abwehr* Documentation; Organization Gehlen Collection. Freiburg, TF.235. See also Gehlen Interrogation Files, United States National Archives, College Park, MD. No. M1270, Roll 24.
Kumm, Otto. Personal Letters, Diaries, courtesy of Kumm.
Stroop, Juergen. *There is No Longer a Jewish Quarter in Warsaw!* Berlin, Germany: Volk und Reich Verlag, 1944.
Wolff, Karl. *Kriegstagebuch, 1939-1945.* Unpublished, courtesy of Wolff.

Militaerarchiv Freiburg/Bundesarchiv Koblenz
Personnel Records (*Indicates Koblenz Location Only)

Hans Frank N-1110
Adolf Hitler N-1128
Georg *Graf* von Manteuffel N-1157
Konstantin von Neurath N-1310
Joachim von Ribbentrop N-1163
(also listed as NL-163 Koblenz)
Albert Speer N-1340*
Fritz-Dietloff *Graf* von der Carl Goerdeler N-1113*
Schulenburg N-1301
(also listed at NL-301 Koblenz)
Eberhard von Mackensen N-581
Wilhelm List N-33 Maximilian
Hermann von Witzleben N-23
Karl Gaisser N-279
Ernst Koestring N-123
Walter Reinhardt N-86
August von Mackensen N-39
Dr. Rudolf Himze N-331
Fedor von Bock N-22

Arthur Seyss-Inquart N-1180
Ludwig Beck N-28
Wilhelm Staedel N-1252
Karl Wever N-1203
Karl Wolff N-1465
Alfred Jodl N-69

Hans Doerr N-29
Wilhelm Keitel N-54
Walter Model N-6
Weichs N-19
Erwin von Witzleben N-231
Kurt Zeitzler N-63
Hans von Seeckt N-247
Paul von Lettow-Vorbeck N-103
Franz Halder N-220
Ferdinand Schoerner N-60
Helmuth Stieff N-114

Wilhelm Willemer N-342
Oskar Niedermayer N-122
Wolfgang Foerster N-121
Heinrich Himmler N-1126
Wilhelm *Ritter* von Leeb N-145
Konstantin *Freiherr* von Neurath N-1310

Erich von Manstein N-507
Hermann Hoth N-503
Wolfgang Kapp N-1309
Dietrich Bonheoffer N-1308
Josef Goebbels N-1118
Bernd *Freiherr* Freytag von Loringhoven N-525

Central Archive of the Russian Federation (GARF)
(Courtesy of Robert Gerd Ridgeway, Reina Pennington and Dr. Ken Slepyan)
Fond 6093: Records of State Radio
Fond 7021: Records of the Extraordinary State Commission on the Determination and Investigation of the Atrocities of the German-Fascist Invaders.
Fond 8355: Records of Osoaviakhim (Auschwitz).
Fond 8581: Record of the Soviet Information Bureau

Central Museum of the Armed Forces of the USSR (TsMVS)
Fond 4: Documents and Objects from the Soviet Partisan Movement.

Russian Center for the Preservation and Study of Documents of Recent History (RTsKhIDNI)
Fond 17: Records of the Central Committee.
Fond 69: Records of the Central Staff of the Partisan Movement.

Scientific Archive of the Institute of History of Russia, Department of Manuscripts (NA IIR ORF)
Fond 2: Records of the Commission on the History of the Great Patriotic War-The Partisan Movement.

Hoover Institution on War, Revolution and Peace
Alexander Dallin Collection: Materials including leaflets and unpublished manuscripts by partisans in the partisan war collected by Dallin.

Ohio State University
Cornelius Ryan Papers, Box 67, Folder 16 (Courtesy of Timothy A. Wray).

United States National Archives at College Park Maryland
Microfilm Publication Collection
M-1019 Roll 23: Post-war interrogation of *Waffen SS Obergruppenfuehrer* Josef "Sepp" Dietrich.
M-1019 Roll 39: Post-war interrogation of *Waffen SS Gruppenfuehrer* Otto Kumm.
M-1019 Roll 80: Post-war interrogation of *Waffen SS Obergruppenfuehrer* Karl Wolff.
M-1270 Rolls 23, Roll 24: Interrogation Reports of *Generalleutnant* Reinhard Gehlen, *Generaloberst* Edmund Gleise von Horstenau (0482), Albert Goering, et al.
T-311, Rolls 167-70, T-313 Roll 488, T-314 Roll 1457, T-315 Roll 2154, T-501 Rolls 247, 249, 264, 265; T-733 Roll 7: Unit records for *1ˢᵗ, 2ⁿᵈ, 3ʳᵈ, 4ᵗʰ, 9ᵗʰ, 10ᵗʰ,* and *12ᵗʰ Waffen SS Panzer* Divisions.

Television Documentaries & Newspapers-Various Dates
Great Britain
Daily Record & Mail. 12 September, 1939; 2, 3 January, 1940.
Manchester Guardian, 5 January, 1940.
Evening Times (Glasgow), various dates.
Forward. 16 September 1939; 9 & 16 March 1940.
The Times (London). 2-3 July 1934; 10 October 1934; 19 June 1936; 1 July 1936; May-July 1940.

The Partisans of Vilna. Documentary Film. Washington D.C.: Euro-American Home Video, 1987.

The Scottish Mail on Sunday. "The Picture that Finally Proves Konrad Kalejs is a Nazi Killer." 9 January 2000, pp. 8-9.

_____. *You*; magazine supplement. "Profile: A Lifetime of Resistance." 23 January 2000 pp. 32-37. Interview with Genevieve deGaulle Anthonioz.

The Daily Record and Mail. Dates of 2, 5, 8, 13, 14,15, 23 September 1939.

Manchester Guardian, various editions.

The Guardian. 30 November, 1998. Article-"Return to Auschwitz: Day Trip to the Death Camps," pp. 2-3

The Sunday Times Magazine. Barbara Wyllie, Paulina Bren and Sam Lowenberg, et al. 22 November 1998. Article-"Goering's List," pp. 44-52.

British Broadcasting Company. Documentary-"Real Lives: Albert Goering," broadcast on 5 December, 1998, BBC Channel 4.

_____. Documentary, "The Death Train." October Films Production, 1997. BBC Channel 4 Broadcast on 18 December 1998.

Jewish Chronicle (London). 28 February; 14 March 1941; 22 November 1940; 31 May 1940; 2 August & 26 July; 11 & 25 October 1940; 10, 24, 31 January; 28 February, 7 March, 15 April, 22 August 1941; 20 March, 17 & 31 July, 25 September 1942;

The Jewish Voice. Various editions.

Jewish Echo. Various editions.

Jewish Evening Times (Yiddish language). Various editions.

The Mail on Sunday

You

Russia

Partizanskaia Mest. Organ of the 5th Leningrad Partisan Brigade.

Partizanskaia Pravda. Organ of the United Partisan Detachments of the Southwestern Districts of Orel Oblast.

Pravda. Various dates.

United States

The New York Times, The Washington Post, The Washington Times.

American Jewish Yearbook, vol. 45, Philadelphia, 1943/5704.

Wilmington Star News.(UPI) "Ex-Nazi Officer Gets 5 Years." 25 July 1997, Sec. A-1, p. 2.

_____. "Ex-Vichy Official to Stand Trial." 27 January 1997, Sec. A-1, p. 2 and follow up story of 30 January 1997, Sec. A-1, p.1. Wilmington, North Carolina.

Germany

Frankfurter Zeitung, Die Welt, Bild am Sonntag, Voelkischer Beobachter (Berlin) April-September 1940; January 1941; December 1942.

_____. (Munich); January-May 1940.

Photograph Credits
U.S. National Archives
(Courtesy of Kevin Hymel and Raymond Denkhaus)
Adolf Hitler, Joachim von Ribbentrop, Wilhelm List, Wilhelm Bittrich, Fedor von Bock, Hasso von Manteuffel, Heinrich Himmler, Hermann Goering, Alfred Jodl, Walter Model, Franz Halder, Ferdinand Schoerner, Erich von Manstein, Georgy Zhukov.

Journals, Book Extracts and Articles
Alberton, Lothar. "German Liberalism and the Foundation of the Weimar Republic: A Missed Opportunity?" Anthony Nichols and Eric Matthias (eds.). *German Democracy and the Triumph of Hitler*, 1971, pp. 29-46.

Ackermann, Josef. "Heinrich Himmler." Ronald Smelser and Rainer Zitelmann (eds.). *The Nazi Elite.* London: New York: Macmillan, 1993.

Astor, D. "Why the Revolt Against Hitler Was Ignored." *Encounter.* Vol. 32. (1969) 3-13.

Asselbergs, W.J.M.A. "Dutch Culture." *Annals of the American Academy of Political and Social Science.* Vol. 245 (1946) 111-112.

Bajohr, Stefan. "WeiBlicher Arbeitsdienst im Dritten Reich: Ein Konflikt Zwischen Ideologie und Oeconomie," *Vierteljahrschaefte Fuer Zeitgeschichte.* Vol. 28, No. 3 (1980) 331-57.

Baldwin, P.M. "Clausewitz in Nazi Germany," *Journal of Contemporary History.* Vol. 16, No. 1 (1981) 5-26.

Balfour, M. "Another Look at Unconditional Surrender." *International Affairs.* Vol. 46 (1970) 258-279.

Barber, John and Mark Harrison. "The Image of Stalin in Propaganda and Public Opinion During World War 2." John and Carrol Gerrard (eds.). *World War 2 and the Soviet People: Selected Papers from the Fourth World Congress for Soviet and East European Studies.* London: Macmillan Press, 1993, pp. 38-49.

Barmin, A. "Kavaler ordena Slavy." *Docheri Rossii.* Cherniaeva, I. (ed.). Moscow: Sovetskaia Rossiia, 1975, pp. 65-70.

Bar-On, Zvi. "On the Position of the Jewish Partisan in the Soviet Partisan Movement." *First International Conference on the History of the Resistance Movements.* New York: Pergamon Press, 1960, pp. 215-247.

Barry, Major General R.H. "Military Balance Within Western Europe, May 1940." *History of the Second World War*, Vol. 1. 1966, pp. 169-177.

Bartov, Omer. "The Conduct of War: Soldiers and the Barbarization of Warfare." *Journal of Modern History*, Vol. 64, No. 4 (December 1992) 532-45.

Begg, H.M. and J.A. Stewart. "The Nationalist Movement in Scotland." *Journal of Contemporary History.* Vol. 6 (1971).

Bell, Kelly. "Costly Capture of Crete," *World War II.* Vol. 14, No. 1 (May 1999) Leesburg, VA: Primedia Publications, Inc., pp. 50-56.

_____. "Darlan Assassination: Death of a Double Dealer." *World War II.* Vol. 13, No. 3. (September 1998) Leesburg, VA: Primedia Publications, pp. 50-56.

Belyakov, Vladimir. "The Route of Death." *World War Two.* Vol. 7, No. 6 (March 1993) Leesburg, VA: Cowles History Group, pp. 22.

_____. "No Retreats Allowed." *World War II.* Vol. 7, No. 3 (September1992) Leesburg, Virginia: Cowles History Group, pp. 22-29, 70-71.

_____. "Stunned by War's Outbreak." *World War II.* Vol. 6, No. 2 (July 1991) Leesburg, Virginia: Cowles History Group, pp. 34-41.

Ben-Israel, H. "Cross Purposes: British Reactions to the German Anti-Nazi Opposition." *Journal of Contemporary History.* Vol. 20 (1985) 423-437.

Bessel, Richard. *The SA in the Eastern Regions of Germany, 1925-1934.* Unpublished Dissertation, Oxford, UK: University of Oxford, 1980.

Biggs, Mark Wayne. "Forty Days at Jotapata." *Military History.* Vol. 16, No. 1 (April 1999) Leesburg, VA: Primedia Publications, pp. 26-33.

Birnbaum, Pierre. "La France aux Francaise." *Histoire des Haines Nationalistes.* Editions du Seuil, Paris (1993).

Bittner, John R. "Undercover," *World War II.* Vol. 5, No. 1 (May 1990) Leesburg, VA: Empire Press, pp. 8, 64-66.

Blackburn, R. "The Break-up of Yugoslavia," *New Left Review* (May-June 1993).

Blair, I.D. "Wartime Problems of English Agriculture," *Agricultural History*, Vol. 15 (January 1941).

Blau, George E. *The German Campaign in Russia: Planning and Operations (1940-42).* Washington, D.C. Department of the Army Pamphlet No. 20-261a (1955).

Blum, J.C.H. "The Second World War and Dutch Society: Continuity and Change," A.C. Duke and C.A. Tamse (eds.). *War and Society.* The Hague: Nijhoff, 1977, pp. 228-249.

Boak, Helen. "National Socialism and Working Class Women Before 1933," Conan Fischer (ed.). *The

Rise of National Socialism and the Working Classes in Weimar Germany. Oxford: Berghahn, 1996, pp. 163-188.

Bock, G. "Anti-Natalism, Maternity, and Paternity in a National Socialist Regime," David Crew, (ed.). *Nazism and German Society*. London, New York: Oxford University Press: Routledge, 1994.

Bodot, Paul. "American Airmen Saved." *World War II*, Vol. 7, No. 6 (March 1993) Leesburg, Virginia: Cowles History Group, pp. 38-44.

Boldin, I. "Popular Reactions in Moscow to the German Invasion of June 22, 1941." *Soviet Union/ Union Sovietique*. Vol. 18, No. 1-3 (1991) 5-18.

Bollmus, R. "Alfred Rosenberg: National Socialism's 'Chief Ideologue?'" Ronald Smelser and Rainer Zitelmann (eds.). *The Nazi Elite*. London: Macmillan, 1993.

Bracher, Karl-Dietrich. "The Technique of the National Socialist Seizure of Power." Translation by Lawrence Wilson. *The Road to Dictatorship*. 2nd ed. London: Wolff, 1964.

Brode, Patrick. "Personality," *World War II*. Vol. 12, No. 6 (February 1998) Leesburg, VA: Primedia Publications, Inc., pp.18-24.

Brooks, Jeffrey. "Official Xenophobia and Popular Cosmopolitanism in Early Soviet Russia," *American Historical Review*. Vol. 97, No. 5. (December 1992) 1431-1448.

Brouwsers, K. "Price of Politics," *Annals of the American Academy of Social and Political Science*. Vol. 245 (1946) 39-47.

Brown, Archie. "Introduction" and "Conclusion." *Political Culture and Communist Studies*. Archie Brown (ed.). New York: M.E. Sharpe, 1985, pp. 2-9; 149-204.

Brown, Demming. "World War II in Soviet Literature." *The Impact of World War II on the Soviet Union*. Susan J. Linz (ed.). Ottawa: Rowman & Allanheld, 1985, pp. 243-251.

Brown, Robert J. "Britain's Bold Strike on the French Fleet," *World War II*. Vol. 12, No. 3 (September 1997) Leesburg, VA: Cowles History Group, pp. 50-56.

Bradford, Richard H. Review of Johann Ewald, *Treatise on Partisan Warfare*; *The Journal of Military History*. Vol. 57, No. 1 (January 1993) 141-42.

Bruins, J.A. "The Resistance," *Annals of the American Academy of Social and Political Sciences*, Vol. 245 (1946) pp. 144-148.

Brustein, William. "Blue-Collar Nazism: The German Working Class and the *Nazi* Party." Conan Fischer (ed.). *The Rise of National Socialism and the Working Classes in Weimar Germany*. Oxford, UK: Berghan, 1996, pp. 137-61.

Buchheim, Hans. "Instrument of Domination." Martin Broszat, et al (eds.). *Anatomy of the SS State*. London: New York: Paladin Press, 1970.

Buchler, Y. "Kommandostab Reichsfuehrer-SS: Himmler's Personal Murder Brigades in 1941," *Holocaust and Genocide*. Vol. 1 (1986) 11-25.

Bullock, Alan. "Hitler and the Origins of the Second World War." *The Origins of the Second World War*. E.M. Robertson (ed.). London: Oxford University Press, 1967.

Bullock, David L. "Reds Versus Whites." *Military History*. Vol. 9, No. 2 (June 1992) Leesburg, VA: Cowles History Group, pp. 42-49.

Burbank, Jane. "Controversies over Stalinism: Searching for a Soviet Society." *Politics and Society*, Vol. 19, No. 3 (1991) 325-340.

Burdett, Paul S., Jr. "Personality: Evelyn Waugh," *World War II*. Vol. 14, No. 1 (May 1999) Leesburg, VA: Primedia Publications, pp. 16-20, 74-6, 80.

Burleigh, Michael. "The German Knights: Making of a Modern Myth." *History Today*. Vol. 35, No. 6 (June 1985).

Caplan, Jane (ed.). Tim Mason, "Women in Germany, 1925-1940: Family, Welfare and Work." *Nazism, Fascism, and the Working Class*. New York: Cambridge University Press, 1995.

Carr, W. "A Final Solution: Nazi Policy Towards the Jews." *History Today*. Vol. 35 No. 11 (November 1985) 665-69.

Chalabian, Antranig. "Personality." *Military History*. Vol. 12, No. 2 (June 1995) Leesburg, VA: Cowles History Group, pp. 10-12, 16.

Chase, J. "Unconditional Surrender Reconsidered." *Political Science Quarterly*. Vol. 70 (1955) 258-279.

Chastain, R. Murray. "Undercover." *World War II*. Vol. 8, No. 3 (September 1993) Leesburg: Empire Press, pp. 14-20, 72-74.

Cherniavsky, Michael. "Corporal Hitler, General Winter and the Russian Peasant." *Yale Review*. No. 51 (1962) 547-558.

Childers, Thomas. "The Middle Class and National Socialism." D. Blackbourne and R.J. Evans. *The German Bourgeoisie. 1919-1933*. London, New York: Routledge, 1990, pp. 318-337.

_____. "The Social Basis of the National Socialist Vote." *Journal of Contemporary History*. Vol. 11, No. 4 (October 1976) 17-42.

Clearwater, John. "Undercover." *World War II*. Vol. 13, No. 6 (February 1999) Leesburg, VA: Primedia Publications, pp. 60-64.

Cohen, Stephen. "Stalin's Terror as Social History." *Russian Review*. Vol. 45, No. 4 (October 1986) 375-384.

Comtois, Pierre. "First Fire of Operation Torch." *World War II*. Vol. 11, No. 4 (November 1996) Leesburg, VA: Cowles History Group, pp. 54-60, 82.

Contey, Frank A. "British Debacle in German East Africa." *Military History*. Vol. 13, No. 5 (December 1996) Leesburg, VA: Cowles History Group, pp. 58-65, 86-87.

Conquest, Robert. "What is Terror?" *Slavic Review*. Vol. 45, No. 2 (Summer 1986) 235-237.

Corni, G. "Richard Walther Darre': The Blood and Soil Ideologue." Ronald Smelser and Rainer Zitelmann (eds.). *The Nazi Elite*. London: Macmillan, 1993.

Cottam, K. Jean. "Soviet Women in Combat in World War II: The Rear Services, Resistance Behind Enemy Lines, and Military Political Workers." *International Journal of Women's Studies*. Vol. 5, No. 4 (1982) 363-378.

Dallin, Alexander and Ralph Mavrogordato. "The Kaminsky Brigade: A Case Study of Soviet Disaffection." *Revolution and Politics in Russia: Essays in Memory of B.I. Nicolaevsky*. Alexander and Janet Rabinowitch (eds.). Bloomington: Indiana University Press, 1972, pp. 243-280.

_____. "Rodianov: A Case Study in Wartime Redefection." *American Slavic and East European Review*. No.18 (1959) 25-33.

D' Angelo, Rudy A. "Perspectives." *World War II*. Vol. 3, No. 3 (September 1999) Leesburg, VA: Primedia History Group, Inc., p. 18

Davenport, John. "Bloody Finale to 'Black Week'." *Military History*, Vol. 12, No. 6 (February 1996) Leesburg, VA: Cowles History Group, pp. 30-36.

Day, R.B. "Probrazhensky and the Theory of the Transition Period." *Soviet Studies*. Vol. 27 No. 2, Cambridge (1975).

Deac, Wilfred P. "Undercover." *World War II*. Vol. 13, No. 3 (September 1998) Leesburg, VA: Primedia Publications, pp. 18-24, 70-72.

_____."City Streets Contested." *World War II*. Vol. 9, No. 3 (September 1994) Leesburg, VA: Cowles History Group, pp. 32-44, 66.

Denkhaus, Raymond A. "Armament," *World War II*. Vol. 8, No. 2 (July 1993) Leesburg, VA: Cowles History Group, pp. 14, 68-69.

Department of the Army Pamphlet No. 20-291. *Effects of Climate on Combat in European Russia*. Washington, D.C., Department of the Army, Department of Defense (February 1952).

_____. Pamphlet No. 20-292. *Warfare in the Far North*. Washington, D.C., Department of the Army, Department of Defense (October 1951).

_____. Pamphlet No. 20-231. *Combat in Russian Forests and Swamps*. Washington, D.C., Department of the Army, Department of Defense (July 1951).

_____. Pamphlet No. 20-230. *Russian Combat Methods in World War Two*. Washington D.C., Department of the Army, Department of Defense (November 1950).

Descher, Guenther. "Reinhard Heydrich." Ronald Smelser and Rainer Zitelmann (eds.). *The Nazi Elite*. London: New York: Macmillan, 1993.

Deutsch, H.C. "The German Resistance: Answered and Unanswered Questions." *Central European History*. Vol. 14 (1981) 322-331.

Deutscher, Isaac. "A View of the Iron Curtain." L. Jay Olivia (ed.). *Russia and the West: From Peter the to Khrushchev*. Boston, Mass: Heath, 1965.

De Zayas, Alfred M. "The Legality of Mass Population Transfers: The German Experience, 1945-48." *East European Quarterly*. Vol. 12, No. 1 (1978).

Dodge, Nicholas. "Revolutionary Upheaval Survived," *Military History*. Vol. 11, No. 5 (December 1994) Leesburg, VA: Cowles History Group, pp. 54-61.

Donovan, Roberta. "Undercover." *World War II*. Vol. 7, No. 4 (November 1992) Leesburg, VA: Cowles History Group, pp. 10-12, 77-80.

Dunn, Walter S. Jr. "Deciphering Soviet Wartime Order of Battle: In Search of a New Methodology." *Journal of Soviet Studies*. Vol. 5 (September 1992) 402-25.

Eden, C. van. "Education of Youth," *Annals of the American Academy of Social and Political Science*. Vol. 245 (1946) 129-143.

Eley, Geoff. "History with the Politics Left out Again?" *Russian Review*. No. 45, No. 4 (October 1986) 385-394.

Ellis, Frank. "Army and Party in Conflict: Soldiers and Commissars in the Prose of Vasily Grossman." *World War 2 and the Soviet People: Selected Papers from the Fourth World Congress for Soviet and East European Studies*. John and Carol Gerrard (eds.). London: Macmillan Press, 1993, pp. 180-201.

Epstein, J. "Die Ausflerung der Wlassow-Truppen," *New Yorker Staatszeitung und Herold* (12 March 1955).

Erickson, John. "Soviet Women at War." *World War 2 and the Soviet People: Selected Papers from the Fourth World Congress for Soviet and East European Studies*. John and Carol Gerrard (eds.). London: Macmillan Press, 1993, pp. 50-76.

Fischer, George. "Vlasov and Hitler." *Journal of Modern History*. Vol. 23, No.1 (March 1951).

_____. "General Vlasov's Official Biography." *Russian Review*. Vol. 21, No. 8 (October 1949).

Fitpatrick, Sheila. "New Perspectives on Stalinism." *Russian Review*. Vol. 45, No. 4 (October 1986) 357-373.

_____. "Postwar Soviet Society: The Return to Normalcy." *The Impact of World War II on the Soviet Union*. Susan J. Linz (ed.). Ottawa: Rowman & Allanheld, 1985, pp. 129-156.

_____. "Stalin and the Making of a New Elite, 1928-1939." *Slavic Review*. Vol. 38, No. 2 (1979) 377-402.

Fleming, Thomas, "Espionage." *Military History*. Vol. 11, No. 1 (April 1994) Leesburg, VA: Cowles History Group, pp. 26-28, 84-86.

Fonner, D. Kent. "Personality," *Military History*. Vol. 12, No. 7 (March 1996) Leesburg, VA: Cowles History Group, pp. 10-12, 16.

Ford, F. "The Twentieth of July in the History of the German Resistance." *American Historical Review*. Vol. 51, No. 3 (June 1946) 609-626.

Fournie, Daniel A. "Intrigue," *Military History*. Vol. 14, No. 7 (March 1998) Leesburg, VA: Primedia Publications, pp. 12, 65.

Fraser, Ronald. "Reconstructing the Spanish Civil War." *New Left Review*. No. 129 (1981).

Friedman, Philip. "Jewish Resistance to Nazism: Its Various Forms and Aspects." *First International Conference on the History of the Resistance Movements*. New York: Pergamon Press, 1960, pp. 195-214.

Frisch, Franz A.P. and Wilbur D. Jones, Jr. "A Panzer Soldier's Story." *World War II*. Vol. 10, No. 3 (September 1995) Leesburg, VA: Cowles History Group, p. 50.

Frohlich, E. "Joseph Goebbels. The Propagandist." Ronald Smelser and Rainer Zitelmann (eds.). *The Nazi Elite*. London: Macmillan, 1993.

Galay, N. "The Partisan Forces." *The Red Army*. B.H. Liddell-Hart (ed.). New York: Harcourt Brace & Co., 1956, pp. 153-176.

Gallately, Robert. "Enforcing Racial Policy in Nazi Germany." Caplan and Childers (eds.). *Reevaluating the Third Reich*. New York: Holmes & Meier, 1993.

_____. "Situating the SS State in a Socio-Historical Context: Recent Histories of the SS, the Police and the Courts in the Third Reich." *Journal of Modern History*. Vol. 64, No. 2 (June 1992).

Gatske, Hans W., "Russo-German Military Collaboration During the Weimar Republic." *The American Historical Review*. Vol.63, No. 3 (April 1958) 565-97.

Gerrard, John and Carol. "Bitter Victory." *World War 2 and the Soviet People: Selected Papers from the Fourth World Congress for Soviet and East European Studies.* John and Carol Gerrard (eds.). London: Macmillan Press, 1993, pp. 1-27.

Getty, J. Arch. "State and Society under Stalin: Constitutions and Elections in the 1930s. " *Slavic Review.* Vol. 50, No. 1 (1991) 18-35.

Geyer, Michael. "German Strategy in the Age of Machine Warfare, 1914-1945." *Makers of Modern Strategy form Machiavelli to the Nuclear Age.* Peter Paret (ed.). Princeton: Princeton University Press, 1986, pp. 527-597.

_____. "The Nazi State: Machine or Morass." *History Today.* Vol. 36 (January 1986) 35-39.

_____. "Professionals and Junkers: German Rearmament and Politics in the Weimar Republic." Bassel, R. and E.J. Feuchtwanger (eds.). *Social Change and Political Development in Weimar Germany.* London: Croom Helm, 1981, pp.7-133.

Gies, Horst. "The NSDAP and Agrarian Organizations in the Final Phase of the Weimar Republic." *Nazism and the Third Reich.* H.A. Turner (ed.). New York: Quadrangle Books, 1972, pp. 45-88.

Gill, Graeme. "Political Myth and Stalin's Quest for Authority in the Party." *Authority, Power and Policy in the USSR: Essays Dedicated to Leonard Shapiro* T.H. Rigby, Archie Brown, and Peter Reddaway (eds.). London: Macmillan Press, 1980, pp. 98-117.

Gingerich, Mark P. "*Waffen SS* Recruitment in the Germanic Lands, 1040-41." *The Historian.* Vol. 59, No. 4 (Summer 1997) 818-30.

Glenn, John M. "Father of the Green Berets." *Military History.* Vol. 14, No. 6 (February 1998) Leesburg, VA: Primedia Publications, p. 50.

Glines, C.V. "The Amazing Bernt Balchen." *Aviation History.* Vol. 8, No. 6 (July 1998) Leesburg, VA: Primedia Publications, pp. 34-40, 74.

Graham, Martin F. "Terrible Lessons Learned." *World War II.* Vol. 8, No. 2 (July 1993) Leesburg, VA: Cowles History Group, pp. 22-28, 70.

Gray, Rebecca. "Perspectives." *World War II.* Vol. 13, No. 5. (January 1999) Leesburg, VA: Primedia Publications, pp.18-24.

Greenberg, Lawrence M. "Rolling Advance Stymied." *World War II.* Vol. 6, No. 2 (July 1991) Leesburg, VA: Empire Press, pp. 26-33.

Gumz, Jonathan. "German Counterinsurgency Policy in Independent Croatia, 1941-1944." *The Historian,* Vol. 61, No. 1 (Fall 1998) 33-50.

Gurian, Waldemar. "From Lenin Through Stalin." *Soviet Society: A Book of Readings.* Alex Inkeles and Kent Geiger (eds.). London: Constable & Co., Ltd., 1961.

Guttman, Jon. "Invasion's Driving Force." *World War II.* Vol. 9, No. 1 (May 1994) Leesburg, VA: Cowles History Group, p. 34.

_____. "Genocide Delayed." *World War II.* Vol. 8, No. 1 (May 1993) Leesburg, VA: Cowles History Group, pp. 44-52.

_____. "Armament." *World War II.* Vol. 7, No. 3 (September 1992) Leesburg, VA: Cowles History Group, p.10.

Gvozdenovic, Dusan. "The Supreme Headquarters of the People's Liberation Army and the Partisan Detachments in Yugoslavia in World War II.*" Revue Internationale d'Histoire Militaire.* No. 47 (1980) 189-206.

Hachtmann, Ruediger. "Industriearbeiten in Der Deutschen Kriegswirtschaft 1936 bis 1944/45." *Geschichte und Gesellschaft.* Vol. 19, No. 3 (1993) 332-366.

von Hagen, Mark: "Soviet Soldiers and Officers on the Eve of the German Invasion: Towards a Deception of Social Psychology and Political Attitudes." *Soviet Union/Union Sovietique.* Vol.18, No.1-3 (1991) 79-101.

Haimson, Leopold. "Civil War and the Problem of Social Identities in Early Twentieth Century Russia." *Party, State, and Society in the Russian Civil War.* Bloomington: Indiana University Press, 1989, pp. 24-47.

Hans, D. "The Legitimate Press," *Annals of the American Academy of Social and Political Sciences.* Vol. 234 (1946) 113-117.

Haskew, Michael E. "Edtorial." *World War II.* Vol. 13, No. 3 (September 1998) Leesburg, VA: Primedia Publications, p. 6.

Hauner, Milan. "Did Hitler Want a World Dominion?" *Journal of Contemporary History.* Vol. 13, No. 1 (1978) 15-32.

Hawes, Stephen. "The Individual and Resistance Community in France." *Resistance in Europe: 1941-1945.* Stephen Hawes and Ralph White (eds.). London: Allen Lane, 1975, pp. 117-134.

Hayostek, Cindy. "Undercover." *World War II.* Vol. 14, No. 1 (May 1999) Leesburg, VA: Primedia Publications, pp. 8-10.

Heaton, Colin D. "*Luftwaffe's* Father of the Night Fighters." *Military History.* Vol. 16, No. 6 (February 2000) Leesburg, VA: Primedia Publications, pp. 42-48.

_____. "The Count: *Luftwaffe* Ace Walter Krupinski." *Military History.* Vol. 15, No. 2 (June 1998) Leesburg, VA: Primedia Publishing Group, Inc., pp. 61-68.

_____. "Taking Belgrade by Bluff." *World War II.* Vol. 12, No. 5 (January 1998) Leesburg, VA: Cowles History Group, pp. 30-36.

_____. "*Luftwaffe* Ace Adolf Galland's Last Interview." *World War II.* Vol. 11, No. 5 (January 1996) Leesburg, VA: Cowles History Group,

_____. "*Luftwaffe* Ace Gunther Rall Remembers." *World War II.* Vol. 9, No. 6 (March 1995) Leesburg, VA: Cowles History Group, pp. 34-40, 77-78.

Heilman, Leo. "Organized Looting: The Basis of Partisan Warfare." *Military Review.* Vol. 45, No. 2 (1965) 61-68.

Hemingway, Al. "Ghost Front Attack." *Military History.* Vol. 9, No. 3 (August 1992) Leesburg, VA: Cowles History Group, pp. 50-57.

Herbert, U. "Labour and Extermintion: Economic Interest and the Primacy of *Weltanschauung* in National Socialism." *Past and Present.* No. 138 (February 1993) 144-195.

Herring, George. "Lend Lease to Russia and the Origins of the Cold War." *Journal of American History.* No. 56 (1969) 93-114.

Hill, L.E. "Towards a New History of the German Resistance to Hitler." *Central European History.* No. 14 (1981) 369-399.

Hines, Fritz. "Undercover," *World War II.* Vol. 8, No. 6 (March 1994) Leesburg, VA: Empire Press, pp. 12-16.

Hirschfeld, G. "Collaboration and Attentism in the Netherlands, 1940-41." Walter Lacquer, (ed.). *The Second World War: Essays in Military and Political History.* London: Sage, 1982, pp. 43-56.

House, Jonathan M. "Personality" *World War II.* Vol. 4, No. 5 (January 1990) Leesburg, VA: Empire Press, pp. 12, 16, 54.

Huchthausen, Peter A. "Perspectives." *World War II.* Vol. 12, No. 4 (November 1997) Leesburg, VA: Cowles History Group, p. 70.

Hull, Michael D. "Reviews." *World War II.* Vol. 12, No. 4 (November 1997) Leesburg, VA: Cowles History Group, p. 64.

_____. "Reviews." *World War II.* Vol. 9, No. 3 (September 1994) Leesburg, VA: Cowles History Group, p. 54.

Jaeckel, Eberhard. "Germany's Way into the Second World War," M. Laffan (ed.). *The Burden of German History, 1919-45.* London: Methuen, 1988, pp. 174-181.

Jennys, David R."D-Days Mighty Host." *World War II.* Vol. 9, No. 1 (May 1994) Leesburg, VA: Cowles History Group, p. 26.

Jones, Charles A. "Perspectives." *World War II.* Vol. 12, No. 1 (May 1997) Leesburg, VA: Cowles History Group, pp. 16-18, 70.

Jones, Gregory T. "Personality." *World War II.* Vol. 6, No. 2. (July 1991) Leesburg, VA: Empire Press, pp. 20, 78-82.

Jones, Larry E. "'The Dying Middle:' Weimar Germany and the Fragmentation of Bourgeois Politics." *Central European History.* Vol. 5 (1972).

Jong, Dr. L. de. "Anti-Nazi Resistance in the Netherlands: European Resistance Movements, 1939-1945," *First International Conference on the History of Resistance Movements.* London: Methuen, 1960, pp. 23-35.

Judt, Tony (ed.). Introduction." *Resistance and Revolution in Mediterranean Europe, 1939-1948.* New York: Routledge, 1989, pp. 1-28.

Kaplan, Cynthia. "The Impact of World War II on the Party." *The Impact of World War II on the Soviet Union.* Susan J. Linz (ed.). Ottawa: Rowman and Allanheld, 1985, pp. 157-187.

Karapalides, Harry J. "Militiaman in the Greek Civil War." *Military History.* Vol. 16, No. 1 (April 1999) Leesburg, VA: Primedia Publications, pp. 51-56.

Karski, Jan. "The Story of a Partisan Doctor." *The Golden-Tressed Soldier.* K. Jean Cottam (ed.) Manhattan, Kansas: Sunflower University Press, 1984., pp. 85-91.

Keesings Contemporary Archives: A Weekly Diary of World Events, 1941-42. London: Keesing, 1941-42.

_____. London: Keesing, 1943-46.

Kedward, H.R. and Roger Austin (eds.). "The Maquis and the Culture of the Outlaw." *Vichy France and the Resistance: Culture and Identity.* London: Croom & Helm, 1985, pp. 232-251.

Keegan, John. "The Race to Holland, August-September 1944." *History of the Second World War.* Vol. 5 (1966) 2101-2107.

Kent, George O. "Pope Pius XII and Germany: Some Aspects of German-Vatican Relations, 1933-1943." *American History Review.* Vol. 70, No.1 (October 1964) 59-68.

Kershaw, Ian. "The 'Hitler Myth': Image and Reality in the Third Reich," David Crew (ed.). *Nazism and German Society.* London: New York: Oxford University Press: Routledge, 1987, pp. 197-213.

_____. "How Effective Was Nazi propaganda?" David Welch (ed.). *Nazi Propaganda: The Power and the Limitations.* London: Croom Helm, 1983, pp. 180-205

_____. "Ideology, Propaganda, and the Rise of the Nazi Party;" Peter Stachura (ed.). *The Nazi Machtergreifung.* London: George Allen and Unwin, 1983, pp. 162-181.

Kettenacker, Lothar. "Hitler's Impact on the Lower Middle Class," David Welch (ed.). *Nazi Propaganda: The Power and the Limitations.* London: Croom Helm, 1983, pp. 10-28.

_____. "The Anglo-Soviet Alliance and the Problem of Germany." *Journal of Contemporary History.* Vol. 17 (no number) (1982) 435-58

Kleinwald, James. "No Relief for Stubborn Volunteers." *World War II.* Vol. 7, No. 1 (May 1992) Leesburg, VA: Cowles History Group, pp. 30-36.

Knox, M. "Conquest, Foreign and Domestic in Fascist Italy and Nazi Germany." *Journal of Modern History.* Vol. 56 (1984) pp. 1-57.

Koch, H.W. "Hitler's 'Programme' and the Genesis of Operation Barbarossa." *The Historical Journal.* Vol. 26, No. 4 (1983) 891-920.

_____. "Hitler and the Origins of the Second World War-Second Thoughts on the Status of Some of the Documents." *The Historical Journal.* Vol. 11, No. 1 (1968) 125-143.

Kocha, J. "German History Before Hitler: The Debate About the German Sonderweg." *Journal of Contemporary History.* Vol. 23, No. 1 (January 1988) 3-17.

Kollewijn, K.D. "Dutch Universities Under Nazi Domination," *Annals of the American Academy of Social and Political Science.* Vol. 245 (1946) 118-128.

Koonz, Claudia. "Ethical Dilemmas and Nazi Eugenics: Single Issue Dissent in Religious Contexts," *Journal of Modern History.* Vol. 64, No. 4 (1992) S8-S31 (supplemental).

Kotik, Ken. "Eagle of the Eastern Front." *Second World War.* Vol. 5, No. 2 (September 1996) Canoga Park, CA: Challenge Publications, Inc., pp. 65-68.

Krop, J.F. "Jews Under the Nazi Regime," *Annals of the American Academy of Social Science.* Vol. 245 (1946) 28-32.

Kumanyev, G.A. "On the Soviet People's Partisan Movement in the Hitlerite Invader's Rear, 1941-1944." *Revue Internationale d' Histoire Militaire.* No. 47 (1980) 180-188.

Kuromiya, Hiroaki. "The Crisis of Proletarian Identity in the Soviet Factory, 1928-1929." *Slavic Review.* Vol. 44, No. 2 (Summer 1985) 280-297.

Laffan, M. (ed.). "Weimar and Versailles: German Foreign Policy, 1919-1933," *The Burden of German History, 1919-45.* London: Methuen, 1988, pp. 81-103.

Lieberman, Sanford. "Crisis Management in the USSR: The Wartime System of Administration and Control." *The Impact of World War II on the Soviet Union.* Susan J. Linz (ed.). Ottawa: Rowman & Allanheld, 1985, pp. 59-76.

Legge, Steven J. "Personality." *World War II.* Vol. 13, No. 2 (July 1998) Leesburg, VA: Cowles History Group, pp. 8-14, 68-70.

Lew, Christopher. "Undercover." *World War II.* Vol. 11, No. 2 (July1996) Leesburg, VA: Cowles History Group, pp. 8, 20

Lewis, Brenda Ralph. "Caesar's Battle for Britannia." *Military History.* Vol. 12, No. 6 (February 1996) Leesburg, VA: Cowles History Group, pp. 46-53.

Lindsey, Brian. "Personality." *World War II*, Vol. 14, No. 2 (July 1999) Leesburg, VA: Primedia Publications, pp. 68-76.

Ludlow, P. "Britain and the Third Reich." H. Bull (ed.). *The Challenge of the Third Reich.* New York: Oxford University Press, 1986, pp. 141-163.

Luedtke, A. "The Appeal of Exterminating 'Others:' German Workers and the Limits of Resistance." *Journal of Modern History.* Vol. 64, No. 4 (December 1992) S46-S67 (supplemental).

Mai, Guenther. "National Socialist Factory Cell Organization and the German Labour Front: National Socialist Labour Policy and Organisations," Conan Fischer (ed.). *The Rise of National Socialism and the Working Classes in Weimar Germany.* Oxford, UK: Berghan, 1996, pp. 117-136.

Maliepaard, C.H.J. "Dutch Agricultural System," *Annals of the American Academy of Social and Political Science.* Vol. 245 (1946) 48-54.

Manne, R. "The Foreign Office and the Failure of Anglo-Soviet Rapprochement." *The Journal of Contemporary History.* Vol. 16, No. 4 (October 1981).

Manning, A.F. "The Position of the Dutch Government in London up to 1942." *Journal of Contemporary History,* Vol. 13 (1978) 117-135..

Marrus, Michael R. and Robert O. Paxton. "The Nazis and the Jews in Nazi Occupied Western Europe, 1940-1944," *Journal of Modern History.* Vol. 54, No. 4 (December 1982) 687-714.

Mason, H.L. "Testing Human Bonds Within Nations: Jews in the Occupied Netherlands." *Political Science Quarterly.* Vol. 99 (1984) 315-353.

_____. "War Comes to the Netherlands, September 1939-May 1940." *Political Science Quarterly.* Vol. 78 (1968) 548-580.

Mason, Tim. "Women in Germany, 1925-1940: Family, Welfare and Work," Jane Caplan (ed.). *Nazism, Fascism, and the Working Class.* New York: Cambridge University Press, 1995, pp. 131-211.

Mason, Tim. "The Workers' Opposition in Nazi Germany." *History Workshop Journal.* Issue 11 (Spring 1981) 120-137.

_____. "Labour in the Third Reich, 1933-1939." *Past and Present.* No. 33 (1966) 112-141.

Matthias, Erich. "Resistance to National Socialism: The Example of Mannheim." *Past and Present.* Vol. 45 (1969) 117-128.

McAuley, Mary. "Political Culture and Communist Policies: One Step Forward and Two Steps Back." Archie Brown (ed.). *Political Culture and Communist Studies.* New York: M.E. Sharpe, 1985, pp. 13-39.

McCaul, Ed. "Hungarian Freedom Fighter." *Military History.* Vol. 15, No. 4 (October 1998) Leesburg, VA: Primedia Publications, pp. 38-44.

McClure, Brooks. "Russia's Hidden Army." Franklin Mark Osanka (ed.). *Modern Guerrilla Warfare: Fighting Communist Guerrilla Movements..* New York: The Free Press, 1962, pp. 80-98.

McNeil, R. "The Decisions of the CPSU and the Great Purge." *Soviet Studies.* Vol. 23 (1971).

McTaggart, Pat. "Winter Tempest at Stalingrad." *World War II.* Vol. 12, No. 4 (November 1997) Leesburg, VA: Cowles History Group, pp. 30-36.

_____. "Desperate Panzer Counterattack at Debreccen." *World War II.* Vol. 11, No. 7 (March 1997) Leesburg, VA: Cowles History Group, pp. 42-48.

_____. "Soviet Encirclement Thwarted." *World War II.* Vol. 8, No. 5 (January 1994) Leesburg, VA: Cowles History Group, p. 34.

_____. "War's Greatest Tank Duel." *World War II*, Vol. 8, No. 2 (July 1993) Leesburg, VA: Cowles History Group, pp. 30-37.

_____. "Personality." *World War II.* Vol. 7, No. 2 (July 1992) Leesburg, VA: Cowles History Group, pp. 10, 67-70.

_____. "City's Death Throes." *World War II*, Vol. 5, No. 5 (January 1991) Leesburg, VA: Empire Press, pp. 22-28.

Michaelis, M. "Fascism, Totalitarianism and the Holocaust: Reflections on Current Interpretations of National Socialist Anti-Semitism." *European History Quarterly*. Vol.19, No. 1 (January 1989) 85-103.

Michel, H. "The Shadow States: Émigré Governments in London, 1940-42." *History of the Second World War*. Vol. 3 (1966) 1118-1120.

Miller, John. "Political Culture: Some Perennial Questions Reopened." *Political Culture and Communist Studies*. Archie Brown (ed.). New York: M.E. Sharpe, 1985, pp.40-61.

Milton, S. "Images of the Holocaust-Part I." *Holocaust and Genocide Studies*. Vol. 1 (1986) 27-61.

_____. "Images of the Holocaust-Part II." *Holocaust and Genocide Studies*. Vol. 1 (1986) 193-216.

Milward, Alan S. "French Labor and the German Economy, 1942-1945: An Essay on the Nature of the Fascist Order." *The Economic History Review*. 2nd series, Vol. 23, No. 2 (August 1970) 343.

Morgan, R.P. "The Political Significance of German-Soviet Trade Relations, 1922-25." *The Historical Journal*, Vol. 6, No. 2 (1963).

Mulligan, Timothy. "Reckoning the Cost of the People's War: The German Experience in the Central USSR." *Russian History/Histoire Russe*. Vol. 9, No.1 (1982) 27-48.

Munoz, Antonio J. "Herakles & The Swastika: Greek Volunteers in the German Army, Police, and *SS*, 1943-1945." *Axis Europa*, Inc., 1997.

Murphy, Jeffrey A. "Personality." *Military History*. Vol. 12, No. 4 (October 1995) Leesburg, VA: Cowles History Group, pp. 20, 24, 28, 80, 81.

Murphy, John F. Jr. "Endless Chain of Battle," *World War II*. Vol. 6, No. 6 (March 1992) Leesburg, VA: Cowles History Group, pp. 38-45.

Nariewicz, Olga. "Soviet Administration and the Grain Crisis of 1927-28." *Soviet Studies*. Vol. 20, No. 2 (1968) 235-41.

_____."Stalin, War, Communism and Collectivization." *Soviet Studies*. Vol. 18, No. 1 (1966) 20-37.

Neal, Larry. "The Economics and Finance of Bilateral Clearing Agreements: Germany, 1934-8." *The Economic History Review*. Vol. 32, No. 3 (August 1979) 392-404.

Nelson, Wayne. "Undercover: Women of the OSS." *World War II*. Vol. 12, No. 2 (July1997) Leesburg, VA: Cowles History Group.

Neumann, Sigmund and Mark von Hagen. "Engels and Marx on Revolution, War, and the Army in Society." *The Makers of Modern Strategy from Machiavelli to the Nuclear Age*. Peter Paret (ed.). Princeton: Princeton University Press, 1986, pp. 262-280.

Noakes, Jeremy. "Social Outcasts in Nazi Germany." *History Today*. Vol. 35 (December 1985) 15-19.

_____. "Conflict and Development in the NSDAP, 1924-1927." *Journal of Contemporary History*. Vol. 1, No. 4 (October 1966) 3-37.

Nolte, Ernst. "Big Business and German Politics: A Comment." *The American Historical Review*. Vol. 75, No. 1 (October 1969) 71-78.

Noordhoek, W.F.H. "The Resistance of the Medical Profession," *Annals of the American Academy of Social and Political Sciences*. Vol. 245 (1946) 162-168.

Nove, Alec. "Socialism, Centralized Planning and the One Party State." *Authority, Power and Policy in the USSR: Essays Dedicated to Leonard Shapiro*. T.H. Rigby, Archie Brown and Peter Reddaway (eds.).London: Macmillan Press, 1980, pp. 77-97.

Noyles, Harry F., III. "Sergeant's Odyssey." *World War II*. Vol. 8, No. 3 (September 1993) Leesburg, VA: Cowles History Group, p. 46.

O'Reilly, Donald. "Besiegers Besieged." *Military History*. Vol. 9. No. 6 (February 1993) Leesburg, VA: Empire Press, pp. 58-65, 94-96.

Orlovsky, Daniel. "Political Clientalism in Russia: The Historical Perspective." *Leadership Selection and patron-Client Relations in the USSR and Yugoslavia*. T.H. Rigby and Bohdan Harasymiw (eds.). London: George Allen & Unwin, 1983, pp. 174-199.

Orlow, Dietrich O. "The Conversion of Myths into Political Power: The Case of the Nazi Party," *The American Historical Review*. Vol. 72, No. 3 (April 1967) 906-924.

Overy, Richard J. "Hitler's War and the German Economy: A Reinterpretation." *Economic History Review*. Vol. 35 (1982) pp. 272-292.

Overy, Richard J., Tim Mason, and D. Kaiser. "Debate-Germany: 'Domestic Crisis' and War in 1939." *Journal of Contemporary History.* Vol. 9 (1974) 23-32. See also *Past and Present.* Vol. 122 (1989) 200-40.

Parker, Danny S. "Ten Percent Chance of Victory." *World War II.* Vol. 7, No. 2 (July 1992) Leesburg, VA: Cowles History Group, pp. 46-52, 62.

Paul, David. "Czechoslovakia's Political Culture Reconsidered." *Political Culture and Communist Studies,* Archie Brown (ed.). New York: M.E. Sharpe, 1985, pp. 134-146.

Paxton, R.O. "The German Opposition to Hitler: a Non-Germanist's View." *Central European History.* Vol. 14 (1981) 362-368.

Perkins, Frank. "Perspectives." *World War II.* Vol. 13, No. 3 (September 1998) Leesburg, VA: Primedia Publications, pp. 60-64.

Peukert, Detlev. "The Genesis of the 'Final Solution' from the Spirit of Science." David Crew (ed.). *Nazism and the German Society: 1933-1945.* London: New York: Routledge, 1994, pp. 274-296.

_____."Young People: For or Against the Nazis?" *History Today.* Vol. 35, No. 10 (October 1985) 15-22.

Posthumus, J.H. "The Structure of the Occupational Government." *The Annals of the American Academy of Social and Political Science.* Vol. 245 (May 1946) 1-2.

Raack, R.C. "Stalin's Plans for World War II." *Journal of Contemporary History.* Vol. 26, No. 2 (April 1991) 215-227.

Reed, Mary E. "The Anti-Fascist Front of Women and the Communist Party in Croatia: Conflicts within the Resistance." *Women in Eastern Europe and the Soviet Union.* Tova Yedlin (ed.). New York: Praeger, 1980, pp. 128-139

Reese, Roger. "The Impact of the Great Purge on the Red Army: Wrestling with the Hard Numbers." *Soviet and Post Soviet Review.* Vol. 19, No.1-3 (1992) 71-90.

Resis, Albert. "Spheres of Influence in Soviet Wartime Diplomacy." *Journal of Modern History.* Vol. 53, No. 3 (September 1981) 417-39.

Reynolds, George A. "Undercover." *World War II.* Vol. 5, No. 5 (January 1991) Leesburg, VA: Empire Press, pp. 16, 62-67.

Rice, Condoleeza. "The Making of Soviet Strategy." *Makers of Modern Strategy from Machiavelli to the Nuclear Age.* Peter Paret (ed.). Princeton: Princeton University Press, 1986, pp. 648-676.

Rigby, T.H. "A Conceptual Approach to Authority, Power and Policy in the Soviet Union." *Authority, Power and Policy in the USSR: Essays Dedicated to Leonard Schapiro.* T.H. Rigby, Archie Brown and Peter Reddaway (eds.). London: Macmillan Press, 1980, pp. 9-31.

Riley, Paul E. "Personality." *World War II.* Vol. 8, No. 1 (May 1993) Leesburg, VA: Empire Press, Inc., pp. 8, 68-72.

Ringer, F.K. "Mosse's Germans and Jews." *Journal of Modern History.* Vol. 44, No. 4 (December 1972) 392-397.

Roper, Hugh Trevor (ed.), introduction; "The Mind of Adolf Hitler." *Hitler's Table Talk.* London: Weidenfeld & Nicolson, 1953.

Ruble, Blair and Edward Bubis. "The Impact of World War II on Leningrad." *The Impact of World War II on the Soviet Union.* Susan J. Linz (ed.). Ottawa: Rowman & Allanheld, 1985, pp. 189-206.

Rupley, Richard M. "Perspectives." *World War II* (July 1993) Leesburg, VA: Cowles History Group, p. 62.

Salone, Ignazio. "Reflection on the Welfare State." *Dissent.* Vol. 8, No. 189 (1961).

Salter, Stephen. "Structures of Consensus and Coercion: Workers' Morale and the Maintenance of Work Discipline, 1939-1945." David Welch (ed.). *Nazi Propaganda: The Power and the Limitations.* London: Croom Helm, 1983, pp. 88-116.

Schartz, Paula. "Redefining Resistance: Women's Activism in Wartime France." *Behind the Lines: Gender and the Two World Wars.* Higonnet, Margaret, et al (eds.). New Haven, CT: Yale University Press, 1987, pp. 141-153.

Seaton, Albert. "Stalin and the Red Army General Staff in the Thirties." Adrian Preston (ed.) *General Staffs and Diplomacy before the Second World War.* London: Croom Helm, 1978.

Shy, John and Thomas W. Collier. "Revolutionary War." *Makers of Modern Strategy from Machiavelli to the Nuclear Age.* Peter Paret (ed.). Princeton: Princeton University Press, 1986, pp. 815-862.

Skilling, H. Gordon. "Czechoslovak Political Culture: Pluralism in an International Context." *Political Culture and Communist Studies*. Archie Brown (ed.). New York: M.E. Sharpe, 1985, 115-133.

Smith, Robert Barr. "Final Verdict at Nuremberg." *World War II*. Vol. 10, No. 4 (November 1995) Leesburg, VA: Cowles History Group, pp. 38-44, 83, 88

_____. "Nuremberg: Final Chapter for the Thousand Year Reich." *World War II* (November 1995) Leesburg, VA: Cowles History Group, p. 38.

Snailham, Richard. "Undercover." *World War II*. Vol. 11, No. 4 (November 1996) Leesburg, VA: Cowles History Group, p. 8.

Sollum, A.H. "Nowhere yet Everywhere." Franklin Mark Osanka (ed.). *Modern Guerrilla Warfare: Fighting Communist Movements*. New York: The Free Press, 1962, pp. 15-24.

Stachura, Peter D. "The *NSDAP* and the German Working Class, 1925-1933." Isador Walliman and Michael N. Dobkowski (eds.). *Towards the Holocaust: Fascism and Anti-Semitism in Weimar Germany*. Westport, CT: Greenwood Press, 1983.

Sternhell, Zeev. "National Socialism and Anti-Semitism: The Case of Maurice Barres," *Journal of Contemporary History*. Vol. 8, No. 4 (October 1973) 47-66.

Stern, G. "Soviet Foreign Policy in Theory and Practice." F.S. Northedge (ed.). *The Foreign Policies of the Powers*. London: Faber & Faber, 1974.

Stevenson, Jill. "Middle Class Women and National Socialist 'Service.'" *History*. Vol. 67, No. 229 (1982) 8.

Stolfi, Russell H.S. "10th Panzer's Lightning Eastern Front Offensive." *World War II*. Vol. 12, No. 3 (September 1997) Leesburg, VA: Cowles History Group, pp. 34-40.

Stout, Robert Joe. "Undercover." *World War II*. Vol. 5, No. 6 (March 1991) Leesburg, VA: Cowles History Group, pp.12-16.

Streit, Christian. "Partisans, Resistance, Prisoners of War." *Soviet Union-Union Sovietique*, Vol. 18, Nos. 1-3 (1991) 260-276.

Strobridge, Truman R. "Personality." *World War II*. Vol. 7, No. 5 (January 1993) Leesburg, VA: Empire Press, 8, pp. 69-72.

Swain, Geoffrey. "The Comintern and Southern Europe, 1938-1943." Tony Judt (ed.). *Resistance and Revolution in Mediterranean Europe, 1949-1948*. London: Routledge, 1989, pp. 29-52.

Szymczak, Robert. "Bolshevik Wave Breaks at Warsaw." *Military History*. Vol. 11, No. 6 (February 1995) Leesburg, VA: Cowles History Group, pp. 54-61, 90.

Talor, Lynne. "The Parti Communiste Francais and the French Resistance in the Second World War." Tony Judt (ed.). *Resistance and Revolution in Mediterranean Europe, 1939-1948*. London: Routledge, 1989, pp. 53-79.

Taylor, Barry. "Personality." *Military History*. Vol. 8, No. 2 (August 1991) Leesburg, VA: Empire Press, pp. 8, 12-16.

Taylor, Blaine. "Perspectives." *World War II*. Vol. 9, No. 1 (May 1994) Leesburg, VA: Cowles History Group, p. 42.

_____. "Personality." *World War II*. Vol. 8, No. 6 (March 1994) Leesburg, Virginia: Cowles History Group, p. 18.

Timmenga, A. "Concentration Camps in the Netherlands," *Annals of the American Academy of Social and Political Science*. Vol. 245 (1946) 19-27.

Thurston, Robert W. "Social Dimension of Stalinist Rule: Humour and Terror in the USSR 1935-1941," *Journal of Social History*. Vol. 24 (1991) 541-62.

_____. "Fear and Belief in the USSR's Great Terror." *Slavic Review*. Vol. 45, No. 2 (1986) 213-234.

Tolz, Vera. "New Information About the Deportation of Ethnic Groups in the USSR during World War 2." *World War 2 and the Soviet People: Selected Papers from the Fourth World Congress for Soviet and East European Studies*. John and Carol Gerrard (ed.). London: Macmillan Press, 1993, pp. 161-179.

Travis, David. "Communism and Resistance in Italy, 1943-1948." Tony Judt (ed.). *Resistance and Revolution in Mediterranean Europe, 1939-1948*. London: Routledge, 1989, pp.80-109.

Trouw, H.C. "The Resistance of the Netherlands' Churches," *Annals of the American Academy of Political and Social Science*. Vol. 245 (1946) 149-161.

Truby, J. David. "Russia's Female Snipers." *Modern Gun*, October (year unknown) pp. 27-29, 73.

Tumarkin, Nina. "Story of a War Memorial." *World War 2 and the Soviet People: Selected Papers from the Fourth World Congress for Soviet and East European Studies*. John and Carol Gerrard (eds.). London: Macmillan Press, 1993, pp. 125-146.

_____. "The Invasion and War as Myth and Reality." *Soviet Union/Union Sovietique*, Vol. 18, No. 1-3 (1991) 277-296.

Turner, Henry Ashby. "Big Business and the Rise of Hitler." *The American Historical Review*. Vol. 75 (1969) 56-70.

Viola, Lynne. "The Peasant Nightmare: Visions of the Apocalypse in the Soviet Countryside." *Journal of Modern History*. Vol. 62, No. 4 (December 1990) 747-770.

Verba, Sidney. "Comparative Political Culture." *Political Culture and Political Development*. Lucien Pye and Sidney Verba (eds.) Princeton: Princeton University Press, 1965, pp. 512-560.

Vonk, K. "The Transportation System," *Annals of the American Academy of Social and Political Science*. Vol. 245 (1946) 70-78.

Ward, James J. " 'Smash the Fascists...' Germany Communist Efforts to Counter the Nazis, 1930-31." *Central European History*. Vol. 14 (1981) 30-62.

Watt, D.C. "New Light on Hitler's Apprenticeship." *History Today*. Vol. 9, No. 11 (November 1959).

Weeks, Albert L. "Perspectives." *Military History*, Vol. 16, No. 1 (November 1998) Leesburg, VA: Primedia Publications, pp. 12-24.

_____. "Personality." *World War II*. Vol. 12, No, 4 (November 1997) Leesburg, VA: Cowles History Group, pp. 8-10.

_____. "Undercover." *World War II*. Vol. 10, No. 3 (September 1994) Leesburg, VA: Cowles History Group, pp. 8-10, 14-16.

Welch, David. "Manufacturing a Consensus: Nazi Propaganda and the Building of a 'National Community' (Volksgemeinschaft)." *Contemporary European History*. Vol. 2, No. 1 (1993) 1-15.

_____. "Propaganda and Indoctrination in the Third Reich: Success or Failure?" *European History Quarterly*. Vol. 17, No. 4 (1987) 403-422.

Wheeler, Mark. "Pariahs to Partisans to Power: The Communist Party of Yugoslavia." Tony Judt, (ed.). *Resistance and Revolution in Mediterranean Europe, 1939-1948*. London: Routledge, 1989, pp. 110-156.

White, Ralph. "The Unity and Diversity of European Resistance." *Resistance in Europe: 1941-1945*. Stephen Hawes and Ralph White (eds.). London: Allen Lane, 1975, pp. 7-23.

White, Stephen. "Soviet Political Culture Reassessed." *Political Culture and Communist Studies*. Archie Brown (ed.). New York: M.E. Sharpe, 1985, pp. 62-99.

Wilke, G. "Village Life in Nazi Germany." *History Today*. Vol. 35 (October 1985) 23-26.

Wilkins, Frederick. "Guerrilla Warfare." Franklin Mark Osanka (ed.). *Modern Guerrilla Warfare: Fighting Communist Guerrilla Movements*. New York: The Free Press, 1962, pp. 3-14.

Winkler, Heinrich August. "German Society, Hitler and the Illusion of Restoration, 1930-33." *Journal of Contemporary History*. Vol. 11, No. 4 (October 1976) 1-16.

Wolf, Thomas H. "Perpsectives." *World War II*. Vol. 10, No. 3 (September 1995) Leesburg, VA: Cowles History Group, pp. 66-72.

X. (Unkown author)."The Sources of Soviet Conduct." *Foreign Affairs*. Vol. 25, No. 4 (July 1947) 566-82.

Zabecki, David T. "Personality," *World War II*. Vol. 12, No.1 (May 1997) Leesburg, VA: Primedia Publications, pp. 8-12, 69.

Zizmond, Egon. "The Collapse of the Yugoslav Economy." *Soviet Studies*. Vol. 44, No. 1 (1992).

And Unpublished Dissertations/Theses

Adams, Catriona. *Stalin: A Popular Leader?* Unpublished Dissertation. Glasgow: University of Strathclyde, Department of History, no date.

Baxter, Julie M. *Church and State in Nazi Germany*. Unpublished Dissertation. Glasgow: University of Strathclyde, Department of History, no date.

Biddiscombe, Alexander P. *The Last Ditch: An Organizational History of the Nazi Werwolf Movement, 1944-45*. London: University of London, 1991.

Bramwell, Anna. "The Resettlement of Ethnic Germans, 1939-41." Unpublished Thesis. Workshop on European and Middle East Refugees in the 20th Century. Oxford University (August 1985).

Breen, John C. *Attitude and Opinion During the Phony War: September 1939-April 1940.* Unpublished Dissertation. Glasgow: University of Strathclyde, 1974.

Breslin, Terese-Marie. *Anti-Semitism in France: In What Circumstances did Anti-Semitism Become a Major Political Force in French Politics?* Unpublished Dissertation. Glasgow: University of Strathclyde, Department of History. 1995.

Brewer, Susan Ann. *Creating the Special Relationship: British Propaganda in the United States during the Second World War.* DA 9204033. Ithaca, New York: Cornell University, February 1992.

Carruthers, June. *Civilian and Military Prisoners in Britain During the Second World War.* Unpublished Dissertation. Glasgow: University of Strathclyde, Department of History, no date.

Chaudry, Bobby. *Factionalism in the NSDAP 1925-1933: A History and Evaluation.* Unpublished Dissertation. Glasgow: University of Strathclyde, Department of History, 1994.

Corum, James Sterling. *The Reichswehr and the Concept of Mobile War in the Era of Hans von Seeckt.* DANN 61452 Canada: Queen's University of Kingston, May 1992.

Davidson, Jaqueline. *The Formation and Social Structure of the NSDAP's Constituency, 1928-1932.* Unpublished Dissertation. Glasgow: University of Strathclyde, Department of History, 1996.

Devaney, Mark. *The Road to Munich.* Unpublished Dissertation. Glasgow: University of Strathclyde, Department of History, no date.

Dickie, Rona. *Were the Western Powers Correct in Insisting Upon Unconditional Surrender or, in the Light of Opposition in Germany to Hitler, did it Prolong the War?"* Unpublished Dissertation. Glasgow: University of Strathclyde, Department of History, 1995.

Dobriansky, Paula J. *The Military Determinants of Soviet Foreign Policy, 1945-1988.* (PS) DA 9207039. Cambridge, Mass. Harvard University, April 1992.

Donnelly, Cameron G.D. *The Nazi-Soviet Pact of 23ʳᵈ August, 1939 and the Relations Between the Two Countries Until the German Invasion of Russia on 22ⁿᵈ June, 1941.*Unpublished Dissertation. Glasgow: University of Strathclyde, Department of History, 1983.

Doran, Laura. *The Nazi Economic Persecution of the Jews: An Interpretation.* Unpublished Dissertation, Glasgow: University of Strathclyde, Department of History, 1996.

De Zayas, Alfred M. *Mass Expulsions: Historical and Ethical Dimensions.* Unpublished Thesis. Workshop on European and Middle East Refugees in the 20ᵗʰ Century. Oxford University (August 1985).

Esnouf, G.N. *British Government War Aims and Attitudes towards a Negotiated Peace, September 1939 to July 1940.* London: University of London, 1988.

Foglesong, David Scott. *Amercia's Secret War against Bolshevism: United States Intervention in the Russian Civil War, 1917-1920.* DA 920561. Berkeley: University of California, Berkeley, 1991.

Forrest, Linda. *The Rise of Nazism.* Unpublished Dissertation. Glasgow: University of Strathclyde, Department of History, 1982.

Gardner, John. *Could the NSDAP Have Attained Power without the Personality and Politics of Adolf Hitler.* Unpublished Dissertation. Glasgow: University of Strathclyde, Department of History, 1992.

Gingerich, Mark P. *Toward a Brotherhood of Arms: Waffen SS Recruitment of Germanic Volunteers, 1940-1945.* DA 9134318. Madison: University of Wisconsin, April 1992.

Giziowski, Richard John. *The Moral Dilemmas of Leadership: The Case of German General Johannes Blaskowitz.* DA 9203046. Illinois State University, February 1992.

Grant, Gavin. *The British Attitude to the Expulsion of the German Population from Those German Territories East of the Oder-Neisse Line That Formed Part of the Polish State

After 1945. Unpublished Dissertation. Glasgow: University of Strathclyde, Department of History, 1986.

Gunn, Gordon. *German Foreign Policy, 1933-39: The Intentionalist-Functionalist Debate in German History*. Unpublished Dissertation. Glasgow: University of Strathclyde, Department of History, no date.

Hand, Claudia. *The Origins and Genesis of Nazi Racial Policy*. Unpublished Dissertation, Glasgow: University of Strathclyde, Department of History, 1996.

Hart, Janet Carol. *Empowering and Political Opportunity: Greek Women in the Resistance, 1941-1964*. DA 9117890. Ithaca, New York: Cornell University, 1991.

Hasselbring, Andrew Strieter. *American Prisoners of War in the Third Reich*. Philadelphia: Temple University, DA 9213970, August 1991.

Hickok, James Neil. *Anglo-French Military Cooperation, 1935-1940*. DA 9124669. Madison: University of Wisconsin, 1991.

Hulse, Melvin Andrew. *Soviet Military Doctrine, 'Militarization' of Industry, and the First Two Five Year Plans: Developing the Military-Economic Mobilization Potential of the Soviet Union for Total War*. DA 9122129. Washington, D.C. Georgetown University, September 1991.

Hutchison, James. *British Food Supply and Distribution Problems during the Second World War*. Unpublished Dissertation. Glasgow: University of Strathclyde, Department of History, 1968.

Joyce, Michael. *Anti-Communism in the USA*. Unpublished Dissertation. Glasgow: University of Strathclyde, Department of History, 1997.

Killen, Christine M. *The Communists and the Popular Front: Spain 1936-1939*. Unpublished Dissertation. Glasgow: University of Strathclyde, Department of History, 1994.

Kirk, Lynsey E.K. *To What Extent Can the French Resistance be Described as a Popular Movement?* Unpublished Dissertation, Glasgow: University of Strathclyde, Department of History, 1996.

Macdonald, Campbell. *Assess the Importance of Gregor Strasser When Accounting for the Success of National Socialism in the 1920s and Early 1930s*. Unpublished Dissertation. Glasgow: University of Strathclyde, Department of History, no date.

McElhone, Louise. *British Society During the Second World War: United or Divided*. Glasgow: University of Strathclyde, Department of History, 1986.

McGrath, Francesca M. *German Political Opposition to National Socialism? 1933-1939*. Unpublished Dissertation. Glasgow: University of Strathclyde, Department of History,1984.

McHugh, Michael Caldwell. *With ailce toward None: The Punishment and Pardon of German War Criminals, 1945-58*. DA 9200975. Florida: Miami University, January 1992.

McIntyre, Roslyn A. *The Emergence of Soviet Dominance in Central Eastern Europe, 1945-1948*. Unpublished Dissertation. Glasgow: University of Strathclyde, 1986.

McKenna, James B. *Hitler and Nazi Germany: Imperialistic Legacy or Revolutionary Dictatorship?* Unpublished Dissertation. Glasgow: University of Strathclyde, Department of History, 1991.

McKie, Graeme. *Was Hitler's Extermination of the Jews Inevitable?* Unpublished Dissertation. Glasgow: University of Strathclyde, Department of History, 1990.

Mills, Stephanie Elizabeth. *The Dutch Experience in World War Two*. Unpublished Dissertation. Glasgow: University of Strathclyde, Department of History, 1997.

Mullaney, Jonathan. *The Soviet Union I the 1920s: The Nature and the Significance of the Economic Controversy Between Probazhensky and Bukharin*. Unpublished Dissertation. Glasgow: University of Strathclyde, Department of History, 1995.

Michael. *The Deficiencies of "Intentionalism" and "Functionalism:" An Examination of Nazi Jewish Policy and the Origins of the "Final Solution."* Unpublished Dissertation, Glasgow: University of Strathclyde, Department of History, 1997.

Osborne, Jodhi. *National Socialism: A Coherent, Relevant Ideology?* Unpublished Dissertation. Glasgow: University of Strathclyde, Department of History, 1996.

Persson, Hansake. "German Refugees: A British Dilemma? The British Policy on the German Refugees at the End of the Second World War." Unpublished Thesis. *Workshop on European and Middle East Refugees in the 20ᵗʰ Century*. Oxford, UK: Oxford University, 1985.

Pott, Tim. *The Yugoslav National Question.* Unpublished Dissertation. Glasgow: University of Strathclyde, Department of History, no date.

Pronin, Alexander. *Guerrilla Warfare in the German-Occupied Soviet Territories, 1941-1944.* Unpublished Dissertation. Washington, D.C.: Georgetown University, 1965.

Reid, Karen J. *Why the Nazi Party Came to Power.* Unpublished Dissertation. Glasgow: University of Strathclyde, Department of History. 1985.

Ridley, Karen. *The Disintegration of the Weimar Republic and the Rise of National Socialism.* Unpublished Dissertation. Glasgow: University of Strathclyde, Department of History, no date.

Russell, Pauline. *The Rise of the SS: Historical Accident or Astute Planning?* Unpublished Dissertation. Glasgow: University of Strathclyde, Department of History, 1994.

Slepyan, Kenneth D. *"The People's Avengers:" Soviet Partisans, Stalinist Society and the Politics of Resistance, 1941-1944."* Unpublished Dissertation. Lansing: University of Michigan, 1994.

Swan, Peter D. *How Influential Were the Economic Considerations in the formation of German Foreign Policy towards the Soviet Union, Poland and Austria During the Weimar Era?* Unpublished Dissertation, Glasgow: University of Strathclyde, Department of History, 1995.

Tait, Alan William . Influence or Significance? "A Critical Assessment of the Importance of Domestic factors in the Timing of Nazi Foreign Policy." Unpublished Dissertation. Glasgow: University of Strathclyde, Department of History, no date.

Waddell, Gordon W.C. *Resistance to National Socialism Within the Wehrmacht: 1939-1945.* Unpublished Honours Dissertation. Glasgow: University of Strathclyde, Department of History, 1977.

Wilson, George. *The Nationalities Question in the Soviet Union, 1917-1938.* Unpublished Dissertation. Glasgow: University of Strathclyde, Department of History, 1996.